DV-Made China

Critical Interventions
Sheldon H. Lu, general editor

Cinema, Space, and Polylocality in a Globalizing China
Yingjin Zhang

Children of Marx and Coca-Cola: Chinese Avant-garde Art and Independent Cinema
Xiaoping Lin

Uneven Modernity: Literature, Film, and Intellectual Discourse in Postsocialist China
Haomin Gong

Remaking Chinese Cinema: Through the Prism of Shanghai, Hong Kong, and Hollywood
Yiman Wang

From Fu Manchu to Kung Fu Panda: Images of China in American Film
Naomi Greene

Fragrant Orchid: The Story of My Early Life
Yamaguchi Yoshiko and Fujiwara Sakuya
Translated, with an Introduction, by Chia-ning Chang

CRITICAL INTERVENTIONS

DV-Made China

Digital Subjects and Social Transformations after Independent Film

**Edited by Zhang Zhen
and Angela Zito**

University of Hawai'i Press
Honolulu

Critical Interventions
Sheldon H. Lu, general editor

Critical Interventions consists of innovative, cutting-edge works with a focus on Asia or the presence of Asia in other continents and regions. Series titles explore a wide range of issues and topics in the modern and contemporary periods, especially those dealing with literature, cinema, art, theater, media, cultural theory, and intellectual history as well as subjects that cross disciplinary boundaries. The series encourages scholarship that combines solid research with an imaginative approach, theoretical sophistication, and stylistic lucidity.

Printed in the United States of America

20 19 18 17 16 15 6 5 4 3 2 1

Library of Congress Cataloging-in-Publication Data
DV-made China : digital subjects and social transformations after independent film / edited by Zhang Zhen and Angela Zito.
pages cm—(Critical interventions)
Includes bibliographical references and index.
ISBN 978-0-8248-4681-7 (cloth : alk. paper)—ISBN 978-0-8248-4682-4 (pbk. : alk. paper)
1. Independent films—China. 2. Digital cinematography—China.
I. Zhang, Zhen, editor. II. Zito, Angela, editor. III. Series: Critical interventions (Honolulu, Hawaii)
PN1993.5.C4D89 2015
791.430951—dc23

2014042674

University of Hawaiʻi Press books are printed on acid-free paper and meet the guidelines for permanence and durability of the Council on Library Resources.

Contents

Acknowledgments

This volume has been long in the making, finding its deep roots in more than a decade of seven editions of Reel China Documentary Biennial screenings and discussions since 2001; in a jointly taught graduate seminar on Chinese independent documentaries (in conjunction with the Biennial in 2008, 2010, and 2012); and more specifically, in a workshop at New York University in December 2010 that produced earlier versions of most of the chapters. More than any other academic work either of us has undertaken in the past, this project has placed us in the midst of a rapidly changing Chinese society and culture in the new century. The nascent, forceful, and increasingly diversified DV movement studied here, with its significant social, political, and aesthetic aspirations, contributes to China's profound social and cultural transformations with a great deal of creative energy as well as urgent critique.

First, and above all, we express our heartfelt thanks to the independent film community in China, which has made the Biennial, the seminar, and the research and development of this volume such an immensely rewarding and enlightening experience. We are especially grateful to the Chinese filmmakers, critics, and curators, including Cong Feng, Cui Weiping, Cui Zi'en, Dong Bingfeng, Du Haibin, Gu Yaping, Hao Jian, He Liren, He Xiaopei, Huang Weikai, Jian Yi, Jiang Juan, Liu Jian, Li Xiaofeng, Lü Xinyu, Luo Bing, Ma Li, Ou Ning, Pema Tsedan, Wang Nanfu, Wang Yuanlong, Wang Wo, Wen Hui, Wu Wenguang, Yang Lina, Yang Rui, Zhang Mengqi, Zhang Xianmin, Zhao Liang, Zou Xueping, Zhu Rikun, as well as Tammy Cheung and Yao Ching of Hong Kong, who came to NYU to share with students, faculty, and the public countless moving images and provocative ideas. We are equally grateful to all filmmakers whose works were screened at the Biennial and other related events.

We are particularly indebted to the Li Xianting Film Fund, which presents the annual Beijing Independent Film Festival, for inviting the two of us in various capacities to take part in BIFF and its related activities. They have shared valuable resources and experiences in our joint effort to promote independent cinema over the past many years. Mr. Li Xianting, Mr. Wang Hongwei, and Ms. Zhang Qi have been most generous and gracious in hosting us and collaborating with us. We gratefully acknowledge as well the collaboration of Mr. Zhang Pingjie and his associates at Rec Foundation. The Asian Cultural Council in New York has, several times over the years, also provided crucial support in bringing filmmakers to the Biennial and the workshop.

At NYU, we are most thankful to our home departments and affiliated institutions, Cinema Studies and the Center for Religion and Media (CRM), which have copresented the Biennial since 2006. The Anthropology and History Departments, the Religious Studies Program, the Center for Media, Culture and History (CMCH), and China House have offered cosponsorship and/or administrative support.

Faye Ginsburg (Anthropology Department), codirector of the CRM and director of CMCH, and Richard Allen, chair of Cinema Studies till recently, have offered moral as well as concrete support over the years. Thanks also go to Dan Streible (Cinema Studies), a constant participant in the Biennial, offering insightful comparative perspectives. Mai Kiang (who left NYU in 2007) and Jeff Richardson, events coordinator at Cinema Studies since 2007, and Catherine Holter, Cinema Studies technical coordinator, and departmental "bookkeeper" Liza Greenfield, along with contingents of student projectionists and volunteers, were indispensible to the successful execution of the Biennial and related events over the last thirteen years. The staff of the CRM, including Laura Terruso, Ann Neumann, and Kali Handelman, along with the staff of CMCH, Barbara Abrash, Pegi Vail, and Cheryl Furjanic, likewise provided constant and excellent support in public programming and coordination of academic events.

For the book itself, we are especially grateful to the NYU Humanities Initiative for a timely collaborative teaching grant that allowed the two of us to further develop the 2010 seminar and the workshop that produced this book. At the workshop three discussants provided a lively chance to further hone the papers: Jennifer Deger, Dan Streible, and Ellen Zweig. The NYU Provost's Office for Global Research Initiative, which has contributed substantially to several editions of the Biennial, also provided a generous subvention for this book's production; our thanks to K. E. Fleming. The Dean of Humanities at NYU, Joy Connelly, dipped into special funds to enable us to hire Shilpa Gupta as a copyediting assistant during the final stage of manuscript preparation. We are grateful to the University of Hawai'i Press's editorial team and to the anonymous readers who offered praises and pressed us for clarifications that strengthened the manuscript. Most importantly, we thank the contributors for their hard and brilliant work (including work revised and updated from a previously published article in

China Perspectives, in the case of Jie Li) and for their patience and cooperation during the long and complicated process of realizing this collective project.

Both of us also received individual support to devote time and energy on research, writing, editing, and filmmaking. Zhen received an NYU Humanities Initiative faculty fellowship in 2009–2010, which allowed her to research and present initial work for her own chapter and develop with Angela the frameworks for the workshop. A fellowship at Hong Kong Baptist University in spring 2012 and a summer fellowship at Fu Dan University's School of Journalism and Broadcasting in 2013 gave her additional time and a number of forums to work further on the project as a whole. A Tisch School of the Arts dean's research grant also enabled her to make multiple trips to China. Angela's turn to thinking about digital media was facilitated by a two-year grant from the Luce Foundation's Henry R. Luce initiative on Religion and International Affairs to study "Digital Religion: Knowledge, Politics, and Practice" at CRM (2011–2013). She relied on research funding from NYU to shoot and edit her own documentary in Beijing, *Writing in Water,* which provided her with an additional perspective on the problem of independent cinema in China.

Saving the best for last, we thank our families for putting up with our insane schedules each time a Biennial was organized and carried out and extend our deep appreciation to the interlocking circles of friends and students who have been sounding boards and the most enthusiastic and loyal audience members. As we say when opening yet another edition of Reel China: "That's enough from us. . . . Now, please enjoy the show!"

ZZ and AZ,
New York, July 21, 2014

Introduction

ZHANG ZHEN AND ANGELA ZITO

Everybody is a director of life.
—Tudou.com (China)

DV-Made China

The title of this volume is inspired by two seemingly unrelated sources—one Chinese, the other American. The first is a documentary called *DV China* (2003), which was shown at the 2nd Reel China Documentary Biennial at New York University in 2004. On New Year's Day 2002, Zheng Dasheng,[1] a young filmmaker from Shanghai, took his small crew and a Sony PD-150 camera to Jingdezhen, the "Porcelain Capital" of China in Jiangxi Province. They made a documentary about an amateur filmmaker (or *DV ren,* "DV person"—Zheng's term) and his locally produced "TV drama series," shot with his home video camera.[2] Less than two weeks into on-location shooting, Zheng decided to call the film "DV China"—referring to the filmmaking on video by both his subject and his own crew, mobilizing the double entendre "China" for both the country and the world-famous porcelain of the city.[3] The film was one of several documentaries made at the cusp of the digital turn in independent or semi-independent filmmaking circles in China at the dawn of the new century. Far more easy to transport than film prints or analog video on bulky industry tapes that are subject to stringent censorship and customs requirements, films on VHS tape (and later burned to DVD) quickly crossed the Pacific to the auditorium of the Cinema Studies department at NYU and other college campuses and public venues in the USA.

The other inspiration for our title comes from the late Bob Sklar, an NYU Cinema Studies professor, and his widely read *Movie-Made America: A Cultural History of American Movies* (Sklar 1975). In popular imagination as well as academic discourse, the history of the United States in the twentieth century, and its status as a superpower, cannot be separated from its domestically robust and globally

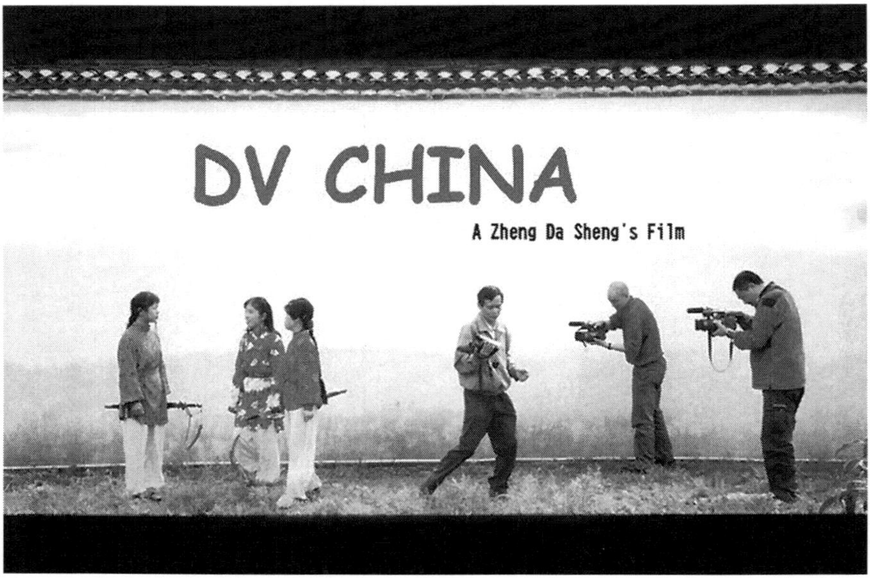

Figure 0.1. Poster for DV China. (courtesy of Zheng Dasheng)

hegemonic film culture. Sklar wrote his book during the decline of the American movie industry, as the vertically integrated Hollywood studio system collapsed and television replaced the movies as the most popular form of mass entertainment. The steady incursion of postwar European art cinema and other alternative attractions (e.g., the *Kung-fu* craze and hard-core pornography) had also created a more segmented and diversified audience with varied tastes, further depressing the box office in mainstream theaters. Interestingly, Sklar ends the book with an enthusiastic introduction to the "future of the movies" via the "New American cinema," or a "personal cinema" (Sklar 1975, 304–306). He finds in it the resuscitated vibrant impulse of early cinema, tracing its emergence in underground film and the "non-representational graphic cinema" or "expanded cinema." This avant-garde film culture experimented with the radical meshing of various opposites: old and new media technology (from super 16mm camera to television to computers), art cinema and home movies, the public and the private, the artistic and amateurish, and fiction and nonfiction (Sklar 1975, 313–314; Youngblood 1970).

However, when Sklar wrote his book, the ideal of a truly democratic cinema allowing the dissemination of affordable technology and the "expansion" of human consciousness for a more humane world was still more constrained. Only corporate interests and a few filmmakers had access to film equipment and specialized knowledge. By the end of the last century, or the "century of cinema," when the most recent and updated edition of *Movie-Made America* was published in 1994, the world of cinema and the cinema of the world had changed enormously. Video and digital technology had radically reshaped both the film industry and the wider visual culture on and off both big and small screens, precipitating a shift analogous to the one so analyzed by Sklar. The kind of "personal cinema" that Sklar observed in the American avant-garde nearly a half century earlier has now entered the domain of everyday life and expanded exponentially in both quantity and variety of formats and modes. Meanwhile, the sense of the "American century" in terms of its movies' pervasive impact on mass culture and modern imagination worldwide has been challenged by a post–Cold War geopolitical world order. The avalanche of new imaging and communicative technologies (especially the Internet and social media) has brought the production and consumption of "personal cinema" within the reach of countless people around the globe, especially in the wake of the digital turn on a mass scale in the past decade. Our updated transnational take on Sklar's term makes space to engage and initiate new conversations on "personal cinema," "expanded cinema," and the relationship between alternative film practice and social change. We also hope that the project will provide comparative perspectives on "new media" and "digital cinema" studies. The juxtaposition of Zheng's *DV China* and Sklar's *Movie-Made America* goes beyond wordplay to function here as a rhetorical and conceptual exchange that sheds light on DV as well as China's increasingly prominent place in the heavily media-saturated world.

In the new century, China, the most populous country in the world with the fastest economic growth and market expansion, appears to be the biggest rival to U.S. status as an economic and media superpower. Since the implementation of Deng Xiaoping's "Open Door" reform agenda in the late 1970s and its subsequent mutations in favor of a party state–mandated capitalist economy, China seems to have recaptured its self-image as the "Middle Kingdom." With a soaring GNP and skyscrapers to match, China produces other indices of spectacular development in both hard infrastructure and soft power, including mass communication and the so-called creative industries. The mainstream Chinese film industry (both official and commercial variants and their hybrids) has revived in terms of rapid expansion in blockbuster production and exhibition sectors, with the deep involvement of transnational capital (Palmer 2006; Curtin 2007; Rosen 2012). Meanwhile, a parallel "personal cinema" and alternative media culture has, against all odds, swept across the country like wildfire, ignited and spread by filmmakers and videographers from all walks of life. Jiang Zhi, one of the independent filmmakers who started with the Hi8 format in the late 1990s, declares,

> DV is not about isms, nor just babbling; DV is not a damage to cinema, nor its savior; DV does not belong to the rich, nor the poor. . . . But DV as a product of [new] technology (not antique), a kind of new imagining tool, has brought to China a nascent creative movement, a generation of image-makers and new topics that have ushered in a new vitality and challenge. (Jiang 2004, 368)

This new image-making movement also includes cineastes, critics, curators, and audiences, comprising cineclubs, art spaces, college campuses, media activist archives or workstations, along with online indie communities whose stomping grounds are everywhere but the big studios and multiplexes. *DV-Made China* focuses on and pays tribute to this other China and its grassroots moving-image practices, specifically the making and sharing of low-cost independent DV and the shaping of an alternative media and public culture. In this other China, cinema production, much like the porcelain of Jingdezhen (scene of Zheng's riotous *DV China*), becomes an artifact of artisanal work that can, thanks to digital tools, be replicated for mass consumption. And like the china of Jingdezhen, this new bottom-up DIY cinema stands at the nexus of traditional artisanal technique and (post)modern mass production. A different kind of product "made in China" with a measure of human touch and creative agency, it is fragile yet reproducible, like the millions of tiny "china" sunflower seeds in an installation work of Ai Weiwei who had them hand-painted in Jingdezhen's workshops and households.[4]

This volume follows on several important works, in English, on Chinese independent or alternative cinema, providing significant updates and more focused perspectives. *From Underground to Independent* (Pickowicz and Zhang 2006), was the first book to broach the subject of unofficial film culture. *The Urban Generation: Chinese Cinema and Society at the Turn of the Twenty-first Century* (Zhang 2007), then examined the Sixth Generation's independent works in conjunction with the New Documentary Movement and an emerging alternative film culture in a rapidly urbanizing China. *The New Chinese Documentary Film Movement* (Berry et al. 2010), is now the major reference point for current scholarship on the New Documentary Movement. These foundational anthologies were followed by two monographs: Paola Voci's *China on Video: Small-Screen Realities* (Voci 2010) and Luke Robinson's *Independent Chinese Documentary: From the Studio to the Street* (Robinson 2012), providing expansion on specific areas. Taken together, these works indicate a rising scholarly interest in nonfiction films and transmedia forms of moving image, in contrast to the previous preoccupation with narrative cinema in Chinese-language film studies in particular and national or world cinema studies in general.[5]

This trend marks a timely response to the blossoming of alternative documentary practices and hybrid forms and their implications for broader transformations in Chinese society and culture. "The new documentary movement" was coined by Shanghai-based scholar Lü Xinyu's path-breaking book, *Jilu Zhongguo: Dangdai Zhongguo xinjilu yundong* (Documenting China: The New Documentary Movement in Contemporary China), a collection of interviews and essays (Lü 2003).[6] Lü later joined American anthropologist Lisa Rofel and British film scholar Chris Berry to edit, in English, *The New Chinese Documentary Film Movement: For the Public Record*. There Berry and Rofel extend previous scholarship and question the designation "independent" for this new cinema, rejecting any notion that it heralds an opening of "civil society" or a "public sphere." Instead, they suggest "alternative" as a designation for the documentary movement, offering a convincing etymology for their choice. In discussing the website for the collective project, www.alternativearchive.com, with filmmaker, artist, and curator Ou Ning, they mulled over its Chinese name Bieguan. The term literally means a side building, but is also homophonic with "leave me alone." The editors added that perhaps the "alternative" does not substitute for or exist in competition with the "main building," but simply grows alongside as something additional and that "this interpretation captures the way in which alternativeness can produce significant change but not through the route of direct opposition" (Berry and Rofel 2010, 137). We agree with Berry and Rofel's parsing of *bieguan,* while continuing to account for the spectrum of designations used by Chinese filmmakers, critics, and curators who occupy varying positions—aesthetically as well as politically—with regard to both independent and mainstream film culture. Some filmmakers such as Jia Zhangke and Pema Tseden (Wanma Caidan in Chinese) operate in the complex border zone between the two, while the majority of independent or amateur DV filmmakers work with far fewer resources but also less reliance on institutionalized domestic and international markets.

Digital Subjects

The digital turn has had such profound impact because of its ability to affect many aspects of image-making and cinema culture (Friedberg 2000; Jenkins 2006; Rees 2011; Bordwell 2012; Dixon 2013). These influences include new forms of *production,* such as in-camera sync sound, extreme portability, and miniaturization, which ironically close the gap between documenting and surveillance; endless cheap reproduction on DV tape and now memory cards; and a ubiquity of shooting possibilities for amateurs on phones. But there are also the new forms of *postproduction* that, through editing on desktop PCs that use software of increasing levels of sophistication, join amateurs and professionals in a kind of postproduction continuum. These are the aspects of the digital medium that would seem to contribute to a sense of "independence." This volume is not concerned with the impact of the digital turn on mainstream cinema and mass culture in China; rather, it is dedicated to an alternative digital culture that is integral to an evolving art and social movement propelled by democratic aspirations and social and aesthetic experiments. While digital technology plays a critical role in the formation of this alternative cultural and social movement, we acknowledge its radical historicity and hybrid nature, paying special attention to how independent, amateur, and activist filmmakers energize the tension between old and new media, performance and representation, fiction and nonfiction, art and politics, China and the world.

Our title and scope also resonate with, while expanding on, Paola Voci's *China on Video: Small-Screen Realities,* which captures the emerging contours of a "mediascape" of digitally induced proliferation of alternative visual and public culture, along with its radical aesthetic potential and political promise. Voci, who contributes a fascinating chapter on vernacular digital animation to this volume, extends the discussion in her book of a number of genres of "light movies" made mostly by anonymous or amateur video-makers and disseminated largely online (often virally and sometimes ephemerally because of online censorship). Alternately connoting "small" and "humorous," she defines the "lightness" of these movies in terms of their "small production costs, distribution ambitions, economic impact, limited audiences, quick and volatile circulation," along with their resistance to "being framed into and validated by either market, art, or political discourse." Voci's examples include both "light" and "heavy" subjects found in independent documentary, experimental animation, amateur cellflix, and online spoofs, all of which share an innovative *personal* use of new media tools and outlets, and the playful intervention "both within and without the borders of legitimate cultures" (Voci 2010, xxi). What she calls "lightness" has a lot in common with Hito Steyerl's "poor images."[7] And the attention to amateurism—and its counterpart with a sharper sociopolitical vision or activism—as a pervasive social and media phenomenon as well as conceptual framework, develops previous observations by filmmakers and scholars (Wu 2002; Wang 2005).

In elaborating what we mean by "digital subjects," we follow Bob Sklar's earlier methodological impulse to link the history of film to both institutions and to people's everyday lives. We also share and hope to amplify Voci's interdisciplinary commitment to "film, media, new media, media anthropology, visual arts, contemporary China area studies, and cultural studies" (Voci 2010, the back cover). The films, videos, and other related media objects in focus here include some "light movies" (or "a light version of cinematic avant-garde"), but also many of their siblings in varying shades between lightness and heaviness in tonal and formal registers, including all kinds of short works, long social documentaries (e.g., Zhao Liang's *Petition*), narrative features (e.g., Pema Tseden's *The Search*), and avant-garde experiments (e.g., Li Ning's *Tape/Jiaodai*) that are dedicated to probing the somber and even tragic fates of their subjects in postsocialist capitalist China. While most of the movies discussed here readily fit in the category of "small screen realities," they are also imbued with a digital flexibility for adapting to a variety of screen sizes and audiences beyond personal computers and cell phones, sometimes receiving consequential reception in large public forums. Indeed, some have even made it to official television (e.g., *DV China*) while others have been shown in festivals and theaters inside and outside China (e.g., *24 City, Last Train Home/Guitu lieche*).

Thus, we feel that the term "digital subjects" works on two registers, inside and outside the DV media itself. On the one hand, we have the multitude of subject matter and subjectivities given expression *in* DV works that often escape the purview of mainstream cinema and state television. On the other hand, there are the creative agents-as-subjects, including filmmakers, critics, curators, and audiences who have formed a loosely connected network on and off line to make, exchange, and consume those objects. Unlike Voci, our primary concerns are not with the stark divide between the sizes of the screens and film formats, or the independent and the official, but with the freedom as well as challenges that portable and affordable digital technology have brought to a new breed of filmmakers traditionally excluded from the institution of cinema. Some of these are professionally trained (Zheng Dasheng, Zhang Yuan, Jia Zhangke, Pema Tseden, Gan Xiao'er), but most are self-taught cineastes, amateurs, and media activists with various backgrounds and agendas. Zhang Xianmin, a prominent independent curator and producer, observes that several years after 1989, "practically everyone, including retired television journalists, fashion magazine editors, college students, long-term laid-off workers, and drifting foreigners in China started making documentaries" (Zhang and Zuo 2012). This widened "art movement" is largely enabled by the popularization of DV.

More importantly, this fast-evolving DV culture has facilitated the making of a "DV China" comprising various film and media communities across different social strata, and "alternative archives" for disenfranchised groups, including ethnic and religious minorities and LGBTQ communities. Luke Robinson's chapter on innovative queer independent documentary, for example, further theorizes Voci's concept of "lightness," finding it perfect for exploring how the capacity for reduplication and recontextualization, along with its quick ubiquity, have made digital media perfect for transacting the business of forging new identities out of old histories. Robert Barnett's ethnographically and historically grounded chapter addresses Tibetan filmmakers (educated elite as well as laymen) and the broader issue of non–Han Chinese cultural and media production not covered by the abovementioned scholarship. His original contribution critically expands the rich and polemical rubric "DV-Made China."

Another important dimension of the DV culture lies in the host of new forms of *distribution* via "diffusion" online, through cheap DVD reproduction and piracy as well as through easy screen projection in public or private places. All these forms have given rise to a new "cinephilia in the age of digital reproduction" (Balcerzak and Sperb 2009). Digital quite naturally acts as an amplifying device, as May Ingawanij observes, in light of Miriam Hansen's seminal study of early cinema's spectatorship (Hansen 1991), for the long-recognized "potential of cinema to constitute a shared public horizon that recognizes experiences elsewhere denied" (Ingawanij and McKay 2011, 9). Ingawanij sees this potential reenergized by the burgeoning Southeast Asian independent cinema and its attendant cinephilia culture. She writes, echoing fellow contributors in the volume she co-edited, *Glimpses of Freedom: Independent Cinema in Southeast Asia,* "the visibility of film festivals and their communitarian air tend to generate the kind of atmosphere conducive to registering the possibility of collective recognition of marginalized groups, and to performing democratic discursive exchange in the 'liminal' space of civic inclusiveness that festivals can sometimes invoke" (Ingawanij and McKay 2011, 9).

This scenario resonates with similar developments in China. Since the First Independent Image Festival held in Beijing and the First Beijing Gay and Lesbian Film Festival (later changed to Beijing Queer Film Festival) in 2001, a host of unofficial or independent film festivals and forums have appeared across the country. They include the Yunfest (Yunnan Multi Culture Visual Festival) in Kunming, the Beijing Independent Film Festival (and a related Documentary Forum until 2009), and the Nanjing Independent Film Festival, all begun around 2003, followed by festivals and showcases in other cities (notably Guangzhou, Shenzhen, Chongqing, Shanghai, Xi'an, Tianjin, Hangzhou, Xiamen, and Lhasa) and at numerous college campuses, cineclubs, galleries, libraries, and newly emerged art houses (Nakajima 2006; Zhang 2007; Nornes 2009; Svensson, 2012; Ma 2012). They are devoted to showcasing and promoting small-budget independent cinema largely made on DV. The festivals and showcases usually include discussion panels and publish catalogs or booklets of critical essays or transcriptions of forum discussions. As with the formation of social and political discussions among netizens fueled by the "power of the Internet" (Yang 2009), a lively online extension of these festivals and events is sustained through web forums and social media such as *weibo* and now *weixin* (Chinese version of WeChat). This evolving, alternative festival and exhibition culture, which is vulnerable due to a volatile political climate in China, connects via transnational linkages with festivals abroad, often second-tier or specialized varieties, that favor and nurture an independent cinema that includes documentary and experimental film.

For moving image cultures, it is the dual capacity of the digital to both form networks and to transmit substantial content in the form of information (in our case, video films) that again collapses older distinctions of infra- and superstructure, production and consumption, creating new human networks that can lead to new forms of agency and empowerment. This mash-up and speed-up of what we might have once called "moments in the dialectical production of social life" (Zito 2008, 78) allows for new social possibilities in the formation of communities that bear with them new aesthetic, political, and ethical challenges and possibilities.

Background of the Project

In the past twenty years, new networks enabled by the Internet and easier transnational travel have allowed independent Chinese films and filmmakers to access international audiences in a way that mainstream Chinese films (both state-sponsored and joint venture) have not, crossing linguistic and financial barriers. The editors of this volume have been involved in one of these efforts for about a decade: the Reel China Documentary Biennial consortium. Established, according to its own website information, in 1997, it was the brainchild of Zhang Pingjie, an art critic and curator based in New York until a few years ago, who started the REC Foundation.[8] During the project's ferment he met Zhang Zhen, who joined forces with him and his associates to produce the first (2001) and second (2004) editions, with Zhang Zhen curating tailored programs for NYU that inaugurated the transnational and multisite Reel China Biennial. Angela Zito joined Zhang Zhen in cocurating the event at NYU in 2006, sampling the larger program from Reel China at large. In the early days, Zhang Pingjie would collect films on VHS and DVD from his contacts on the mainland and look for screening occasions in the United States, dubbing and bundling them to travel around to colleges. NYU's Cinema Studies Department, along with the Center for Media, Culture, and History in the Anthropology Department, has provided the permanent screening home, as well as funding, for Reel China since 2006.[9] We later developed a close curatorial relationship with Zhu Rikun, founder of Fanhall Cinema and mainstay of the Li Xianting Film Fund in Songzhuang, Beijing until 2011 when Zhu left the fund. Zhu is a leading curatorial and now producing presence in independent documentary in China, having organized eight Beijing Independent Film Festivals along with a separate documentary forum each spring, called DOC China, until 2011. Reel China @NYU has continued and expanded partnership with Li Xianting's Film Fund in recent years, including inviting its artistic director Dong Bingfeng to guest-curate and introduce a shorts program for the 7th Reel China in spring 2014. We have also served as jury members and organized or participated in forums at several of these venues.

The idea of the volume stems therefore from a more than decade-long involvement in screening, teaching, and writing about Chinese new documentary and alternative cinema,[10] crystallized in the workshop dedicated to the subject at NYU in December 2010. For brainstorming collectively, we provided the group with the following opening questions: How has the adoption of digital media changed the perception and practice of filmmaking in China? In what ways do DV works—in production, distribution, and reception—differ from traditional forms and formats of cinema? For example, how has the relationship between the filmmaker and his or her subject changed in adopting the portable DV camera? What kinds of new subject matter and new subjects have entered the filmmakers' viewfinder or LCD? Is there a digital aesthetic that's markedly different from previous modes of cinema? Where is DV culture located in relation to mainstream media as well as independent cinema and art? To what extent has DV become a viable mode of social and political advocacy while probing the moral fabric of a rapidly changing society?

This volume materializes the fruits of the workshop collaboration, drawing on a few more contributors. The workshop then, and the volume now, are informed by a polyphonic spectrum of perspectives, intersecting disciplines, and methodologies crossing humanities and social sciences, including cinema and media studies, anthropology, history, comparative literature, religious studies, and Asian studies. Many of the contributors are also active practitioners as filmmakers and curators, which brings firsthand experiences to bear on academic approaches. We hope that this introduction and chapters to follow address our original questions and raise new ones in the Chinese context. We also hope to extend the implications of our conceptual frameworks to media culture and its everyday life in the new century of a world that both contains, and is influenced by, China.

Ethical and Political Stakes

The volume comprises two parts of six chapters each, "Ethical and Political Stakes" and "Aesthetic and Activist Experiments," respectively. Admittedly, the four terms or dimensions in the two rubrics are inseparable in many of the films, videos, and related practices covered in the volume. While the authors' references and approaches resonate throughout the volume, each part gathers a group of contributions that share similar emphases or overlapping concerns. By starting with the vital questions of ethics and power relations in image-making and dissemination, we highlight the critical affinity of independent documentary and alternative cinema's role in a burgeoning social movement for a more open and humanitarian society. The democratic aspirations of the DV culture are intimately intertwined with and articulated through formal experiments that challenge parameters in traditional cinema studies. These are touched upon in Part One, but will be pursued in considerable depth in Part Two, to account more fully for the political and aesthetic significance of the DV culture in a related "citizen's documentation movement."

Part One opens with Abé Mark Nornes' "Marking the Body: The Axiographics of the Visible Hidden Camera." A senior scholar of documentary studies and Japanese cinema, Nornes finds contemporary China to be "[o]ne of the most exciting documentary scenes on the planet," yet, invoking Bill Nichols, fraught with problems of the "axiographics" through which a filmmaker's ethics are inscribed in the representation of time and space on-screen. He examines the roots of direct cinema documentary in China, contemplating the ethical dimensions of the specific brand of observational cinema in China. Frederick Wiseman's direct cinema style—most popular in China—attempts to repress completely the presence of the camera from the profilmic scene. A quintessential lone-wolf maker, intent on optimizing all tools to defend his independence as an artist, Wiseman epitomizes the "independent" possibilities of the digital turn. A few Chinese directors, however, have followed Shinsuke Ogawa into cinema verité, where the camera's intervention is recognized. Ogawa emphasized the networking of exhibition and reception into the act of filmmaking itself, avoiding the Wisemanesque narcissism that Nornes sees plaguing most Chinese documentary. As the relationship between a filmmaker and his or her subjects increasingly becomes a major subject itself within documentary, it comes under heavier scrutiny. Nornes feels that many Chinese filmmakers have failed to uphold this trust, as evidenced in films such as *Wheat Harvest* (*Mai Shou* 2008), *Toxicosis* (2010), and *Martian Syndrome* (*Huoxing yao zonghezheng*, 2009). For example, Xu Tong, director of *Wheat Harvest,* never told the prostitute who was the subject of the film about his intentions—she discovered accidentally online that her life story was making the international festival rounds. In this sense, while filmmakers' cameras are perfectly visible, they are also hidden, enabling directors to capture "life unawares," as if people were being shot by a secret camera. Nornes notes that ultimately, the lack of an established distribution system or reception context for the independent documentary in China means that people are virtually unaware of their existence. In this context, he contends, many directors, while identifying with their powerless subjects, ignore the ethical implications of shooting people without being up front about their intentions or asking for consent, ironically replicating the violent power structure of state surveillance cameras.

J. P. Sniadecki offers a different view. In his chapter, "The Cruelty of the Social: *Xianchang,* Intersubjectivity, and Interobjectivity," he defends the observational aesthetic in Chinese documentary as a "moral and potentially therapeutic response" in a society suffused with violence and trauma. This move aligns the "cruelty of the social" reenacted in the independent documentary with, at least in spirit, Artaud's "theater of cruelty" aimed at relieving repression and liberating instinctual energy. Sniadecki does this by widening the context of the suffering to include filmmakers themselves by reintroducing for this volume the unique Chinese cinematic term, *xianchang*, usually translated as "on the scene." Carrying an aesthetic and ethical weight beyond the sense of "location shooting," however, a commitment to *xianchang* entails emphasizing openness to contingency, and thus " 'the real,' in contradistinction to the staged artificiality of state propaganda documentary films" (Robinson 2010, 180–181). Everyone is always already in *xianchang*, on the scene, and this deeper truth encompasses any local strategies and claims for objectivity of observation. Instead of surrendering to the obvious shortcomings of observational cinema, Sniadecki renames it in the Chinese case and pries open its reflexive possibilities. He explores the formal, haptic elements that render *xianchang* aesthetics fertile ground for both *intersubjective* and *interobjective* experiences, which energize cinematic space for the witnessing of social suffering. To establish the possibility of "intersubjectivity," Sniadecki calls on a tradition of critique maintaining that, no matter what claims might be made on behalf of objectivity in observational or direct cinema, the work of the camera is always embodied and hence subjective.[11] He is willing to grant more faith in filmmakers' intentions to share in (or at least recognize themselves within) the stories they craft with their subjects, as in the case of Xue Jianqiang's works, which Nornes criticizes. Sniadecki notes that the DV camera, handheld and set on autofocus, enables this sweeping across surfaces and sliding between film subjects. Such an intimate and embodied camera, in turn, works to foster a valuable cinematic space of *intersubjectivity* between film subject, filmmaker, and audience.

Nornes and Sniadecki engage in a debate with no easy answers. Indeed, the opportunities of extreme portability that digital technology provides for intimacy clash with the growing use of digital surveillance in the service of the state. How can people accustomed to having the state's eyes on them defend themselves from an enforced sense of intimacy even by the most well-intentioned cameraman? Most Chinese filmmakers are from social strata more economically and educationally privileged than those they film. Filming, like ethnography, is famously easier when practiced "downward" from a higher (class) vantage.

Jie Li joins the conversation between Nornes and Sniadecki over the triangulated power relations between the state, the filmmaker, and the filmed marginal subject. In her chapter "Filming Power and the Powerless: Zhao Liang's *Crime and Punishment* (2007) and *Petition* (2009)," Li rescues Zhao's work as a welcome exception to what she identifies as a creeping problem of independent documentary in China. She offers an analysis of two complementary filmic portraits of representatives of state power and the powerless: *Crime and Punishment* (*Zui yu fa*) follows police; *Petition* (*Shangfang*) follows those who feel deeply wronged by the system. She argues that Zhao's films provide "seeing lessons" for the audience in three senses: by rendering visible those who are un(der)represented; by exposing and critiquing the deception of official media images; and by showing various complex ways that power is connected to surveillance and visibility. Thus the filmmaker, his camera, and the spectators all become implicated in power relationships as we cast voyeuristic, panoptic, activist, empathetic, or critical gazes on the documentary subjects. Digital ubiquity does not offer the same possibilities to everyone; yet we are all implicated in the networked results of such filmmaking efforts. Toward the end, Li discusses Zhao Liang's recent above-ground turn, specifically with the making of a government-sponsored documentary on AIDS, finding it illustrative of the evolving power relations with which Zhao and other independent filmmakers, as well as their subjects and spectators, have to constantly negotiate in China today.

The representational, iconic power of digital video for social and political mediation is pursued further by Shuang Shen, working with a different set of motifs and issues, in "The Spectacular Crowd: Representing the Masses in DV Documentary." The "powerless" multitude in independent film is here reconsidered and reimagined through the shifting configuration of the crowd—the crowds thought of as harbingers of modernity by theorists like Gustave LeBon. When thinking of online media worlds in the digital era, it is perhaps too easy to ignore the vast numbers of living human beings that are affected by these technologies. We might give an impression that Schnapp and Tiews are correct in noting that the postindustrial political economy in the West is "characterized by the coexistence of media aggregation and bodily disaggregation" and that crowds of actually sweating people, "real" crowds, are gone (Schnapp and Tiews 2006, xi, cited by Shen in this volume). However, the resurgence of the Occupy movement globally gives lie to this postmodernist cliché. And in China, certainly, crowds remain important enough for Shen to take up the DV documentary politics and ethics of picturing the changing face and form of the "masses." She asks: How does contemporary Chinese documentary represent and make crowds? How does the documentary filmmaker define her increasingly self-conscious alternative position in relation to the crowds as both subject of representation and audience?

Shuang Shen broaches socialist political and aesthetic legacies for the post-Reform alternative film scene by linking crowd representation in contemporary China to the political history of representing the masses through abstract notions such as "the people" (*renmin*) or "the masses" (*qunzhong*) in the post-1949 socialist era. Shen sensitively places filmmakers right into the crowds they film, reminding us that those who make media occupy "media worlds" even as they construct them. The crowds present a problem of representation in two senses: mimesis and the politics of delegation and election. She traces the changing figure of the crowd, from the disciplined, postsocialist crowd to the more fluid or "humanized" kind (read Western individuation), as seen in Zhang Yuan's *Crazy English* (1999) and Fan Lixin's *Last Train Home* (2009). Shen underscores the significance of the crowd as a medium of renewed political expression as DV becomes the preferred medium of artistic expression in transnational neoliberal China. Echoing Nornes, Shen cautions against a romantic celebration of DV's egalitarian promise in representing the masses on-screen. Her insight also has implications for understanding the shape and nature of the audience-as-crowd in the context of transmediation within the specific history of Chinese socialism and postsocialism.

In "DV-made Tibet: Domestic Videos, Elite Films and the Work of Pema Tseden," Robert Barnett tackles with a great deal of historical sensitivity and ethnographic acuity the problem of representation and self-representation alongside the complex relationship between digital technology and sociopolitical change in the Tibetan context. Because it coincided with rapid growth in personal incomes, the arrival of digital technology in the Tibetan areas of China in the mid-2000s enabled a significant number of Tibetans to produce songs and videos of their own. Constructing an elaborate cultural history of what he identifies as a Tibetan New Wave, which finds its fullest expression in Pema Tseden's work, Barnett traces the introduction and dissemination—domestic and transnational—of five types of DV production by Tibetans in China. These include home videos that record family and religious events; civic videos made to benefit broader communities and construct an indigenous political discourse; export videos made by the authorities or by dissidents to win support in China and from abroad; independent documentaries of various persuasions (and their tenuous links with the New Chinese Documentary); and fiction films that build on and resonate with other kinds of technology and representation. He argues that the practice of recording religious teachings—the creation of private cultural archives of Tibetaneity—lies at the core of all these works. Three variants of this same project, which he identifies as the inquiry into what it means to be a contemporary Tibetan, are found in digital documentaries and fiction films: studies of the pain experienced in the tradition-modernity encounter; portraits showing pride in nomadic culture; and stories about the loss of selfhood and its rediscovery. Behind these variants lies not so much concern about encroachment by the Chinese state, as might be expected, but a recurrent anxiety about contemporary Tibetan masculinity in the face of modernity. These works are threaded through with variations on the story of Milarepa, an eleventh-century hermit deprived of his inheritance who finally rejects recourse to revenge, and the symbolic figure of the elder as the moral example and source for peaceful reconciliation and communal cohesion.

Among the numerous educated elite as well as laymen filmmakers discussed, Barnett highlights the ways in which two leading filmmakers, Chenaktshang Dorje Tsering and Pema Tseden, have gone beyond binary approaches to questions of identity and culture. Both were also well-known poets and fiction writers from the Amdo region before taking up filming as a supplementary and more effective medium. Dorje Tsering was connected with and inspired by Chinese documentarians working in Tibet in the early 1990s. He made documentaries about ordinary Tibetans and their cultural predicament that challenged both exoticist and objectivist trends in Chinese representation of Tibet. Pema Tseden's career and work is both representative and distinctive with regard to this Tibetan New Wave. While deeply embedded in the broad literary and cultural ferment of Amdo, he was also trained professionally at the prestigious Beijing Film Academy and was able to successfully launch his filmmaking career within the Chinese film system. He made documentary and fiction films on 35mm that won Chinese and international accolades, which were followed by censorship restrictions. Pema then moved on to make the low-budget independent digital film, *The Search* (2009), about a small film crew on the road in search of actors for a film based on a Buddhist legend-inspired Tibetan opera *Drime Kundan* about compassion and sacrifice. Barnett finds the film to be a reflexive work on the difficult condition of Tibetan filmmaking and (self) representation, a perfect embodiment of a rigorous formal approach combining documentary realism and Tibetan storytelling and of cultural introspection through the vehicle of the road movie found in films by other filmmakers (including *The Driver and the Lama* [2009], a short by the first Amdo woman director, Rinchen Drolma). The thematic and stylistic emphases on loss, absence, reticence, and emasculated masculinity in these films articulate a "politics of recovery and reconstruction" rather than militant nationalism. Exhaustively researched and ethnographically informed, Barnett's chapter offers a poignant story of the making of an alternative, transmediated DV culture whose significance amounts to an emerging regional cinema, critically amplifying and complicating the framework of a "DV-made China."

Returning to a China remade in the digitally networked era that lies both within and beyond its geographic borders, Dan Gao's chapter, "Chinese Independent Cinema in the Age of 'Digital Distribution,'" deals with the ethics of distribution touched on fleetingly in other chapters. How the promiscuous ease with which the digital forms of cinematic art can circulate creates a not undeserved sense of unease. Gao analyzes various scenes of exhibition, calling the post-digital film scene in China an "institutionalizing enterprise." She thinks of "distribution" as "*a set of* heterogeneous practices that generally help to 'spread' (and in the meantime, also 'sculpt') the cultural product and its discourse." She encourages us to widen the process "to designate duplication, transmission, dissemination, and proliferation of messages *of* and *about* the film—a series of processes that involve various organizations and individuals." Moving from domestic exhibition practices enabled by cheap digital projection that opened up new social spaces to cultural production (e.g., bars and coffeehouses), to online forums—many of which are closed down now—she takes us abroad to film festivals and a U.S. company founded in 2008 that takes as its main business the commercial representation of Chinese independent films in North America.[12] Gao, wary of this new form of connection that ties filmmakers to international resources, analyzes four film entities—Practice Society (Shijian she), Fanhall Studio (Xianxiang Gongzuoshi), the New York–based REC Foundation/Reel China Documentary Biennial, and the dGenerate distribution company. She argues that these entities, which cooperate and part company here and there, do not just play neutral roles of bridging the production and reception scenes of independent cinema, but also have a delimiting and regulatory function on social discourse's formation. They all assume important interpretative and constructive powers that may bring into the notion of Chinese independent cinema elements from existing and far more established rules and concepts.

Aesthetic and Activist Experiments

Part Two widens the ethical and political frameworks through a more thoroughgoing examination of the experimental impulses and representational strategies found in documentary, fiction, docu-fiction, performance-on-camera, animation, activist video, and other forms of DV work. Where do these varied high-stakes aesthetic adventures lead us? What are the dangers and the delights? We open with Bérénice Reynaud's important expansion of an original catalog essay for a showcase of Chinese independent films under the rubric "Chinese Digital Shadows" (*Sombras digitales: Cine chino de última generación*) at the Festival Internacional de Cine in San Sebastian, Spain, in 2010, which she curated. Her chapter, "*Chinese Digital Shadows*: Hybrid Forms, Bodily Archives, and Transnational Visions," expresses perfectly several themes we have already opened, especially digital media's capacity to induce adventures in border-crossing and hybridization of all sorts. Reynaud writes, based on her decades of curating and writing about independent cinema in China and elsewhere, on the aesthetic consequences of the eradication of the boundaries between documentary and fiction—boundaries broken down through the fluid, easily accessible modes of production enabled by digital tools. Replacing this ethically driven binary, she describes instead how, in the films within and beyond the "Chinese Digital Shadows" program (such as Hao Jie's *Single Man* [*Guanggun'er,* 2010] and Emily Tang's *Perfect Life* [*Wanmei shenghuo,* 2008]), "fecund aesthetic tension has emerged between 'a desire for cinema' and 'a desire for documentation.'" Filmmakers' use of the digital medium as either a cheaper substitute for celluloid or as a handy tool for recording "reality" both indicate an "implicit belief in the transparency of the digital." This perception breaks down or reconciles the divide between stylized art cinema and cinema with a documentary impulse, or between montage and archive, the cut and the long take, as seen in the use of cinemascope ratio in independent digital film.

Reynaud enlarges on these observations to suggest that DV has replaced the celluloid of the founding dreams of the cinematic, opening up a host of aesthetic possibilities with consequential social and cultural implications. This is most visibly seen in the creation of "bodily archives" in documentary (notably by Yang Lina, Wu Wenguang, and Wen Hui) and by nonprofessional actors in independent fiction films such as Liu Jiayin's *Oxhide* cycle and Hao Jie's rural sex comedy, which function as embodied carriers of alternative communal and individual histories and memories. Reynaud's decidedly transnational perspective directs our attention to a critical element in the construction of the hybrid digital aesthetic: editing. The difficulty of "cutting" the long take, or the archive of what Sniadecki sees as the "intersubjectivities" of the cruel *xianchang,* for international festivals and distributors has been tackled in some instances by the hands of non-Chinese editors, notably Adam Kerby (for Wang Bing) and Mary Stephen (for Du Haibin). These collaborations also extend to economic and financial areas, further complicating the idea of "DV-made China" as not the same as DV made in China.

Qi Wang, inspired by performance studies' approaches to embodiment, takes up questions of hybrid aesthetics and bodily archive directly in "The Recalcitrance of Reality: Performances, Subjects, and Filmmakers in *24 City* and *Tape.*" While noting that they continue the archiving of underprivileged existences for which independent documentary is much lauded, she points out that Jia Zhangke's *24 City,* about a factory closing, and Li Ning's *Tape,* a personal account of the performance artist's life and times, differ greatly in their testing of the resilient yet treacherous boundary between performance and documentary. Wang uses "performance" in its literal sense of the theatricality of staged action: Jia's *24 City* famously inserts well-known actors in a film shot as a documentary, whereas Li Ning includes documentation of several of his works with his troupe. She does not blame Jia for using actors as much as for his "confusion of fiction and nonfiction in order to produce an effect of historicity that can only come from the real." Wang contends that the film fabricates an "organic" relationship between two distinct categories of representation, thereby orchestrating "an echoing effect between fiction and nonfiction."

Tape, however, shifts regularly between three types of nonfiction specifically enabled by DV cameras: home video, performance documentation, and footage showing Li's actual working process in creating the current film on video. Wang objects to *24 City*'s attempt at using fiction to copy nonfiction, eliding their difference to give us a unified narrative and interpretation. She prefers *Tape*'s overt interest in baring the boundaries between the two modes of representation and exploring the rich dynamic when performance and reality encounter each other or even clash.

Zito also writes about the crossover or tension between fiction and nonfiction in a nested pair of films by a single director, in "Crossing Cameras in China: Christian Aesthetics and Realized Fictions." The fiction feature *Raised from Dust* (*Juzi chentu,* 2007) by Gan Xiao'er uses mostly members of the community as actors. His documentary *Church Cinema* (*Jiaotang dianying,* 2008) intercuts a chronicle of community screenings of *Raised from Dust* in churches with extensive postproduction debriefing with its nonprofessional actors about their participation in making the feature. The community argued that more mobilization of feeling would enhance the fiction feature, whose purpose was, according to them, to spread the gospel. Although he was himself a member of the church, Gan differed, intent on pursuing his own agenda as writer and director with a modernist art-house sensibility. In Gan's double project, Zito sees a form of filmmaking enabled by the turn to the small, intimate formats of video that resides between two of its most obvious generic innovations—"first person documentary" and "vernacular video"—but not quite fitting either.

Zito thinks of Gan as a fabulator[13] who collaborates across his minoritized community, a community that overtly understands media as bearing the gospel good news out of any frame and into the world. For them, "representation" *is* a form of "participation." And in fact, it is his film-objects that Gan offers to them as tokens of his own participation in their community, despite their aesthetic differences. Zito frames their differences as less contradictory and more as examples of how the dialectical mediation of social life requires, in fact, just such distinct moments of live performance and materialized objectification. How the digital turn facilitates, remakes, or ruptures mediated social production is exactly what is under question here.

Paola Voci finds in digital media new possibilities for creativity and connectivity beyond documentary or narrative film, strongholds of traditional cinema studies. In "DV and the *Animateur* Cinema in China," she writes about short digital animations made by and/or circulated for online (or on-mobile) moviemakers and/or viewers. These animations are described and conceptualized as *animateur* cinema that, the author suggests, makes a distinctive and largely unrecognized contribution to alternative cultural spaces, broadly defined by noninstitutional and unofficial locations. These simple, short animations, such as the famous "Grassmud, horse" (*caonima*)[14] cartoons, take the visually digital beyond the DV camera and its indexical connection to extra-filmic reality. Their very nonrealism allows the presentation (rather than representation) of social, thoughtful, and political realities that could never be "seen" otherwise.

Voci notes how these short works turn us back to cinema's exhibitionist beginnings, when film did not attach itself to the world as its faithful narrator but instead surprised viewers with the medium's own capacity to "do things." They often require considerable decoding skills to understand their political point or their hilarious puns, placing the audience outside the text of the film itself. The goal is not to be absorbed into a narrative-induced forgetfulness of participation in the storyline, but to actively contribute interpretation by understanding the larger social context. The networks formed through *animateur* films are the opposite of those commodifying or regulatory ones discussed by Gao. They are premised on unregulated gifting, remixing, mash-up, and forwarding and citation on social media, blogging and video-sharing sites, often to the point that, once viral, their original point of creation is invisible. Their pleasure and triumph lies in a "noninstitutionalized alternative space" in which fleeting, nomadic attempts to escape the fixity of ideological demands and commercial interests are made through an adherence to an aesthetic of "lightness."

The materiality of new, digitally facilitated aesthetic choices that have begun to undermine the boundary between "fiction" and "nonfiction" filmmaking underlies other possibilities of mediation, especially in activist practices. The digital turn has been crucial in an evolving social activist movement in China. In it we see that the long-cultivated sense of *xianchang* ultimately lends itself to a commitment to an embodied cinema—once you grant that the filmmaker must be there, it is only a matter of time before he or she actively intervenes. This turn to activist filmmaking provides a perfect storm of new aesthetic, political, and ethical potential and challenge.

For example, the networking possibilities provided by new forms of digital circulation may face daunting state-controlled online censorship in China proper, but they nevertheless also create opportunities for both community-building at home and opening the way to transnational identifications with communities offshore. The filmmaking commitments of several directors whose works appear in this volume allow Buddhists (Pema Tseden in Barnett), Chinese Christians (Gan Xiao'er in Zito), LGBT activists (Cui Zi'en in Robinson), and human rights advocates (Ai Xiaoming and others in Zhang) to contribute to the making of grassroots communities while reaching out and finding transnational networks that exceed the bounds of the nation.

Luke Robinson stresses the importance of the digital transformations undergone by the corporeal drama of embodied sensuality in his chapter, "'To Whom Do Our Bodies Belong?' Being Queer in Chinese DV Documentary." Independently produced digital documentaries about the Chinese queer community have been available since the late 1990s. But the earliest documentaries represented homosexuals as on-screen spectacles, especially in the several accounts of drag queens, while the films themselves "performed" a theatricality so close to feature fiction that genres blurred. Robinson notes a shift, however, as ". . . these documentaries make use of the body of the queer performer to interrogate specific understandings of the digital in its Chinese context," specifically linking to the practice of *xianchang*, where, we have noted performance and embodiment have been central. Filmmakers who are themselves gay have moved beyond sympathetic portrayals of others' performances of queerness to incorporating themselves as queer members of a community through the very making of that community's shared media.

Robinson focuses on Fan Popo and David Cheng's *New Beijing, New Marriage* (*Xin Qianmen dajie*), Cui Zi'en's *Queer China, "Comrade" China* (*Zhi Tongzhi*), and the webcast *Queer Comrades* to demonstrate how contemporary queer nonfiction production embraces the "light" qualities of remediation and low impedance. In the process, he refashions the relationship of the Chinese queer community to visual representation. Robinson's rich account weaves between the specific aesthetic choices that allow for what he calls a shift in the metaphorical construction of queer male subjectivity in these works, where the function of representation ("inscription") gives over to participatory "incorporation" and sexuality as performance becomes identity as network.

In the final chapter, "Toward a Digital Political Mimesis: Aesthetic of Affect and Activist Video," Zhang Zhen identifies the activist turn or extension in independent documentary. She notes that many activist video works squarely fit within "engaged documentary" by virtue of their singularly sympathetic preoccupation with subaltern, marginal, or activist subjects—products of an unjust judicial system and contradiction-ridden social and political order. Yet they are also markedly different in terms of modes of production, distribution, spectatorial address, "authorship," and more. Building on Michael Renov's four-tiered template of documentary poetics, or "poesis as active making," Zhang stresses the power of affect and embodied emotion in most activist documentary. The various forms of "active making," especially in more playful forms that go "beyond pathos," offer building blocks for an emergent mode of perception and civic ethical discourse of rights aided by DV and its networks of dissemination.

Synthesizing the ideas of Jane Gaines and Philip Rosen on the "radical historicity" and affective power in traditional social documentary and digital hybridity, Zhang develops an experimental conceptual frame, *digital political mimesis*, to sharpen our understanding of political and activist videos produced in postsocialist China, as they circulate locally, transnationally, and virtually. She compares several key figures, such as Ai Xiaoming, Ai Weiwei, and Wu Wenguang, as well as works by other grassroots activists (such as Yang Lihong) or collectives. Zhang makes a strong case that activist documentary and citizen documentation are crucial components and extensions of new "structures of feeling." While part and parcel of the living experience and everyday struggle now increasingly taking place in cyberspace or mediated by new digital tools, the filmmakers and activists explore an evolving expressive form straddling and breaking the boundaries of old and new media and traditional and alternative film practices and institutions.

In Conclusion: Digital "In Dependence"

May Adadol Ingawanij and other contributors in *Glimpses of Freedom: Independent Cinema in Southeast Asia* explore the ambiguous usefulness of the ubiquitous category "independent cinema" in another global context. In her introduction, Ingawanij expands upon "the dialectics of independence," greatly enriching the term and pointing us along the way to a Chinese film culture that, since 1989, has moved in "directions away from 'underground' and toward semi-independence or 'in dependence.'"[15] In its original usage by Pickowicz and Zhang, the term rightly refers to a film scene that can never wholly escape the state in China to be wholly on its own, hence it is "in dependence" on the state. But the way that we are using the term here, taking our cue from Ingawanij, widens far beyond the government and the network of dependencies that have organically formed in China after the digital turn.

Indeed, at every turn we confront the irony that the digital, on the one hand, facilitates forms of radically *private* film production and audience habits of small-screen consumption while simultaneously linking up makers and consumers, curators and censors ever more swiftly into wider *publics*. These publics allow for speedier circulation of films made in digital video, more discussion, and quicker formations of public political and aesthetic discourses. While the personalization may provide a *sense of independence* (which, to be sure, has profound creative results), the spreading and tightening of networking surely bespeaks a growing *actual interdependence* among writers, directors, producers, distribution entrepreneurs, and audiences.

The digital turn seems to install itself precisely in this fruitful contradiction, allowing for hybridization, boundary breaking, and experimentations that are both socially and aesthetically distinctive. Digital video provides a particularly lucid example of how social life is constantly mediated into being through its materialization, even if that materiality is ironically, even maddeningly, ephemeral. Most of us have been involved in intensive curatorial collaboration with mainland Chinese alternative documentary participants (filmmakers, producers, curators, critics, scholars) for the past decade of its international "outbreak." We have found ourselves part of the "next round"—a post-digital round—of the emergence of Chinese "in-dependent" film into new publics. Finding ourselves part of the network we study has given us a keen sense of the profound connectedness fostered by digital capabilities in the world of exhibition, reception, and interpretation.

Notes

1. Zheng studied experimental film at the Art Institute of Chicago and then returned to his native Shanghai. He is the grandson of the late Huang Zuoling, the famous film and theater director, and the son of Huang Shuqin, a leading Fourth Generation female director. Before and after *DV China,* he made several narrative films.

2. The film belongs to the part of the new Chinese documentary that has state sponsorship and public broadcasting access. Independently conceived, the project was partly funded by China Film Group and the film was later shown on China Central Television in 2004. Its original Chinese title, *Yige nongmin daoyande shengya*, literally means "The Career of a Peasant Director." Zhang Zhen obtained a VHS tape of the film from the director during a research trip in Shanghai in Summer 2004.

3. Zheng Dasheng, *DV China* (DV China production log) http://www.douban.com/note/118929788/.

4. Tate bought eight million pieces of the porcelain seeds for its collection, about a tenth of the total (Kennedy 2012). For a video about the conception of the project and the installation of Ai Weiwei's *Sunflower Seeds* in the Tate Modern Turbine Hall in Mar. 2012, see http://www.youtube.com/watch?v=PueYywpkJW8.

5. As we finalize the manuscript, a new anthology, *China's iGeneration: Cinema and Moving Image Culture for the Twenty-First Century* (Johnson et al. 2014) has just been published. While its use of digital cinema seems broader and covers 3D and IMAX films as well as documentary and experimental film, our volume is informed by a rigorous historiographic framework and is more invested in alternative DV culture and its dynamic relationships to social and political transformations.

6. Chinese filmmakers and critics have taken issues with the term "movement" and pointed to the heterogeneous origins of the new documentary. See, for example, Wang Xiaolu's article from 2010.

7. "Poor images are the contemporary Wretched of the Screen, the debris of audiovisual production, the trash that washes up on the digital economies' shores. They testify to the violent dislocation, transferals, and displacement of images—their acceleration and circulation within the vicious cycles of audiovisual capitalism. Poor images are dragged around the globe as commodities or their effigies, as gifts or as bounty. They spread pleasure or death threats, conspiracy theories or bootlegs, resistance or stultification" (Steyerl 2009).

8. http://www.reelchina.net/index.html. The account that follows is written from the perspective of the editors. Dan Gao's chapter also discusses the role of Reel China in the festival circuit.

9. In 2006 and 2008, at Zhang Pingjie's suggestion, juries of academics and practitioners were formed to give three prizes in Shanghai. This seems to have led, in 2008, to a backlash among the mainland-based filmmakers who objected to REC Foundation's nonpayment of screening fees. There was a flap online and at that point the NYU team began producing its own curated versions of Reel China @NYU 5th Biennial (2010), Reel China @NYU 6th Biennial (2012), and Reel China @NYU 7th Biennial (2014), partnering with the Li Xianting Film Fund. The two teams now curate separately, and NYU pays screening fees directly to filmmakers. No prizes have been awarded since 2008.

10. One fruit of this process is a special issue of *Chinese Independent Cinema (Zhongguo duli yingxiang)* on independent documentaries, edited by Zhang Zhen (2013) and consisting of articles by us and several graduate students who participated in the seminar on the "Chinese independent documentary" taught in conjunction with the Reel China Biennial at NYU between 2008 and 2012.

11. Sniadecki uses David MacDougall's work on the "corporeal image" to make this point, though one could look in other places as well, to Vivian Sobchack, for example.

12. Zhang Zhen and Angela Zito provided extensive counsel and other tangible help to the organization at its inception and later on. dGenerate sold its catalog to Icarus Films in 2012.

13. Zito found Ilona Hongisto's idea of "documentary fabulation" from Deleuze useful. She quotes Deleuze, saying that "fabulation is the becoming of the real character when he himself starts to 'make fiction,' when he enters into the 'flagrant offense of making up legends' and so contributes to the invention of his people" (Hongisto 2011a; 2011b, 9).

14. *Caonima* is the phrase "f*ck your mother" that is written alternatively with the homophonic characters for grass, mud, and horse.

15. Taken from the preface to Pickowicz and Zhang (2006, vii).

Bibliography

Balcerzak, Scott, and Jason Sperb, eds. 2009. *Cinephilia in the Age of Digital Reproduction.* New York: Wallflower.

Berry, Chris, Lü Xinyu, and Lisa Rofel, eds. 2010. *The New Chinese Documentary Film Movement: For the Public Record.* Hong Kong: Hong Kong University Press.

Berry, Chris, and Lisa Rofel. 2010. "Alternative Archive: China's Independent Film Culture." In *The New Chinese Documentary Film Movement: For the Public Record,* edited by Chris Berry, Lü Xinyu, and Lisa Rofel, 135–157. Hong Kong: Hong Kong University Press.

Bordwell, David. 2012. *Pandora's Digital Box: Films, Files, and the Future of Movies.* http://www.davidbordwell.net/books/pandora.php.

Curtin, Michael. 2007. *Playing to the World's Biggest Audience: The Globalization of Chinese Film and TV.* Berkeley: University of California Press.

Dixon, Wheeler. 2013. *Streaming: Movies, Media, and Instant Access.* Lexington: University Press of Kentucky.

Friedberg, Anne. 2000. "The End of Cinema: Multimedia and Technological Change." In *Reinventing Film Studies,* edited by Christine Gledhill and Linda Williams, 438–452. London: Arnold.

Hansen, Miriam. 1991. *Babel and Babylon: Spectatorship in American Silent Film.* Cambridge, MA: Harvard University Press.

Hongisto, Ilona. 2011a. "Soul of the Documentary: Expression and the Capture of the Real." Unpublished PhD dissertation, University of Turku, Finland.

———. 2011b. "Documentary Fabulation and the Creation of Collectivity." Paper presented at Visible Evidence, New York University, New York, Aug. 11–14.

Ingawanij, May Adadol, and Benjamin McKay, eds. 2011. *Glimpses of Freedom: Independent Cinema in Southeast Asia.* Ithaca, NY: Southeast Asia Program Publications, Cornell University Press.

Jenkins, Henry. 2006. *Convergence Culture: Where Old and New Media Collide.* New York: New York University Press.

Jiang, Zhi 蒋志. 2004. "DV bushi shenma (ji qita)—Jiang Zhi ziji shuo DV不是什么（及其他—蒋志自己说" (DV is not something [and other things]—According to Jiang Zhi himself). In *Zhongguo duli jilupian dang'an* 中国独立纪录片档案 (Chinese Independent Documentary Archive), edited by Mei Bing 梅冰 and Zhu Jingjiang 朱靖江。. Shanxi shifan daxue chubanshe.

Johnson, Matthew, Keith B. Wagner, Kiki Tianqi Yu, and Luke Vulpiani, eds. 2014. *China's iGeneration: Cinema and Moving Image Culture for the Twenty-first Century.* London: Bloomsbury.

Kennedy, Maev. 2012. "Tate Buys Eight Million Ai Weiwei Sunflower Seeds." *The Guardian,* Mar. 5. http://www.theguardian.com/artanddesign/2012/mar/05/tate-ai-weiwei-sunflower-seeds.

Lü, Xinyu 吕新雨. 2003. *Jilu Zhongguo: Dangdai Zhongguo xinjilu yundong* 纪录中国：当代中国新纪录运动 (Documenting China: The New Documentary Movement in Contemporary China). Beijing: Sanlian shudian.

Ma, Ran 马然. 2012. *Lunji Zhongguo minjian dianyingjie* 论及中国民间独立电影节 (About Chinese Independent Film Festivals). *Zhongguo duli yingxiang* 中国独立影像 (Chinese Independent Cinema) 9. Beijing: Li Xianting Film Fund.

Nakajima, Seio. 2006. "Film Clubs in Beijing: The Cultural Consumption of Chinese Independent Films." In *From Underground to Independent: Alternative Film Culture in Contemporary China,* edited by Paul G. Pickowicz and Yingjin Zhang, 161–187. Lanham, MD: Rowman & Littlefield.

Nichols, Bill. 1992. *Representing Reality: Issues and Concepts in Documentary.* Bloomington: Indiana University Press.

Nornes, Abé Markus. 2009. "Bulldozers, Bibles, and Very Sharp Knives: The Chinese Independent Documentary Scene." *Film Quarterly* 63 (1): 50–55.

Palmer, Augusta. 2006. "Mainland Cinema: Public Square to Shopping Mall and the New Entertainment Film." In *Contemporary Asian Cinema,* edited by Anne Tereska Ciecko, 144–155. Oxford, New York: Berg.

Pickowicz, Paul G., and Yingjin Zhang, eds. 2006. *From Underground to Independent: Alternative Film Culture in Contemporary China.* Lanham, MD: Rowman & Littlefield.

Rees, A. L. 2011. *Expanded Cinema: Art, Performance, Film.* Tate Gallery Publications.

Robinson, Luke. 2010. "From 'Public' to 'Private': Chinese Documentary and the Logic of *Xianchang.*" In *The New Chinese Documentary Film Movement: For the Public*

Record, edited by Chris Berry, Lü Xinyu, and Lisa Rofel, 177–194. Hong Kong: Hong Kong University Press.

———. 2012. *Independent Chinese Documentary: From the Studio to the Street.* London: Palgrave Macmillan.

Rosen, Stanley. 2012. "Film and Society in China: The Logic of the Market." In *A Companion to Chinese Cinema,* edited by Yingjin Zhang, 197–217. Chichester, West Sussex: Blackwell.

Sklar, Robert. 1975/1994. *Movie-Made America: A Cultural History of American Movies.* New York: Vintage.

Steyerl, Hito. 2009. "In Defense of the Poor Image." *E-flux journal* 10 (Nov.). http://www.e-flux.com/journal/in-defense-of-the-poor-image/.

———. 2012. *The Wretched of the Screen.* New York: Sternberg.

Su Qiqi 苏七七. 2004. "Youzai jingzhong: ji Zheng Dasheng 犹在镜中：纪郑大圣" (In the Mirror: About Zheng Dasheng), Feb. 18. http://www.samdeha.appspot.com/t/29962.

Svensson, Marina. 2012. "Independent Documentary Film in China: The Birth of an Independent Documentary Film Industry." The 35th Gothenburg Film Festival Catalogue, 13–20.

Voci, Paola. 2010. *China on Video: Small-Screen Realities.* New York: Routledge.

Wang, Xiaolu 王小鲁. 2010. "Zhuti jianxian—20nian Zhongguo duli jilupian de guancha 主题渐显—20年中国独立纪录片的观察" (The Gradual Revelation of Subjectivity—Observations on 20 Years of Development in the Independent Documentary). *Dianying Yishu* 电影艺术 (Film Art) 6: 72–78.

Wang, Yiman. 2005. "The Amateur's Lightning Rod: DV Documentary in Postsocialist China." *Film Quarterly* 58 (4): 16–26.

Wu, Wenguang. 2002. "Just on the Road: A Description of the Individual Way of Recording Images in the 1990s." In *The First Guangzhou Triennial Catalogue, Reinterpretation: A Decade of Experimental Chinese Art* (1900–2000), edited by Wu Hung et al., 132–138. Guangdong Museum of Art.

Yang, Guobin. 2009. *The Power of the Internet in China: Citizen Online Activism.* New York: Columbia University Press.

Youngblood, Gene. 1970. *Expanded Cinema.* New York: Dutton.

Zhang, Xianmin 张献民 and Zuo Jing 左靖. 2012. "Yishu yundong cunzai ma? 艺术运动存在吗" (Does an Art Movement Exist?). *Yingxiang zhongde Zhongguo dangdai yishu* 影像中的中国当代艺术 (Chinese contemporary art in moving image). Indie Screening Alliance of Art Space, screening season two, pamphlet.

Zhang, Zhen. 2007. "Introduction: Bearing Witness: Chinese Cinema in the Era of Transformation (*Zhuanxing*)." In *The Urban Generation: Chinese Cinema and Society at the Turn of the Twenty-first Century,* edited by Zhang Zhen, 1–45. Durham, NC: Duke University Press.

Zhang Zhen 张真, ed. 2013. Special issue on independent documentary. *Zhongguo duli yingxiang* 中国独立影像 (Chinese Independent Cinema) 12 (Aug.). Beijing: Li Xianting Film Fund.

Zheng Dasheng 郑大圣. n.d. *DV China* Hanghai rizhi (xuanzhai) 航海日志（选摘） (DV China production log–excerpts). http://www.douban.com/note/118929788/.

Zito, Angela. 2008. "Culture." In *Keywords in Religion, Media and Culture,* edited by David Morgan, 69–82. New York: Routledge.

PART ONE

Ethical and Political Stakes

CHAPTER 1

Marking the Body

The Axiographics of the Visible Hidden Camera

ABÉ MARK NORNES

One of the most exciting documentary scenes on the planet has appeared in the People's Republic of China. One reason is that there is no lack of compelling subject matter. The scale of the problems and transformations facing this society are consonant with the vastness of the geographical space the filmmakers work within. Just as important is the stance these filmmakers take in the face of the historical world. It is a place where anything goes, and filmmakers clearly believe they can do anything. No holds barred. Nothing will hold them back, even if they possess only the most rudimentary of skill sets for making films, or if they have little knowledge of or access to the long history of the documentary form.

In such a situation, it comes as no surprise that some filmmakers cross discomforting boundaries. This is, after all, the point. One of the most exciting aspects of contemporary Chinese documentary is the fact that it operates in an authoritarian national space where state power is exerted across a set of spectra of geography, class, occupation, and subject matter. On this complex ideological terrain, these filmmakers and their exhibitors confront line after line laid down by the state, readily stepping right over and forging ahead to capture their personal vision on video.

Most of these taboos are constructs imposed by the government and most of them deserve challenge by the filmmakers—someone has to do it. Admirable though this is, other lines they cross relate to notions such as privacy, informed consent, and other issues that are more ethical than political. This chapter attempts to delineate some of these problems through historical comparison and a set of revealing examples. It conducts what Bill Nichols called "axiographics" in *Representing Reality*. This involves an inquiry into the ethical stances filmmakers take when they enter the historical world, camera in hand, to render real people (or animals) in moving image media. Nichols argues they also inscribe their ethics into the representation itself, in every camera angle, cut, or sound recording. He writes,

> How do the visual representations of the camera place the filmmaker in relation to the historical world? The presence (and absence) of the filmmaker in the image, in off-screen space, in the acoustic folds of voice-on and voice-off, in titles and graphics, constitute an ethics, and a politics, of considerable importance to the viewer. Axiographics extends those classic tropes of ethical debate—the nature of consent; proprietary rights to the recorded images; the right to know vs. the right to privacy; the responsibilities of the filmmaker to his or her subject as well as audience, or employer; codes of conduct and the complexities of legal recourse—to include the ethical implications conveyed by the representations of time and space itself. (Nichols 1992, 77)

Nichols poses this as a challenge to spectators as much as to filmmakers themselves. When the lights dim on a movie theater, the audience comes into relation with the time and space of other sentient beings, both human and animal. The filmmaker has taken a stance in that historical space, a positionality that is rendered graphically and sonically in the anterior space of the movie theater. Nichols argues that as spectators, we must ask ourselves how a given filmmaker has "acquitted" him- or herself in the face of the historical world and consider what ethics or politics adheres to this moving image representation. This is because we in turn adhere to the filmmaker's look on the historical world.

This chapter examines the axiographics of Chinese documentary, paying special attention to the films made in the style of direct cinema—which is to say, the majority of them. Its approach is analytical, historical, and comparative. The comparisons are mainly between China and Japan, which has been both a site of discovery and a sounding board for documentary praxis on the continent. It begins in the mountains of Yamagata, with Asia's first documentary film festival. It was here that the first Chinese documentarists encountered two titans of the documentary: Frederick Wiseman and Ogawa Shinsuke. I wish to think through the implications of the situational differences between Japan and China and their consequences for creative praxis, particularly when it comes to ethical concerns. What happens when an independent documentary film culture appears out of thin air, with little sense of history (with no common sense, as it were)? What happens when it then conceptualizes documentary primarily as a (creative?) process in opposition to an oppressive mainstream—yet disregards questions of distribution and reception? There are some vexing ethical conundrums linked to these conditions. We can tease them out through another comparison, this between the double-edged impact these two foreign filmmakers have had on the Chinese independent film scene. This approach will prepare us to explore the axiographics of the present-day scene through three compelling films. We will find that these renegade filmmakers too often reproduce the intrusive politics they are so intent on fighting.

But first to Japan.

Japan/China—Ogawa/Wiseman

Ask a Chinese filmmaker about the documentarists they admire and the answer is inevitably Wiseman and Ogawa. All this started in Japan in 1991. Ogawa Shinsuke hit their radar when Wu Wenguang brought his first film to the 1991 Fukuoka Asian Film Festival (in August) and the Yamagata International Documentary Film Festival (in October). This was the first outing for the Fukuoka festival, and Yamagata, the lone documentary film festival in Asia, was issuing only its second edition. The first was in 1989, when there were no Chinese documentary filmmakers working outside of official media (they did invite fiction filmmaker Tian Zhuangzhuang, but he was prevented from attending in the wake of the Tiananmen Square incident). Between the two festivals, Wu and feature film director Peng Xiaolian were invited to Ogawa Productions on three or four occasions. After each screening, Ogawa would sit down with them to chat. Wu was enchanted by Ogawa's famous charisma and his enthusiasm for Chinese documentary's future. Ogawa was a consummate cheerleader, and Wu left charged up and with luggage filled with VHS tapes of several Ogawa films.

We can pinpoint Wiseman's entrance onto the Chinese documentary scene even more precisely. Wu returned to the next Yamagata festival in 1993 with Duan Jinchuan and Hao Zhiqiang in tow. Unfortunately, Ogawa had passed away after the previous festival; however, his influence continued to be felt by all subsequent festival participants. But Wiseman was there to present *Zoo* (1993). Here is the moment of contact as described by intellectual historian Akiyama Tamako, who served as the Chinese interpreter attached to the three directors. She accompanied them to the screening of *Zoo* and describes what happened after the film:

> No sooner had the lights gone up than someone behind me suddenly began shaking my shoulder. "Oi! Tamako! Did you see that!?" Wu, speaking faster than ever, raised his voice in excitement. Slightly taken aback, I mustered my best Chinese and said, "Um, well, it was a strange film. It's a zoo, with nothing out of the ordinary. Yet both the people and the animals feel like they are part of a single system . . ." This drew a winking smile from Wu. "Oh, you were watching closely, weren't you? I wondered if you were sleeping," he said with an air of satisfaction, and then stood up. When we left the confusion of

> spectators in the theater, it was dark out. Rejoining each other on the street outside the theater, the three Chinese directors were itching to talk about the film they had just seen. The evening air of Yamagata had started to feel chilly, but their faces were flushed and slightly sweaty. Wu Wenguang, Duan Jinchuan, and Hao Zhiqiang stepped on each other's sentences in excitement, striding through the evening darkness like a herd of buffalo—me chasing behind them, trying to keep up. After that screening, Chinese documentary filmmakers came to line up Frederick Wiseman next to Ogawa Shinsuke when they spoke of the directors they particularly admired. (Nornes 2014, 256–257)

Wu went home after the 1993 film festival with yet another armload of videotapes, which included the works of both Wiseman and Ogawa. He held intimate screenings in his Beijing apartment for friends, many of whom were equally startled by both filmmakers' work. They started making their own films, and most of this work took the form of direct cinema. For whatever reason, only a few took Ogawa to heart.

When we consider these two filmmakers, the fact that they are mentioned in the same breath as the foundation for Chinese documentary seems rather perplexing. Ogawa predicated his cinema on a deep identification with his subjects, which were almost always groups of people. The films were the product of years of study and, more importantly, *intimacy* with their subjects. Furthermore, he favored a collective production mode and never once worked alone. He even lived with his crew, who lived with their subjects. Their cinema was conceptualized as one collective representing another . . . for yet another (the audience). Significantly, when queried about their "film movement," the Ogawa Productions filmmakers assumed they were being asked about *distribution* and not the point of production. For example, when he left the PR company Iwanami, the first thing Ogawa did was build a collective called the Independent Screening Organization (*Jishu Joei Soshiki no Kai*, or Jieiso for short). They created a network of sites across Japan that could step around the mainstream film circuit, which locked out independent producers. This organization eventually turned into Ogawa Productions in 1968. Ogawa saw production, distribution, and exhibition as inextricably linked. At a fundamental level, these links were *conceptual*: this was about creating a new human who was a social being, and they theorized a mimetic relationship on the part of the spectator vis-à-vis the historical actors on-screen. Also, the links were *practical*: 16mm production was remarkably expensive and required a steady flow of donations and ticket sales from the reception context to ensure the continuity of the collective and, by extension, the social movements they took part in.[1]

Wiseman, in contrast, may work with crews but they are anonymous and he presents himself as the lone filmmaker and subject of his praxis. He took on this appearance from the beginning of his career, when the other high-profile direct cinema outfit was Drew Associates. Subsequently, most of the other major figures working in this style were in partnerships: Albert and David Maysles, D. A. Pennebaker and Chris Hegedus, or Joe Berlinger and Bruce Sinofsky. Wiseman also pays close attention to the issue of distribution. He is well known as a crafty businessman and keeps the strictest of holds on the distribution of his work. For example, before the age of DVDs he sold exhibition rights to the education market only for the short term, later recharging at a new rate adjusted for inflation (in both the economic and cultural capital senses). Now exhibition rates are linked to expensive library sales. While he does enjoy wide theatrical distribution for his films, it is likely that theatrical and festival screenings essentially function as PR for television sales around the world. Wiseman has been the most obstinate proponent of the direct cinema style. He never appears in the films, and there are few gestures in the films to his presence. He spends enough time with his subjects for them to disregard his presence, but takes leave of them upon the completion of the film.

While most Chinese documentarists follow Wiseman in lock-step, Ogawa did make his mark on a handful of filmmakers, at least when it comes to developing and maintaining intimate relationships to the subject and devoting oneself to long-term study. Prominent examples are Feng Yan (*Bing'Ai* 2007), Zhao Liang (*Petition* 2009), Cong Feng (*Dr. Ma's Country Clinic* 2008), Mao Chenyu (*I Have What? Chinese Peasants War: The Rhetoric to Justice* 2013), and Gu Tao (*Yuguo and His Mother* 2011).[2] However, starting with the film Duan Jinchuan and Zhang Yuan made immediately after Yamagata—*The Square* (1993)—it is Wiseman who informed the documentary practice that was swiftly spreading across China. The overwhelming majority of films are in direct cinema style, eschewing voice-over narration, intertitles, and obtrusive editing. They avoid argumentation and work hard to reproduce the time and space of history, rendering the very present filmmaker rhetorically absent. They conceive of their work as personal and individual, and their technical tools enable them to work alone. Finally, they promote and distribute their films themselves.

On this last point, there are differences from Wiseman that have profound consequences, precisely because the situation on the ground today is remarkably similar to the one that Japanese filmmakers like Ogawa and Tsuchimoto Noriaki confronted in the early 1960s. Unlike Wiseman, the Chinese filmmakers do not enjoy well-developed circulation systems for their films. There are no distribution companies, and television is not an option. It is mostly unclear where films can be shown publicly, aside from a handful of domestic festivals and a ragtag collection of galleries, bars, and cafes. And unlike Ogawa, none of the filmmakers seized the opportunity of this vacuum to build a distribution network from the ground up. This leaves the Chinese directors on their own.

What happens in a situation where a documentary film culture appears so suddenly in the vacuum created by propagandistic nonfiction media, and then conceptualizes documentary primarily as an individual, creative process in opposition to an oppressive mass media—disregarding the question of distribution and reception? This is the question to which I will turn in the remainder of this chapter.

The Visible Hidden Camera

That there is a connection between the lack of a distribution system and documentary practice is evidenced by the remarkable length of so many films. We may treat this in a symptomatic fashion, as an index of their larger production context. It is possible in the first place because there are no distributors or exhibitors breathing down their backs, demanding short running times for the sake of profit. Indeed, the filmmakers are proud that they calculate the proper running times of their films with profit extracted from the equation. At the same time, it indicates that they are also making those calculations without consideration of the audience. This is about their vision and what the film supposedly requires—and by "film" they mean production, a creative practice cut off from reception. That is to say, they operate with a conception of documentary utterly different than that of Ogawa Shinsuke.

In the rest of the world, lengthy documentaries are almost always conceived for televisual distribution. Ken Burns and Wiseman are exemplary in this regard. When these filmmakers began distributing their films on television, the running times swiftly expanded to multi-night affairs. Other long-form documentaries tend to be about impossibly huge topics (e.g., *The Sorrow and the Pity* 1969, *Shoah* 1985). Ogawa's films also became longer and longer over the course of his career, even though he never had access to television; however, it is significant that this happened only when the student movement came to an end and his independent distribution system disintegrated. This case only proves my point: in the absence of pressure from the distribution/reception context, running times tend to soar.

Outside of these examples, filmmakers generally avoid long running times because distributors will not touch the work, spectators fall asleep, and cultural conventions inform their sense of "proper" running times. As a consequence, every filmmaker struggles with the pain of cutting hard-won scenes to achieve the most powerful shape and length for their work. However, Chinese documentary filmmakers do not struggle over this; they keep everything. I am a fan of long-form documentary, but I can think of few Chinese films that deserve running times over 120 minutes. The length of Chinese documentaries is mainly a sign of a lack of rigor (Wiseman's photography is pedestrian, but his editing is masterful) and a narcissistic concentration on the production to the exclusion of reception.

More importantly, ignoring the reception context enables the Chinese filmmakers adopting the direct cinema approach to think outside of ethical responsibilities as they walk into the historical world with camera in hand. They devote their energies to reproducing the time and space of the profilmic scene with remarkably little regard for the people they encounter. This is probably one attraction of the direct cinema approach, because it hardly demands filmmakers to think too hard about what they are doing. Everything can be for the sake of the film. (In contrast, the filmmakers following Ogawa's example follow their subjects over the long term, developing respectful—and thus "contractual"—relationships that demand thinking from the other's position, and thus tapping into other kinds of power.)[3]

We can tease out the implications of all this by considering the poster for the 2010 Songzhuang Film Festival, which was designed by film director Wang Wo. It symbolizes the situation in Chinese documentary, and not in entirely conscious ways. The poster features a weathered pole ornamented with a collection of surveillance cameras pointing this way and that. A traditional tiled roof ornaments the background. The poster has an attractive red-orange palette, and Wang has given a worn look to the image with virtual defects and scratches. The sheer number of cameras on this single pole is striking and initially grabs one's attention; however, the eye eventually strays from this dominant feature to the bottom corner and notices a very famous forehead edging its way into the photograph. It is Mao, and this is Tiananmen Square. The overt meaning of the poster is clear. Above and beyond the comment on state surveillance, the filmmakers represented at Songzhuang are renegades. Their cameras are aboveboard and about capturing reality as it is, not exerting power over behavior to mold the world into a preconceived vision or ideology.

This poster made me wonder about the camera in the hands of independent filmmakers. In an ideal sense, their camera is identical to Wiseman's: these are films about institutions where life is caught "unawares," as if what happens there would have taken place whether or not the camera was present. The conventional trope we use to describe this direct cinema approach is the "fly on the wall." The filmmaker remains so discreet and out-of-the-way that his or her subjects stop noticing the camera and act "naturally." This stance would allow the filmmakers to capture the *reality* of China, which has never been recorded on moving-image media before. The aim is to capture the behavior of subjects as though a camera were not present; the only gaze these

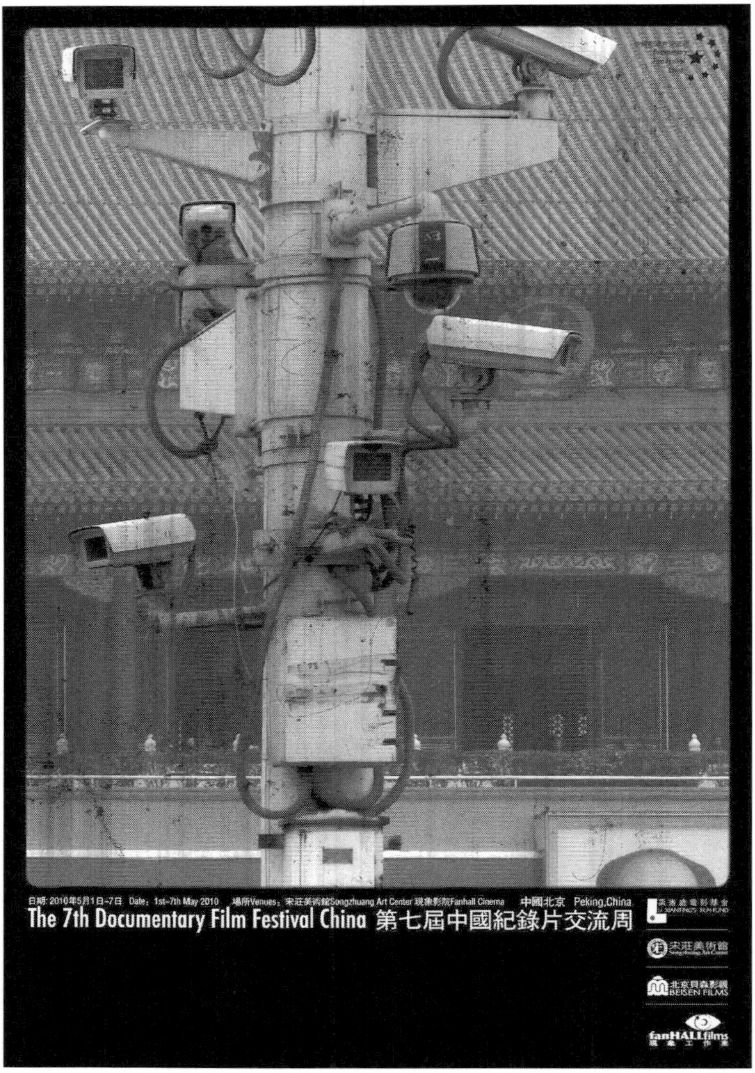

Figure 1.1. Poster for the Songzhuang film festival: they surveil the state, hiding their cameras in the black margins. (courtesy of Wang Wo)

subjects deal with is that of the state, and if anything is the main theme of the independent documentary it is precisely that. And this is, indeed, the effect of these films. It explains why so many scholars of China have gravitated to the documentary, and also why their work tends to be focused resolutely on text over context.

However, there is another way to read this poster from Songzhuang's film festival. The black frame and the photograph it contains express two ends of a spectrum within Chinese moving-image culture. When I look at that poster, I see the vague contours of the Songzhuang documentarists themselves—*their cameras*—built into its structure. Their camera is the frame, that black edge that (very visibly) attempts to hide from view yet organizes the structure and meaning of the image. The surveillance camera must be seen, or its omnipresence must be assumed, in order to have the desired effect: the exertion of power over and control of behavior, and the internal installation of the state's gaze. In contrast, the camcorders of independent documentary hide in the pitch black of that poster's frame. Out in the real world, those camcorders may be visible, but the point is for the filmmakers to behave as though they are invisible. Unless one is looking to the margin and thinking about the black border, the contrivances of the filmmakers, their framing, goes unnoticed.

Ideally, these filmmakers would be hidden . . . and, in fact, they are. Theirs is the "visible hidden camera." This is not "fly on the wall" cinema, but rather the cinema of the hidden camera. And that hidden camera is, ironically enough, visible to all. It explains the extraordinarily "natural" scenes these filmmakers manage to capture. Yet acknowledging the camera's paradoxical *visible invisibility* draws our attention to the relations of power that this cinema generally disavows, and a set of discomforting ethical issues emerges for both filmmakers and viewers.

We can most easily draw out the implications of the visible hidden camera by investigating how it pivots around (real) human bodies. It is in his discussion of the body where Nichols' axiographics provides powerful footing for thinking about the Chinese documentary and the treatment of its subjects. Nichols introduces two powerful terms as the basis for axiographics: magnitude and vivification. Documentaries are always at pains to point beyond themselves to the historical world where, as Fredric Jameson suggests, there is hurt. One cannot reduce nonfiction film to mere textuality because it is always about the world we live in. And no matter how "direct" an approach filmmakers take, there will always be an ample measure of excess—a magnitude of historical excess that the film can only hope to gesture to. A fundamental question for filmmakers is how to use the tools of cinema to achieve a representation of the historical world that is adequate to the magnitude we sense living in it.

"The issue of magnitude," writes Nichols, "involves a tension between the representation and the represented as experienced by the viewer" (Nichols 1992, 232). Without this tension, we are no longer dealing with documentary but rather a fictive world of fantasies. Vivification refers to the ways that filmmakers evoke the emotional, experiential, and visceral within that gap between representation and the historical world. Through vivification, they "render *felt* what representations only allude to" (Nichols 1992, 234). Some filmmakers make overt use of cinematic techniques to accomplish this. Interesting, if overt, examples might include the work of Errol Morris or Stan Brakhage. However, direct cinema filmmakers downplay form to call our attention to the object plane, the historical world itself.

Chinese direct cinema adherents would seem to benefit from China itself. It is such a vast place—geographically, culturally, linguistically. The Chinese documentaries display an incredible variety of landscapes, many of which are epic in scale. Visual and aural difference is inherently spectacular, from the clothes people wear and the food they eat to the subtitled dialects they communicate in. One palpably senses the magnitude of China in these films' direct and simple imagery, seemingly rendering the imperative of vivification moot.

While the enormity of China itself may make it easy for China's documentary filmmakers to give their simple, direct cinema films the weight of history, this could not be enough. Otherwise, the documentaries would amount to little more than travelogues. The other, crucial, added ingredient is violence. Many of these films center on the brutality of the state, scenes of abject poverty, personal viciousness, or the cruelty of indifference. Occasionally, there is also the violence of our intrusion into the personal zones of history. We can get a handle on this by focusing on how these filmmakers treat the human body—how we experience the historical, human body. Nichols writes,

> Documentary film insists on the presence of the body. It exerts a relentless demand of *habeas corpus*. Like the legal system, documentary discourse insists on the principle that we must be presented with the body. Witness and testimony, deposition and refutation, accusation and denial—all depend on direct encounter and physical presence. The cinema in general cannot leave the incarnation of characters or social actors to the viewer's imagination. An indexical bond prevails between the photographic image of the human body and the more abstract concept of historical or narrative agency . . . a photographic likeness offers evidence of a life as it was lived and experienced in the flesh, within the constraints of the historical, physical body itself. And yet that likeness in and of itself is insufficient evidence. It is but a frozen moment, an artifact, that requires the animating force of time, narrative and history to gain experiential meaning. An *awareness* of the tension between representation and that which is represented, of magnitudes beyond representation, is the foundation for praxis informed by a text.
>
> (Nichols 1992, 233)

It is our recognition of the mortality of the human body—our cognizance of those organs grinding away inside us—that is the ultimate stuff of magnitude. When we watch a documentary we assume the referent is as fragile as us. What filmmakers "do" is emplace the bodies of their subjects in the paradoxes, conflicts, and contradictions of an historical moment. "The body is the battle site of contending values and their ends," asserts Nichols, and the formations of that battle are embodied in the sum of technical and formal choices the filmmakers have made in the course of production (Nichols 1992, 238). The choices are written into the fabric of the film. It is our responsibility as viewers to consider how the filmmakers conduct themselves, particularly considering how these particular documentarists deploy a camera that is visible, yet somehow hidden, from the historical actors before them.

How does the visible hidden camera work? First, it is predicated on the nonexistence of a distribution system for independent documentary. One curious scene from Du Haibin's *1428* (2009) reveals the nature of the profilmic scene of the Chinese documentary. A woman approaches the filmmakers and asks, "Are you filming for the government or yourself?" Without missing a beat the filmmaker answers, "For ourselves." Du Haibin may have been speaking for the entire community of Chinese documentary filmmakers; as I will argue, too many will do anything for the sake of their films. The image world of China is either official or it is thoroughly private. It is either broadcast television or home video. Those are the only options Du's interrogator can imagine; Du is neither, but he does not enlighten her regarding his more public intentions. Without distribution through companies or television, only a select and very small community among the billion are aware that an independent documentary exists. This means that unless a filmmaker reveals his or her intentions, the subjects have no idea their lives are headed toward international distribution and the accumulation of capital—cultural and sometimes monetary. After all, the filmmakers are rarely working in crews, and camcorders are now ubiquitous consumer products embedded in the fabric of daily life. They look no different than anyone else shooting home movies. Since the filmmakers generally aren't given tutorials on the history of documentary, and they hardly look like TV crews, the subjects of these films are oblivious to what is going on. The camcorders may be visible, but these secret motives render the cameras invisible.

This is as close to capturing "life unawares" as is imaginable, and surely one of the reasons the films are so powerful. It is roughly analogous to the shooting conditions of the ethnographic film before consumer video penetrated the village and experiments in self-representation, most famously the various projects with the Amazonian Kayapo, called attention to the ethics and politics of ethnographic capture and exhibition. The Chinese documentary offers a similar scene, and by pushing the "camera" from the blackness of that frame into the light we can see an array of prickly ethical implications that rarely get aired. In the remainder of this chapter, I wish to explore some of these issues through three quite revealing films: *Wheat Harvest* (2008), *Toxicosis* (2010), and *Martian Syndrome* (*Huoxing yao zonghezheng* 2009). These films each pivot around the treatment of bodies in space and thus lend themselves to an investigation of the axiographics of Chinese documentary.

However, before that, it is worth noting we are mainly dealing with the filmmakers that have stepped into the legacy of Wiseman here. The filmmakers that admire Ogawa work aboveboard. They develop long-term relationships with their subjects, who are collaborators and not merely objects of the camera's gaze. For example, the people that appear in films like Zhao Liang's *Petition* (2009), Feng Yan's *Bing'Ai* (2007), or Xu Xin's *Karamay* (2010) clearly understand what these films are about. They are collaborations and this, along with the virtues of long-term relationship building, is an important source of their power. Indeed, Ogawa and his collaborators used a hidden camera in one early film and then renounced the practice. The film was called *Forest of Oppression* (*Assatsu no mori* 1967), and the scene involved a member telling a leader that he wanted to quit. It was a delicate situation, so the filmmakers shot the scene from outside the room with a telephoto lens. Cameraman Otsu Koshiro explains what happened after that.

> Later on when the rushes were done the staff were all holding their heads saying, "We shouldn't have done it like this . . ." I think Ogawa and Tsuchimoto both stopped using "hidden camera" techniques after that. That was some pretty bitter medicine, to be honest. There was a debate over whether or not to use the shot, but in the end we did use it. It was a strange shot. Let's say we had a camera here with us as we're talking, with a cameraman to do the shooting. If there is no mutual trust—not necessarily a contract, but an agreement with the person being photographed that there will be a camera present—we probably shouldn't be filming. The problem is whether or not that question was considered, and in this case it wasn't. We weren't serious enough about building a relationship between the camera and the subject. (Nornes 2007, 81)

Borrowing Otsu's term, we could say that the direct cinema directors of China are not serious enough. Furthermore, anyone appearing before an Ogawa Productions camera knew precisely how the film was going to be shown, whether they were farmers, students, or riot police. It is clear this is not the case for the majority of the people appearing in Chinese documentaries—the subjects of these films shot with perfectly visible hidden cameras.

Consider *Toxicosis*, a competently made record of the traffic at the Manhai Border Post on the China-Burma border funded by the Busan International Film Festival's Asian Network of Documentary (AND) Fund. The post is the primary setting of the film; it essentially serves as a customs and immigration station with interrogation rooms and a jail. Director Wang Baochun was originally a television producer, although the film is in the direct cinema style and contains content that could probably not be broadcast in China. Presumably because of his connections to official television, Wang is granted extraordinary access to the police. They seem to allow the filmmaker to shoot freely in the jail and interrogation chambers. Although the police here surely deal with all sorts of crime, Wang is interested in drug trafficking and concentrates primarily on three women who have been arrested. One is an older mother of nine who was caught carrying and is interrogated at length. Her scenes are intercut with two young women who were smuggling heroin and are awaiting trial in a holding cell. Wang shoots their conversations through a barred window.

The indisputable climax of the film arrives when two new female suspects are led into the station for questioning. The scene starts like any other in the film and then takes a nasty turn. Suspicious that one of the women is carrying heroin in her body, the police insert a camera in her vagina to investigate. Seeing strange shapes that shouldn't be there, they subject her to a full body cavity search—which the filmmaker shows in its entirety.

Two policewomen force the woman onto the floor and pin her down. The position puts the suspect's head at the feet of the cameraman. One policewoman holds the woman on the ground as the other pulls up her dress, reaches inside her vagina, and starts pulling out bag after bag of heroin. The scene is shocking and slightly chaotic, and after tossing ten bags next to her head the police demand to know how many she inserted. The woman tilts her head to count the pile as if to stop the attack, but they push her face back to prevent her from looking. Not satisfied with her answer, they reach in and pull out more bags.

At first glance, this might remind one of Zhao Liang's *Crime and Punishment* (*Zui yu fa* 2007). This kind of torture and rape would seem to be such a normalized interaction between police and citizenry that the officials don't think twice about letting someone film it. How else to explain the photography of such brutality? Indeed, the parading of criminals being punished is something of a genre in news programming on Chinese television. Since we come to these films with some sense of individual rights vis-à-vis the state, we are aghast at the treatment of suspects and prisoners. This is certainly the position from which Zhao shot *Crime and Punishment*, a position that becomes crystal clear at the end of the film when he awkwardly inserts Christian imagery as a symbol of hope that is incapable of being coopted by the state. Likewise, his audience at the Songzhuang festival shouted at the screen in uncontrollable anger. However, the axiographics of Wang's *Toxicosis* are, thanks to his use of the visible hidden camera, exceedingly vague.

Nichols' description of axiographics argues that a filmmaker's ethics are inscribed in the representation of time and space on-screen. The body cavity search hints at Wang's positioning in relation to the historical world—in relation to these historical beings he photographs. In the course of the search, as the woman screams and cries for help, the director makes two revealing edits. Apparently dissatisfied with his mise-en-scène, the director cuts to circle the woman's body forty-five degrees. After a moment, this view is evidently inadequate, and the director cuts once again to move another forty-five degrees to the woman's feet. (In all probability, this was one long shot orbiting the woman's body, with the camera moves expunged by the edits. Perhaps that was "too much"?) Now he is finally able to shoot straight up the woman's spread legs as the officer penetrates and fishes around her vagina. Finally, when the rape is over, he offers what might be a site for mimetic identification for the spectator: the officer that did the dirty work bends over and vomits violently on the floor. Suddenly (finally?) self-conscious at being filmed, she flees the building and bends over a barrel in the courtyard to vomit more—Wang's visible hidden camera running after her the entire way.

One imagines a couple lines of defense for the inclusion of this scene. First, it did, after all, *happen*. The whole point of direct cinema is to show life as it is, as if the camera were never present in the first place. This is an important part of life for both suspects and guards on the border. It happened to take place while the filmmaker was present, so he shot it. Secondly, one could assert it is an event that *should not* be elided, considering the violence of the act (and perhaps even the official's nonchalant willingness to allow its filming—by a male director no less). As I mentioned previously, the screening of *Crime and Punishment* actually incited angry shouting at every blow of the police when shown in Songzhuang, and it is easy to imagine a similar reaction to this film. Spectators might greet the scene with anger; however, the axiographics of the scene undermine a claim on the director's part that he had an ethical responsibility to shoot and include this violent act. That is because of all the ways he could have rendered the incident—aurally, through voice-over narration, with a carefully written intertitle, or even retreating to a long shot, or simply looking the other way—he chose to get a "better view." The camera's 180-degree pivot around the woman's body gives the film a revolting ambivalence; it remains ambivalent precisely because of the absence of context in the direct cinema style. Of the viewing positions available—independent exposé of state violence or official televisual spectacle of criminals being punished—either seems possible.

Although an excessive example, *Toxicosis* provides us with two basic lessons. First, it invites us to ask direct cinema filmmakers about their relationships to their subjects, because they so often seem incapable of affiliating with others in compromised situations. Secondly, it reveals the way axiographics typically revolve around representations of the body. *Toxicosis* is an extreme example of the tendency of Chinese direct cinema films to concentrate on discomforting situations of personal exposure of one sort or another; but there are countless films showing people living amidst abject poverty. Many center on lives spinning spectacularly out of control because of alcoholism and mental illness. Before engaging more ethical considerations, it is important to first recognize how cinematic treatments of the corporeal *function* in direct cinema, for the impressive reality effect of this style is deeply connected to how human bodies are rendered in the time and space of the documentary.

It may be useful to bring English-language reality television in as a foil. This is because there are special moments in reality television where the palpable artifice of the situations that the "actors" have been inserted in falls away and something overwhelmingly real infuses the show. These are usually scenes featuring turbulent emotions, people in the throes of one passion or another. Laura Grindstaff has likened these moments to the "money shot" of hard-core pornography. For her, the money shot of reality television is where

> joy, sorrow, rage, or remorse [are] expressed in visible, bodily terms. It is the moment when tears well up in a woman's eyes and her voice catches in sadness and pain as she describes having lost her child to a preventable disease; when a man tells his girlfriend that he's been sleeping with another woman and her jaw drops in rage and disbelief. . . . These moments have become the hallmark of the genre, central to its claim to authenticity as well as to its negative reputation. According to producers, the more emotional and volatile the guests and audience members, the more real (and the more "ordinary") they are. . . . Like the orgasmic cum shot of pornographic films, the money shot of talk shows makes visible the precise moment of letting go, of losing control, of surrendering to the body and its "animal" emotions. It is the loss of the "civilized" self that occurs when the body transcends social and cultural control. (Grindstaff 2002, 19–20)

There are countless moments like this in the independent Chinese documentary. One entire subgenre where bodies often lose emotional control is the rubble film, where people protest land expropriation to make way for national modernization. Some films have money shots that remain the durable images of the films. After watching Gu Tao's *Aoluguya . . . Aoluguya* (2007), the very title evokes the memory of the main character wasted on liquor and completely incapable of controlling her body. Or there is the final, insane dance of the mentally handicapped

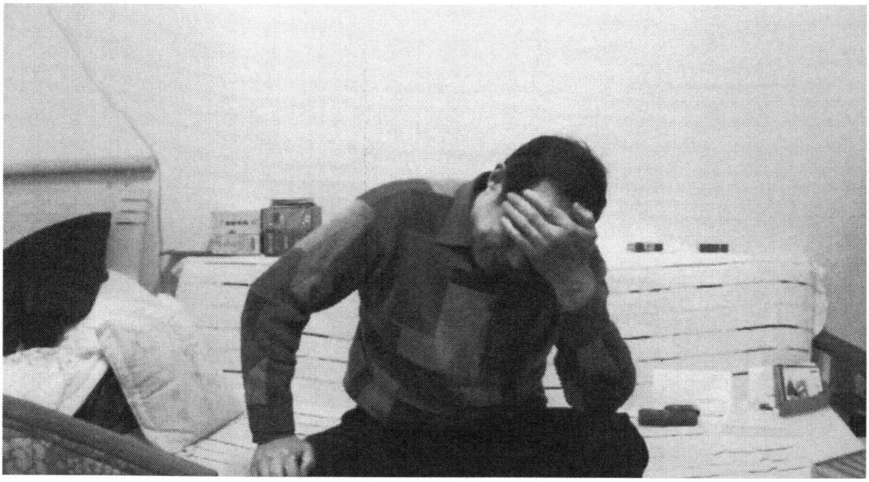

Figure 1.2. *Karamay*. Money shot: Xu Xin strings together parent after parent, sitting on similar couches telling similarly heartbreaking stories about losing their children in a school fire.

man in *Survival Song* (Yu Guangyi, 2008), his seizure-like movement seemingly purging the pressures of the world. It is precisely at these moments where the authenticity of the sober direct cinema style is guaranteed.

Furthermore, it's not always a money shot. Direct cinema also has its meat shot, which is not so much an analogue of the hard-core trope as a variation. For example, director He Yuan literally shoots *Apuda* (2011) with a surveillance camera. Unlike other direct cinema directors, he seems to be something of a formalist. Much of the film is shot in a small one-room home in the Burma and Tibet borderlands. Apuda is a dirt-poor farmer and his father lies on his deathbed; Apuda's bed sits on the other side of the room. The 145-minute film patiently follows the father's inexorable slide toward death. Most of the film is shot from one of two corners of the tiny room, using unwavering forty-five-degree angles on each bed. The director clearly set up the camera, hit record, and left the home. This surveillance camera style has its own strong reality effect, but there is also the moment when the father struggles mightily to sit up in bed. His robes fall open and out pops his penis.

This wasn't the first meat shot in Chinese documentary. The most famous is probably Wang Bing's 2013 *Till Madness Do Us Part* (*Feng ai*), one of the most ethically dubious films of the independent Chinese documentary. Before this, his *West of the Tracks* (*Tiexi qu* 2003) had already featured full frontal male nudity, including shower scenes. *In Till Madness Do Us Part,* Wang constantly shows inmates of a mental hospital wandering around naked and urinating in bathrooms,

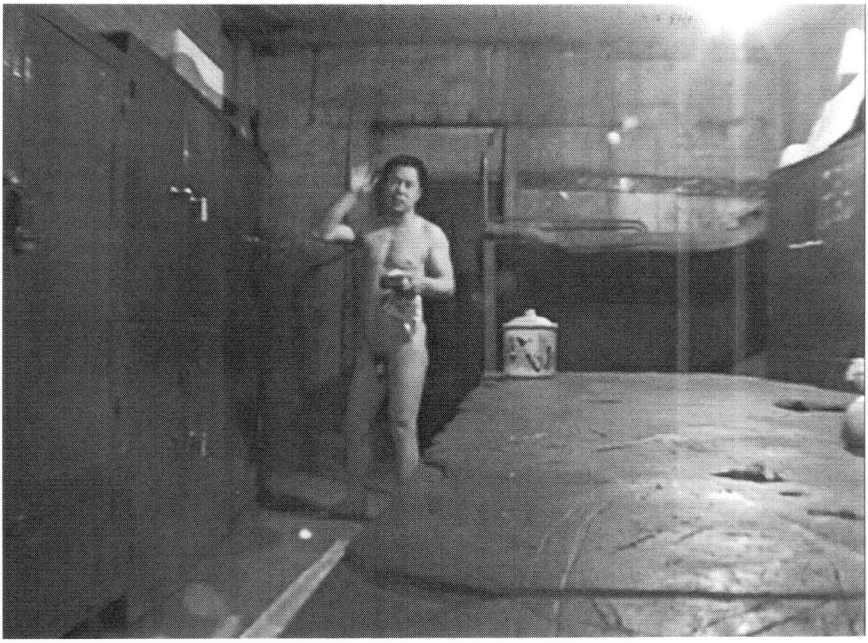

Figure 1.3. *West of the Tracks.* Meat shot from Wang Bing, who shoots swinging dicks discreetly at genitals level.

cells, and hallways. One scene in particular powerfully reveals Wang's axiographic position. An old man crouches over a plastic bowl relieving himself, his penis in full view. When he realizes Wang is photographing him, he uncomfortably shuffles around the bowl in order to obtain some modicum of privacy—effectively turning his back on the camera, without spilling a drop of urine. Wang cruelly disregards this awkward but perfectly legible gesture of humiliation and defiance, continuing to shoot the man and ultimately including the scene in the final film.

The meat shot is unusual in documentary. The few examples I can think of all come from queer work, ethnographic documentary, or films shot in the heyday of the 1960s counterculture. The key difference with the Chinese examples is that they are all shot with the visible hidden camera. The people in these Chinese documentaries surely have no idea that the camera in the room will circulate their personal lives around the world and compete in competitions for cash prizes and fame. One wonders if they would have thrown a hand in the camera or a towel over their crotch if they had known that their genitalia would be projected and enlarged for public consumption from Japanese film festivals to the classrooms of Harvard University. In any case, like the money shots exhibiting intense bodily responses that punctuate the Chinese documentary, these meat shots are strong markers of authenticity. To borrow Linda Williams' words, "This aspect of the genre is characterized by a cinema vérité devotion to the revelation-confession of real bodies caught in the act of sexual pleasure—in, for example, the 'meat shot.' Here . . . is irrefutable, visible evidence of penetration, really taking place, with no possible faking" (Williams 1993, 241). Our Chinese documentarists punctuate their penetration of Chinese reality with their own meat and money shots, and incidentally with a decidedly masculine bravado as well.

Axiographics invites us to see these deployments of the human body as more than the mark of the authentic. Indeed, while pornography and documentary have a variety of curious points of contact, Nichols points out how the use of narrative and actors renders the opposition of fiction and documentary a difference between erotics and ethics, "a difference that continues to mark out the movement of the ideological through the aesthetic" (Nichols 1992, 76). Let us now explore this issue through two more complex examples that raise questions about filming-filmed relations and the cinematic deployment of real human bodies.

The first of these two films is Xu Tong's *Wheat Harvest.* It was celebrated as one of the first, or perhaps *the* first, Chinese film to deal with prostitution without merely condemning it. Xu follows a young woman, named Miaomiao, between her workplace in Beijing and her rural home. She prostitutes herself to help support family and her ill father. Xu began his project as a novel and he used video as a form of visual note-taking. He received the consent of Miaomiao for this research (it's never clear if he's a "participant observer," as it were). However, after a while his novel morphed into a documentary film project, something he neglected to tell Miaomiao and the men and women around her. They merely thought it was Xu's habit to carry around a video camcorder and shoot constantly. It appeared woven into his daily life.

He premiered *Wheat Harvest* at the 3rd Beijing Independent Film Forum and then shortly thereafter at Yunfest in Kunming. At the Yunfest Q and A, he mentioned that Miaomiao had no idea he was making a film. This was probably the worst place to make such a revelation, as the participants of this particular festival include many activists from NGOs who are dedicating their lives to social issues like prostitution, sexual slavery, AIDS, and the like. He was roundly attacked, and then the dialogue became so heated that the festival scheduled a separate discussion. It lasted several hours. Xu was—and remains—unrepentant, much to the furious frustration of his critics. The controversy follows him wherever he goes, although it has rarely if ever prevented a festival from showing the film.

Miaomiao eventually stumbled on the controversy in an online forum. Not surprisingly, she was rather surprised to discover that Xu had made a film about her life without telling her, and also that it was being shown around the world. She raised objections and proffered a set of conditions for the film's continued screening:

1. Delete all the negative information about her on the Internet, where possible.
2. No more domestic screenings of the film, although foreign screenings would be acceptable.
3. Cover the identities of everyone in the film but her.
4. And she wanted to see the film.

Xu accepted all but one of the conditions. For some inexplicable reason, he refused to accept the last condition. He doesn't have a terribly good explanation for why. I finally asked him directly, and he parried questions with vague assertions that they have a good and long-term relationship, and that the relationship is not predicated on showing her the film. She stopped asking about it; he says she was primarily concerned about the publicity about her life.[4]

Wheat Harvest is quite a good film. At the same time, Xu Tong's deployment of the visible hidden camera remains troubling, and he would likely argue that the film wouldn't have been possible in the first place had he not made it surreptitiously. Needless to say, this was at the expense of Miaomiao's privacy; and, notably, the terms of their relationship were also somewhat vague in the end (i.e., it is difficult to ascertain whether this was, as I have mentioned before, participant observation). In comparison, what makes an equally controversial film like *The Good Woman of Bangkok* (1991) quite admirable is precisely that Dennis O'Rourke started shooting Aoi with her explicit cooperation and exposed his motivations and the terms of their relationship within the film itself.[5] In other words, O'Rourke's camera was anything but hidden; he does shoot one scene with a hidden camera, but it is reserved for drunken Europeans and their misogynist reviews concerning the women of Patpong.

The next film, Xue Jianqiang's *Martian Syndrome,* discovers a novel way of hiding the fully visible camera—simply lie about its ability to "see." Xue is one of those young directors for whom the camera is an extra appendage. It is always with him, and he is always shooting. *Martian Syndrome* documents a single evening shared by four young men. They are from rural areas, budding artists attracted to the cutting-edge art scenes of 798 and Songzhuang. They also seem to be gay, or at least experimenting with their sexuality. However, they remain bitterly on the outside edges of the art world they desperately want to enter. The film literally takes place on either side of the front door of one artist. He cowers inside, afraid of a new arrival that enjoyed his body and food earlier in the week. The new man is starving and homeless and keeps knocking on the front door, leaving the artist feeling harassed. The man is a bundle of contradictions, highly aware that he doesn't fit in; he calls himself a "Martian," which provides Xue his title. The artist refuses to answer his front door and keeps his lights off. Another friend calms the man down, stroking his arm and chest. After eighty-three minutes of traumatized hemming and hawing inside, the Martian is finally rejected and retreats into the night.

The filmmaker tags along all evening, shooting the conversations on either side of the door with the infrared setting of his camcorder. This gives it an otherworldly feeling, leeching the color from the image. It has the grainy gray palette of Pixelvision. And thanks to the infrared, everyone's eyes transform into glowing orbs. One film festival called it a "bravura night poem," but this would be like calling the tortured grammar of Google Translate poetry. The film consists of only five shots.[6] The first is a short, introductory image of a woman, possibly drunk, stumbling through the streets at night. The next four shots, each between fifteen and twenty-five minutes in length, capture the conversations inside and outside the apartment in real time. Whatever chunks of time are excised in the editing are short. There are brief flashbacks that interrupt the continuous flow of time of the five shots; each insert is rendered in negative and recalls a snatch of conversation from earlier in the film—some bit of hypocrisy, contradiction, or outright lie. Outside of this, it is the simple record of an evening of interaction, a tedious adolescent drama and not much more.

Through the evening, Xue carries his camera loosely. For the most part he points the camera in the general direction of people, but not with much "accuracy" because, after all, he is trying to hide the fact that he is shooting them. In the first shot after the introduction, the Martian points at the camera after a moment and asks, "Hey man, can you shoot?" (Meaning, can you shoot in the darkness?). Xue lies, "No, I can only record sound." The conversation continues—three young men shooting the breeze in the dark. Five minutes into the second shot they go inside after the Martian takes leave; when the apartment owner finally calms down he notices that Xue is shooting video. "Who is that? Is he with you? Can he see?" he asks. His companion replies, "Yes, it's an advanced camera." The owner says, "Oh, this will be classic." With this acknowledgment of the camera, the film would seem to shift modes as it moves from outside to inside the apartment. Outside, Xue's lie rendered his camcorder into a visible hidden camera and was firmly recording in the direct cinema mode. Once inside, when the photography is properly acknowledged, the film apparently shifts to something akin to the interactive, interventional style of cinema verité.

The work would seem to maintain this mode when Xue returns outside in the next shot, now a half-hour into the film. The Martian is back, and a third man

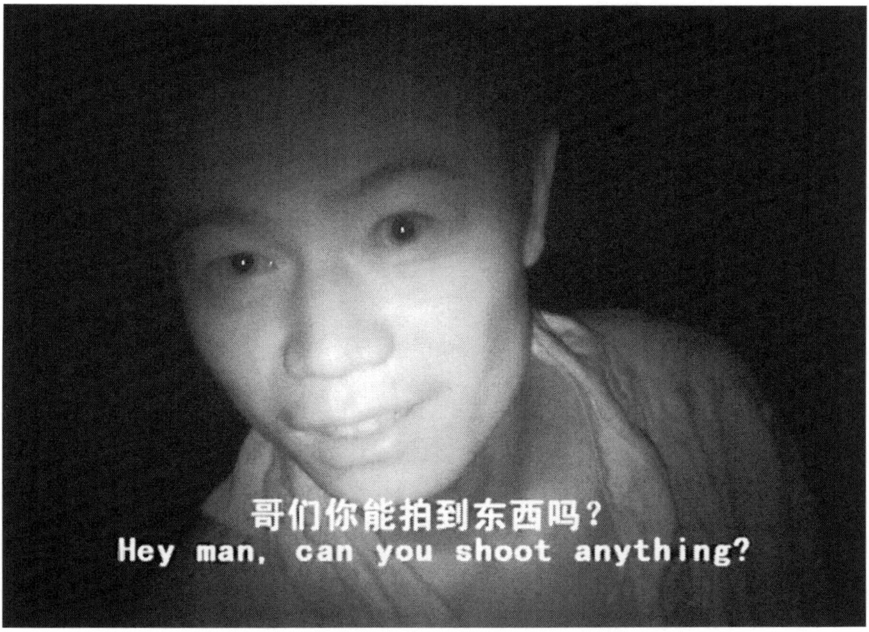

Figure 1.4. Martian Syndrome. Rendering the camera invisible: the director responds with a lie—"No, I can only record sound."

has arrived to ask Xue about editing his film. The third man knows enough about cameras to realize Xue is shooting their conversation. He demands repeatedly that the camera be turned off, pushing his hand into the camera lens. Xue dodges, ignores him, and continues shooting. When he leaves, Xue turns to the Martian and says, "Now it's your turn." Xue berates the Martian for harassing the artist inside the apartment. The Martian is only half-listening. He now realizes that Xue has been photographing their entire conversation, tells Xue to stop, and repeatedly demands the tape. The crux of the film, such as it is, finally arrives: *the director drops his camera onto the ground and beats the Martian into submission.*

Camcorder abandoned on the sidewalk, the horizon canted at an impossible angle, we *hear* but do not see the fight. Now the camera records sound but cannot see. The image is strikingly similar to the famous scene from *The Battle of Chile* (*La batalla de Chile* 1979), where the camera falls to the ground when the cinematographer is fatally shot and records his own death. Significantly, the power dynamic is completely reversed. Here, the cameraman is the agent of violence. When the Martian flees, Xue picks up the camera and returns inside to the accolades of his companions: "Was the camera on or off? On? That'll be a famous banned film!"

Actually, the film has enjoyed some success, as evidenced by a 2011 London screening and an award in 2010 at Songzhuang (as discussed in chapter 2 by J. P. Sniadecki). The acclaim at Songzhuang was not universal. Xue faced tough questions about the ethics of beating his subject in the post-film Q and A. He was unable to articulate a response. In fact, his explanation was so incoherent that some audience members left convinced that the entire film was a brilliant staging of that evening's events in the mock documentary tradition. Others felt this was giving Xue a bit too much credit, that it looked more like an "accidental" documentary—his camera was on and merely pointing in the general direction of the action, with only five or six edits needed to keep the running length reasonable. At the nearby festival lounge the conversations brought Xue in and he dispelled any notion that it was a skillfully executed, fictional set piece. Xue happened to have his camera running while something interesting happened and, aside from a few snide flashbacks, he made an attention-grabbing film despite himself. In other words, while Xue's approach would seem to be interventional at first glance, it is actually an observational, direct cinema documentary about his own life and self. We usually associate autobiography with the essayistic rather than direct cinema, but it is possible here because the director described the position from which he filmed—his position, his self—as "empty."

Perhaps this is why he so desperately tries to fill that empty self, at least with his next film, *When I Was Young I Also Beat a Tiger* (2010). This is essentially a self-shot record of Xue confronting veteran filmmakers like Wu Wenguang, condemning them as old hat to their faces, and claiming the mantle of a new and improved generation of documentary filmmakers. He was shooting this film at the same time as a visit to CCD Workstation's May Festival by Hara Kazuo, which I organized with Wu Wenguang. Hara gave long talks there and at Songzhuang. Xue was present, and apparently left deeply impressed by what Hara called his "action documentary." He identified with Hara's interventional approach, which he thought he was doing as well.

However, this is a gross misreading of Hara's "action documentary," which involves a complex interplay of ethics and politics and serves as an excellent counterpoint to the direct cinema filmmakers of China. After all, Hara conceived his approach in reaction to Ogawa and the collective approach he stood for. Furthermore, many of his films may be in direct cinema style, but they are deeply informed by the axiographic praxis of filmmakers like Ogawa and Tsuchimoto Noriaki. Hara worked as an assertive, individual filmmaker moving through—and thus influencing—the historical world; however, he was an individual filmmaker carefully working through webs of relationships. His innovation was to make "private film," but he conceived of the private as a place thoroughly supplemented by and inseparable from the social. This is to say, it naturally had a politics about it.

For example, one can contrast the meat shots of Chinese documentary or Xu Tong's surreptitious capture of Miaomiao's body with Hara's *Extreme Private Eros: Love Song 1974* (*Kyokushiteki erosu koiuta 1974*). The nudity in Hara's film was part of the fabric of the times and entirely consensual. The women he shot were actually collaborators on the film. Moreover, the difference between Xu Tong and Hara is most obvious in the climactic scene of *Extreme Private Eros,* when Hara's lover (and producer) and his ex-wife both give birth at home, on the kitchen floor. They explain that this method of giving life was an expression of their independence as women. Having Hara shoot it was a way of amplifying this expression. In contrast, Xu Tong surreptitiously uses Miaomiao's body for his own ends.

We could also compare Xue Jianqiang's *Martian Syndrome* to Hara's *Emperor's Naked Army Marches On* (*Yuki yukite shingun* 1987). The latter film was very much about the director's relationship to Okazaki and his patent insanity, a WWII veteran who beats his interviewees into revealing their shared history of wartime atrocity. Thus, this film also revolves around the mortal bodies before the camera. These are old men, and the beatings are quite real; one of Okazaki's victims (who participated in the horrific massacre and violence during the war) was recovering from surgery and required a visit to the hospital after the film crew's visit. Indeed, unlike Xue's bravura attack, Okazaki called the ambulance and accompanied the old man to the hospital. Where to draw the line was Hara's constant question, a political one considering the societal consequences of erasing war memory. The power of Hara's film comes precisely from this intersection of ethics and politics that is rendered with great sophistication in cinematic space and time. This is something Hara spoke eloquently about in the Q and A's Xue heard in Beijing. Hara would agree with Bill Nichols' assertion that any interventional style involves an "ethic of responsibility." He would also agree with Nichols that one can also imagine an "ethic of irresponsibility," a camera gaze that "actively sides with the agency of death, legitimates itself through the same code that legitimates the taking of life in the first place" (Nichols 1992, 85). Notably, Taiwanese documentary is quite self-conscious about these issues. Kuei-fen Chiu writes,

> The filming act is represented as a controversial activity that generates unexpected and unwanted impacts on human relationships during the filming process. In this kind of documentary, we often find an oscillation between the desire to use the camera and the urge to put it down. The question that continues to weigh upon the filmmaker's mind is no longer "How can I use my camera to represent them?", but "Should I put down the camera?" (Chiu 2012, 148)

Filmmakers on the mainland might find this no more than naval gazing. They will film anyone doing anything. It may be unfair to claim that this means the

Chinese disciples of Wiseman "actively" align themselves with the side of dominance and control in the hierarchies they confront with their cameras. The Songzhuang poster, bristling with surveillance cameras before the forehead of Mao, obviously asserts the opposite. In scenes of official corruption, state violence, and other abuses of power, they are not simply catching life unawares; they are catching criminals in the act. In this sense, that battery of surveillance cameras directly symbolizes their camcorders—surveilling "Mao" and all the things done in his name.

Indeed, the attraction to Wiseman's cinema is not only its "objective" feel (in contrast to state television), but also the way it offers an easy route to identify with the powerless side of the hierarchies of Chinese society. Perhaps the problem is that it is too easy a route. In *Ideology and the Image,* Nichols called Wiseman's cinema "tactless" for the way it eschews "etiquette and taboo," even if it relentlessly draws our attention to areas of society that normally get pushed out of view (Nichols 1981, 140). Chinese documentary filmmakers have inherited this ethical ambivalence; however, with no checks from the distribution or exhibition contexts, and a daring cinema driven by an anything-for-the-sake-of-the-film narcissism, that ambivalence ends up amplified and edging toward a troubling ethics of irresponsibility in too many works.

Where does that leave *us?* Yiman Wang has also noted the questionable practices of Chinese directors in a fascinating essay published in *Film Quarterly.* The essay takes virtually the opposite stance I have suggested here. After analyzing several films, she writes,

> The amateur documentarians' recurring emphasis on the "cruelty" of documentation suggests their awareness of a conventional documentary ethic *and* their decision to go against it in order to deliver what they see as the truth. In these terms, the question one should ask is not simply what is the bottom line of DV documentary making, or how far it can go without becoming too intrusive and exhibitionistic; *but rather whether it is necessary* [my emphasis] and possible to justify the "guilty" ethics of deliberately cutting into the private realm of everyday reality and exposing it with unbearable clarity.
>
> (Wang 2005, 22)

Wang does ask some tough questions of the filmmakers she examines. Whether they are cognizant of the ethical conundrums of documentary practice (I remain unsure what she means by a "conventional ethics") is a matter of debate. Nevertheless, this quote demonstrates Wang's alignment with their values. Intrusiveness and exhibitionism are at the heart of it all. And this is because the ultimate goal of the independent documentary is, for both filmmaker and viewer, to be "seared" or "wounded" by the cruelty before the camera (or inflicted by the camera). As for the films' subjects, they are curiously left in brackets. They are mainly necessary for "teasing out neglected but important social issues" (Wang 2005, 23).

By way of contrast, Nichols challenges we spectators of the Chinese documentary to ask how filmmakers acquit themselves in relationship to the historical world as they commit it to video, give it form through editing, and then re-present it in theaters, cafes, universities, and art museums. What ethics or politics come to play in this process? What ethics adhering to a work might actually undermine its politics? Should a film like *Martian Syndrome* be awarded a prestigious prize? Should *Wheat Harvest* still be shown in China? In other words, I am suggesting there is an ethics of exhibition to consider as well, something the programmers at Songzhuang appear to be especially self-conscious about. The poster for this year's festival features a cinema clapboard in the form of a meat cleaver.

Unfortunately, it was a festival that never took place. In the summer of 2011, there was a government crackdown reaction to the Arab Spring and in anticipation of the change of leadership. Ai Weiwei had been arrested in April and his whereabouts were unknown. This strategic arrest chilled the film, art, and architecture scenes. Around the same time, the sudden disappearance of the websites for Li Xianting Film Fund and Yunfest portended trouble. Yunfest endured, despite some official interference and a financial crisis. CCD Workstation's May Festival went without a hitch, although early visits by police made them wonder if they'd get to the finish line. The year before, Iberia let its film archivist and programmer go, supposedly because independent film brought no added value or accumulation of wealth to the gallery; finally, in the summer of 2011, the owner of the high-profile gallery Ullens announced he was selling everything, pulling out of 798 and moving to India.

In the summer of 2011, things were worst at the epicenter of the independent documentary film scene, the Li Xianting Film Fund and its film festivals. After the vice-mayor of Beijing visited Li to demand all the festival selections for inspection, the organizers decided to pull back and cancel the event rather than submit to inevitable censorship. In the past, they had met such interference with bullheaded resistance; they would simply move to a secondary space and show the films anyway. This year, according to Li, the pressure was different. He felt that to proceed with the festival would mean going head-to-head with the most powerful adversaries they had dealt with thus far, and that it could very well mean losing everything. Better to take one or two steps back and then proceed with caution for a while. He invited people to watch films on TV or computer monitors, which a few people did in the first couple days. However, they were followed in the streets, and Mark Peranson, the Canadian juror and programmer from the Locarno International Film Festival, was even questioned at his hotel. The director

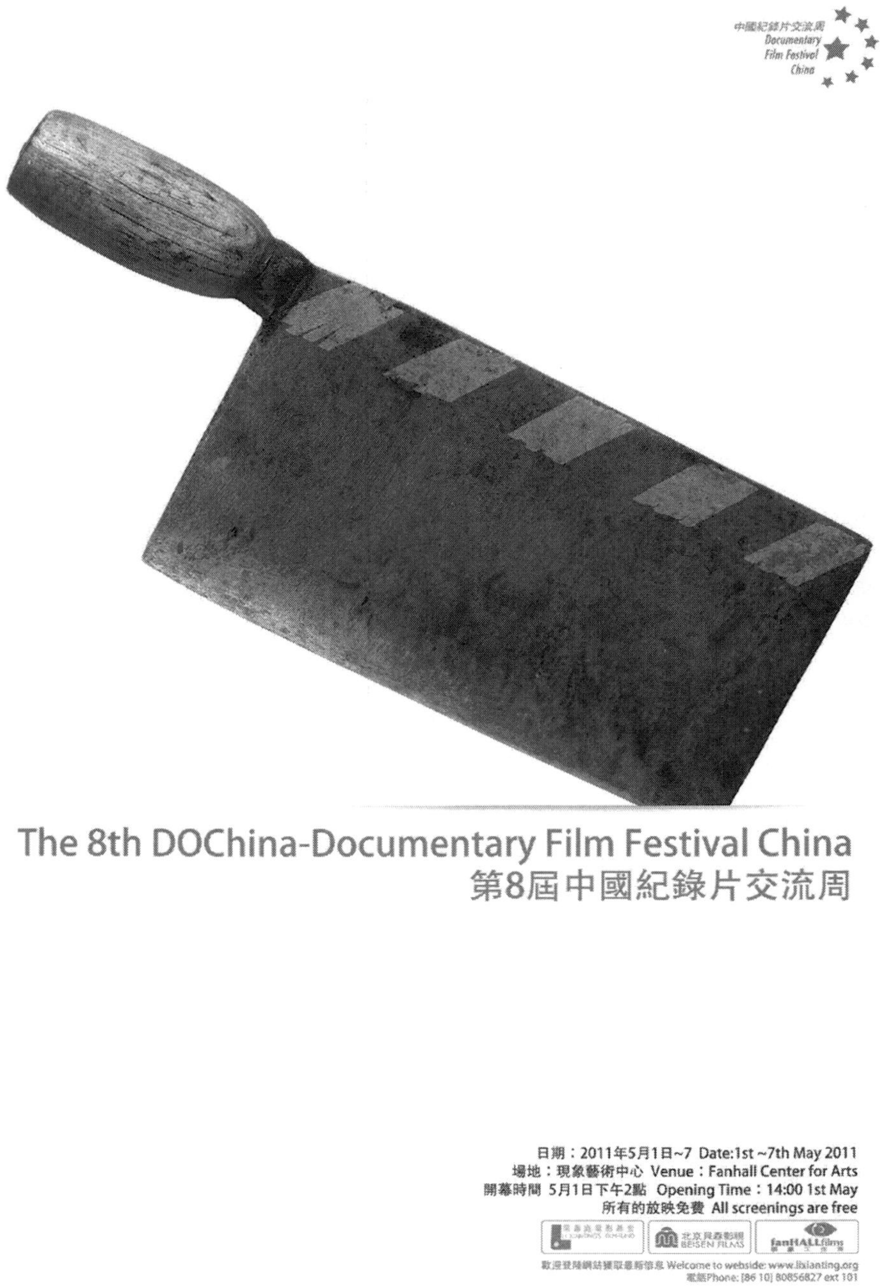

Figure 1.5. Poster of the 8th Documentary Film Festival in China. (design: Wang Wo)

of the institute, Zhu Rikun, resigned from his position and announced that he would return to his hometown to become a farmer (that didn't last long).

Amidst this chilly atmosphere, there was a significant bright spot. Indie Workshop, the outfit run by Beijing Film Academy professor Zhang Xianming, established the Indie Screening Alliance of Art Space. They will curate packages of films and circulate them through a formal network of screening sites around the country. Their first package of twenty-three films, *To Live—in China*, was assembled in the spring of 2011. The package did not include the most daring films, but this is hardly surprising under the circumstances. It initially circulated through ten venues. Happily, more sites were added as time went on. In other words, the Chinese documentary film movement, such as it is, was finally building the reception context into its ethics of exhibition. It was finally tackling what Ogawa in Japan took as his starting point when he left Iwanami and established Jieiso. However, in subsequent years government pressure has only intensified, culminating in the total suppression of both Yunfest and Songzhuang's Beijing Independent Film Festival in 2014. This basically leaves personal DVD hand-offs and the Internet as the only means of distribution and exhibition for the independent documentary. In this situation, it is hard to imagine the filmmakers looking to someone like Hara Kazuo and combining the best of Wiseman and Ogawa.

Notes

This chapter was written with the support of the State Innovative Institute for the Studies of Journalism & Communication and Media Society at Fudan University and the University of Michigan's Center for Chinese Studies and Confucius Institute.

1. I describe and analyze these conceptual and practical aspects, at length, in Nornes 2007.

2. These filmmakers follow Ogawa's example of long-term interaction with their subjects, but in terms of style they opt for the Ogawa of the mid-career Sanrizuka Series and not the more formally innovative films of the Magino Village Story.

3. One can palpably understand this dynamic by considering the experience of watching Gu Tao's work, which invites one to think from the perspective of the ethnic minority family that is pushed off their ancestral hunting lands to live in awful tract housing. Watching their abject poverty, profound misery, and embarrassing drinking binges in *Aoluguya . . . Aoluguya* (2007) and *The Last Moose of Aoluguya* (2013), one wonders about the role of the director. The films feel objectifying and almost unbearably exploitative. By way of contrast, it is difficult to feel this way with Gu's 2011 follow-up, *Yuguo and His Mother.* We now see the same family in many of the same situations, but he follows them for years and their relationship is obviously close. The style of the films is similar, but there is a pronounced shift from a Wiseman

to an Ogawa mode. Still, it is unclear if the stumble-drunk mother has the slightest idea her life is winning awards on the international film festival circuit (the second film won the Ogawa Shinsuke Award at the 2011 Yamagata International Documentary Film Festival).

4. The following website has information about the controversy: http://www.mvage.com/space.php?uid=4&do=thread&id=208.

5. I was involved in the programming of this film for the competition at Yamagata International Film Festival in 1991, where it caused a controversy equal to that of *Wheat Harvest* (although mainly among foreign viewers). The festival stood by its choice in terms similar to Linda Williams' defense of the film in "The Ethics of Documentary Intervention: Dennis O'Rourke's *The Good Woman of Bangkok*" (Williams 1997).

6. This is an analysis of the original version shown at the Beijing Independent Documentary Film Festival; the version J. P. Sniadecki writes about elsewhere in this volume seems to have a coda added after the fact.

Bibliography

Chiu, Kuei-fen. 2012. "'Should I Put Down the Camera?'—Ethics in Contemporary Taiwanese Documentary Films." In *Documenting Taiwan on Film: Issues and Methods in New Documentaries,* edited by Sylvia Li-chun Lin and Tze-la Deborah Sang, 138–154. New York: Routledge.

Grindstaff, Laura. 2002. *The Money Shot: Trash, Class, and the Making of TV Talk Shows.* Chicago: University of Chicago Press.

Nichols, Bill. 1981. *Ideology and the Image: Representation in the Cinema and Other Media.* Bloomington: Indiana University Press.

———. 1992. *Representing Reality: Issues and Concepts in Documentary.* Bloomington: Indiana University Press.

Nornes, Abé Mark. 2007. *Forest of Pressure: Ogawa Shinsuke and Postwar Japanese Documentary.* Minneapolis: University of Minnesota Press.

———. 2014. "Yamagata—Asia—Europe: The International Film Festival Short Circuit." In *The Oxford Handbook of Japanese Cinema,* edited by Daisuke Miyao, 245–262. New York: Oxford University Press.

Wang, Yiman. 2005. "The Amateur's Lightning Rod: DV Documentary in Postsocialist China." *Film Quarterly* 58 (4): 16–26.

Williams, Linda. 1993. "Pornographies On/Scene, or Diff'rent Strokes for Diff'rent Folks." In *Sex Exposed: Sexuality and the Pornography Debate,* edited by Lynn Segal and Mary McIntosh, 233–265. New Brunswick, NJ: Rutgers University Press.

———. 1997. "The Ethics of Documentary Intervention: Dennis O'Rourke's *The Good Woman of Bangkok.*" In *The Good Woman of Bangkok,* edited by Chris Berry, Laleen Jayamanne, and Annette Hamilton. 79–90. Sydney: Power Institute Press.

CHAPTER 2

The Cruelty of the Social

Xianchang, Intersubjectivity, and Interobjectivity

J. P. SNIADECKI

At the closing awards ceremony for the 7th Annual DOChina Festival held in May 2010 in Songzhuang—a gentrified artists' village at the far eastern edge of the Beijing municipality—young animator, poet, and filmmaker Xue Jianqiang was recognized with an honorable mention for his haunting documentary *Martian Syndrome*. The award came with 2000 RMB, a Panasonic DV camera (the jury's official comments noted that Xue lacked his own camcorder and had to borrow one to make his film), and the chance to speak before a gathering of who's who in Chinese independent documentary filmmaking. He no sooner got his hands on the microphone than had these words to share with his peers and elders:

> Now it's time to criticize you, you idiotic documentary directors. You only fucking know how to use TV stories and TV aesthetics to make films. You think of yourself as a blemish on your film, and so you cut yourself out and lose many secrets that lie behind your documentary. I can see clearly every cut you make. You want society to be open. You want every person you film to be open, but you yourself are not open and cut yourself out. You are dictators. . . . Since you shoot people, you should let other people shoot you. Only like this is it OK. Otherwise your logic is a violent logic. Thank you.[1]

This unexpected outburst, captured by Xue's friend on a Handycam, also appears in the first few minutes of Xue's follow-up feature, *When I Was Young I Also Beat a Tiger* (2010). In a bold move of self-reflexivity—as well as a testament to the ubiquity of DV cameras capturing live all moments great and small within the Chinese documentary world—*Tiger* arguably marks a first, albeit awkward, step toward a metadiscourse on the Chinese independent film scene itself. The film is a naive yet cutting romp through Beijing's notable alternative documentary centers and organizations—namely, Caochangdi Workstation, Fanhall Films, and the Li Xianting Film Fund. It features Xue as a self-styled provocateur using his critique of the "logic of violence" to make multiple attacks on, and pursue multiple inquiries into, the methods employed by an older generation of filmmakers. In perhaps the film's most shocking moment, Xue barges in on Wu Wenguang, the figure often cited as the father of independent documentary in China, and asks to chat. Wu, obviously annoyed and wary of the brash intruder, blows off Xue's repeated attempts to know his opinion on the young director's films and personal character. Xue retreats from the gated Caochangdi Workstation, but then later returns with fiction director Ying Liang, a well-respected figure with whom Wu apparently has time to sit down and talk. Omitting the content of their chat with a quick and artless cross-fade, Xue's film cuts right to his chance to pounce on the patriarch. He thrusts the camera into Wu's face and insists: "I've seen all your films, and only *Fuck Cinema* is OK. . . . Your village documentary project is good, but your time is over. You shouldn't make films anymore."

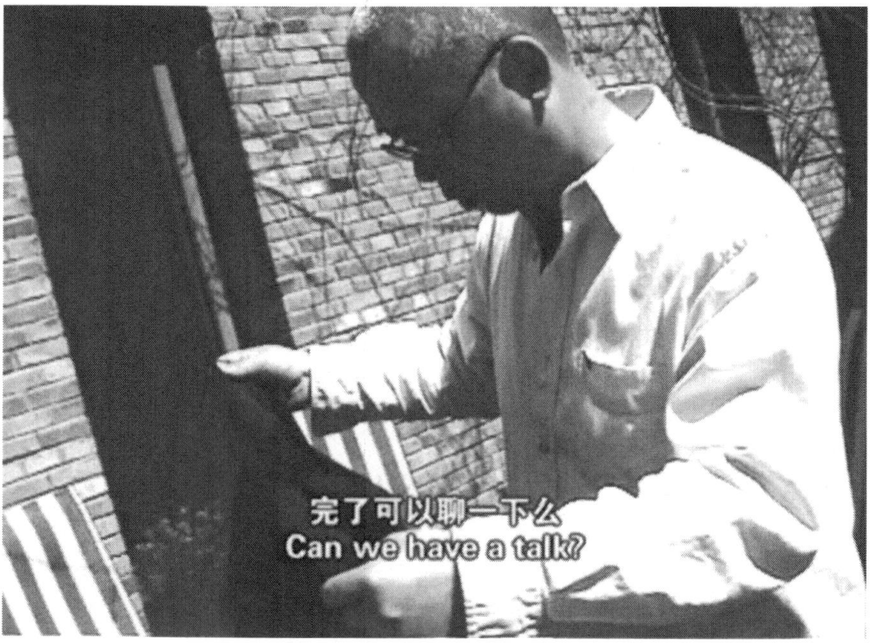

Figure 2.1. *When I Was Young I Also Beat a Tiger.* Xue Jianqiang confronts filmmaker Wu Wenguang in his studio home, Caochangdi Workstation. (image by Xue Jianqiang)

In these outbursts, is Xue driven by genuine concern for the "logic of violence" underlying the filmmaker–film subject relationship in the works of his peers, or is he perhaps an ambitious upstart motivated by a desire to revolt against the more established order of filmmakers? Holding a thorough exploration of these speculations in abeyance, it is nonetheless interesting to consider how Xue's attack resonates with formal and ethical concerns persistently raised by scholars and critics tracking the scene. These concerns hinge on a sense that a particular observational filmmaking style not only holds reign in Chinese independent documentary but also raises ethical questions that tend to be pushed aside, if addressed at all.[2]

Two reports of independent festivals held in different Chinese cities in 2009 express just these concerns. Abé Mark Nornes' report on the Yunnan Multicultural Visual Festival (Yunfest) in Kunming and the 6th DOChina Festival in Songzhuang portrays the documentary world as flourishing and vibrant, but ultimately faults the Chinese directors for their "renegade" approach to documentary ethics and for falling short of formal innovation. He concludes that "having tired of their conservative devotion to direct cinema, not to mention roughshod camerawork and sound for otherwise amazing films, I look forward to something new" (Nornes 2009, 55). Similarly disappointed in the documentary output at the 6th China Independent Film Festival held the same year in Nanjing, Chris Berry demurs: "listening to a forum of documentary filmmakers, it was clear that observational cinema still predominates in Chinese independent documentary" (Chris Berry 2009).

This is not to say that other approaches to documentary filmmaking have been entirely absent. Xue's deviation from straight and strict vérité is not an anomaly: from Ju Anqi's voxpop-styled *There's a Strong Wind in Beijing* (2000) to Hu Xinyu's exploration of his own domestic realm in *The Man* (2003) and *Sister* (2008) to Wu Haohao's provocateur "action cinema" (*xingdong dianying*), best exemplified in his *Action/Kun 1* (2009), there has been a range of experimentation and shifts away from the observational. In addition, Luke Robinson has pointed out how the heterogeneity of formal elements that operate *within* the films themselves renders them fairly resistant to the categories we may try to thrust upon them (Robinson 2010). In fact, more than a few documentaries that would for the most part fall under the rubric of observational cinema also seamlessly incorporate informal interviews and moments of self-reflexivity to varying degrees, as seen in Feng Yan's *Bing'Ai* (2007), Zhao Liang's *Petition* (2009), and Wang Bing's *West of the Tracks* (2003).[3]

Yet, by and large, the dominant mode of filmmaking in the independent documentary world continues to reveal the "real face" of Chinese society—as opposed to the state-approved programs of mainstream media—through a formal approach that scholars and critics have alternately called *xianchang,* cinema verité, the observational mode, or direct cinema.[4] The standard lineage of this approach enshrines Frederick Wiseman and Shinsuke Ogawa as totem gods (see chapter 1, by Abé Mark Nornes, in this volume) and espouses an austere and spontaneous filmmaking style (no voice-over, no extradiegetic music, no staging, no formal interviews) that records the sufferings and hardships of individuals who find no place in the official narrative of China's triumphant rise to global ascendancy. The goal is to record the flow of lived-experience as it unfolds, only rarely including overt self-reflexivity, and almost never turning the gaze of the camera directly back on the filmmaker. In other words, Lou Ye's famous line in *Suzhou River* (1999) that "my camera doesn't lie," which over the years has often been cited in the context of Chinese independent cinema, may be expanded to describe the current dominant approach to documentary: "my camera doesn't lie, and its lens never turns back on me."

However, no matter where directed, every act of pointing a camera carries the subjective imprint of the operator.

Filmmaker-anthropologist David MacDougall has described how image-making, whether photographic or cinematic, entails a reflexive dimension, because the decisions that go into framing an image "refer back" to the image-maker and his/her own subjective and embodied point of view" (MacDougall 2005, 4). Thus, image-making is always corporeal, and "corporeal images are not just the images of other bodies; they are also images of the body behind the camera and its relation to the world" (MacDougall 2005, 3). Understood thus, a *xianchang* or observational approach admits of self-reflexivity in that it entails an embodied camera.[5] Furthermore, attached to the embodied camera is the filmmaker's own subjectivity, which contends and connects first with the subjectivities of film subjects in the filmmaking encounter and then with those of audience members in the multivalent process of reception.

It is a key argument of my chapter that by attending not only to these revelatory traces of authorial subjectivity, but also to the individual traumas and broader violence that compel the content and production of many Chinese independent documentaries, we may witness how social suffering and violence play a major role in shaping the filmmaker's relation to the world and direct his/her image-making. In this reading, then, Xue's cry against the "logic of violence" and the scholarly critiques of a default observational style, while useful, fail to consider violence and suffering as a larger social process suffusing the profilmic of independent documentary and the affective fabric of Chinese society in general. Indeed, many independent filmmakers in China are social individuals not only marked by the massive changes and repressed injustices of the nation's recent history, but also possessed of the sensitivity and sense of responsibility to represent them. From the ripples of psychic damage that weigh down on both the film subjects and filmmaker Wu Wenguang himself in his early and seminal *Bumming in*

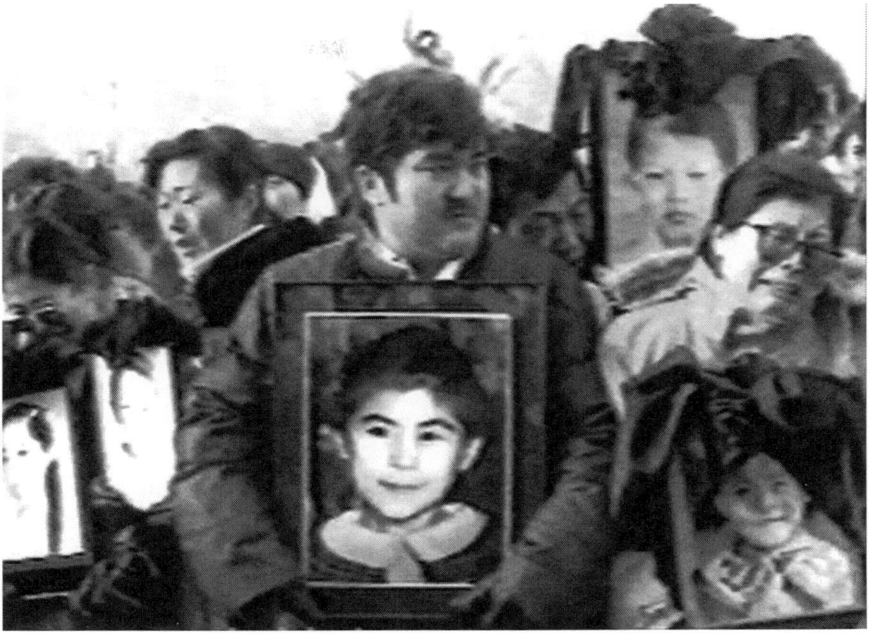

Figure 2.2. *Karamay*. Mourning parents holding portraits of their children who died in the Karamay fire. (image by Xu Xin)

Beijing (1990) to the expressions of extreme grief and anger by parents who lost their children in the 1994 fire that stands as the centerpiece of *Karamay* (2010), Xu Xin's six-hour exposé of the suppressed tragedy, countless independent Chinese documentaries have not only served as testimonies to the overlooked and often actively denied narratives of pain and injustice suffusing Chinese society today, but also doubled as a creative process through which the filmmaker may work out his/her own experience of social suffering. With these observations as a point of departure, my aim in this chapter is to elucidate how the *xianchang* aesthetic is able to open up various cinematic spaces that, rather than necessarily adding up to a logic of violence, may potentially serve as responses to violence and injustice experienced in the social world. I begin with an overview of *xianchang* and then explore some of the formal elements—including its relationship to the profilmic—that render it fertile ground for both *intersubjective* and *interobjective* experience. These observations then lead to a closing discussion of how the appeal of many of today's independent documentaries lies in their capacity to constitute a powerful form of witnessing trauma and suffering.

Xianchang and Documentary Cruelty

Those tracking Chinese independent documentary often contextualize the aesthetic commitment to *xianchang*—which translates as "live" and "on the scene"—as possible only within a postsocialist era of media reform and, perhaps more importantly, as reactions to both the didacticism of socialist realism and the lavish films of the Fifth Generation (Lü 2003; Chris Berry 2007; Johnson 2006). Further, in contrast to official and commercial productions, independent filmmakers are seen as able to bridge the gap between mainstream media and the everyday experience of Chinese people by turning their DV lenses to the marginalized corners of society, thereby contributing to an unofficial and ever-expanding archive of counterdiscourse. They aim to expose the hardships and complexities of China's shifting social landscape and render visible the injustices that transpire in the dark, overlooked corners of the nation's economic miracle. In terms of production, filmmakers tend toward an ethnographic model, investing considerable stretches of time living among their film subjects and, in most cases, working solo for all phases of production. DV technology has allowed them to pursue low-budget, individual efforts that remain unadorned by smooth camerawork or postproduction polish, but also unfettered by government censorship. Raw reality thus serves as an antidote to official and commercial gloss. And the antidote has been celebrated and pursued with increasing gusto since affordable digital video cameras hit Chinese markets in the 1990s. Indeed, there has been a boom of amateur video production as people from all walks of life pick up camcorders and adopt the title of independent director.

While the popularization of documentary filmmaking has built a dynamic alternative sphere of cultural production, it has also led to a saturation of copycat productions and, perhaps more alarming, serious ethical questions regarding the exploitation of film subjects and the politics of representation. Yiman Wang employs the term "the documentary of cruelty" as a label for those DV works that are produced in "deliberate violation of the codes of decorum, or the documentary ethic, that help to maintain the subjects' dignity." For Wang, filmmakers see these transgressions as necessary and justified in the pursuit of footage capable of "cutting into the private realm of everyday reality and exposing it with unbearable clarity" (Wang 2005, 17).

In *Jilu Zhongguo* (Documenting China), Lü Xinyu points out that the film subjects of Li Hong's feminist classic *Out of Phoenix Bridge* (1997) were not only denied a chance to see the finished film but were also unaware of its exhibition success. Even the fact that their images, voices, and personal stories have made their way to festival and university audiences around the world remains unknown to these four migrant women from Anhui. Li Hong herself confessed that documentary filmmaking is a cruel, unbalanced process and that she felt her film amounted to stealing from her subjects, who stood to gain nothing from their participation in the film (Lü 2003). Another example is the informed consent controversy at the 2009 Yunfest that erupted around Xu Tong's *Wheat Harvest,* a portrait of a young woman from Hebei province earning money in Beijing as a prostitute in order to pay for her father's medical expenses back home on the farm. During the festival it was discovered that the protagonist, Hongmiao, was not aware that Xu was making a film destined for exhibition both domestically and internationally. One of the festival's sponsors, upon learning this, protested the two awards given to the film. Xu argued that his subject both knew and accepted that he was taking footage—the level of intimacy he achieves would be practically impossible if she did not—and, further, that at the time of shooting even he himself did not know what would become of the rushes. Following an eight-hour discussion the pressure relented and Xu was allowed to keep the awards. However, the lively debate from this incident that ensued on Internet blogs caused Hongmiao tremendous alarm—it was through the online discussion that she, in fact, first learned of the film's existence. She contacted Xu and demanded to see the film. Xu refused, fearing she would have a negative reaction. The two of them eventually agreed that, in order to keep her occupation a secret from her parents, the film would no longer be screened in mainland China. This incident is an example of the kinds of trangressions that compel Nornes' critique of "renegade" behavior and serve as instances of Wang's "documentary of cruelty."

While hoping for greater accountability toward film subjects, many critics also anticipate that the ever-increasing number of legibly more personal and self-reflexive films will refresh the scene. This expectation may arise from a comparison, all too tempting to draw, between the documentary scene in China and earlier ones in Europe, the US, and Japan. That is, similar to the shift away from cinema verité and direct cinema that dominated the 1960s toward more autobiographical and personal documentary in the 1980s that took place outside China, an eventual decline of the dominant aesthetic is seen as inevitable within China. While the introduction of more self-critical elements in representing the Other may help soften the contentious tactics employed by some directors today, one objection to this prognosis is that neither self-reflexivity nor the use of other documentary modes necessarily ensures ethical filmmaking. In Xue's overtly self-reflexive *Martian Syndrome,* for example, one of his film subjects makes repeated requests not to be filmed and at one point even asks for the DV tape in Xue's camera. Xue not only continues filming and refuses to hand over the tape but also, at the climax of the conflict, puts down his camera—still rolling—in order to chase and thrash his unwilling film subject. For Xue, it is the decision to include this eruption of violence that exempts his work from trafficking in the "logic of violence." In this case, as also for the numerous verbal lashings Xue unleashes in *Tiger,* this justification is satisfying perhaps only to Xue himself. The mere fact of the filmmaker's appearance before the camera lens—which is often, in any case, a guarded performance of the self—does not absolve him from criticism for abusing film subjects. In fact, no mode of documentary can claim the moral high ground over others, since what constitutes responsible filmmaking is never fixed, always shaped not by external ethical prescriptions but rather by the specific dynamics of the filmmaking encounter and the uses to which the resulting footage is put.

HAPTIC CINEMA AND INTERSUBJECTIVITY

Thus, while speculating about what is on the horizon remains a worthwhile endeavor, it is also vital to continue to consider some of the reasons why *xianchang* cinema has generated excitement both overseas and within China's own borders as an aesthetic with its own unique properties that simply cannot be understood as wholly derivative of an earlier style as construed by a Euro-centric formulation of documentary film's evolution. By virtue of their amateur and independent status, these films do not usually screen to mass audiences; however, they do generate impassioned responses from their growing number of viewers. The energy in the theater (or gallery or cafe or classroom) during screenings is often intoxicating. Perhaps, in more cases than we would like to admit, this excitement is a result of a digitally mediated Orientalism, both external and internal; that is, audience members are so enlivened because they share with the filmmakers a curiosity about the social and cultural "Other," whether it be a young prostitute, a Tibetan nomad, or a mentally handicapped drifter.[6] Or perhaps it is the suspenseful thrill of what Dai Vaughan has called the "horror of a documentary," which "can lie in our being required to conceptualize (or—if there were such a word—*per*ceptualize) the world in a certain way and being, at least for the duration of the film, powerless to intervene in it" (Vaughan 1999, 188).

Another hypothesis is that the lo-fi and observational DV aesthetic, in its creation of an unrehearsed and digitally visceral copresence, substantiates what Laura Marks calls "haptic visuality," a viewing experience that, in immersing the spectator in a rich sensorial field of textures and movements, departs from the more detached stance often associated with optical visuality (Marks 2000, 162). In contrast to the "logic of violence" critique leveled by Xue, MacDougall has shown how observational cinema in fact possesses the potential to empower both film subjects and audiences because of its insistence on the autonomy of the profilmic (MacDougall 2005). In this view, the material world—including other human beings—is self-sufficient and autonomous, with an agency beyond that of the filmmaker's.

Autobiographical documentary, on the other hand, grants us access to a self-authorized "thick" description of the filmmaker's subjectivity but, in doing so, tends to work toward constraining the profilmic and may even eclipse the subjectivities of others appearing in the film. In Li Ning's *Tape* (2010), for example, we are privy to the narrative of personal hardship that Li constructs as a struggling performance artist and avant-garde dance troupe leader in Shandong, but are left more or less in the dark when it comes to the lives of those who supported him and performed with him. Thus, the *xianchang* approach may more readily acquiesce to the fact that reality always exceeds the intentions of the filmmaker rather than attempting to bend the profilmic—and by consequence the alterity of the film subjects—to one particular subjectivity. The filmmaker's sensibility and agenda weigh down on the world the filmmaker depicts, but they can never succeed in fully becoming its master. Such a formulation of *xianchang* as caught up with the *flesh* of the world destabilizes the popular critique that it aspires to pure objectivity and a mere duplication of the scientific gaze. As Zhang Zhen has observed, Chinese independent cinema provides "a new cinema anchored in the social and the now but also, in aesthetic terms, an alternative cinematic space that is haptic rather than optic, sensuous and open rather than abstract and closed" (Zhang 2007, 21).

This viewing experience also has much to do with the amateur style of almost exclusively handheld shooting, with cameras set on autofocus, sweeping across surfaces and sliding between film subjects. Such an intimate and embodied camera, in turn, works to foster a valuable cinematic space of *intersubjectivity* between film subject, filmmaker, and audience. Intersubjectivity is constituted by the ever-shifting ways of social interaction and communication between subjects that accommodate both accordance and discordance, what anthropologist Michael D. Jackson has described more generally as the "interplay of subject and object, ego and alter. Singular selves are simultaneously part of a commonality, sole but also several, not only islands but parts of the main" (Jackson 1998, 6). Jackson's description echoes director Wu Wenguang's account of the intimate, interconnected filmmaker–film subject relations he experienced in the production of his film *Life on the Road* (*Jianghu* 2000) (Lü 2003).

A focus on this field of relationships and encounters engendered not only by the actual filmmaking encounter but also by the receiving audience opens an intricate, co-constituted nexus of relations, emotions, agendas, and ideologies that animate documentary filmmaking and viewing. Thus, despite the fact that certain dubious truth claims might go unquestioned, or that the observational style employed by primarily male middle-class directors carries the risk of merely reinforcing existing power relations, these films nonetheless often succeed at not only acquainting people who might never have meaningful contact with one another, but also in committing to digitally record the hardships and sufferings of others. This is not necessarily just a matter of raising awareness; the production process entwines the film subject and filmmaker, and the viewer's cinematic immersion into that encounter—revealed in digital fragments on-screen—connects him/her to the subjective experience of both.

Zhao Liang's *Petition* (2009), which he filmed over the course of twelve years from 1996 to 2008, provides an example of the primacy of intersubjective cinematic space within the dominant formal mode of Chinese documentary. *Petition* focuses on a community of petitioners who have come to Beijing from the provinces to seek justice in the Chinese court system. In 1996, when still a student at the Beijing Film Academy, Zhao's search for a documentary subject came to an end when a friend directed him to the Petitioner's Village near Beijing South Train Station. The petitioners, struggling for survival along the railroad tracks in shacks made from scraps of metal and wood, had left their homes in the provinces in order to bring their unresolved cases and bitter grievances to the attention of the central government. Enduring the opaque machinations of the Petition Bureau

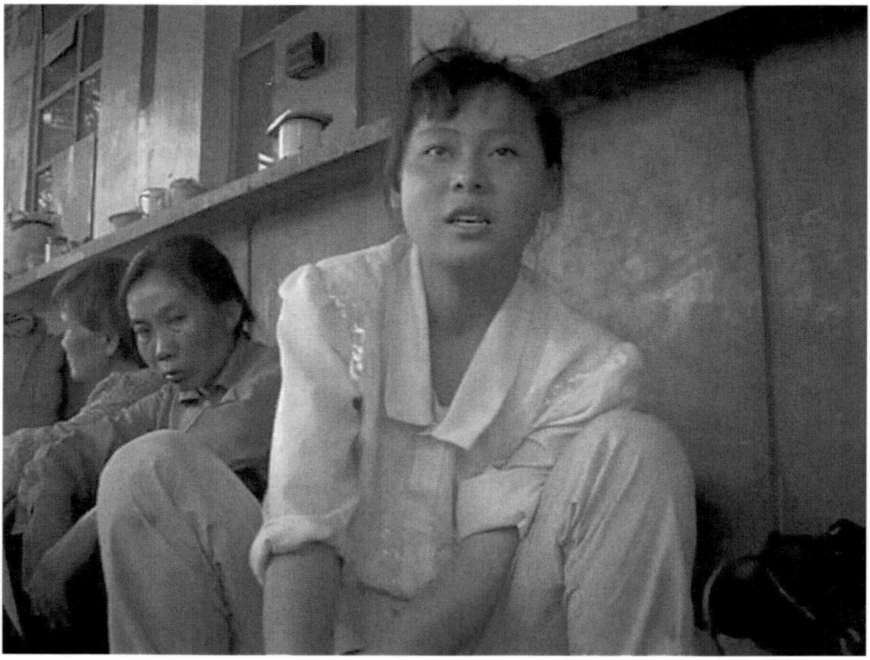

Figure 2.3. Petition. Xiaojuan speaks with filmmaker Zhao Liang about her petitioning mother. (image by Zhao Liang)

for years without any substantial response to their appeals, the petitioners' Sisyphean struggle reflected an admirable tenacity and tragic desperation that immediately appealed to Zhao.[7]

As Jie Li observes in her chapter on the work of Zhao Liang, throughout *Petition* his camera adopts a variety of styles: from direct address serving as a conduit for the petitioners' vehement anger; to a humane observer of individual and collective suffering; to an embodied and self-reflexive engagement with his film subjects (Li 2010). As the petitioners wait in vain for justice and eke out a living with Zhao in tow, we witness several meaningful and complex relationships unfold. Foremost among them is Zhao's relationship with Xiaojuan and her adoptive mother, who have been petitioning since Xiaojuan was a young girl. Despite allowing herself and her daughter to be filmed, the mother remains suspicious of Zhao and, in one unforgettable scene after Xiaojuan abandons her, rails against him for his intrusion into their lives. She shouts and pushes Zhao away. By contrast, as Xiaojuan grows into a young woman and Zhao matures as a filmmaker, we witness mutual trust develop. This deepening connection unfolds not only profilmically between subject and filmmaker but is also refracted through our engagement with the film as audience members. Like Zhao, we as viewers are situated within the petitioner milieu, even if the irreducible opacity of each individual's deep subjectivity remains intact and we are unable to fully experience their torment and indignation. It is these varying kinds of intersubjective dynamics involving the spectator that Vivian Sobchack, in developing a phenomenology of nonfiction film reception, describes as her central concept of the address of the eye: "It is a visual address always housed in a situated body experienced as 'mine' and yet always also able to extend itself to where that body is not. It is able to reflectively connect that body both with its own future and past situations and with the bodily situations of others."[8]

INTEROBJECTIVITY AND WITNESSING

Sobchack's evocation of the role of the body in relation to intersubjective cinematic space is important here because a large number of Chinese documentaries, like *Petition,* depict the aftermath of actual physical trauma and represent experiences of suffering that constitute the dark side of China's ecomonic development. In one particularly striking scene of *Petition,* Zhao's tracking camera allows us to sense his body-in-motion and, more importantly, his body-in-shock as one among a group of petitioners searching a railroad line for the clothes and body parts of an elderly petitioner who was chased to her death along the tracks. Suddenly, his camera fixes on the meager material remains of the pursued woman: a piece of skull and her severed hand. What is revealed in Zhao's decision to linger over the skull bone and the severed hand is the horror of encountering the evidence of death, which Sobchack argues is experienced by subjects like us as other than we are and as an object (Sobchack 2004).

While death remains an extreme beyond verifiable comprehension, the experience of the body as a suffering object is one we all share in common. *Petition* puts forward a steady stream of disturbing images of the suffering body, of the body as an object that can be acted upon and mangled: from the man beaten so heavily that his eyes turn bloodshot black to the coroner-like photos of severely injured loved ones that petitioners thrust toward the camera as evidence. Different from the confrontation with death, what strikes us as viewers in these moments, Sobchack explains, is the surprisingly intimate experience of the body—both our own body and the body of the Other in the film—as an object. By depicting maimed, mutilated, and disfigured bodies on-screen and expressing the filmmaker's embodied way of looking, *Petition* and many of its contemporaries make possible an ethically charged cinematic space, supplementary to intersubjectivity, that Sobchack terms "interobjectivity," the "co-constitutive experience we have of ourselves and others as material objects," as bodies that can suffer, that can be vulnerable to external forces (Sobchack 2004, 296).

Resonating with Veena Das' philosophical contemplation of "how my pain may reside in your body," Sobchack's notion of interobjectivity forms the ground for ethical response to the pain and suffering of others (Das 2007, 40). Thus, there is a kind of social engagement at work in Chinese independent cinema that helps to further contextualize the persistence of the raw and the observational. Simply put, this kind of filmmaking serves as a humanizing response to trauma. Of course, films that testify to suffering through the structured interview format, such as Hu Jie's *In Search of Lin Zhao's Soul* (2004) and *Though I Am Gone* (2007), Wang Bing's *Fengming: A Chinese Memoir* (2007), all three of which focus on the excesses of the Mao period, are also powerful oral histories of injustice and trauma. The activist mode, championed by Ai Xiaoming and artist Ai Weiwei, is another powerful way to marshal forth a protest against injustice. Yet, with *xianchang* understood as another, more open-ended form of witnessing, such an approach offers an experiential receptivity to register the pain and suffering of others. Although less directly engaged than the activist mode, this process is still political in China, if not explicitly then implicitly, as the anguish depicted is often the result of state violence, corruption, or negligence—precisely that which goes unaddressed by government authorities and official media. Such accounts, committed to sound and image, become what James Scott has called "hidden transcripts," the secret discourse shared by members of the public behind the Party's back (Scott 2008).

The filmmaker Xu Xin, in his six-hour documentary *Karamay* (2010), also makes extensive use of these hidden transcripts and delivers them in austere fashion to not only criticize the Party but also show how trauma—especially when suppressed—affects individuals and ripples out into a community. *Karamay* recounts a tragic fire on December 8, 1994, in Karamay, an oil town in northern Xinjiang, which broke out when primary and middle school students held a performance to honor a delegation of officials. Very few students made it to safety and, in the end, the fire claimed the lives of 323 people, 288 of whom were children. The exact details of what happened remain unclear, but one thing is certain: all the city officials escaped to safety without suffering any serious injury.

The film's contemplative long-take introduction of an early December sunrise over the graveyard of students' tombs on the thirteenth anniversary of the tragedy gives way to cinema verité scenes of director Xu Xin approaching tomb after tomb, caressing the cold stone and faded photos with his handheld camera. A handful of grieving parents who have come to mourn their children begin to talk to Xu, speaking out their anger and sadness. The film then moves into its main formal register, which is a skillful interweaving of interviews with parents and archival footage from local newscasts and home videos to shed light on the community's experience of trauma as well as the chain of events. When the stage curtains first caught fire, the students were instructed to "stay seated" and "let the leaders go first." But the fire spread quickly and claimed hundreds of lives due to startling oversights on the parts of the local leadership. Rescue attempts were delayed and, inexplicably, the fire trucks arrived on the scene more than forty-five minutes after first being called. After promising martyr status for the victims and paying off the families, officials turned their backs on the traumatized citizens and intervened only to prevent them from reaching out to media or petitioning in Beijing.

When Xu began production exactly thirteen years later in December 2007, the situation was still tense. The bulk of shooting had to be conducted in the homes of the grieving families, out of sight of local authorities. Although the interview format lies outside the conventions of observational cinema, Xu's open-ended shooting style registers the lived and embodied experience of prolonged, unacknowledged suffering and at the same time constructs a new historical document. Indeed, Xu has stated these scenes are not easily definable as interviews; he refrained from posing a set of questions but rather created a space not only for testimony and disclosure, but also for the parents' grief to be heard. During these intimate moments where Xu adopts a self-effacing and receptive mode of filming by placing the camera on a tripod and allowing the parents to speak freely at length, the duration of the long takes opens the possibility for meaningful contact between film subject, filmmaker, and viewer.

While the tragedy in Karamay resonates with other cases of injustice that today call for exposure—the frequent cover-up of mining accidents or the collapsed schools in the Sichuan earthquake come to mind—what is most striking about

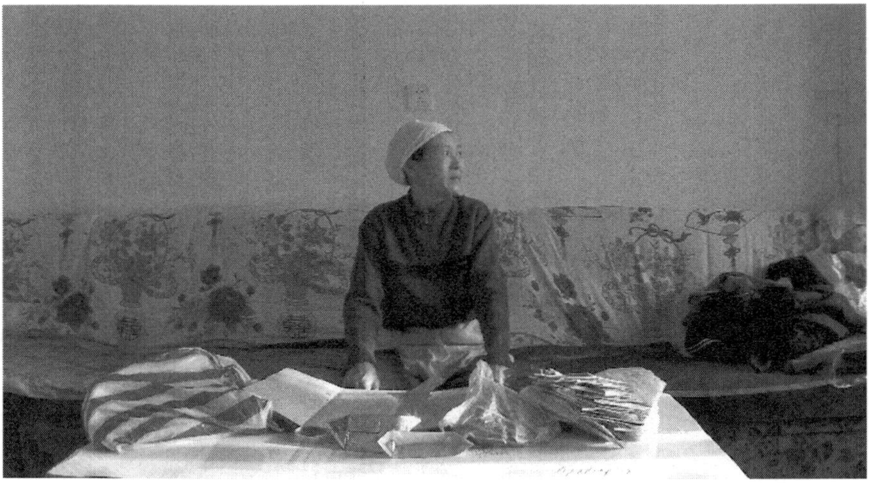

Figure 2.4. *Karamay*. A mother shares her experience of losing her child in the Karamay fire. (image by Xu Xin)

Karamay is that it not only gives voice to multiple narratives, but also depicts various embodiments of pain through its careful attention to gesture, speech, and comportment. There are certainly numerous emotional scenes as parents shed tears in memory of their children. Similar to the scenes of direct address in Zhao Liang's film, some parents even unleash their outrage at the government—in an act of *suku,* or "speaking bitterness"—directly into the lens. Xu also makes use of archival VHS footage of emergency staff and volunteer rescuers carrying the severely burned bodies of the children through hospital hallways and placing them onto hospital beds. Witnessing these small, charred, and deformed human forms plopped in piles onto hospital beds, some perhaps still breathing yet with no doctors in sight, we as viewers feel the charge of interobjectivity wherein, as Sobchack writes, "the body-subject 'suffers' a *diminution of subjectivity* and, in this diminution, comes to experience—within subjectivity—an increased awareness of *what it is to be a material object*" (Sobchack 2004, 288). Other less dramatic moments reveal more subtle expressions of suffering. After an aging mother finishes speaking, for example, the shot lingers as she stands next to her son's framed photo. Rather than cutting on this pause, Xu is compelled by the mother's wistful posture to continue filming as a witness to her pain. Eventually she begins wiping the portrait not with affected melancholy but with quotidian caresses that express her everyday experience of loss.

Zhao Liang and Xu Xin are not the direct victims of the pain and trauma their films strive to depict, and there is substantial scholarship that argues for making a clear distinction between the firsthand experience of trauma and its vicarious representation. Exploring the role of literature in representing social suffering, David Morris writes that "perhaps the most important thing that literature has to tell us about suffering concerns the need for respect in the face of an experience that always holds back part of its truth, inaccessible and alien" (Morris, 1997, 42). Nonetheless, Michael Berry has pointed out that cultural texts—whether literary or cinematic—focused on the experience of pain and violence such as these films are no less powerful in the construction of cultural memory and national psyche (Michael Berry 2008). They achieve for the filmmakers, for the body of the film, and for us, what Veena Das, writing about another nation's history of violence, hopes she achieves in her anthropological project: letting the pain of the Other happen to her (Das 2007, 41).

Conclusion: The Cruelty of the Social

What are we to make of this project to reflect social suffering and the experience of trauma, to allow the pain of the Other to mark us? Independent directors have used such imagery as "double-edged swords" and descriptions of the production process as a mutual "searing" or "wounding" to express that documentary is not only damaging to the film subject but also to the filmmaker him/herself (Wang 2005). Similarly, Yiman Wang has employed the metaphor of a lightning rod held up in a thunderstorm to describe the role of the DV director. She warns against the inappropriateness of casting independent directors as political activists and asserts that they view themselves more as individual witnesses producing subjective yet honest accounts of Chinese society. Wang likens them to ethnographers who expose themselves to the "multivalent material circumstances" of their surroundings and states that "it is only by allowing him/herself to be seared by the environment that the documentary maker is able to channel and manifest an electrifying reality" (Wang 2005, 24).

I think this is an illuminating metaphor, not only for the reasons Yiman Wang explores in the space of her essay, but also for how it might, in turn, modify her own concept of "the documentary of cruelty." That is, I argue that the cruelty she describes exists not only within the confines of the filmmaker–film subject relationship: it also exists beyond the body of the film as a diffuse social force acting on and shaping the filmmaker, the film subject, and the audience members. This cruelty of the social—one of the key formative aspects, in my reading, of the "multivalent material circumstances" for Chinese filmmakers today—is the offspring of the hardships and injustices pervading Chinese society today and the legacy of an intensely violent and tumultuous twentieth century. Thus, an important and formative element of the reality the independent filmmaker reflects by raising high the lightning rod is both social and personal suffering. Against the assumption that only careerist ambitions motivate independent filmmakers, I argue that many filmmakers are actually compelled by both social responsibility and self-examination to use DV cinema to make sense of this very experience of suffering, whether it be their own or that of the Other. Xu Xin, for example, has expressed that although he cannot claim to have faced the same trauma as the families in Karamay, his act of recording their verbalized and embodied experience of suppressed grief and pain was also a method for him to register and work through his own experience of trauma as a social being. In this way, Wang's concept of the "documentary of cruelty" can be extended and modified to characterize the DV works that serve as a response to the pain and trauma shaping the social.

By way of conclusion, I return to Xue Jianqiang. In the introduction, I raised the question of generational dynamics but held it temporarily out of bounds. I lack the space here to explore it fully, but would like to at least acknowledge—and then destabilize—concerns regarding the younger generation of filmmakers that are relevant to the foregoing. In short, a prevailing assessment of the 1980s and 1990s generation in China casts this age group as self-absorbed consumers driven by material desires and cut off from full awareness of the less whitewashed elements not only of China's recent history but also, if their guardians have their way, of the massive social changes taking place around them. In terms of filmmaking, then, the concern is that these young filmmakers are only capable of producing narcissistic works that lack the political and historical consciousness of their elders and fail to critically respond to social suffering.

The selective amnesia induced by Chinese authorities is indeed a genuine concern, and the works thus far produced do evince a high degree of egotism, but the effects of China's tumultuous twentieth-century history and uncertain present nonetheless remain embedded within the social fabric and are readily reflected through DV cinema. Xue's *Martian Syndrome* is a prime example of a film that is shaped by the cruelty of the social. In addition to its use of the long take and its incisive interventions into the film's temporality, *Martian Syndrome* stands out precisely because it registers—in a vague and ambivalent manner appropriate to its themes—the social dislocation and everyday violence of Chinese society. Shot on a summer evening in the outskirts of Beijing on only two sixty-minute DV tapes, *Martian Syndrome* unfolds with the power of Beckett's later works as its Sony Night-Shot aesthetic envelops the viewer in a world of desperation, confusion, fear, and nihilism. Indeed, the dialogues in *Martin Syndrome* are on par with any piece of absurdist theater, yet it was filmed utterly spontaneously, without any preplanning.

The film begins with Xue and his friend Yang walking along a quiet street. On the way to the home of their friend Xiao Dong, a stranger around their age, Wang Xi, stops them and inquires if Xiao Dong is home. Xue and Yang, intrigued by the shabbily clothed stranger or perhaps just utterly bored, continue talking with him. Another depressive young man who is later described as "lonely" joins the discussion. Their conversation drifts from Wang Xi's new routine of asking their friend Xiao Dong for food, to the hardships of their shared experience as outsiders in Beijing, to incomplete statements about art and philosophy. Forlorn Wang Xi mumbles, "I am from Mars," and Xue responds with alacrity, "I'm from Mars too." Eventually, Xue and Yang leave the two needy interlopers and step into Xiao Dong's home. They find Xiao Dong alone, shirtless, shaking in sheer terror due to the harassment he has experienced at the hands of the stranger they just encountered, Wang Xi. Yang begins to caress and calm his friend as Xue continues filming, panning around the room to a bedside knife. Eventually, Xue steps outside again and begins to argue with Wang Xi about the DV tapes. Their tempers escalate until Xue suddenly drops his camera to the ground and attacks Wang Xi. After we hear the audio of the beating (we only see the dark dusty lane where the camera was set down), Xue collects his camera and goes back indoors. Some time later, Wang Xi returns and stands outside the door asking for a chance to take revenge on Xue. This NightShot section, which constitutes the bulk of the film, closes with a long take of the frightened yet fed-up Xiao Dong lecturing the remorseful Wang Xi through the screen door, which serves as a textural metaphor for their tense communication. The film's final shot removes us from this nightscape and places us in daylight for the first time in the film: we are suddenly at the Fanhall Films complex in Songzhuang where scores of people are milling about the courtyard. A festival must be happening and the crowd is ostensibly waiting for the next film screening. Suddenly, Xue's camera pans to a young man seated at one of the courtyard tables: it is Wang Xi no longer captured shirtless in Sony NightShot but now clothed in broad daylight and seated among the festival milieu of directors, students, critics, and cinephiles who make up the Chinese independent documentary community.

Through his openness to letting a film take shape around him—and for allowing the desperation of Wang Xi, the trembling fear of Xiao Dong, and the sudden violence he himself exhibits to mark the videotape—Xue has brought forth a unique chronicle of the experience not only of migrants in the capital, but also of the social surround of violence, suffering, and desperation in China. Demonstrating that the everyday can be brutal, he makes the inherent cruelty of the social the very fabric of his work. Just as his film disturbs us with its haunting imagery, it should also compel us toward a deeper engagement with the cruelty of the social—and the documentary impulse to reflect and re-create that cruelty—as we approach the diverse imbrications of aesthetics and ethics emerging from Chinese independent documentary today.

Notes

1. Transcribed from author's personal recording.

2. These questions are akin to the 1970s backlash against Direct Cinema's supposed goal of a detached observer recording the lives of those who remain powerless in the shaping of their own representation. See Johnston 1999, 31–40.

3. Academic publications have championed the rise of a second wave of independent documentary, characterized as foregrounding the poetic, the participatory, and the performative against the first wave of "public," observational documentaries. The 7th DOChina, with the buzz created by Xue's *Martian Syndrome* and Li Ning's autobiographical documentary *Tape*—discussed by Qi Wang in chapter 8—as well as the special section of "Private Portraits" devoted to Wu Wenguang's three most recent works, may indeed mark a watershed moment for "private" documentary in China.

4. The fact that scholars have employed an alternation of these terms highlights not only the overall complexity of Chinese independent documentary output, but also the inherent shortcomings entailed in academic definitions of artistic practices, as well as the multiple perspectives on documentary form.

5. It is also for this reason that one of the main proponents of *xianchang*, director Wu Wenguang, has emphasized that his fiercely individual and independent form of filmmaking resembles a personal "diary of images" (Wu 2010, 47).

6. For a discussion of "internal Orientalism," see Schein 1997.

7. Personal Interview with Zhao Liang. There are two versions of the film, a two-hour version for international festival programming and a five-hour trilogy version for the "domestic" audience in China. The two-hour *Petition* premiered in Cannes in 2009 and the longer version took the top documentary award at both the 2009 DOChina festival and at the 2010 Hong Kong International Film Festival.

8. In Sobchack's project to construct a film theory on the basis of phenomenological thought, she asserts that "as a philosophy of conscious experience, phenomenology systematically grounds the attempt of this study to make explicit the phenomenon of signification in the cinema as it is lived through and embodied in an enworlded subject of vision, that is, as it occurs existentially and directly for us and before us, rather than abstracted from us or posited against us" (Sobchack 1992, 27–28).

Bibliography

Berry, Chris. 2007. "Getting Real: Chinese Documentary, Chinese Postsocialism." In *The Urban Generation: Chinese Cinema and Society at the Turn of the Twenty-first Century*, edited by Zhang Zhen, 115–136. Durham, NC: Duke University Press.

———. 2009. "When is a film festival not a festival?: The 6th China Independent Film Festival." *Senses of Cinema,* Issue 53. Available at http://sensesofcinema.com/2009/festival-reports/when-is-a-film-festival-not-a-festival-the-6th-china-independent-film-festival/.

Berry, Michael. 2008. *A History of Pain: Trauma in Modern Chinese Literature.* New York: Columbia University Press.

Das, Veena. 1998. "Wittgenstein and Anthropology." *Annual Review of Anthropology* 27: 171–195.

———. 2007. *Life and Words.* Berkeley: University of California Press.

Jackson, Michael. 1998. *Minima Ethnographica: Intersubjectivity and the Anthropological Project.* Chicago: Chicago University Press.

Johnson, Matthew David. 2006. "'A Scene Beyond Our Line of Sight': Wu Wenguang and New Documentary China's Politics of Independence." In *From Underground to Independent: Alternative Film Culture in Contemporary China,* edited by Paul G. Pickowicz and Yingjin Zhang, 47–76. Lanham, MD: Rowman & Littlefield.

Johnston, Claire. 1999. "Women's Cinema as Counter-Cinema." In *Feminist Film Theory: A Reader,* edited by Sue Thornham, 31–40. Edinburgh: Edinburgh University Press.

Li, Jie. 2010. "Filming Power and the Powerless: Zhao Liang's *Crime and Punishment.*" China Perspectives. http://chinaperspectives.revues.org/5053.

Lü, Xinyu. 2003. *Documenting China* (Jilu Zhongguo). Beijing: Sanlian Publishing, 2003.

MacDougall, David. 2005. *The Corporeal Image.* Princeton, NJ: Princeton University Press.

Marks, Laura. 2000. *The Skin of the Film: Intercultural Cinema, Embodiment, and the Senses.* Durham, NC: Duke University Press.

Morris, David. 1997. "Voice, Genre, and the Moral Community." In *Social Suffering,* edited by Arthur Kleinman, Veena Das, and Margaret Lock, 25–46. Berkeley: University of California Press.

Nornes, Abé Mark. 2009. "Bulldozers, Bibles, and Very Sharp Knives: The Chinese Independent Documentary Scene." *Film Quarterly* 63 (1): 50–55.

Robinson, Luke. 2010. "From 'Public' to 'Private': Chinese Documentary and the Logic of *Xianchang.*" In *The New Chinese Documentary Film Movement: For the Public Record,* edited by Chris Berry, Lü Xinyu, and Lisa Rofel, 177–194. Hong Kong: Hong Kong University Press.

Schein, Louisa. 1997. "Gender and Internal Orientalism in China." *Modern China* 23 (1): 69–98.

Scott, James. 2008. *The Weapons of the Weak.* New Haven, CT: Yale University Press.

Sobchack, Vivian. 1992. *The Address of the Eye.* Princeton, NJ: Princeton University Press.

———. 2004. *Carnal Thoughts: Embodiment and Moving Image Culture.* Berkeley: University of California Press.

Vaughan, Dai. 1999. *For Documentary: Twelve Essays.* Berkeley: University of California Press.

Wang, Yiman. 2005. "The Amateur's Lightning Rod: DV Documentary in Postsocialist China." *Film Quarterly* 58 (4): 16–26.

Wu, Wenguang. 2010. "Program for the 7th Documentary Film Festival China" (DOChina): 47.

Zhang, Zhen, ed. 2007. *The Urban Generation: Chinese Cinema and Society at the Turn of the Twenty-first Century.* Durham, NC: Duke University Press.

CHAPTER 3

Filming Power and the Powerless

Zhao Liang's Crime and Punishment (2007) and Petition (2009)

JIE LI

In the autumn of 1996, Zhao Liang, an aspiring filmmaker from Liaoning and recent graduate from the Lu Xun Arts Academy, was living in Beijing with other young artists and looking for a new documentary subject. One day, a photographer friend came over for a drink and suggested that he go take a look at "the spectacle of petitioners at South Railway Station" who came from all over China to complain about the abuses and injustices committed by their local authorities (Zhao 2009). The following day, Zhao Liang took a bicycle and rode over with a DV camera. For the next twelve years, he would return many times to document the plights of these disenfranchised people, their confrontations with state power, as well as his own evolving relationship to his subjects, a process that parallels the development of Chinese independent documentaries.

The 1990s and the new millennium saw the rise of the New Documentary Movement in China, which left behind official, grand narratives for more personal narratives about ordinary people in contemporary society (Lü 2003, 8–9). Early films focused on vagabond young artists, such as freelancers in Wu Wenguang's *Bumming in Beijing* (*Liulang Beijing* 1990), experimental drama in Jiang Yue's *The Other Bank* (*Bi'an* 1995), and the punk rock musicians in Zhao Liang's first film *Paper Airplane* (*Zhi feiji* 2001). Soon enough, new documentary filmmakers also began turning their cameras away from their marginalized *selves* onto marginalized *others* (Jaffee 2006, 102), featuring figures as diverse as migrant workers, prostitutes, coal miners, homosexuals, Christians, AIDS villages, and suppressed voices from the dustbin of history. Such a shift in subject matter in the last decade produced unsanctioned memories and alternative histories such as Wang Bing's nine-hour epic *West of the Tracks* (*Tiexi qu* 2003), Ying Weiwei's *The Box* (*Hezi* 2001), Li Yifan's *Before the Flood* (*Yanmo* 2005), Hu Jie's *In Search of Lin Zhao's*

Soul (*Xunzhao Linzhao de linghun* 2004), and Zhao Dayong's *Ghost Town* (*Fei Cheng* 2008).

In its de-emphasis of dominant ideologies, however, the New Documentary Movement has only rarely confronted the mechanisms of state power in the present,[1] as if the initial turn away from politics *to* the everyday has obscured the politics *of* the everyday. In this regard, Zhao Liang's works present a welcome exception in their penetrating observations of state-society relations in contemporary China, showing both their human and dehumanizing aspects: *Crime and Punishment* (*Zui yu fa* 2007) documents the everyday operations of a police station in a small town in Liaoning; whereas *Petition* (*Shangfang* 2009) chronicles the perseverant appeals for justice by the disenfranchised over more than a decade. This chapter offers an analysis of these two complementary portraits of representatives of state power and of the powerless. I argue that these films provide "seeing lessons" for the audience in three senses: by rendering visible those who are un(der)represented; by exposing and critiquing the deception of official media images; and by showing various complex ways power is connected to surveillance and visibility. Thus, the filmmaker, his camera, and the spectators become implicated in power relationships as we cast voyeuristic, panoptic, activist, empathetic, or critical gazes on the documentary subjects. As *Petition* rose to international visibility while being banned in China, however, Zhao Liang has gone on to transform his relationship with the Chinese authorities by making an officially commissioned "public announcement film," *Together* (*Zai yi qi* 2010). My conclusion will briefly discuss this recent turn of events in ways that defy stark dichotomies between resistance and collaboration with power.

The "Human" Faces of Power: Crime and Punishment

Shot near the filmmaker's hometown at China's border to North Korea, *Crime and Punishment* follows a few young officers at the local police station as they carry out their law enforcement duties. Unlike the crime police miniseries that one might watch on television, Zhao Liang's two-hour documentary features cases too insignificant and absurd to be reported in the media: A mentally ill man calls the police for a "corpse" he has found in his bed, which turns out to be a pile of blankets. An apparently mute robbery suspect refuses to admit his crime even after suffering physical abuse. A scrap collector without a license is detained at the police station and, after his son insults an officer on the phone, is forced to make a humiliating apology. Finally, the police catch three peasants driving a truck loaded with stolen lumber and force them to confess with on-screen and off-screen violence.

Police officers featured in a handful of Chinese feature films in the 1990s made in the style of documentary realism, among them Ning Ying's *On the Beat* (*Minjing gushi* 1995), Zhang Yuan's *East Palace, West Palace* (*Donggong Xigong* 1996), and Jia Zhangke's *Xiao Wu* (1997). Shot on location with a cast of real Beijing local police officers, *On the Beat* is particularly comparable to *Crime and Punishment* in showing the daily routines of overworked officers, garrulous interrogations of intransigent petty criminals, bland and long meetings, and dog killings (Shi 2007, 316–343). As a documentarist, however, Zhao Liang does not have perfect control over his subjects, who follow the contingencies of the moment rather than a given script and mise-en-scène. Though abounding in amusing and absurd details, *Crime and Punishment* is not deliberately satiric, but rather has a directorial stance of sympathy and critical distance that shows both the human faces of state power and the way power could render both its exercisers and victims inhuman.

The opening sequence shows three policemen making their beds, one after another, kneading, folding, and manicuring their blankets into perfect cubes with straight parallel lines and right angles at all corners. As a reviewer comments, "nothing better conveys how the cop-soldiers strive for exactitude, no matter how pointless the activity" (Koehler 2008). At the same time, we can behold the human effort and an almost-endearing handicraft that pour into the cultivation of uniformity. It is a process that comes at a cost, as we soon learn that many officers in their twenties are already losing hair from stress at work. They also become impetuous and easy to offend, thus abusing power under the facade of maintaining law and order.

Embodying standards of regimentation, the policemen, walking in a single file though there are just two or three of them, go out to town and try to straighten out whatever disorder they see. Turning a corner, they find a scrap collector and ask to see his permit.

SCRAP COLLECTOR: My permit's on file. Go check at the police station.

POLICE OFFICER: We're from the police station. How come we've never seen your file?

SCRAP COLLECTOR: You don't even know me.

The officer claims to be an embodiment of the surveillance system that oversees the town's population, whereas the scrap collector points out the impossibility for such "omniscience" to *know* even an insignificant man like himself. Sure enough, the police win and bring him back to the station. Claiming that his permit is at home, the scrap collector borrows a policeman's cell phone to call his son, who lets loose a string of curses at the police, not knowing that the police are overhearing his "hidden transcript" at the other end of the line.[2] To retaliate, the police exploit the labyrinth of bureaucratic contradictions to detain the old man's donkey cart and make him walk several miles home to get his permit, which turns out to have expired. They also demand a personal apology from his son—a show of submission to their authority to compensate for his brief, unwitting rebellion.

For the most part, the camera is aligned with the police's point of view during arrests, house searches, and interrogations. The police obviously gave their permission to film, whereas the others appear neither to understand nor to dare question the camera's presence. Thus, the camera is *complicit* with police surveillance and occasionally seems to contribute to the intimidation of the suspects. The mute man accused of robbery, for instance, is ordered into a stress position somewhere between standing and squatting, and the camera films him in a six-minute take, during which the guarding officer goes in and out of sight.

Without the camera, it is reasonable to conjecture, the man could find temporary relief when the officer is out of the room. A slight shakiness in the shot suggests handheld work whereby the cameraman is also in a kind of "stress position"—something that a sympathetic audience can vicariously experience in tedious real-time. In this sense, the panoptic gaze turns into an empathetic gaze, confirmed by the considerably more relaxed manners of the arrested when they are alone with the camera than when the police are watching. Sometimes they would even speak of their difficult lives to the camera, placed at a low angle to suggest respect rather than condescension.

At once *complicit* and *compassionate,* Zhao Liang's long takes remain faithful to what André Bazin has called the "ambiguity of reality" revealed through the continuity of space and time (Bazin 2005, 68), which requires more participatory modes of viewing than montage that guide our attention at every moment. As Dudley Andrew elucidates the concept: "The spectator *should* be forced to wrestle with the meanings of a filmed event because he *should* wrestle with the meanings of events in empirical reality in his daily life" (Andrew 1976, 163). *Crime and Punishment* fosters critical viewing without dissecting the event and interpreting it for us; meanwhile, it is sympathetic without suturing the viewers to overidentify with any of the filmed subjects.

Not only is the filmmaker's position vis-à-vis his subjects ambiguous; as the film unfolds, the relationship between the police and those they arrest, detain, and even torture also transforms. In the last and most elaborate case of the illegal lumbering by three peasants, the police force them to confess after an all-night session of interrogation and beating. The next day, two officers accompany the main culprit back home to collect a fine and to the nearby forest to collect photographic evidence at the "scene of crime." As they approach the man's clearly impoverished household, the officer takes off his handcuffs so that he "wouldn't lose face in front of your wife." Yet his wife spots right away that something is wrong: "Why is your face all red and swollen?" Without answering her, the culprit takes the police and Zhao Liang on a long hike through the forest to find the stumps for the trees that he had cut down so that the police could take pictures. The physical exhaustion and shared shame over the night's violence, however, seemed to have forged a strange bond between the police and the illegal lumberjack, who asks the officers to stay for lunch, while the police promise to persuade their captain to reduce his fine. The lumberjack also shares with the police the reason why he stole the wood—he wanted to buy his children some presents on market day.

As the police discover in their "criminal suspect" a husband, a son, and a father, the tortured man sees in the police officers ordinary fellows with the capacity for compassion, who are also just trying to make a living. After such mutual recognition, the police photography of the suspect with handcuffs next to the tree stumps seems closer to photographic souvenirs than the mug shots taken of him and his accomplices the night before. As they return to the man's home and collect the fine, however, the wife follows them, insisting that "the police can't just go around hitting people, even if they broke the law." An intertitle tells us that for fear of the family filing a complaint, the men were fined a token amount and allowed to keep the lumber they cut down. As police surveillance meets with the sharp sight of the illegal lumberjack's wife, both decide to turn a blind eye to the other's violation of laws and regulations.

With patient long takes and an ambivalent gaze that is in turn complicit, compassionate, or critical, *Crime and Punishment* shows us the human beings in military uniforms—their capacity for rage, sympathy, and fear—as well as how the power authorized by these uniforms might dehumanize, through violence and humiliation, not only those suspected to be criminals, but also the police officers themselves. Apart from discipline and punishment, much police power resides with surveillance, though a sustained look at the other could also generate empathetic recognition, and returning the gaze may well be the first step for the powerless to empower themselves.

From Voyeurism to Empathy: *Petition* as a Seeing Lesson

Just as *Crime and Punishment* takes up a subject matter treated in earlier feature films, *Petition* can also find a genealogical precedent in Zhang Yimou's *Story of Qiuju* (1992), about a pregnant peasant woman determined to seek justice at ever-higher administrative levels after the village chief kicked her husband in the groin. Shot in cinema verité style, Zhang's low-budget feature is a comedy and fable of "be careful what you ask for"—since the village chief does get arrested, but only after he saved the lives of Qiuju and her baby in a complicated childbirth. Even earlier in 1977, documentary photographer Li Xiaobin took about a thousand photographs of petitioners, often victims of the Cultural Revolution unable to find redress through their local judiciary systems. Acclaimed as "the most poignant work of Chinese documentary photography from this period," one of these pictures shows a haggard and disoriented petitioner in Tiananmen Square, with several large Mao buttons pinned on his tattered clothes (Wu 2008, 101–102). Made three decades later in a different medium and genre, Zhao Liang's *Petition* presents not only a sequel, but one that has been called "epic in scope and profound in its implications, as its critique expands to challenge the foundations of China's current political system" (Kraicer 2009). There are two versions of the film, a two-hour version for international festival programming and a five-hour trilogy version for the "domestic" audience in China, with a slower pace and many more details. Except otherwise noted, this paper refers to the more widely screened two-hour version.

Petition opens with an unimpressive, even prosaic establishing shot of the old Beijing South Railway Station, a bird's-eye panorama featuring a busy highway and an arriving train in the backdrop. Toward the end of the film, we will see a panoramic view of the same site taken from the same angle, showing the futuristic curved roofs of the newly constructed South Railway Station—the largest in Asia—that opened on the eve of the 2008 Beijing Olympics. Like the opening shot, no human figure is visible, and all we can hear are station loudspeakers announcing the arrival of the high-speed Beijing-Tianjin Intercity Train. What the film has taught us between these two impersonal shots at the beginning and end, however, is to *see* the petitioners who used to live in the nooks and crannies of this place and who were *made to disappear* from view to fulfill the state's image of itself as a modern and harmonious nation.

Shot between 1996 and 2008, *Petition* is also a document of Zhao Liang's own development as a filmmaker and his evolving relationship to his film subjects. He first began filming petitioners out of voyeuristic interest—after all, the petitioners live in open, public spaces and have nowhere to hide if someone turns a camera on their apparently abject existences. We can see glimpses of such intrusive and unethical shooting in some early footage where, for instance, the director films a man sleeping under piles of cardboard before the station on a snowy night. In the shot, the cardboard is lifted momentarily from the man's face and a flashlight or video light wakes him up so that he stares confusedly into the camera.

The filmmaker's initial alienation from his subjects is also manifested in his inability at times to understand their heavy accents and awkward questions such as: "Doesn't writing a petition feel like writing an essay for school?" Even as the director becomes familiar with several petitioners, many shots continue to suggest common "viewing positions" from which the film's target audience *might* have seen the petitioners. As passengers arriving in Beijing we might see the shabby shacks the petitioners built along the tracks; as we walk out of the station we might brush aside their attempts to sell us maps; at Tiananmen Square we might see a petitioner being arrested by the police for giving out flyers. By showing us these familiar locales, Zhao Liang reminds us of occasions when we rubbed shoulders with petitioners and either turned a blind eye to their suffering or watched them as curious spectacles.

Following the voyeuristic mode is what might be called an "activist-exposé" mode of filming, which preoccupies the first eight minutes, where petitioners present their complaints succinctly and forcefully to the camera, often accompanied by written petitions on paper, cloth, or clothing, or against the backdrop of physical evidence such as mutilated bodies or demolished homes. A farmer accuses his county cadres of the effective confiscation of a harvest. A worker was laid off without living expenses. A woman pleads for the innocence of her imprisoned husband. A mother indicts her son's military superiors for disabling him physically and mentally. These petitioners' bombastic words and unflinching bodies almost spring out of the screen with fervent outrage, and the montage sequence of their complaints ends with several group portraits: a long shot of two dozen people holding up papers and photographs—some standing and others kneeling—and a tracking shot that "swims" through another crowd who cry "unfair" in cacophony (Figure 3.1).

Such frontal, demonstrative, and unaestheticized "activist-exposé mode" of filming is not atypical of human rights activist videos around the world and is practiced more consistently in China by Ai Xiaoming, who documented grassroots struggles against local power in videos such as *Taishi Village* (*Taishi cun* 2005). Such filmmaking seems to borrow from the Communist revolutionary tradition of speaking bitterness (*suku*), occasions where "oppressed members of the 'old society' took center stage to vent their rage in a compelling performance that made the working of history palpably 'real'" (Anagnost 1997, 17). Many films of the Maoist era also dramatized such *suku* performances, where peasants, workers, and soldiers recall their suffering at the hands of landlords, capitalists, or Nationalists. In *Petition,* however, the families of peasants, workers, and soldiers decry against abuses of power by Communist Party cadres instead, using the director's camera as a possible channel for their complaints.[3] While such on-screen performances of indictment can invoke outrage and pity, they do not always bring us closer to understanding or even recognizing the pain and humanity of the petitioners.

In the course of filming and within the film's duration, Zhao Liang begins to adopt a third, *empathetic* mode of filming that probably has a more profound

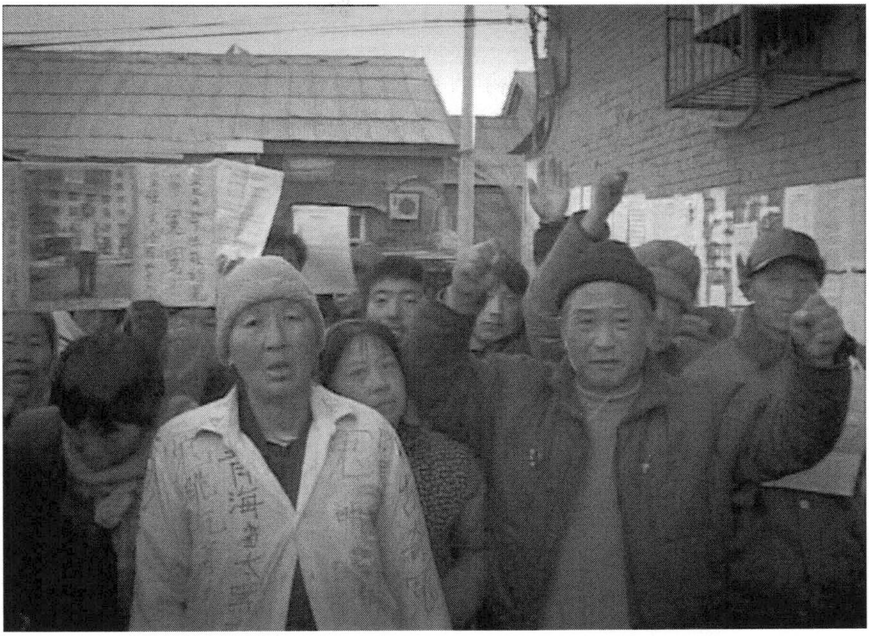

Figure 3.1. Petition. An "activist-exposé mode" of filming: petitioners cry "unfair" before the camera.

impact on the audience than a litany of injustices. Similar to Wang Bing's unobtrusive, tactful cinematography in *West of the Tracks* (Li 2008), Zhao Liang and his camera keep on returning to the same places and befriending the community of petitioners. As they become comfortable with his camera, Zhao Liang's shots also grow calmer, steadier, and more deferential. He records their everyday lives, their love and laughter as well as tears and protests. For instance, one sequence begins with a bedridden man telling the camera how he had been paralyzed by the arbitrary violence of his local police, who went on to beat his father, wife, and brother when they came to petition in Beijing—a narrative illustrated with photographic evidence and still shots of his whole family in a makeshift and leaking shelter (Figure 3.2). Far more moving, however, is the ensuing NightShot scene where his wife, a toddler in one arm, puts a bottle of water with a straw to her husband's lips. Then we see the toddler feeding the father his meal with a spoon and then giving him a massage afterward, while the sound of a passing train rattles by and a single candle illuminates their small world (Figure 3.3). If the earlier scene of accusations make us pity the family, then this scene of affection and resilience moves us to respect them, and our

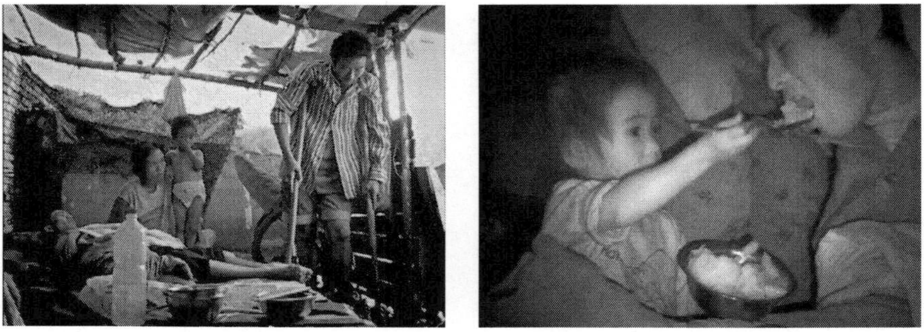

Figures 3.2 & 3.3. Petition. Zhao Liang captures both the misery (3.2) and resilience (3.3) of a petitioning family.

indignity at what happened to this family is transformed into a deeper recognition of their human dignity.

The empathetic mode of filming could also be compared to what film theorist Vivian Sobchack calls "the humane gaze" in filming death or extreme human suffering. Marked by "extended duration" and a "relatively steady camera," the humane gaze "visibly and significantly encodes in the image its own subjective responsiveness to what it sees" (Sobchack 2004, 252). This is particularly applicable to one scene as Zhao Liang and other petitioners—for the sake of burial and evidence—gather the scattered clothing and body parts of an elderly female petitioner run over by a train as she escaped from the authorities. First the camera follows other petitioners as they pick up a jacket, a shoe, a jawbone, a skull piece, and an identity card. Then it stops at the tracks, holds still, as though taking a deep breath, and very slowly zooms onto a mutilated hand, with tendons still sticking to the rail. The frozen quality of the camera's stare here, to borrow Sobchack's words, "suggests the ethical recognition that there is no tolerable point of view from which to gaze at such a death yet that such horror must be witnessed and attested to" (Sobchack 2004, 253).

To identify in such a shot the humane gaze, however, is to take into account the filmmaker's other interactions with his subjects. Even though Zhao Liang himself never appears on-screen, his presence is unmistakably felt as a human witness to their testimonies rather than as an indifferent mechanical device. On several occasions he also serves as a messenger, entrusted with delivering letters and even donation money. At the petition office and other spaces of power, where "cameras are strictly forbidden," Zhao Liang's hidden camera is held at belly level, vulnerable to being attacked or confiscated. When filming at the petition office he dresses like a petitioner, but beyond this camouflage, his filmmaking act is also mimetic of the petitioners' struggle. Along these lines, a *Variety* reviewer praises

Zhao Liang for lobbying "on behalf of those who have lobbied in vain" (Chang 2009), and Chinese public intellectual Cui Weiping gave this film the alternative title "The Children of Sisyphus," which describes not only the petitioners themselves but also Zhao Liang the filmmaker (Fanhall Films 2009).

Like the petitioners, Zhao Liang wishes to show with oral testimonies and photographic evidence that injustice has taken place. Like them, he must be perseverant and undertake various physical, psychological, political, and legal risks. Also somewhat like petitioners, the film is not pristine or polished, yet the viewer can easily recognize that even the most dimly lit, shaky, tilted, or otherwise precariously composed shots did not come easily. In these ways, *Petition* is not only a portrait of petitioners but also in itself a petition for political reform in China, extended toward a domestic and international public. "Signed" by commoners at the bottom of the political, economic, social, and educational hierarchies, this film petition weaves together their faces and wisps of narratives into a larger tapestry showing the sinking bodies and dark sides of China's rise into global visibility.

Petitioning Spaces and Communities

The previous section analyzed Zhao Liang's growing relationship to his subjects through the voyeuristic, activist-exposé, and empathetic modes, which guide the audience to *see* the petitioners in a state where power and visibility are intricately connected. As Ann Anagnost points out: "The tower at the center is not entirely a darkened space inhabited by an invisible gaze but an illumined stage from which the party calls, 'Look at me! I make myself visible to you. Your return gaze completes me and realizes my power' " (Anagnost 1997, 116). That illuminated stage is the Tiananmen Square Rostrum where generations of PRC leaders from Mao Zedong to Hu Jintao have greeted the people. It is also the square itself and, by extension, the city of Beijing. Thus, the petitioners' struggle for justice is also one of struggling for visibility in the nation's capital. This section examines the specific *sites* in Beijing where the film is set: the South Railway Station and the nearby shantytowns where petitioners live, as well as the petition office and other official spaces with symbolic power. In these sites, petitioners are shown to wrestle with the many faces of power—from a centralized bureaucratic labyrinth to the lackeys of local authorities, from the pristine facades of the national government to the state-controlled mass media—only to be swept away by the inexorable logic of progress, modernization, and economic development.

Connecting regions with the center, the South Railway Station is where petitioners first arrive in Beijing after a long journey from home, after having tried and failed to appeal to local courts. Yet the Beijing offices often force them to return home under the escort of the interceptors or retrievers (*jiefangren*) sent by the regional or local authorities. Even so, they would not have come entirely in vain because encounters with other petitioners expand their perspectives beyond their personal grievances, for as one petitioner puts it in the film: "I was secluded in my region, but once I reached [the capital] I realized that there are numerous cases of injustice, so my thoughts turned to the government and the nation."

Apart from a contact zone between the region and the center, the railway station also features the tug and pull of the "old" and the "new," the "backward" and the "modern," the "past" and the "future." While demolition is among the "three inevitabilities in Chinese independent documentary" (Nornes 2009, 50–55), it is all the more poignant in *Petition* because those who lose their footing in this place are marginalized and adrift to begin with. The train station and its surroundings are a camping ground for the petitioners, providing a roof over their heads or, failing that, a patch of ground where they could put down their blankets. Even a plastic sheet can be a petitioner's precious belonging, for it keeps the dews from drenching his blanket. When the bulldozers push together what appears to be mere rubbish, we can detect within the debris the artifacts of livelihood and, often at the end of a long pan, a person or an entire family at the rubble's margins. The ruin of the "petition village" forces petitioners to camp outdoors, to move to faraway suburbs or into the dark cracks in the abutment of beam bridges over a shallow canal. Thus, the great leap into the future—the largest station in Asia with the fastest conventional trains in the world—rendered the existences of these petitioners into that of prehistoric "cavemen."

Since some people have been petitioning for decades, their grievances are also old, historical, and anachronistic, including remnant cases from the Cultural Revolution with no contemporary legal solutions. The petition system also has a long historical pedigree in China turning citizens into supplicants at the feet of power (Fang 2009, 1105–1135). A few intellectuals featured in the film call for the system's abolition because "it is a lie" and a "dead end." Yet for the lack of better alternatives, desperate individuals and communities continue to turn to petitioning as "the preferred, and sometimes the only available, route" (Dillon 2009, 88). So they gather about the gray, nondescript building of the petition office, first seen in the film through railings. Inside, filmed with a hidden camera, the officials operate behind iron bars and petitioners are busy filling out forms. Power takes the visual appearance of various bureaucratic grids onto which minds and bodies, lives and deaths are mapped, inscribed, and reduced. Yet this bureaucracy is less functional than Kafkaesque—people come to the petition office with cases that their local courts turned down, only to have the petition officers tell them to take the cases back to the local courts. The petitioners confront the grid of laws and regu-

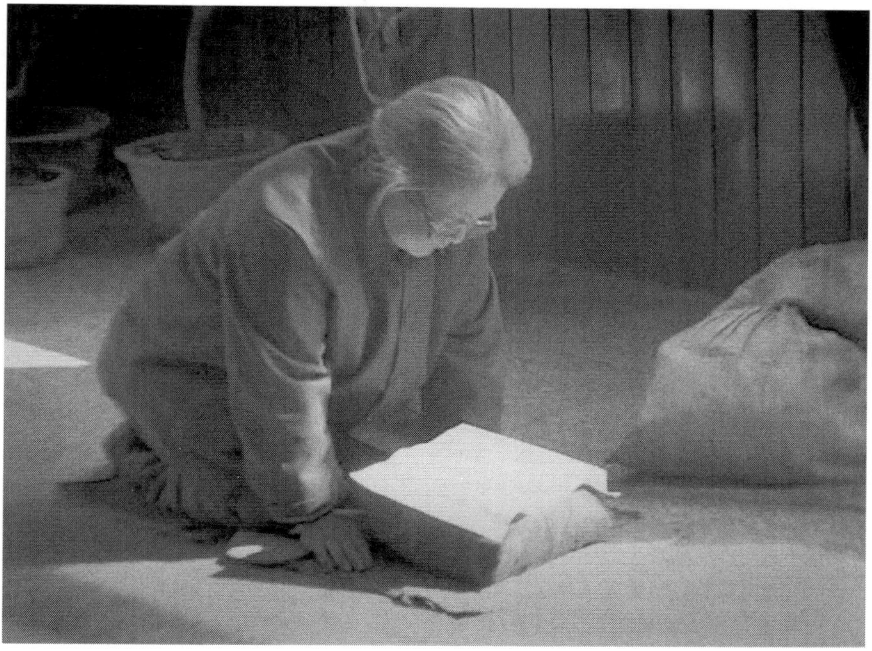

Figure 3.4. Petition. A petitioner kneels like a devout pilgrim before the authorities at the petition office.

lations with their pleading narratives, photographs, tears, and bodies that refuse to budge—that is, until the police expel them by force or hand them over to the "retrievers."[4]

The bureaucratic grids of the petition office also have a strange power to enthrall those caught in its labyrinth: the petitioners treat this place almost as a site of divine power. The first scene inside the petition office shows an old woman kneeling in the center, facing the authorities behind the bars. A beam of sunshine falls on her white hair and the white paper, giving her the air of a devout pilgrim who prays to a god (Figure 3.4). Indeed, many petitioners are Buddhists who donate money to the local temples and Christians who thank God before their humble meals, gleaned from other people's leftovers. But even petitioners without subscription to a particular faith seem to undergo a sort of "religious" experience as they wait in endless queues to receive forms that would then put them in another queue to meet with the authorities. For one petitioner in the film, the long wait makes the paper form feel like a holy imperial edict (*shengzhi*):

> Finally I got it! How my heart aches with joy! When filling out the form, I keep telling myself: "Don't make a mistake." In my mouth and in my heart I pray: "Cadre, cadre, could you say a sentence or just a word that would make the local authorities solve my case so that I don't have to come back?" Eventually I meet with the cadre, who gives me a piece of paper. I take it home with me, and there the holy paper turns into wastepaper. Then the process starts all over again.[5]

The petition system presents petitioners with a constant tug and pull between hope and cynicism, between faith and despair. Whereas the central petition office is represented as at once a darkened panopticon and a sacred temple, outside its thresholds is a wild frontier where local and provincial levels of power appear as bloodhound-like retrievers. Filmed with a hidden camera, these men dress in suits or leather jackets and have cars parked nearby, ready to seize the petitioners from their respective regions to be incarcerated in detention centers or mental hospitals. One telling scene shows three "retrievers" cornering a woman petitioner on crutches in a back alley: "Our city has millions of people," said one of men with a sinister, gangster-like aura. "We don't care if one person disappears."

Caught between the bureaucratic grids of the petition office and the "wild frontier" outside it, desperate petitioners try to enhance the visibility of their cases by performing various forms of protest at Tiananmen Square, including collective kneeling and wailing, distributing pamphlets, or transgressing into the forbidden empty space around the Monument of the People. Such attempts to call attention to themselves are nipped in the bud, for the police, within minutes or seconds, would have arrested these stray bodies and confiscated their scattered papers, meanwhile telling spectators that "there's nothing to look at!" At such sites of symbolic power, the petitioners appear as stains on the face of power and are supposed to "disappear" as if they had never existed, especially during national congresses or events such as Hong Kong's return in 1997 or the Olympics in 2008—all occasions for the self-display of state power in the eyes of the nation or the world, occasions where the symbolic spaces of power multiply their effects through the state-controlled mass media. Keenly aware of the connection of their destinies to national or even international affairs, the petitioners often seek public attention shortly before these important media events. After all, there are only two ways to make them disappear—solve their problems or arrest them by force, which entails at least a momentary loss of face for the regime.

Without reporting by the mass media, the effect of these petitioner-staged spectacles is quite limited. But since the petitioners tell Zhao Liang ahead of time about their guerrilla battles, he can record them at the right place and time. His film thereby helps to enhance the visibility of their struggle on a global festival circuit as well as through independent film distribution in China.[6] Whereas the camera in *Crime and Punishment* is aligned with the agents of state power, *Petition* is filmed entirely from the perspective of the powerless, and the director's solidarity with the petitioners is unambiguous. In this sense, this documentary does not pretend to be a neutral, balanced, and impartial representation of the Chinese complaint system as a whole. At no point does Zhao Liang try to interview officials at the petition office or to find out from local courts their rationales for rejecting the cases of given petitioners. We do not learn of any successful petitioning cases; nor do we learn of the government's dilemmas. The state appears as a monolith of evil, and the only "good" officials featured in the film are ones who quit or were dismissed from office due to their uncompromised sense of justice. Meanwhile, the film momentarily suggests, but does not further explore, the nostalgia among many petitioners for the Mao era, remembered to be free of corruption and inequality. A petitioner in the five-hour version expresses his longing for a Maoist-style political campaign to avenge corrupt bureaucrats—for him at least, revolutionary violence would be equivalent to justice, a sentiment that could probably find echoes among as many petitioners as calls for liberal democracy.

While such complexities went missing, the film does render the petitioners' struggles *visible* to a broader audience so that the latter might be able to see *through*

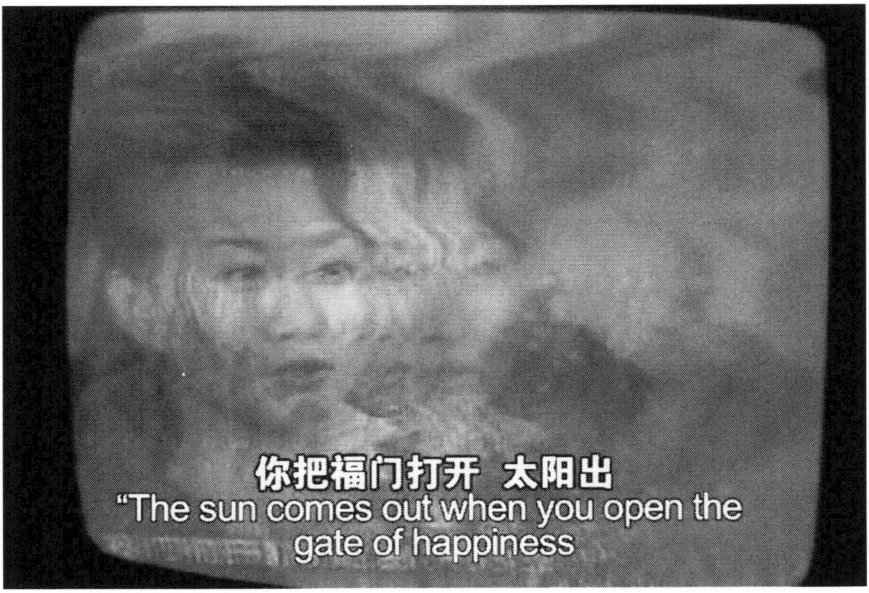

Figure 3.5. Petition. On Chinese New Year's Eve, a few petitioners watch the Spring Festival Gala on an old television from a Dumpster.

the more hegemonic images on television. In a powerful scene, several petitioners camping outdoors watch the Spring Festival Gala on an old television picked from a Dumpster (Figure 3.5). As fireworks explode in the backdrop, they cook with a makeshift stove and sit amid their scattered belongings in the demolition rubble. We hear the off-screen television speak: "Dishes of sweet rice cakes and bowls of hot rice wine are on the table now. Premier Hu Jintao is joining the family's New Year's Eve Supper." Hu's voice says: "I'm happy to see that your life is getting better." In a little while, the sweet voice of Song Zuying, a popular singer of patriotic and folk songs, fills the soundtrack: "The sun comes out when you open the gate of happiness." Here, the film finally cuts from the dimly lit but captivated faces of the petitioner-audience to a point-of-view shot of the black and white television screen, which has such poor signals that Song's beautiful face is twisted by the white noise.

The television set in the rubble is analogous to the famous Taoist mirror in the classical Chinese novel *The Story of the Stone,* a mirror showing an attractive woman in the front and a grinning skull in the back—the truth of the illusory front (Cao 1987, 252). Official propaganda continues to hold its appeal for even these marginalized petitioners, but its sublime pronouncements can only arrive in their lives in the most ironic and even grotesque forms. This scene offers an incisive criticism of the official media as hypocritical illusion. It is against such a luminous backdrop that the darker realities of independent Chinese documentaries are defined.

The Fiction and Authenticity of Kinship and Image

Over twelve years of filming petitioners, Zhao Liang chose to focus on a mother and daughter from Jiangsu to give a sustained identification point for the film. Qi's husband died inexplicably during a medical checkup at work and was cremated without Qi's permission, so she took their daughter Juan to petition in Beijing. Twelve when Zhao Liang first met her in 1996, Juan did not attend school but accompanied her mother day in and day out in the shantytown. At age 18, she decides to leave her mother and start a new life with a boyfriend, not to return until six years later with a child of her own. Since the two-hour version omits some important reasons for her departure as well as the intervening six years, this section deals with the five-hour version and addresses the ethics of kinship and the politics of representation, as this story both explores the power dynamics among the powerless and exposes the benevolent mask of a paternalist state.

Structured as flashbacks framed by Juan's return to Beijing, "Mother and Daughter" in the five-hour version shows Juan's growth from an innocent girl attached to her mother to a savvy and rebellious adolescent. As she begins receiving attention from young men, Juan feels that she needs one of them to defend her from the rest as much as her mother wants to protect her against them all. Juan only decides to leave Qi and the petitioner lifestyle, however, when she finds out from relatives that Qi and the "father" for whose death they have been petitioning were not her biological parents but rather adopted her as a baby. The knowledge releases Juan from the obligations she thought were her destiny. Angry at the waste of her youth and her mother's deception and tyranny, she speaks cynically of all human relationships in terms of "using" and "being used," and how she would "use" her boyfriend to help her leave.[7]

When Juan reappears in the film three years later, she is living under the custody of Zhang Chunquan, her prefecture petition bureau chief, who had "adopted" her to propagate his own image in the press as a "parental official" who turned an unkempt, anti-social riffraff with a crazy mother and lots of fleas into a healthy, cleanly dressed, and school-attending young lady who would never again make trouble by petitioning in Beijing. Though fully aware of being used, Juan continues to play along and lets Zhang sponsor her wedding two years later. Excerpts from her wedding home video would be broadcast on China Central Television (CCTV). Also reported in *The People's Daily,* the story was naturally known to Qi, who speaks of her sense of being betrayed to Zhao Liang's camera. Juan's collaboration with state power has rendered Qi's cause absurd and "drawn a clear line of demarcation" that placed her in the category of the mad. And as we know from Michel Foucault, only by incarcerating petitioners like Qi in mental institutions could society call itself "sane" and "harmonious" (Foucault 1973). Thus, Qi vows never to stop petitioning in Beijing, for otherwise "Zhang Chunquan would be promoted to come to Beijing." Her cause has transformed from petitioning for her husband to petitioning to keep what she considers an embodiment of evil hypocrisy from taking power.

A year later, however, Juan would return and ask for her foster mother's forgiveness in a poignant and melodramatic scene of reconciliation,[8] where Juan recalls the affection and care Qi had bestowed on her since childhood, all of which had nothing to do with "use" or "profit." Here Juan, and we, are able to reclaim kinship as something based neither on genes nor mutual "use" value, but rather "a last vestige of morality (and of humanity) left in an utterly amoral world" (Chow 2007, 178). Twice adopted, first by a powerless petitioner and then by powerful official who rose through the ranks, Juan's story could also be understood allegorically: she is a child of all petitioners who cared for her in turn, who brought her up with their legends of injustice; but she is also a child of the provincial and central powers who sought to "educate" her in a myth of the "harmonious society." When we compare the "hidden transcripts" of the weak and the public pronouncements of the strong, or the face of the mother and the mask of the Party, however, it is not difficult to see which is the greater lie.

Just as Qi turns out to be a more "authentic" parent to Juan than Zhang Chunquan, Zhao Liang's documentary is also more "true" than CCTV's televised propaganda, even if both are fragmentary mediations and do not tell the "whole story." By framing the televised story of Juan and her powerful benefactor/exploiter within the twelve-year reportage on the mother and daughter, *Petition* offers a trenchant critique of the official media as a fabricator of lies that have real-life impacts. This film thus brings forth with clarity what Rey Chow has insightfully discerned in Zhang Yimou's *Not One Less* (*Yige dou bushao* 1999), namely, the "usurpatory nature of the mediatized image." In Zhang's film, a thirteen-year-old substitute teacher Wei Minzhi goes looking for a missing student in the big city. Despite her strenuous physical efforts, it is when she "turns herself into an image on metropolitan television that she finally and *effortlessly* accomplishes her mission" (Chow 2007, 160–161). Therefore, Chow points out, "it is to the mediatized image that people will give their concern and compassion, and it is such images, rather than actual suffering human bodies, that now generate capital and, with it, social influence and political power" (Chow 2007, 164). In the story of the mother and daughter, we can see how a seemingly innocent "human interest" story in the mass media can generate political symbolic capital and give moral high ground to the already powerful, meanwhile delegitimizing the struggles of the powerless as harmful to society. While showing the gap between representation and reality, however, *Petition* also demonstrates a more *faithful* way of representing reality, where the relationship between the filmmaker and his subject must be nurtured over time and relatively disinterested, where the film is the construction of a fictive kinship based on authentic feelings and honest dealings.

Conclusion: Power of the Powerless

In his seminal essay "Power of the Powerless," Czech writer Václav Havel writes of a greengrocer who hangs a sign in his shop window that says "Workers of the world, unite!" Although he does not believe in these words, the sign makes him feel safe, and so out of fear he lives in a lie along with everyone else. But what would happen, Havel goes on to ask, if this greengrocer were to remove the slogan, speak his mind, and start to "live in truth"? Then he must pay for it dearly, for he would have "shattered the world of appearances" and the "exalted façade of the system" by showing an alternative to "living a lie" (Havel 1985, 23–40).

The petitioners in Zhao Liang's film do not much resemble Havel's greengrocer who decided to give up the "lie" of ideology in order to "live in truth." Instead, they borrow heavily from the official ideological discourse and seek to hold the government to its own promises. They are what Kevin O'Brien and Lianjiang Li call "rightful resisters" who exercise "critique within the hegemony" by employing "the rhetoric and commitments of the powerful to curb the exercise of power" (O'Brien and Li 2006, 2). Nevertheless, like Havel's greengrocer, the power of their petitioning act does not reside in the formation of political parties but rather "*in the light it casts* on those pillars of the system and on its unstable foundations" (my emphasis, Havel 1985, 40). As one petitioner in the film explains her cause beyond her specific case, "I do not want to hold or struggle for power; nor do I have any ulterior motives. I petition to give a soul-stirring warning to the leaders who have made mistakes." Rather than an oppositional group seeking to overthrow the government and replace it with an alternative political model, the petitioners render visible the profound darkness beneath immaculate appearances.

Just as the political impact of these petitioners consists of simultaneously undoing appearances and becoming visible, Zhao Liang's documentary, as I have argued in this chapter, shares in such "power of the powerless" by illuminating injustices that the official media keeps in the shadows. As Jane Gaines points out, while there is little evidence that any documentary has "changed the world," the representation can take on and magnify the power of the represented, extending the community of their sympathizers (Gaines 1999, 84–102). When petitioners struggle for visibility, it is already a political act to see, to acknowledge, and to empathize with their pain, perhaps also to engage in some critical questioning: What drove these people to such desperation? What can be done to resolve their problems? To what extent might we be complicit in the political system that perpetuates such injustice by pretending that it doesn't exist? Under what circumstances might "simply doing our job," like the police officers in *Crime and Punishment* who look like perfectly nice chaps, partake in the state's structural violence?

Ideally, such questions should be going through the minds of Zhao Liang's domestic audiences. However, whereas *Petition* screened at major international film festivals and art cinemas to critical acclaim, it was banned after just one public screening in China at the 2009 China Documentary Festival in Songzhuang in Beijing's suburb. Frustrated with the failure to reach a broader Chinese audience, Zhao Liang accepted an official commission from the Ministry of Health to make a documentary that aimed at countering discrimination against people with HIV and AIDS. *Together* was to be the companion piece and "public service announcement" to the dramatic feature *Love for Life* (*Zui ai* 2011), directed by Gu Changwei and starring Zhang Ziyi and Aaron Kwok. Gu Changwei adapted the story from Yan Lianke's 2006 banned novel *Dream of Ding Village* about villagers who contracted AIDS by selling their blood. However, despite its social commitment, government sponsorship also means submission to censorship and avoidance of political critique, which in turn gives this project the aura of propaganda. Edward Wong's extended profile of Zhao Liang in *The New York Times*, titled

"From Rebel to Insider," cites a "Chinese film expert" and Zhao's former friends as they indict him for "going over to the other side." Zhao Liang defends his pragmatic decision to work within Chinese borders and to deliver his films to Chinese audiences even if it involves some compromises (Wong 2011).

Rather than seeing Zhao Liang's transition "above ground" as a betrayal of his cause and a fall from integrity, we might remember that many petitioners in his previous film profoundly wished for an official venue to express their grievances and to win social sympathy, even though, as *Petition* showed us, official media could also misrepresent and hijack their stories for state propaganda. Neither Zhao Liang's documentary nor Gu Changwei's feature film mention any governmental responsibility for the exacerbation of the AIDS crisis through various cover-ups. However, in educating the public about HIV and in promoting social sympathy for patients, they still mark "a U-turn for the government, which has leapt from censoring media covering of AIDS to backing a blockbuster detailing the disease's murky past" (Davison 2011). Such a turn owes at least something to the wave of unsanctioned activism, writing, and documentary filmmaking on AIDS in China,[9] testifying to the power of the images of powerless people—via the roundtrip of international circulation—to push forbidden and invisible issues into a sanctioned domestic arena. Ultimately, however, Zhao Liang's negotiations with the authorities show that no one living in China can break free from the nets and circuits of state control. In this sense, his career development since *Petition* mirrors all too well the shifting points of view between the powerful and the powerless in his previous work. His films—as well as stories of their production and reception—help the audience recognize our own complex entanglements in power relations.

Notes

1. Notable exceptions are Ai Xiaoming and Hu Jia, who are considered activist-dissidents before they are considered filmmakers, as well as Duan Jinchuan, whose *No. 16 Barkhor South Street* (*Barkhor nan jie 16 hao,* 1996) deals with the day-to-day implementation of government policies by a Neighborhood Committee in Lhasa.

2. Coined by James Scott, "hidden transcript" refers to defiant discourse by subordinate groups that takes place "offstage," in contrast to the more deferent "public transcript" performed in the presence of powerholders. Bordering on a public declaration of the hidden transcript, the scrap collector's son has not only insulted the police but also shaken their secure sense of domination (Scott 1990, 4, 202).

3. As Zhao Liang reveals in his interview with Fanhall Films, many petitioners initially took him to be a television reporter (Zhao 2009).

4. For the central government, the number of petitioners coming from the regions becomes a measurement of local government's disciplinary conduct. Many local government agents, called "retrievers," are then present at the petition offices in Beijing to intercept the petitioners. See also "Human Rights Watch, We Could Disappear Anytime," http://www.hrw.org/reports/2005/china1205/2.htm.

5. This interview appears only in the five-hour version.

6. *Petition* premiered at the prestigious Cannes Film Festival and has gone on to screen at other major international festivals such as Vancouver, Hawaii, Locarno, and AFI. It also screened and won the top award at the 2009 China Documentary Film Festival in Beijing.

7. To what extent she feels "used" by the director or finds him "useful" is not entirely revealed, though an intertitle tells us that two months after leaving, Juan calls up Zhao Liang and asks him to wire her some money for a train ticket back to Jiangsu.

8. Without the story's complex details in the film's short version, however, the intimacy of the reconciliation scene made many audience members I spoke with feel as if it should never have been filmed or shown to a larger public.

9. Among the most prominent Chinese activists who have campaigned against AIDS are Gao Yaojie and Hu Jia. Documentary films that deal with HIV/AIDS in China include Chen Weijun's *To Live Is Better Than to Die* (*Haosi buru lai huozhe* 2003), Ai Xiaoming's *The Epic of Central Plains* (*Zhongyuan jishi* 2005), and Ruby Yang's *The Blood of Yingzhou* (2006).

Bibliography

Anagnost, Ann. 1997. *National Past-Times: Narrative, Representation, and Power in Modern China.* Durham, NC: Duke University Press.

Andrew, Dudley. 1976. *The Major Film Theories: An Introduction.* New York: Oxford University Press.

Bazin, André. 2005. *What Is Cinema?* vol. 2, translated by Hugh Gray. Berkeley: University of California Press.

Cao Xueqin. 1987. *The Story of the Stone,* vol. 1, translated by David Hawkes. Bloomington: Indiana University Press.

Chang, Justin. 2009. "Review of *Petition.*" *Variety,* June 11. http://www.variety.com/review/VE1117940368.html?categoryid=31&cs=1.

Chow, Rey. 2007. *Sentimental Fabulations, Contemporary Chinese Films: Attachment in the Age of Global Visibility.* New York: Columbia University Press.

Davison, Nicola. 2011. "Interview with Gu Changwei." *Time Out Shanghai,* June 30. http://www.timeoutshanghai.com/features/Books__Film-Film_features/1537/Interview-Gu-Changwei.html.

Dillon, Michael. 2009. *Contemporary China: An Introduction.* New York: Routledge.

Fang, Qiang. 2009. "Hot Potatoes: Chinese Complaint Systems from Early Times to the Late Qing (1898)." *The Journal of Asian Studies* 68 (4): 1105–1135.

Fanhall Films. 2009. "Jilupian yu shehui xianshi: Zhao Liang Shangfang zai CDFF2009 fangying hou de xianchang yantaohui jiaoliu shilu" 纪录片与社会显示：赵亮上

访在放映后的现场研讨会交流实录 (Documentary and Social Reality: Transcript of the Discussion Following the Screening of Zhao Liang's *Petition* at the 2009 China Documentary Film Festival). http://fanhall.com/group/thread/14776.html. Accessed Nov. 13, 2009.

Foucault, Michel. 1973. *Madness and Civilization: A History of Insanity in the Age of Reason.* New York: Vintage Books.

Gaines, Jane. 1999. "Political Mimesis." In *Collecting Visible Evidence,* edited by Jane Gaines and Michael Renov, 84–102. Minneapolis: University of Minnesota Press.

Havel, Václav. 1985. *The Power of the Powerless: Citizens against the State in Central-Eastern Europe.* Armonk, NY: M. E. Sharpe.

Jaffee, Valerie. 2006. "'Every Man a Star': The Ambivalent Cult of Amateur Art in New Chinese Documentaries." In *From Underground to Independent: Alternative Film Culture in Contemporary China,* edited by Paul G. Pickowicz and Yingjin Zhang, 77–208. Lanham, MD: Rowman & Littlefield.

Koehler, Robert. 2008. "Review of *Crime and Punishment.*" *Variety,* May 12. http://www.variety.com/review/VE1117936924.html?categoryid=31&cs=1.

Kraicer, Shelly. 2009. "Finding Ways to Fit: Mainland Chinese Films at Toronto and Vancouver." *dGenerate Films.* http://dgeneratefilms.com/chinese-cinema-events/finding-ways-to-fit-mainland-chinese-films-at-toronto-and-vancouver/.

Li, Jie. 2008. "Wang Bing's *West of the Tracks*: Salvaging the Rubble of Utopia." *Jump Cut: A Review of Contemporary Media* 50 (Spring). http://www.ejumpcut.org/archive/jc50.2008/WestofTracks/index.html.

Lü, Xinyu 吕新雨. 2003. *Jilu Zhongguo: Dangdai Zhongguo xinjilu yundong* 纪录中国：当代中国新纪录运动 (Documenting China: The New Documentary Movement in Contemporary China). Beijing: Sanlian shudian.

Nornes, Abé Mark. 2009. "Bulldozers, Bibles, and Very Sharp Knives: The Chinese Independent Documentary Scene." *Film Quarterly* 63 (1): 50–55.

O'Brien, Kevin and Lianjiang Li. 2006. *Rightful Resistance in Rural China.* New York: Cambridge University Press.

Scott, James. 1990. *Domination and the Arts of Resistance: Hidden Transcripts.* New Haven, CT: Yale University Press.

Shi, Yaohua. 2007. "Maintaining Law and Order in the City: New Tales of the People's Police." In *The Urban Generation: Chinese Cinema and Society at the Turn of the Twenty-first Century,* edited by Zhang Zhen, 316–343. Durham, NC: Duke University Press.

Sobchack, Vivian. 2004. *Carnal Thoughts: Embodiment and Moving Image Culture.* Berkeley: University of California Press.

Wong, Edward. 2011. "Chinese Director's Path from Rebel to Insider." *New York Times,* Aug. 13.

Wu, Hung. 2008. *Making History: Wu Hung on Contemporary Art.* Hong Kong: Timezone 8.

Zhao Liang 赵亮. 2009. "Guanyu Shangfang: Xianxiangwang Zhuanfang" 关于上访：现象望专访 (About *Petition:* Interview with Fanhall Films). Accessed Nov. 13, 2009. http://fanhall.com/news/entry/17025.html. Reposted. Accessed Oct. 13, 2011. http://www.douban.com/note/39656677/.

CHAPTER 4

The Spectacular Crowd

Representing the Masses in DV Documentary

SHUANG SHEN

In their introduction to a collaborative study of crowds organized by the Stanford Humanities Lab in 2000, Jeffrey T. Schnapp and Matthew Tiews observe that while the first half of the twentieth century witnessed a rise of collective social action and various forms of mass assembly, the second half was a period of the decline of collective political formations and the replacement by virtual and media-based assemblies for physical crowds (Schnapp and Tiews 2006, xi). The postindustrial political economy in the West is "characterized by the coexistence of media aggregation and bodily disaggregation," Schnapp and Tiews claim (xi). What is the situation like in contemporary China? Judging from some recent DV productions, it seems we cannot disassociate "media aggregation" with "bodily aggregation" so unambiguously and pronounce the death of crowds in contemporary China so quickly. Indeed, some proponents of the New Documentary Movement, such as Wu Wenguang, advocated individuation and proposed the principle of "individual filmmaking" in terms of mode of production, subject matter, and aesthetic style (Wu 2010, 49). Yet it was also Wu who, concerned with the relationship between the masses and the camera, created a project that gave cameras to peasants for them to film their own lives. Even though contemporary Chinese documentaries are turning away from big public events toward the private lives of individuals, and some filmmakers reject allegorical interpretations of their films,[1] the narcissistic attention to subjectivity in some films is countered by an equally obsessive dedication to the representation of accidental crowds, mobs, the crowded existence of those living in the "village in the city," and those unexpected collective eruptions that the mainstream Chinese-language media call *tufa shijian* (sudden eruptive incidents). Some examples of this second category include Ning Ying's *Railroad of Hope* (2002), Ai Xiaoming's *Taishi Village* (2005),

Ai Weiwei's *Lao Ma Ti Hua* (2009), Cao Fei and Ou Ning's *San Yuanli* (2003), Huang Weikai's *Disorder* (2009), and Fan Lixin's *Last Train Home* (2009). How does contemporary Chinese documentary represent and make crowds? How does the documentary filmmaker define her increasingly self-conscious alternative position in relation to the crowds as both subject of representation and audience?

The subject of crowds in contemporary DV documentaries has an additional historical dimension related to the indexing of China's transition from socialist to postsocialist modernity. The existence of crowds in human societies is by no means restricted to a specific time or location, but the critical approach to crowds as an index of historical transition was already defined in one of the earliest studies of the subject, *The Crowd* by Gustave Le Bon (1895). Dubbing modernity as "the era of crowds," Le Bon justified the timeliness of his study of this transhistorical topic by observing the increasing importance of organized crowds in the political, economic, and social lives of modern times (Le Bon 1960, 14–15). He predicted, rather hyperbolically, that if the barbaric nature of crowds was not properly understood and managed, we would meet the "dissolution" of "our civilization" in the hands of "unconscious and brutal crowds," which was how he had imagined the fates of ancient civilizations (Le Bon 1960, 18). Le Bon's attitude toward crowds was not atypical among crowd theorists. Gabriel Tarde and Freud both perceived the suggestibility of crowds as a threat toward individuality and rationality. For them, the contagious quality of crowd experience encouraged blind imitation and made individual members of a crowd sink back to the stage of primitivism or the hypnotic state of the unconscious. Yet theories about crowds are themselves formed in specific historical contexts. Michael Tratner states that "the concern about crowds . . . is in part a concern about the politics of mass movement," and in different "political systems based on representing masses [vs.] representing individuals," the perceptions of crowds and crowd management are bound to be different (Tratner 2003, 56).

Classical crowd theories present crowds as something to be feared and managed, but China not only has its own tradition of Confucianism that presents a discourse of the individual and the collective in rather different ways from the Western liberal tradition of individualism and the general will; it also has a socialist tradition that elevates the masses and puts them at the center of its political imagination. Maoism upholds the mass line (*qunzhong luxian*), a theory that recognizes the importance of the masses (*qunzhong*) in shaping the political theory and practice of the Communist Party. This elevation of the masses by Maoism and the Communist Party does not mean that China after 1949 did not develop its own mechanisms of crowd control or that key terms in reference to crowds such as the masses and the people (*renmin*) are unconditionally inclusive of everyone. The history of the realpolitik in China since the 1940s shows that the masses have not just been celebrated and idealized, but also fetishized and instrumentalized. Elicited by Mao as a political weapon to get rid of what he perceived to be the usurpers of the Communist Party, the masses were repeatedly involved in political struggles whose outcome hardly had much to do with their own lives and interests. The mass gatherings of Red Guards at Tiananmen Square during the Cultural Revolution could not represent the "true" voice of the people; rather, they represented occasions of ideological indoctrination and rituals of Mao worship. Socialist realism as an aesthetic practice developed alongside the political theory of the "mass line" is concerned more with creating model characters and typical incidents (*dianxing renwu, dianxing shijian*) illustrating the party line and the dominant ideology than with representing the real conditions of the masses.

The use of the term "postsocialism" to describe what is also referred to as the "post–New Era" or "post-Tiananmen" period in China does not automatically lead to any clear understanding of how the cultural logic or aesthetics of the contemporary era differentiates from or remains continuous with the socialist period.[2] The vexed relationship between socialist and postsocialist aesthetics is registered in crowd representations in contemporary documentaries. As the state rolled back and the market stepped in after the economic reforms began in the early 1980s, emergent crowds and new forms of mass gathering have appeared in both cities and the countryside. These crowds do not fit comfortably into the socialist political economic structure or the existing discourses of the masses and the people inherited from the socialist era. Some crowds, such as the migrant workers depicted in the movies by Fan Lixin, Ning Ying, and Ai Xiaoming, are a new type of mobile and unorganized crowd, nonexistent and unseen in cultural representations before the 1980s. Other mass gatherings, such as the confrontations between citizens and the law enforcement depicted by activist filmmakers such as Ai Xiaoming and Ai Weiwei, were not visible before the emergence of independent films and the popularity of DV technology. The fact that these crowds are ambiguous in nature—that is, whether they are "good" or "bad" crowds and from whose perspective these judgments can be made remain open questions—poses a challenge to existing legal infrastructures and mechanisms of crowd control, and fuels many documentary filmmakers' creative and political imaginations.

Thus, crowds in contemporary Chinese documentaries present a problem of representation—"in both the sense suggesting literary-aesthetic operation (mimesis) and that tied to the political process of delegation" (Ertürk 2010, 684). Although the New Documentary Movement in the early 1990s defined its raison d'être in terms of a subversive gesture toward socialist realism and the official mode of documentary practice, the connections that contemporary documentary films bear with socialist concerns, socialist institutions, and even socialist aesthetics and modes of representation are myriad and complex. The fascination with crowds among new documentarians is one example. "Crowds" as a trope and theme thus offers a lens for defining the politics of contemporary documentaries as well as for understanding the nature of the postsocialist transition China is now undergoing. Contemporary documentaries do not just represent crowds in an objective or detached manner; they search for crowds, generate crowds, and sometimes empower crowds. By investigating crowds as an index to the mode of relationality of individual filmmakers with the multitude that, on the one hand, contextualizes filmmakers' life and work as, on the other hand, it is the very material they seek to represent, we look into the kind of social action imagined and enabled by documentary filmmakers.

Emphasizing the sociality and performativity of contemporary documentaries vis-à-vis crowds does not mean that a singular and uniform political stance can be discerned in these documentaries. If digital technology is a new medium of artistic expression, crowds in China can be considered a renewed medium of political expression. Yet, the political aesthetics of contemporary documentaries as problematic of transmediation, as Chris Berry and Lisa Rofel rightly remind us, do not yield a singular stance of alternativeness or subversion in the practice of contemporary DV documentary.[3] A deeper historical perspective that situates crowd representations in socialist political and aesthetic practices of earlier decades will allow us to see that the thorny question of the relationship between the leader and the led remains a central issue in contemporary DV documentary practices. The convenience of the digital technology does not automatically allow the filmmaker to blend into the masses. Rather, the relationship between the filmmaker and the crowd, the camera and the crowd, is an ethical and political issue that has to be defined actively by the filmmaker. The capability of DV technology for allowing the filmmaker to immerse herself in crowds only facilitates the articulation of these ethical concerns; it cannot serve as a technological substitute.

Building on my discussion of the transformation of the aesthetics of crowd representation in official and independent documentary filmmaking from the 1960s to the present era, I focus in particular on the spectacular crowds in independent and DV documentaries.[4] A comparison between Zhang Yuan's *Crazy English* (1999) and Fan Lixin's DV work *Last Train Home* (2009) allows us to see that the crowd as spectacle is one of the favored tropes of representation of China's postsocialist transformation. Yet these spectacular crowds constantly raise the question of where the filmmaker and her camera position themselves vis-à-vis the masses. *Crazy English* is important because as a self-funded independent documentary film, it signaled both transition from and continuity with the socialist realist aesthetics of mainstream documentary filmmaking of the 1950s and the 1960s. This is particularly evident in the movie's representation of the leader-crowd relationship through its depiction of ambitious English teacher Li Yang. Ten years after Zhang's film, Fan Lixin's *Last Train Home* is a DV documentary, funded by international sources and made with international art house audiences in mind, that garnered much attention from film festivals and global media on public release. If the ten-year span from Zhang's *Crazy English* to Fan's *Last Train Home* can represent roughly the journey undertaken by Chinese independent documentary, crowd representation allows us to view this decade in more complicated terms than a linear progression from the underground to the international, from the local to the global. Indeed, the broader social context of neoliberal globalization that frames contemporary documentary practice has also brought renewed attention to the ethics and politics in the representation of masses.

Hailing the Crowds in Post-1949 China: The Masses (Qunzhong) and the People (Renmin)

Crowds become a medium of political governance only when they undergo certain symbolic transformations such as naming. In the Chinese context, the post-1949 nation-state hails crowds with terms such as *qunzhong* (masses) and *renmin* (people). The uses of these terms in the second half of twentieth-century China have their precedents in the first half, making this century a particular kind of "era of crowds," but not exactly in the same sense as Le Bon's discussion of modernity and crowds.

In his study of popular cultural movements in the 1930s, Li Hsiao-t'i notes the changes in the word for "people" that reflect different perceptions and modes of management of the masses by the rulers in different periods of history.[5] The distinction between *min* and *zhong* (and the related term *qun*) was crucial in the late Qing to early Republican transition. While late-Qing intellectuals such as Yan Fu approached the masses in a top-down elitist manner by constructing discourses such as *Kai minzhi* (to develop people's intelligence) or *Jiaohua* (to transform the people), the enlightened intellectuals of the 1920s and the 1930s constructed discourses of mass mobilization and mass movement, which were embraced by both the left (such as Qu Qiubai) and certain sectors of the non-left (such as Gu Jiegang).

The Communist Party inherited these discourses of mass movement of the 1930s, particularly the leftist perception of the masses as a potentially radical political force. Mao's theory of the "mass line" is an ultimate example of the left's elevation of the masses even though this elevation did not mean the culture of the masses was accepted without the mediation of politics. Mass culture for the left was, from the very beginning, an ideological construction of the proletariat, as we can see from the writings of the Communist theorist Qu Qiubai. The theory of the "mass line" is a principle that emphasizes reciprocal exchange between the party and the masses and encourages the continuous refinement of theory through practice.[6] Yet the actual practice of this principle encountered a number of difficulties. Rebecca Karl cites problems such as the increasing bureaucratization of the Communist Party and the growing cult status of Mao in the 1940s, which resulted in the canonization of Mao's texts for the purpose of ensuring a uniform ideology and the instrumentalization of the masses as a weapon of political and ideological struggles (Karl 2010, 67–68). The term *qunzhong* in the communist vocabulary became a political construction closely connected with repeated political movements launched by Mao. Connotations of hierarchy and marginalization were retained in usages of the term *qunzhong* in the daily political parlance of the CCP. For instance, party members who deviated from the party line were sometimes asked to undertake a "reeducation by the masses," which referred to the removal of these deviators from their official positions and their marginalization in the political structure.

If *qunzhong* refers to the reciprocal relationship of the party with the masses in theory and political practice, *renmin* is a concept that has to do with the representation of the masses by the political structure of the state. Both concepts are not unconditionally inclusive of every Chinese. The inclusiveness of *qunzhong* was dependent on the situation of political struggles engaged by the CCP. When Mao first formulated his theory of the mass line in the early 1940s, he defined the masses as revolutionary masses, which, in the context of the War of Resistance against Japan, pretty much included every anti-Japanese person (Karl 2010, 62). The establishment of the People's Republic called for a new configuration of the masses in relation to the particular form of popular sovereignty of the PRC, which is officially called a "people's democratic dictatorship." This concept implies that not everyone belongs to the category of people, as we can see from Mao's 1957 essay "On the Correct Handling of Contradictions Among the People." A crucial distinction in this essay is contradictions "among the people" (*renmin neibu*) and those "outside the people" (*renmin waibu*), indicating clearly that "the people" (*renmin*) is a concept with boundaries. Mao maintains that contradictions among the people are nonantagonistic, whereas contradictions outside the people are antagonistic and "must be dealt with dictatorially" (Karl 2010, 95). "The people," the revolutionary force on which the party and the state rely to define their legitimacy and ensure that they retain their revolutionariness, can participate in the democratic political life of the nation-state, but "the 'non-people' were not permitted to participate in the life of the socialist nation, until their 'reeducation' by the people was completed" (Karl 2010, 74–76). While "the people" are managed through the mechanism of democratic centralism, "non-people" are dealt with dictatorially with force.

During political movements in post-1949 China such as the Anti-Rightist Movement and the Cultural Revolution, the distinction between "the people" and "non-people" was reinforced and manifested in representations of organized mass gatherings for the political purpose of reaffirming and implementing people's democratic dictatorship. In his study of propaganda posters during the Cultural Revolution, Haun Saussy discerns a pattern of contrast between "anonymous, but recognizable, 'functional constituencies'" and "contorted, insect like individuals who have fallen from grace and must be expunged" (Saussy 2006, 262). While the first category, consisting of "groups of distinctively attired ethnic figures, or the professional groups each in the costume appropriate to its work, for example, soldiers, sailors, airmen, farmers, scientists," represent "the people," the second category clearly refers to the "non-people," even the nonhuman (Saussy 2006, 261). These pictorial representations of people vs. non-people, situated in their context of exhibition, generated crowds of viewers whose identity was produced through vicarious (dis)identification with the (non)people. Cultural Revolution posters thus form a close intertextual relationship with their linguistic counterparts—the political slogans and big-character posters, which contained explicit messages that exposed and criticized the antirevolutionary thoughts and behavior of one's fellow workers and party leaders. The crowd culture of the Cultural Revolution period presented itself as a multilayered phenomenon, where the polarized logic of "the people" and "non-people" became increasingly blurred, as dogmatic representations of crowds reached the actual masses who voluntarily or involuntarily participated in mass politics.

Representations of crowds in post-1949 visual culture have a direct connection with the socialist conceptions of the role of the intellectual and the political function of cultural work. Mao formulated his theory of the "mass line" around the same time as he delivered the famous "Yan'an Talks," where he extended the left's proposal of the massification of culture further in the direction of relating culture closely to the political and ideological struggles of the Communist Party. From Mao's perspective, the function of revolutionary culture was to serve not just the people, but the purpose of political struggles undertaken by the people and the party. This set the tone of cultural work as vehicle for propaganda or for the ideological interpellation of the masses.

Documentary films produced by the Central Newsreel and Documentary Film Studio in the 1950s and the 1960s consciously fashion the filmmaker and the camera as the mechanisms of propaganda for party ideology and the views of the state. This is particularly evident in the crowd scenes of the movies of the time. In some documentary footage that depicts one of Chairman Mao's several meetings with the Red Guards at Tiananmen Square in 1966, we can find a complex trajectory of multiple perspectives woven together to solidify the seamless unity of the masses and their leader. This documentary footage begins with an aerial view of the crowds on the square shot by a camera positioned on top of the Tiananmen Gate. This representation of the crowds is followed by a close-up image of the tall and heroic figure of Mao captured by another camera right next to him. Since the position of the camera shooting Mao is clearly visible in the frame, we can assume there must be more than one camera positioned on top of the Tiananmen Gate. Next we see more of this camera following Mao's every move and trying to capture all the subtle expressions of the leader's face. Seconds later, the film cuts to a close-up of the face of a member of the crowd, which must have been captured by a different but invisible camera positioned in the midst of the crowds on the square. This image shows the excited expressions on the woman's face, as if suggesting a response to Mao's presence on the Tiananmen Gate.

The articulation between the cameras high above on the Tiananmen Gate and those down below on the square emphasizes the communication between the leader and the crowds and conveys a dialectic that Jeffrey Schnapp calls an "oceanic" model of crowd representation—that is, the representation of the sovereign individual "to emerge while being immersed in the mob, to control while being controlled" (Schnapp and Tiews 2006, 8). This oceanic model of mass representation derived inspiration from the eighteenth-century imagination of the sea as the sublime, according to Schnapp. In the Chinese context, oceanic representations of masses serve the purpose of defining the political sublime by emphasizing the unity of the leader and the crowds. This purpose is facilitated by multiple carefully placed cameras and editing techniques that define the documentary as a genre of filmmaking as state mechanism. The representations of crowd scenes in this footage remind us that crowds are never an exterior social "reality" passively waiting to be captured by the camera. They exist to be viewed from specific perspectives, angles, and positions. Crowds gathered for the National Day Parade, for instance, are meant to be viewed by the party leadership positioned high up on the Tiananmen Gate, embodying the perspective of what Haiyan Lee calls the "egocrat," the "head" of "militaristic body politic" (Lee 2011, 403). Virtually creating the crowds for the state and the party, these documentary images defined the position of the cultural worker within the socialist state.

Other narrations from the point of view of individual, former Red Guards deconstruct official documentary representations of Mao's meetings in Tiananmen Square in 1966 by emphasizing the negative aspects of crowd experience. They note that documentary representations only capture the spectacular quality of the crowds of Red Guards gathered at Tiananmen before and during Mao's visit. They complain that such films hardly concern themselves with the journeys individuals traveled to gather at Tiananmen, or the actual experience of individuals be-

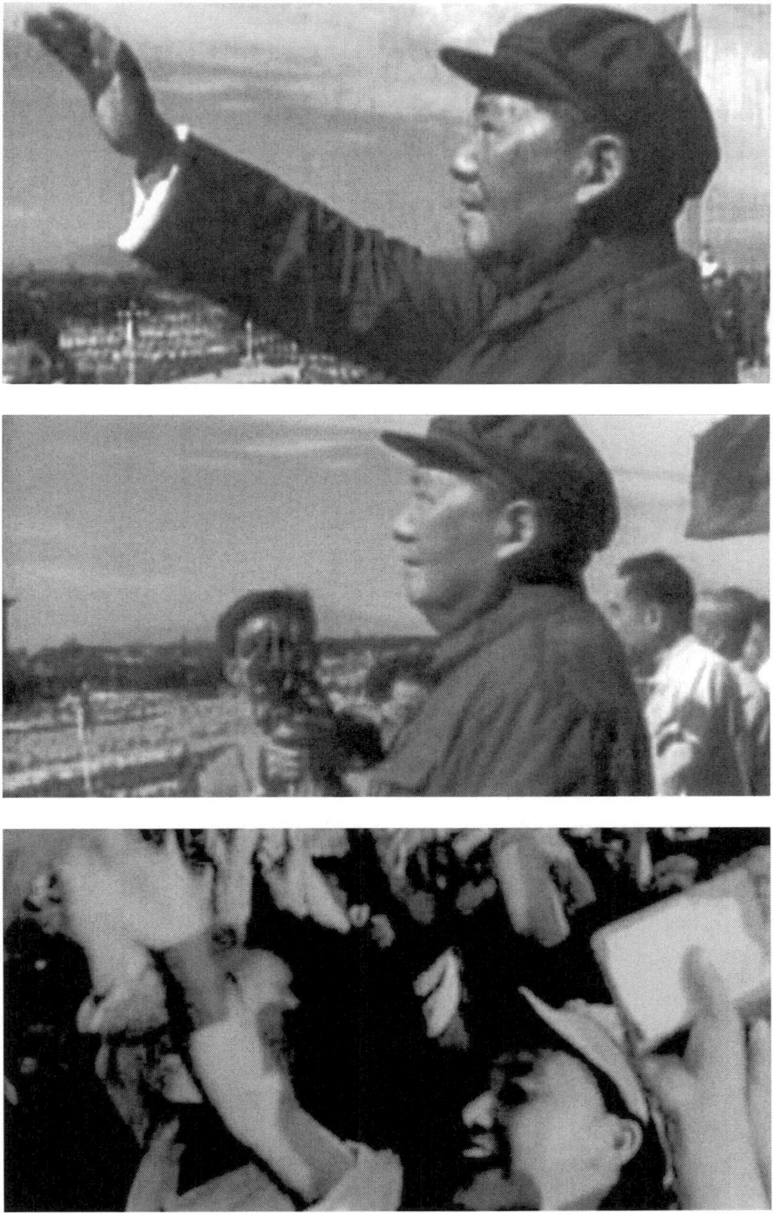

Figures 4.1–4.3. Meeting the Red Guards. Camera work and the cut to the crowd.

fore and while they became a part of the crowd. In his memoir about the Big Propaganda Tours (*Da Chuanlian*) in 1966,[7] Bei Dao remembers that the crowds gathered at railway stations and on the trains were far from harmonious and peaceful. Fear and anxiety experienced by individual members of the crowds were more pronounced than excitement in anticipation of meeting a great leader. As Bei Dao recalls,

> Each car severely exceeded its capacity limit. It was supposed to take in one hundred and eight people, but three times of that number crammed into the car. People sat or lay on luggage racks, on the back of seats, or on the floor. Even toilets were crammed with people so that they were no longer available for the designated use. The train had many stop-and-goes, sometimes stopping for several hours. People took turns to get off and release themselves, look for food or water. There was often no alarm to tell you when the train would move again. Those off the train often had to run to climb up through the windows if they saw the train moving. . . . My seat was on the back of a chair. When I finally could not fight off sleep and dozed off with my head perched in between two coat hooks, I dreamt two dreams, one about going home, the other about exile. (Bei Dao 2010, 171; my translation)

Notice how this narrative moves from the multitude to the singular, the exterior to the interior, conveying an attempt to create the interior space of an individual member of the crowd. The last sentence locates this space in the speaker's dreams, transcending the boundary between the historical past and the present of narration and establishing a subject who is physically within the crowd but emotionally apart. Yet, this representation of crowd experience during the Cultural Revolution is not to be taken as historical truth representative of everyone's experience. We can easily find many other narratives written during the Cultural Revolution that echo Le Bon's argument about the contagious nature of crowd experience and the death of the individual in crowds. Juxtaposing Bei Dao's narrative with the documentary footage created by the cameras of the official media is not meant to suggest that one representation is more true than the other, but to emphasize that crowd representations largely depend on the self-understanding of the artist's role vis-à-vis the crowds, as well as the technology of representation, linguistic or visual. Because of Bei Dao's involvement in the underground poetry movements in the 1970s, his understanding of the technology of representation resisted the ideological interpellation of the crowds as either "masses" or "people." In the case of visual culture, this kind of resistance would have to wait longer, until the New Documentary Movement in the early 1990s, to create new images of crowds and crowd experience.

The Leader and the Led in *Crazy English*

Comparing the crowds in Zhang Yuan's *Crazy English* with the documentaries of the Cultural Revolution period, we can see both similarities and differences. We can thus position Zhang's film as a self-consciously transitional work from mainstream documentary to the New Documentary. Both *Crazy English* and the documentary footage of Mao's reception of the Red Guards at Tiananmen focus on the relationship between the leader and the led and portray the crowd experience as an essentially positive one. Both stress, consciously or unconsciously, the ideological work performed by mass gatherings in specific historical contexts. Although the protagonist of *Crazy English,* Li Yang, is an English teacher, the speeches he delivers in front of various crowds are not linguistic lessons but performances akin to Louis Althusser's notion of hailing or ideological indoctrination, thus harkening back to our memories of the Cultural Revolution period. The many crowd scenes in *Crazy English* resemble Mao's meetings with the Red Guards at Tiananmen, but they are also different because of a different context of market economy that frames the dynamics of the exchange between the leader and the crowds in the case of *Crazy English.*

Crazy English puts a great deal of emphasis on the self-formation of Li and the proactive role of this leader in motivating and energizing the crowds. From the stories told to foreign and Chinese reporters, we know that Li's success is measured by a different set of standards of popularization than during the era of Mao. Li is different from Mao in that he is a self-made man and distinguished from most Chinese by such personal qualities as over-the-top confidence and aggressiveness. Unlike the political leader whose public image was shrouded in the mystique of cultish worship, Li's personal stories represented in the movie were carefully constructed but every inch human, inviting the audience's identification with the newly minted market hero. In terms of his relationship with crowds, Li has to work much harder than Mao, providing them with psychological inspiration while commodifying himself and his product, which includes the ideology of globalization and a new discourse of Chineseness, along with English as a cosmopolitan language.

The crowds gathered to hear Li Yang's speeches have an ambiguous identity if read in relation to the conventional discourses of the masses during the socialist era. They are different from both the masses or the people, but they are also not the conventional market crowds of shoppers or speculators, either. It is unclear whether people have gathered together voluntarily or have been ordered to come by their employers, superiors, or teachers, but many of Li Yang's audiences make homogenous and well-disciplined crowds: some of them are People's Liberation Army (PLA) soldiers; others are primary and secondary students or hotel employees. The highly organized nature of these crowds brings back memories of tighter crowd control and more direct ideological indoctrination through mass gatherings.

The ambiguous nature of the crowds presented in this movie is useful for representing the time warp in which postsocialist China is situated. Ackbar Abbas takes note of the weight of history that contextualizes the stories of the individual and the crowds in this movie. Abbas states that the crowds here manifest a collective desire to be "generic," "liberated from character and affect," "from the awkwardness and messiness, the clumsiness and naiveté of historical questions—for example, questions of cultural identity and the burden of the historical past" (Abbas 2010, 30). While registering "awkwardness and messiness" even in the articulations of the desire for liberation, *Crazy English* remains nonetheless deeply embedded in the socialist realist narrative convention. Situating Li's personal experience in relation to the master narratives of Chinese Revolution and Chinese Enlightenment, this film depicts Li according to the socialist realist logic of typicality (*Dianxing*), emphasizing that these histories haunt the individual development of Li, even as they appear only as representative settings and symbolic icons, such as the Huang Hua Gang Tomb of revolutionary martyrs, the Great Wall, or the impressive presence of the uniformed PLA soldiers. In a seemingly casual way, Li tells us that he used to live in close proximity to the tombs of revolutionary martyrs and he would practice English by shouting to the dead souls of the revolutionaries. This remark alludes to an entire history of revolutionary struggles, against which this current story is juxtaposed. Another indication of Li Yang's embeddedness in history is his narrative of needing to overcome the physical flaws and mental weakness of the Chinese, by building up "Chinese muscle" or changing Chinese personality. This narrative harkens back to the discourse of the "sick man of Asia" and the twisted logic of self-improvement through self-criticism of the discourse of the Chinese Enlightenment that we see in the writings of many early twentieth-century intellectuals such as Lu Xun, Hu Shi, and others.

Although the crowd experience depicted in the movie belongs to the present, the present is also a site of personal and collective memories and history. Crowds become a symbol of an individual's success and the success of individualism over history. The juxtaposition of the mass gatherings in the present against the historical past enables a complex depiction of crowd psychology in ways that bear some similarities to the psychological discussions of crowd experience by theorists such as Le Bon and Freud but takes them further. This crowd psychology is punctuated by the word "crazy," which carries multiple meanings: being crazed about something, acting crazy, and looking crazy. The movie contains many depictions of the "craziness" of Li and the crowds, and the fascination of the crowds toward the leader, but we as audience do not feel that we are sucked into the mania. Rather, we are mildly amused by these individual and mass performances. Why?

Le Bon and Freud both argue that craziness in the sense of irrationality is intrinsic to crowd experience. Crowd experience is dangerous because it exposes the hidden primitiveness of human beings. Freud explains that a group maintains its collectivity through the identification of its members with each other only because they share the same object of love—their leader as the ego ideal. Yet the love bestowed onto the ego ideal is by nature unfulfilled. The infatuation that group members have for their leader more resembles hypnosis than love, since "the hypnotic relation is the devotion of someone in love to an unlimited degree but with sexual satisfaction excluded, whereas in the case of being in love this kind of satisfaction is only temporarily held back, remains in the background as a possible aim at some later time" (Freud 1922). In the movie, Li can be considered as a collective ego ideal. He works the crowd by using crowd psychology; that is, by asking his audiences to repeat English phrases after him and imitate his demeanor and style, he tries to make the crowds fall in love with the traits of Chineseness embodied by him: outspokenness, self-assertiveness, and ambition. In Freud's formulation, the ego ideal is by nature inaccessible to the crowds. The unfulfilled love for the leader is introjected and transformed into identification of group members with each other, according to Freud. Here, Zhang Yuan's depiction of crowd experience parts way with Freud's psychoanalytic interpretation by shifting attention from the members of the group to the leader. The movie never provides any confirmation about whether the characteristics Li cherishes are reproduced in the individual students he has taught. Instead, we get many narcissistic accounts of Li himself through the interviews given to reporters. This turning of attention to Li Yang demystifies the ego ideal, making it more accessible to us than the typical crowd experience described by Freud. In other words, it is as though the director decided to interrupt the chain of suggestibility and contagion between the crowds depicted in the movie and those of us who watch the movie. We, the audience crowds, become amused by or even judgmental toward the crowd performance by considering it as comedy, but we do not participate in the craziness. The film apparatus, in other words, does not attempt to perform hypnosis on the movie audience.

Through a self-reflective representation of the camera as a medium of infatuation and propagation, this movie lends itself to being read as simultaneously continuing while subverting the socialist mode of documentary filmmaking. The film is not a DV production and makes no pretense that the crowd scenes are spontaneous events that the cameras happen to capture. Rather, the opening scene of *Crazy English* already sets the tone of theatricality that is sustained throughout the entire movie. This scene suggests that the craziness of Li Yang and the crowds, although infectious, is staged and designed for the camera. In this sequence, we first see a close-up of the protagonist of the film, Li Yang, shouting repeatedly to the camera, "Crazy English, crazy work, crazy study, I love this crazy game." The camera then pulls away to present the film crew, including the director himself, joining in and chanting enthusiastically. The dramatic introduction of Li Yang ends with comic relief when a member of the crew trips over the wires and falls on the ground. Exposing the fourth wall of the crowd experience as performance, this sequence breaks the spell of the larger-than-life Li over his audiences. Such self-reflexiveness can be read as yet another indication of the director's self-positioning vis-à-vis the mainstream state-sponsored documentary practice, in a similar way that *The Square* seeks to frame and subvert this state-sponsored tradition.

Many scenes in *Crazy English* present highly visible cameras, with TV and radio reporters crowding around together and constituting the mechanism that makes Li Yang into a star. In another documentary, *The Square,* codirected by Zhang and Duan Jinchuan, the artifice of mainstream filmmaking is exposed in a scene when the CCTV documentary film director coaxes his subjects into representing a certain version of "reality" he desires. There is a similar scene in *Crazy English,* where Gu Changwei, the photographer for several movies by Fifth Generation directors Zhang Yimou and Chen Kaige, gives verbal instructions to Li about how to perform in front of the camera. This detail adds another layer of intertextuality, linking this documentary with mainstream blockbuster films of the same period. The cameras, media technology, and media workers constitute another type of crowd before whom Li Yang is not the leader, but a performer. Just like the magnetic power he commands over his audience, Li is himself hypnotized by the power of this technological crowding. This exchangeability between the leader and the led reinforces the self-consciousness of this movie's representation of crowds as performance, conveying a great deal of ambivalence toward the convention of socialist agitprop that we found in the Tiananmen documentary footage of the 1960s.

The film presents Li Yang's "Crazy English" lessons largely as comedy and pokes fun at Li's market success as a form of ideological self-indoctrination. Yet this deconstructive take on crowd dynamics does not automatically lead to the construction of a more egalitarian relationship between the leader and the group. The scandal of domestic abuse in which Li was subsequently involved offers the public a glimpse of the tendencies of violence and exploitation beneath the surface of Li's iconic image. In a 2011 TV interview about the domestic violence case, Li confessed to wife beating but showed no remorse whatsoever toward his behavior.[8] Highlighting and critiquing the spectacular crowd effect of Li Yang's "Crazy English" pedagogy, the filmmaker Zhang has left the iconic status of Li intact. We can argue that while the crowd as spectacle is exploited by Li Yang as a strategy for self-advancement, Zhang Yang also exploits these spectacles to present a prototypical and iconic image of China undergoing neoliberal globalization. What this representation elides is the individual identity and voice of the members of the crowds.

Last Train Home: Humanizing the Crowds

The advent of the DV technology brought at least two major changes to contemporary Chinese documentary as far as crowd representation is concerned. One change has to do with self-conscious representation of the growing popularity of DV cameras, not in the hands of professional filmmakers, but of ordinary people. In documentaries such as Ai Xiaoming's *Our Children* (2009), we encounter not just human crowds, but also the "crowding" of everyday life with digital cameras. The second change is the increasing intractability of crowds, accompanied by new terms used by mainstream Chinese-language media in reference to these new crowds, such as *qunti shijian* (mass events) or *tufa shijia* (incidents of sudden eruption). These terms, drawing attention to the unpredictability of mass gatherings or collective incidents, underscore the fear of eruption toward existing frameworks of mass representation and mechanisms of crowd control. The authorities' reluctance to classify these crowds as either good or bad testifies to the dangerous suggestibility of these crowds in terms of challenging existing frameworks of political representation. The independent filmmaker's willingness to represent these emergent marginalized groups in China's economic development and globalization, as Berry and Rofel note, precisely manifests the "alternativeness" of this genre (Berry and Rofel 2010). Yet the spectacular presentation of the crowd may undercut the effectiveness of documentary activism. This spectacular effect can be generated not solely by the filmmaker's camera, but also by the iconic status of individuals at the center of a crowd or by some protest groups' strategic utilization of mass media. Individual filmmakers' self-reflection on this spectacular effect often constitutes a major difference in how each filmmaker understands and approaches documentary activism.

Take as an example the subject matter of migrant peasants in Chinese cities looking for work. These crowds are not fixed and stable groups, but mobile and unstable gatherings highly contingent on specific times and places as well as the authorities' mechanism of crowd control and management. DV documentary's representations of these crowds in fact blur the distinction between what Luke Robinson calls the metonymic and the unexpected or idiosyncratic in documentary filmmaking, since in the films by Ning Ying, Ai Xiaoming, and Fan Lixin, we can see a style of representation of "documentary events" that is both intentional and random (Robinson 2010). Whereas in *Crazy English,* crowd scenes resemble predesigned and well-rehearsed theater, the documentaries by Ai Xiaoming and Fan Lixin prefer to represent crowds that do not have a fixed organizational structure and they maintain a fluid form of communication between the camera and crowds in the course of the filmmaking. I argue that the works of the activist-conscious filmmaker Ai Xiaoming signal a deliberate transformation from the deconstructive to activist approach to crowd representation, but what remains unexplored is the spectacular crowd effect.[9] In fact, comparing the works by Ai, Ning, and Fan in conjunction with the much-discussed celebrity-activist Ai Weiwei, we can discern an increasing degree of the artist's consciousness of the interaction between crowd formation and spectacle construction. Ai Weiwei's documentary *Lao Ma Ti Hua,* for instance, shows clearly that it is the celebrity status of the artist-filmmaker that draws a crowd around him at a scene when Ai and his crew have dinner in an open-air restaurant in the city of Chengdu. Although these crowds gathered by a celebrity figure can convey powerful political messages, the question still remains: How are they related to the actual victimized communities for whom Ai supposedly speaks?

Ai Weiwei's celebrity status and Fan Lixin's award-winning documentary *Last Train Home* draw attention to the role played by international media vis-à-vis representations of marginalized groups in China. The migrant worker crowds depicted by Fan's film are not an uncommon subject matter for Chinese documentary filmmakers. Ai Xiaoming's *The Train to My Hometown,* for instance, depicts migrant workers stranded at Guangzhou Railroad Station, waiting to go home during the Chinese New Year in 2008. Yet Fan frames these crowd scenes differently from Ai. He contextualizes the representation of crowds in a larger narrative that provides an in-depth portrayal of one particular migrant family, following its members for three years traveling back and forth between the city where the parents work and the countryside where the children and grandparents live. Even though Ai's film also goes to the hometown of a victim of the train station stampede, Ai's portrayal of her emphasizes her victimhood more than her individual personhood.

Fan's humanistic touch and emphasis on individual stories allow *Last Train Home* to present Chinese migrant workers as a spectacle for consumption by art house audiences both Chinese and foreign. The fact that these audience groups are generally located in urban centers in China or abroad means that they are far removed from the actual migrant groups. The movie was an instant hit when it was shown in major film festivals in North America and Europe, winning several prestigious awards and gaining public release rights in many art house cinemas outside China. The easy availability of the DVD of this film for sale and rent on Amzon.com is a sure sign of the relatively lucrative profit return uncommon for a documentary that makes little attempt to lighten up a serious subject matter. When the movie started shooting in 2006, Fan gained Canadian residency, an identity that gave him readier access to international funding sources for independent filmmakers. Although this pattern of circulation is not uncommon for contemporary Chinese documentaries, Fan's film can be considered more successful than most other films with the same path of circulation, and there are certainly other documentaries, such as those by Ai Xiaoming, that are almost completely buried with relatively few chances of screening at international film festivals. Ai made a point of sending her films to the people represented in her movies,[10] but it is unclear whether *Last Train Home* has had a similar kind of reciprocal exchange with the family represented in the film.

The movie's attraction for international film audiences can be accounted for partly by the step-by-step training it provides to the audiences in terms of how to understand and empathize with Chinese crowds. In Fan's film, representations of migrant workers taking the train back home appear at least three times, and as we get to know this migrant family better, the crowds seem increasingly less intimidating. In contrast to mixed feelings of barrenness and awe elicited by the beginning of the movie, where alternating shots depict an empty piece of concrete ground and crowds of people lined up to catch the train, crowds depicted in the middle and toward the end of the film gradually elicit empathy and identification from the viewer. The camera also changes position in relation to the crowds in the course of the movie. At the beginning, the camera is placed outside and above the crowds, but it is placed in the midst of crowds in the middle of the film. At the beginning of the movie, the crowd scene is shot from one end of an empty tunnel at a railway station where the camera is stationary and distanced from the crowds. From this angle, migrant workers rushing to catch the train seem like an undistinguishable, almost nonhuman, mass seized by anxiety and fear. The viewer of this scene is invited to pay attention to the feelings of the crowds without being able to identify with any individual member in the crowd. The viewer remains emotionally detached from the crowd, perceiving it as an object of knowledge and, to a certain extent, exoticization.

This relationship changes as the narrative develops and the camera inserts itself more and more into the private lives of the Zhang family, following the parents on their journeys between the city and the country and depicting interpersonal relations within the family. We might say that the film utilizes the division between the individual and the multitude, the private and the public, effectively to humanize the crowds of migrant workers. But to use the term "humanize" implies a specific understanding of the human as an autonomous individual with fully developed interiority. By contrast, Ai Xiaoming's film *Taishi Village* does not necessarily subscribe to the same understandings of the human. There, we also encounter an attempt to humanize the crowds of villagers, but this is accomplished by giving voice to their demands as a collective subject and their feelings only in relation to their collective struggles.

The most fully developed figure of the individual human in Fan's film is the daughter Ya Qin. The film does not just depict the social conditions in which she grows up but also her feelings, aspirations, and desires. We know that she yearns for more love from her parents who left home several years ago. We also know that she has ambivalent feelings about leaving home and working in the city herself since, while she yearns for the urbane lifestyle, she feels lonely and exploited as a young migrant worker in the city. Because of her work in a modern and glitzy bar catering to the new urban middle class, economic disparity in the city becomes more visible to her and the audience compared to the sweatshop environment where her parents work. So when the movie shows a group of workers at the bar gathering in front of the TV to watch the opening ceremony of the Olympics, we can sense the distance between the carefully orchestrated performance of crowds in Beijing as a symbol of China and the living crowd of migrant workers in front of the television set.

This movie is shot in a style similar to Frederick Wiseman's practice of direct cinema.[11] Yet although we cannot spot explicit intervention by the director, some monologues that express the inner thoughts of the characters are clearly prompted by members of the film crew. The documentary betrays little evidence of itself as a film, except at one moment when Ya Qin breaks into a fight with her father after he hits her, and she screams to the camera, "Shoot this! Please shoot this! You want reality? This is reality." Yet this moment of self-referentiality hardly suffices to deconstruct the wholeness of the film's constructed reality, since ambivalence and internal conflicts are consistent with the personality of Ya Qin and only serve to make her characterization fuller. In many scenes of the movie, the camera captures the Zhang family members in their private moments when they are alone and appear to be in a self-reflective mood. This emphasis on interiority helps the viewers of *Last Train Home* (mostly international art house movie viewers) to identify with the characters as individuals presented in the movie.

The emphasis on individual rather than mass subject makes the crowd scenes toward the end of the movie less alienating and threatening. Fan's film does not intentionally utilize crowd scenes as an occasion to articulate a political message or fashion them as alternative or counter publics. His film does not treat issues of freedom of expression or democracy as their central concerns. In fact, Fan renders a rather depoliticized understanding of "freedom" compared to other documentaries, such as Ai Xiaoming's *Taishi Village*. In Fan's movie, Ya Qin makes a statement that is arguably the most important message in the entire movie: "To us, freedom is happiness." In this statement, she expresses a yearning for individual autonomy, a notion that is complicated and undercut by the movie's representations of the many constraints over the lives of the migrant workers and the compromises they must make from time to time. In Ai's movies, however, individual autonomy is not taken as a premise or justification for freedom of expression, whether it pertains to the Taishi villagers' desire to keep their democratically elected officers in power or the migrant workers' wish to go home and spend the Chinese New Year with their families.

Conclusion

According to Bérénice Reynaud, Zhang Yuan's 1999 film *Crazy English* signaled the director's attempt "to reoccupy the center" after he had finished a succession of films that were made illegally and forbidden public release in China (Reynaud 2007, 281). The film, embodying the ambivalent and precarious status of the individualistic independent filmmaker, captures the tension between art and the masses, the camera and crowds, mediated by the representation of narcissistic English teacher Li Yang. The conflictual desire to focus on the leader vs. the masses, the impulse to be simultaneously realistic and theatrical, determines the position of the camera vis-à-vis the subject of representation. With the increasing popularity of DV cameras not just for filmmakers but also among the general public, the very nature and function of "crowd" will certainly change in ways yet unforeseen. Yet we should be careful with overly romanticizing the power of DV technology or new media in terms of their interventions in mass formations and politics in contemporary China. As socially conscious documentary filmmakers make visible underrepresented communities with the help of digital technology, either existing structures of political representation or new structures of commercialism will continue to exert their forces and shape the filmmakers' aesthetics of crowd representation. Digital technology, with its promise of open access, does not guarantee egalitarian or ethical representation of the masses. Recognizing this paradox should be the first step for socially conscious documentary filmmakers to engage in some self-reflection on their art and politics.

For one thing, this chapter has focused more on crowds as represented on the screen than on crowds in the audience watching, although circulation plays an unignorable role in terms of shaping the relationship between the filmmaker and the masses. Even though "alternative minority cinema remains very much a minority and intellectual pursuit," as Berry and Rofel claim (2010, 151), the success of Fan's *Last Train Home* in international art houses indicates that transnational audiences are increasingly drawn toward some DV documentaries from China. This insight, however, does not take into account the virtual circulation of documentaries over the Internet. Audience crowds for DV documentaries are not necessarily concentrated in the physical sites of a few alternative viewing venues in China's major cities. Those who watch the documentaries on the Internet may not even be considered "crowds" in the conventional sense of the word, although virtual communities revolving around certain films are certainly conceivable. In this context of transmediation, "crowd," as a transhistorical form of collectivity and certainly a term that carries specific connotations in the history of Chinese socialism, proves to be a symbolic site of cultural configuration that continuously redefines art's relationship with power and politics.

Notes

1. Luke Robinson offers some good analysis of what some people claim to be a transition of Chinese documentaries from the public to the private (see Robinson 2010). He argues that more focused attention should be given to the mode of representation of individuals in relation to the social context depicted in the movies. Chinese documentaries of the early 1990s and more recent documentaries construct documentary events in different ways depending on how documentary filmmakers approach profilm events.

2. See chapter 1 of McGrath 2008 for a discussion of the condition of post-socialist modernity in China.

3. See Berry and Rofel 2010. They argue that contemporary Chinese documentary embodies different kinds of alternativeness in theme, form, and viewing culture. Often the more sensitive the subject matter of a documentary film, the more ambivalent is its message.

4. See my article "From Deconstruction to Activism: The Chinese Independent Documentary and the Crowd" in *Modern China*, January 2015, 1–24.

5. Li explains that "[i]n imperial times they [the people] were called ignorant people (*wuzhi yumin*), ignorant men and women (*yufu* and *yufu*), small people (*xiaomin*), or commoners (*shumin*). In the late Qing and early Republican period they were called citizens (*guomin*), the people (*renmin*), or ordinary people (*pinmin*). Starting in the 1920s, the mass character of the people was emphasized. The terms *minzhong* (literally 'people grouped'), *dazhong* (literally 'large group') or '*qunzhong*' (the masses) became the standard designation, not only in political arenas but also in cultural affairs" (Li Hsiao-t'i 2001, 45–46).

6. For discussion of Mao's formulation of the "mass line," see Karl 2010, ch. 5.

7. During the Cultural Revolution, Mao encouraged Red Guards to travel to other cities and revolutionary sites and spread the messages of the Cultural Revolution. These journeys, usually taken by train, are referred to as Da Chuanlian or the Big Propaganda Tours.

8. See Li Yang's TV interview with CCTV reporter Chai Jing on Sept. 25, 2011, http://www.youtube.com/watch?v=2BpLfIOyDd4.

9. "From Deconstruction to Activism: The Chinese Independent Documentary and the Crowd," *Modern China,* January 2015, 1–24.

10. This information was provided by Ai Xiaoming during my meeting with her in May 2009.

11. Frederick Wiseman's style of direct cinema refers to the method of direct and unobtrusive observation of the subject of representation. This approach to documentary filmmaking has been rather influential among Chinese documentary filmmakers, along with the French documentary school of cinema verité.

Bibliography

Abbas, Ackbar. 2010. "Affective Spaces in Hong Kong/Chinese Cinema." In *Cinema at the City's Edge: Film and Urban Networks in East Asia,* edited by Yomi Braester and James Tweedie, 25–36. Hong Kong: Hong Kong University Press.

Bei Dao. 2010. *Cheng Men Kai* (The Gate Opens). Xianggang: Niujin Daxue Chubanshe.

Berry, Chris and Lisa Rofel. 2010. "Alternative Archive: China's Independent Documentary Culture." In *The New Chinese Documentary Movement: for the Public Record,* edited by Chris Berry, Lü Xinyu, and Lisa Rofel, 135–154. Hong Kong: Hong Kong University Press.

Connolly, Joy. 2006. "Crowd Politics: The Myth of the 'Populus Romanus.'" In *Crowds,* edited by Jeffrey T. Schnapp and Matthew Tiews, 77–97. Stanford: Stanford University Press.

Ertürk, Nergis. 2010. "Those Outside the Scene: Snow in the World Republic of Letters." *New Literary History* 41 (3): 633–651.

Freud, Sigmund. 1922. *Group Psychology and the Analysis of Ego,* translated by James Strachey. Available online at the Guttenberg Project. https://archive.org/details/grouppsychologya35877gut.

Karl, Rebecca. 2010. *Mao Zedong and China in the Twentieth-Century World.* Durham, NC: Duke University Press.

Le Bon, Gustave. 1960. *The Crowd: A Study of the Popular Mind.* Mineola, NY: Dover Publications.

Lee, Haiyan. 2011. "The Charisma of Power and the Military Sublime in Tiananmen Square." *Journal of Asian Studies* 70 (2): 397–424.

Li Hsiao-t'i. 2001. "Making a Name and a Culture for the Masses in Modern China." *positions: east asia cultures critique* 9 (1): 29–68.

McGrath, Jason. 2008. *Postsocialist Modernity: Chinese Cinema, Literature, and Criticism in the Market Age.* Stanford, CA: Stanford University Press, 2008.

Reynaud, Bérénice. 2007. "Zhang Yuan's Imaginary Cities and the Theatricalization of the Chinese 'Bastards.'" In *The Urban Generation: Chinese Cinema and Society at the Turn of the Twenty-first Century,* edited by Zhang Zhen, 264–294. Durham, NC: Duke University Press.

Robinson, Luke. 2010. "From 'Public' to 'Private': Chinese Documentary and the Logic of *Xianchang.*" In *The New Chinese Documentary Movement: For the Public Record,* edited by Chris Berry, Lü Xinyu, and Lisa Rofel, 177–195. Hong Kong: Hong Kong University Press.

Saussy, Haun. 2006. "Crowds, Numbers, and Mass in China." In *Crowds,* edited by Jeffrey T. Schnapp and Matthew Tiews, 249–261. Stanford, CA: Stanford University Press.

Schnapp, Jeffrey T. and Matthew Tiews. 2006. "Introduction: A Book of Crowds." In *Crowds,* edited by Jeffrey T. Schnapp and Matthew Tiews, ix–xvi. Stanford, CA: Stanford University Press.

Shen, Shuang. 2015. "From Deconstruction to Activism: The Chinese Independent Documentary and the Crowd." *Modern China* (Jan.): 1–24.

Tratner, Michael. 2003. "Working the Crowd: Movies and Mass Politics." *Criticism* 45 (1): 53–73.

Wu, Wenguang. 2010. "DV: Individual Filmmaking." In *The New Chinese Documentary Movement: For the Public Record,* edited by Chris Berry, Lü Xinyu, and Lisa Rofel, 49–54. Hong Kong: Hong Kong University Press.

CHAPTER 5

DV-made Tibet

Domestic Videos, Elite Films, and the Work of Pema Tseden

ROBERT BARNETT

> In all, this phenomenon derives from the West,
> from digital technology!
> —Chenagtshang Dorje Tsering

In the three decades after 1980, major changes took place in the ways in which culture in Tibet was produced, transmitted, and consumed.[1] These changes, however, were not evidence of the radical transformation often claimed as the result of digitization, but were brought about by earlier forms of technological development. In terms of music and radio, it was the arrival of cheap cassette players and recorders in Tibet in the late 1980s that allowed Tibetans to choose for the first time when to listen and, within the limits allowed by the market and the government, what to listen to (Dhondup 2008). Well before digital possibilities emerged, Tibetan musicians had begun to produce cassettes of their own music in significant quantities (Morcom 2008), sometimes using them to challenge dominant representations of their culture (Baranovitch 2003, 3) or even to communicate lightly coded nationalist messages (Wangdu 2011). It was much the same with film and video: it was the arrival of the videocassette that allowed Tibetans for the first time to watch any market-available products, including those from Hong Kong and Taiwan, first in semiprivate spaces such as teahouses and video parlors, and later, once living standards had improved, in private homes. Digitization had significant impact in one area of cultural consumption—it made the music video a major feature of Tibetan cultural life—and it vastly improved the quality of the listening experience in music, much as it improved the capacity of cell phones and cameras. But in Tibet, the structural changes that define modern cultural practice had taken place before the digital arrived.

It is in more specialist areas that digital technology has had significant impact. It enabled wealthier Tibetans in Tibet to produce and circulate raw video footage within their families and private networks, and it led to a wave of independent film and video production by Tibetan artists and intellectuals. These remain a drop in the ocean of production and consumption compared to music videos, and for the most part they are made and viewed by the educated elite or are homemade products that remain within small communities or the family. But they have proved formative among Tibetans in enabling people "to escape the centralized and homogenizing control of the state," as Baranovitch put it (2003, 3). As a vector of discursive change, popular music has played an important role among Tibetans in enhancing cultural pride and national feeling. But it is a short-form medium, limited in the range of concepts that can be raised: when songs touch on social or political issues, they tend to adhere to what Abu-Lughod (1990) and Bulag (2002) described as "the romance of resistance," a binary saga that narrativizes social and political conflicts as a single-minded struggle of the oppressed against heartless domination.

The conversations within and around the new Tibetan DV movement, however, represent a discursive development of significance and complexity. They suggest, for example, that Tibetans do not define themselves purely by the presence of the Chinese state—indeed, the most striking feature of these works is that China and the Chinese are almost never mentioned. These works in many cases require us to recalibrate notions of how social tension is experienced, conceptualized, and debated in a context such as Tibet. It is these notions, as reflected in the unofficial films and videos made by Tibetans in Tibet in the digital era, with particular focus on documentaries and fiction films, that I discuss in this chapter.

From Cassette to DV

By the early 1980s, thirty years after the People's Liberation Army had moved into Tibetan areas, Chinese modernity had brought little change to Tibetans in terms of domestic technology. Most urban dwellers probably had electricity and an indoor toilet, and perhaps a radio and a bicycle, but little else that stood for technological modernity. Eighty-five percent or more of the population lived in the countryside and would have seen little evidence of the modern in their homes until near the end of the twentieth century, even if their village was near a town. Even by 1990, only a third of Tibetan households in the countryside had a radio.[2] For almost all Tibetans, their experience of public art and culture after the early 1950s would have been mainly limited to government radio programs broadcast via loudspeaker systems in their village or commune, plus rare performances of traditional arts considered sufficiently proletarian to be permitted to take place in the more moderate periods. There would have been occasional visits by traveling projectionists who would screen Chinese films, usually about communist soldiers fighting Japanese invaders or Chinese nationalists in the 1940s,[3] plus rare performances by traveling drama troupes of official plays and sketches with heavy moral and political messages, still the staple feature of all theater in Tibet today.

This changed only when audiocassette players became a common household item in the urban areas in the late 1980s. By 1996, a third of rural households in the TAR had a cassette recorder, making it often the first and only media appliance to be found in rural homes. By that time digital technology had already arrived in China, with DVDs becoming widespread there from about 2000. Technological change had always reached Tibet years later than in the ethnic Chinese areas, and by 2004 still only a third of rural households in the TAR had television sets. But a policy of vast government subsidies in this period boosted incomes in Tibet (Fischer 2009), just as new technology was entering the market. By 2006, a third of rural Tibetans in the TAR had acquired digital disk players (VCDs) and mobile phones, and in the urban areas a significant number of Tibetans were able to afford stereo systems and DVD players as well as smartphones. It was this development that led to an upturn in unofficial film and video production by Tibetans in Tibet. A small number of Tibetans were already making unofficial films and videos before this time, but digitization led to a marked increase in their output and range. That output can be divided into five main types—home, civic, and export videos, plus documentaries and dramas.

HOME AND CIVIC VIDEOS

Home videos are products made domestically by those wealthy enough to afford a camera,[4] probably for showing only to family members and friends. Of the five categories, this is the one least changed by digitization, because rich Tibetans who could afford analog video cameras in the 1990s were already making such films for home viewing then. But the Tibetan middle class is now far wealthier and larger than twenty years ago, and the practice of making home videos will have increased accordingly. These videos typically capture important or memorable moments in family or communal life, particularly those that are seen as distinctively Tibetan. According to one Tibetan from a village near Rebkong in Amdo (Qinghai), if someone in his village has a video camera, "they film rituals and events like those at *Losar* [New Year], or dancing. Otherwise they film the mountains and the scenery" (interview, June 26, 2011). Picnics, regarded as an important marker of Tibetan identity, are also common subjects for domestic videos. By 2004 many Tibetans had mobile phones with video capacity, and a much greater number of them were able to record such events.

These practices represent a domestic form of cultural reconstruction and recovery, the creation of a sort of archive of Tibetaneity for the household. Often, as Françoise Robin has noted, they specifically commemorate works representing what she has termed "endo-compassion"—reaffirmations of the central role in Tibetan culture of the notion of compassion (Robin 2009, 43). As we shall see, cultural reconstruction and collective redefinition in one form or another underlie all unofficial and independent film and video production by Tibetans, no matter what category they belong to.

Such works take on a new and acute significance when those social and identity-marking practices are contested by the state or are seen as under threat or dying out. The videos then constitute a part of communal memory; they become potential public records, not just domestic ones. This becomes clearer if we consider the practice of recording religious teachings, probably the most important and prominent form of domestic video in Tibet. Tibetan tradition does not expect a lama (a term used in Tibetan to refer to a highly regarded religious teacher) to teach regularly or to be available whenever a student needs advice, as in some Western religions: a lama is not a priest or a minister. Each visit or teaching by a lama could be the last and only opportunity to hear a particular teaching, receive a ritual transmission, or get that lama's spiritual or practical advice. The precariousness of receiving teachings is compounded in Tibet, given that government permission is required for public teachings and in some areas (most notably the TAR) is rarely given. The informal recording of religious teachings is thus a highly valued practice among Tibetans who have cameras or camera-phones.

Tibetans who work for the government have since the mid-1990s been forbidden by the authorities from attending religious ceremonies or practicing religion, at least in the TAR (Barnett 2003). So those who make video recordings of Buddhist teachings will usually be Tibetans whose wealth has come from trading, farming, or herding, rather than members of the urban elite, who are mostly government employees. Some will have limited education or will be semiliterate; for them, oral teachings are especially important. Often the people who make these recordings are also the sponsors of the ritual: they will have invited the lama to their locality to hold the ceremony for the community and will have covered all the costs of the event, which are often vast. Such forms of giving are seen as important forms of lay religiosity and community history, and recordings of these events thus capture the ritual participation of the community as well as the teachings given by the lamas. The recordings often circulate within society, either through informal distribution among friends, relatives, and others, or as lightly packaged products for purchase in the market.

This creation of unofficial and private video archives of Tibetan Buddhist teachings and ceremonies is, I would argue, the defining practice at the core of all

Tibetan video production, as well as other forms of cultural activity. It has uncontested meaning and value within Tibetan society, and all forms of filmmaking and record-keeping, at least in the Tibetan context, can be said to derive their worth and significance from their relation and proximity to that practice. This link is sometimes disguised for strategic reasons: independent Tibetan film-directors, for example, are usually not allowed by government censors to portray religion beyond a token level,[5] and so they seek other ways to represent the core values that are demonstrated unambiguously in home videos of lamas giving teachings or performing rituals. In other areas of contemporary Tibetan culture, the linkage is present but unstated, an expression of the same value that lies behind the practice of recording and sharing religious teachings and traditions.

This can be seen with what I call *civic videos*, which express in a modernist and sometimes secular form a similar sense that the Tibetan heritage or community needs defending from various forces of challenge or decay. These videos, which were scarcely feasible before the advent of digital technology, focus on such issues as environmental preservation, cultural heritage, and social education. The producers are often Tibetans who were able to establish local NGOs once such organizations were permitted to function in the late 1990s, or who have more recently set up businesses or social enterprises instead, since these are treated by officials as less sensitive than NGOs (Yeh 2011, 15). Some civic video-producers use the language and concepts of contemporary global debates in their projects, which can be seen as "import" initiatives, inspired or supported by foreigners or Chinese who advocate for the social value of community filmmaking. They often document their own work in public, post their films on their websites as motivational or publicity products, or teach video-production skills to others as a form of community capacity building. One such project, Rabsel, based in Kham, the eastern part of the Tibetan plateau mainly within Sichuan province, teaches young Tibetans to make documentaries in or about their community.[6] In Lhasa, a group of young Tibetans led by Lobsang (Blo bzang) produces shorts that dramatize the risks of addiction or discrimination, such as the damage caused by gambling (*The Bet*, 2008) or by prejudice toward the disabled (*A Foolish Brother*, 2008). A third example is Amilolo Films, formed in 2011 by a group of Tibetan students in Siling (Zi ling, Ch.: Xining) in Qinghai with the aim of "educating young Tibetans about digital video production and encouraging a new generation of Tibetan filmmakers."[7]

Other civic initiatives are completely indigenous: they are aimed inwardly toward the Tibetan community and have little or no relation with outsiders. As Yeh has shown (2011), these are sometimes based on emic, Tibetan notions of environment and society that are linked to religious practices and beliefs. An example can be seen in the video footage produced by an environmental protection project established by two Tibetans, Rinchen Samdrup and his brother Chime Namgyal, in a remote village in Chamdo prefecture, TAR. The videos showed the group's activities, such as tree planting, and were distributed to other villagers as a celebration of the community's work and a demonstration of their collective achievement.[8] Civic uses of digital video of this kind to sustain or record communal initiatives are probably quite widespread in Tibet, but are rarely known to outsiders.

MADE FOR EXPORT

A third type of digital video is intended partly or entirely for audiences who are not Tibetans. Some are touristic travelogues offering exotic or picturesque views of Tibetan culture and landscape, often aimed primarily at Chinese audiences, domestic or overseas, as well as foreigners. Usually produced by government offices or commercial enterprises, and similar to the videos that Robin has described as forms of "exo-performance" (Robin 2009, 45), these resemble romanticist travel videos typical of Western tourists, travel companies, and commercial-ethnographic endeavors like National Geographic and the Discovery Channel; they show exotic landscapes, colorful customs, and distinctive monasteries and temples. They are no doubt similar in ethos to the images shot for private use by Chinese and other tourists during their visits to Tibet. Commercial videos of this type are produced by Tibetan companies too, but these generally celebrate cultural richness, folk arts, architecture, or landscape. These videos are typically sold in shops and market stalls as gifts for friends or visitors, especially those from outside Tibet.

Another type of export video comes from Chinese governmental offices responsible for propaganda work. These products are usually documentaries that either demonstrate the progress China has brought to Tibet or document the evils of the former society from which it is supposed to have liberated Tibetans in the 1950s (such as *Tibet in the Past,* c. 2007 and *Dalai Lama,* c. 2008). In 2008, the Chinese authorities realized the potential of raw digital video for instant news management: it broadcast and distributed footage from its security cameras that showed savage beatings of ethnic Chinese by a number of Tibetan rioters during a protest in Lhasa that March. These images were replayed constantly on national television within China as well as sold to broadcasters worldwide. This saturation portrayal of Tibetan violence transformed the general perception both within China and abroad of Tibetans as pacifist or virtuous (Barnett 2009b).

At the same time, unofficial images that aimed to criticize the Chinese government and to document abuses by the state were increasingly recorded and distributed by Tibetans in Tibet. These examples of digital "citizen activism" first emerged during the 150 or so protests that spread across the Tibetan plateau following the Lhasa riot of March 2008. The recordings consisted of brief shots of Tibetan protests taken by participants on cell phones and then somehow transmitted secretly abroad, almost always to exile Tibetans in India or Nepal. Because digital communication allows such images to reach the outside world within hours, they have significant potential news value. In one case, still images that showed the bodies of Tibetans who had been shot dead, presumably by Chinese troops during the protests, reached exile activists in India within a day of the protests.[9] But most such images of protest were taken before the security forces arrived and so did not show violence by the state, making them less effective as counters to the raw footage circulated by the Chinese authorities. Digitization is still subject to the hierarchies of market preference and value: the international media place a premium on video footage of violence, especially if it appears to be unedited, rather than on film of peaceful protests. Stills have news value in the digital age only as a last resort, and the photographs of Tibetan corpses were rarely used by broadcasters.[10]

When a wave of self-immolations by Tibetan protestors began to spread across eastern Tibetan areas in March 2011, local bystanders began regularly to send cell phone footage of the burnings to other Tibetans or to exiles in India.[11] They aimed presumably to provide video that would be used by international broadcasters, and to some extent they succeeded. Since that time, the Chinese authorities have routinely shut down Internet access and other communications systems in localities where a protest or self-immolation has occurred so that activists can only transmit footage for a brief period after an incident. Since at least 2007, when a Tibetan monk called Adak Lopoe was given a ten-year sentence for trying to send a photograph of a protest to an exile news organization, Tibetans have faced stiff punishment if caught distributing or exporting images of protest.

In rare cases, some political videos have emerged within Tibet that were edited or planned products, rather than raw footage. Some of these were produced and distributed as DVDs using the basic format of the music video, such as *Red Fragment* or *Red Prophecy*, a collection of songs celebrating the Tibetan protests of 2008 and lamenting the victims. These were reportedly produced in about 2009 by a group of monks from Tshakho and Khakhor monasteries in Golok Matoe (Rma stod, Ch.: Madoi), a Tibetan area of Qinghai; eleven people were arrested in December 2009 for producing the DVD and making 5,000 copies (TCHRD 2009).[12] Other videos of this kind have been based on the format of the documentary rather than on that of the music album, intended for the exile or international communities. The best known of these, *Leaving Fear Behind* (2008), had a transnational aspect. It was made by Dondrub Wangchen (Don grub dbang chen), a thirty-five-year-old Tibetan from Hualong in Haidong prefecture, Qinghai, after he returned from a visit to Europe. He bought a DV camera and traveled around Qinghai in the spring of 2008, asking Tibetans to state, on camera, their views of the forthcoming Olympics in Beijing and government policy in general. He then smuggled the tapes via a visiting overseas Tibetan to a cousin in Switzerland, who edited them into the film (Pemba 2009). In December 2009, Dondrub Wangchen received a six-year sentence for making the film (Walsh 2010).[13]

Another speech-based video intended for an outside audience was the statement given on camera in 2008 by a senior Tibetan monk, Jigme Gyatso ('Jigs med rgyal mtsho) from Labrang monastery (Bla brang, Ch.: Labulengsi) in Gansu, in which he described the conditions of his detention by local police a few weeks earlier. His statement was delivered straight to camera, at the instigation of the speaker and not as a response to a question or an interview. It was filmed by a friend from Beijing, who then posted it online via YouTube (which cannot be accessed within China).

These works were not unique products of the digital moment. Similar films, in some ways even better ones, had been produced by Tibetan "guerilla" documentarians in the age of the videocassette. In 1996, a Tibetan, with no background in film or political activism, contacted me from Tibet through an intermediary and asked to be given training secretly in video technique. He was able to travel to Kathmandu, where I arranged for Witness, a U.S.-based NGO that promotes the use of videography in human rights, to give him a camcorder and to provide him with basic training in using it. We made no suggestions as to what he might use the camera and his training for, and it seemed that he already had decided on his subject matter before approaching us. A few months later I received two tapes that showed some seventy trucks over a seven-hour period traveling along a mountain road somewhere in southern Tibet, each one carrying tree trunks of enormous girth. The secret filmmaker had hidden himself high up on a mountain slope and filmed each truck that passed along the road on the far side of the valley that day, along with his comments as he watched. At one point, he says to the camera, "I'm very nervous, in case somebody sees me, so this film is not so good. Sometimes I'm afraid, and sometimes I'm not afraid, and then I think that I am doing this for Tibet. Sometimes I think even if I die, I'm dying for Tibet." Apart from masking the filmmaker's voice, the footage needed nothing to be added for it to serve as a study of deforestation in Tibet, and it was broadcast unedited by the BBC (*Cutting Down Tibet,* 1996). But analog video has many limitations, as became evident when the filmmaker smuggled out a second tape involving more sensitive and complex material. This time, he had filmed two Tibetan families discussing their situation in their homes in a rural village. This interior setting was much harder to film on analog video using available light, the discussions were often diffuse and hard to hear, more work was needed to conceal the identities of the speakers, and it was harder to get interest from the media.

The filming involved major risks for the Tibetan—he was of the wrong social class to own a camera at that time, and if discovered he would have been liable to charges of espionage as well as of what was then termed "counterrevolution."[14] The digital age and the improvement in personal incomes in Tibet reduced the first difficulty, making cameras affordable for many Tibetans. It also made them easier to use, with much smaller tapes that can be hidden easily—Dondrub Wangchen was able to send out some 120 mini-DV tapes, through his overseas Tibetan friend, just days before he was detained—as well as sensors that can operate in low-light conditions, and effective, in-line microphones. But even with these advantages, few guerilla documentaries of the type demonstrated by the 1996 logging film were made by Tibetans in the first digital decade.

Momentary incident recordings and preplanned interviews and documentaries by activists aim to persuade a foreign public about a principle or an argument rather than record or archive the condition of a community's culture or environment. From a Tibetan perspective, they derive from the notion of truth-telling, a concept of great force that has recurred repeatedly in Tibetan political discourse over the last century or more and is still dominant today. It suggests that in the end, "truth" will always triumph in the political or national domain, just as it does by definition in the religious sphere: it links religious and national purpose when faced with an outside threat. This was largely how the Tibetan state had theorized popular opposition to China's actions in the early 1950s, and in many exile schools a prayer called the *Bden mtshig smon lam* or "Prayer of Words of Truth," written by the present Dalai Lama in 1960, is still recited daily, calling for an end to the "*rivers of blood and tears*" (*ngan dgus 'joms pa'i khrag dang mchi ma'i rgyun*) that result from being *conquered "by barbaric forces of evil"* (nag phyogs kla klo'i dpung gis). The Tibetan practice of resting political arguments on the assertion of truth makes "the camera that does not lie" the medium of choice for the people or the cause that does not lie; the Chinese authorities have long followed a similar principle in their propaganda work, namely, that "seeing is believing." The basic political practice among Tibetans in the 1990s, as Margaret McLagan showed in her study of exile self-representation (McLagan 1996), reflected the same notion of truth-telling: it was one of testimony, giving verbal witness to suffering. In the contemporary mediatized environment, the digital video and the recording of dissent—in the form mainly of snatched cell phone footage of protests and incidents—is replacing speech as the principal form of political discourse among Tibetan activists, but the underlying principle remains the same.

FORMAL DIGITAL DOCUMENTARIES AND THE WORK OF DORJE TSERING

Only a very small proportion of cultural production in Tibet deals directly with political questions. The fourth type of output—unofficial documentaries—consists of highly crafted, self-conscious works of art and intellectual enquiry, intended for broadcast rather than political activism. Production of this type was significantly boosted by the advent of digital technology. Mainly associated with former students and intellectuals, these documentaries present an important alternative to the use of film as testimony or "truth-telling." The majority come from the northeastern Tibetan area known as Amdo, mostly administered by Qinghai province, and are made by filmmakers who have worked or studied with foreigners. Several of the nonfiction filmmakers are graduates of an English-language program at Qinghai Normal University in Xining who decided to produce their own documentaries, most notably Phagpa Dondrub ('Phags pa don grub, Ch.: Puhua Dunzhu), who made three full-length documentaries about Tibetan culture in 2005–2006.[15] Tsering Perlo, founder of the community-filmmaking organization Rabsel, worked with two filmmakers from the United States, Nelson Walker and Lynn True, to produce their semiofficial coproduction *Summer Pasture* (2011), a prize-winning study of a nomad family in Kham. In Lhasa, where Tibetan intellectuals have found it easier to express themselves through fine art rather than filmmaking as in Amdo, the young conceptual artist Penchung used video in 2006 to record one of the first installation pieces in Tibet: he created a ground-painting in chalk (a traditional practice for weddings and consecrations and for greeting important visitors) during the night at a normally busy crossroads in the city. His DV of the installation shows its gradual erosion by the traffic.

In the early 2000s, a number of major Tibetan intellectuals from Amdo had already turned to making documentaries. One of the best known was the poet and short story writer Chenagtshang Dorje Tsering (Lce nag tshang Rdo rje tshe ring), who writes under the pen name Jangbu (Ljang bu) and comes from Sokpo (Sog po, Ch.: Henan) county in Qinghai. Since 2002 he has held a position as a lecturer at the Institut national des langues et civilisations orientales in Paris, but his decision to shift from writing to filmmaking came long before his contact with foreigners and before the digital era. In a 2007 lecture in New York, he described that decision as a response to early documentaries about Tibet made by members of the famous, or infamous, coterie of Chinese artists who lived in Lhasa in the 1980s (see Zhang Ziyang et al. 2004), who sometimes called themselves the *liumang* or "hooligans." In particular, his move toward filmmaking was a response to Wang Huaixin's documentary *Tibetan Seductions* (1988), which told the stories of a Chinese journalist from Anhui, a prominent painter (Han Shuli) from Beijing, and a Japanese musician, all of whom had come to Tibet because of its cultural or artistic offerings. The film, in Jangbu's words, led to a "hot wave of documentary filmmaking" about Tibet. But in his view, it

> showcased the beautiful and grand scenarios of Tibet totally from the perspective of outsiders without relating with the subjects shown. The first time

> I saw this film brought forth a strong feeling in me: indigenous Tibetan people who were so lively didn't appear in the film as major characters; on the contrary, they were only contrasts and embellishments. So I raised such questions as these for myself: are we forever the kind of people who came from a marginal and concealed world and who served only as a foil or contrast, waiting to be discovered? (Chenagtshang 2007, 3)[16]

In about 1989, Dorje Tsering resigned from his position in a prestigious government office (the TAR People's Congress) and, with funds raised from other Tibetans—mostly college and high school students—bought a still-camera with the aim to capture "from my own perspective the Tibet that was neglected by outsiders, that was happening, and disappearing, with form and realism" (Chenagtshang 2007, 4). But he never had enough money or expertise to develop the film or complete the project. Not long after, Dorje Tsering met the leading Chinese artist and documentary maker Wen Pulin and was asked to draft a proposal for a documentary. "That very night I wrote a project for a documentary on a popular ceremony held in Rebkong, Amdo. Before that, I had no clue about what documentary filmmaking was," he wrote (Chenagtshang 2009a, 72). From 1993 he worked as a writer, researcher, and second director on a series of projects with Wen, and from 1999–2002 he helped the Chinese filmmaker Chen Zhen on *Potala*, a documentary about the Potala Palace, a collaboration he described as "my greatest opportunity as an artist."

It was only in 2003 that the affordability of digital equipment allowed him finally to make his own documentaries, by which time he was mostly living abroad. He showed or distributed these works unofficially in Tibet as well as publicly abroad—*The Tantric Yogi* (2005), *Lhacham—A Tibetan Nun* (2007), and *Kokonor Lake* (2008), along with a partly dramatized study of illegal fungus collection, *Yartsa Rinpoche* (2013).

Dorje Tsering's film work has something in common with the complex and difficult *rab rib* (misty) style for which his poetry is famous (see Jangbu and Stoddard 2010), not in terms of textual obscurity, reference, or even lyricism, but in the avoidance of moral judgment and of resolution-reaching narrative. The films are not ethnographies or transparency-endowing studies of a culture by an outside eye. They are unfinished conversations by their subjects with the director, who is unseen but sometimes heard, and clearly viewed as a member of their own community. The subjects are Tibetans from the countryside, *mi phal pa,* ordinary people, "nobodies." Their talk is characterized by laughter and gentle self-mockery, often by failure, and never by any claim to significance. The tantric adepts in his first film have no pretensions to spiritual proficiency; their concern is baking a giant loaf of bread to give to their community—they cannot quite work out how

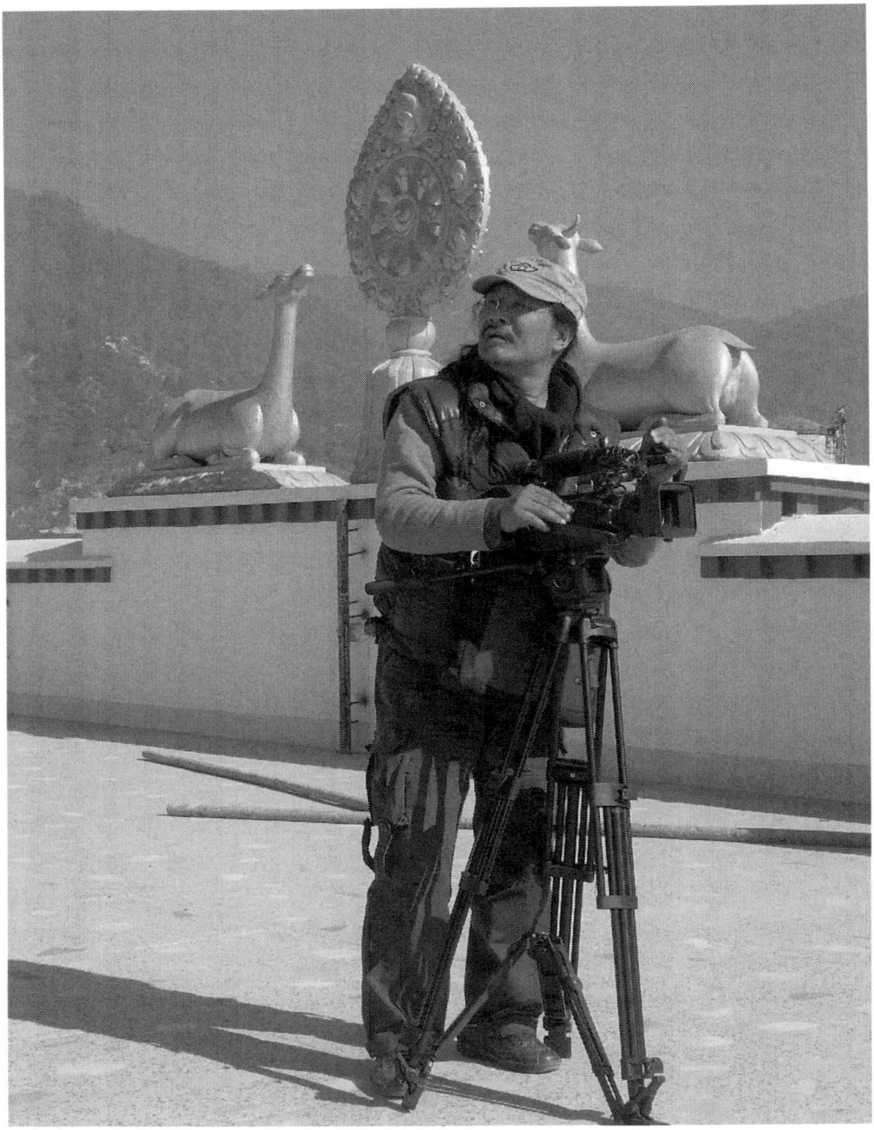

Figure 5.1. The poet and filmmaker Chenagtshang Dorje Tsering (Jangbu).

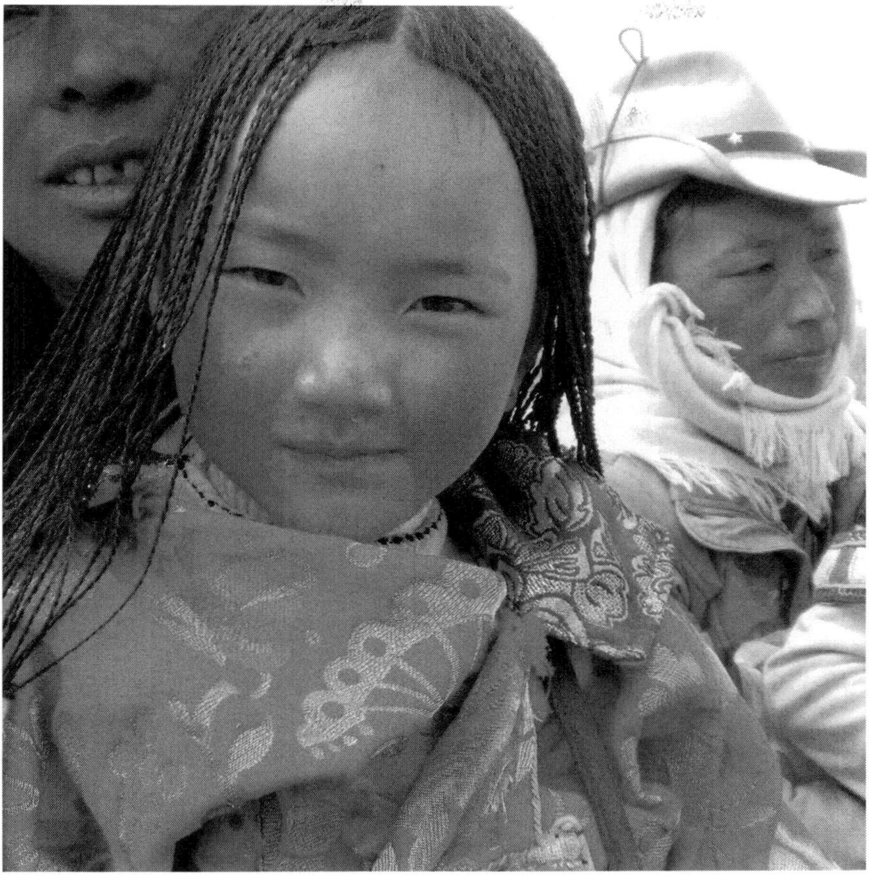

Figure 5.2. Kokonor Lake. Culture for sale: Tibetan children hoping to be paid to be photographed with Chinese tourists at Qinghai Lake. (still photo by Dorje Tsering, from his 2008 film)

to get the local bus drivers to deliver it to a festival on time, almost get lost on the way, and have difficulty working out how to lift the bread onto the roof of the bus without it breaking. The camera work is roughly made, like the bread, and there is no resort to exoticism, lyricism, or drama: everything is pervaded by a kind of incomplete, drab modernity, which is neither judged nor commented on. Viewers are left to relate to the often difficult, morally unclear, and unresolved predicament of the subjects.

Dorje Tsering's work thus presents the direct opposite of the glossy finish and narrative certainties of exoticist and nature-loving documentaries about Tibet, whether made by the Chinese government or the international corporate media.

But it also differs from the assertions of the political truth-tellers, whether Chinese officials or political activists opposed to them. It has closer links to the New Documentary Movement in China, a movement that had deep ties to Tibet. The leaders of that movement in its earliest phase from 1989–1993 were Wu Wenguang, Wen Pulin, Duan Jinchuan, Jiang Yue, and nine others (Lü Xinyu 2010, 19). The last three of those named here, plus at least two others (Chen Zhen and Fu Hongxing), joined the successors of the *liumang* in Lhasa in the early 1990s, which is when Dorje Tsering came to know them. Lü Xinyu critiques the group for similar reasons to those of Dorje Tsering, describing them all, apart from Duan Jinchuan, as having failed to learn from Duan's unsentimental study of Lhasa administration, *No. 16 Barkor South Street* (1996). That film, she says, "neither romanticizes nor mysticizes Tibetan life but rather depicts ordinary Tibetans in their ongoing engagements with the Chinese government." But of the other Chinese filmmakers in Tibet at that time she adds, "I have discovered that this utopian impulse never really ended . . . Tibet still serves as a symbol of distant lands and as the sign of difference from modern civilization." Many other Chinese documentarians, including those based in inland China, she adds, "embraced nostalgia" and continued "the search for utopia in distant places" (Lü Xinyu 2010, 36–37).

Dorje Tsering's films are more than a rejection of exoticism: unlike Duan's work, they are not objectivist reporting. They reject the use of formal aesthetics in their approach to composition and narrative, and they do not choose subjects who are, as individuals, socially marginal or ostracized. Rather, they are from ordinary Tibet, neither the elite nor the dispossessed. Not exotic or even strange, they are fully human and without auras. But they are not faceless victims of modernity either: we are made to glimpse in each of them an energetic but lightly sketched individuality and humanity.

His films are thus about engagement with the nonelite, portraits of the messy, undefined, and erratically structured confusion that is the hallmark of sociality and of people who have common purpose by virtue of some indistinct shared attribute such as nationality. His camera always stands for the filmmaker in conversation with his subjects, rather than as an outsider gazing at them or explaining them. The films demonstrate a commonality between the elite Tibetan intellectual and the ordinary rural or small-town Tibetan farmer, monk, policeman, scavenger, or nun. If the Chinese new documentaries show individuals as marginal to modernity or to urban society, Dorje Tsering's work shows not individuals on the fringes of society, but a collective that as a whole seems marginal, a collective constituted by unexceptional Tibetans in conjunction with intellectuals like himself. This condition of collective marginality is not described or pointed to, no reason is suggested for it, and no emotional or political response is invited or induced.[17] His films resist interpretation, not through formal difficulty as in his poetry, but through refusal to adopt a morally delineated narrative structure or conclusion.

In a similar way, Dorje Tsering himself ignores questions about his ethnicity—like the leading writer and novelist Tsering Dondrub (Tshe ring don grub), he comes from a community defined as Mongolian but which expresses itself culturally as Tibetan. His camera is used to demonstrate full engagement with the subject as both the method and final purpose of the filmmaking project. It is in itself constitutive of the act of making a community, a bond between Tibetans on either side of the camera.[18]

After the unrest of 2008, a new type of digital video appeared in Tibet, lying somewhere between the formal documentary and citizen journalism, but aimed at the community within Tibet rather than outsiders. These videos consisted of short, simple pieces made as part of intellectual and cultural debates within the community, sometimes with editing and commentary. They were much simpler and shorter than the political DVDs, *Red Fragment* and *Hope from Disaster* (2011), and avoided any specifically political statement or criticism of the state. Instead, they focused on cultural issues, expressing pride in Tibetan identity or culture. Two were posted on the Chinese video-sharing site, tudou.com, and appear to have had some impact within Tibet. The authors are unknown. One piece, *Let's Speak in Pure Tibetan* (c. 2008), consists of a montage of still images taken from websites showing iconic features of Tibetan culture—snow mountains, monks, the Potala Palace, a Tibetan mastiff, and so on—while a professional narrator recites a poem about using Tibetan language. Unlike most videos, films, or documentaries described here, it uses Lhasa or Central Tibetan dialect, rather than a dialect from Kham or Amdo. An echo effect has been added to the speaker's voice, and a Tibetan folk song is played underneath:

> The Tibetan alphabet is the heart and soul of my existence.
> For the sake of continued survival, let's all speak this Tibetan language of ours.
> Let's speak in pure Tibetan.
> If you are a descendant of the Land of Snowy Ranges who loves and cares about your nation,
> Then let's not use any hybrid language when conversing in our day-to-day life,
> People of the Land of Snows![19]

The poem and the video spread to numerous Tibetan websites during 2008 and 2009. A second, more risky and creative piece came from Amdo and first appeared on December 19, 2009. It was called *I Am Tibetan* (2009) and also circulated widely. The anonymous video, carefully composed and formally precise, consists solely of single headshots of interviewees speaking directly to the camera.

Each shot is one sentence long, with speed cutting and no additional sequences or context. It is mostly shot in small towns and villages in Amdo or in vehicles traveling between them. Each sentence begins with the phrase "I am Tibetan because. . . ." The answers are each offered by a different person:

> I am Tibetan because I grew up on this grassland.
> I am Tibetan because I wear these Tibetan clothes.
> I am Tibetan because my mother is Tibetan.
> I am Tibetan because I know how to recite *ma Ni* [the six-syllable mantra].
> I am Tibetan because I always eat *rtsam pa* [parched barley flour].
> I am Tibetan because I'm a nomad who looks after sheep.
> I am Tibetan because I'm a shepherd from Tibet.

The video, which included no explicitly political statements and no explanation, led to a series of poems and writings on the same topic by Tibetan writers on the Web.

Other videos were already circulating that encouraged certain forms of behavior associated with Buddhist ideals. One appeared in 2006 that urged Tibetans to respect endangered species by burning the fur pelts used as trimmings for traditional robes (Robin 2009, 43). In 2007, a DVD circulated widely in Tibet showed gory pictures of abattoirs in order to promote vegetarianism; it was financed by a wealthy trader from the northern Tibetan town of Nagchu (Robin 2009, 44) and is part of a growing identity-affirming movement in Tibet.

These digital products, from online poem-videos to formal documentaries, were matched by a marked increase in lightly veiled discussions and debates among Tibetans on Internet forums and websites. Together they encapsulate the impulse driving the new Tibetan documentary movement: engagement with the question of identity and the cultural future of Tibetans. In these videos we see digital technology facilitating discussions about collective meaning that are too sensitive to convey in written form without attracting censorship. The very ephemerality and variety of digital products made them safer and more convenient as platforms for discussion than the formats of the predigital age.

Independent Tibetan Fiction Films

The shape of this conversation among Tibetans in Tibet becomes clearer and more nuanced if we look at the dramas and fiction films made by independent Tibetan DV filmmakers from 2005 to 2011. Digital technology led to the production of some twenty-five or more of these films. Of these, at least four were distributed internationally for theater screenings (three by Pema Tseden and one by Sonthar Gyal, plus Tsering Perlo's documentary coproduction with Walker and True) and won awards, while the others were circulated on the Web or sold unofficially as DVDs. Most of these filmmakers came from Amdo, the heartland of the renaissance in modern Tibetan literature and poetry that began in the early 1980s with the work of the Amdowan writer Dondrub Gyal (Don grub rgyal, 1982). Affordable digital technology made it possible to extend the concepts and questions of that movement to film and video. It also allowed short films to be circulated online or as DVDs, obviating the need for a cinema release or a television broadcast, both of which require government approval for the script as well as for the final product.

Independent Tibetan film in China can be divided into three periods: the pioneer work of Phagmo Tashi (Phag mo bkra shis) in the early 1990s on Beta SP, the 35mm films of Pema Tseden (Pema rtshe brtan, Ch.: Wanmacaidan) from 2004, and the surge of digital films from 2005.[20] The work produced in these three periods can also be divided roughly according to its subject matter, again into three categories: dramas about the tension between modernity and tradition; nomadic romance dramas; and dramas of religious biography and redemption. As we shall see, they share a commonality in their treatment of gender and masculinity.

THE PIONEER PHASE: PHAGMO TASHI'S LONGING

The first Tibetan director to shoot a full-length fiction film in China (or anywhere) in his own language was the Amdo intellectual Phagmo Tashi, head of the main Tibetan-language dubbing and translation company for the local government in Qinghai.[21] In 1992, he used a Beta SP camera to make *Longing*, the story of a nomad youth who has received a modern education in the city of Xining and has remained there to take up work as a clerk. Four years later, when he returns to the grasslands to ask his fiancée to marry him, he finds that her family has already settled her marriage to another man.

The film laments the loss of innocence and cultural certainty in the face of modernity. It stands out for its style of dialogue, which is highly formalized: the speech of the main characters is framed by narration that is recited by an off-screen voice in verse or poetic prose. Chanted, lyrical narration is an important feature of Amdo film and video and is found in online educational videos on Tibetan language and culture, as well as in one of the first state-produced television drama series set in Tibet, *Suru Flower* (1984). Phagmo Tashi's pioneering film was remarkable because it was made entirely by Tibetans, written and performed only in Tibetan language, and because it studied a critical issue at the center of communal life: families ruptured by the demands of modern urban life, education, and the loss of traditional cultural norms. It was shown on Qinghai TV, but for many viewers, the production must soon have seemed dated and mannered, with the hero wearing a dapper suit whilst in the city and a long-since out-of-fashion hairstyle. The director later disavowed the work, reluctant to have it shown again because of what he considered to be a lack of technical quality and professionalism. Neither he nor any other Tibetan in Tibet made an independent fiction film or drama in their own language for twelve years, when Pema Tseden's first film was completed.[22]

The years in between saw increasing tensions in the Tibetan areas, first in Lhasa and then in the eastern areas of Kham and Amdo in the later 1990s, as new policies were gradually imposed following a meeting in Beijing in 1994 called the Third National Forum on Tibet Work. Probably as a preventive measure following the collapse of communism in the Soviet Union, this forum explicitly attacked certain elements of Tibetan culture seen as linked to irredentist nationalism, most notably the religious standing of the Dalai Lama and the social role of monks and monasteries (Barnett and Spiegel 1996). The most important attempt ever made by a Chinese director to make a credible film about Tibetan history, Zhang Yi's *The Secret History of the Potala Palace* (1989), a study of seventeenth-century Tibetan history told partly from a Tibetan point of view, had already been banned five years earlier. There was no further sign of any effort to make a serious Chinese-language fiction film set in Tibet, let alone one by a Tibetan, until the release of Xie Fei's *Yeshe Drolma* (2000; see Barnett 2002), if not Lu Chuan's *Mountain Patrol* in 2004.[23] Until then, it seems that the intellectual and political climate was too restrictive for a serious representation of Tibet in fiction cinema.

THE ARRIVAL OF PEMA TSEDEN

Tibetan-language cinema reemerged only after Pema Tseden entered the Beijing Film Academy in 2002, the first Tibetan to do so.[24] Already well established in his native Amdo as a short story writer, and fluent in both Tibetan and Chinese, he first trained at the academy as an actor before deciding to study directing under the leading Chinese film directors Tian Zhuangzhuang and Xie Fei. His motivation was very similar to that of another leading Amdo writer, Dorje Tsering, ten years earlier, as discussed previously. It also emanated from a concern about rescuing Tibet from hegemonic mainstream representations:

> My main motivation behind making films? Well, my friends or other acquaintances and I have all seen many films on Tibet and Tibetan culture. However, most of these films do not portray Tibetan culture, the Tibetan way of life, or value-systems properly. So, all of us feel saddened. We felt that it would be very good to see someone who has lived and experienced that culture himself, to make a film representing that real experience. Everyone shared that view. I also feel the same way. (Pema Tseden 2010)

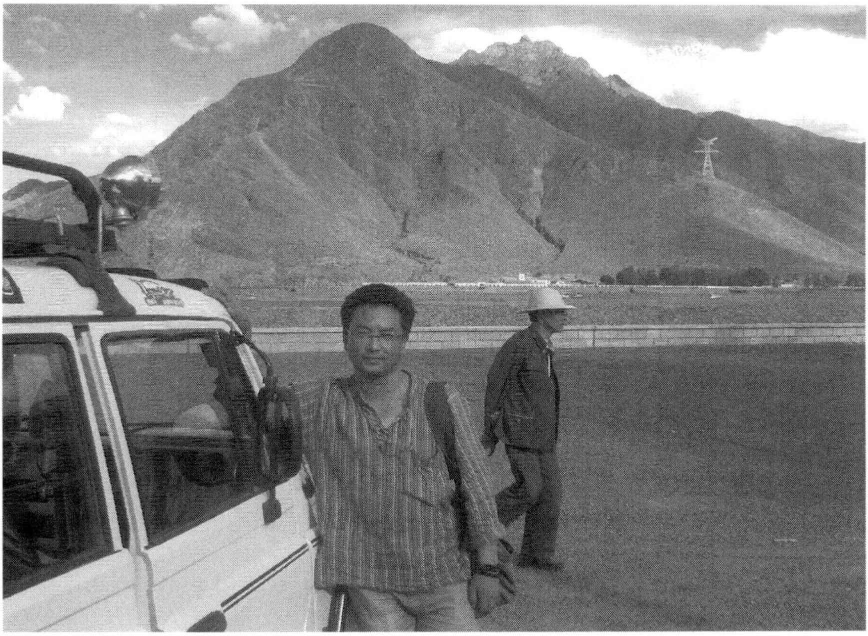

Figure 5.3. Pema Tseden in Lhasa, 2007. (photo by the author)

Pema Tseden's work belongs to the social-engagement movement that had swept Chinese cinema in the 1990s, as described by Lü Xinyu (2010), and is related to the Sixth Generation filmmakers and the documentary realism found in China at the time. But as Zhang Zhen has noted,[25] his work also represents a preoccupation with poetics, though in a very different way from Phagmo Tashi's lyrical narration. Instead, it focuses on paying strict attention to visual and narrative formalism. His first film, a student graduation piece called *The Grassland* (2004), shot on 35mm, was relatively conventional in story terms, with narrative tension that leads to a satisfying resolution: two older Tibetan nomads find a traditional and conciliatory way to resolve a dispute with a younger Tibetan over the theft of a yak. The film used landscape as an index for emotion and as a form of value statement, a device found in standard exoticist film about Tibet, including his teacher Tian Zhuangzhuang's pathbreaking film set in Tibet, *Horse Thief* (1986). But *The Grassland* retained a distance from its characters, resisting the temptation to craft heroic figures or to use the close-up as a device for psychological interpretation.

Pema Tseden's first major work, the longer version of *The Silent Holy Stones* (2005), was shot on 35mm and won him the Golden Rooster Award as the most promising new director in Chinese cinema for 2006. Like his first film, it attempted to construct an authentic representation of the culture, what Françoise Robin has called "staging Tibetanness from within" (Robin 2006, 5–9). In this work, influenced by the formal restraint of the Iranian director Abbas Kiarostami, Pema Tseden went much further in stylistic discipline, never using a push-in, a close-up of the human face, or a tracking shot, and almost abandoning the conventional narrative arc.[26]

The film is an observational study of three days in the life of a young Tibetan monk in an Amdo village who wants to watch the television series *Xiyouji* (*Journey to the West,* also known as *The Monkey King*) both while at his monastery and while visiting his family in their village. There, the locals watch a performance by other villagers of the traditional Tibetan opera *Drime Kunden* (*Dri med kun ldan*), an ancient Buddhist parable of a king who gives even his eyes away as an act of charity. But the boy is more interested in watching television and in buying a garishly colored plastic mask of the Monkey King from a local hawker. At the end of the film, the little monk is left in the monastery without the television or the videocassette. But, holding the mask and the empty box of the *Xiyouji* VCD, he runs off to join the other monks and to chant with them the prayers that mark the beginning of the Tibetan year.

The film takes up some of the same core issues raised by Phagmo Tashi a decade before: the tension between the modern and the traditional, the urban and the rural, the Tibetan and the outside worlds. But instead of using romance as the backcloth against which these tensions are played out, Pema Tseden takes the commodity as the locus of disruptive desire and modernity, in this case the videocassette of the television drama. (In a later, digital film, *Old Dog* [2010], he uses the Tibetan mastiff as a key, divisive commodity in a Tibetan family, the desire for which encapsulates the relationship between the nomadic and urban worlds.) *The Silent Holy Stones* shows the consumption of commercial video and the pursuit of the monastic life as in tension but not conflict. As the director put it, "Some critics have interpreted my film as showing the conflict (*'gal zla*) between tradition and modernity. This is a misunderstanding: it deals with their intermingling (*bsres pa*)" (Robin 2006, 7). We can see a similarity with the documentaries of Dorje Tsering and their resistance to polar narrative, which we might define as the distinctive feature of Amdowan filmic sensibility.

The third phase of Tibetan fiction filmmaking began in 2005, when a number of other Amdo Tibetans, galvanized by the achievement of *The Silent Holy Stones* as the first effective, self-determined representation of Tibetan culture on film, started to make films using digital equipment and online distribution.[27] Two distinct groups emerged among these new Tibetan filmmakers—those who were, like Phagmo Tashi and Pema Tseden, already well-known authors, performers, artists, or poets, and those who were students at one or other of the *minzu daxue* or "nationality universities" established across China to provide higher education for members of China's official minorities and for those Chinese destined to administer them. The work of the student group, which included women, began to emerge from about 2008. By that time a third or middle group had come to light in Amdo, formed by Tibetan men who were neither writers nor students and not widely known but who were independently making fiction films and posting them online, with their focus mainly on stories of nomad culture.

The first group to emerge after Pema Tseden's early work was that of socially established cultural figures—writers, poets, and performers, plus one painter and a lama. Among the best-known poets and authors who started to make films, according to Dorje Tsering, were Nyima Dondrub (Nyi ma don grub), Tenpa Yargye (Bstan pa yar rgyas), Tashi Palden (Bkra shis dpal ldan), Tsering Dondrub (Tshe ring don grub), Gangshon (Gangs zhun), Rigdan Gyatso (Rig ldan rgya mtsho), Shide Nyima (Zhi bde nyi ma), Jone Yum Tsering (Co ne Yum tshe ring), and Dodrag (Rdo grags, Ch.: Duo zhi he). The first three are important writers from Lhasa whose film work I have not yet been able to trace, but the others are from Amdo; the last three of them are noted for having written and directed television drama series rather than cinema films. Dorje Tsering himself moved from documentary to fiction film in 2006 when he worked as one of the main writers on *Prince of the Himalayas* (2006), a major Chinese film with international impact that consisted of a powerful and nuanced setting of Shakespeare's *Hamlet* in Tibetan prehistory.

PROBING THE MODERNITY-TRADITION DIVIDE

The Tibetan writers and artists who turned to film focused mainly on producing pieces about the modernity-tradition divide, resuming the discussions and the issues presented in the work of Phagmo Tashi in 1992 and Pema Tseden from 2004. In *The Coral Necklace* (2006), the performer, poet, and comedian Shide Nyima showed both the romantic idyll, symbolized by the innocence of a young nomad woman playing with her younger brother on the grassland, and the difficult choices facing her nomad father when he goes to a nearby town to buy a necklace for her. Tibetan rural culture is represented as innocent and female, and as facing a challenge from modernity and the disruptive impact of desire, symbolized by the necklace and the marketplace. As in *The Silent Holy Stones*, the locus of desire and the intersection of modernity and tradition are represented through a single fetishized commodity, not by ruptured romance as in *Longing*.

Shide Nyima's film has touches of realism, particularly in a scene of a wealthy urban Tibetan couple who, although surrounded by Tibetan artifacts in their home, are highly sinicized in dress and appearance. This was unusual: until 2011, independent Tibetan films, and even state productions about Tibet, rarely if ever showed a Chinese character or even a sinicized Tibetan, and generally avoided scenes set in Tibetan towns. For most independent Tibetan filmmakers, this was probably because their overriding objective was to demonstrate a pristine Tibetan essence imagined as existing only in the countryside, primarily among nomads. For the intellectuals, urban settings in their films are probably absent because no representation of modern city life could easily avoid suggesting tension between Tibetans and their Chinese fellow citizens—and, technically at least, it is a political problem in China, if not a crime, to show or suggest lack of harmony among the nationalities.[28] In the predigital era just four state-produced fiction films or dramas had been set in Lhasa—Xie Fei's romantic feature, *Yeshe Drolma* (2000), and three drama series: *Longing for Lhasa* (1997), *The Eight-Petalled Kelsang Flower* (2001), and *A Happy Life* (2008)—but none had shown any Chinese characters or even any sign of Chinese language or signage in the city: they had been made by Chinese directors or government studios and were urban idylls of an imaginary Lhasa without Chinese presence. The avoidance by Tibetan filmmakers and artists of any Chinese-Tibetan encounter, and of urban settings generally, is a sign

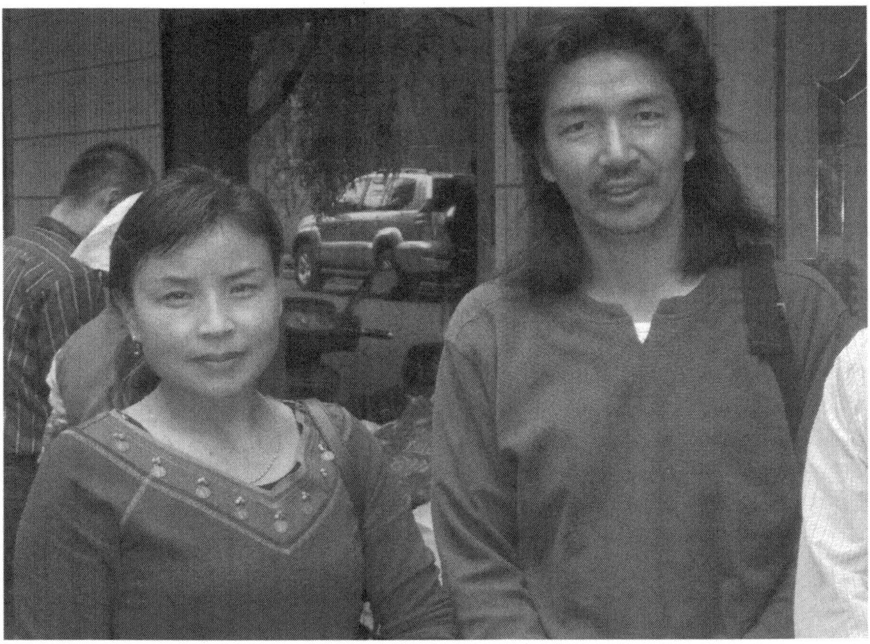

Figure 5.4. Khamo Gya, writer of The Girl Lhari, probably the first DV fiction film by a Tibetan in Tibet, with director Rigdan Gyatso. (photo by the author, Xining, 2007)

of the underlying tensions in the Tibetan world, and a major reason why the work of the Tibetan filmmakers is so often rural—and why, by omission, their work is often powerful for a Tibetan-speaking audience.

In 2005, the writer Rigdan Gyatso, who had graduated from the Qinghai Nationalities College in 1992, made his first film, a short called *Bu mo Lha ris* (*The Girl Lhari*), probably the first digital fiction film made by a Tibetan in Tibet. Written by Khamo Gya (Mkha' mo rgyal), founder of the first Tibetan magazine about women, it examined the modernity-tradition divide in Tibetan society from an entirely new perspective—that of gender. A dramatization of a Tibetan folktale about a young woman exploited by her new husband's family, it explores contemporary questions about the treatment of women in rural society—issues that had been raised in the short stories of the leading Tibetan modern writer, Dondrub Gyal, two decades earlier (Dondrub Gyal 2000 [1982]).

Rigdan's second short film for adults, *Fierce Turquoise Mountain* (2007), was also innovative in that it dealt with contemporary commerce and trade, rather than the rural or religious communities. It illustrated the tension between the modern and the traditional within commodity culture by showing a nomad family's response to a businessman's plan to build a hotel in their valley. As in Pema Tseden's *The Grassland* three years earlier, the film ends with the settlement of an intergenerational dispute by a traditional process of conciliation within the community. *Fierce Turquoise Mountain* was also the first Tibetan film to use the road journey: it opens with its characters traveling by car through a rural setting, as a signifier for the liminality of Tibetans within modernity. This motif would later be developed into entire films by Rinchen Drolma (Rin chen sgrol ma), Pema Tseden, and Sonthar Gyal (Zon mthar rgyal).[29]

Concern about the impact of modernity and the commodity culture on the Tibetan sense of community also emerged among the writers who moved to television drama rather than to film. The eight-part series *Stories of Yesterday* (2009), written and directed by the writer Dodrag, is described in its publicity materials as having been written "out of regret at the crisis facing nationality folk culture" (Tibetan Cultural Network 2009). But it goes further than that, presenting a parable of the modernity-tradition conflict told through the history of domestic technology in Tibet: the arrival of the radio, the television set, and the video player in a Tibetan household. The series follows a boy called Sonam who is brought up listening to the stories of his grandfather and who yearns to be a monk when he is old enough. One day, a shepherd brings a radio to the village, and people gather round it to listen to Tibetan songs and stories; some years later a television arrives. It is soon followed by a VCR. The grandfather and his stories of yesterday are forgotten, along with Sonam's childhood idealism: he decides to go to college in the city rather than to a monastery. Later he comes to realize the importance of cultural heritage and returns to the village with a digital recorder to tape the stories, but finds his grandfather dying: he has arrived too late. In this version of the parable, unlike in *The Silent Holy Stones,* modernity is a source of threat that education and the digital recorder can mollify but not negate. This is another reworking of Phagmo Tashi's original tale of a young and troubled male in the modern city struggling to find a way back to his original Tibetan community, a community riven by commoditization. As in many of these films, the essence of heritage and community is personified by an elderly Tibetan man.

At about the same time, another Tibetan independent filmmaker emerged in Kham: Sonam (Bsod nams), a *trulku* or reincarnated lama based in Chengdu. Like Rigdan Gyatso, he had lived for some time with Tibetan exiles in India and had no training or knowledge of film or theater apart from what he had seen in Indian and Chinese cinemas. Already a figure of some cultural standing as a lama, but without any artistic experience, he had come to see film as a way to explain Buddhist ethical ideas in the country to which he had returned. His first work, *Milarepa,* completed in 2006, was the first of several Tibetan films to develop the genre of religious biography, in which a wayward person finds redemption through a return to spiritual commitment.

In Buddhism, redemption and return to faith do not imply any intervention by a monotheistic deity, but are closer to the modernist concept of self-discovery. Sonam presents this inner journey through the story of the most famous poet-hermit in Tibetan history, whose vengeance-filled youth was eventually transformed by dedication to religion. The film represented a journey for the director too, since *Milarepa* was written, filmed, directed, crewed, and edited by him, entirely on his own, with no training, experience, or outside guidance, using local villagers from Gonjo in Kham as actors. Sonam told me that to edit the film he bought a computer and some software and just followed the instructions in the manual. The result was the first full-length feature film by a Tibetan within Tibet to be shot on digital video.[30]

Other Tibetans followed Sonam's initiative in using DV technology to celebrate this core story within Tibetan religious history. An eighteen-part drama series about the same story—the life of Milarepa—was written and directed by Choedar Gyatso (Chos dar rgya mtsho) and released on DVD in 2010, also in Kham dialect.[31] The same theme appears in later Tibetan films, such as *Deji from the Town of Tawa* (2011) directed by Tsewang Norbu (Ch.: Caiwang Naoru), a member of the student group of digital filmmakers and cofounder of the leading Chinese website on Tibetan issues, tibetcul.com.[32] Norbu's parable tells the story of Deji, a fallen woman who later becomes a religious paragon, one of many treatments of redemption and rediscovery in Tibetan cinema.

TIBETAN MASCULINITIES ON THE ROAD

It was Rinchen Drolma and Sonthar Gyal, members of the student group, who decisively reworked the theme of redemption into an effective filmic format. Both used the device of the road film to dramatize the inner transformation of the protagonist. *The Driver and the Lama* (2009), directed by Rinchen Drolma, the first Tibetan woman film director in Amdo, is the first Tibetan road movie, drawing consciously on Western cinematic tradition. The film follows a deeply withdrawn Tibetan truck driver tormented by childhood memories of the murder of his father; he is on a journey to find and kill the murderer.[33] On the way, he gives a lift to a young, lighthearted Tibetan monk who carries a Tibetan lute. At the end of the film, finally face-to-face with his quarry, the driver at the last moment abandons his quest for revenge: a transformation has taken place. The vector of change is the lute-playing monk and his Buddhist insights, but religion is represented not so much as a particular faith or practice as an internalized, contemporary journey toward self-knowledge.

Sonthar Gyal develops this form further in *The Sun-beaten Path* (2010), his first feature-length film. He had studied at the Beijing Film Academy with Pema Tseden and worked with him as cameraman or art director on all his films, but was also known as a modern artist in Amdo, having begun painting in 1994. In *The Sun-beaten Path* there is no explicit reference, visual or verbal, to Buddhism or any other religion and little visual indication of anything specifically Tibetan—only open, barren plains and hillsides on either side of a modern highway. We gather that the central figure, a young Tibetan, has prostrated from his home all the way to Lhasa, many hundreds of kilometers to the west, in order to appease his guilt at having caused his mother's death in a motor accident. He is now making his way back by foot to his home in Amdo. We see no sign of the months he must have spent prostrating on the road except for the marks of sunburn on his left cheek. The director described his choice in this way:

> For Tibetans, faith has a supreme value, which is why I first tried to find redemption for the brothers in religion, but it was a cliché, it brought nothing new. I thought that if they found relief in life itself, the film would be stronger. . . . I focused on the main narrative frame of mind of the protagonist as he just finished his pilgrimage, on his way out of the mist towards the sun, from self-forgetfulness to the assertion of self.
>
> (Veg 2011, 42; my translation from the French)

The religious journey is reshaped into a road film: the protagonist has to come to terms with his guilt while hitchhiking or walking along the road back to his home, as massive trucks and buses thunder by. The only person he meets is an old man who reappears by chance at different points in the journey, sensing the boy's inner torment and showing him ways of reconciliation through small acts of kindness. The film illustrates Katie Mills' argument in her study of road movies that "the very communities whose movements and spontaneity have been restricted by dominant regimes . . . have deployed the language of mobility . . . crafting tales of agency regardless of the restrictions on their movement" (Mills 2006, 13). This story is, however, a Tibetan version of agency and self-discovery, for the journey represents not the American search for individual fulfillment, or "modernist rebellion," as Mills puts it, but the Tibetan effort to reconcile modernity with tradition and to adapt modern male subjectivity to traditional family obligations. Visually, *The Sun-beaten Path* is boldly new: there is nothing idyllic about its vision of the Tibetan countryside. And while it is a road movie, it is a distinctively Tibetan one: the old man is a modern version of the *mkha' 'gro ma* of Tibetan fable, the *dakini* or sky-going goddess who appears from time to time as a hag on the roadside when people are in need of help.

Rinchen Drolma's and Sonthar Gyal's road movies are both about a young, unmarried male who is deeply conflicted, ridden by guilt, and unable to communicate or to enter into his community. The sullen, isolated central figure in these films is a wounded creature, damaged by his past, emasculated and uncertain. He is not a Tibetan rebel or an equivalent of the men found in classical American road movies. Never presented as a hero, he is not seeking a recovery of self in the sense of individualistic agency and the ability to act. Instead, he searches for collective selfhood, the restitution of his membership in his own community—more specifically, the capacity to be Tibetan in practice by readmission to the group. These figures stand for all Tibetan men lost in the wasteland of the new Tibet that is neither fully city nor completely countryside, deeply fissured by the changes and the history that have shaped their lives and split them from their families and their homes. This perception of contemporary Tibetan masculinity—muted, almost tragic men who carry silent burdens of cultural destiny on their shoulders, with the only possible resolution to their condition being the task of reintegrating with the Tibetan community—is visible in almost all the work of the new Tibetan filmmakers. It allows us to see that what some writers refer to loosely as a crisis of identity, usually depicted as a struggle within the self, is shown more precisely in these films as an effort to retain that distinctive feature of Tibetan religion and culture that resists the fracturing of self from the collective, a fracturing that is endemic to late socialist modernity in China and to neoliberal society in general.

As digital cameras became more accessible in the first years of the new century, several Tibetans who belonged neither to the literary or the student group set out to produce short fiction films. With little or no training or experience, they usually circulated their films on the Web or locally on DVDs rather than through cinemas or local television, still less internationally. These films were also about men trapped by a larger force, but in their dramas that force is tradition rather than modernity. These romances or romantic tragedies—among them are Tsedup Karko's *Hornig: Beat the Dog* (2005), Dobha's *Wailing at Dusk* (2009), Lodroe's *The Oath, Part 1* (2009), and Nordreng's *Blood on the Grassland* (2010)—are set in nomad encampments and feature often violent rivalry among men, where a young woman is the object of attention and desire.[34] They follow another strand within Phagmo Tashi's film from fifteen years earlier, celebrating the often tragic crisis of Tibetan masculinity and unfulfilled emotion.

These dramas depict a world in which there are only Tibetans and in which Tibetans pursue lifestyles or practices that are seen as uniquely or distinctively Tibetan, such as the love-feud. *Hornig: Beat the Dog,* for example, takes as its motif the so-called nocturnal courting rituals that, like the many Chinese documentaries and writings about the Mosuo people in Yunnan, are presented as premodern, sexually liberal, and exhilarating.[35] In dealing with the tragic outcomes of love in rural Tibetan society, these directors were returning to themes found in the short stories of Dondrub Gyal that had helped initiate Tibetan literary modernism in the early 1980s. But his stories were about unromanticized village life rather than idealized nomad culture and were presented within the context of communist or modernist critiques of tradition and its repressions. The nomadism in these later films stands not for the complexity of the encounter with modernity but for the reassertion of a rough Tibetan masculinity, with women as pure, downtrodden objects of male love and vengeance. These dramas nevertheless share a strong affinity with the other new Tibetan films: these men can neither escape their past nor express their dilemmas, and their masculinity remains largely tragic, burdened, and inarticulate.

By 2008, signs of a more critical approach were emerging within the writers' group. Shide Nyima's four-minute short, *Shepherd Song* (2008), despite its name and pastoral context, offered a lighthearted critique of modern urban Tibetan masculinity, in which digital technology serves as a marker of invasive voyeurism rather than of progress. We see a confident Tibetan youth in expensive modern clothes picnicking on the grasslands like a tourist, and through the viewfinder of his digital camera we see that he is taking pictures of a young nomad woman in the distance. A nomad child in traditional clothes sees that the urban Tibetan has taken some eggs from the nearby nest of an endangered species of bird and angrily prevents the urban Tibetan from eating them. Criticism of the urban sophisticate is a staple feature of Tibetan television comedy—a particularly biting example is *Gesar's Horseherders* (2004), a *xiaoping* or comic sketch written and directed by the Tibetan comedian and writer Manla Kyab (Sman lha skyabs).[36] Like *Shepherd Song,* it shows an educated Tibetan as no match for a rural, unmodernized Tibetan with his far greater understanding of Tibet's environment and heritage.

From about 2008, a student group of Tibetan DV filmmakers began to produce a series of short films about contemporary social tensions. *The Smile of Xesrob* (2011), made by students from the Central Nationalities University in Beijing, shows the inner struggle of a young teacher working in a remote rural school; the same theme is treated in *Leaving* (2011). In these films, the urban educated Tibetan is celebrated for his dedication to serving the rural community. But other student films show Tibetan failure and complexity. In *The Way Out* (2011), a young Tibetan woman tries unsuccessfully to find a religious solution to the failure of her marriage. *Sunday* (2011), made by Lhamo Tashi and a group of fellow Tibetan students in Chengdu and elsewhere, shows the contemporary university as a site of moral disintegration for Tibetan students. It follows a young student who eventually gives up his studies to spend his time in heavy drinking with his fellow students, all Tibetan men.[37] Probably the first film by a Tibetan filmmaker to be shot entirely in an urban setting, it shows this failure as gendered: the protagonist discards his more educated Tibetan girlfriend in favor of alcoholic masculinity. The lonely, displaced but virtuous Tibetan town dweller who represented Tibetan modernity in *Longing,* Phagmo Tashi's film from nineteen years earlier, has been replaced by outgoing, gregarious, but depraved men. Unlike the road movies, *Sunday* offers no promise of spiritual resolution or reconciliation with the community.[38] At the center of all these films is the crisis of Tibetan manhood in the modern context.[39]

The Search

These issues and approaches were addressed at a new and stunningly inventive level in Pema Tseden's second feature, *The Search* (2009). That film marked his shift from 35mm to digital video, but he used that equipment to do more than just record the film: it became its central metaphor, a deep reworking of the concept behind *Stories of Yesterday.* After *Silent Holy Stones,* he had been refused permission by the authorities to shoot the next scripts that he had submitted, which had aimed to follow the little monk with the Monkey King mask on a pilgrimage to Lhasa. *The Search* is the result of that refusal: instead of continuing the story of an earlier film, it is a film about the difficulty of making a Tibetan film—an arcane, unstated comment by an artist to his censors that what they do not allow to be said can be shown even more effectively through omission.

The Search has only incidental references to religion, presumably as the censor might have wanted, and its story line is slender, almost imperceptible. The nameless central character, who rarely speaks, is a Tibetan film director, played with powerful restraint by Manla Kyab, who had written *Gesar's Horseherders* six years before. The film follows his search for young performers to play the lead roles in a film he plans to make of the traditional Tibetan opera, *Drime Kunden*, the same quintessentially Buddhist legend about compassion and self-sacrifice that the villagers had been shown watching in a key section of *The Silent Holy Stones.*

The Search follows the director's journey with his unnamed cameraman (played by Rigdan Gyatso, who had made the first digital Tibetan short, *The Girl Lhari*) and his producer, a local businessman (played by Tsondru, Brtson 'grus). The three are driven from village to village across Amdo seeking young Tibetans who still know how to sing the arias of the traditional opera. In between, they stop in small-town bars and school halls to hold impromptu auditions of random would-be actors. Meanwhile, the cameraman, who never speaks, films everything that is seen in the film with his own digital camera. Eventually the group is led to a village girl (played by Lumo tso, Klu mo mtsho) who is completely conversant with the female lead in *Drime Kunden.* However, she will not show the visitors her face, which throughout the film remains covered by a scarf, one which is garish pink in color rather than traditional. She agrees to act for the director and the producer only if they first drive her to meet her former boyfriend, who has become a teacher in a nearby town.

As they drive, the film producer tells the others in the car a long story about his decision in his youth to abandon his life as a monk in order to seek out a girl with whom he had fallen in love at a bus station years before. His search for the girl was unsuccessful, but he has turned that experience into a rich and active life. The producer is a type of male character rarely seen in Tibetan film: he is not burdened by tragic failure or reticence in the face of modernity and its deprivations. The group finds the boyfriend and sees that he too is skilled in the role of *Drime Kunden.* But it remains unclear if he will return to his ancestral village to take part in the annual opera, if he will reunite with the girl with the scarf, or if the film will ever be made. In the end, we learn that the unnamed girl was profoundly affected by the producer's story but has disappeared. The film ends with the discovery on the road of the scarf with which she had concealed her face throughout the film.

If the veiled girl is Tibetan culture, and the search is for its essence, what survives the labyrinth of modernity are traces or signs of culture. These are the empty videocassette cover and the plastic mask shown at the conclusion of *The Silent Holy Stones* and the vague aspirations voiced by Tibetans in their stories and auditions in *The Search.* The essence of Tibetan culture, its content, is never shown. "Is it that hard to see a beautiful woman's face?" asks the businessman in the final scene.

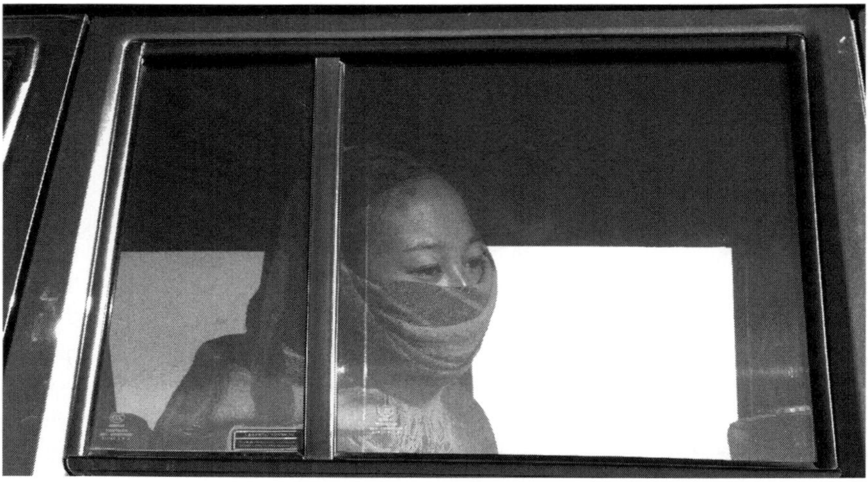

Figure 5.5. The girl with the scarf, from Pema Tseden's first digital feature, The Search.

But *The Search* is not a lament for lost culture. Instead, it is a rejection of positivist descriptions of it and, implicitly, of statist demarcations of Tibetan culture that present it in terms of the singing, dancing, colorful clothes, and long-haired, swarthy nomads shown on endless television shows, music videos, and concert stages throughout China. Instead, just as the businessman's love story had implied, it is the search, the journey, the inconclusive encounters among Tibetans and the questions that they ask each other that remain the core constituents of culture, not the answers that they wait for. Rather than a mystical statement about the spiritual nature of the journey, the film is a highly sophisticated discussion about the constructive nature of culture and the way that once it takes embodied, finished form, it is already in the past. Thus the car and the digital camera, both of them vehicles that travel and recycle, are the vectors through which that culture can be known in the modern world, not the finished and commoditized forms in which it sometimes manifests.

This point of view reflects the emphasis in Buddhist epistemology on reality coming into existence at the moment of contact with consciousness rather than being a self-existing entity. The film suggests that the process of capturing on camera the quotidian journey of the film director and his crew through modernity is Tibetan culture-in-action, although we never see what it is that the camera within the film has recorded. Not a rejection of the modern, it provides instead a radical restatement of the cultural project, one that offers a difficult but discernible resolution of the modernity-tradition tension.

Pema Tseden's work thus moved through and redefined all the main genres found so far in Tibetan independent and digital film. His first short, *The Grassland,* transformed the rural idyll into a serious discussion of its sociality, valuing Tibetan Buddhist culture not for its religious content as such but for its capacity to resolve communal and generational conflict through indigenous traditions. His first feature, *The Silent Holy Stones,* used the videocassette and the television drama to present the modernity-tradition and urban-rural dyads as encounters rather than conflicts, ones in which the Tibetan subject consumes modern Chinese mass culture without being destroyed by it. His second feature transformed the widespread anxiety among Tibetans about cultural loss by taking the digital camera as a metaphor for the active engagement of the Tibetan subject in cultural production under conditions of modernity. The small, affordable, silent camera stands for the process of seeking and transmitting knowledge of the community in which one lives. It suggests that a Tibetan is formed through the inquiry into what it is to be a Tibetan, just as the businessman has transformed his destiny and his tradition by his pursuit of a wholly felt and articulated desire, even though he did not attain it, and just as the brightly modern scarf is transformed into a placeholder for a larger, unseen cultural essence.

Conclusion

Pema Tseden's later films used the opportunity offered by digital technology to demonstrate a new and highly nuanced approach to the crisis of representation in Tibetan cultural circles. It also addressed the long-running anxiety among Tibetans about the threat posed by modernity. In doing so, he drew on a surprisingly vigorous body of work by other independent Tibetan filmmakers which he had also in large part inspired. His exploration of the modernity question followed the direction marked out by Phagmo Tashi over a decade earlier, as well as by earlier writers like Dondrub Gyal, and was to be taken up by much of the Tibetan film community. His use of the road, the vehicle, and the journey as structuring metaphors developed the earlier efforts of Rigdan Gyatso and Rinchen Drolma and was to be further explored by Sonthar Gyal in *The Sun-beaten Path.* His extraordinarily restrained and quiet characters, almost without dialogue, related to yet radically transformed a persistent feature in all the other Tibetan films: the trope of muted, troubled masculinity among the younger generation of Tibetans shown in this movement. That anxiety can be seen in the jilted city lover in *Longing,* the yak-stealing son of the nomad chieftain in *The Grassland,* the weak new husband in *The Girl Lhari,* the distracted boy-monk in *The Silent Holy Stones,* the jealous and murdering youths in the nomad romance films, the forgetful hero and his alcoholic neighbor in *Stories of Yesterday,* the vengeance-seeking driver in *The Driver and the Lama,* the guilt-ridden boy in *The Sun-beaten Path,* the anger-prone teacher in *The Smile of Xesrob,* and the binge-drinking students in *Sunday.* Only in Pema Tseden's films do we find lead characters—the boy-monk, the film director, the businessman, the girl with the scarf—who, while equally driven by troubling questions, are not tormented by them. They too speak very little and reveal little of their inner lives, but they appear comfortable with the elusiveness of answers. They point through their reticence and restraint to an unseen world through the use of an elusiveness that is both culturally rich, distinctively Tibetan, and strategically productive in a colonized society.

The trope of the troubled male seeker in independent Tibetan films of the digital era brings together all the types of story that we have encountered in this movement. It unites the narratives of modernity-tradition tension with the nomad romances, showing that both are at a deeper level reworkings of the religious biographies of redemption found in classical Tibetan literature. As filmic artifacts, they are offshoots of what can be considered the central practice in Tibetan film, the use of cameras by ordinary Tibetans to archive and distribute religious teachings, which in turn fuels the truth-telling practices of the political activists and citizen journalists. In home videos the most important figures are religious teachers, aged in years or lifetimes, and usually men; in the independent fiction films the dominant figures are also men with a spiritual mission, albeit usually troubled and uncertain. These modern men are in effect all contemporary versions of Milarepa, the eleventh-century hermit whose story has already been filmed at least three times in the short history of film and television within Tibet. His is the archetypal account in Tibetan literature of a tormented youth who seeks to avenge the theft of his family's heritage, but who finally recovers moral purpose in his life through hardship, error, suffering, and an inner journey of discovery. Although the Milarepa story is usually thought of as a vindication of the importance of Buddhist faith, it is also an account of a cultural exemplar, a figure who sacrifices everything for the sake of a lost legacy. Atonement and recovery of one's heritage come, the Milarepa tale suggests, not through violence or revenge, but through a largely silent and inward process of rediscovery made possible by memory, reflection, art, and, especially, listening to elders.

In these contemporary Tibetan tales of failed manhood, the legacy that has been betrayed or lost is culture, the most precious possession of the protagonist and his or her community. But who in the modern stories is the enemy who has crushed the mother or stolen the family's heritage? In the original Milarepa story, the antagonist is internal to the community: it is Milarepa's uncle who steals the family's land and their belongings. In contemporary Tibetan films, too, we do not find an external enemy. Some might expect the threat to Tibetan heritage to be shown as having come from China or from some outside force representing it; others might expect it to be described in terms of colonialism, occupation, or oppression. But these forces are nowhere suggested in the works produced by this movement. There, as we have seen, almost all reference to China and its political history in Tibet has been erased, and only modernity is depicted as the source of threat, along with the internal, Buddhist enemies within the mind, which Rinchen Drolma has referred to as "one's demons."

The People's Republic has always insisted to its subjects and to Tibetans in particular that it is the giver of modernity, and that "good" or beneficial modernity is Chinese. We find this view most pithily in the song that China's leaders and singers often repeat when visiting Tibet or appearing in television shows there: *Meiyou Gongchandang, meiyou xin Xizang* (If there is no Communist Party, there is no new Tibet).[40] We do not know how many Tibetans see China as an oppressive force, but the form and pace of modernity imposed on Tibet have clearly been shaped by Chinese policy, inseparable from China's role there. Yet even the documentaries produced by independent Tibetan filmmakers in Tibet, apart from such openly political and forbidden works as those of Dondrub Wangchen and Jigme Gyatso, rarely if ever refer to the role of Chinese policy or culture in the current crisis, and even less to China's history in Tibet, just as they omit the presence of Chinese people there.

It is not enough to call this reluctance to show Chinese presence forced: all these filmmakers would be certainly welcomed by the state if they showed Chinese-Tibetan interaction in a positive light—indeed, at least nineteen feature films have been made in China by Chinese directors since 1985 that show interethnic romance. In this sense, it is Tibetan filmmakers who are extraordinarily reticent and muted, not just the characters they create: they choose to be silent about the subject that may be most present to them. This largely self-imposed politics of silence is hard not to consider a standard feature of colonial life. Only in music videos, and even then quite rarely, do we see explicit references to this issue: they include coded remarks about deep dissatisfaction with the current situation, although rarely stating what that situation is (Wangdu 2011). But looked at overall, digital production by Tibetans is not marked by indirect concern with China's role in Tibet, but by a deeper sense of absence, whether it is expressed by the missing father-mother figure of their culture, the current Dalai Lama, as in the music videos, or by the fear of cultural erosion, as in the civic videos, documentaries, and fiction films. This pressing and pervasive sense of Tibetan loss, threat, and failure unites the music, documentaries, and the fiction films of non-state digital production in Tibet and allows us to see it as a movement.

Even the most explicitly political of these products do not speak of revenge, an important indicator of current political thinking among Tibetans involved in cultural production. Just as in the Milarepa story, their emphasis is first on loss and emasculation and, second, on the search for a form of personal and collective restitution and rediscovery. The concern with depleted masculinity in the fiction films differs from that ascribed by Sheldon Lu to Chinese cinema and television of the 1980s and early 1990s (Lu 2000): in the Tibetan case, it relates not to personal anxiety about individual growth but to uncertainty about how Tibetans as a community should resolve collective loss. Almost all the Tibetan works go further than lamenting loss to also offer or imply solutions. In the songs and videos of political lament, the solution is the return of the Dalai Lama. In most music videos and the more idyllic films, completion is represented by absorption in a totally Tibetan cultural experience. In the fiction films, we find discussions of other possibilities: *The Grassland* and *Fierce Turquoise Mountain* recommend traditional forms of conflict resolution by the older generation. For Shide Nyima, resolution is to be found in the Buddhistic recognition of inner value over commodity desire. For Rinchen Drolma, modern Buddhist insights offer a solution through reconciliation with one's internal pain. For Dodrag, an answer can be found in the conscious act of respecting and recording Tibetan cultural heritage before it is too late. For Sonthar Gyal, the future lies in the self-abnegation of cleansing ritual and the ability to hear the teaching of the older man, the wisdom of the *dakini* encountered by the wayside.

In most of these films, the younger Tibetan relives the role of the Milarepa figure burdened with the obligation to restore or pay his cultural dues, while usually an older Tibetan provides the turning point leading that figure from a violent search for revenge toward a resolution. In the Milarepa story, that figure is Marpa, the tantric master. In the music videos of political lament, the Dalai Lama is ascribed that role. In *The Girl Lhari,* a Tibetan protector-deity appears in traditional *sambhogakaya* form to advise the abandoned heroine. But few of the other films, apart from the explicitly religious ones, show religious figures or offer a vision of complete redemption for the hero. Instead, the protector figure who provides guidance at a turning point in the narrative appears in many of these works in modern, semi-secular form: the nomad chieftains in *The Grassland* and *Fierce Turquoise Mountain* with their skills in dispute settlement, the hitchhiking, lute-playing monk who transforms the driver in *The Driver and the Lama,* the unnamed old man who meets the guilt-plagued boy on the road in *The Sun-beaten Path,* the aging grandfather in *Stories of Yesterday,* and the businessman in *The Search* whose story releases the veiled girl from her burden. Older men, this seems to say, sometimes can resolve the burdens felt by youth in Tibetan society; they are contemporary equivalents of Marpa and of protector-deities. The role of women has yet to be explored by filmmakers in Tibet apart from Rigdan Gyatso, but judging by their portrayal in *The Search,* they are sometimes seen as the carriers of the culture, if not the culture itself, as of greatest value and at greatest risk.

This sense of pervasive loss and guilt has to be placed within Dorje Tsering's view of Tibetan cultural history as a long trajectory within which Chinese socialism represented an imposed hiatus: "Although indigenous Tibetans had started to make documentaries in the 1940s, later they were interrupted," he wrote in his account of Tibetan film history (Chenagtshang 2007, 5). Elsewhere he has made clear his view of Chinese modernism, art, and culture even after the 1980s as also a hiatus, a period of aggressive counter- and misrepresentation of Tibetan culture (Chenagtshang 2008; Robin 2006). This rejects the implicit notion that Tibetans had to evolve or be guided toward the achievement of expressive capacity in the modern world: even in his predigital writings he states that it had been the cost of film equipment and processing that prevented the earlier emergence of indigenous Tibetan filmmakers (Chenagtshang 2008, written in 2003). Once digital technology arrived, it "decreased the cost of production and offered more information, and also provided non-professionals with desire and confidence, hope and possibility" (Chenagtshang 2007, 5). The possibility was delayed by cost and technology, not by a failure of essence.

Dorje Tsering's repeated emphasis on the loss of confidence and cultural pride among Tibetans is a crucial insight. Intellectuals of this rank focus not on the idea that China has deprived them of an object that they must recover or avenge, but on the fact that they have suffered internal wounds—primarily the loss of belief that they are already modern. These are wounds, he seems to say, that they themselves must heal in order to make their own growth possible, if they are to determine their own cultural agenda. This links directly with the portrayal of loss so evident in Tibetan films and song and has to be considered as the greatest cost for Tibetans of Chinese versions of modernity. The final sentence of his 2007 lecture on the emergence of Tibetan filmmakers and documentarians—"in all, this phenomenon derives from the West, from digital technology!"—thus referred most likely not just to the opportunity created by the new technology for Tibetan artists, or to the fact the audiocassette had given Tibetans the chance to become producers of music rather than just consumers. His exclamation mark surely does not indicate surprise or excitement about the achievements of the West, or a vindication of claims that digitization leads to modern liberation. Most likely, it conveys a sense of irony and perhaps relief that, for once, an important and influential form of modernity cannot be claimed by China as its gift to backward Tibetans.

As we have seen, Chinese modernity had produced surprisingly little for Tibetans in terms of domestic technology in the first thirty years of Chinese rule, and even less for those in the countryside until near the end of the twentieth century, apart from the loudspeaker and the traveling projectionist. Digital technology enhanced the practice of listening to music and watching films, but its greater innovation was providing ordinary Tibetans with the capacity to produce and circulate raw footage on the camera-phone and to have given elite Tibetan filmmakers the means to become producers as well as consumers of finished cultural product. In that sense, it can surely be said that the digital era has helped Tibetans to challenge dominant representations of themselves and their culture.

But those challenges are more convulsions of pain at the loss and depletion that has been experienced rather than any celebration of the emancipatory possibilities implicit in academic and journalistic discourse about the promise of digital technology. The focus of home videos on the archiving and circulation of religious teachings, together with other ways of recording cultural specificity, reminds us that the central practice in Tibetan use of the digital camera is a decision to pursue a politics of recovery and reconstruction rather than one of revenge or militarism, just as is found in the Milarepa story. In these works, we see that the more important threats to culture are internal: the failure of the colonized to recognize the richness and potential of their own practices, a misplaced acceptance of modernity as an external gift, and a craving for essence instead of process. The digital dividend has produced in Tibet, especially in Amdo, and most notably in the work of Pema Tseden and Dorje Tsering, an important space for the development of increasingly thoughtful reflections on the condition of Tibetan cultural life and the role of Tibetans given the predicament they face, some of which are of artistic significance well beyond their own community.

Notes

Epigraph. Chenagtshang 2007.

1. I have used the term "Tibet" in this chapter loosely to refer to all the Tibetan-inhabited areas within the PRC, sometimes called "Cultural Tibet" or "Ethnographic Tibet." This term includes central and western Tibet, which is now called the "Tibet Autonomous Region" (the TAR), plus the twelve "Tibetan autonomous areas" in the eastern part of the Tibetan plateau. The latter are administered by the provincial governments of Sichuan, Qinghai, Gansu, and Yunnan. Chinese texts use the term "Tibet" to refer only to the TAR, the area directly ruled by Lhasa and the Dalai Lama's government in 1950. The work of Tibetans living in exile is not included in this study.

2. These figures are based on various tables in the successive volumes of the TAR Statistical Yearbook (*Xizang zizhiqu tongji nianjian*), 1990–2009.

3. Rural film projection in Tibet was still a governmental priority in 2002 and apparently remained so even in 2007: "the National Bureau of Radio Broadcasting and TV has bought for Tibetan people 47 sets of 16mm film projection equipment, 35

mobile film projection vehicles and 848 film copies, organized 478 projection teams in the farming and pastoral areas, which are distributed in 7,679 projection spots in Tibet with the annual projection volume of 123.82 times. As a result, 90 percent of farmers and herdsmen can see a film once a month" (*China's Tibet*, 2007). Presumably the authorities hoped that these efforts would expose Tibetans in the countryside to officially approved films, or they had not realized that digital technology would reach Tibetan rural homes so quickly.

4. Less than 8 percent of urban households in China had video cameras (digital or otherwise) by 2009. The number in the Chinese countryside or in urban parts of the TAR was too small to be included in government statistics.

5. See La Frances Hui's interview with Pema Tseden at Asia Society, New York, Apr. 10, 2010, http://asiasociety.org/arts/film/pema-tseden-tibetan-films-tibetan-people.

6. Rabsel's English-language website is at http://rabsal.org/about.html. The project uses "multimedia technology to creatively capture aspects of Tibetan culture and to invigorate interest among young Tibetan people in their representations and regeneration of their culture." Although this language reflects foreign involvement in these projects and the need to seek funding overseas, the project was indigenous, having been initiated by a young Tibetan filmmaker from Dzachuka, Tsering Perlo, after working for some years with foreign development projects in Tibetan areas.

7. http://amilolofilm.weebly.com/.

8. The group, the Voluntary Association for the Protection of the Environment of Domed Anchung Sengge Namzong, was closed down in 2010. The two brothers were detained and later convicted on charges of political subversion, almost certainly fabricated by local officials (Jacobs 2010a; 2010b; Yeh 2011). The closure and arrests were triggered by a visit to the village by a Tibetan cameraman from a local NGO in Sichuan who aimed to make a small film about the project's work for outside or foreign use, an indication of the acute sensitivity of export forms of digital production.

9. The stills came from only one location, Ngawa (Ch.: Aba) in Sichuan, where between eight and twenty-four Tibetans are said to have been shot dead by security forces during a protest on Mar. 16, 2008, depending on which reports are credited. The photographs from Ngawa reached India immediately, meaning they must have been transmitted digitally. Cell phone videos made by Tibetans started to reach exiles in India only some months later, having presumably been smuggled out by hand. They showed protests at Labrang Tashikyil monastery at Xiahe in Gansu on Mar. 14–16, in Ngawa in Sichuan on Mar. 16, at the Nationalities University in Beijing on Mar. 17, in Ragya in Qinghai on Mar. 21, and in Tsigorthang in Qinghai that same month (see http://www.uprisingarchive.org/video.html). One video, an official internal record leaked to Tibetans, showed extensive beatings of protestors by police in Lhasa, apparently in March 2008. But it arrived too late to attract the interest of foreign broadcasters.

10. I base this statement partly on an editorial meeting I attended at the BBC World Service in March 2008. The editors decided only to use the Chinese government's video footage of Tibetan violence, although they had already used that footage

repeatedly, rather than still photographs distributed by Tibetan exile organizations that showed the corpses of Tibetans shot in protests.

11. In March 2011, raw footage emerged within a month of a monk from Ngawa, Phuntsog Jarutsang, setting himself on fire to mark the third anniversary of the 2008 shootings there; he died the following day. Since then Ngawa has become not only the most active site of protest in Tibet, but one of the few locations with a functioning network of people consistently transmitting digital images of protests and information in real time to exiles in India, despite government restrictions. This made it an important political center with some impact on China's international reputation. This could only have been accomplished by using digital communication.

12. Another guerilla documentary, called *Hope from Disaster* (2011), was a compilation of speeches and songs by leading Tibetan cultural figures in Sichuan criticizing the government's response to the earthquake in Jyeku (Yushu in Qinghai) in April 2010. It was produced anonymously for unofficial circulation within Tibet.

13. Dondrub Wangchen assumed the film would lead to his arrest and, before beginning the film, moved his wife and family to India to protect them. Somewhat controversially, the faces of all the interviewees were shown in the final film.

14. A Tibetan exile, Ngawang Choephel, who had been brought up in India and had studied in the United States, had been given an eighteen-year prison sentence in China for espionage in 1995 after he traveled to Tibet with an expensive video camera to record footage of Tibetan singers and musicians there. He was accompanied there at times by foreigners and spoke no Chinese, and his filming activity was quickly noticed. After extensive international pressure he was released in 2002. He later produced a documentary about the Tibetan political situation (*Tibet in Song*, 2009), using some of the footage he had sent out before his arrest.

15. Phagpa Dondrub later studied film in the United Kingdom, making a series of ethnographic studies of Tibetan life, focusing on rural or monastic settings, including *Tibetan Village Wedding* (2005), *The Perfection of Wisdom* (2006), and *A Tibetan Woman's Life* (2006). His films are mainly distributed online via Lulu.com or shown abroad, and like many digital documentaries in China are usually not broadcast there.

16. In 2003, Chenagtshang Dorje Tsering wrote what was probably the most scathing critique written by any Tibetan of the work and thinking of the Chinese *liumang* artists who lived in Lhasa in the 1980s, describing them as "all people who had been unable to make the grade, or who went to Tibet just to make a living, or else who went in search of inspiration for their art, looking for a mother. They went to Tibet and then somehow managed to come out again with some good results. And it is difficult to count any in this group who really rubbed shoulders with Tibetans apart from Tashi Dawa and Alai [who were half-Tibetan or not fluent in Tibetan]" (Chenagtshang 2008, 278–279). This criticism seems not to have been intended to include those who maintained some distance from the mainstream exoticization and exploitation of Tibetan culture, notably Wen Pulin. Lü Xinyu distinguishes Duan Jinchuan's work from the majority of Chinese filmmakers for similar reasons (2010, 36).

17. Dorje Tsering's films are not completely "understated": the state is shown in some films, but without comment and usually at a distance. In *Yartsa Rinpoche*, for example, it is not clear if we should sympathize with or be disturbed by the police raids on illicit fungus harvesters. Dorje Tsering's study of nomad land appropriation, *Kokonor Lake*, is an exception in that it directly deals with a political issue, including the arrest and jailing of nomads who had protested against the loss of their land.

18. From about 2005, a number of other Amdo Tibetans turned to documentary, many of them already well established as literary or artistic figures in other fields. Pema Tseden made *The Weatherman's Legacy* about the work of a ritualist in a small Tibetan village (2005). Other documentaries have been made by the leading rock singer Yadong, who directed a study of environmental protection in Zorge (Ch.: Ruo'ergai), a county in Ngawa (Ch.: Aba) Prefecture in Sichuan Province, and by the researcher and scholar Yangdrol Tsongkha, whose *Life Among the People of Choni* (2008–2009) compares the current situation in a former Tibetan principality in Amdo with records of a visit there by the American botanist Joseph Rock eighty years earlier. The poet Dodrag has made a series of documentaries, and two of the leading Tibetan writers of the younger generation that emerged in the 1990s, Kyabchen Dedrol (Skyabs chen bde grol; see Robin 2011) and Chungthargyal (Khyung mthar rgyal), have made studies of Tibetan nomadism and the government's settlement policies.

19. The original of "Let's Speak in Pure Tibetan" was posted at http://www.tudou.com/programs/view/xpN7dQbKHKE/ but had been removed by Nov. 6, 2010. For the translation of both this poem and the following poem and commentary, see the "High Peaks Pure Earth" website at www.highpeakspureearth.com/2010/02/i-am-tibetan.html. The original of *I am Tibetan* was at http://www.tudou.com/programs/view/6RGfyb0I9-s/ and was accessible on Nov. 6, 2011.

20. I have not included in this study the work of Tibetans involved in producing in-house television dramas in Tibetan language such as *The Fiancé* (also translatable as *The Son-in-Law,* 1991) and other plays, which were short amateur film pieces made for Tibet TV (Xizang dianshitai), or the work of the first Tibetan woman television director, Drolkar (Sgrol dkar, Ch.: Zhuoga), such as *The Grave-digger* (1988), *Snow Will Not Forget* (2006), and *Return to Lhasa* (2008; not distributed). Drolkar is a director for Tibet TV and worked on *Tibet Wind and Clouds* (CCTV series, 1999) and *Red River Valley* (Fei Xiaoning, 1997) as an assistant director. Her last two films are classified in the official press as independent, but the subject matter of *Snow* (Chinese military heroism in Tibet) is mainstream and "main melody" (expressing the main Party propaganda objectives of the time). The subject of *Return to Lhasa* is interethnic romance, but it has not been allowed distribution and I have not been able to obtain a copy.

21. The exile Tibetan writer Jamyang Norbu has noted that an exile Tibetan, Gungthang Tsultrim, may have made a fiction film in the 1970s in India, but it is not known to have survived.

22. An exception was a short fiction film shot on video in English by Tibetan students in the late 1990s at the English training/teaching program run by Kevin Stuart

at Qinghai Normal University in Xining. It dealt with the same issues of displacement as in Phagmo Tashi's *Longing*, many of the students having themselves come to the city from the countryside. It seems not to have been widely circulated and I cite it from memory here, as I have not been able to obtain a copy since I first saw it.

23. The Chinese film industry continued to produce Tibet-related films and drama series during this time, but they were either formulaic, populist "main melody" works by Chinese directors, such as *Red River Valley* (Fei Xiaoning, 1997) and *Princess Wencheng* (CCTV, 2000), or heavily laden with political content, as with *Tibet Wind and Clouds* (CCTV, 1999). However, Chinese-language television drama series about Tibet recovered from the 1990s cultural freeze earlier than did Chinese-language films—*Longing for Lhasa* (1997), *The Eight-Petalled Kelsang Flower* (2001), and, outstandingly, *Tales of Lhasa's Past* (2002) showed an increasing commitment to contemporary realism and to a reduction in political messaging (see Barnett 2009a).

24. Pema Tseden was born in December 1969 in Trikha (Khri kha, Ch.: Guide) in Tsholho (Mtsho lho, Ch.: Hainan) Tibetan Autonomous Prefecture in Qinghai. After graduating from high school, he taught Tibetan and Chinese at a local school until 1991, when he went to study in the Tibetan department of the Northwest Nationalities Institute in Lanzhou (Gansu). After graduation, he worked as a translator (Tibetan-Chinese) before rejoining the Northwest Nationalities Institute as a research student. He graduated in 2002 with a dissertation dedicated to technical translation (Tib.: *tshan rtsal lo tsa*). He had already published some thirty stories before deciding to go to Beijing to study film in 2004.

25. Zhang Zhen made these observations at a post-screening Q and A with Pema Tseden as part of the Reel China @NYU 6th Biennial, New York University, Oct. 27, 2012. See also Zhang Zhen 2007, introduction.

26. Speaking as the chair of the jury at the Busan International Film Festival in 2006, Kiarostami praised the film and described Pema Tseden's work as in the tradition of Bresson and Ozu. Pema Tseden gave this explanation of his approach: "From the very beginning when we [Tibetan filmmakers] made films, we have intentionally avoided succumbing to those images . . . of an exoticized Tibet you see in other films. We emphasize reflecting the basic condition of people in Tibet as well as their basic emotional life." He added, "For me, I want to create a new system of culture. . . . So, be it exhibiting Tibetan culture, or contemporary Tibetan lifestyles, or Tibetan wisdom, the art of filmmaking should become the basic system of presenting the contemporary culture." He emphasized that "presenting" is an interpretive not a mechanical process and thus depends on culturally specific knowledge: "Actually there are many movies on Tibet and Tibetan culture. But I think the main difference is in expression and interpretation. If you are a Tibetan, you have your own interpretation. . . . So in terms of interpretation and expression, between a Tibetan and someone else making a movie on Tibet, I think there will be a big difference. That is the main thing" (Pema Tseden 2010).

27. Tibetans in exile in India and Bhutan had been active in producing feature films since Dzongsar Khyentse Norbu directed *The Cup* (*Phur ba*) in 1999.

28. In Chinese-made films set in Tibet, Chinese characters appear as revolutionary leaders and comrades; as loyal but mute servants; and more recently as lovers. In political drama series set in Tibet, such as *The Uprising of Alag Tsugu* (1989), *Suru Flower* (1991), *Tibet Wind and Clouds* (CCTV, 1999), and *Getag Living Buddha* (CCTV, 2005), Chinese characters are flawless revolutionaries or paragons and are reticent or largely silent. This is similar to the most famous of socialist realist films about Tibet, *The Serf* (1963), the archetype of Chinese state-message films about Tibet, in which the Chinese characters are perfect and rarely speak. The CCTV series *Love Song of Kangding* (2004) and *Tales of Lhasa's Past* each have a single Chinese character, but in both cases that character is a loyal servant to Tibetan aristocrats and again is largely silent. In the new wave of mainstream romances set in Tibet from the late 1990s onward, such as *Red River Valley* (1997), *My Lucky Flower* (2002), and *Ganglamedo* (2006), Chinese appear as lovers, usually male, who are loyal, dedicated, and almost feminized.

29. Rigdan Gyatso, who was self-taught, focused mainly on producing children's films for Tibetans. These works were restagings, as mask dramas, of a number of folk-stories he remembered hearing from his grandparents as a child. They included *The Ewe Goes to Central Tibet* (2007), *Taming the Wolf* (2008), and *Deceive the Text-reciter* (2008).

30. Sonam's *Milarepa* was distributed internationally on DVD by a company in Taiwan.

31. For the eighteen-episode drama series *The Biography of the Noble Milarepa*, intended for television or for direct sales, see www.tudou.com/programs/view/ScgHqUI-Vtg/. An exile lama, Nyeten Chokling, born in Bhutan, produced a 35mm exile biopic entitled *Milarepa* in 2006; several digital versions of the Milarepa story have been produced in exile, such as the multi-episode filmed staging by Khenpo Sonam Topgyal and Khenpo Konchok Thupten from Dehra Dun. A stage version was written and directed by the 17th Karmapa Urgyen Thinley (U rgyan 'phrin las) in exile in India in 2010.

32. Norbu's story is more explicitly devotional than most of those made by the student group, perhaps because he speaks little Tibetan, having been brought up in a largely sinicized area on the far northeastern fringe of the Tibetan plateau (Pari or Tianzhu in Gansu).

33. The story of a Tibetan seeking to avenge patricide is also found with the character "pock-faced Sonam" in Tashi Dawa's story "A Soul Knitted with a Leather Thong" (*Xizang, jizai pisheng koushang de hun*, 1985).

34. Tsedup Karko is an Amdowan who moved to the UK as a youth and studied at the National Film School in London. He had access to digital equipment earlier than his Tibetan counterparts and traveled back to his native area of Amdo in 2005 to make the film unofficially. Karko's own romantic history is told in an autobiographic account by his wife, Kate Karko, *Namma: A Tibetan Love Story* (London: Sceptre, 2001).

35. On the use of such motifs in Chinese films, see Gladney 2004, 43ff. Scenes of naked female ethnic bathing can be found in *Sacrificed Youth* (*Qingchunji*, Zhang Nuanxin, 1985), *Red River Valley* (1997), the pretitle credits for the documentary *Potala*

(2005), the main mural at Gongkar airport outside Lhasa, and the main mural at Beijing airport in the early 1980s. Karko's film has no features of this kind, but the UK publicity for the film played on a similar theme, describing it as "a rare glimpse of a unique, remote, and inaccessible culture."

36. Other examples of sketches that satirize modern urban Tibetans are *The Fiancé* (*Mag pa*) (1991) and *This Is Not a Joking Matter* (c. 1991), both written by Phuntsog Tashi (Phun tshogs bkra shis).

37. Phuntsog Tashi's *This Is Not a Joking Matter*, popularly known as *Drunk Lhagpa* (c. 1991), shows the comic antics of an alcoholic Tibetan doctor and his patient and could be said to be celebrating their excesses. A study of alcoholism among urban youth in Lhasa by Tenchar in his online short, *So I Think* (2012), links self-abuse to doubts about virility and sexual identity.

38. Other digital shorts by Tibetan students from nationality universities include *Love on the Grassland* (2011), *Shepherd Pig Year* (c. 2011), and *The Way Out* (2011). The first formal discussion of shorts by Tibetan filmmakers was held at the Central Nationalities University in Beijing in March 2011 (see Jamdrug [Byams phrug], 2011).

39. Pema Tseden's third feature, *Old Dog*, came out after I finished the first draft of this paper and so is not discussed in detail here. It deals explicitly with the issue of failed masculinity. The main plot of the film describes a Tibetan farmer who tries to stop his son from selling the family mastiff to a Chinese trader, but the subplot, which has no direct link to the main story, follows the son's slow and painful discovery that he is impotent.

40. This is, of course, a variant on the more common version of the song, which says that there is no new China without the Chinese Communist Party. The Tibetan version was sung during the celebrations led by Vice President Xi Jinping in Lhasa on July 19, 2011, to mark the ninetieth anniversary of the founding of the Chinese Communist Party and the sixtieth anniversary of the "Peaceful Liberation" of Tibet.

Bibliography

Abu-Lughod, Lila. 1990. "The Romance of Resistance: Tracing Transformations of Power Through Bedouin Women." *American Ethnologist* 17 (1): 41–55.

Baranovitch, Nimrod. 2003. *China's New Voices: Popular Music, Ethnicity, Gender, and Politics, 1978–1997*. Berkeley: University of California Press.

Barnett, Robert. 2002. "The Secret Secret: Cinema, Ethnicity, and Seventeenth Century Tibetan-Mongolian Relations." *Inner Asia* 4 (2): 277–346.

———. 2003. "Chen Kuiyuan and the Marketisation of Policy." In *Tibet and Her Neighbours*, edited by Alex McKay, 207ff. London: Edition Hansjörg Mayer.

———. 2009a. "Television in Tibet and the Drama Series." In *Tibetan Arts in Transition: A Journey through Theatre, Cinema, and Painting*, edited by Valeria Donati, 51–70. Rome: Asia Onlus.

———. 2009b. "The Tibet Protests of Spring, 2008: Conflict between the Nation and the State." *China Perspectives* 3 (Guest Editor: Françoise Robin): 6–23.

Barnett, Robert, with Mickey Spiegel. 1996. *Cutting Off the Serpent's Head: Tightening Control in Tibet, 1994–95.* London: TIN; New York: Human Rights Watch.

Bulag, Uradyn E. 2002 [1999]. "Models and Moralities: The Parable of the Two Heroic Little Sisters of the Grassland." In *The Mongols at China's Edge: History and the Politics of National Unity,* 183–205. Lanham, MD: Rowman & Littlefield.

Chenagtshang Dorje Tsering (Lce nag tshang Dorje Tsering). 2007. "From Pen to Camera: Jottings on Tibet Today." Lecture delivered at the Weatherhead East Asian Institute, Columbia University, New York, Oct. 31. See also under Jangbu.

———. 2009a. "An Introduction to My Experience as a Documentarist." In *Tibetan Arts in Transition: A Journey through Theatre, Cinema, and Painting,* edited by Valeria Donati, 71–73. Rome: Asia Onlus.

———. 2009b."On the Relationship between Literature and Cinema in Tibet." In *Tibetan Arts in Transition: A Journey through Theatre, Cinema, and Painting,* edited by Valeria Donati, 75–78. Rome: Asia Onlus.

Chenagtshang Dorje Tsering (Lce nag tshang Dorje Tsering, aka Jangbu). 2008 [2003]. "Reflections on Tibetan Film." In *Tibetan Modernities,* edited by Robert Barnett and Ronald Schwartz, 267–281. Leiden: Brill.

China's Tibet. 2007. "Projects Forming a Bridge between Tibet and the Outside World." *China's Tibet,* Dec. 26. See http://en.tibetculture.net/art/movie/200712/t20071226_304390.htm.

Dhondup, Yangdon. 2008. "Dancing to the Beat of Modernity: The Rise and Development of Tibetan Pop Music." In *Tibetan Modernities: Notes from the Field,* edited by Robert Barnett and Ronald Schwartz, 285–304. Leiden: Brill.

Dondrub Gyal (Don grub rgyal). 2000 [1982]. "A Blighted Flower" (*Sad kyis bcom pa'i me tog*). In *A Blighted Flower and Other Stories: Portraits of Women in Modern Tibetan Literature,* edited and translated by Riika J. Virtaanen, 31–74. Dharamsala, India: Library of Tibetan Works and Archives.

Fischer, Andrew Martin. 2009. "The Political Economy of Boomerang Aid in China's Tibet." *China Perspectives* 3 (Guest Editor: Françoise Robin): 38–54.

Gladney, Dru C. 2004. *Dislocating China: Reflections on Muslims, Minorities, and Other Subaltern Subjects.* Chicago: University of Chicago.

Jacobs, Andrew. 2010a. "Tibetans Fear a Broader Crackdown." *New York Times,* June 23.

———. 2010b. "Tibetan Environmentalist Receives 15-Year Sentence." *New York Times,* June 24.

Jamdrug (Byams phrug). 2011. "First Collected Showing of Tibetan Short Films at Central Nationalities University," Mar. 22. Published on "Offering Lamp" (*Mchod me*) website at http://www.tibetcm.com/html/news/201103223017.html.

Jangbu (Chenagtshang Dorje Tsering) and Heather Stoddard. 2010. *The Nine-Eyed Agate: Poems and Stories by Jangbu.* London: Lexington Books. See also Chenagtshang.

Lu, Sheldon H. 2000. "Soap Opera in China: The Transnational Politics of Visuality, Sexuality, and Masculinity." *Cinema Journal* 40 (1): 25–47

Lü Xinyu. 2010. "Rethinking China's New Documentary Movement: Engagement with the Social." In *The New Chinese Documentary Film Movement: For the Public Record,* edited by Chris Berry, Lü Xinyu, and Lisa Rofel, 15–48. Hong Kong: Hong Kong University Press.

McLagan, Margaret. 1996. "Mobilizing for Tibet: Transnational Politics and Diaspora Culture in the Post-Cold War Era." PhD dissertation, New York University, New York.

Mills, Katie. 2006. *The Story and the Rebel: Moving Through Film, Fiction, and Television.* Carbondale: Southern Illinois University Press.

Morcom, Anna. 2008. "Getting Heard in Tibet: Music, Media, and Markets." *Consumption Markets & Culture* 11 (4): 259–285.

Pema Tseden (Padma Tsedan, Wanmacaidan). 2010. "Creating a Modern Thankga [*sic*]: An Interview with Director Pema Tseden." New York: Trace Foundation, Interview. Video. http://wn.com/TraceFoundation and http://www.youtube.com/watch?v=hvtmMV40Jgg.

Pemba, Dechen. 2009. "The story of Dhondup Wangchen, filmmaker jailed in China." Committee to Protect Journalists, Dec. 10. http://cpj.org/blog/2009/12/the-story-of-dhondup-wangchen-a-filmmaker-jailed-i.php.

Robin, Françoise. 2006. "*Silent Stones* as Minority Discourse: Agency and Representation in Pema Tseden's *The Silent Holy Stones* (*Lhing 'jags kyi ma ni rdo 'bum*)." Paper delivered at the 11th Seminar of the International Association on Tibetan Studies, Bonn, Germany.

———. 2009. "Performing Compassion: A Counter-Hegemonic Strategy in Tibetan Cinema?" In *Tibetan Arts in Transition: A Journey through Theatre, Cinema, and Painting,* edited by Valeria Donati, 37–49. Rome: Asia Onlus.

———. 2011. "Littérature contemporaine du Tibet." *Siècle 21* 18 (Mar.). http://www.scopalto.com/siecle-21/18/litterature-contemporaine-du-tibet.

TCHRD (Tibetan Centre for Human Rights and Democracy). 2009. "China arrests eleven Tibetans in Golog over subversive VCD." Dharamsala, Dec. 8. http://www.tchrd.org/press/2009/pr20091208.html.

Tibetan Cultural Network. 2009. "Independent film 'Stories of Yesterday' director—Qinghai TV eight-episode TV series 'Stories of Yesterday' film success." Mar. 12. http://www.douban.com/group/topic/5681713/.

Veg, Sebastien. 2011. "Naissance du Cinema Tibétain: Lettre de Chine. Au Festival de Hongkong, Deux Films Révèlent L'émergence Fragile du Cinéma Tibétain." *Cahiers du Cinema* (July): 42–43.

Walsh, Michael. 2010. "Dhondup Wangchen jailed for *Leaving Fear Behind.*" *Moviemaker,* Dec. 18.

Wangdu, Kalsang. 2011. "The triple jewel of sun, moon, and star: New millennium's Tibetan cultural expression through pop music." MA Research Paper, Teacher's College, Columbia University, New York.

Yeh, Emily T. 2011. "The Harmonious Society vs. Contingent Collaborations: The Rise and Fall of the Green Tibetan." Paper presented at seminar on "Challenging the Harmonious Society: Tibetans and Uyghurs in Socialist China," University of Copenhagen, May 20–21.

Zhang, Zhen, ed. 2007. *The Urban Generation: Chinese Cinema and Society at the Turn of the Twenty-first Century.* Durham, NC: Duke University Press.

Zhang Ziyang et al. 2004. "Ganbei Xizang" (Drink to Tibet). *Xizang renwen dili* (Tibet Geographic, Tib.: *Bod kyi snod bchud*), July: 82–140.

CHAPTER 6

Chinese Independent Cinema in the Age of "Digital Distribution"

DAN GAO

> . . . the sociology of cultural products must take as its object the whole set of relationships (objective ones and also those effected in the form of interactions) between the artist and other artists, and beyond them, the whole set of agents engaged in the production of the work, or, at least, of the *social value* of the work (critics, gallery directors, patrons, etc.).
>
> —Pierre Bourdieu

My chapter looks at Chinese independent cinema as an institutionalizing enterprise. In other words, although many filmmakers keep emphasizing the individualistic quality of their agenda or the idiosyncrasy of their film works, independent films have developed things in common, such as certain thematics, addresses, formalistic styles, and modes of production. Their survival is also predicated more and more on shared infrastructures of film communities, distribution agents, and exhibition networks. Of course, this does not mean that the institution of Chinese independent cinema is settled and finalized; it isn't like a breed of crops circled by impermeable ideological or physical fences. Rather, the formation of what counts as "independent cinema" has been constantly subjected to various influences—the state apparatus, filmmakers, funding sources, distributing agents, exhibitions, film critics, academics, and the audiences, both domestic and foreign. Noticing this historical complexity, at the conjuncture when Chinese independent cinema steps into its third decade of practice, I will explore some of the conflicts and changes in its institutionalizing process by foregrounding the significant role digital distribution has played in transforming and diversifying this enterprise.

In the following section, I will first define and elaborate what I mean by "digital distribution" in the case of Chinese independent cinema. After that, I will spend two sections discussing the emergence of domestic exhibition and online film forums that were fueled by new digital technologies. These practices have contributed to the promulgation of independent cinema and, practically speaking, brought it into public space since the early 2000s. A fourth section will introduce Chinese independent cinema's commercial digital distribution abroad, taking the United States as an example in order to discuss how what is, domestically, a politically cutting-edge film culture carves itself another facade through its gradual commodification internationally. To be more specific, this chapter talks about four distributing/exhibiting entities that specialize in Chinese contemporary independent cinema. The first, Practice Society (aka Touchfilm), was one of the earliest cineclubs initiated in 2000 in Beijing. Fanhall Studio, another well-known film club established in 2001, soon followed. Fanhall quickly evolved into a comprehensive film organization that produces, exhibits, and distributes independent films. It also hosted a web forum, fanhall.com, which served the independent community for ten years. The website used to be a major platform where issues about independent films got publicized, discussed, and debated liberally by different people, including filmmakers, self-taught critics, festival curators, and ordinary spectators. In April 2011, it was forced to shut down and did not recover until a year later with the new domain name fanhall.net. The third, Reel China Documentary Biennial, is a New York–based nonprofit independent film festival established in 1997 by REC Foundation.[1] Since 2006, a core part of the festival program began to be sponsored by and housed at the Department of Cinema Studies of New York University (and later joined by the Center for Religion and Media). Finally, dGenerate Films is a small New York–based commercial distributing company started in 2008. I argue that these entities, which constitute agents of the "digital distribution" I am talking about, do not just play a neutral role that bridges between the scenes of production and reception, but also have delimiting and regulatory functions on the formations of social discourse. More importantly, they all assume interpretative and constructive powers that may bring into the notion of Chinese independent cinema elements from existing and far more established rules and concepts.[2]

Digital Distribution

Distribution has been a persisting problem plaguing the independents since the beginning; yet it also appears to be an identifying facet of this enterprise. Chinese independent cinema used to be dubbed "invisible images," "banned pictures," or "underground films"[3] due to various political and cultural factors.[4] It has been

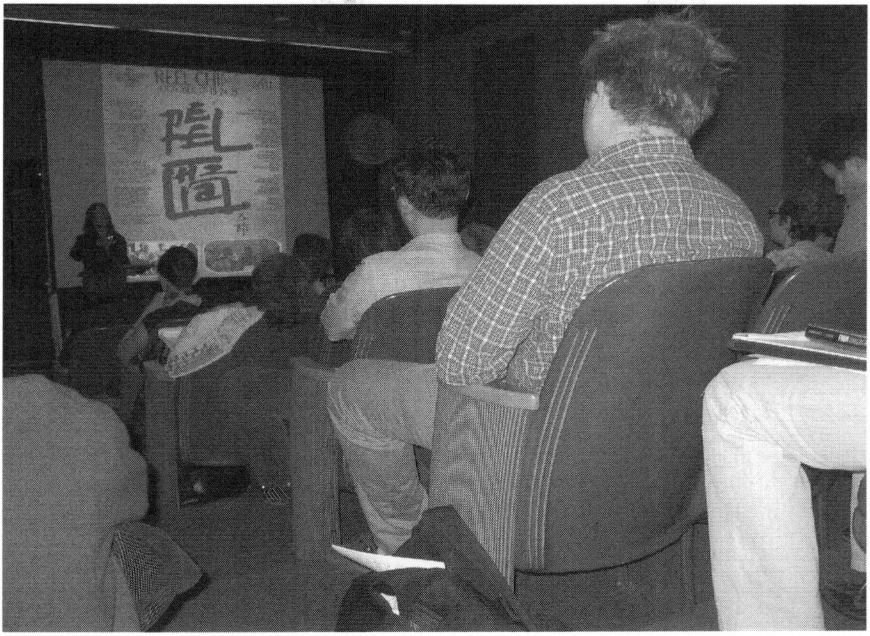

Figure 6.1. The fourth edition of Reel China, New York University, Oct. 17, 2008. (photo by the author)

widely observed that most of the Chinese films made "independently" rarely get systematic and legal domestic distribution at all.[5] There are commentators, Abé Mark Nornes in this volume, for instance, who go as far as to claim that many Chinese independent documentary makers indeed "calculate" some aspects of their products (such as running time) "without consideration of the audience" since there is no pressure from the distributor at all. This is sharply ironic considering the level of social or personal gravity many films struggle to carry, which can only be delivered when facing an engaged and *engaging* audience. However, I argue that these observations do not necessarily lead to a conclusion that a study of Chinese independent cinema can disregard its distribution. Rather, we should indeed pay closer attention to how independent cinema spreads and finds its promulgator and audience in its own way, by jumping out of the framework of traditional distribution forms. For despite harsh censorship and the absence of theatrical, broadcasting, or home entertainment markets, Chinese independent film does get around, gaining its own peculiar kinds of visibilities. In some scholarship, film festivals and other types of organized public screenings are observed to be the major venues in which independent films get watched and discussed by a public audience.

Moreover, independent works have been flowing from hand to hand in a "manuscript" or "underground" manner among film academics, students, interest groups, and cinephiles since the 1990s (Cheng and Huang 2002, 10). Popular indie films such as Lou Ye's *Suzhou River* (1999) and Jia Zhangke's *Xiao Wu* (1997) were later sold in the form of CD-R, usually wrapped in brown bags, by pirated disc vendors, along with other illegal copies of commercial or art films, to anyone browsing their catalogs. Although in these copies, the audiovisual quality of the original film gets degraded to different degrees due to the technological limitations of the bootlegger, these forms of visibility cannot be forgotten and go uncredited.

Another form of circulation easily neglected is the *discourse about* the independent films. Even while full filmic or visual texts were not easily accessible in most cases, the films did not disappear completely from public vision. They have been talked about in different ways, in various public forums (including but not limited to publicity about screening events; debates initiated by distributors, exhibitors, film professionals, or academics; even newspaper announcements about banning certain works). This visibility has gotten a significant boost since new and digital media emerged onto the scene in the late 1990s.

In response to this complex sort of context, I propose that, in order to take into account all these conditions, we should expand the commonsense definition of "distribution" in film studies, which is usually production-centered and inflected with the connotation of a market economy. Instead, I think it will be productive here to look at distribution as *a set of* heterogeneous practices that generally help to "spread" (and in the meantime, also "sculpt") the cultural product and its discourse. In other words, as far as Chinese independent cinema is concerned, I use the term "distribution" to designate duplication, transmission, dissemination, and proliferation of messages *of* and *about* the film—a series of processes that involve various organizations and individuals. With this conceptual move, then, we will be able to talk about all the above-mentioned aspects of Chinese independent cinema at the same time, without leaving some of them behind because they do not fit into the prior theoretical framework.

This new take on distribution will further be joined, and in a sense structured, by a critical rethinking of the changes brought about by the "digital" in the realm of marginal media. Critics and scholars of Chinese cinema have reached a consensus that the increasing use of digital video cameras (plus their less popularized analog precursors) and digital methods (including data conversion and nonlinear editing) in film production outside of the state-sanctioned media system have transformed independent film. The digital turn has contributed to both new modes of production and formal qualities on-screen, such as documentary or home-video aesthetics, introducing more personalized, intimate, or democratizing addresses, as well as amateurism. Nevertheless, innovative applications of digital technologies to the arena of distribution remain largely understudied.

The neologism "digital distribution" has gained considerable currency in the post-Internet media trade to indicate new models of content delivery in digital forms (as opposed to transmission via physical mediums)—for example, online streaming and downloading. Here, however, I will also use it to cover the experimental forms of distribution developed by Chinese independent film communities since 2000 that take advantage of other digital or digitizing technologies as tactical responses to the local media ecology. Seeking public exposure and discursive response both domestically and abroad are the ever-greater imperatives for Chinese independent cinema both psychologically and economically. Indeed, as my chapter will show, changes in distribution mode and technique have been acting as major driving forces in modifying the role of independent cinema within the national film culture and society at large. Distribution is key for understanding these films as well as the agents and institutions that produce them.

"Digital Independent Theater" and Amateur Projection

> . . . although the name of this organization—"Practice Society (*shijian she*)"—manifests its initial intention to encourage production (*chuangzuo*) . . . viewed from today, it accomplished less in terms of production than promulgation (*chuanbo*).
>
> —Wang Xiaolu (2010)

Despite their glamorous award-winning moments abroad, in China, independent films and video arts were either circulated in small circuits (usually consisting of the same persons who produced them) from hand to hand or, by the late 1990s, sold as pirated discs. Theatrical release was beyond imagination, which means if there was any chance to bring a work to a *public*, it had to occur in an essentially *private* space, as Wu Wenguang once recalled:

> This film [*Jianghu: Life on the Road*] and my other films had only been shown on VCR in my own home; the audience were just a couple of friends—the number never exceeded ten each time. Usually they would watch the film while I was cooking in the kitchen. The film finished when the dinner was ready. The entree was usually my specialty—Chinese-styled beef stew. Of course there wouldn't be any formal response or discussion session—and I would rather not to be such a killjoy asking for any—I would just say, "come, come eat!" There was once when Zhang Yuan and Old Lin (Lin Xudong, nicknamed "the Godfather

> of Underground Film") came to watch *My 1966*. . . . Having watched the film, the only words Lin threw out at it were: "This is a film to listen to." The other time, Liu Zhenyun and Yu Hua . . . made another comment while eating, "the beef is REALLY yummy!" (quoted in Wang 2010, emphasis mine)

This description may only apply to Wu Wenguang at that time, as a part-time video artist experimenting with unattractive and outside-of-the-system documentaries, who had never been enlisted into the usual hierarchy of Chinese film directors arranged in "generations." However, it still captures the essence of a "dining room theater," where the audience was put into an intimate milieu and their desire to engage intellectually with what they watched on-screen was apparently *displaced* by what their stomachs moved for.[6] This scene makes a dramatic contrast to another exhibition mode, pulled together soon by various technological and institutional factors, as well as personal passion. Around 2000, independent cinema began to find its way into various newly available public "theatrical" spaces, especially in urban centers like Beijing, Guangzhou, and Shanghai, where thousands of "small screens" were installed in the late 1990s.

When LCD projection systems initially entered China as high-tech, high-cost gadgets in the early 1980s, they were preserved exclusively for military and administrative uses. In the meantime, China had already felt the need for multimedia assistance in educational settings and experienced booms in the sales of other audiovisual and IT equipment to the mushrooming public entertainment businesses such as karaoke booths, clubs, bars, and coffee shops. Therefore, as the video projector's price dropped in the 1990s, it soon filled in the market need, got generally adopted by most higher education institutions, and became a leisure gimmick in major urban centers. Market reports publicized at that time happily announced that, from 1996 to 1998, domestic need for LCD projectors had tripled, rising from 5,000 to 15,000 units. They observed that the expansion of the market had a lot to do with the improvement of the new projector's computing capability, which made the equipment compatible with digital signal input and thus capable of being directly hooked up with computers—a must-have for both organizations and individuals in the end of the last century (Tang and Zhou 1998).

Around then, many renowned universities and professional schools started video/digital media production programs in response to the new possibilities of cinema brought by the digital age. They thus competed with the more entrenched film school—Beijing Film Academy (BFA). College-based film societies also grew more popular by organizing various kinds of digital screenings and taking advantage of the multimedia-equipped classrooms or library conference rooms during their "after-hours."[7] At the same time, transplanting a leisure cultural form from abroad, certain fashionable bar owners either sought cooperation with non-state (*minjian*) film organizations or incorporated screenings as an additional attraction themselves. The well-known partnership between Practice Society and the bar owner of Huang Tingzi No. 50 was initiated at that time. Wu Wenguang's story continues with a thrilling experience at the first projection of his own work in this bar, located near BFA:

> Therefore when *Jiang Hu* was screened at Huang Tingzi, I was excited. Despite being a simple and dim bar, this is a *public* space. A *screening* is established when you put up a small projector and cast the images onto a screen that is 100 cm [wide]. I felt heavenly already. . . . The audience size was beyond a hundred, crowding the bar . . . I finished the film in the dark. Hearing the Henan dialect sounding in a public space, I felt much happier than when I was at the Amsterdam Film Festival a while ago. This was a *screening* of my own film in China which I had been awaiting for a long time. (Wang 2010, emphasis mine)

Wu Wenguang's experience is full of symbolic implications. The story can be playfully interpreted into a social melodrama of the dinner table, in which Chinese independent video works finally transformed from an "appetizer" (adding something extra to the beef stew) to the "entree" (the main dish accompanied by wine, coffee, and sides) of the night. They made their debut at bars and coffee shops, coming out to the public.[8] Indeed, it also marks the "revival" of a screening tradition of alternative and small cinemas. Public screening making use of smaller, amateur, and portable projection equipment may seem newborn in China, but it had actually been practiced in other places of the world for a long time. In European and U.S. contexts, a 16mm projector was used to show films in local and semi-public settings as a more flexible and affordable alternative to theatrical film projection systems as early as the 1920s. Historians of amateur and home movies point out that the abundance and price drop in secondhand film equipment as a result of the Second World War triggered a boom of amateur 16mm filmmaking and cineclub-style screenings. In the following years, film projection (utilizing either 16mm or the later dominant 8mm projector) remained the mainstream screening form for amateurs and independents until the video system (camcorder, TV set, and VCR) took its place in the early 1980s (Szczelkun 2000, 96). Historians remark on the *projecting* milieu, in comparison to screening on a CRT TV set, stating that the "ritual" of projection not only "had a sense of occasion marked by its association with the cinema show," but also let the audience "be much more active [in] providing a running commentary on the footage shown" (Szczelkun 2000, 96). Although this tradition of smaller yet essentially theatrical projection practice was never popularized physically in China before, when digital projection system matured at the turn of the century, it did take up a new incarnation in this country's urban centers and become the key channel through which Chinese independent films were "distributed" into public spaces.

The simple LCD projector, though, only cost the bar owner of "Huang Tingzi No. 50" 10,000 RMB and he did not need to bother with rights clearance. In exchange, the screenings not only promulgated independent film, but also successfully brought in businesses for the bar—hundreds of customers filled up the space, which in the past would probably have been empty by 9:30 p.m.—a cheap but fabulous promotional gimmick for sure. According to common practices in the late 1990s, the "newly born public entertainment businesses (*xinxing gonggong yule shiye*)," such as bars and cafes, enjoyed relative freedom with the little "theatrical spaces" they provided. Technically, they were able to put on a show (and screening, supposedly) as part of their attractions if they got a general permit from the local cultural bureau at the time of registration. Similarly, screenings on campus were very much locally regulated practices as well. Events organized by student societies were open to the general public and could be realized easily as long as they acquired permissions from the Students' Union or the Youth League, both of which were mainly self-governed by work-study graduate students or junior staff. These newly emergent venues were therefore "independent" too, since their "shows" were basically exempt from the state's governing mechanism, under which any theatrical release or TV broadcasting of material designated as "film" needs to undergo several rounds of censors. They became "small digital theaters" where events centering on rarely seen independent film, art cinema, or experimental video works were staged. Screening was usually followed by a conversation between the director and his audience—it seems the kind of "public cinematic space" that Wu Wenguang, Practice Society, and their contemporary cohorts envisioned was generally put into reality. This initial wave of film groups and screenings soon multiplied and evolved into an alternative film culture accentuated by independent film festivals.

Festivals and Online Forums

> A lot of film critics were brought along in their *careers* by DVDs; the desire to *talk* arises from the experience of watching DVD. In the meantime, my own longing for talking [about film] was incited by the Internet.
>
> —Zhang Xianmin (2005, 1; emphasis mine)

While it is still hard to bring independent film into the general public vision in normative ways, many critics claim that the most dynamic transformation of Chinese independent cinema that happened in the last decade was located in its reception scene. When asked about the differences of Chinese independent cinema in 2010 compared to ten years ago, veteran producer and curator Zhu Rikun summarized two points: first, the diversification of filmmakers in terms of their background experience; second, a prominent improvement in terms of exhibition—more venues in different cities, more visibility, more dynamism all around. These exhibitions fostered exchanges among filmmakers and enhanced communication between producers and the audience.[9] Most of them are organized as civil events (not sponsored by the state, *minjian huodong*) with miscellaneous funding sources. The organizers still have to operate within a gray area and adopt guerrilla tactics (thanks to the mobility of digital video storage and projecting devices) to elude the state administrator's intervention. Nonetheless, the number of domestic venues devoted to independent film kept growing quickly during these years. A decade's practices have also created festival "brands" such as Beijing Independent Film Festival (BIFF, Beijing), Documentary Film Festival China (DOChina, Beijing), Yunfest (Kunming), Chongqing Independent Film and Video Festival (CIFVF, Chongqing), and China Independent Film Festival (CIFF, Nanjing), as well as several other smaller and more occasional festivals in second-tier cities. Some traditional print media have built up nice relationships with the independents,[10] but it is the Internet that has turned into the major location for new voices of independent cinema to diversify, redefine, or defend their identities against each other or the stale definitions and theoretical grids imposed by academics and critics. Both Zhang Xianmin and Zhu Rikun, two radical fighters for independent cinema (and arguably the helmsmen of two camps[11]), also designate importance to their discoveries of the Internet.[12]

Physical festivals (driven by digital technologies) and virtual forums on new media platforms were both devoted to carrying on the mission of "promulgating" independent cinema against all odds and providing spaces for participatory public discussion. From the start, the production and screening practices of Practice Society were accompanied by avid publications of online film criticisms, mainly on discussion boards such as "Film Nocturn-pedia (*dianying yehangchuan*)."[13] Zhu Rikun's fanhall.com (*xianxiang wang*) came slightly later, in 2001, and claimed to be a comprehensive web forum devoted solely to Chinese independent cinema. While mingling in these virtual film communities, the youngsters also honed their skills as self-taught public intellectuals and writers. Criticism writing certainly gave birth to a generation of independent film critics, journalists, and curators who continue to accumulate discursive power and practice free speech. These new breeds soon populated the "independent" landscape, bringing more energy and different accents to it.

In a post from 2010 on fanhall.com, filmmaker Mao Chenyu envisioned a utopian (and purist) future for Chinese independent cinema that could be realized through further consolidation of a bipartite digital distribution structure—physical screening plus virtual online "projection":

> We really don't need "independent film fans"; what we need is *production force*. This poses a more difficult request upon the exhibitors in the "new age." . . . The key for now is the construction of a *media system* for independent cinema's promulgation: digital logistics (web 2.0, interactive space . . .). Then, the task of *screenings* is merely critiquing the labor force and [creating] an embodied concept of reality, since the space of live [screening] can also be converted into *digital data* and *projected* onto the media system. To really exert the impact and energy onto the social level, [we need to] break the quantity set limit [by the screenings], to reach a possible population of 1.3 billion. This is *the* approach that fits the rules of Free Society; this is the key to solve the problem. (Mao 2010)

Mao's original post caused more contradictions among the online discussants rather than being representative of their common agreement. For me, the most interesting part of this post is that he consciously used the "projection" metaphor to signify the role of the Internet—as an extension of the LCD projector I discussed earlier—to further digitize and therefore multiply and broadcast limited cinematic texts, the social texts of screenings, and the literary texts of their writings to an extremely large and ideally engaged public. In this prophecy about Chinese independent cinema, it is as if the small-screen–mediated cinematic experience (projection) has to hand over its mission to a more comprehensive and powerful Internet-mediated social activism. As far as I can tell, this vision does capture one function of some film websites, blogs, and miniblogs (*weibo*) (for example, fanhall.com, sinoreel.com, cifvf.org, and many other institutional sites based on douban.com or Sina's miniblog): to "record" and represent on the multimedia platform and in great detail each event and any relevant news it perceives as the worthwhile topics in its discourse.

Nevertheless, festival and web forums do not always work as their initiators imagine and may have paradoxical effects. The problem may be common to all kinds of "one-way" projections. On the one hand, these experiments are motivated by the longing for free society, free speech, and conversation. On the other hand, in practice, they also help to build discursive camps and fences that defend against each other and exorcise unwanted voices. Certain websites and festival organizations were criticized as more intimidating than inviting for many people interested in Chinese independent cinema, especially the less radical participants, some junior filmmakers or film students, and certain critics or academics who have no direct experience of video production (not to mention that female voices were collectively absent from most of the online debates).[14]

Concerns about the film festival's role as a public forum in relation to issues about commonality/publicness (*gonggong xing/gongzhong xing*) were also constantly placed at the center of some debates, on and off the Internet. For example, in a discussion that occurred on fanhall.com at the end of 2010, CIFF 7 and BIFF 5 were raised as representative samples of two different festival modes that deserve comparison and critical interrogation. Organizers of BIFF, CIFF, and CIFVF such as Zhu Rikun, Zhang Xianmin, and Ying Liang and independent film activists such as Xu Xin participated in this online debate. One central critique posed against the Songzhuang independent film community near Beijing noted that it had intentionally built itself into a "mount (*shantou*)" or "small circuit" of its own (Zhu 2010), and the film fests (BIFF and DOChina) it hosts are suspected of having become mere "carnivals of the circuit itself, for its own members to cuddle each other internally" (Niba 2010). As I mentioned earlier, backed up by Fanhall Studio and the Li Xianting Film Fund, the independent film community in Songzhuang was quite self-sufficient and self-contained. By 2010, Fanhall had gathered the necessary resources and personnel for film production over the years, from financing to distribution; it had its own voice and public forum (fanhall.com and reporters); hosted two film festivals; owned an economic but professional theater; partnered with a cafe and restaurant, and at that time, thought it might even open a hostel in the future. As a nonprofit art institute, Li Xianting Film Fund also owns a growing video archive of Chinese independent cinema and was experimenting with a short-term film production training program. Although the Songzhuang film institutions had been addressing broad social issues and exerting an influence, even internationally, located at the far eastern end of the city of Beijing, they were also observed to be consciously building boundaries and defenses against an "imagined" outside. This was deemed very problematic by Zhang Xianmin, who led the Indie Workshop (*yingdi gongzuoshi*) and had been playing a major role in CIFF's operation. Compared to Songzhuang's community mode, which I shall call a "vertical mode," CIFF's recent development appears to be more "horizontal."[15] Its seventh edition in Nanjing drew together resources from educational institutions, commercial financers, mainstream media, and even the local government. It has the ambition to pull together strategic alliances across diverse entities. In an interview with *Contemporary Art & Investment* as the initiator of Indie, Zhang says, "institution (*tizhi*)" does not have to be "either black or white"; thus, the kind of screening Indie tries to realize should be "itinerant," should "charge for ticket," and be oriented toward creating "screening leagues"[16] (Zhang, Dong, and Dai 2009). It is observed that the seventh edition of CIFF was able to attract more students and white-collar people to attend. As opposed to the low-key and self-exilic sensibility of the Songzhuang fests, CIFF certainly has become a pretty high-key local cultural event.

The debate on fanhall.com, while it addressed the merits and problems of both modes, did not reach any consensus on how to balance internal community bonding and the construction of a public openness in independent film festivals. Rather, they only generally acknowledged that film fests may have different personalities according to target audience, size, format, or political stance.[17]

Of course, these unresolved worries and arguments aside, Chinese independent cinema has developed a healthy heterogeneity to date. The emergence of ISAAS (Indie Screening Alliance of Art Space) in March 2011 marked the entry of another new type of screening society (or, conversely, the entry of independent film into a new constellation of screening spaces). This time the members of the alliance were not individuals passionate about producing and promulgating rarely seen films, but film or art institutes who were willing to devote their theatrical resources (and more) to independent cinema.[18] Besides the independents' own ever-institutionalized distribution model, a greater number of filmmakers also seek to take advantage of the limited amount of exposure mass-media channels, such as TV broadcasting and theatrical release, started to offer. Although experiences of this kind of boundary-crossing and cooperation vary for different filmmakers and projects in terms of level of satisfaction, issues of cultural capital, economic right, social mobility, and consciousness about professionalism loom large in all these new distribution forms.

Capitalization: Digital Distributor of the "Reel China"

> Why We Call ourselves dGenerate . . . One, independent filmmakers in China are often labeled "degenerates" by the government. Two, Chinese filmmakers historically are grouped by their "generation"; our filmmakers fall into the sixth and post-sixth generation. Three, "d" for Digital, that being the medium our filmmakers utilize and the *distribution channels* we deploy.
>
> —dGenerate (2009, emphasis mine)

In the past decades, digital technology and new media (especially those associated with the Internet) have revolutionized traditional modes of distribution with both promises and challenges on a global scale. They have also changed the technological ecology and revenue source for independent practitioners working for marginal and smaller media. For example, in the field of documentary, Vladica and Davis observe the rise of cooperation between documentarist and the producing/distributing organization in order to reengineer this type of marginalized media product into desirable and innovative "experience goods" (Vladica and Davis 2009, ii, 1). They further identify several business strategies in both modeling and practice, ranging from installing trendy content forms and catering to new customer needs in the age of Internet to stylizing the online transaction interface. They claim that these strategic changes have already brought about the "renaissance" of this genre in many local and transnational markets and will be helpful for other small, new media entrepreneurs to apply.

It is clear that Vladica and Davis' vision is shared by many commercial distributors on the transnational market who are anxiously seeking their buckets of gold from many newly uncovered margins. In a neoliberal atmosphere of free competition, new terrains are gradually integrated into the global cultural market, voluntarily or unconsciously. As for China, economic concern manifests ever more openly in the production and distribution of independent films. Matthew David Johnson points out that even for the most radical and antithetical pioneers of independent cinema, the space of "the independent" found itself awkwardly positioned with the official media system's new trends of outsourcing and profit pursuit since the 1980s (Johnson 2006, 53). While independent filmmakers and exhibitors were still gaining little monetary payoff (even suffering economically when compared to their counterparts, Chinese artists) in the late 1990s and early 2000s, they were accumulating considerable symbolic capital (at least) through campus, cineclub, and international festival exposures (Nakajima 2006). Moreover, Johnson also sharply perceives that the *generic* concept of independent documentary, as the case of Wu Wenguang's early works show, was more consciously and rhetorically framed by multiple agents in order to enhance its collective reputation. This enhancement of reputation benefited filmmakers themselves in the first place. Then the international film festival that joined in with its own cultural and political agendas ran into domestic exhibitors, and its situation was further complicated by a parallel populist and commercial turn in the official media system itself in China. These arguments are all gaining renewed significance in the age of "digital distribution," especially when independent filmmakers collectively reach out for digital distributors abroad. As many newly formed actors of the domestic independent film community were maturing and constructing an independent film culture in the fashion of a non-state, civil society and not-for-profit enlightenment enterprise, Chinese independent cinema was also establishing its status as a cultural product and proving its viability on the international film market. Therefore, its "dependency" on international resources becomes an ever more suspicious problem.

This kind of "interdependence" started with international film festivals. Both Sixth Generation filmmakers, such as Zhang Yuan and Jia Zhangke, and the new Chinese documentary makers, such as Wu Wenguang, were accepted into the auteur's pantheon of world cinema through Cannes, Berlin, or Yamagata. The awards made to singular films also extended further invitation to a group of filmmakers and their works, as a collective, on behalf of the international "distribution house" that is busy discovering and cultivating artistic gems from the marginal, underrepresented, and controversial. It is part of a cultural industry where honor, publicity, and advertisement are to a large extent interchangeable. So far, the international cultural industry remains the place to which Chinese independent cinema reaches out for economic return, financial investment (if there is any), discursive authorization, and applause. However, rather than genuinely caring for the agenda of these institutions abroad, filmmakers are becoming more and more disenchanted and critical of either the international festivals or the distributing opportunities they provide, especially when domestic circuits of independent cinema are arriving at their own maturity and acquiring more transnational agency themselves. Consciousness about copyright and fair (contractual) partnership also arises.

At the end of 2008, thirteen Chinese documentary filmmakers publicized three open letters (probably pulled together by *Bing' ai*'s director Feng Yan, with the support of her critic friends) in an accusation aimed at the New York–based Reel China Documentary festival on filmmaker Zhou Hao's website sinoreel.com. The group of thirteen formally denied Reel China as a legitimate distributor of their works, demanding that the festival's organizer immediately cease any unauthorized future screening of their films, including an ongoing one in Germany.[19] Considering Reel China's long-term and benign relationship with Chinese independent documentarists for almost a decade by then, and the festival's role as one of the most avid promoters of the Chinese new documentary in the United States, it is a rather embarrassing yet not unreasonable accusation. Ignited by a series of careless copyright infringements by their domestic and foreign distributing partners, the signed filmmakers felt it urgent to ask for respect and the monetary compensation they deserved. In this sense, "Reel China" and "rights abuse" might have been but two straw men targeted by the independent cohort at one of their own thresholds of transformation. The filmmakers picked on this non-profit organization in particular also because it is registered in the United States—"where copyright protection is most eminent"—therefore there should not be any excuse for it to "not understand the most fundamental academic and legal standards of these practices [clearing rights]"(Shu et al. 2008). As Abé Mark Nornes grasps in a precise way, "[these filmmakers] were demanding contractual relationships, hinting at a sea change about to take place" (Nornes 2009, 55). This also explains why these correspondences between the filmmakers and Reel China were exposed in an online "public" space (though indeed, the website is actually part of the independent's own discursive territory, as I discussed earlier), rather than through private email exchanges—which Reel China (REC Foundation) would have preferred.

The call for "professionalism" was reflected in the emergence of dGenerate Films as a new choice for many Chinese independent filmmakers as their North American distributor, probably not just coincidentally, also at the end of 2008. Despite the company's small size and its status as a rather new player with a small budget in the market, the nontheatrical distributor dGenerate successfully compiled a catalog of some twenty titles through one single acquisition trip to China in September, 2008.[20] Unlike the "unprofessional" and nonprofit Reel China, or other North American distributors who usually only pick up titles that are winners of prestigious awards or of anthropological concern, dGenerate is interested in bringing solely any cutting-edge Chinese independent film into the nontheatrical market in the United States. Moreover, its commitment to profit return makes it a suitable (though not ideal) business partner for the filmmakers and their rights holders (if there are any).

dGenerate's founder Karin Chien envisions a distribution model predicated on "digital channels"—a structure not unlike the domestic one I described earlier: physical informational events backed up by a comprehensive website that serves the multiple functions of publicity, criticism, networking, and consumer cultivation. This structure is then supplemented by "traditional" marketing tools such as postcards, posters, and direct mail catalogs (Infinicine 2008). Like many of its peers speculating on niche media markets, dGenerate is versed in the game of bundling and branding. In this slogan, carefully framed from the standpoint of marketing, not only are the films intentionally coded in relation to "porn" and "degeneracy"—two very sexy catchwords familiar to many Asian film lovers (considering a similar image cast and reified by distributor-created film brands such as "Asian Extreme"), the filmmaker and the distributor are also tied up intimately via the "digital" approach they share. Similar marketing tactics can also be found in the company's recent promotional tours to U.S. university campuses, where the digital independent filmmakers are dubbed as "the d-generation." This smart wordplay merges the meaning of digital-generation and de-generation, implicating that for this new Chinese cinema powered by the digital apparatus, it is no longer necessary to talk about them in terms of "generation." Thus, these marketing tactics playfully liquidate a long-standing paradigm in postmodern fashion. Moreover, similarly lurking in this renaming campaign is a hidden declaration of the distributor's "ownership" of these filmmakers—the d-generation can be acquired through a line of mere commercial actions—discovery, collecting, branding, then marketing and selling for profit. This kind of acquisition deal is of course not a new tale for the film biz; nevertheless, thanks to the Internet and digital delivery technologies, the cost for pulling all these processes together is now cut to the minimum, not to mention the extra discursive power the website is able to provide. Integrating journalistic reports, introductory essays on Chinese culture and politics, film reviews, promotional articles, and columns hosted by known critics, dGenerate is presented as not only a company specializing in distributing Chinese independent cinema, but also a *specialist* of it.

These critiques aside, however, judging from its own standpoint as a professional commercial distributor, dGenerate's achievements to date can still be said to be innovative and cost-efficient. To my knowledge, the amount of effort its operators put into promoting these films is motivated not just by the desire to make money, but also by a certain level of sincere appreciation of the works and their signification in society as well. However, sticking to a mainstream business model and its basic rules of exploitation may have made this type of distribution an objectifying and alienating process.[21]

Similar ambivalence is also present in the domestic scene. Seeking contractual and legal partnership, on the one hand, reflects the filmmakers' legitimate longing for respect for their labor and authorship; on the other hand, this new relationship will certainly bring in new power dynamics that separate the producers from the control over their products (i.e., the right to distribution and interpretation). We can probably expect other kinds of transformation on the part of independent filmmakers soon, since more and more of them have begun to be accepted by legitimate or bigger screens. (Several independent films were released in the emerging art cinemas or launched onto commercial video websites such as tudou.com in China; many are being shown in the theaters of ISAAS members.) At the same time, we have also seen the gradual withdrawal (voluntarily or forced) of some radical players from the scene. For example, fanhall.com was shut down after being warned by a web administrator in April 2011.[22] Though it returned in the form of fanhall.net a year later, the latter site could never regain the same importance after being "castrated" once by the censors. Do these new changes foreshadow that the independents will eventually lose their elasticity and radicality, getting professionalized and converting collectively to the rising neoliberalism in China today?

At this threshold moment, many people suspect Chinese independent cinema will be ringing down its curtain soon. Wu Leilei, a veteran film critic, summarizes the disillusion: "The importance of capital has clearly been heightened for independent cinema. The prosperity of all kinds of screenings helped it to promulgate, and socialization pushed it to step further into the arena of fashion and power" (Wu Leilei 2011). This observation precisely captures both the past achievement and the future trap of Chinese independent film. In the past two decades, thanks to digital distribution, it got out of the individual cinephile's or filmmaker's dining room, created new types of public cinematic-social spaces, and cultivated an increasing number of constituent communities and participants. But to emerge from repression and to open up is a gradual and "two-way" process, which entails transformation of both sides. As soon as awareness of copyright, authorship, and discursive power takes the place of their shared initial desire to merely spread the images, the various agents of Chinese independent cinema—filmmakers, curators, critics, academics, audiences, and even the subjects of the films, once allied in building and enlarging this circuit, became more and more sensitive to the complicated power relationships among them. Which concern will become the stone that eventually breaks the temporary solidarity, modifies the parameter of independent production, sets the new normative, or even puts an end to it? Will it be the imperative of professionalization? Will it be the economy of theatrical exhibition? Or the right to interpret, to judge, to criticize, or make norms?

The main body of this chapter was initially formed between the winter of 2010 and the spring of 2011. Since then, several updates in terms of arguments and supportive material have been made to accommodate new changes within the institutions, collectives of Chinese independent cinema, and individual filmmakers. As this chapter has shown, during these years, the different agents involved in the digital distributing endeavor cooperate, part company, and then may be prepared to reconvene at a later moment. Fanhall's web forum perished and reincarnated like a haunting phantom; documentary festivals and filmmaking workshops in Songzhuang and elsewhere struggled with the local regulator or censor like guerilla fighters; dGenerate has made a change in its way of business, holding hands with Icarus Films and many more universities; Reel China is able to draw more critical thinking from the academy and gain more importance year by year; ISAAS seems to have downplayed the element of Chinese independent film in its new season, while Qifang—Cinephile Collective Screening Program—has successfully promulgated independent works in many second-tier cities such as Hangzhou and Kunming. As I noticed in 2010, the landscape keeps altering its shape with the rhythm of digital music we hear at a nightclub. Without knowing where these changes are bringing us, I feel it appropriate to borrow the title of an essay Jia Zhangke wrote in 2010 and to end this chapter with it here (although his reference was about the fate of the Sixth Generation, while mine is about that of the digital generation): "I don't believe you can guess how we're gonna end up."

No, of course we can't. Not yet.

Notes

Epigraph. Bourdieu 1993, 140.

1. For a brief introduction to Reel China, see http://reelchina.net/english.htm.

2. These concepts include, for example, social activism, academic disciplines (ethnography, film studies, history, etc.), commodity and market economy, as well as the ethos of neoliberalism that is merging onto the scene.

3. "Invisible images (*kanbujian de yingxiang*)" is a term coined by Chinese film critic and scholar Zhang Xianmin at around 2001, when he wrote a series of essays on

rarely seen art or underground films for the magazine *Book Town* (*shu cheng*) and on the Internet. These film criticisms were published as a collection in 2005, also titled *kanbujian de yingxiang* (translated as "images banned from watching" when it was introduced into English-speaking context). Independent film was also known as "underground film" by the early 2000s. The year 2003 is deemed as the turning point when independent filmmakers changed their status from underground to independent, after being acknowledged and thereafter supervised by the Film Bureau (Jia 2010). Contrary to Zhang's viewpoint, Jia Zhangke points out that owing to film piracy and the advance of digital technology, art films and independent works were already popularized before the status change (Jia 2003). The essay's more recent revision is titled "Images That Cannot Be Banned" (interestingly echoing with Zhang's phrase) (Jia 2005).

4. Monopolizing or close monitoring the sector of cultural production is one prominent characteristic of Mao's socialist cultural policy. Although this total control was loosened up slightly when the Economic Reform started, ideological riot soon broke out in 1989. Since then the state's cultural control has evolved into a novel format in which the propaganda machine is combined with market economy.

5. See Nakajima 2006. Besides domestic visibility, there are several professional distributors for independent cinema abroad. But choices are very limited. These distributors include First Run/Icarus, D.E.R. (Documentary Educational Resources), dGenerate Films, and Asiapacificfilms.com. In 2012, dGenerate sold its China collection to Icarus Films. http://icarusfilms.com/subjects/dgendoc.html.

6. I use the word "displace" because according to Wu, it was not the audience's intention not to talk about their opinion or critique. Instead, it was the "zero distance" between them and the screen that repressed their desire to express directly nothing but a desire to eat (Wu Wenguang 2000).

7. For example, film societies at Peking University and Beijing Normal University held screenings of this kind. Fanhall Studio also started renting space from National Library, Wangfujing Bookstore, and college theaters for some of their video screenings since 2002.

8. For four detailed sample lists of these kinds of serial screenings, see appendices 8.1–8.4, in Nakajima 2006, 189–203.

9. Panel discussion at Reel China Documentary Biennial 2010, New York University, Oct. 16, 2010.

10. For example, *Southern Weekend,* a renowned weekly newspaper, has been closely following and sponsoring independent film exhibitions since its cooperation with Practice Society in 2000.

11. In 2010, Zhu described the confronting "camps" (in his own words, "*shantou*") that BIFF and CIFF represent in a post on fanhall.com, in response to Zhang's "friendly attack" on the "small circuit (*xiao quan zi*)" built by the website, "its" film festival, and "its" leader Zhu Rikun (Zhu 2010). Nevertheless, as Zhu resigned from his post at Li Xianting Film Fund in 2013, this confrontation seems to have dissolved.

12. Zhang started his "career" as a film critic (in addition to being a literary professor at BFA) by posting film reviews on xici.net's "Rear Window (*houchuang kan*

dianying)" film forum at the end of the 1990s. Zhu Rikun also pioneered in taking advantage of the new media platform the Internet offers. Before settling down as a curator and promoter of Chinese independent cinema, Zhu started his film rental "business" with an initial interest in web design and electronic business. He was thus scorned by the BFA film students-turned-organizers of Practice Society as lacking "constructive meaning [for society]" beyond merely showing films: "his thinking is 'industrialization,' which may not be a good word, but they want to make money by showing films. I don't think doing it that way is a bad thing. But their thinking is mixed. They just have fun, but later nothing remains" (see Nakajima 2006, 170–171). Though Seio Nakajima uses pseudonyms for the clubs he investigates and hides the organizers' names, it is easy to identify Zhu through the detailed biographical information Nakajima's essay gives out.

13. More details about this online forum and criticism-writing culture, which developed between 1998 and 2005, are recollected in a journal essay (Zhang Xiaoqi 2011).

14. A critique of Songzhuang filmmakers as a "small circuit" and BIFF as "internal screening" appeared in a heated debate on fanhall.com between Zhang Xianmin, Xu Xin, Zhu Rikun, and an anonymous post-1980s (80 *hou*) film student (Zhang Xianmin 2010).

15. The vertical and horizontal modes are usually used to signify two organizational forms Hollywood studios took before and after the Paramount antitrust case. After the lawsuit, the studios were practically forbidden from owning theater chains and had to integrate businesses across multiple media (horizontal). Here I borrow these terms, though with new connotations, to describe the Songzhuang and CIFF circuits, respectively, in order to underscore their organizational difference.

16. The initiation of the "Cinephile Collective [Qifang] Screening Program" and ISAAS (Indie Screening Alliance of Art Space) in early 2011 have put some of Zhang's ideas into practice.

17. For example, for CIFVF, what they would insist is the festival's slogan—"Just Cinema (*dianying eryi*)."

18. Though, up to spring 2014, ISAAS had expanded its screening repertoire to Asian documentaries. The films shown as part of the "Third Season" of ISAAS's program included *In Search of Riyal* (Nepal, 2009), *The Cat That Lived a Million Times* (Japan, 2012), and *Five Broken Cameras* (France, Palestine, and Israel, 2013).

19. The first and second open letters as well as Reel China's first response can be found on sinoreel.com: http://sinoreel.com/?mid=news&page=45&document_srl=594&sort_in; http://sinoreel.com/?document_srl=606&mid=news&sort_index=regda; http://sinoreel.com/595. The third open letter can be found at Zhang Xianmin's blog (with English translation): http://blog.sina.com.cn/s/blog_474b3e2a0100bbvv.html.

20. A documentary of this trip is available on dGenerate's website (Tejada 2008).

21. As some of my director friends (whose works were under contract with dGenerate and a couple of European distributors alike) mentioned to me, a feeling of

alienation from his/her own work and its "independent spirit" frequently arose, when promotion activities associated with commercial benefit were arranged by the distributor.

22. The reason for shutting down fanhall.com is not clear. It may have been discussions and videos posted on this website about the film *Petition* (Zhao Liang, 2009), according to a staff member's online statement, which appeared on his own blog soon after the website's closure. Someone else also implied to me that the website had been suspected of involvement in the "Jasmine Revolution" in China. (Jasmine Revolution originally referred to a Tunisian political protest started at the end of 2010. In February, 2011, China also saw a wave of street demonstrations that were called the Jasmine Revolution by the participants themselves.)

Bibliography

All URLs from fanhall.com are no longer retrievable, but as of May 2014, many of the posts could be found by searching on fanhall.net.

Bourdieu, Pierre. 1993. *Sociology in Question*. London: Sage.

Cheng, Qingsong and Ou Huang 程青松、黄鸥. 2002. *Wo de sheyingji bu sahuang: xianfeng dianyingren dang'an—Shengyu 1961–1970* 我的摄影机不撒谎：先锋电影人档案—生于 *1961–1970* (My Camera Doesn't Lie: The Profiles of Avant-garde Filmmakers—Born in 1961–1970). Beijing: Zhongguo Youyi Chuban Gongsi.

dGenerate. 2009. "Why We Call Ourselves dGenerate." Mar. 31. http://dgeneratefilms.com/category/why-we-call-ourselves-dgenerate/.

Infinicine. 2008. "Interview—Karin Chien—dGeneration." *Infinicine* (June 8). http://infinicine.com/2008/06/the-dgeneration.html.

Jia Zhangke 贾樟柯. 2003. "Wei yingxiang shidai de daolai er huanhu 为影像时代的到来而欢呼 (Hooray for the arrival of an age of images)." In *Tao die* 淘碟 (Panning out Disks), edited by Yunlei Li. Nanchang: Baihuazhou Wenyi Chubanshe.

———. 2005. "Wufa jinzhi de yingxiang 无法禁止的影像 (Images that cannot be banned)." In *Jia Zhangke dianying shijie teji* 贾樟柯电影世界特辑 (All about the World of Jia Zhangke), edited by Teri Chan and Xiaoyi Li. Hong Kong: Hong Kong Art Center.

———. 2010. "Wo bu xiangxin, ni neng caidui women de jieju 我不相信，你能猜对我们的结局 (I don't believe you can guess how we're gonna end up)." *Southern Weekend* 南方周末 (July 21). http://www.infzm.com/content/47901.

Johnson, Matthew David. 2006. "'A Scene beyond Our Line of Sight': Wu Wenguang and New Documentary Cinema's Politics of Independence." In *From Underground to Independent: Alternative Film Culture in Contemporary China,* edited by Paul G. Pickowicz and Yingjin Zhang, 47–76. Lanham, MD: Rowman & Littlefield.

Mao Chenyu 毛晨雨. 2010. "Wo dui shanghai de suowei duli dianying wenhua shi jibu manyi de 我对上海的所谓独立电影文化是极不满意的 (I am extremely unsatisfied with Shanghai's so-called independent film culture)." Fanhall.com, Aug. 24. http://fanhall.com/group/thread/17654?page=2.

Nakajima, Seio. 2006. "Film Clubs in Beijing: The Cultural Consumption of Chinese Independent Films." In *From Underground to Independent: Alternative Film Cul-*

ture in Contemporary China, edited by Paul G. Pickowicz and Yingjin Zhang, 161–208. Lanham, MD: Rowman & Littlefield.

Niba 泥巴. 2010. "CIFF yu BiFF: Duli jingshen yu gonggongxing & guanzhong shi yizhong minyi ma? CIFF 与 BiFF：独立精神与公共性 & 观众是一种民意吗？(CIFF and BIFF: Independent Spirit, Commonality and Does Audience Count as Public?)." Fanhall.com, Oct. 31. http://fanhall.com/group/thread/20449.html.

Nornes, Abé Mark. 2009. "Bulldozers, Bibles, and Very Sharp Knives: The Chinese Independent Documentary Scene." *Film Quarterly* 63 (1): 50–55.

Shu, Haolun, Hao Zhou, Weikai Huang, Yan Feng, and others. 2008. "A Response to the Response of the Reel China Program Committee." Dec. 3. http://blog.sina.com.cn/s/blog_474b3e2a0100bbvv.html.

Szczelkun, Stefan. 2000. "The Value of Home Movies." *Oral History* 28 (2): 94–98.

Tang, Nan and He Zhou 唐楠、周贺. 1998. "Touying chunqiu: 1998 Nian shangbannian zhongguo duomeiti yejing touyingji shichang yanjiu baogao 投影春秋：1998年上半年中国多媒体液晶投影机市场研究报告 (The Spring and Autumn period of projection system: A report on the multimedia LCD projector market in China, the first half of the year of 1998)." *CCID* 336: 61–62.

Tejada, Rachel. 2008. *Digital Underground in the People's Republic* [video]. dGenerate Films. http://dgeneratefilms.com/digital-underground/.

Vladica, F. and C. H. Davis. 2009. "Business Innovation and New Media Practices in Documentary Film Production and Distribution: Conceptual Framework and Review of Evidence." In *The Media as a Driver of the Information Society (8th World Media Economics and Management Conference)*, edited by A. Albarran, P. Faustino, and R. Santos. Lisbon: Media XXI/Formal Press and Universidade Católica Editora.

Wang Xiaolu 王小鲁. 2010. "Shijianshe wangshi 实践社往事 (The Bygones of practice society)." June 26. http://wxiaolu999.blog.163.com/blog/static/1353341472010526112325325/.

Wu Leilei 吴蕾蕾. 2011. "Duli dianying de laishi jinsheng 独立电影的来世今生 (The afterlife and this life of independent film)." Indicine.org, May 9. http://www.indicine.org/cntextdetails.aspx?id=21.

Wu Wenguang 吴文光. 2000. "Zouchu dianshi hezi de jilupian 走出电视盒子的纪录片 (Documentary that steps out of the TV Box)." http://www.ccdworkstation.com/archivewuarticle34.html.

Zhang Xianmin 张献民. 2005. *Kanbujian de yingxiang* 看不见的影像 (The invisible images). Shanghai: San lian press.

———. 2010. "Gongji Tie 攻击帖 (Attack)." Fanhall.com, Nov. 1, 2010. http://fanhall.com/group/thread/21055.

Zhang Xianmin, Bingfeng Dong, and Zhanglun Dai 张献民、董冰峰、戴章伦. 2009. "影弟工作室 Indie Workshop." *Contemporary Art & Investment* 2009 (4): 18–9.

Zhang, Xiaoqi 张晓琦. 2011. "Hun zai luntan de rizi 混在论坛的日子 (The Days When We Commingled on the Forums)." *Dianying Shijie* 电影世界 *(Film World)* 2011 (9): 24–29.

Zhu, Rikun 朱日坤. 2010. "Yige meiyou zui qima de changshi de gongmin shi kebei de; zhengge guomin ruci juedui shi beiju 一个没有最起码的常识的国民是可悲的；整个国民如此绝对是悲剧 (A citizen with no bottom-line common sense is pathetic; a whole population like this is definitely tragedy)." Fanhall.com, Nov. 5. http://fanhall.com/group/thread/21911.html.

PART TWO

Aesthetic and Activist Experiments

CHAPTER 7

Chinese Digital Shadows

Hybrid Forms, Bodily Archives, and Transnational Visions

BÉRÉNICE REYNAUD

Introduction: An Impure Text for Hybrid Practices

In September 2010, in the picturesque streets and shell-shaped beaches of the city of San Sebastian in Spain, three elderly Chinese peasants (Yang Zhenjun, Liang Youzhong, and Liang Chunying) were walking about in their village clothes, their feet encased in identical pairs of black cloth shoes, gathering attention from the locals and the cosmopolitan visitors attending the *Festival Internacional de Cine*. They were flanked by a slim young man (first-time director Hao Jie) and two young women (actress Ye Lan and publicist Yan Na). Except for a brief stopover in Beijing, they had never ventured outside their village or seen the sea. If they were puzzled by Western food and had to struggle with knives and forks, they were gracious about it, demonstrated a fondness for Spanish red wine, and Yang Zhenjun went surfing over the gray-green waves of the Atlantic. They were attending the international premiere of the digital feature *Single Man* (*Guanggun'er* 2010), in which they were playing fictionalized versions of themselves.

The film had been produced, on a modest budget, by a Beijing-based company, Heaven Pictures Culture & Media Co. Ltd., founded in 2009 by a businessman intent on giving young filmmakers the chance to make personal movies. Zhang Xianmin, Hao Jie's former professor at the Beijing Film Academy, organized its world premiere in the 139-seat auditorium of the Ullens Center for Contemporary Art (UCCA), on June 5, 2010. This marked the launching of a new program, "Indie Film Forum," between UCCA—founded as a nonprofit organization by two Belgian collectors, Baron Guy and Myriam Ullens, in the 798 Art Zone (*798 Yìshuqu*)[1]—and Zhang's own production/distribution structure, Indie Workshop.[2]

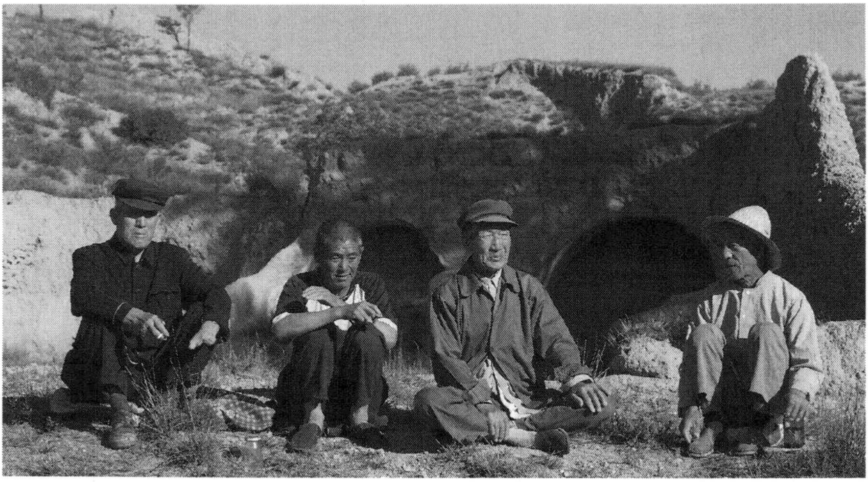

Figure 7.1. *Single Man*. The Four "Single Men" in Hao Jie's film. Notice Bighead Liang's stump.

Zhang Xianmin had invited a couple of international curators, which is how the film got invited to San Sebastian and Vancouver. (Later it went to Tokyo Filmex, where it received the Kodak Vision Award; the Hong Kong International Film Festival; and Jeonju in South Korea, where it won the NETPAC Award.) Since *Single Man* was an "independent" (i.e., not officially accredited) production, it couldn't be distributed in China, and could only have semi-confidential screenings in alternative spaces, universities, or non-official festivals or clubs. The international film network could play a crucial role to increase its visibility.

I was one of the curators invited to the UCCA screening. My practice as a cultural worker has been to bring independent Chinese media to some European film festivals—and to program "New Chinese Cinema" Film/Video series in Europe and the United States. I am a non-impartial witness, as well as a facilitator, of the role played by Chinese digital media in the interaction between China and the rest of the world. This chapter, therefore, bears the marks of the conditions in which it was initiated. To quote André Bazin, it is an "impure text," or "a text of mixed means"[3] (Bazin 1975). The "impurity" I acknowledge and reclaim, however, is not only in the eye of the beholder, the curator, and the exhibitor—it is, more essentially, a reflection of the "hybrid conditions" in which Chinese digital cinema is produced. It is, on the one hand, an indigenous art form, born out of the domestic media landscape. On the other hand, at an aesthetic, political, and technological level, the filmmakers are involved in a dialogue with manifold transnational film networks—be it in Asia or the West.[4] Due to the systemic failure of the domestic market to support such work, it tends to be produced as either a "cottage industry" with low production values and self-financing from the makers' savings or within financial strategies that involve a combination of local and transnational producers, financiers, and distributors.

A "Desire for Cinema?" Montage vs. Archive

Looking at the hundreds of digital films produced amounts to taking a roller-coaster ride into a multiplicity of cinematic strategies. As in the labyrinthine novel dreamed by Jorge Luis Borges in "The Garden of Forking Paths" (Borges 2000), any twist or turn *not* taken by one filmmaker will be followed by another; every choice will be made; every formal strategy embraced; every mode of distribution adopted; a multifarious array of alternatives will be simultaneously explored. A fecund aesthetic tension has emerged between "a desire for cinema" and "a desire for documentation." In the first case, there is a tendency to ignore the formal properties of the new medium and shoot as one would on film—but more cheaply and without some of the censorship issues pertaining to film production.[5] In the second case, the possibilities offered by the new toys are embraced with gusto, as producing better means of recording "reality." Both positions reflect an implicit belief in the transparency of the digital medium as either a cheaper substitute for celluloid or a mere recording tool.

The distinction between "digital art cinema" and "digital cinema with a documentary impulse" does *not* follow the traditional fracture lines between fiction and documentary. Hybridity has become a salient feature. Digital modes of production render the distinction between "art cinema" and "cinema with a documentary impulse" somewhat obsolete, or at least paradoxical, as *all* digital media present the same crucial feature: they are *not* structured around "the alternation between an exposure of 1/48 seconds, and a dark phase of 1/48 seconds" (Ekardt 2011, 126) on which cinema relies—a technological trait that generated the concept of montage. With digital media "the material base for this montage concept . . . disappears, unless you produce it artificially" (Ekardt 2011, 126). For "digital art films" the quintessential digital possibility to shoot extremely long takes fulfills an old cinema dream hitherto foreclosed by the limited size of film magazines. There is no need to cut, and a long-shot sequence can unfold without having to mask the cuts as in Alfred Hitchcock's *The Rope* (1948). For documentary, archival, as well as surveillance purposes, the camera can be kept on for hours and record while being held by an untrained hand or even without being monitored. As an essential scansion of cinematic discourse, the cut is under threat. "Through the mutual destruction of two images in montage, there emerges a third term, an epiphany. And this epiphany has now been separated from technical necessity" (Ekardt 2011, 126).

Usually, DV filmmakers are more on the side of the image and its (archival) accumulation than its destruction via montage. The suturing effect produced by the alternation of shots in classical cinema (Oudart 1977) now follows a novel pattern, as suggested by Francesco Casetti: "Since realism is still associated with the idea of a direct gaze at reality . . . a 'suturing point' may be represented by the presence of 'raw shooting' like that provided by surveillance cameras or cell phones. These devices are seemingly still devoted to capturing the world as it is" (Casetti 2011, 106). This passion to document "the world as it is" is motivated by a sense of urgency. Entire landscapes may be destroyed, whole populations displaced or simply made to vanish before being visually represented. So there is a burning desire to record, preserve, and show every image that could be possibly be shot—houses threatened with demolition, country roads, illegal coal mines, underfunded schools for migrant children, mom-and-pop workshops, gay bars, disused factories, massage parlor back rooms, police stations and jails. DV practitioners act *politically* to saturate the visual field, to "occupy" the terrain with their productions, and to find as many ways as possible to exhibit and disseminate them. So the tension between the "desire for cinema" and "the documentary impulse" articulates the way the conjoint aesthetic issues of editing and off-screen space are handled. A "cinematic" approach will aim at creating a dialectic between the visible and the invisible and composing discrete units that amount to a signifying chain, while a "documentarian" approach tends to spill over on the side of "surveillance camera" (i.e., I film whatever I can, nonstop, whether my subject is aware of it or not), and further, to create a repertory and archive of manifold situations, human types, ethno-cultural differences, sites, urban destructions, government injustices, police brutalities, social inequities, etc. . . .

The use of cinemascope lenses, so pervasive in digital cinema yet so paradoxical when using a tiny camera, is a symptom of this tension. From a documentary perspective, the cinemascope format seems an excellent tool, allowing one to see "more" of the visual field without resorting to lateral camera movements or reverse angle shots. It implies the utopian dream of a machine that could record "reality" without human interference—that is, without much editing. Trinh T. Minh-ha eloquently deconstructs this "lure of authenticity," as it manifests itself, most prominently, in classical anthropology: "THIS IS HOW IT IS. Or was. . . . And the ideology adopted is no other than of *capturing* movements (objects) of *life* or restituting it (them) in a raw manner and revealing the authentic reality by a neutral camera as well as a neutral cineaste. . . . Human interventions in the filming and editing process are . . . reduced to a minimum. The cineaste . . . should . . . avoid

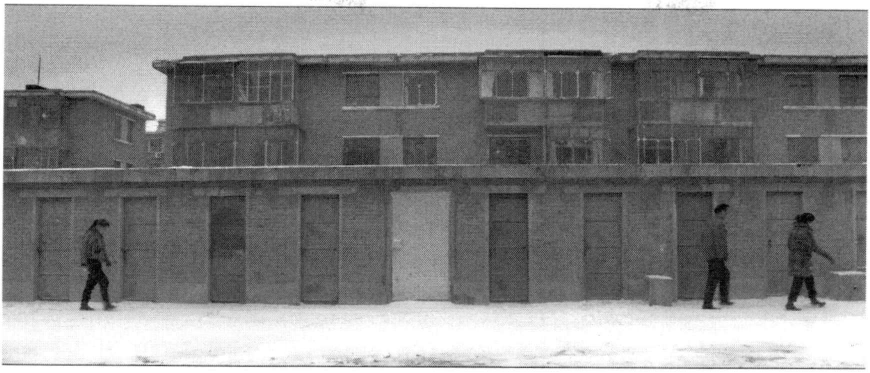

Figure 7.2. Winter Vacation. Winter landscape. No sky, no depth.

all montage—regarded as an artifice likely to compromise the authenticity of the work" (Trinh 1991, 54–56). She insightfully connects the belief in the value of long takes ("the longer, the truer") with the fondness for wide lenses.

A number of independent digital films resort to the cinemascope ratio to rigorously compose images in which each action is choreographed, taking the frame as a canvas for sweeping visual experiments. Li Hongqi's *Winter Vacation* (*Hanjia* 2010) unfolds one-shot sequences filmed frontally—with the occasional interruption of a close-up or a reverse angle. There is no sky, no depth, and Li uses the same crisp imagery (no shadow, no fuzziness, no chiaroscuro) when filming the drab interiors, which creates a disturbing theatricality (with *alienation effect*). In *Oxhide* (*Niupi* 2004) and *Oxhide II* (*Niupi er* 2009), Liu Jiayin breaks down the cramped space of a fifty-square-meter Beijing apartment into a limited number of shots (twenty-three for the first film, nine for the second) without reverse angle. In *Oxhide II,* Mom, Dad, and the filmmaker-daughter make and eat dumplings in real time. Tension is rigorously contained within the frame and every gesture; every verbal exchange reorganizes the balance of power between the three protagonists. In *The Other Half* (*Ling Yiban* 2006) Ying Liang and Peng Shan construct a fractured narration that alternates tightly designed frontal shots devoid of reverse angle with a fly-on-the-wall, pseudo-documentary shooting mode. This approach is echoed in Zhao Ye's *Jalainur* (*Zhalai nuo'er* 2008), albeit with a wildly different visual style (lush and painterly with Zhao, who extracts the hard beauty of remote Inner Mongolian landscapes in the dead of winter, while Ying and Peng stress the mundane and casual aspects of a small industrial Sichuan town). In *Little Moth* (*Xue chan* 2007), Peng Tao follows the lives of professional beggars in Hubei province and the children they exploit. The film ends on a paralyzed little girl, abandoned on a roadside, staring at the off-screen void. Pema Tseden's *The Search* (*Xunzhao zhimei gengdeng* 2009) also makes a suspenseful use of the off-screen space: as a film crew scouts the area of Amdo in search of actors for a Tibetan opera film, a young woman stubbornly keeps her face hidden and is shot at a distance, her back to the camera, at the moment she removes her scarf.

An interesting case of mélange between fiction and documentary, a film whose narration is entirely constructed through an editing process *en abyme*, is Emily Tang's second feature, *Perfect Life* (*Wanmei shenghuo* 2008), which intertwines the destinies of two women. Li Yueying, born in the dreary northeastern town of Fushun (Liaoning Province) is uneducated, unskilled, and repressed—but, in her burning desire for change, hops on trains, switches jobs, and tempts fate. Tang spliced her fictional heroine's story with documentary footage following Jenny, a Mainlander whose marriage to a Hong Kong man was ending in divorce and financial hardship. As Yueying flees toward the south, Jenny returns north, to the city of her youth, in the Special Economic Zone of Shenzhen. For a fleeting moment documentary and fiction collide, as the two women briefly meet in a street market. Around them, in the city of broken dreams and mysterious survival, thousands of young women from all parts of China are working for minimum wage in toy factories. The camera glides over the assembly lines, sometimes capturing a defiant smile amid the boredom and fatigue. . . .

In the complex texture she weaves between different layers of representation, different temporalities, Tang cross-pollinates fictional and documentary spaces; in addition, her characters keep projecting themselves in the two-dimensionality of the still image, a form of self-archiving that represents yet another form of fiction. Yueying spends money to have her picture taken in front of a fake, glamorous background; the man she befriends, at the moment of being shot by gangsters, props a little camera to take a last image of himself; Jenny indulges in the contemplation of photos of her dead sister and herself when they were younger; and the film ends on a wedding picture, which is both the record of a past moment and a masquerade—the frozen, delusional image of an impossible dream.

These films are structured around formal strategies pertaining to framing and editing. They are hybrid dramatic features courting a neorealist approach: a documentary-like way of shooting in real location and with available light, and using mostly nonprofessional actors, or in the case of Tang, mixing "actors" with "real people" whose life is "documented" (which implies a certain level of self-awareness and performance for the camera). And it is the mixture of aesthetic ("auteurist") rigor and the capacity of functioning as a "window" opening onto China's reality that made them attractive to international audiences. *Winter Vacation* received the Golden Leopard award in Locarno and was shown theatrically in France. After *Oxhide* received a FIPRESCI Prize in Berlin, it was acquired by a

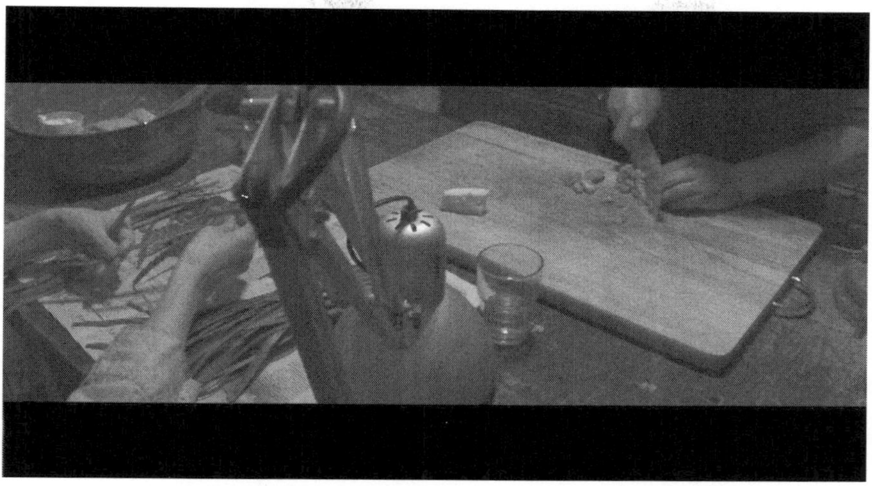

Figure 7.3. *Oxhide II*. Cinemascopic/claustrophobic balance of power: the daughter cuts scallions, the father chops meat.

prestigious French distributor (MK2) and *Oxhide II* was shown at Cannes. *The Other Half* received multiple awards in Tokyo Filmex, Jeonju, and Singapore; *Jalainur* also received prizes in Busan and Shanghai. *Little Moth* was shown in Locarno and released in France. *The Search* was awarded an International Jury Prize in Shanghai. *Perfect Life* was shown in San Sebastian and Tokyo Filmex, and received the Dragons and Tigers Prize in Vancouver.

This flurry of international recognition didn't happen by chance, but reflects a coherent strategy on the part of the filmmakers, their producers, and "agents," as well as the efforts of international critics, curators, and distributors. However, Abé Mark Nornes (see chapter 1 in this volume) is correct in asserting that Chinese *documentary* filmmakers are less invested in the issue of distribution and can shoot in a utopian manner, as they please, with a certain disregard for potential audiences and, therefore, for the ethics of representation. The "construction" of audiences—at an aesthetic, theoretical, but also financial and economic level—responds to different norms if the film is labeled as "narrative," "documentary," or "experimental." Major film festivals show few documentaries, while documentary film festivals have different sets of norms and rules and present stakes that are not as high in terms of prestige and commercial gains. On the other hand, while there are film festivals specialized in documentaries in China, most "independent" events mix narrative and documentaries as coming from the same ilk. This is an acute example of the insidious reshuffling caused by the sanction of the international exhibition/distribution networks where films identified as "documentaries" and "narratives" are treated differently, which is not true to the same extent within the Chinese independent sector.[6]

Huang Weikai's *Disorder* (*Xianshi shi guoqu de weila* 2009) presents a salient counter-example to the tendency of stitching together as many images as possible "stolen" from "reality" without organizing them through a coherent editing strategy. Not surprisingly, the film garnered major prizes in festivals devoted to *experimental,* innovative, and documentary cinema (Cinéma du Réel and Belfort in France, Ann Arbor in the United States, China Visual Festival in London) and was later distributed in France as an "auteur film." Trained as a painter at the Guangdong Academy of Fine Arts, Huang had, for his first feature documentary, *Floating* (*Piao* 2005), devised original shooting and editing methods to depict the life of a "vagrant" street musician. *Disorder* goes one step further and takes the archival as well as the image-sharing potential of digital media to their logical conclusion. Huang collected more than 1,000 hours of footage shot by a group of amateur videographers in the streets of his hometown, Guangzhou. He then selected twenty-odd incidents, reworked the images into quasi-surreal grainy black and white, and montaged them to create a kaleidoscopic view of the great southern metropolis: traffic accidents; scuffles with the police; bitter arguments about counterfeit money and restaurant health regulations; a flooded neighborhood; a bunch of pigs, and later, a madman, running in the streets. In addition to the disturbing picture it offers on contemporary urban chaos, *Disorder* can be read as a statement on the current state of digital documentary filmmaking: garrulous, untrained, cumulative shooting—turned into a superior filmic text (and texture) through the reprocessing of the original material and an expert montage/collage strategy.

Huang participated in collective projects spearheaded by the multimedia artist Ou Ning—himself a staunch advocate of digital media, in which he saw the possibility of "an unprecedented 'image democracy'" (Ou 2004a). In the late 1990s, Ou created U-theque to show digital independent work (Berry and Rofel 2010, 145–148). Through the Hong Kong critic/film director Shu Kei, he "was able to get the license to distribute a lot of films in China. The screenings we organized were very successful and U-theque grew very big" (Edwards 2011). In addition, U-theque became the conduit to receive funding for multimedia projects. The Chinese curator Hou Hanru, who had moved to Paris in 1990, commissioned *San Yuanli* (2002), an experimental electronic portrait of a Guangzhou "village-in-the-city," for the 2003 Venice Biennial. Huang is credited as the main cinematographer for the film. In 2004, an investigative newspaper, *The Southern Metropolis Daily* (*Nanfang dushi bao*) sponsored a Jia Zhangke retrospective at U-theque. The daily, however, was in hot water for reporting the case of the student Sun Zhigang, who had been beaten to death by the Guangzhou police for not carrying his residency permit with him.[7] The newspaper's support, coupled with the Guangzhou's government suspicion toward *San Yuanli,* ended up in U-theque being closed down in 2004. The same year, Ou founded The Alternative Archive, in collaboration with the installation artist Cao Fei.[8] Huang worked as the main cinematographer and editor for *Meishi Street* (*Mei Shi Jie* 2006), the video component of Ou's next endeavor, *The Dazhalan Project,* which he described as part of a "a series of research and creative practice concerning urbanization and impoverished communities in cities in China" (Ou 2005). Named after a Beijing popular neighborhood slated for demolition before the 2008 Olympics, and commissioned by two German arts organizations (Kulturstiftung des Bundes in Zusammenarbeit and the Goethe-Institut in Beijing), *The Dazhalan Project* is one of the most ambitious examples of digital archiving to date, as it has taken, in space and time, different forms: a website; a photographic and (more originally) sound archive (to preserve the everyday sounds of streets about to be demolished); publications; several fine arts exhibitions/installations; and the digital video. The website lists nineteen artistic collaborators: in addition to Ou, Cao, and Huang, one finds the sound artist Yan Jun, the experimental filmmaker Tan Tan, and the Belgium documentarist Olivier Meys; there is also footage taken by neighborhood activist Zhang Jinli to

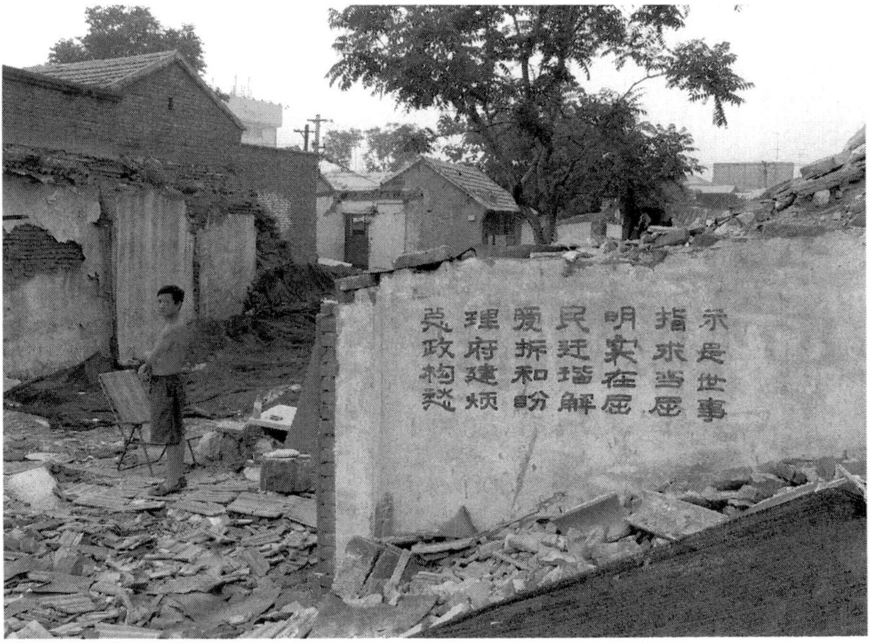

Figure 7.4. Meishi Street. Urban destruction.

document his fight to prevent the demolition of his family home and restaurant. The different components of the project are self-contained but acquire additional meaning depending on the combination in which they are apprehended by the viewer/reader/listener. This montage strategy foregrounds the contradictions of point of view, interest, and agency between the "artistic team" and the neighborhood activists: the former are mastering the image, the latter are losing their homes. It is through a very filmic sense of editing that the project holds together and makes sense. Its tentacular, multi/mixed/hybrid media approach represents, on the other hand, an innovative way of bridging the distance all-too-often noticed between the art world and the film world.

Body as Living Archive

However, the development of independent digital media took a turn toward a more intimate approach. First, light, compact, and easy-to-use digital cameras made it possible to shoot everywhere—close to the body of the subjects, in cramped quarters, with very little available light—but also far away from the urban centers in which the first phase of the New Documentary Movement was centered. Second, the availability of at-home-editing software allowed everybody to edit without formal training—a bit like a rookie DJ in a student party. Yang Lina and Wu Wenguang were among the first to take full advantage of the possibilities offered by the new technology. An actress trained at the People's Liberation Army Art Academy, Yang Lina had become tired of the propagandist aspect of the roles offered to her,[9] but when she picked up a DV camera and started filming, she retained an acute awareness of her physical presence in space. In a distant echo of Ross McElwee's *Sherman's March* (1986), she uses the camera as a tool to facilitate, orchestrate, and mediate her encounters with the people that fascinate her. Her debut film, *Old Men* (*Lao Tou* 1999), was touted as the first "Chinese personal documentary" when it was awarded a major prize at the Cinéma du Réel Festival in Paris in 2000 and then shown on the French-German cultural channel ARTE. This international accolade reflects the Western perception that the representation of "the intimate" is problematic in Chinese culture. As discussed elsewhere (Hemelryk Donald 2000; Robinson 2010; Braester 2010, 207–211), the evolution of cinema in China, and more specifically, of the documentary, can be read as the fractured history of the construction/deconstruction, revelation/obfuscation of the personal sphere. What made Yang Lina's experiments seem "novel" in the West (and sometimes "scandalous" in China) was her foregrounding of the gendered persona of the filmmaker, integrating her theatrical background into a sophisticated variation on the actor's narcissism: she keeps her image out of the frame, but tantaliz-

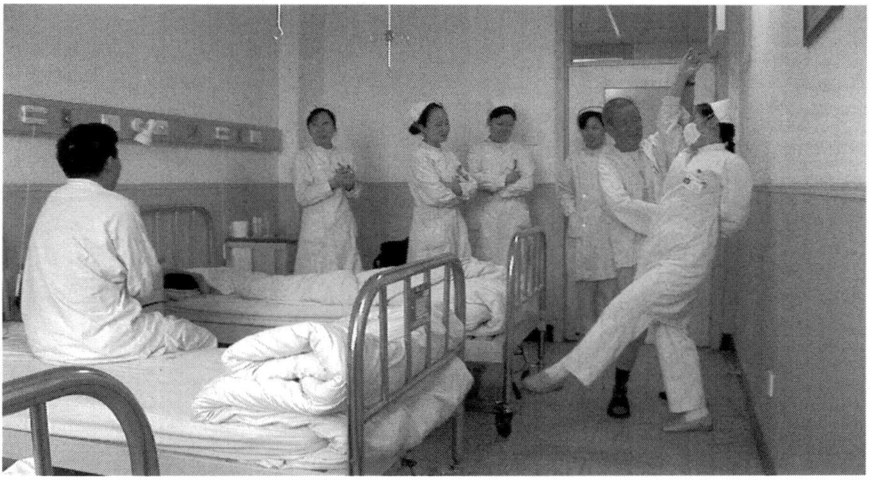

Figure 7.5. Old Men. Even in the hospital, Lao An yields to his love for dancing.

ingly close, at the border, in the same diegetic space as her subjects with whom she converses in her melodious, highly recognizable voice. She gracefully inserts herself in the aural texture of her films through a mix of vérité and diaristic style that projects an aura of quiet seduction—whether she tries to understand the disintegration of her parents' marriage from different points of view (*Home Video* 2001), unfolds the extramarital love affair of a grandfather addicted to dancing in the park (*The Love of Mr. An/Lao an* 2008), speaks with her elderly neighbors about their memories of the war with Japan (*My Neighbors and Their Japanese Ghosts/Wo de linju shuo guizi* 2008), or follows young boys abandoned in an orphanage over a twelve-year period (*Wild Grass* 2009). She is a confidante, a friend, sometimes an object of flirtation; her advice is sought or rejected, her presence is acknowledged.

Wu acquired a portable DV camera during one of his trips to show his films in Hong Kong in 1998,[10] and immediately appreciated the impact the new technology would have on the field of documentary filmmaking. For his first digital film, *Jianghu: Life on the Road* (*Jianghu* 2000), "I just carried the DV camera with me like a pen . . . ," he said (Wu 2010, 49). The liberation experienced during the shooting, as he was recording image and sound by himself, was matched by the autonomy offered by comparatively affordable at-home editing systems. He became enthusiastic at the possibility of discarding a "professional approach" to documentary—an attitude he took to heart, setting up a production center, Caochangdi Workstation, in which he teaches villagers, students, young people from all walks of life, and artists from other disciplines to use video to tell their own stories.[11] "You don't decide on a subject before you start shooting, you find your subject *as you are shooting*."[12] When Wu returned to directing after a gap of several years devoted to training nonprofessional filmmakers, he made "personal cinema" pieces. *Treatment* (*Zhiliao* 2010) was triggered by the emotions caused by the death of his mother in 2007. Drawing a parallel between a decaying building serving as hospice (old people are sent there to die, not to be "treated") and his own attempts to "treat" his sense of loss and guilt, Wu digs through his personal archives. First, there are the letters, notebooks, and photos from the time of the Cultural Revolution when, as a teenager and young adult, he lived alone with his mother in Kunming. Second, he retrieves video footage taken during his mother's trip to Beijing. Due to the exiguity of the apartment he was sharing with his girlfriend, choreographer Wen Hui, he found it inconvenient to let his mother stay too long and convinced her to return home. Three years after her death, Wu films himself in front of his monitor, revisiting the footage and recounting the experience of driving her back to the airport, aware of her reluctance to leave.

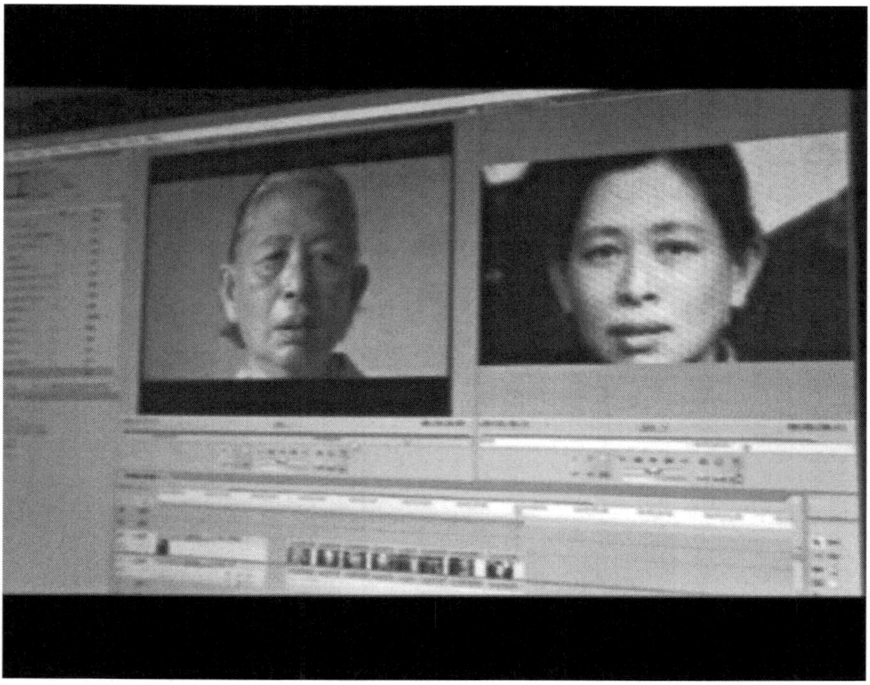

Figure 7.6. Treatment. Video *en abyme* in Wu Wenguang's work.

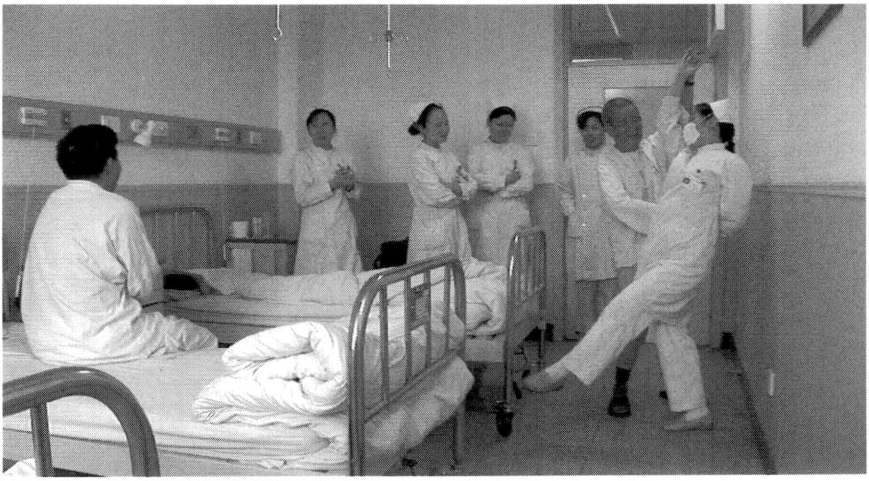

Figure 7.5. Old Men. Even in the hospital, Lao An yields to his love for dancing.

ingly close, at the border, in the same diegetic space as her subjects with whom she converses in her melodious, highly recognizable voice. She gracefully inserts herself in the aural texture of her films through a mix of vérité and diaristic style that projects an aura of quiet seduction—whether she tries to understand the disintegration of her parents' marriage from different points of view (*Home Video* 2001), unfolds the extramarital love affair of a grandfather addicted to dancing in the park (*The Love of Mr. An/Lao an* 2008), speaks with her elderly neighbors about their memories of the war with Japan (*My Neighbors and Their Japanese Ghosts/Wo de linju shuo guizi* 2008), or follows young boys abandoned in an orphanage over a twelve-year period (*Wild Grass* 2009). She is a confidante, a friend, sometimes an object of flirtation; her advice is sought or rejected, her presence is acknowledged.

Wu acquired a portable DV camera during one of his trips to show his films in Hong Kong in 1998,[10] and immediately appreciated the impact the new technology would have on the field of documentary filmmaking. For his first digital film, *Jianghu: Life on the Road* (*Jianghu* 2000), "I just carried the DV camera with me like a pen . . . ," he said (Wu 2010, 49). The liberation experienced during the shooting, as he was recording image and sound by himself, was matched by the autonomy offered by comparatively affordable at-home editing systems. He became enthusiastic at the possibility of discarding a "professional approach" to documentary—an attitude he took to heart, setting up a production center, Caochangdi Workstation, in which he teaches villagers, students, young people from all walks of life, and artists from other disciplines to use video to tell their own stories.[11] "You don't decide on a subject before you start shooting, you find your subject *as you are shooting*."[12] When Wu returned to directing after a gap of several years devoted to training nonprofessional filmmakers, he made "personal cinema" pieces. *Treatment* (*Zhiliao* 2010) was triggered by the emotions caused by the death of his mother in 2007. Drawing a parallel between a decaying building serving as hospice (old people are sent there to die, not to be "treated") and his own attempts to "treat" his sense of loss and guilt, Wu digs through his personal archives. First, there are the letters, notebooks, and photos from the time of the Cultural Revolution when, as a teenager and young adult, he lived alone with his mother in Kunming. Second, he retrieves video footage taken during his mother's trip to Beijing. Due to the exiguity of the apartment he was sharing with his girlfriend, choreographer Wen Hui, he found it inconvenient to let his mother stay too long and convinced her to return home. Three years after her death, Wu films himself in front of his monitor, revisiting the footage and recounting the experience of driving her back to the airport, aware of her reluctance to leave.

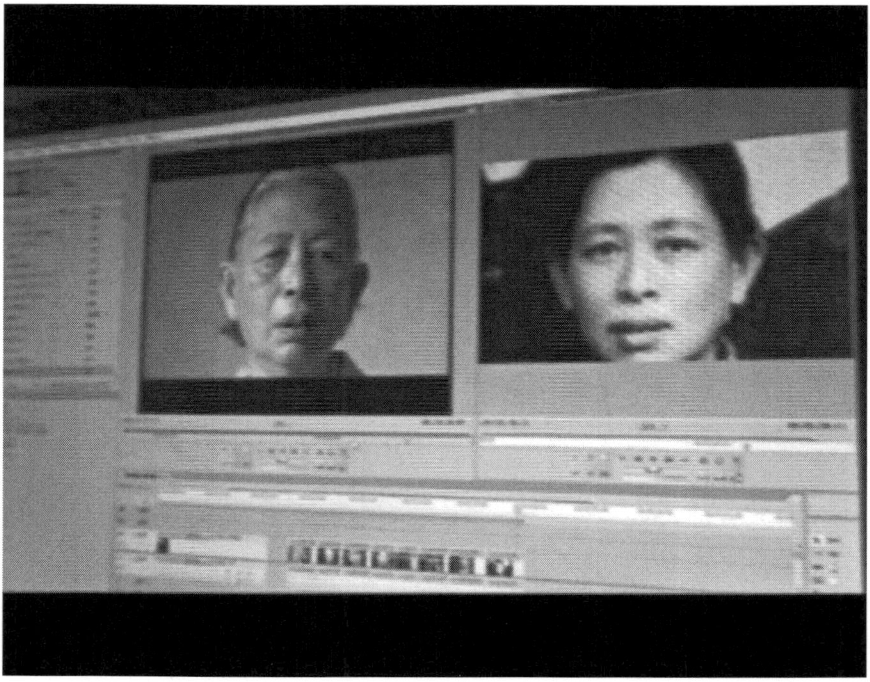

Figure 7.6. Treatment. Video *en abyme* in Wu Wenguang's work.

Video has strong connections to performance art, often playing with the "immediate feedback" effect. From the onset, through his relationship with Wen Hui and avant-garde theater director Mou Sen, Wu has been involved in performances. While his art has benefited from his collaboration in Wen Hui's choreographies, the dancers working at Caochangdi Workstation were given cameras and started to make their own films, including Wen Hui herself, with *Listening to Third Grand-Mother's Stories* (*Ting sannainai jian congqian de shiqing* 2011). The piece sprouted from a multimedia performance, *Memory* (2009), which toured a number of international venues. Exploring the concept of "body as living archive," Wen Hui delved into her childhood memories during the Cultural Revolution. From her research, a figure emerged. To avoid being branded with a "bad family background," her father, a schoolteacher, had never mentioned the existence of a "third grandmother"—a child bride, uneducated but coming from a landowning family, who had married his mother's brother. Decades later, this woman is an old peasant hiding her long white hair under a little cap, with twinkles in her eyes. To trigger Third Grandmother's memories, Wen involves her entire body, in a sort of improvised choreography. By sharing gestures (the two women sleep side by side, comb each other's hair, cook and eat together, and perform some little "dances"), she creates an intimate space between her and her subject. This graceful approach springs a small miracle, giving the floor to this resilient senior, uncovering a side of history as it was experienced by a woman: being brought to her in-laws' house without knowing anything about life or domestic work; the birth of her son; her divorcing a charming, educated, but philandering husband; the persecutions suffered during the Land Reform. . . .

The relationship between "the body" and "the archive" is complex, as outlined by Allan Sekula: photography was first used as criminal evidence, as well as a way of imposing a taxonomy on human types to make it easier to spot "criminal features" in suspects. "Can any connection be traced between the archival mode of photography and the emergence of photographic modernism?" (Sekula 1986, 58). Documentary practices modeled on the idea of "surveillance camera" reshuffle the question. Since surveillance, originally, is on the side of the state, is it possible to turn it inside out and direct the camera at the injustices of the state—or is every instance of surveillance camera fraught with the possibility of alienation and repression? The concept of "photographic realism" is originally a repressive one, designed to solidify the status quo and the domination of the ruling class. However, Sekula suggests,

> We would be wise to avoid an overtly monolithic conception of realism. Not all realisms necessarily play into the hands of the police. . . . If we are to listen to, and act in solidarity with, the polyphonic testimony of the oppressed and

> exploited, we should recognize that some of this testimony . . . will take the ambiguous form of visual documents, documents of the "microphysics" of barbarism. . . . Our problem as artists and intellectuals . . . will be to help prevent the cancellation of that testimony by more authoritative and official texts. (Sekula 1986, 64)

One way to prevent the "cancellation of that testimony" is not to look at the "archiving of bodies," but at bodies themselves as "living archive." This concept, borrowed from dance theory, gives its value to the collaboration between a documentary filmmaker and a choreographer in the "Memory Project" and can also be transposed to the notions of "reenactment" and "performance for the camera" that have been at stake whenever documentary filmmaking is discussed since Robert Flaherty's *Nanook of the North* (1922).[13] André Lepecki proposes the concept of "[the] will to archive," which he defines as "specifically choreographic" (Lepecki 2010, 29), but can be applied to other time-based, kinetic arts such as cinema. "Is it at all possible to affirm a past that is not always already 'misplaced'? . . . Is archiving, as Foucault . . . suggests in *The Archaeology of Knowledge* (1972), a system of *transforming simultaneously* past, present, and future—that is, a system for recreating a whole economy of the temporal?" (Lepecki 2010, 30). Quoting Jessica Santone (2008), it is not, he advances, the "past that is incomplete" but "history that is incomplete" (Lepecki 2010, 30), which "echoes Rebecca Schneider's provocative notions of re-enactments as 'counter-memory' and 're-documenting' " (Lepecki 2010, 31, citing Schneider 2001). So, "in dance re-enactments there will be no distinctions left between archive and body. The body is archive and archive a body," concludes Lepecki (2010, 31). His theses prompt us to reevaluate the use of "nonprofessional actors" in the narrative films mentioned at the beginning. Indeed, they stage fictional, scripted (or semi-scripted) situations, but the feeling of "truth" we experience by looking at these films is embedded in the performances of the nonactors, not so much in the way they deliver their lines, but how they move their bodies in the cinematic space. They can "act true" because of the memories stored in their bodies which, in turn, create a different kind of filmic time, a new "economy of the temporal." This is particularly salient in the *Oxhide* cycle, as well as in the character of the legal secretary of *The Other Half,* the coal miners of *Jalainur,* the teenagers of *Winter Vacation,* or the Tibetan peasants of *The Search.* Why, asks Lepecki, "recur to the most moving support, the most precarious support, a human body, in order to archive?" (Lepecki 2010, 34). This is a good question for dance, but an even better question for cinema, where we are no longer dealing with "the body" itself, but its reproduced image, "preserved" in space and time on a photographic medium. It is because each body, having an individual shape, idiosyncratic flaws, and a specific history, resists the systematization of official history. "In its

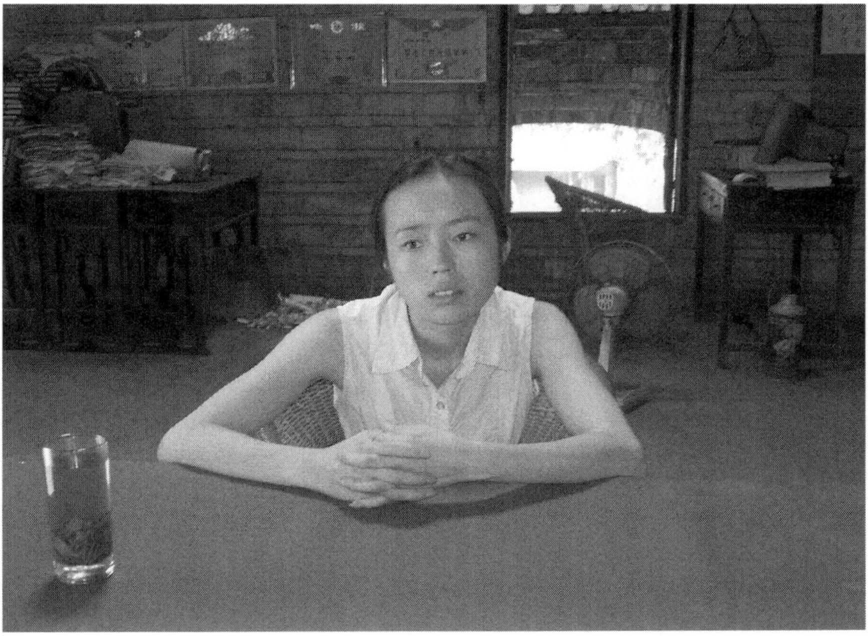

Figure 7.7. The Other Half. Absence of reverse angle: the legal secretary.

constitutive precariousness, perceptual blind-spots, linguistic indeterminations, muscular tremors, memory lapses, bleedings, rages, and passions, the body as archive re-places and diverts notions of archive away from a documental deposit or a bureaucratic agency dedicated to the (mis)management of 'the past,'" concludes Lepecki (2010, 34). So the significance of the aforementioned films lies in their capability to look at imperfect bodies as site of resistance—and thus as encoding the signs of a counter-history.

Sex, Village Songs, and Video

In this wake, the way Hao Jie makes use of "reenactments" and treats the bodies of his protagonists/performers as "living archives," turns *Single Man* into a multilayered filmic text—posited at yet another critical boundary between documentary and fiction. The film brings to light the repressed energy, the secret longings hidden in the bodies of elderly bachelors from the mountainous village of Gujiagou, in one of the poorest areas of Hebei Province. As in many rural communities, men outnumber women. Some buy wives from Sichuan, while others remain bachelors—which does not imply (and this is where the film becomes wickedly original) a total lack of sex life. History has inscribed itself in the physical appearance, the gait, the gestures, the wrinkles, the mutilations of the four antiheroes—such as Liang Youzhong's stump (*you can't fake this; it is the trace, the proof that something has happened to this man*). During the Cultural Revolution, Bighead Liang (Liang Youzhong) lost a hand while flirting with a girl dangerously close to a threshing machine. In 1945, Gu Lin (Du Tianguang) was kicked out of his house for trying to seduce his sister-in-law. In 1942, Liu Ruan (Liang Chunying), then a mere boy of twelve, was forced into an arranged marriage with an older girl. As for Lao Yang (Yang Zhenjun), he is still in love with Eryatou, the girl he was forbidden to marry as a young man; she is now the middle-aged wife of the village head, but they sneak out for secret trysts. Eryatou (Wang Suzhen) exudes an easygoing, fun-loving sensuality while being a practical woman. She extends her kindness to the other bachelors, and her frolicking is rewarded by financial gifts; she saves the money toward the college tuition needed by her older son, Hao Jiangen (played by the filmmaker). So far, so good. The peasants sing bawdy songs during village fairs, joke about whose son so-and-so is, and gang up against the watermelon traders who exploit them. One day Gu Lin convinces Lao Yang that, more than an occasional roll in the hay, what he needs is a wife. . . .

Born in Gujiagou, Hao Jie designed the story in close collaboration with his relatives and neighbors, and he inserted autobiographical elements, such as his character's departure for the university—echoing the concerns of the New Chinese documentary, especially in its development in the "personal" works of Wu Wenguang and Wen Hui. However, these artists are currently leaning toward a more formalist approach/reorganization of "the real" either via a *mise en abyme* of the video image (Wu) or a stylization of dance/performance art–inspired movements (Wen)—while Hao Jie combines the codes of neorealism with the new digital aesthetics: handheld camera, seemingly improvised composition of the image. It also contains elements of other genres, such the village farce, which counteracts the somber "gritty-realistic" tone of many Sixth Generation films. For example, it seems to offer a nonchalant point of view on the issue of bride trafficking in rural communities, miles apart from its melodramatic treatment in Li Yang's *Blind Mountain* (*Mang shan* 2007). Lao Yang spends his life savings (6,000 RMB) to buy a pretty Sichuan bride (played by the only professional actress, Le Yan, an outsider to the village, just like her character). Yet the victim is given agency. She states loud and clear that she does not like her husband, cries when forced to perform her conjugal duties during her wedding night, and tries to escape. When a young man, Qiaosan (the son of Bighead Liang's youthful love in-

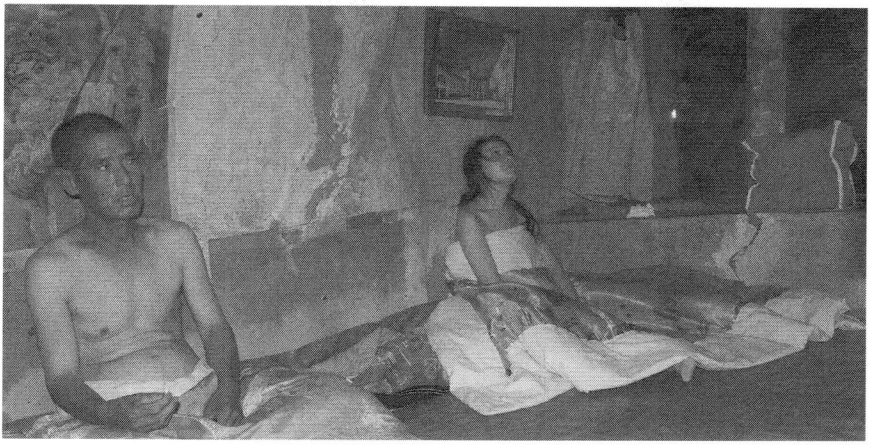

Figure 7.8. Single Man. The sexual impasse: Lao Yang and the Sichuan bride.

terest), catches her eye, she decides she wants to marry *him*. Qiaosan, smitten with her, convinces his parents to buy the bride from Lao Yang for him.

At key moments, Hao directs the film as a musical: traditional ribald songs or contemporary rock comment on the plight of the single man—his freedom, desires, frustrations, and need for cash (*without money, she will not undress for you*), often playing on double entendres, as *guanggun* (bachelor) also means "rascal." Unlike the traditional musical, though, in which the soundtrack, no matter how carefully lip-synced, is clearly prerecorded and overlaid over the visuals, the songs featured in *Single Man* are anchored in the diegetic space. Traveling entertainers and locals sing at village fairs; various tunes are heard from television monitors, transistor radios, or record players that are foregrounded in the composition of the image.

The film wittily combines these "genre" elements with frank, fluid, and open-minded treatment of sexuality—presented as *the language* these bodies are speaking. Here the content is a result of the technology. Before small digital cameras that can store a seemingly unlimited amount of tape, staging a sex scene was a much more dramatic affair—due to the size and obtrusive quality of the camera, the presence of a crew, and the necessity to reload the camera mid-action. A new generation of filmmakers is now able to stage and record sex scenes with an unprecedented amount of spontaneity, which produces, maybe, the innocence early cinema had been longing for. Hao Jie's mode of filming echoes similar experiments, or trends, taking place all over the world, such as the U.S. "mumblecore,"[14] in which the reshuffling of the boundaries between "being" and "performing" allows for a matter-of-fact, non-melodramatic representation of sexuality.

Two scenes strike by their boldness and their modernity. After Lao Yang sells his bride to Qiaosan's parents, Eryatou is still mad at him, so he finds himself without a sex partner. He goes to the next town, where he makes quite an impression on the receptionists of a luxury hotel asking for "millet" (local slang for prostitute), then wanders through a seedy street, where a lightly clad girl offers him "lodgings" (another code word for prostitution). Hao cuts to a medium shot of Lao Yang and the hooker sitting on the pink coverlet of a bed surrounded by pink drapes, bathed in a pinkish light coming from a cheap string of lights; on the wall are *Playboy*-type posters of naked women—one Asian, one blonde. Lao Yang negotiates the price, gets a rebate, draws his 100 RMB bill out of his pocket, and gets his 20 RMB back. Off-screen, while the camera focuses on the string of lights, the sex takes place. "This is not what I expected," complains Lao Yang. Another cut brings the handheld camera onto the girl's naked shoulder (she's wearing a tank top), with half of her face off-screen on the left. The camera moves down, and, from the contractions of the girl's arm muscles, one can guess the movement of her left hand (still in the off-screen space below). An invisible Lao Yang continues to complain: "Not as comfortable as lying on your belly. . . . Oh no, fucking is not like this."

After two cuts in rapid succession, the situation is resolved in a very mobile medium shot lasting one minute and twenty seconds. Lao Yang, on the bed with his pants partially pulled down, tries to kiss the girl. She refuses.

HOOKER: Here we all do it like this.
LAO YANG: But I cannot fuck this way. . . . Give me back my money.
H: Give back?
LY: Yeah.
H: I can't (meanwhile she removes a transparent plastic glove from her left hand and starts crumbling it into a ball).
LY: Can.
H: I can't.
LY: You can. Please. I didn't fuck you. Just like massage (gesture of the hands).
H: Next time, brother. OK? Next time I'll give you a better price. (Her hands continue to crumble the plastic glove.)
LY: No, I didn't even touch you.
H: Whom was I serving for such a long time?
LY: Eh . . . then I will pay you less. Ten.
H: Impossible (Lao Yang starts getting up). It's pretty hard for me.
LY: It's pretty hard for me as well. (Lao Yang, back to the camera, seen from the waist up, pulls his pants back up). Give me back my money and then

I'll go. (He gets up and goes around the bed; we hear his shoes' shuffling noise.) It's dark. Give me back my money. I need to go. (He is now standing in the background, behind the bed, dominating the girl who is still sitting on the bed. She takes a cigarette and lights it. We hear the click of the lighter.) Give it back!

H: No. (She smokes).

LY: Give it back! (He tries to grab her hands.)

H: I did my job!

LY: You must give it back to me! . . .

H: No. (shouting) Big Boss!

(Cut to Lao Yang running away in the dark street.)

This one-shot-sequence, obviously choreographed while giving the impression of an improvised spontaneity made possible by the DV recording, is a brilliant illustration of the Lacanian adage that "the sexual relationship does not exist." As the pitiful ejaculation in the gloved hand remains off-screen, Hao Jie films the after-sex—getting dressed up, getting up, talking about it—as what really happens between men and women. Lao Yang pleads ardently, repeatedly, not for sex (and we know he can be very passionate about it) but for his money back. His longing for physical intimacy has been transmuted into longing for money. Besides, this is the only thing he can talk about with the girl, and his verbal exchange with her is the longest one-on-one conversation he has with any of the protagonists of the film.

What makes the scene so arresting is Yang Zhenjun's physical presence: the line between "reenactment" and "fictionalization" is very thin. The body of the performer becomes the "living archive" through which the plight of these "single men," their erotic longings, their loneliness, can be represented on the screen.

The elegant long shot ending the encounter with the hooker starkly contrasts with the minute decoupage in which Hao Jie presents another sexual situation. After returning from the city, Lao Yang receives the visit of the Sichuan bride (now married to Qiaosan) who, in dire need of money to visit her hometown where her father has just died, comes to offer herself to him. What we may have perceived as a "light" treatment of human trafficking is recontextualized here. Real damage was done to the young woman: no matter whom she likes or does not, she perceives herself a commodity for sale.

An elliptical montage brings us promptly to Lao Yang all bloodied and battered (the result of Qiaosan's jealous rage), seeking refuge in Liu Ruan's home. The latter tends to his wounds and offers him hospitality for the night. The moon shines in the sky, the TV is on, reporting on French President Nicolas Sarkozy's visit with Chinese President Hu Jintao. The reverse angle is a tight close-up of what happens when the two men are in bed: a hand touching a flabby belly. This is followed by a series of close-ups isolating body parts, heads, intertwined legs, arms; Liu Ruan kisses Lao Yang's naked shoulder. Lao Yang keeps complaining: "Don't push me.... If you have money, find a woman. Don't annoy me." A medium shot reveals Liu Ruan embracing Lao Yang, who has his back turned to him. Finally Lao Yang gets up. The camera stays on Liu Ruan lying on the mattress, his face turned toward the left. Off-screen, the noise of a door shutting down. The following shot is a medium close-up of Liu Ruan, fully dressed in a white shirt, looking melancholy, as his face dissolves into that of his twelve-year-old self.

In these two instances of thwarted desire, Lao Yang is the one who flees. With the young hooker, he couldn't face his erotic disappointment and stubbornly refused to understand what the girl's labor meant to her. With Liu Ruan, not only is he unable to face the desire of the Other, but he fails to see in the other man's longing a mirror image of his own. The social texture observed by Hao Jie in Gujiagou village is a mixture of permissiveness, bawdiness, frustration, jealousy, open-mindedness, and petty resentments. The availability of small DV cameras allows for a form of representation in which various examples of non-normative sexuality (adultery, sex outside marriage, sex coerced through human trafficking, prostitution, homosexuality) coexist and overlap with a non-melodramatic, non-prurient fluidity rarely seen in Chinese cinema since the 1930s.[15] The night encounter between Liu Ruan and Lao Yang could fall into the (mainstream heterocentrist) tropes of the "tragic homosexual," fated to a lonely life, if *all* forms of desire were not presented in the film as the result of a difficult negotiation between a rampant frustration and an all-too-rare satisfaction, in moments snatched from the order of the social fabric, in ordinary instances of the "sexual impasse." The rural "single man" becomes the prism through which Hao Jie looks at contemporary sexuality in China and produces images about what was not hitherto visible. It is, however, because it shows such forbidden situations that *Single Man* cannot have a theatrical release in China, in spite of the international accolades it has received.

The Role of the Editor in a Globalized Context

So the tension identified at the beginning of this chapter between the "desire for cinema" and "documentary impulse" has been subsumed into the tension between the "will to archive" and "the necessity to edit," with "the body" as a vector for this dilemma. Archiving is a cumulative process, especially poignant in the case of "counter-archiving" (i.e., presenting an alternative record against official history). Editing is, at best, a form of sculpting; it involves countless instances of subtractions. Can elements be eliminated from the archive without destroying its very nature? Many independent documentary filmmakers seem to be leaning toward keeping what they probably view as the "integrity" of the accumulative archival process—which may explain their suspicion against, or their resistance to, montage. Documentarist Du Haibin reports that most of his colleagues tend to shoot a lot (a ratio of 100 to 1 is the norm) and edit alone, on a home computer, without feedback.[16] There is, however, a major difference with the "non-interventionist" ideology described by Trinh. Classical anthropological films document "the Other" from the point of view of the dominant culture. Chinese independent filmmakers document "others" with whom they share a similar territory. In the case of filmmakers belonging to ethnic or sexual minorities (for instance, Tibetans or queer subjects), the distance between the artist and his/her subject is reduced to the minimum. Pema Tseden and queer activist Fan Popo speak from within their communities. Yu Guanyi, a former lumberjack, describes people who could have been his coworkers in *Timber Gang* (*Mu bang* 2006). The body of the filmmaker and those of the people in front of the camera *belong to the same field*: it is a relationship of contiguity, generating what I have tried to define, in another text, as a "sidelong glance, . . . a partial, sympathetic gaze: the director is pointing his camera at a reality in which he is a part" (Reynaud, 2007, 268). To the moment in Du Haibin's *1428* (*1428* 2009) discussed by Nornes in chapter 1 ("Are you filming for the government or yourself?"—"For ourselves."), I will add another, no less telling, moment. A young butcher whom Du is filming talks back to him: "You and I are from the same generation. You remember how terrible it was in 1979!" In other words "You are behind the camera and I in front of it, but you and I share a common experience." So I will slightly differ with Nornes' interpretation of the identity of these "ourselves." I do not think they represent "the entire community of Chinese documentary filmmakers," but you my subject and I the maker, *we,* the Chinese people, are in the same boat together.

This is why the editing of independent Chinese documentaries is difficult—it is hard to cut a part of one's own body. This is why, more and more frequently, a "third eye" is called to the rescue. It is at this crucial junction that the question of the audience must be reintroduced. Who is the archive for? Domestic audiences, in their desire to see "their" reality represented, may display patience for "self-indulgently long, roughly edited films" (Shaffer 2010). International audiences may not. So the problematic of editing is ultimately tied up to issues of globalized reception. Wang Bing may be the most famous case of this connection, as his career has grown in parallel with a proactive attitude toward digital media displayed at international film festivals from the early 2000s on.

At first, non-analog films had a hard time showing in international venues that only accepted 35mm and 16mm in the most generous cases. The first Chinese digital feature, Zhu Wen's *Seafood* (*Hai xian* 2001), had to be blown to 35mm in an Australian laboratory to do the run of the festivals (starting in Venice, where it received an award). Gradually festivals opened themselves to the new formats. In addition, they made production and completion funds available for digital projects, and Wang's *West of the Tracks* (*Tiexi qu* 2003), a film that drastically affected the status of the documentary and the digital image (Lü 2010, 57–76), received such support. Having immersed himself for almost two years in a community in crisis (factory workers of an industrial complex in the process of being dismantled), Wang had become a "filming body" and brought back an enormous amount of footage.[17] A grant from the Dutch Hubert Bals Fund allowed him a whole year to rework the material with a British editor (Adam Kerby) and produce the nine-hour version, world premiered in Rotterdam. The fourteen-hour-long *Crude Oil* (*Yuan you* 2008) was commissioned as an installation piece by the Rotterdam Film Festival, while Wang's next projects—*Fengming: A Chinese Memoir* (*He Fengming* 2007), *Coal Money* (*Meitan qian* 2008), *The Man with No Name* (*Wu ming zhe* 2009), his first narrative feature *The Ditch* (*Jiabiangou* 2010), *Three Sisters* (*San Zimei* 2012), and *Till Madness Do Us Part* (*Feng ai* 2013)—were French productions or coproductions benefiting from European talent (sound, editing). Wang continued working with Kerby for *Fengming, Three Sisters,* and *Till Madness.*[18]

Another significant example is that of Du Haibin. Having made a number of successful documentaries, he tackled a more ambitious project, *Umbrella* (*San* 2007), that went beyond a pure vérité approach. It exposed discrepancies of lifestyle and income throughout China, taking the making, selling, and circulating of the ubiquitous umbrella as a signifier for these disparities. The film showed workers assembling umbrellas in a factory in the Pearl River Delta: a woman from the Zhejiang countryside who gave up peasant life to become an umbrella manufacturer in the city of Yiwu; recent graduates looking for jobs in Shanghai—carrying umbrellas under the rain. The umbrella then migrates to be seen with street vendors and professional shoe polishers struggling to make a living, young peasants signing up to become soldiers, and old peasants left alone in their deserted village. Sharp, rigorous editing was the only way to make the film work. *Umbrella* had been produced by a Beijing-based Foundation, CNEX, which aimed to submit it to festivals (*Umbrella* eventually went to Venice, Cinéma du Réel, and a number of Asian or Asian-themed events). So, for the international version, CNEX hired a second editor, Hong Kong-born Mary Stephen, who had been Eric Rohmer's collaborator from *The Aviator's Wife* (*La Femme de l'aviateur* 1980) till his death in 2010. Du worked again with Stephen on *1428,* about the aftermath of the Sichuan earthquake. The film received an award in Venice and is distributed by small companies in France and the United States. At the time these lines are written, Du and Stephen are completing their third collaboration. The input of a foreign editor goes beyond the aesthetic realm; it has financial and economic consequences. "Independent filmmakers don't have much money; the editing takes months, and I am not independently wealthy, so I need to find a way to cover my living expenses," says Stephen. "So I have to get involved in fundraising, and I become a coproducer."[19]

In other cases, it is the Chinese (co-)producer who looks for a foreign editor. For Hao Jie's second feature, *The Love Songs of Tiedan* (*Mei jie* 2012), Chow Keung hired the Korean editor Baek Seung Hoon—who had already edited Han Jie's *Hello, Mr. Tree, Hello!* (*Shu xiansheng* 2011) produced by Jia Zhangke. No less bawdy, brave, comical, and sensual than *Single Man, Tiedan* is the story of a romantic obsession that spans several decades. Growing up in a poor Shanxi village, six-year-old Tiedan falls in love with Sister May, the beautiful neighbor who practices a traditional form of singing, *Er-ren tai,* with his father. Folk singing is persecuted during the Cultural Revolution, and Tiedan, as a grown man, encounters Sister May's daughters with heartbreaking results, but the desire, the longing, and the music survive all twists of fate. . . . The film passed censorship and enjoyed a modest theatrical run. Even when administrative obstacles are removed, the domestic market may not be the ideal arena for these works. The dilemma of "auteur cinema" that receives a warmer reception abroad than at home predates, of course, digital modes of production, blurring further the line between the national and the international.

In the case of hybrid documentary/fictions that take a de facto oppositional stance, foreign sources of funding and exhibition may become a necessary conduit. In 2011, the Jeonju Festival invited Ying Liang (who at the time was teaching at the Hong Kong Academy of Performing Arts) to make a short digital film, which he eventually expanded to seventy minutes. *When Night Falls* (*Wo hai you hua yao shuo* 2012) is inspired by a notorious case (already the subject of an Ai Weiwei documentary). In 2007, Yang Jia, a young Beijinger on a trip to Shanghai, was beaten up by the police for riding an unlicensed bicycle. Later, according to authorities, Yang knifed six policemen to death in a police station—becoming a folk hero for thousands of netizens.

His mother, Wang Jingmei, was kidnapped and locked under an assumed name in a mental hospital for months, which prevented her from acting as legal representative for her son. Ying Liang starts the film when Wang is released from the psychiatric ward, the day before her son's scheduled execution. He interweaves material downloaded from the Internet with fictional reconstitutions of the mother's lonely fight. *When Night Falls* struck a raw nerve with the censors, and, at the time I am writing this chapter, Ying has not been able to return to the PRC. The film, however, received two prizes in Locarno, Best Director for Ying and Best Actress for Nei An (a noted television actress who is also one of China's best independent film producers), and it has been widely written about in the Western press.[20] Beyond the dramatic turn of events that it triggered, what is most significant about *When Night Falls* is the questions it poses to the aesthetics of the digital medium—as a space in-between the heritage of classical cinematic mise en scène and the vanishing point represented by the ever-fluid forms of Internet posting.

The Owl in the Garden of Forking Paths

Chinese digital cinema embodies a utopia, which Ou Ning connects with other forms of activism, such as land reclamation in urban or rural settings (Ou 2011). This is also why it has become the tool of choice for some disenfranchised populations, such as the LGBT community. Cui Zi'en's impressive output is a good example: make one film after another, after another; something will remain, something will be seen. . . .

Borges' "Garden of Forking Paths," however, outlined an aesthetic impossibility. The utopian construction of simultaneous forms of representation keeps abutting against the unsavory realities of politics and market economy. International circuits of exhibition and distribution are growing tepid toward the forms of digital neorealism they had embraced enthusiastically when it was the new thing on the block.

The gap between mainstream and alternative cinema has widened. Prosperous production companies invest in commercial "products" and turn away from Sixth Generation auteurs or new independent filmmakers. While the independent digital cinema is becoming the object of serious academic discourse, its distribution prospects at home and abroad have grown dimmer. As "the owl of Minerva begins its flight" (Hegel 1991), are Chinese independent digital media at the onset of dusk?

The question that has haunted digital cinema since its origins—is it cinema or not?—may have been inadequate, and maybe Alexander Kluge is right when he asserts that "cinema is lost" (Ekardt 2011). Like the filmmaker who points his/her camera at a building being demolished, the function of digital media is precisely to document this societal/technological/aesthetic process through which we are losing cinema—at the very moment an archaic cinematic longing for unbroken shots and ubiquitous cameras is being fulfilled. And so, as a redoubling/deconstruction/refashioning of the cinematic image, occupying a no man's land between reality and its recording, DV films have the uncanny potential for articulating these moments of rupture, these breaks in the *episteme,* through which societies and cultures are evolving.

Notes

1. http://www.artspeakchina.org/mediawiki/index.php/Baron_Guy_and _Myriam_Ullens_盖•尤伦斯男爵夫妇, retrieved Sept. 10, 2011.

2. http://short-stays.org/news/zhang-xianmin-hosts-indie-film-forum -saturday-june-5, retrieved Sept. 10, 2011.

3. Bazin, André. 1975."Pour un cinéma impur—Défense de l'adaptation." in André Bazin, *Qu'est-ce que le cinéma—Edition définitive,* 81–106. Paris: Editions du Cerf. The title, which means *For an Impure Cinema—In Defense of Adaptation,* was translated by Hugh Gray as "In Defense of a Mixed Cinema" in *What Is Cinema,* vol. 1, Berkeley and Los Angeles: University of California Press, 1967 and 2007, 53–75. I consider this translation to be a slight misinterpretation of Bazin's argument—that cinema was enriched by borrowing from literature, theater, and the other arts. In this chapter I am hoping that theory can be enriched and reflection stimulated by practices external to a purely theoretical field.

4. As engagingly described in Abé Mark Nornes' chapter, the role of Asia has been quite significant in this domain: not only the festivals of Tokyo, Osaka, Yamagata, Pusan, Jeonju, and Hong Kong have shown many such works, but Jeonju has commissioned works by Jia Zhangke, Zhang Yuan, Ying Liang, and others for its series "Short Digital Films," with Hong Kong recently following suit with its series "Beautiful," for which Zhang Yuan directed *I Love You, Boss* (2014). The sanction of the international film network, therefore, is not couched in terms of "Orientalist gaze" vs. "Chinese authenticity" but is part and parcel of a complex interplay of negotiations, some of it being intra-Asian or pan-Asian.

5. The Film and Television Bureau resulted from a merging of several government agencies in 1986 and submitted all film productions to a three-tier censorship system (screenplay, rough cut, and export visa). Independent videos and digital media were not under its supervision and were generally ignored; shot outside the sanctioned "production units," they *had no legal existence*; ignored and semi-invisible in China, they could be sent or screened abroad without major hassle. In 1998, the Bureau reorganized as the State Administration of Radio, Film, and Television (SARFT) and seems to have finally caught up with the importance of digital media. On March 30, 2009, SARFT prohibited thirteen categories of content online—including time travel, gambling, prostitution, and adultery. Effective July 1, 2010, it has become forbidden to send abroad tapes or DVDs of *all* media work not having received official sanction.

6. This may also explain why Wang Bing, Yang Lina, and now Huang Weikai, who are respected documentary filmmakers, have all tried their hand at making narratives.

7. This death was also reported in digital documentaries. The feminist academic Ai Xiaoming, one of the first Chinese intellectuals to use digital media as a form of political protest, made *White Ribbon* (*Bai sidai*) in 2004. And Huang Weikai inserts a mention of the Sun Zhigang case at the end of *Floating*.

8. "Alternative Archive is founded in January 2004 by Ou Ning and Cao Fei, as a platform that connects contemporary art, film, music, theater, design, city study, and publishing. At the same time, it archives all the works in all these areas. The space itself is not opened to public, but all the archives can be shared with people via this website in digital format" (Ou, 2004b). http://www.alternativearchive.com/en/introduction/introduction.htm.

9. Conversation with Yang Lina, Beijing, June 3, 2011.

10. Interview with Wu Wenguang, Beijing, May 30, 2011.

11. See http://www.ccdworkstation.com/english/homepage-e.htm.

12. Interview with Wu Wenguang, Beijing, May 30, 2011.

13. Flaherty asked Nanook to build an igloo in which his cumbersome 35mm camera could enter, or to take his time when harpooning a seal so that the camera could capture "how it was done."

14. Here I define "mumblecore" as low-budget films shot on DV that focus more on a faux-improvised rendition of contemporary relationships among young people than on plot, as in work of Joe Swanberg, Sophia Takal, or Alex Ross Perry (Hoberman 2007; Lim 2007).

15. Sun Yu's *The Big Road* (*Dalu* 1934) has been noted for the freedom and generosity in which it represented the bodies and physical interaction of its male and female protagonists.

16. Interview with Du Haibin, Beijing, June 7, 2011.

17. A first version of the film was shown in the "Focus on China" Panorama section of the 2002 Berlin Film Festival. Wang worked two months with his first editor to compress the film to the five-hour version required by Berlin. Interview with Wang Bing, DVD supplement, *A l'Ouest des Rails,* Paris: MK2 edition, 2004.

18. Adam Kerby also contributed as editor to the success of Zhao Liang's *Crime and Punishment* (*Zui yu fa,* 2007), a German coproduction.

19. Conversation with Mary Stephen, Beijing, June 12, 2013.

20. See in particular, and for more details about the case, Richard Brody's *New Yorker* blog: http://www.newyorker.com/online/blogs/movies/2012/10/when-night-falls-ying-liang.html, retrieved Apr. 28, 2013.

Bibliography

Bazin, André. 1975."Pour un cinéma impur—Défense de l'adaptation." In *Qu'est-ce que le cinéma—Edition définitive,* by André Bazin, 81–106. Paris: Editions du Cerf.

Berry, Chris and Rofel, Lisa. 2010. "Alternative Archive: China's Independent Documentary Culture." In *The New Chinese Documentary Film Movement: For the Public Record,* edited by Chris Berry, Lü Xinyu, and Lisa Rofel, 135–154. Hong Kong: Hong Kong University Press.

Borges, Jorge Luis. 2000. "The Garden of Forking Paths." In *Labyrinths—Selected Stories and Other Writings,* edited by Donald Yates and James E. Irby, translated by James E. Irby, 44–54. London: Penguin.

Braester, Yomi. 2010. "Excuse Me, Your Camera Is in My Face: Autorial Interventions in PRC New Documentary." In *The New Documentary Film Movement: For the Public Record,* edited by Chris Berry, Lü Xinyu, and Lisa Rofel, 195–215. Hong Kong: Hong Kong University Press.

Casetti, Francesco. 2011. "Sutured Reality: Film from Photographic to Digital." *October* 138: 95–106.

Edwards, Dan. 2011. "CinemaTalk: A Conversation with Ou Ning." *Ou Ning's Blog.* http://www.alternativearchive.com/ouning/article.asp?id=821.

Ekardt, Philip. 2011. "Return of the Archaic, Reserves for the Future: A Conversation with Alexander Kluge." *October* 138: 120–132.

Foucault, Michel. 1972. *The Archaeology of Knowledge.* Translated by A. M. S. Smith. New York: Pantheon.

Gray, Hugh, trans. 1967. "In Defense of a Mixed Cinema." In *What Is Cinema* 1: 53–75. Berkeley: University of California Press.

Hegel, Georg Wilhelm Friedrich. 1991. *Elements of the Philosophy of Right,* edited by Allen W. Wood. Cambridge: Cambridge University Press.

Hemelryk Donald, Stephanie. 2000. *Public Secrets, Public Spaces—Cinema and Civility in China.* Lanham and Oxford: Rowman & Littlefield.

Hoberman, Jim. 2007. "It's Mumblecore!" *Village Voice,* Aug. 24. http://www.villagevoice.com/2007-08-14/film/it-s-mumblecore/.

Lepecki, André. 2010. "The Body as Archive: Will to Re-Enact and the Afterlives of Dances." *Dance Research Journal* 42: 28–48.

Lim, Dennis. 2007. "A Generation Finds Its Mumble." *New York Times,* Aug. 19. http://www.nytimes.com/2007/08/19/movies/19lim.html?pagewanted=1&8dpc.

Lü Xinyu. 2010. "*West of the Tracks*: History and Class Consciousness." In *The New Chinese Documentary Film Movement: For the Public Record,* edited by Chris Berry, Lü Xinyu, and Lisa Rofel, 57–76. Hong Kong: Hong Kong University Press.

Ou Ning. 2004a. "Digital Images and Civic Consciousness." Argos Festival publication, Brussels. http://www.alternativearchive.com/ouning/article.asp?id=102.

———. 2004b. "Introduction." Alternative Archive website. http://www.alternativearchive.com/en/introduction/introduction.htm.

———. 2005. "Introduction." *The Dazhalan Project.* http://www.dazhalan-project.org/introduction-en/introduction-en.htm.

———. 2011. "Agrarian Utopia: An Artistic Experiment in Chiang Mai." Translated by Shumei Roan. *Chutzpah* 1: 3–13.

Oudart, Jean-Pierre. 1977. "Cinema and Suture." *Screen* 18 (4): 35–47.

Reynaud, Bérénice. 2007. "Zhang Yuan's Imaginary Cities and the Theatricalization of the Chinese 'Bastards.'" In *The Urban Generation: Chinese Cinema and Society at the Turn of the Twenty-first Century,* edited by Zhang Zhen, 264–294. Durham, NC: Duke University Press.

Robinson, Luke. 2010. "From 'Public' to 'Private': Chinese Documentary and the Logic of *Xianchang.*" In *The New Chinese Documentary Film Movement: For the Public Record,* edited by Chris Berry, Lü Xinyu, and Lisa Rofel, 177–194. Hong Kong: Hong Kong University Press.

Santone, Jessica. 2008. "Marina Abramovic's *Seven Easy Pieces:* Critical Documentation Strategies for Preserving Art's History." *Leonardo* 41 (2): 147–152.

Schneider, Rebecca. 2001. "Archives Performance Remains." *Performance Research* 6 (2): 100–108.

Sekula, Allan. 1986. "The Body and the Archive," *October* 39: 3–64.

Shaffer, Benny. 2010. "The Films of Huang Weikai: Towards an Urban Documentary Surreal." *Leap—The International Art Magazine of Contemporary China*. http://leapleapleap.com/2010/12/huangweikai/.

Trinh T. Minh-ha. 1991. "Mechanical Eye, Electronic Ear, and the Lure of Authenticity." In *When the Moon Waxes Red*, 53–62. New York and London: Routledge.

Wu Wenguang. 2010. "DV: Individual Filmmaking." In *The New Documentary Film Movement: For the Public Record*, edited by Chris Berry, Lü Xinyu, and Lisa Rofel, 49–54. Hong Kong: Hong Kong University Press.

CHAPTER 8

The Recalcitrance of Reality

Performances, Subjects, and Filmmakers in *24 City* and *Tape*

QI WANG

Since its beginning in the early 1990s, independent Chinese documentary has steadily built a reputation with its unflinching presentation of the underbelly of China's economic boom and social sea changes. Individuals and groups whose experiences register the drastic costs of this process have become the most natural and common subject matter of independent documentaries. From the struggling artists who were among the first to quit state employment and go independent in *Bumming in Beijing* (Wu Wenguang 1990) to the art-aspiring young migrants from the rural area in *The Other Bank* (Jiang Yue 1995), from the homeless youngsters in *Along the Railroad* (Du Haibin 2000) to the laid-off state-factory workers and their equally lost younger generation in *West of the Tracks* (Wang Bing 2003), from the homosexuals and transvestites in *The Box* (Ying Weiwei 2001) and *Meimei* (Gao Tian 2005) to, most recently, the wronged-many-times but still recalcitrant petitioners for justice in *Petition* (Zhao Liang 2009)—Chinese independent documentary has truly created a precious alternative archive of visible evidence and human existences that testifies to the irreducibility of those sides of reality and history not quite admissible in official representation. Apart from their historical value as alternative records of contemporary China, these documentaries, through some of the more experimental approaches that highlight the constructed nature of (cinematic) representation and foreground the illusory boundary between observational vérité and participatory performance, also challenge the ways in which we understand issues like truth, authenticity, and ethics in documentary and other related forms of visual historiography. Exemplary works of this kind include *The Other Bank, Nightingale, Not the Only Voice* (Tang Danhong 2000), *Dance with the Farm Workers* (Wu Wenguang 2001), *Night Scene* (Cui Zi'en 2004), *Fuck Cinema* (Wu Wenguang 2005), and *Women Fifty Minutes* (Shi Tou

2006). All of these unconventional documentaries feature performances either through the explicit staging of theatrical or fictional projects or through the active participation of the filmmaker, often accompanied by a highly embodied camera. Thus testing the boundary between fiction and nonfiction by exploring the complex relationship between performance and reality, these works exemplify an intriguingly cautious and reflexive attitude toward ethics, subjectivity, and documentary filmmaking as a particular mode of visual historiography that has its own advantages and loopholes in terms of authenticity and narrative "emplotment" (White 1973). This thoughtful and wary exploration in the form—and the problematic—of representing reality through the movie camera contains, I suspect, the most important contribution of independent documentary to the writing of history in contemporary China.[1]

In this chapter I want to look at two recent documentaries—*24 City* (Jia Zhangke 2008) and *Tape* (Li Ning 2009)—that in many aspects summarize and highlight the achievements as well as problems independent documentary has garnered in this exploration. Both works continue the practice of documenting underprivileged existences, one as a group portrait of workers abandoned by the state, their factory sold and developed into a new real estate complex, the other as an individual self-portrait spanning five years of the director's life and work as an artist outside the mainstream with dreams to realize, a family to consider, and a challenging reality to face. Both pieces foreground not only the concept but also the fact of performance to such an extent that they qualify only partly as documentaries. *24 City* enlists performances from professional actors; at least one-third of *Tape* consists of video recordings of site-specific performances by the director and his independent theater troupe called "J Town Body Guerilla Troupe." By highlighting the resilient boundary between performance and documentary, both works cultivate an intriguingly porous relationship between fiction and nonfiction, whose epistemological commitments and practices of historiography, however, seem quite different. Through the connection and difference in their cinematic portraits of Chinese life, and particularly through a critique of *24 City* as compared to *Tape*, I argue for increasing reflexivity on the complex relationship between subjectivity, historiography, and documentary ethics in order to produce a more thoughtful and accurate approach to reality and history.

A Smooth Crafting of Collective Memory in 24 City

Like *West of the Tracks* early in the decade, *24 City* presents drastic transformations in the state economic system through the closing of a state-run factory—in this case Factory 420, a military factory built in Chengdu, Sichuan Province, in the late 1950s against a Cold War background. Following the end of the Cultural Revolution and the implementation of paradigmatic changes in Chinese politics and economy, Factory 420 had tried to adapt itself to the manufacture of consumer appliances such as television sets and refrigerators in the 1980s and 1990s. Eventually it failed and the film recounts its final liquidation and purchase by private real estate developers. Rather than relying solely on spontaneous footage taken directly from the phenomenal world, Jia Zhangke incorporates performances by four professional actors and himself, inserts textual quotes by famous poets, and demonstrates his signature virtuosity through a meticulously realist mise-en-scène and a highly effective soundtrack. Nonfictional material includes interviews with five real subjects (four former workers and a young teenage girl who comes from the family of a Factory 420 worker), cinematic portraits of unidentified workers and their families, and footage of the actual factory space. Throughout the film, these fictional and nonfictional materials cycle in an orderly fashion as establishing and reestablishing shots (in the space of the factory complex), portrait moments, interviews (with real subjects or fictional characters), and poetic texts. The resulting narrative structure thus neatly moves from the general and the collective to the specific and the individual, and then concludes with a transcendental and impersonal poetic vision.

Jia Zhangke describes *24 City* as a gesture of respect for a disappearing collective socialist past and its impact on the human elements, specifically the working class of socialist China who had once benefited but now were dropped from state protection (Jia 2009b). For such a historical mission, what is gained through the current specific form of juxtaposing fiction and nonfiction and what might also be lost and even sacrificed? To answer these questions, I find it particularly productive to look at where the two distinct modes of representation encounter and overlap with each other. My discovery shows that, in his attempt to create a group portrait of the Chinese working class, the director tends toward a deliberate evocation of a sense of commonality across the ontologically discrete categories of fiction and nonfiction. To achieve this goal, he implements a series of strategies ranging from narrative assimilation to visual uniformity and constructs a smooth blend of reality and performance.

Performance exists on two explicit levels in *24 City:* that of professional actors and that of the director himself when he communicates with actors from off-screen. Four actors in the roles of former workers (Lü Liping, Joan Chen, Chen Jianbin) and the daughter from a worker's family (Zhao Tao) deliver full-length narrations scripted by Jia and Zhai Yongming, a famous female poet from Chengdu. According to Jia, the scripted narrations are based on field research among workers of Factory 420 and derive from "condensing a lot of documentary material" (Jia 2010, 63). To overcome the cognitive gap between the readily recognizable faces

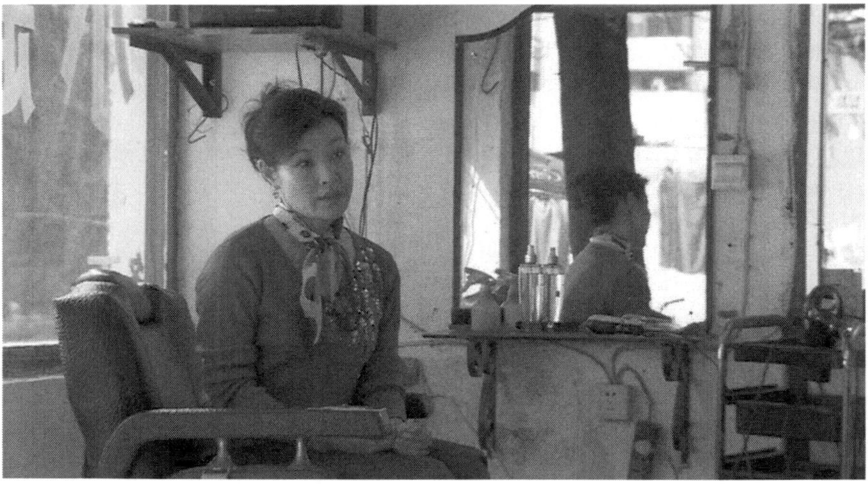

Figure 8.1. 24 City. Movie star Joan Chen posing as a former worker of Factory 420.

of the star actors and the next-to-anonymous visages of the real workers, Jia orders naturalistic acting from his professionals and places them in realistic settings (e.g., a typical worker home, a low-grade hair salon, a characterless front-desk area of a company, and an emptied classroom). Thanks to the medium shots used in framing the interviewees, real and fictional, they all look about the same size on-screen. Almost all of them are arranged in a sitting position slightly off the center of the frame, facing faintly sideways in conversation with the director who listens and occasionally speaks from off-screen. Even the facial expressions demonstrate an uncanny coherence. Notwithstanding their obvious physiognomic distinctions, everyone displays a set of facial features that are evenly held, thus looking poised and even peaceful despite the sad nature of their various accounts of sacrifice and loss. The female worker Hou Lijun is the only exception, and interestingly, she is also the only one who, on the one hand, demonstrates the most obvious emotions, and on the other hand, avoids eye contact most of the time with the director-interlocutor off-screen.

Jia mentions the presence of fury and drama (*jilie*) in the over fifty interviews conducted during his field research, but he chose to "cut off all those [parts] and kept only some commonsense (*changshixing*) experiences" (Jia 2009a, 254). In his opinion, while the latter body of information might not appear so theatrically riveting, such commonsense or mundane narrations tend to be more effective in providing "a larger space for imagination onto which [the audience] can project and invest their own experiences." He further states that "this is not an individual case,

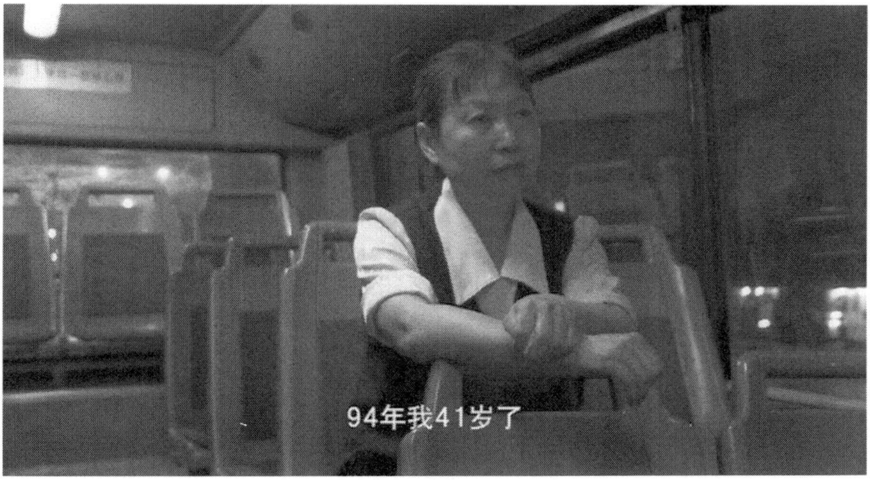

Figure 8.2. 24 City. Hou Lijun, a real former worker at Factory 420.

this is collective memory" (Jia 2009a, 254). Jia's particular working process highlights the subtleties and challenges when collective memory is produced out of individual experiences. In his practice of cutting out and leaving behind the specificities as material unfitting for a particularly conceived narrative, we do not exactly know, for example, how much of the deletion actually accounts for a form of collective memory that might differ from the version Jia distills and crafts in the current film. Jia's drive for a smooth and coherent historical narrative, despite its humanistic intellectual intent, is disturbing in its lack of critical angles that allow visibility to the complications and contradictions often present in the process when individual experiences are woven and written into collective memory and history. In fact, the idea of an essential or accurate single version of collective memory is ultimately a myth.

Interviews of real subjects are selected for their presentation of small but concrete "commonsense" moments of life. The workers' memories tend to take an essayistic form, meandering around details such as a worker's deep appreciation for his tool, a family trip back to Shenyang, and the goodbye party for laid-off workers, which have had an important role in the narrators' lives but do not necessarily give rise to a thematic climax or summary. However, the stories told by the fictional characters have a more complete structure and more definite core of drama that tends to go against the "commonsense" quality that Jia emphasizes: Dali (Lü Liping) loses her eldest child while relocating from Shenyang to Chengdu; for Xiaohua (Joan Chen), the most memorable romantic memory is her falling for the photograph of a dead young man (which particularly stands out since she never marries); Song Weidong (Chen Jianbin) is saved from a beating by the fact that Premier Zhou Enlai has just passed away on the day he runs into the local gang; for Nana (Zhao Tao), her estranged relationship with her parents starts to change from the moment she observes the humble anonymity of a worker's existence embodied by her mother. Despite the absence of clear narrative closure, each fictional narration has a climax or a central message as befits classical narrative structure.

To act convincingly, invariably all the actors enlist realistic behaviors such as coughing, throat clearing, stuttering, repeating, pausing, and in the case of Joan Chen and Zhao Tao, even assuming a deliberately accented Mandarin (with a heavy touch of Shanghainese) or an imitation of the local Sichuan dialect.[2] These acting strategies all mean to communicate a sense of interruption and obstruction in the narration of difficult memories that Jia observed during interviewing workers: "Outside the[ir] narration, when they stopped narrating and fell silent, how many heartrending and spirit-shaking memories were left hidden in the silence. Perhaps those silences are the most important" (Jia 2009a, 6). To further accentuate this sense of dropping off narration and falling in silence, Jia regularly employs "black leader," a technique that uses a strip of undeveloped opaque black film, or black frames in digital editing, to communicate a period of no action. Whereas its use is justified for allowing privacy to the portending emotional breakdown of real subjects such as Hou Lijun, its appearances in the performed narrations are much more arbitrary and even forced. For example, whereas Dali appears obviously articulate through Lü Liping's performance, insertions of black leaders in her narration create a semblance of essayistic remembrance or a suggestion of emotional difficulty, even though the latter effect is not necessarily justified by the content of the performed memory. The distribution of black leaders throughout all the interviews, real or fictional, helps give rise to a deliberately uniform structure of feeling characterized by difficulties of remembrance and fluctuations in the flow of narration.

The deliberate and problematic staging of remembrance is also detectable on the second layer of performance, that of the director himself. Through his own presence off-screen and complicity in narrative construction, Jia enacts yet another strategy in smoothing over the gap between fiction and nonfiction. In the role of an interviewer and interlocutor, he allows his voice to be heard occasionally through a question directed at the interviewees. For example, as Hou Lijun speaks about her parents' relocation from Shenyang to Chengdu in 1958 when Factory 420 had just opened, Jia asks from off-screen, "Do you still remember your trip back to Shenyang?" To this Hou responds with one of the most emotionally charged remembrances in the film, which is about her and her mother's trip to Shenyang in 1972 after fourteen years of separation. However, if this need to make his presence felt as an interlocutor with the interviewee is a normal situation in documentary, its occurrence in the fictional sections—such as asking Dali, "In which year did you enter the factory?" or asking Xiaohua, "What do you mean by 'standard piece' (*biaozhun jian*)?"—can only be understood as a motivation for simulating documentary realism. After all, the fictional narrations and Jia's questions are scripted. Apart from creating a narrative coherence between reality and fiction and reinforcing the historical narrative the director has already conceived and scripted, it is not entirely clear what extra dimensions of knowledge are intended through such a faithful imitation of documentary techniques. It can neither pass as authentic experience for the emotive goal of moving the audience nor achieve an effect of difference and distance for the benefit of critical reflexivity. Other than simulating reality to the effect of reinforcing a heavily controlled and uniformly interpreted structure of feeling—one about sacrifice and loss—the fictional sections in *24 City* beg for stronger reasons to justify themselves.

To be sure, the problem with *24 City* does not lie in its commensuration of fiction and nonfiction. After all, this is a classical practice that has been constantly exercised in the history of both narrative film and documentary. *24 City*'s problem lies in its implicit demand of the viewer to derive a rather uniform structure of feeling from what is essentially a specific choreography of fiction and nonfiction. More specifically, its emotional empathy toward the vicissitudes of the Chinese working class is essentially predicated on the viewer's epistemological acceptance of the historical veracity of all of its materials. This goal conflicts with the very confusion of the sources of information exercised through the genre mix. In such a circumstance, however humanistic the filmmaker's intention is, the resulting viewing experience and audience identification might pose an epistemologically and historically consequential challenge to our truthful understanding of the past.

In a meticulous discussion of the presence of documentary moments in fiction films and our embodied knowledge of what is real and what is not on-screen, Vivian Sobchack differentiates this knowledge as our "documentary consciousness" and "fictional consciousness" (Sobchack 2004, 261, 272–274). For instance, she contemplates the experiential instance when one becomes, often subtly and sometimes suddenly, aware of the implication of real-world existence during the viewing of a fictional film, such as her own realization of the real death of a real rabbit in (and for) Jean Renoir's film classic *Rules of the Game* (1939). On such an occasion, our illusionistic immersion in the representational world (e.g., a fictional film) is both breached and potentially enriched by the "charge of the real" that exudes from the phenomenal world. In other words, our relationship to the representational world on-screen is transformed by a shift from a trusting embrace of fiction to a more (self-)aware "documentary consciousness." In certain extraordinary instances, such as the realization of a rabbit really dying in and for the film that we are watching, this documentary consciousness charges spectatorship with a heightened sense of our implicated responsibility for the watching. While Sobchack's discussion is mainly about the presence of documentary space and consciousness in fictional films, it is of great relevance and significance to our current discussion because of her clarification of the ethically resonant connection between film, spectatorship, cinematic consciousness, and ethical responsibility in the contemporary moving image culture. In the case of *24 City*, while its genre mix offers a salient opportunity for the activation of our documentary consciousness and fictional consciousness, it seems intent, problematically, on cultivating a rather impoverished knowledge and uniform reaction toward the represented past. In this process, the distinction between the two types of cinematic consciousness is first activated but eventually encouraged to disappear and make way for a coherent narrative.

In *24 City*, fiction and nonfiction are systematically tailored and adjusted to move closer to each other. On the one hand, the real interviewees are subjected to directorial manipulation and presented through regular cinematic strategies of framing, mise-en-scène, and editing to give an impression of well-controlled, even tonality. On the other hand, the fictional sections try hard to simulate reality through deliberately naturalistic acting, costumes, and makeup. However, because of the discrete differences innate in these two modes of representation and particularly because of the recognizability of the star actors' faces—at least for a Chinese viewer—one can hardly accept the combination of two obvious jarring modes as an organic, coherent whole.[3] It then makes one ponder what might be their justification other than that of making believe (or evidencing the actors' virtuoso performance as this seems to be an important highlight for the marketing of the film). The reason for such harmonization might lie in the director's desire to produce a *typical* image of the subjects as a working class rather than as unique workers whose personal experiences and independent visions are specifically contingent, therefore not necessarily in good accordance with a master narrative.[4] If the director's goal is historical veracity, his scripting through condensation and rewriting renders it debatable. If his goal is emotional authenticity, the professional rendition of experiences and feelings can only fake it. If his goal is to experiment for greater historiographic accuracy and reflexivity, his many strategies of assimilating documentary and fiction into each other, based on a principle of coherence and smoothness, speak of the opposite. Such a goal would be better achieved through an effect of incongruence and polyphony between the discrete elements.

Overall, the relationship of fiction and nonfiction in *24 City* seems loaded with the director's desire for a particular narrative order. Instead of having the two ontologically different modes of representation enter into a provocative collision and set off the complexity of memory, history, and narrative, *24 City* prioritizes smoothness over incongruence, interpretation over truth, and art over reality. The quotes of poetry by contemporary and historical literary luminaries including William B. Yates, Cao Xueqin, and Ouyang Jianghe further punctuate the film with textual voices that do not belong to the workers. Matching with this disembodied intervention are cinematographic strategies like the use of digital tinting with a nostalgic green color (Jia 2009a, 251, 261) and black leader. Applied regularly and evenly in both real and performed narrations, such strategies allow the fiction to emulate a rhythm found in real narration although devoid of the emotional justification of the latter. The director's desire to present a cinematic equivalent of a sepia-toned, nostalgic portrait of, through, and for the disappearing socialist working class overrides the workers' autonomy over their own lived experiences as conscious historical subjects, thus tending to close off opportunities for personal alternative interpretations.

Throughout the whole film, the parts that contain the least amount of manipulation seem to be the six cinematic portraits of various subjects collected from the time-space of the disappearing Factory 420: workers, their family members, and even peasants hired to demolish the factory. Each of these portraits presents a frontal view of the people, their facial expressions between expressionless and faintly smiling, giving an effect both vague and mysterious. The shots range from medium to medium long, lasting from five to thirty-six seconds. Although it is not clear exactly what instructions they received from the director, the subjects look like they are posing to be photographed, waiting for the camera to finish its job. Many of them make an obvious effort to hold still and maintain a fixed expression. As indicated by psychological research on facial expressions such as a smile, a prolonged length of time in holding an expression tends to make it "difficult to determine if it should be treated as a single expressive event or as more than one event" (Ekman et al. 2005, 205). In the case of these cinematic portraits in *24 City*, the facial expressions, even though mostly neutral and perhaps started as an expressive event in response to the camera, gradually become rendered into more conscious performances because of their unusual prolongation.

While I fully appreciate the ontological significance and poetic historicity of these cinematic portraits, for which ample theoretical support can be found in Roland Barthes' *Camera Lucida* (1982), I contend that their precise meaning needs to be understood within the context of the whole film. Often appearing between establishing or reestablishing shots of the factory (or related spaces) and the fictional sequences, these portraits—ranging from the massive group portrait to family, coworker, or single portrait containing one to three subjects—function like transitions from the spatial to the human, from the general to the specific, and from documentary to fiction. All the four fictional sequences, while preceded by documentary portraits of this kind, also end with their own enactment of similar portraiture complete with more narrative support from a carefully prepared mise-en-scène: Dali eats alone in her humble home; Xiaohua watches on TV the classical 1979 film that bears her (nick)name and that made the current actress Joan Chen into a star; Song holds a basketball, the same game he was playing when his girlfriend broke up with him years ago; and Nana thoughtfully overlooks a misty cityscape of Chengdu. Again, similar to the portraits of the real workers, the facial expressions of these fictional characters look mostly neutral. What purpose might such deliberate imitations serve other than that of enhancing structural balance? If they are meant to evoke a comparable effect of historicity that we find in the portraits of the real people, that would be a significant breach of the epistemological acceptance and emotional empathy of the viewer because these reactions are predicated on a recognition of real time having passed and real experiences having been lived. That essential *real*ity is absent from the current feigned and performed lives on-screen. One wants to feel touched, but at the same time, one feels awkward because we know Lü Liping, who plays Dali, has not lost her child, and Joan Chen is famous and married, etc. In other words, in face of the film's conflation of fiction and nonfiction, the viewer's "documentary consciousness" and "fictional consciousness" (Sobchack 2004) are equally present and active in experiencing the film. Such a mixture of cognitive modes has great potential for exploring the complex dynamic between topics of history such as testimony, memory, and historiography as narrative. However, the current form in which *24 City* organizes the fictional and nonfictional modes of representing reality tends to close off the opportunities for critical thinking it has just opened up. In the case of the two types of cinematic portraits, the film relies on the viewer's documentary consciousness for identification of and consequent compassion for the historical vicissitudes of the workers. Yet the same order of documentary consciousness, when becoming activated in regard to the real-world status of the star actors, presents a (potentially productive) "obstacle" for the viewer's acceptance of the performed sequences as true accounts of history. Whereas such a natural and necessary differentiation between nonfiction and fiction is already present, the imposition of (yet) another round of fiction mimicking nonfiction—such as the performed portraits—seems to demand of the viewer a surprisingly uniform (and forced) historiographical consciousness, asking him to accept the fiction in the same cognitive order and emotional register we often reserve for real history and time. The feel and the fact of time-fullness that the viewer gathers from the cinematic portraits of real subjects are essentially absent from the fictional equivalents rendered by the actors.

A related and telling example is detectable in the ambiguous "ontological status of the cinematic space" (Sobchack 2004, 272) featured in the fictional portraits.

In a slow pan of the camera that moves across Dali's bedroom, we see quotidian traces and objects of a typical worker's home: old furniture, bedding with mismatching colors and designs, an outmoded radio, an alarm clock, and old family picture frames. The panning camera stops on Dali who is watching TV and eating noodles in the kitchen. This is again a curious moment blending fiction and nonfiction. If Dali is an invented textual component of the particular narrative that the director distills and re-creates from field research, what about the "home" this character currently inhabits and its furniture or domestic objects? Given that the introduction of each fictional character including Dali is bracketed in a consistent manner by shots of documentary space—the factory and its living quarters as these are in real life—I would argue that Dali's cinematic home is meant as a collage construct, providing narrative support as setting for the particular character without foregoing its advantage as being suggested as part of the real lived space of Factory 420. But here the director's cinematographic signature—the patient and graceful panning of the camera featured frequently in Jia's films including *In Public, Unknown Pleasures,* and *Still Life*—presents a problem.

In *24 City,* the camera pan is used several times to introduce documentary spaces related to real workers, effectively creating a mood of contemplation and appreciation of the suggested plenitude of time, history, and experience in the lived space of Factory 420. This effect is similar to the power of the portraits of real subjects, as both are justified by the factual knowledge of such lives having been really lived, such time really spent, and such places really occupied as live documents of historical change. When used across the home of Dali, however, the panning shot is trying to suggest the presence of something ontologically nonexistent. The home space and its domestic objects, while possibly a real location with props borrowed from a local worker's home, has not been *real*ly used by Dali because she is not real. This home space belongs neither to the character Dali nor the actress Lü Liping. In the absence of this indexical relationship between reality and representation, which is crucial for our experience and acceptance of the historicity of the nonfictional cinematic image, the insistent panning of the camera turns out to be a performance on the part of the director. It is a faked caressing of endured time and lived life that is not there. The problem lies not so much in the fact of the performance as in the confusion of fiction and nonfiction in order to produce an effect of historicity that can only come from the real. By thus suggesting an "organic" relationship between the two distinct categories of representation, the director orchestrates an echoing effect between fiction and nonfiction. As traces of the encounters between materials of ontologically discrete categories tend to be covered up, the resulting picture of the Chinese working class is indeed both smooth and "superficial."[5]

Ultimately, *24 City* must confront the question of its legitimacy as a historical document of its proclaimed subject. Implementing a number of strategies that craft verisimilitude and subsume the nonfictional in service of a fictional narrative order, the film produces a smooth narrative and a normative collective portrait of the multiple characters and experiences. Though it claims to be a document of the collective memory of the Chinese working class, the current group portrait it produces seems to be closer to the director's vision on this topic than to the worker subjects' own understanding. I deeply respect the film's historical vision and artistic accomplishment in throwing light on an important social body whose experiences in the past few decades are among the most powerful evidence of change in Chinese society. However, I argue that a deeper sense of reflexivity on the implications of documentation and historiography, including baring some of the film's implicit problems despite the filmmaker's good intention, would contribute to a more conscientious attitude to the writing of history. A more considerate and accurate way of representing others, particularly when it involves sensitive experiences such as trauma and loss, would have as its goal maintaining the integrity of the connection between experience, subjectivity, and agency. In such a historiography, the historian or artist would take care to bare his own involvement in the construction of the current historical document, assist the subjects to navigate on their own, travel along with them, and document their journey from the side instead of mapping their experience and drawing a conclusion for them. Although Jia Zhangke acknowledges the significance of the many silences he observed during interviews, *24 City* goes in a different direction. It mobilizes various strategies to simulate or fill out those very silences. The resultant smooth historical narrative about "the Chinese working class" tends to mute the irreducible specificity and rich diversity of the workers as not only connected, but also individual historical subjects.

Art Overwhelmed by Reality in *Tape*

Turning now to *Tape* (2009), directed by Li Ning, a new filmmaker who is also a dancer, choreographer, and director of physical theater, we find a contrasting attempt at navigating the boundary between fiction and nonfiction, performance and documentary. Running through Li's life and work from 2005 to early 2010, this self-portrait video presents another hybrid of portraiture, performance, and documentary, though of a very different nature and temperament. *Tape* shifts regularly between three types of nonfiction: home video, performance documentation, and footage showing Li's actual working process in creating the current video. There are about twenty-four sequences that feature Li's family life, including his interactions with wife, kid, and mother. There are also video recordings of the various rehearsals and site-specific performances enacted by "J Town Body Guerrilla," Li's independent physical theater troupe. Furthermore, we see footage of Li in the middle of editing *Tape* on computer and him vehemently creasing an entangled mass of plastic to create sound effects that we have just heard at an earlier point in *Tape*. Because of its constant shift between these various kinds of material, *Tape* gives the impression of being cyclical and even endless, despite its largely chronological order.[6] While it is apparent that Li tends to arrange the sequences in the order they occurred in real time, the obvious difference and apparent irrelevance of their contents, such as his baby boy being born and his troupe practicing avant-garde physical theater in the street, brings an essayistic logic of organization to replace a conventional narrative impulse. Thematically unruly in texture and tone, the various materials are structured around the filmmaker's subjectivity as well as physicality. What emerges is, on the one hand, a cubistic cinematic portrait of the artist Li Ning, and on the other hand, a video collage of different places, events, and people of the social world to which Li happens to be present, participating and documenting.

Throughout *Tape*, the staging of explicit performance is intimately embedded in the midst of reality. All of Li's physical theater performances are site-specific and take place in real time. For example, two components of a performance project also called *Tape* are staged on busy streets in the actual urban space of Jinan, the capital of Shandong Province. In these performances, Li Ning explores the various physical, emotional, and philosophical qualities of tape, the familiar sticky material used in stationery, postal office, moving service, and other places and occasions that need to connect, mend, seal, and package things. He experiments by transferring the physical quality of tape onto contacts and relationships of all sorts. For example, he has tape put onto and then peeled from his own body. Through choreographed bodily moves staged in real space, members of Li's troupe render typical and often unpleasant relations found in modern existence: careerism, the anonymous urban space and its disorienting traffic, as well as the random but forceful interpersonal relationships found in big cities. A performer dressed like an office lady has her face taped to a laptop. Life-sized photo prints of people are pasted on the streets and run over by city traffic. Performers act like passersby on the sidewalks, run into each other and, once in physical contact, they can no longer break free from each other however hard they try. Stickiness, arbitrariness, and forcefulness are some of the qualities of tape that Li notes while fanning his pregnant wife at the beginning of the video. Apart from these explicit performances, tape also becomes a metaphor of relationship and relevance made possible by technology and media, including Li's current digital video. Through the insistent presence of Li's camera, sometimes to the discomfort of the subjects such as his wife, whatever parts of the social world that become recorded, arbitrarily or purposefully, can be used or, in Li's words, "manipulated" in the creation of "new connections" with others.

In comparison with *24 City,* in which fiction tries to copy nonfiction and the use of performance is driven by a desire for a unified narrative and interpretation, *Tape* seems more interested in baring the boundary between the two modes of representation and exploring the rich dynamic when performance and reality co-occur or even clash. The traces of such coming in contact through the medium of digital video—literally video*taping*—are always visible as well as accountable back to the role of the filmmaker, thus allowing the audience to engage with their own reactions or independent opinions. With Li's person intimately attached to the device, human and technology become an embodied video*tape* that not only makes spontaneous contact with the phenomenal world but also allows contact to be made or elicited between the various visible elements, existences, and phenomena that appear on camera. The DV screen becomes a sticky palette for a collage of life, mixing performance with spontaneity and presenting an almost endless opportunity for interpretation. The resulting video portrait of the filmmaker might look disorderly due to the rich diversity of the materials used and the lack of a singular narrative structure in organizing them. At the same time, this apparent disorder is accompanied by a conscientious unambiguity as to the distinct ontological statuses of fiction and nonfiction, performance and reality. In contrast to *24 City, Tape* mobilizes a much greater diversity of shot compositions as well as arbitrary or even off-putting editing decisions. These strategies are accompanied by a constant exploration in the advantages of the DV technology in evoking effects of "intimacy, immediacy, and weightlessness" made possible by an extremely mobile and embodied camera (Landesman 2008, 42). Together with the rich diversity of the materials, *Tape* creates a roller coaster of a viewing experience during which the viewer constantly needs to adjust his epistemological consciousness in order to figure out his own independent position in the face of this dynamic confusion.

As a video self-portrait, *Tape* definitely has its creator as the constant factor around whose subjectivity the materials gather. However, Li's subjectivity, while evident in his authorial status and his physical presence behind and in front of the camera, is not mobilized as the producer of one particular uniform interpretation. More intriguingly, rather than having authority over the documented subjects and materials, Li's camera tends to become solicited by the referential historical world and is asked to serve as witness of the subjects' own enunciations. In moments like this, uncontrolled events invade representation (including both filmmaking and performance) and almost render the latter superficial and laughable as they reveal reality's own surreal and shocking dimensions. One such sequence happens at the time of the Beijing 2008 Olympic torch relay. Against the sound of TV coverage, Li presents a performance of the torch relay on a site of demolition ruins, a common sight of contemporary urban development in China. We see an almost completely naked Li climbing and crawling on the ruins in front of a crane truck as if being chased by it. This image then cuts to a shot of Li and others doing a sort of primitive ritual and licking their own informal version of an Olympic torch. With an added soundtrack from a sex video that invades the official reportage of the games, the performance of obscene and absurd acts is in deliberate discordant counterpoint to the official spectacle that costs the mobility and visibility of many citizens, including migrant workers, political dissidents, and petitioners. As this scene cuts back to Li's continuing climb on the ruins, as if he were measuring the site with the length of his body, two onlookers intervene and ask Li, "Is this performance art? Do you want to see some real performance? Please go to the other side. The performance there is more infuriating." We next see another side of the place where former residents have put up a banner protesting against the developers' violation of their private property. Li, whose performance has since been interrupted, speaks with a middle-aged man who is sitting next to the ruins. The man is one of the onlookers of Li's earlier crawling. It turns out that the man is a former resident of this place who apparently has been forcefully evicted, like many others, to make room for new housing projects. As their exchange goes on, we learn that the man actually has prepared gasoline for self-immolation, an extreme form of protest used in similar situations in various parts of China. Now the onlooker in the earlier scene turns out to be an activist and "performer" himself, only his kind of performance would completely overshadow Li's artistic gesture because of the macabre seriousness and realness of its contingency. Thus, at the solicitation of those who normally remain as either subjects or background, Li's camera changes from a recorder of the artist's creativity to a witness of larger-than-art life. At such a moment, art, instead of occupying a vantage position and using reality as its source material, finds itself being mirrored and overwhelmed in exceptional dimensions by life. The artist Li Ning and his representational device are brought down to earth, playing the role of a participating witness for reality to come forth in its own most honest, yet also strangest, form.

In another equally powerful moment, Li's camera is even forced to move out of its apparent neutral mode of documenting reality when a subject explicitly demands and directs it to serve as active testimony to her situation. At the time, Li is on a hired videotaping mission by a school that seems to be in the process of closing or relocating. Unexpectedly, we see a scene of violence as a woman—apparently a former employee of the school who comes to seek redress for some matter involving perhaps payment disputes—is being held on the ground by some

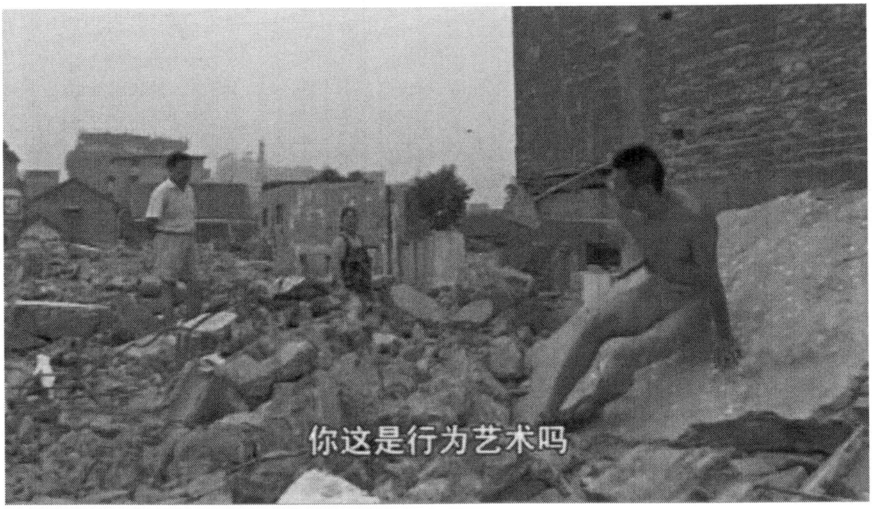

Figure 8.3. *Tape*. Art demanded by reality.

male staff. She screams and kicks to no avail. For a second, because of lack of narrative introduction and the unusual dramatic force of this scene, it appears almost like yet another performance by Li's troupe. Adding to the surreal theatricality of this occurrence is an emptied classroom building on whose walls are painted the phrase "law of the jungle," a relatively outlandish Darwinist hard line that comments quite fittingly on the violent scene taking place on the ground. However, instead of being another project of Li's physical theater, this is, sadly, reality revealing its extreme dimension. Kicking desperately and trying fruitlessly to break free from the powerful grip of the men, the woman calls out at Li's camera: "You film this and you keep it! If you don't, just be careful. . . ." With reality thus bulging forth and requiring the active participation of the filmmaker through the presence of his running camera, the "passive" subject is able to direct and render a video indictment of the current violence and injustice inflicted on her. The fact that Li does include this moment in the final cut of *Tape* evidences her at least partial triumph.

In these sequences, reality, and particularly the filmed subjects, stops serving as raw material for the expressive desire of the artist and take "back" their agency. They present themselves as, if not in full control of the representation, at least recalcitrant and resistant to a completely passive status. Instead of remaining docile beneath the surface of representation, they demonstrate an able agency in the expression, interpretation, and action toward their particular social or historical

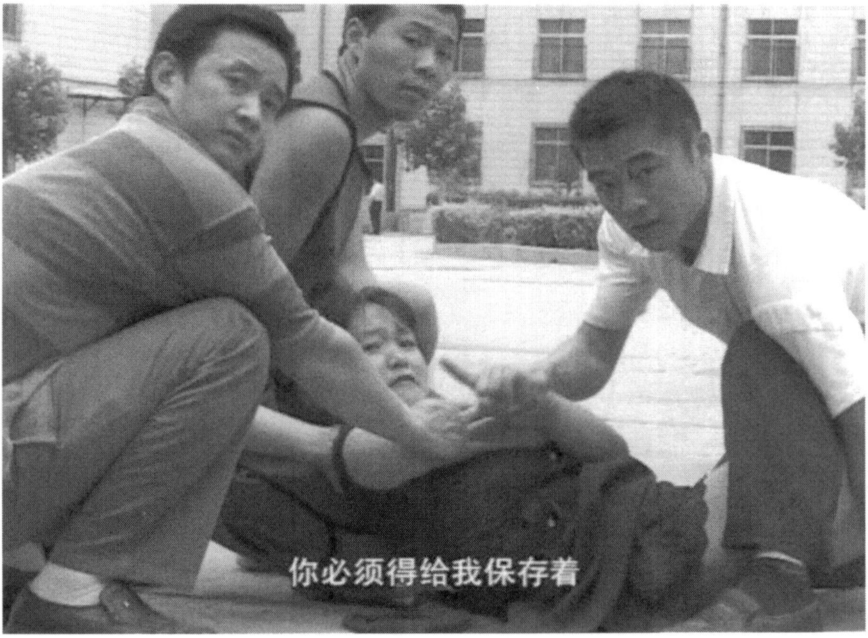

Figure 8.4. *Tape*. Representation interpellated by the filmed subject.

situation. The position of the artist here is both respectful and indispensible because reality is able to demonstrate its powerfully theatrical side exactly through the artist's presence by way of his DV camera as well as performances. Rather than assuming the director's role and having reality at his command (and when he has tried, he shows himself failing to do so), Li constantly tests the validity of representation against reality. On the one hand, his site-specific performances are reliant on the lived space of the social world for their completion and meaning. With exaggerated gestures and a rhythm frequently out of sync with the flow in the surrounding real world, Li's performances are like a distorting mirror, changing the normative dimensions of reality and rendering them both more familiar and more strange. On the other hand, when we are already accustomed to the regular appearance of these performances in the video, reality is able to acquire an effect of augmented theatricality when it unexpectedly stops being background material, comes forth, and demands the camera. As the two abovementioned cases demonstrate, when the local resident of the demolition site and the manhandled woman address Li directly and guide his camera onto their respective real-life scenarios, by extension they also call on the viewer to adjust to an even more active documentary consciousness because now reality speaks for itself.

Neither Li's performance nor his camera is able to maintain a cool, non-involving distance or occupy a vantage point from which to manipulate the phenomenon of the historical world for artistic use. As a matter of fact, the filmmaker becomes so provocatively vulnerable on camera that we even witness another occasion of forceful address, this time communicated through violence directed at Li himself. In what appears to be a hotel lobby, Li is seen wearing from head to toe a futuristic silver costume in preparation for a commercial performance. He starts protesting against the unsolicited attention of an onlooker's camera. The verbal exchange soon gets out of hand into a melee between the two men. Li emerges with a bloody scalp. The onlooker even hits the running camera that is being held by Li's assistant to prevent her from filming. The violent jolt of the camera relays a feeling of being assaulted to the viewer who watches this scene. At such a moment, like the two previous examples, both filmmaker and viewer lose their usual privileged status of being in control and non-involved. Being thus attacked, physically or virtually, they are instead forced into a more intimate, though less comfortable, relationship with the unruly forces in the real world. Rather than plucking what seems fit from the social world and incorporating it into artistic creation, the artist tends to lose control or even "lose face"—as in the words of Wu Wenguang who, with all his own tendency for planting performance in the midst of documentary, unsurprisingly savors such a scene—so that reality will emerge forth from the mundane background and show its most macabre, absurd yet painfully real size.[7]

Compared to Jia Zhangke's propensity for a controlled surface of phenomena in *24 City,* Li Ning's engagement with reality is more subjective, embodied, and allows itself to get out of control and be messed up. As a portrait film, *Tape* allows the filmed subjects to assert their own autonomy, to flesh out their own experience through the presence of the artist's camera as well as his performance. In contrast, *24 City* as a group portrait organizes real experiences into a coherent narrative according to the director's understanding and interpretation, distilling history and reality into a "common" structure of feeling for the audience. Curiously, two instances in *24 City* demonstrate what Walter Benjamin calls the "recalcitrant mystery" of old photography (Phillips 1994, 32). Different from the other interviewees, real or fictional, who all maintain eye contact with the director off-screen during their narrations, Hou Lijun almost never looks at him. In a contemplative pose reminding one of Marilou in *Chronicle of a Summer* (Jean Rouch 1960), where the latter reminisces about her personal experience of Gestapo persecution, Hou either looks down at her own hands or out of the bus window as if she were speaking to herself or to the mystic past itself. The second case of recalcitrance comes from the heartwarming moment of two coworkers who pose for thirty-six seconds in front of the camera. During the long pose, one worker visibly succumbs to his desire for movement, starts to tickle the cheek of his co-worker, amusing them both into smiling. If we envision the whole film of *24 City* as a symbolic and condensed group portrait on which the images of the various interviewees, real and fictional, are juxtaposed with or superimposed onto each other, we would probably see a glossed picture as the overall principle of coherence and smoothness has adjusted and aligned the possible incongruences. However, these two cases of recalcitrance might not be so easily absorbed into this summary group portrait of the Chinese working class. Hou, keeping her gaze away and only in contact with her inner self, and the two anonymous workers enacting gestures and expressions of their own volition would tend to stand out and speak for their own specificity. Although one should not deny the power of the movie camera in eliciting these behaviors, they first and foremost belong to the subjects themselves. They are close to the property that Walter Benjamin sees admiringly in old photographs ". . . of a real person of the past," a property "that does not testify merely to the art of the photographer . . . something that is not to be silenced, something demanding the name of the person who lived then, who even now is still real and will never entirely perish into *art*" (Phillips 1994, 32; Benjamin 1980, 202). It is not entirely clear to what extent such moments of incoherence might be intended by the director, but in contrast to the overall smooth texture of *24 City,* they do point to fissures in the collective narrative composed in the film and rip open a little space for more reflexive engagement with the productive tension between representation and reality. It is, in contrast, such fissures in the hybrid of documentary and performance that provide for the charm and power in Li Ning's *Tape.*

Notes

1. For exemplary critical interventions in this issue, see Leary 2003; Reynaud 2003; Chao 2010; Berry et al. 2010; and Wang 2012 and 2013. Among these, *The New Chinese Documentary Film Movement* (Berry et al. 2010) devotes a total of five articles to this topic (see "Part IV: Between Filmmaker and Subject: Re-creating Realism," 77–96, 157–236). Most recently, this topic was featured in "Just Images: Ethics and Chinese Documentary," a one-day symposium that took place on April 30, 2011, at the Fairbank Center for Chinese Studies, Harvard University (see http://fairbank.fas.harvard.edu/event/documentary-lens-and-chinese-rural-subject).

2. The most obvious trace of professionalism—the perfect Mandarin spoken by Lü Liping despite her otherwise realistic performance—actually becomes an example of incongruence to which Jia admits as an imperfect compromise between realism and professionalism (Jia 2009b, 258–259).

3. It is even more problematic when the film is indeed "coherently" taken as a documentary and the fictional characters successfully pass for real ones. This point is testified by the comment of an American reviewer of an early version of this chapter: Not equipped to immediately identify the stars, she was not aware of the fictional status of the professional performances and instead found those characters "incredibly articulate."

4. Vivian Sobchack (2004, 281–284) provides an illuminating discussion of the subtle distinction between "typical particulars" and "unique particulars" as well as our cinematic experiences of these two concepts. Also relevant, as mentioned by Sobchack, would be the chapter "Generalizing" in *The Language and Logic of Philosophy* (Alexander 1972, 230–256).

5. Jia's artistic exploration of the concept of "surface" deserves a full-length discussion. I provide a study of this concept and its fascinating application in Jia's narrative films elsewhere (Wang 2014, 93–114). For the current discussion, I want to quickly point out some of the relevant references. Jia's admitted infatuation with the surface dates back to *Xiao Wu* (1997): "I don't want the camera to penetrate beneath the surface because when you enter a character's inner world with the camera—I mean the kind of subjective entry—you already start to make interpretations about the character. Nobody has the right to give instructions about other people's life. I hope my film stays on the track of non-involvement. Of course cinema cannot avoid involvement because when you choose to shoot in a certain way you are already involved and start to make decisions of filming what and not filming what. I hope I can restrain myself" ("Jia Zhangke" 1999, cover story). Apparently this attitude of self-discipline through staying at a distance continues into his recent discussion of documentary films:

"In documentary, I feel distance is important as it creates the relationship between the filmmaker and the filmed subject. I always stay at a certain distance, trying my best not to talk or have any relationship to the subject. I rarely use interviews, and keep my camera invisible. This is a matter of aesthetic taste. I feel that the stuff on the surface is very informative. There is no need to get into the concrete details in his life. Those details about his state [of mind], [such as] his creasing his brows, his silence, his smoking, his walking . . . [are enough]. Looking at him from a distance, one can organize his face/look (*mianmao*) through fragments and such an appearance will invite the audience to understand and feel, investing with their own life experiences. This process of mobilization (*diaodong*) is particularly interesting. The images we provide have the power to mobilize others' memories." (Jia 2009a, 242–243)

"The critic Lü Xinyu finds this stand of staying on the surface deliberate and 'limiting' so much so that the director seems to be 'besieged' by it" (Jia 2009a, 258).

6. Writing about portraiture in American avant-garde film and documentary from the seventies, Paul Arthur points out the apparent floating, endless quality of cinematic portraits as a temporal concept: "All portraits struggle to establish some inner logic for beginning and ending that is without recourse to devices of narrative

anticipation or resolution, a struggle in which closure itself is instated as both formal conundrum and biological destiny" (Arthur 2003, 114). *Tape* as Li's self-portrait certainly demonstrates that nonlinear quality, pursuing an order outside narrative. The piece starts with Li in the midst of work (writing down notes on the various qualities of sticky tape) and family life (fanning his pregnant wife at the same time) and ends with Li's apparent submission to the demand of reality by dressing up normally and joining a waiting line at a job market. However, this act of giving up turns out to be perhaps another performance because Li immediately follows it up with a performance—him sitting in an office, pasting his snapshot onto a job application form, and dropping unconscious from the desk—that comments on what a normal professional life might do to him. Therefore, what almost seems like a thematic (and dramatic) conclusion of the film is again rendered relative and ineffective by the performance.

7. Correspondence between Li Ning and Wu Wenguang, http://blog.sina.com.cn/s/blog_539086f70100h1n5.html. Given Wu's own fascination and indefatigable experiment with performance in documentary, it is not surprising to note Wu's excitement over such provocative humiliation of the artist by what he sees as a "hard and cold" real world that never fails to produce extraordinary, "beyond-imagination" real materials for artistic creation. For a discussion of Wu's performative documentary, see Wang (2012).

Bibliography

Alexander, Hubert G. 1972. *The Language and Logic of Philosophy.* Albuquerque: University of New Mexico Press.

Arthur, Paul. 2003. "No Longer Absolute: Portraiture in American Avant-Garde and Documentary Films of the Sixties." In *Rites of Realism: Essays on Corporeal Cinema,* edited by Ivone Margulies, 93–118. Durham, NC: Duke University Press.

Barthes, Roland. 1982. *Camera Lucida: Reflections on Photography.* New York: Hill and Wang.

Benjamin, Walter. 1980. "A Short History of Photography." In *Classic Essays on Photography,* edited by Alan Trachtenberg, 199–217. New Haven, CT: Leete's Island Books.

Berry, Chris, Lü Xinyu, and Lisa Rofel, eds. 2010. *The New Chinese Documentary Film Movement: For the Public Record.* Hong Kong: Hong Kong University Press.

Chao, Shi-yan. 2010. "Performing Gender, Performing Documentary in Post-socialist China." In *As Normal as Possible: Negotiating Sexuality and Gender in Mainland China and Hong Kong,* edited by Yau Chine, 151–175. Hong Kong: Hong Kong University Press.

Ekman, Paul, Wallace V. Friesen, and Maureen O'Sullivan. 2005. "Smiles When Lying." In *What the Face Reveals: Basic and Applied Studies of Spontaneous Expression Using the Facial Action Coding System (FACS),* 2nd ed., edited by Paul Ekman and Erika L. Rosenberg, 201–214.

Jia, Zhangke 贾樟柯. 2009a. *Jia Xiang, 1996–2008: Jia Zhangke Dianying Shouji* 贾想 1996–2008: 贾樟柯电影收集 (Jia's Thoughts, 1996–2008: Jia Zhangke's Notes on Film). Beijing: Peking University Press.

———. 2009b. *Zhongguo gongren fangtan lu: ershisi cheng ji* 中国工人访谈录：二十四成绩 (A Collective Memory of Chinese Working Class: 24 City), Jinan: Shangdong Pictorial Press.

———. 2010. "Building a Public Consciousness: A Conversation with Jia Zhangke." *China Perspectives* 1: 58–64.

"Jia Zhangke: *Pickpocket* Director." 1999. *Beijing Scene Online* 5 (23). http://www.beijingscene.com/V05I023/feature/feature.htm.

Landesman, Ohad. 2008. "In and Out of This World: Digital Video and the Aesthetics of Realism in the New Hybrid Documentary." *Studies in Documentary Film* 2 (1): 33–45.

Leary, Charles. 2003. "Performing Documentary, or Making It to the Other Bank." *Senses of Cinema* (July). http://sensesofcinema.com/2003/feature-articles/performing_documentary/.

Phillips, Sandra S. 1994. "Meditations on the Document." In *Public Information: Desire, Disaster, Document.* San Francisco Museum of Modern Art, 27–37. New York: Art Publishers.

Reynaud, Bérénice. 2003. "Dancing with Myself, Drifting with My Camera: The Emotional Vagabonds of China's New Documentary." *Senses of Cinema* (Oct.). http://sensesofcinema.com/2003/feature-articles/chinas_new_documentary/.

Sobchack, Vivian. 2004. *Carnal Thoughts: Embodiment and Moving Image Culture.* Berkeley and Los Angeles: University of California Press, 2004.

Wang, Qi. 2012. "Performing Documentation: Wu Wenguang and the Performative Turn of New Chinese Documentary." In *A Companion to Chinese Cinema*, edited by Yingjin Zhang, 299–317. New York: Wiley-Blackwell.

———. 2013. "Embodied Visions: Chinese Queer Experimental Documentaries by Shi Tou and Cui Zi'en," *positions: east asia cultures critique* 21 (3): 659–681.

———. 2014. *Memory, Subjectivity, and Independent Chinese Cinema.* Edinburgh: Edinburgh University Press.

White, Hayden. 1973. *Metahistory: The Historical Imagination in Nineteenth-Century Europe.* Baltimore: Johns Hopkins University Press.

CHAPTER 9

Crossing Cameras in China

Christian Aesthetics and Realized Fictions

ANGELA ZITO

> There haven't been any films that deal with this cultural phenomenon, this religious feeling, while these things happen under everybody's nose.
>
> —Gan Xiao'er

The films of director Gan Xiao'er are the first narrative features to take up Chinese Christians in their everyday concerns. This chapter discusses a pair of his films, one a fiction feature, the other a documentary made about taking that feature on the road and showing it in churches. It is about filmmaking practice—and especially documentary—as social occasion, as the concatenation between people of self-reflective moments of cultural creativity and critique. By social occasion, I mean that Gan has documented in the second film the moments of self-conscious "participation" in the fiction feature and in the documentary itself. Thinking of his work as creative of social occasions makes it particularly susceptible to forms of analysis honed in anthropology through ethnography.

As is typical in ethnographical analysis, the specific, the local, the small is taken up in order to illuminate larger issues. As is also usual in writing based on ethnographic encounter (and in this case, *about* encounters that are quite ethnographic themselves, Gan's relationship with his films' subjects), I will use personal interview material, mimicking in this text the empirical bias fundamental to documentary-as-social-occasion. However, besides the emphasis on encounter and performance in the acts of making, this chapter also discusses the video product itself, the films, as the objectified precipitate of this ongoing process, taking us into the realm of its aesthetic particulars.

Gan's pair of films were both shot in digital video. The fiction feature, *Raised from Dust* (*Juzi chentu* 2007), uses mostly members of the religious community as actors. Gan's documentary, *Church Cinema* (*Jiaotang dianying* 2008), intercuts a chronicle of screenings of *Raised from Dust* with extensive postproduction discussion about the community's participation in making the feature.[1] In it we see the sense of ownership various church members developed about the original project. Gan mobilizes from within the interest of the community in seeing itself represented in various ways—thus inciting and securing the community's participation. We see in his work an example of the shift in general in documentary making from representation to recording impulses of self-reflexive participation (Nichols 1994; MacDougall 1998). In turn, once the bounds of "objectivity" are breached by filmmakers stepping into the lens and subjects talking back to it, considerations of aesthetics come into play across the board—at issue in Gan's fiction feature and discussed at length in his documentary. Gan successfully challenges the boundary between scripted fiction feature and what Bill Nichols would call "sober documentary," with its automatic claim on unvarnished, direct truth.[2]

Gan's films provide a rich case for investigation because of the differing aesthetic positions taken up in the materialization of this project: the community argued that more mobilization of feeling would enhance the fiction feature, whose purpose was, according to them, to spread the gospel. Although he was himself a member of the church, Gan differed, intent on pursuing his own agenda as writer and director with a modernist art-house sensibility. Their differing aesthetic regards point to differences of urban/rural sensibilities and of class distinctions of education, but also to a division within Protestant sensibilities about "sensibilities" themselves. Gan's restraint about what can be "shown" contrasts with his fellow congregants' affective enthusiasm about "liveness." I have been thinking about their differences as less contradictory and more as examples of how the dialectical mediation of social life requires, in fact, just such distinct moments of emphasis on objectifications in contrast with liveness /performance. In short, their differing investments in what Ilona Hongisto, borrowing from Gilles Deleuze, calls "fabulation," or self-conscious myth making, point us to interesting conclusions about documentary in general and in China today (Hongisto 2011b).

Of Christians in China

Being Christian in China has become more complex and interesting beyond the ever-present matter of dealing with the state in your religious business. Catholics and Protestants in China have parallel histories. Both originated in outside missionary activity from Europe and North America, both were enfolded into the

Chinese state via governing bureaus after the success of the Communist-led revolution in 1949, and both suffered splits within their own ranks as many refused to join up with the Three-Self Patriotic Movement (TSPM)[3] and went underground. The Catholics went into secret parishes that maintained tenuous connection with Rome, refusing to recognize state-sanctioned bishops ordained in China; the Protestants into "House Churches" or *jiating jiaohui.* All such churches are considered illegal and must meet quietly, often secretly, in people's homes. There are five large House Church systems in China, mostly rural in location, four in Henan and one in Anhui (Qi 2009, 92). This simple formula of mostly rural and very different from the TSPM state churches has become more complex. House Church life in the cities has developed and gone more public[4] with the rising urban middle class providing a widening pool for conversion.[5]

Gan Xiao'er has attended urban house churches since he left his small country town. But the churches you will see in his films are not "underground"; they are registered with the state's Bureau of Religious Affairs and are open and legal TSPM churches. However, their liturgical and theological sensibilities are saturated with the underground house churches that began in Henan, where Gan's films are located. He estimates that about 15 percent of his hometown population is Christian (Kwok 2007). Religious groups in China play an elaborate hide and seek, "now you see me, now you don't" high-stakes game with the state. Falungong lost that game; Christians are only getting started.

Of Chinese Independent Documentary

> [There is a] move away from attempts to speak from mind to mind, in the discourse of scientific sobriety, and toward a politics and epistemology of experience spoken from body to body.
>
> —Nichols (1994, 82)

The Chinese independent documentary makers who took their start after Tiananmen in 1989 have cultivated a style of watching closely, allowing things to unfold at a leisurely pace before the lens, a style that has been called "direct cinema" and that, in the land of performative films by people like Michael Moore, seems quaintly retro.[6]

However, this direct gaze does not naively serve up simple "objectivity" in the sense of letting events speak for themselves. Neither is it about an absence of subjective feeling. So what might look like direct cinema's wish to find a kind of objectivity in a realism that's treated as scientifically drained of subjective taint (what Nichols criticizes) remains more complicated for Chinese filmmakers.[7] If "reality" is being invited to speak up and have a voice, this invitation must be understood in the context of the major competing voice this new "reality" might possibly encounter. For filmmakers, that unwelcome voice would be emanating from state-run, mainstream media in its many forms. Their quiet gaze acts as more of a ground-clearing gesture, a preemptive announcement of neutrality that nonetheless, in their context, carries more political heft than Wiseman's.[8]

Yet, coming from a tradition deep within the demands of building socialism through media forms of TV, film, and radio, all in control of the Communist Party, many filmmakers gained their technical chops in those same venues, and some still work for them (Johnson 2006, 51–52; Lin Xu-dong 2004). Many more of them now graduate from state-run college and university media and film departments. These filmmakers nonetheless continue to plant themselves in the outside world, turning away from those familiar institutions as much as they can. The world they wish to see—and thus invite viewers to reimagine—is felt and constructed beyond the gaze of the state, as a kind of newly neutral territory.

Once their (aesthetic) ground is defended against the state's tropes of voice-over, scripted action, and added-in music to cue emotion, this neutral territory is found to be waiting to be infused with a new feeling. What do they hope will arrive in this objectified space? I'd venture it is new subjects in all senses of that word.

In front of the lens, filmmakers find subjects to shoot in the territory beyond the state's gaze by usually concentrating on the marginalized, the neglected, the overlooked, the willfully ignored, or the uncategorizable.[9] This choice has often brought down on them criticism for showing only misery and corruption—for airing dirty national laundry and pandering to foreign voyeuristic curiosity. Yet it has also enlarged the map of social life in China, making visible and available for historical archiving people's lives heretofore neglected or prettified by mainstream media (whether censored by politics or the market).

And what of the subjects behind the lens? What are filmmakers becoming themselves? Making a movie often changes them, reworks their own subjectivities, as much as it changes the subjects they shoot. Thus, instead of subject versus object, what we have is a matter of "intersubjectivity" (Wang 2010; Zito 2014). Scholar Paola Voci says of documentary in China today: "*Authenticity* is better described as the subjective *striving to achieve* truthful representations of reality than the objective claim of capturing and explaining the only true meaning of reality" (italics mine, Voci 2004, 103). These realities are presented as implicitly shared and intersubjectively produced, rather like the "social subjectivity" that Bill Nichols discusses in *Blurred Boundaries*.[10] I would amplify Voci's point by venturing that Chinese filmmakers have begun spending more effort documenting their own "striving" at the social process of production, making those scenes an ever more important and integral part of filming the social world around them.

Thus, one fresh thing in Chinese documentary is how it brilliantly works through, and contributes by its uses of social subjectivity to, a current shift in documentary in general from "representation" as the major trope to an impulse of "participation." This self-reflexive effort is still harnessed to an old documentary rhetorical imperative: its ability to persuade people that what they are seeing/hearing is so important that audiences might change their minds or take action. Or, as Sarah Elder puts it, respond to the empathy created by the documentary (Elder 1995).[11] However, nowadays, films marshal not only the rhetoric of evidential representations; they also tend to display the filmmakers' own sincerity and tactics on-screen. The rise of first-person video, directly related to portable camcorder availability, filled the U.S. documentary scene from the mid-1980s until now (Aufderheide 1995, 1997; Sherman 2007). Such films thus reveal that the first level of persuasion of authenticity occurs for the people making the film, and that we might participate in their transformation as we watch it happening, as they strive to achieve their truthful representation. It is, as it were, the thoughtful effort that has begun to count with audiences as much, or more than, the evidence. Or, to put it another way, the evidence of their effort, and of the filmmaker's sincere emotion, is as important as any other evidence.

New Chinese documentary,[12] since its inception in the early 1990s, has often been highly collaborative in its social production, which interferes with an automatic sense of auteur representational authority. Instead of filmmakers automatically claiming, or being given, full control over what is going to be represented on the screen, subjects often seek filmmakers to shoot them. For example, we have the family documented by Zhang Yuan in *Sons* (1996); Zhang Zanbo's classmate-turned-local-official in his film *The Interceptor from My Hometown* (2011); or sometimes the subjects themselves picking up a camera during the production and contributing their own footage, as in Ou Ning's *Meishi jie* (2006).

Gan Xiao'er's films fully exploit this turn to participatory, performative style at the level of production and consumption in their combination of fiction and documentary feature films: the narrative film *Raised from Dust* is the second in a projected series of seven narrative films around Christian themes, through which Gan hopes to illuminate a Chinese life of the spirit (Gan, interview, June 2007). After its completion, Gan took *Raised from Dust* on the road in Henan and showed it "at about 10 sites, only one of which was in a house, the others all churches. Roughly about 4000 people saw the film, and we got forms filled out by over 1000, and filmed their opinions and feelings. The crew altogether shot about 80 hours of footage, and collected 1000 photos" (personal communication, Sept. 7, 2007). The resulting documentary, taken together with the feature film, provides a pioneering glimpse of a post-Reform community of Christians in Henan using film to mediate itself to itself and to the world. That effort, thanks to Christian aesthetics that emphasize media to spread the gospel, actually takes us even further, where representation becomes a form of participation itself in a wider world.

A Story "Uncovering Itself": *Raised from Dust* and Representation

> I think this fiction film can function as a documentary film that records the lives of Chinese peasants nowadays, and their Christian lives. The story uncovers itself as it develops.
>
> —Gan Xiao'er, director's statement

Gan graduated from the Beijing Film Academy's Literary/Critical Department, where he majored in film theory and turned to actual production after graduation. In this unorthodox route he was preceded by the director Jia Zhangke. Gan was born in 1970, in Henan Province, Xinxiang township, in Qiyiling—the village made famous by Mao's pronouncement in 1958 that "Communes are good!" He returned there to shoot *Raised from Dust.* His great-uncle had studied with missionaries and passed on the gospel to Gan's father, but Gan himself did not convert until his father's death in 1997.

> My father's liver illness lasted for 18 years. My mother nursed him continually until there was no hope. By the end he could not move, but they were singing praise hymns together, him trying to raise himself up because he felt it not proper to sing lying down. It was wrenching. Suddenly I saw my parents in a completely different light—as though they were strangers. My mother offered up my father's life to God, right in front of me. I had to rethink my own relationship to them—and it was then that I realized this was a wonderful religion. (Gan, interview, June 2007)

An illness lovingly nursed forms the plot for *Raised from Dust.* A young woman's husband lies dying of silicosis in a hospital, in a freezing corridor because the family is so poor.

We follow Xiaoli as she rides her three-wheeler around the village, scavenging for bricks and coal, to-and-fro carrying meals to her desperately ill husband, helped by her sunny, young daughter whose school fees are hanging hostage alongside the hospital bills. Xiaoli is Christian, and her life in the church band and choir forms the counterpoint to her desperate poverty. Her husband is finally released into her care in a wrenching scene where the medical team helps load him into the back of the tricycle on his quilt, putting his shoes on at the last, as his feet dangle over the edge. He gasps without his oxygen tank. The sound of his painful,

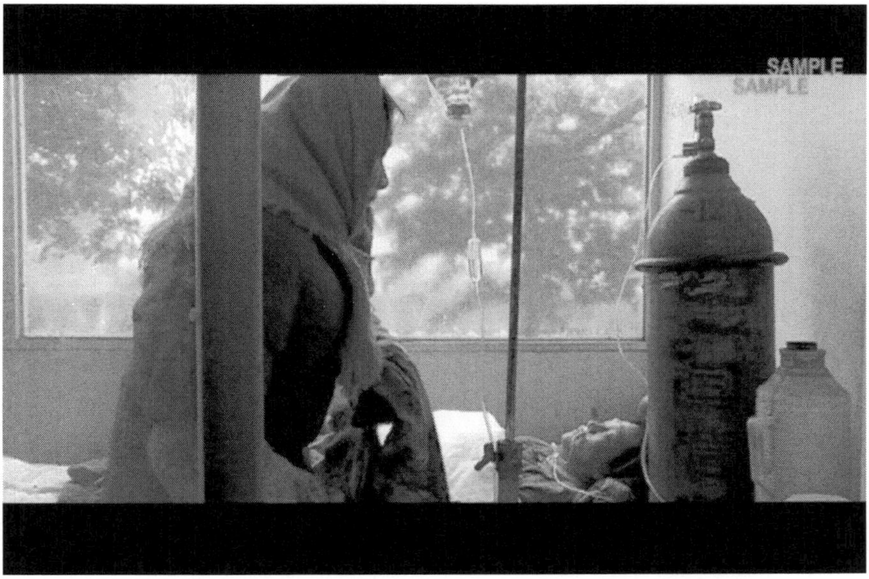

Figure 9.1. *Raised from Dust*. Xiao Li visiting her husband, who is dying from lung disease in the hospital.

labored breathing cuts out as the camera's point of view shifts to the barren ground. Suddenly, the frame silently fills with Xiaoli's smiling face; it is spring, she carries a pink paper flower. Her husband is driving the tricycle—she is being carried. They are joyful in a silence finally broken by the wheel rumbling along the hard, cold ground, seen from above. The very next scene shows that ground being dug up by several of the village men—it is a grave, her husband's grave.

Let us backtrack.

The film opens mysteriously with a fixed, wide shot of two men whom we slowly realize are surveying the flat land. We learn a railroad will be coming through, and people begin rushing to build structures so that the government will be forced to pay them off to demolish them. The final scene takes us out to the same fields, where people are still building the rickety fake structure. Xiaoli is still delivering the bricks that will ultimately return to rubble. We hear faintly a faraway train. This is the only hint of the presence of the state as outside presence, a framed disavowal that makes way for the institution that Gan is most interested in capturing in this film—the Christian community and its large church.[13]

When the state does appear, it is borne in the conversations and prayers of the members. At several junctures, they are led in public prayer for the nation and

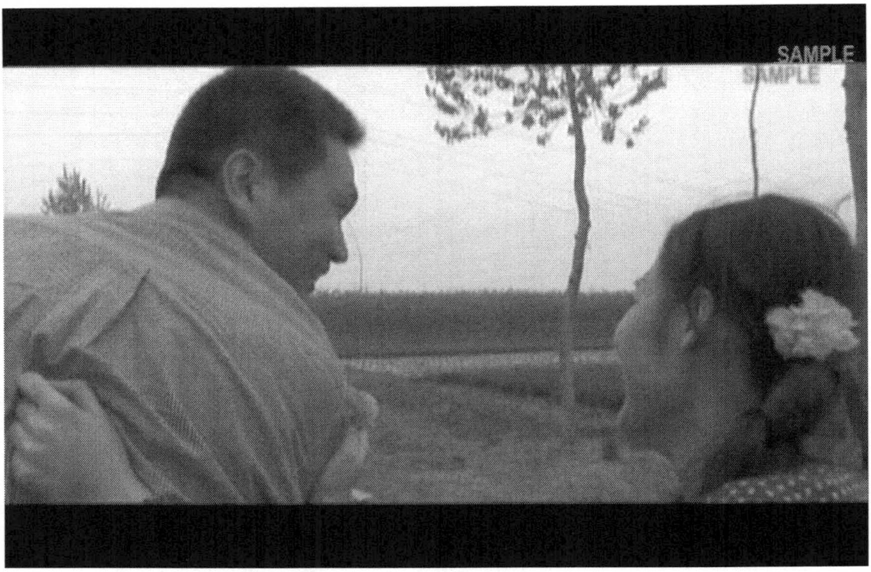

Figure 9.2. Raised from Dust. Xiao Li's memory of riding home with her young husband after the wedding.

its leaders. Xiaoli is a member of the choir (*changshiban*), which is accompanied by a muscular, Salvation Army–style brass drum and bugle corps complete with uniforms. An old drummer explains that, though they call it a choir, outsiders will not understand this term. So he recommends calling it a "propaganda team." "Right," pipes in the choir leader. "A propaganda team for Jesus." Laughter all round, as the drummer breaks into song. In this moment, two things become evident: first, that Gan is shooting his fiction feature deliberately in an improvised documentary style, sweeping up commentary on details of Christian life, and second, that everyday life accommodates multiple tropes for action on the part of its subjects, both Christian and communist/socialist.

Gan used only two professional actors in the film: Hu Shuli performed the role of Xiaoli and Zhang Xianmin the role of her husband. Everyone else played roles close to their own lives, as the later documentary shows at length. In this choice, Gan follows a long line of independent filmmakers, including Jia Zhangke who used amateurs in his first, pathbreaking narrative feature, *Xiao Wu* (Wu 2000, 194–198). Gan said of his own films' *jishi fengge* style,[14] "Documentaries and narrative films both share 'documenting.' What we call fiction is also a form of 'documenting' [*jiu shuo fiction ye shi zai jilu*]" (Gan, interview, June 2007, English in original).

Scholars and critics have noted this bleed between fiction and documentary in Chinese independent film (Zhang Zhen 2010; 2007, 3, 7, 17). Gan has compared *Raised from Dust* to Jia Zhangke's fiction feature *Still Life* (*Sanxia haoren* 2006). Before Zhang made *Still Life,* there was a documentary by Li Yifan about the Three Gorges Dam project that highlighted its destructive dislocation of people: *Before the Flood* (*Yanmo* 2005). But according to Gan, Jia Zhangke's feature film was much better known; only a fraction of Jia's audience numbers would ever see, or even hear of, *Before the Flood.* So if we are talking about the documentary mission of empathetically moving people to grasp a social critical point, or even to feel that they have participated in an authentic effort to provide an experience of some particular reality, then according to Gan, Jia's fiction feature will go further in fulfilling that function. In this way, Gan feels that the gap and difference between fiction feature and documentary is easily broached.

Gan thinks he and Jia used similar methods: "[There is a] using of fiction feature as documentary. Both stories are boring. The films are definitely not about telling you a story. They are about documenting the bigger things . . . in my case I wanted to document the larger background. Storyline is like a melody, but the background provides the structure. These films are about structure" (Gan, interview, June 2007).

Gan's slow camera and spare dialogue present us with a sideways, almost diffident narrative. The camera is used with indirection, like an eye that restlessly cannot take in all it sees yet remains coolly engaged. Gan himself performs a role as the returning bridegroom that locates him inside the film as a participating element, a piece of the whole that he is trying to glimpse. Gan also starred in his first film, *The Only Sons* (2002), as the fictional protagonist, but the biographical nature of his role in *Raised from Dust* brings it closer to a docudrama sensibility. The film treads between improvisation and tight directorial control—and certain aspects of how affect was used and portrayed became a source of debate between Gan and his local "actors."

Perception and Feeling: Church Cinema as Participation

> Every time I face this subject, I know perception is secondary. I just trust my feelings.
>
> —Gan, director's statement, *Raised from Dust*

In 2007, Gan committed himself and a small crew to building a grassroots audience and exposing more people to his feature film by taking it on the road. I have already noted the shift from representation to participation as key to understanding current documentary. This participation takes place in several ways: between the filmmaker and the subjects of the film; among the subjects of the film; between the audience and the film; among the audience members. In other words, the heretofore hierarchized interaction between auteur/maker and subject, along with spectacular, representational film and audience, is intercut with horizontal forms of participation. His documentary of the screening road trip, *Church Cinema,* is replete with examples of this mixture of participatory agendas as it displays at its heart the feature film process that brought the community together. Gan appears on-screen in both the feature and the documentary alongside the community that provides context, actors, and eventually the audience for both projects.

Gan's documentary accomplished several things. First, he used the occasion of *Raised from Dust* to introduce some of its cast in person, in their lives as Christians—we are introduced to them in their film roles through quick clips first, and then we follow them into their daily lives where they talk theology, religious commitment, and church politics while going about their business feeding pigs, playing mahjong, or eating dinner. Second, we see the film being shown in the very church where it was shot; the church that served as the set for the film now becomes a cinema, but an unusual one, where watching the film is a religious act. After we see the screen raised and the projector being set up by Gan and his star

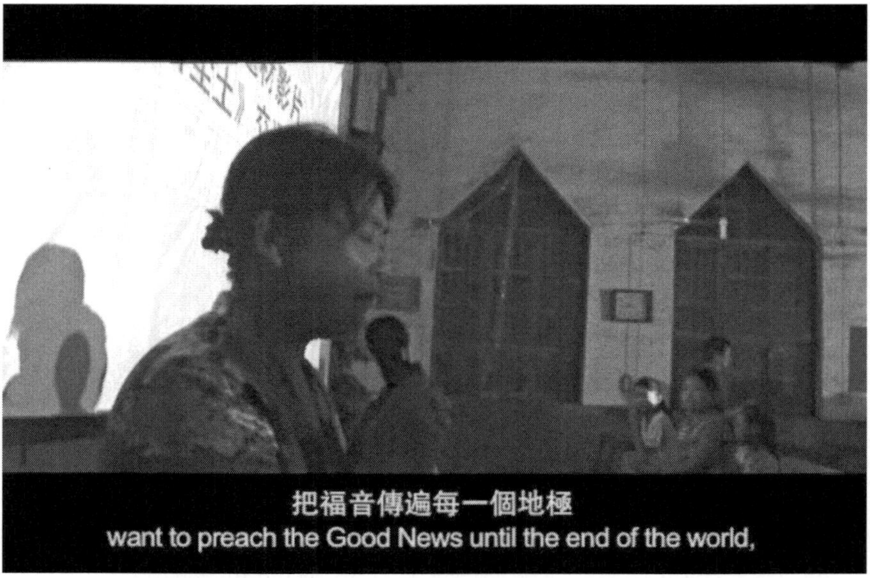

Figure 9.3. Church Cinema. A thankful exhortation to go forth and preach in the wake of Gan's feature film release.

Zhang Xianmin, we cut to a panning shot of the congregation, each person praying aloud with eyes closed. Then a member leads a public prayer in which God is thanked for having answered their entreaties. She declares that "in their hearts each brother and sister is willing to preach the Gospel," providing a list of media that includes everything but the Internet: newspapers, magazines, TV, and movies. We begin to suspect that their notion of what the fiction feature was designed to do might differ from Gan's.

This suspicion proves true in a long scene where the members discuss and criticize *Raised from Dust*. Their passionate engagement of the process and the final product reveals how deeply invested they are. The discussion raises sharp aesthetic differences between the director and the church members—who often refer to the film as *zamende dianying*, "our film." Gan sits at the table with them.

One woman worries that non-Christians will not understand, feeling that the film is very particular, which contrasts with Gan's universalizing ambition of showing Christians as Chinese people. Then the woman beside her bluntly says that he did not succeed in his mission of documentation. She says that "real life was not embodied forth." Frankly, I thought he succeeded richly at this goal, but began to realize that her definition of "real life" is not a material one. When she says, "He didn't show how Christians live . . . ," the problem seems to be a failure at depicting a Christian *ethical* life. She accused him of ambiguity in staging the husband's death, and she was also confused by the silent, joyful scene on the way back: Only slowly did she realize it was memory. Then someone else interjected that music was needed and a veritable clamor for music is heard around the table—"music and spoken parts." The first woman actually reminds Gan that "this is not a documentary [using the old state TV term *zhuanti pian*] and as a feature film it needs a musical atmosphere. Even if you are preaching the good news [which seems to suggest that she thinks that is the movie's point] you can add hymns."

Following the yearning for music comes the yearning for more indications of feeling—Xiaoli's heart is breaking with her husband's dying, and what she needs, as a Christian, is words of God or an inspirational poem or someone singing to her. This drive to melodrama is certainly anathema to Gan, who is in the scene taking notes, lips literally sealed. It casts his opening remarks (as quoted above) in an ironic light: To what feelings in himself is he turning? I'd venture they are artistic sensibilities, not Christian urges to evangelize.

In a series of interviews we conducted in New York City in February 2008, Gan talked about the relationship between religion and art for himself as a filmmaker. He noted that, although he found art before Jesus, it was his religious commitment that eventually formed his own artistic direction. In China, Christian filmmakers are very rare. Even as he hungers to find a way to represent the

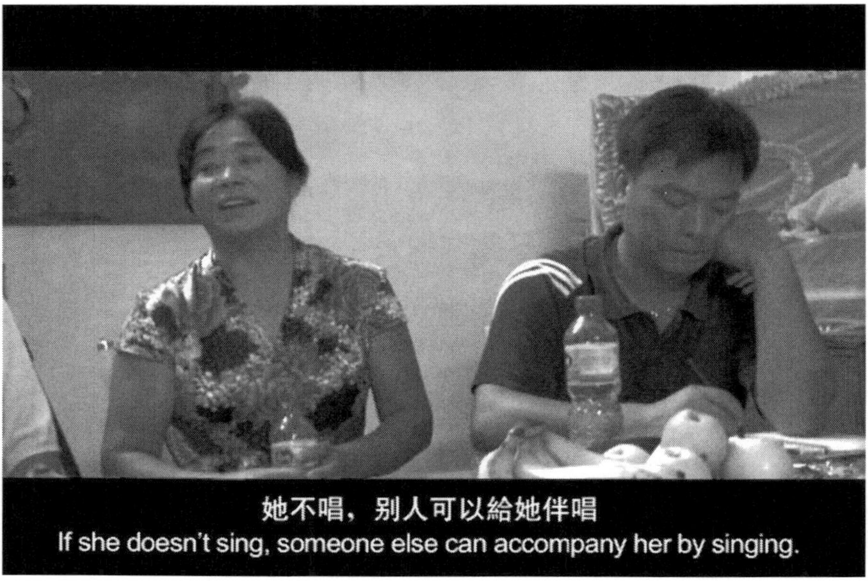

Figure 9.4. Church Cinema. Meeting of his church community with Gan (on right), discussing how his film *Raised from Dust* might have been improved.

nature of spirituality in his films, he finds himself on unfamiliar ground. Loving Bergman's films, he at first thought that he would have the heroine of *Raised from Dust* say nothing beyond the occasional "Praise the Lord!"

> But when we actually started shooting, we realized that was wrong! In China, when someone comes to your home, you must speak to them. Otherwise, it would be impolite. I see Europeans films where people can refuse to speak and no one thinks it strange. But in China, if you don't talk, people think it really weird. This is quite serious. As I said, Chinese films have not yet found a way to express the nature of spirituality, not a good way. Silence is not a method; at first I thought, not letting them speak was good. I wanted to make a quiet, very interior thing, and I could not figure out a better way.
>
> (interview, Feb. 25, part two, 2008)

This sense of interiority seems to be a key component for Gan in understanding people's relationship to God—he pointed out that, lacking as it does a theological tradition, Chinese films are replete with stories about relationships among people, but none about humanity's relationship with deity. In that craving for silence and quiet we find Gan's aesthetic most at odds with the collective enthusiasm of his fellow congregants. He laid it out in terms of historical contingency:

> I have to say that the reason I am not "crazier" about religion is mostly because all the historical experience of New China has been of a sort of special "crazy fanaticism." [The term here is *kuangre,* which means mad, crazy, wild, unrestrained, with overtones of arrogance, hence a favorite translation of "fanaticism."] And that situation made us very resistant toward such craziness, very resistant. Which seems quite reasonable.
>
> (interview, Feb. 25, part two, 2008)

He used the Chinese term *kezhi* ("restrained") to describe not only his own directorial style, but even his personal demeanor:

> And showing feeling was like that: If you liked someone, you would not be especially fanatical. Everything was done in a whisper. The entirety of historical experience of that period influenced people of my cohort this way. When we watched films as kids, and a person died, there was always someone wailing, "Oh, Mama . . . Mama. . . ." That sort of expression is unbearable; not bad per se because sometimes they are necessary. But we cannot produce them!

Instead, Gan hopes to "express the nature of religion, spirituality and emotion through the trembling body and the peaceful heart"—an aesthetic of restraint, not melodrama. He noted ruefully that his film suffered criticism for not being more intense (*jilie*) and passionate (*jiqing*).

In this context, Gan brought up Yuan Zhiming, the eventual producer and director of a highly melodramatic testimonial documentary *The Cross: Jesus in China.* Yuan's initial reactions to enthusiastic Christianity in Princeton after he fled to America following the Tiananmen incident of 1989 were, according to Gan, emblematic of intellectuals' attitudes: "He went to a service and everyone was holding a little book—wasn't this just like Mao's sayings? And they were singing from it, and using its own words to understand it? Hadn't we been struggling mightily to get past this kind of thing? What were the Americans doing?" Even more importantly, Gan felt that many people in his cohort (he was born in 1970), artists and directors, living as they have with the results of political excess even if they were not participants, now tend to shy from "fanaticism" or "obsessiveness," being very restrained in their emotional expression.

But melodrama is precisely what Gan's critics featured in the documentary *Church Cinema* seem to want. And we can turn to Yuan Zhiming's tour-de-force of the genre for a glimpse of that aesthetic. *The Cross: Jesus in China* is a famous

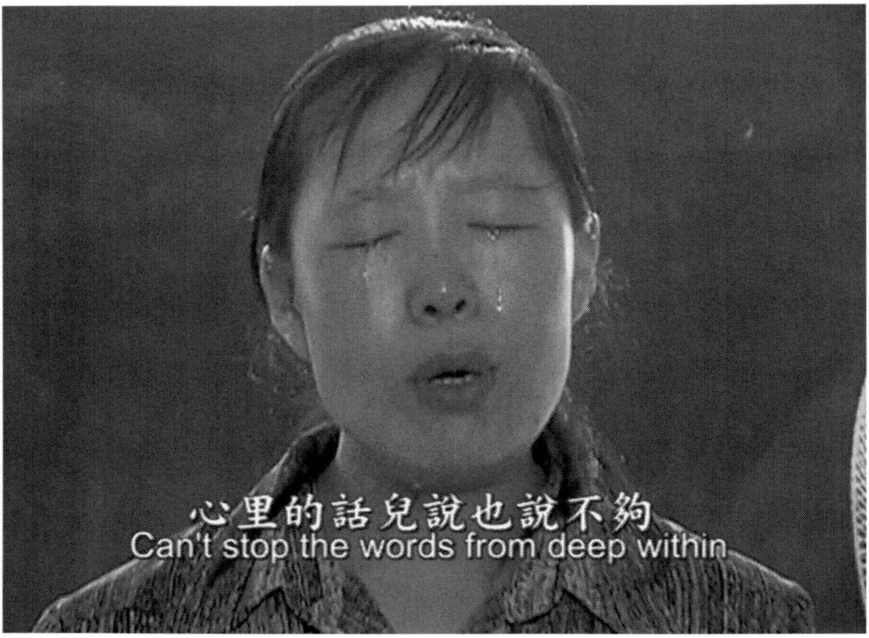

Figure 9.5. The Cross: Jesus in China: Part 3, The Bitter Cup. Choral music swelling in the background provides the soundtrack for close-ups.

Christian four-video set that has been circulating underground in China on DVD since it was made in 2003 by Chinese in exile.[15] It provides a history of Protestant missionary churches in China, along with the current state of the underground House Church movement. It is full of witnessing for the Lord through stories of conversion and trials in prison. Every so often the interviewing and voice-over narration is interrupted by hymns and extreme displays of emotion.

In a report in the *China Soul* newsletter, Pastor Yuan writes of how extraordinary people find the video: "We have received countless letters and emails, and the most common phrase we see is: 'It is just too moving! We cried straight through to the end!' In Europe and North America at tens of screening venues, thousands of people have come forward to witness for Christ, hundreds giving their bodies to the Way." On the mainland, people are warned to bring hankies: "Countless numbers of copies of *The Cross* are spreading across China. Christians that are spread across China in all four directions crowd themselves into homes for a first viewing. In some villages they stop the film while people sop their tears, and then resume the screening" (Yuan 2004).

I suspect that is more what Gan's critics had in mind—the tears, the emotional excess, the music, all call forth a response in the viewer that is involving in its intensity. These DVDs circulate as encouraged piracy in China. "People have made thousands of copies of [the first of the four DVDs] "Springs of Life" and passed them out on the street, at curbsides, in markets . . . No wonder *The Cross* has sparked a preaching movement on the mainland, a renaissance in the Churches" (Yuan 2004).

The DVDs also act as fund-raisers and prods to piety among evangelical groups abroad, such as the Voice of the Martyrs. "*The Cross* incites our Brothers and Sisters in America and elsewhere, and as more [DVDs] of the English versions of the film are produced, more translation versions are being made including the eight languages of Europe, Arabic, Korean, and Japanese—all done by volunteers and most nearly finished" (Yuan 2004).

We are left to contrast Gan's wish to make a film that would function more as a restrained, representational, and objectified artistic text with the congregation's wish to create something more like pretext for melodramatic feeling and action. I am reminded of a useful distinction David Morgan draws in his book *Visual Piety: A History and Theory of Popular Religious Images*. Morgan muses that Warner Sallman's immensely popular, and very sweet, head of Christ can never be taken as "high art" because it fails the test of what he calls an "aesthetic of disinterestedness" or "beauty characterized by a non-instrumental enjoyment . . . that incites no desire for a thing, but enjoys only its representation in the mind." Instead, he notes that "a popular response to images often merges form and physical existence, representation and object, in order to experience the presence of Jesus himself" (Morgan 1998, 26). In the case of *Raised from Dust,* I would amend that formula to say that the congregation longed "to experience the presence of another Christian experience."

In Conclusion: Tarkovsky Says

> How does time make itself felt in a shot? It becomes tangible when you sense something significant, truthful, going on beyond the events on the screen; when you realize, quite consciously, that what you see in the frame is not limited to the visual depiction, but is a pointer to something stretching out beyond the frame to infinity; a pointer to life.
>
> —Andrei Tarkovsky, *Sculpting in Time* (1989, 117–118)

As we noted, other filmmakers in China (and elsewhere to be sure) experiment with the boundary between documentary and fiction narratives. Such blurring has been a signature move of Jia Zhangke who, while making *Still Life,* his brilliant feature about several dislocated by the Yangtze River dam project, also shot a documentary in the same location (Kraicer 2007; McGrath 2008). The documentary was about the artist Liu Xiaodong (entitled *Dong* [2006], it was packaged together with *Still Life* for DVD sale). Jia and Gan share the ongoing formation of a self-reflexive, participatory, and performative cinema aesthetic, but use it for quite different ends. Both projects, literally, represent collaborations, but they have different consequences in how they point to the world outside the screen. Rather than sharing the project as an artist within his own community (the case with Gan), Jia and Liu share a project as two artists. In Jia's documentary we notice that one of his favorite actors, who played the worker protagonist in *Still Life,* casually joins the actual workers posing in their underwear for the painter Liu. But in Gan's project, people step into the fiction film from their lived world, embodying a kind of imaginative extension of everyday life in a specific intention of Christian mission projected into this artistic form. In Jia's documentary, an actor joins the people; in Gan's feature, real people act.

Jia Zhangke's projects still hew closely to older, non-digital forms of cinema: tightly controlled by his directorial vision, the performative aspects are relegated to a kind of art-circle in-joke. In Gan's double project, I see a form of filmmaking enabled by the turn to the small, intimate formats of video that resides between two of its most obvious genre innovations—between "first-person documentary" and "vernacular video," and yet not quite fitting either.

Though Gan appears in his films, these are not exactly "first person" efforts reflecting the filmmaker's own life. Gan's project resembles neither Ross McElwee's *Sherman's March* nor Jonathan Caouette's *Tarnation,* where the filmmaker truly becomes the object of his own subject (Lebow 2012). The only part of his life that Gan allows is his role in making these films—as an actor and as a director.

However, neither is his project exactly the vernacular video that Pat Aufderheide predicted in 1995 would proliferate as "personal journalism by camcorder." She presciently asked nearly twenty years ago—before the rise of the interwebs, YouTube, social media—"Will the genre largely circumvent the traditional middlemen of journalism, letting people tell their own stories their own way?" (Aufderheide 1995, 46). Gan's participants did not pick up cameras, nor did they contribute actual footage. Their contributions were, instead, opinions and performances.

Ilona Hongisto's idea of "documentary fabulation" borrowed from Deleuze is useful here: She quotes Deleuze saying that "fabulation is the becoming of the real character when he himself starts to 'make fiction,' when he enters into the 'flagrant offense of making up legends' and so contributes to the invention of his people" (Hongisto 2011a, 9; 2011b). Gan is a fabulator who collaborates across his minoritized community—a community that overtly understands media as bearing the gospel good news out of any frame and into the world. For them, "representation" *is* a form of "participation." And in fact, Gan offers his films to them as tokens of his own participation in their community, despite their aesthetic differences.

If we take seriously the notion that culture is not a *thing,* but a *process*—even though it may seem like a congeries of things, and even though we can analyze only through the materiality of things—we must get it in analytic motion.[16] Much in human life—including "the social"—remains empirically directly unavailable. Yet we know it is "there"—in fact, a good deal of human life is about making the invisible visible, that is, *mediating and materializing it.*

Marx's own dialectical vocabulary consistently "views things as moments in their own development in, with and through other things" (Ollman 1977, 52), leading to the Frankfurt School's view of culture as that which "mediates the interaction between the material and the mental, the economic and the socio-political" (Mendieta 2006, 5). By emphasizing the marvelous slippage between "media" and "mediation," I want to focus our attention on the paradox of *materializing process* (Zito 2008). For analysis, this comes down to grasping the importance of the choices we make of which moments we focus on in the general dialectical construction of social reality. Like many things, a film is only sometimes an object—it strains to become a thing that can exist, be circulated, and not decay with undue speed. But it is also much more: a pause in an ongoing and ensemble process of making, of social production, that takes a certain materialized form, one that can be heard, seen, portably carried, or emailed.

In the case of Gan's films, we are presented with intersecting angles of performance and objectification, moving at possible cross-purposes. Gan wants to make artistically significant films that can be shown in European and American art houses and festivals. In his eyes, that is the finest gift he can make to his community. Yet he cuts his documentary *Church Cinema* to include their long critiques and discussions of their own hopes for *Raised from Dust* as an intentional vehicle for the Gospel—even though he disagrees and has no intention of changing the feature. He claims his role as objectifier even as his respect for their performances is, at every level, exemplary.

Community members trade their own performances wholeheartedly in this joint enterprise, but wish to prolong their own moments of participatory, emotional connection to create an extension that will draw in audiences mimetically to feel moved toward religious fervor and Christ. In this hope, they have an aesthetic that closely resembles that of West African Pentecostal video dramas. As Brian Larkin sums up: "These are genres designed to generate physical effects. Like the Holy Spirit, they come in to take over your body" (Larkin 2008, 190).[17]

They wish to close a gap that Gan perforce seeks to hold open for the spectatorial aesthetic pleasure that will gain audience for his object. For the congregants, the ideal audience would be made of people who would star in the next feature about Christian life—even, and especially, if it meant conversion. In a more politically sensitive reading of the clash of aesthetics, their objections to the semiotically complicated and yet stylistically unguided viewing of the husband's painful, wheezing death in the tricycle as not evoking Christian emotions might also be registering subliminal anxieties. One could, left unguided, see the ways in which that scene (indeed all the scenes of grinding poverty) indicate the failures of socialism after reform and the resultant inadequacy of community. Those vexing, politically provoking readings would be precluded, or at least forestalled, with more sensory direction through obviously Christian music or poetry.

Rather than naming one kind of object as "documentary," the term might be better theorized as a disposition toward the world, a creation of something that points outside itself toward the next social engagement in its life as an object being circulated. In that sense—that is, in the sense of acting as a prompt to empathy, as the basis for future social occasions—Gan's religious community ironically may have a more avant-garde and highly developed sense of "documentary" than he does! But they do need him to make one.

Notes

Epigraph. Kwok 2007.

1. Two other documentaries about Christians in China were made around the same time as Gan's: *Fangshan Church* (*Fangshan Jiaotang*) by Xu Xin and *Faith* (*Xinxin*) by Wei Xueqi. Simply considering the three documentaries, as outsiders, both Xu and Wei bring different agendas and perspectives from Gan's insider one. Gan himself thinks of his work as important to religious life inside China. I cannot say. I chose his work for its formal qualities that, as I will argue, actually do hinge to some extent on his engagement with certain Christian aesthetic forms. Embroiled in them himself, he provides an occasion for the unfolding of something intimate: his vision of Christian ways of thinking among themselves in the midst of life. I did not choose Gan's pair of films because of what they can "tell" us about Christian life in the context of state pressure—prominent features of the other two films. I found looking closely at his pairing of fiction and documentary in the same project to be also interesting and useful for considering documentary in general.

2. Bill Nichols analyzes this trend in his brilliant *Blurred Boundaries: Questions of Meaning in Contemporary Culture.* One of the more basic boundaries to be worked over and through, according to Nichols, is that between "confirmation" of an interpretive frame and "evidence" from the historical world (Nichols 1994, see especially chapter 2).

3. TSPM emphasizes self-governance, self-support, self-governance (Xu 2004, 107).

4. The state has eased up on them considerably in recent years to the point that one famous house church in Beijing reached a membership of 1,000 and collected $4 million for its own building. However, around April 10, 2011, "Shouwang" or "Lighthouse" was evicted by state order from their rental hall. In a show of willingness to stand their ground, they neither disbanded nor dispersed back into private living rooms (Jacobs 2011). This congregation is middle class, well-educated, and rich enough.

5. The number of Chinese Christians (including Catholics and Protestants) is estimated to range from 54 million to over 100 million. See Weilander (2009, 850, n2) for a discussion of how various accountings are made. Figures on Christians in China are hard to come by. They range widely from the most recent government census available as 4 million Roman Catholics and 10 million Protestants to the figure of 130 million by the end of 2006, including 20 million Catholics, from State Administration for Religious Affairs Director Ye Xiaowen's in-house report to universities, subsequently denied by the Foreign Ministry (personal xerox copy). On the other hand, an American Christian organization called ChinaPartners.org sent thirty-one survey teams around China over a thirteen-month period; these teams interviewed a total of about 5,500 people and concluded there are 39 million Protestants in China (Ellis 2007).

6. Filmmakers were introduced to the work of Frederick Wiseman and Ogawa Shinsuke at workshops and have acknowledged this debt; see Wu Wenguang (2010).

7. They also tend not to be interested in "realism" per se because, again, that is a trope of old state socialist aesthetics (Zhang Yingjin 2006, 27). Of course, since an older generation grew up on those aesthetics, their influences, conscious or not, may remain profound.

8. "Politically neutral" translates in the Chinese case as "not state-owned or operated." One might read this as a convenient, even necessary, appropriation of neoliberal market impulses. But it should not at all be seen as some kind of capitulation to that idea. Caught between a critique of the state and a critique of capitalist excess, what is a filmmaker to do? Evading the state might be thought of as an impossible, utopic fantasy. Nonetheless, and even though post-Olympics, the state's new surveillance apparatus remains in place, looking *away* from the state's purview, to see things it refuses to see, still remains a very powerful motivation for documentary in China, I think.

9. Here are just a few examples of things that go unseen in mass media: *West of the Tracks* by Wang Bing (2001) about *displaced workers;* several films by Du Haibin, including *Umbrella* (2007), an omnibus that presents vignettes of *people struggling in a small-town rural setting* to overcome rurality and get somewhere else, including workers, army recruits, and students; and Du's *1428* (2009) on *survivors* of the Sichuan earthquake of 2008; the robust queer cinema on its community's difficulties and edges, such as *Meimei* by Gao Tian (2005) on a *down-and-out drag queen,* until quite recently with the attempt at historicizing a queer presence and giving it media visibility (e.g., *Queer China* by Cui Zi'en [2008]; see also chapter 11, by Luke Robinson, in this

volume). A veritable documentary genre has grown up around contested property rights and local corruption: *Petition* by Zhao Liang (2009) and *Taishi Village* by Ai Xiaoming (2005) are examples of activist filmmaking discussed by Zhang Zhen in chapter 12 this volume.

10. "Social subjectivity would link not only the doer and the done to, in self-constituting action, but the state of 'does/done to'" experienced by one and that experienced by others. Social subjectivity, like the social imaginary that it transcends, is a category of collective consciousness (Nichols 1994, 105). See also Yingjin Zhang on subjectivity and performance in Chinese cinema (2009, 103–169).

11. Documentary film has long served a "social purpose," given a "call to action." But in the past this was accomplished more by providing a "greater sense of knowledge or even a more fully elaborated sense of social structure and historical process" (Nichols 1994, 47). Here I am talking about the mobilization of affect.

12. "New Documentary Movement" is how Lü Xinyu characterizes the films I am discussing (Lü 2003, 1–23; Lü 2010, 15–48). How to categorize the films produced, not uncoincidentally, in the wake of Tiananmen in 1989 remains somewhat fraught. Are they underground and on their way to independent? (Pickowicz and Zhang 2006, vii–xi) That is, are they constantly evading state censorship and made by people who rigorously eschew the state-media apparatus? Not exactly. Still underground? Not really. See the American distribution company website that confides to the world "dGenerate Films brings uncensored, unprecedented, and visionary content from deep within mainland China's independent, and underground, film scene to the U.S. market" (http://dgeneratefilms.com/about/, accessed 12/9/10). For more arguments, see Johnson 2006 and especially Berry and Rofel, who argue against "independent" and for "alternative" as a designation (2010, 135–137). Berry and Rofel are particularly persuasive in noting that these films form an "alternative archive." I feel they are indeed "new" in both their aesthetic reach and their social impetus, and that this performance of "newness" at this juncture will be deeply appreciated at a future time.

13. Rural Henan and Anhui provinces have seen the most rapid growth of the evangelical, Protestant Christianity that has recovered fairly rapidly since the close of the Cultural Revolution and the beginning of Reform in the late 1970s. More recent figures from Pew Research (2011) put the number of total Christians at 67 million while the latest report by the U.S. State Department's International Religious Freedom Report (2012) says, "The 2011 Blue Book of Religions, produced by the Institute of World Religions at the Chinese Academy of Social Sciences (CASS), a research institution directly under the State Council, reports the number of Protestant Christians to be between 23 and 40 million." One can certainly note the striking fact that there were only about 700,000 Protestants in the country in 1949 when the Communist Party came to power after the civil war.

14. Chris Berry and Lisa Rofel translate this term, which refers to a spontaneous style devoted to sync sound and natural light, as "on-the-spot realism" (Berry and Rofel 2010, 5).

15. It is also available for download online, but not in the mainland (Wong 2004). Yuan Zhiming (b. 1955) fled China after Tiananmen and was one of the writers of the critically acclaimed and popular TV series, *River Elegy*. He converted to Evangelical Christianity in the United States and now has a ministry based in Petaluma, CA. It produces a lot of gospel media. Its website is http://www.chinasoul.org/.

16. Theodore Schatzki offers this useful formulation of "practices as embodied, materially *mediated* arrays of human activity centrally organized around shared practical understanding" (Schatzki et al. 2001, 2, italics mine). See also Zito 2008.

17. There is a rich literature on Pentecostal videos in Africa. See Katrien Pype (2012) on Kinshasa in the Democratic Republic of the Congo and Birgit Meyer (2006) on Ghana.

Bibliography

Aufderheide, Pat. 1995. "Vernacular Video: For the Growing Genre of Camcorder Journalism, Nothing Is Too Personal." *Columbia Journalism Review* 33 (5): 46–48.

———. 1997. "Public Intimacy: The Development of First-Person Documentary." *Afterimage* 25 (1): 16–18.

Berry, Chris and Lisa Rofel. 2010. "Introduction." In *The New Chinese Documentary Film Movement: For the Public Record,* edited by Chris Berry, Lü Xinyu, and Lisa Rofel, 3–14. Hong Kong: Hong Kong University Press.

Elder, Sarah. 1995. "Collaborative Filmmaking: An Open Space for Making Meaning, a Moral Ground for Ethnographic Film." *Visual Anthropology Review* 11 (2): 94–101.

Ellis, Mark. 2007. "China Survey reveals fewer Christians than some Evangelicals want to believe." *Assist News Service,* Oct. 1. http://www.assistnews.net/STORIES/2007/s07100011.htm.

Hongisto, Ilona. 2011a. "Documentary Fabulation and the Creation of Collectivity." Paper presented at Visible Evidence, New York University, New York, Aug. 11–14.

———. 2011b. "Soul of the Documentary: Expression and the Capture of the Real." PhD dissertation, University of Turku, Finland.

Jacobs, Andrew. 2011. "Illicit Church, Evicted, Tries to Buck Beijing." *New York Times,* Apr. 17. http://www.nytimes.com/2011/04/18/world/asia/18beijing.html?_r=1&emc=tnt&tntemail0=y.

Johnson, Matthew David. 2006. "'A Scene beyond Our Line of Sight': Wu Wenguang and New Documentary Cinema's Politics of Independence." In *From Underground to Independent: Alternative Film Culture in Contemporary China,* edited by Paul G. Pickowicz and Yingjin Zhang, 47–76. Lanham, MD: Rowman & Littlefield.

Kraicer, Shelly. 2007. "China's Wasteland: Jia Zhangke's *Still Life*." *Cinema Angle* 29. http://www.cinema-scope.com/cs29/feat_kraicer_still.html.

Kwok, Yenni. 2007. "The Passion of Gan." *Asia Sentinel,* July 20. http://www.asiasentinel.com/index.php?option=com_content&task=view&id=590&Itemid=34.

Larkin, Brian. 2008. *Signal and Noise: Media, Infrastructure, and Urban Culture in Nigeria.* Durham, NC: Duke University Press.

Lebow, Alisa. 2012. *The Cinema of Me: The Self and Subjectivity in First Person Documentary.* London: Wallflower Press.
Lin Xu-dong. 2004. "Documentary in Mainland China." *Documentary Box* 26: 24–36.
Lü, Xinyu 吕新雨. 2003. *Jilu Zhongguo: Dangdai Zhongguo xinjilu yundong* 纪录中国：当代中国新纪录运动 (Documenting China: The New Documentary Movement in Contemporary China). Beijing: Sanlian shudian.
———. 2010. "Rethinking China's New Documentary Movement: Engagement with the Social." In *The New Chinese Documentary Film Movement: For the Public Record,* edited by Chris Berry, Lü Xinyu and Lisa Rofel, 15–48. Hong Kong: Hong Kong University Press.
MacDougall, David. 1998. *Transcultural Cinema.* Princeton NJ: Princeton University Press.
McGrath, Jason. 2008. "The Cinema of Displacement: The Three Gorges Project in Feature Film and Video." In *Displacement: The Three Gorges Dam and Contemporary Chinese Art,* edited by Wu Hung, 33–46. Chicago: Smart Museum of Art, University of Chicago.
Mendieta, Eduardo. 2006. "Introduction." *The Frankfurt School on Religion: Key Writings by the Major Thinkers,* 1–17. New York: Routledge.
Meyer, Birgit. 2006. "Impossible Representations: Pentecostalism, Vision, and Video Technology in Ghana." In *Religion, Media, and the Public Sphere,* edited by Birgit Meyer and Annelies Moors, 290–312. Bloomington: Indiana University Press.
Morgan, David. 1998. *Visual Piety: A History and Theory of Popular Religious Images.* Berkeley: University of California Press.
Nichols, Bill. 1994. *Blurred Boundaries: Questions of Meaning in Contemporary Culture.* Bloomington: Indiana University Press.
Ollman, Bertell. 1977. *Alienation: Marx's Conception of Man in a Capitalist Society.* New York: Cambridge University Press.
Pew Research, Religion, and Public Life Project. 2011. "Global Christianity: A Report on the Size and Distribution of the World's Christian Population—Spotlight on China." Accessed Apr. 8, 2014. http://www.pewforum.org/2011/12/19/global-christianity-regions/#asia.
Pickowicz, Paul G. and Yingjin Zhang, eds. 2006. *From Underground to Independent: Alternative Film Culture in Contemporary China.* Lanham, MD: Rowman & Littlefield.
Pype, Katrien. 2012. *The Making of Pentecostal Melodrama.* New York: Berghahn Books.
Qi, Liu. 2009. "Field Notes: A Close Look into an Immigrant Workers' Church in Beijing." *Nova Religio: The Journal of Alternative and Emergent Religions* 12 (4): 91–98.
Schatzki, Theodore, Karin Knorr Cetina, and Eike von Savigny, eds. 2001. *The Practice Turn in Contemporary Theory.* London and New York: Routledge.
Sherman, Tom. 2007. "Vernacular Video." *Wired,* Jan. 28, 2007. Accessed May 12, 2013. http://www.wired.com/beyond_the_beyond/2007/01/vernacular_vide/.
Tarkovsky, Andrei. 1989. *Sculpting in Time: The Great Russian Filmaker Discusses His Art.* Austin, TX: University of Texas Press.
U.S. Government International Religious Freedom Report for 2012, China. Accessed Apr. 8, 2014. http://www.state.gov/j/drl/rls/irf/religiousfreedom/index.htm?dlid#wrapper.

Voci, Paola. 2004. "From the Center to the Periphery: Chinese Documentary's Visual Conjectures." *Modern Chinese Literature and Culture* 16 (1): 65–113.

Wang, Yiman. 2010. "'I Am One of Them' and 'They Are My Actors': Performing, Witnessing, and DV Image-Making in Plebian China." In *The New Chinese Documentary Film Movement: For the Public Record,* edited by Chris Berry, Lü Xinyu, and Lisa Rofel, 217–236. Hong Kong: Hong Kong University Press.

Weilander, Gerda. 2009. "Bridging the Gap? An Investigation of Beijing Intellectual House Church Activities and Their Implications for China's Democratization." *Journal of Contemporary China* 18 (62): 849–864.

Wong, Joanna S. 2004. "The Cross: Jesus in China." *Christianity Today,* Feb. 29. http://www.christiantoday.com/article/the.cross.jesus.in.china/136.htm.

Wu Wenguang 吴文光. 2000. "Fangwen Xiaowu daoyan Jia Zhangke" 访问小武导演贾樟柯 (Interviewing the director of *The Thief,* Jia Zhangke). Document/Xianchang 1 (1): 184–213.

Xu, Yi-hua. 2004. "Patriotic Protestants: The Making of an Official Church." In *God and Caesar in China: Policy Implications of Church-State Tensions,* edited by Jason Kindopp and Carol Lee Hamrin, 107–121. Washington, DC: Brookings Institution Press.

Yuan Zhiming 远志明. 2004. *Shizi jia: Yesu zai Zhongguo jianbao* 十字架：耶稣在中国简报 (A Short Report on *The Cross: Jesus in China*). Shenzhou Chuanbo xiehui (China Soul for Christ Foundation Newsletter), July 20. http://christiantimes.org.hk/Common/Reader/News/ShowNews.jsp?Nid=24787&Pid=2&Version=886&Cid=105&Charset=gb2312.

Zhang, Yingjin. 2006. "My Camera Doesn't Lie? Truth, Subjectivity, and Audience in Chinese Independent Film and Video." In *From Underground to Independent: Alternative Film Culture in Contemporary China,* edited by Paul G. Pickowicz and Yingjin Zhang, 23–46. Lanham, MD: Rowman & Littlefield.

———. 2009. *Cinema, Space, and Polylocality in a Globalizing China.* Honolulu: University of Hawai'i Press.

Zhang Zhen. 2007. "Introduction." In *The Urban Generation,* edited by Zhang Zhen. Durham, NC: Duke University Press.

———. 2010. "Transfiguring the Postsocialist City: Experimental Image-Making in Contemporary China." In *Cinema at the City's Edge: Film and Urban Networks in East Asia,* edited by Yomi Braester and James Tweedie, 95–118. Hong Kong: Hong Kong University Press.

Zito, Angela. 2008. "Culture." In *Key Words in Religion, Media and Culture,* edited by David Morgan, 69–82. New York: Routledge.

———. 2014. "*Writing in Water,* or, Evanescence, Enchantment and Ethnography in a Chinese Urban Park." *Visual Anthropology Review* 30 (1): 10–22.

CHAPTER 10

DV and the *Animateur* Cinema in China

PAOLA VOCI

Film scholarship on the movie-making, movie-viewing, and movie-circulating practices that have developed since the mid-1990s in China has appropriately emphasized the role played by the rise of digital video (DV) and its impact on independent and, in particular, documentary filmmaking.[1] In this chapter, I want to explore one line of development in DV independent production that has received much less attention—what I call *animateur* cinema—which concerns short digital animations that are made by and/or circulated for online (or on-mobile) moviemakers/viewers.[2] Fan-originated digital animation or *egao* animation can also be found online, but my focus is on *animateur* cinema that, while it may have some reference to popular mass-consumed animations, does not construct itself simply as a fan response or a parodic remake and commentary on mass media events or celebrities, but rather as an independent and creative cultural practice. More specifically, this chapter explores *animateur* cinema's distinctive contribution to "alternative" cultural spaces, broadly defined by noninstitutional and unofficial locations.

My personal journey into *animateur* cinema began when I first stumbled on *Xiaoxiao,* a little man drawn as a black stick figure who is the protagonist of a series of parodic revisitations of one of the most popular national culture icons: the martial arts hero (Voci 2010, 55–56).[3] In a series of flash animations, *Xiaoxiao* fights enemies (who are his exact replicas but in different colors) and humorously but also quite violently defeats them. While nothing in *Xiaoxiao* is obviously "Chinese," his Chinese-sounding name, his martial arts skills, and the Chinese characters that at times appear to comment on his actions all contribute to make him a parody of the officially promoted Chinese-branded animation.

This chapter focuses on digital animations such as *Xiaoxiao,* which are located outside the more structured and regulated animation industry and its traditional distribution outlets of movie theaters and TV (including their official Internet sites). While not necessarily antiestablishment or dissenting, these animations—like other practices in Chinese popular culture—have opted for

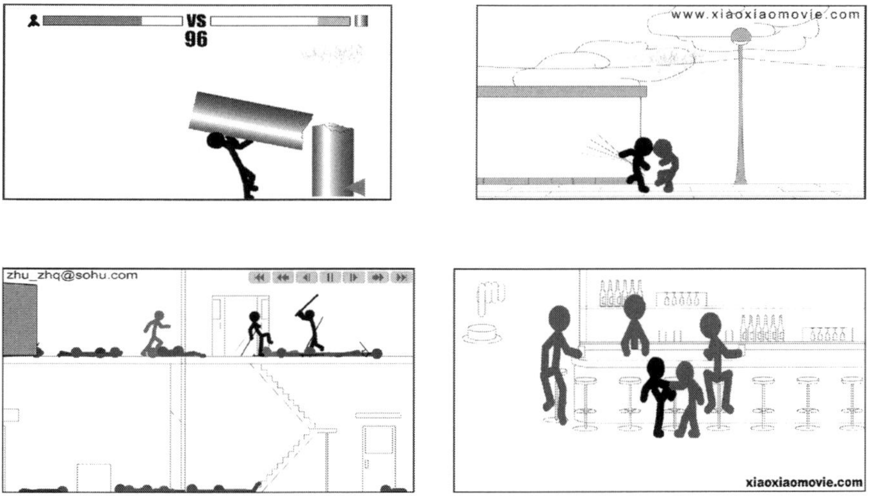

Figure 10.1. *Xiaoxiao*. A small *animateur* saga: scenes from four different Xiaoxiao animations.

unregulated and shared (rather than marketed) productions that rely on individual, and often amateur, creativity. Mostly (but not exclusively) produced in China by Chinese animators, *animateur* cinema in each individual instance only reaches relatively small audiences that may sometimes include foreign viewers (as in *Xiaoxiao*'s case). In all cases, unlike the more popular and state-supported nationally branded digital animation, *animateur* cinema is better understood as a nonmainstream, albeit widely circulating, cultural product.

Chinese *animateur* cinema is one of the least studied applications of digital technology.[4] It may be a consequence of the fact that Chinese animation film has been traditionally isolated from all other genres broadly fitting into the live-action film context. Animation film has very rarely had more than a marginal location in Chinese film histories and theories, in either the Chinese or English language. Furthermore, as compared to other independent DV practitioners, who often are filmmakers by training or ambition, independent animators inhabit a separate, on the surface less cinematic, cultural space that is characterized by hyperfragmented, unregulated, and often even hardly traceable production and distribution practices that take place almost exclusively on computer or mobile small screens.

It is precisely *animateur* cinema's small-screen location, which is also at the root of its marginalization (if not exclusion altogether) from Chinese film studies, that I set out to investigate and reassess. I propose that *animateur* cinema is quite distant from (and even oppositional to) the larger screens inhabited by Chinese mass-consumed institutionalized animation and, instead, needs to be framed within the same context in which independent and experimental DV practices have developed in China. In this context, we can recognize that *animateur* cinema originally contributes to the broader expropriation, reappropriation, and redefinition of the cinematic medium and its expressive potential that DV has certainly facilitated but has not initiated. Its creative and artistic modality presents (rather than represents) realities that, because of their intangible, invisible, or taboo nature, the DV camera cannot capture and that can only become visible as animated realities.

I begin by noting *animateur* cinema's dislocation from mainstream Chinese animation and national creative industries policies and rhetoric (Keane 2006). In this context, animation is mostly defined by an overall concern with Chinese branding and its national and transnational marketing. *Animateur* cinema's dislocation originates from its resistance to branding and marketing and is further emphasized by its content and format, which I analyze in a necessarily limited selection of animations. Within their great variety, *animateur* movies share some common traits. They are brief and their narrative is mostly nonevent driven and often fragmented. As for their style, they never aim at realistic representations. Instead, their all-is-allowed format includes genre mix, pastiche, and insertion of live-action images. They invite the notions of spectacle and exhibitionist pleasure, rather than diegetic absorption. It is precisely this type of exhibitionist engagement with the cinematic experience, amplified by the transient, mobile, and noninstitutional locations of its producers and viewers, that makes *animateur* cinema too volatile, too escapist, too raw, too small—or, in one word, too *light*—to warrant film scholars' attention (Voci 2010, 12–13).

In my conclusion, I suggest that we understand *animateur* cinema as being located not only in the Chinese cultural context but also in other cultural spaces that transcend Chinese borders both spatially and temporally. The larger context to which I refer is not the widely evoked, analyzed, and problematized cultural space of global production and consumption, from which *animateur* cinema in fact remains largely outside. Rather, I refer to the liminal space of cultural practices that can only originate in and be defined by *transitional* temporalities. Besides being an important and yet still quite undervalued development of DV culture in the contemporary Chinese context, I argue that Chinese *animateur* cinema's modalities of production and distribution also establish important lines of connection with early cinematic practices and therefore contribute a new perspective to the broader rethinking of cinema in the digital age.

Chinese-branded Animation: The "Official" Discourse and Its Variations/Deviations

While animation as a visual art form can and should be also examined in aesthetic and theoretical terms, mainstream animation has instead been mostly discussed in relation to its commercial value. Academic scholarship on Chinese animation (in Chinese as well as other languages) is still limited to historical overviews in Chinese (Jing and Wang 2005; Wu and Han 2009; Yan and Suo 2005; Zhang, H. 2002) and only a handful of studies in English (Ehrlich and Jin 2001; Kang 2006; Lent and Ying 2003; Quiquemelle 1985). Hopeful signs of a renewed critical interest in this important cinematic practice are found in the work of Wu Weihua—whose dissertation focuses on the study on animation in postsocialist China (Wu 2006) and, more recently, Du Yan, who has looked at earlier Chinese animation from the 1940s to the 1970s (Du 2012). With these two notable exceptions, most of the available analysis on contemporary animators and animation-producing companies has not been produced by researchers working within the broader areas of art history or visual culture, but mostly, and often only tangentially, by researchers focusing on the growth of creative industries in China from socio-economic and political perspectives.

It is useful here to provide a brief summary of how Chinese animation, as a leading creative industry, has been described from both state policy and market perspectives. In the creative industry framework, as Michael Keane has noted, the artist/entrepreneur is assumed to cooperate with the government to realize the common goal of making capitalism work for socialism (Keane 2006). Needless to say, this alliance is not a straightforward one, but is complicated by transnational factors, since the primary and secondary actors (e.g., production companies and audiences) and the controlling institutions are not necessarily all located within the same geopolitical context (Liu and White 2001).[5] In other words, local economy and politics as well as global markets impact on animation marketing strategies, distribution practices, and creative choices.

In light of this alliance, state and animation companies have joined forces and succeeded in making capitalism work for socialism. The media often report on how the animation market is growing incredibly fast.[6] The partnership between animation industries and the state can be traced back to governmental policies that consistently have supported the animation industry since the early 2000s. Beginning in 2002, the government began to actively develop China's animation industry, and a series of policies testified to its attitude and determination. Between 2004 and 2005, the government approved the establishment of nineteen animation production and research centers, awarding prizes for outstanding cartoon films and exempting the industry from taxes (Zhang, X. 2008, 16).

Most of the investment and workforce in this area continues to be directed toward either feature-length animated films or, even more prominently, TV animation series that have Chinese audiences as their main targets. Even with the huge popularity of the *Pleasant Goat and Big Bad Wolf*, aka *Happy Sheep and Grey Wolf* (*Xi yangyang yu huitai lang*), TV series and feature films, Chinese animation has not yet reached global audiences. This is not to say that in China animation is inherently a locally defined cultural practice; however, at this stage it has not yet developed the same global soft power that, for instance, resides in the long-established American Disney or Japanese Studio Ghibli animation.

In terms of contents and forms, in this domestic-oriented and state-supported mainstream animation, a softer and more diluted definition of national belonging—a Chinese branding—has increasingly displaced the earlier focus on the promotion of a "national style" (Farquhar 1993; Voci 2010, 44; Wu 2010; Yi 1988). For instance, the relatively good box office success of the 2D animation *The Legend of a Countryside Hero* (*Chi Song Wei Long* 2008) seems to indicate that the adaptability of this branding might have allowed animators to gain audiences' favors while still satisfying official directives. While the drawing style follows the conventions of Japanese anime, the company (Hangzhou Hui Huang Animation) that produced *The Legend of a Countryside Hero* clearly brands it as "Chinese" and describes itself as a company that engages "in the development of a new generation of original animation with Chinese national characteristics, and creates productions of cartoon and animation with connotation of national culture, fresh and humor, as well as entertainment" (Hangzhou Hui Huang 2010).

Indeed, *The Legend of a Countryside Hero* includes many elements that could be easily identified as Chinese. Most noticeably, it takes place in a Chinese village around 800 CE, where the narrative centers on the fight against evil superstition and its protagonist, Chi Song, embodies many traits of the martial arts hero. The co-protagonist is Diao Man, the general's spoiled daughter for whom Chi Song's mother works as a maid, who appears to be at first hostile but then falls for him and becomes his ally. At the start of the movie Chi Song is a student of master Lü Yi. After angering his master, as a punishment Chi Song is sent away on a long journey around the world. When he comes back to his village, he notices that his parents' house has been rearranged according to *fengshui*. He immediately shows his suspicion against this superstition by purposely breaking the *fengshui* arrangement. He soon finds out that almost the whole village has fallen under the control of an evil wizard and his cult. Chi Song later confronts him and opposes his tricks and superstitions with science, angering him to the point that the wizard decides to get rid of Chi Song. The wizard secretly poisons the water of the well, causing the villagers to fall sick; he then blames Chi Song's disruption of the *fengshui* equilibrium for the inexplicable sickness of so many people. The villagers believe the evil wizard and chase Chi Song away; when he is about to leave, however, the local general—also under a spell of the evil wizard—has him arrested and sentenced to be burnt. Diao Man saves him and together they decide to find an antidote to the poison that has sickened their fellow villagers. A series of misadventures follow: Diao Man loses her memory, then regains it, and finally Chi Song frees the general from the wizard's spell, saving all the villagers.

While in the animation many obvious branding elements are recognizable as Chinese (such as the location, the ethnicity of the characters, the reference to *fengshui*), there is no direct homage to a Chinese historical figure or literary character from either traditional or socialist classics.[7] One could also easily see how the tropes for the hero, the heroine, and their enemies are rooted in non-Chinese and in fact arguably Hollywood archetypes. For instance, the hero fighting against evil magic and oppressive superstition and the heroine who evolves from a spoiled antagonist to an ally and a companion are also found in *Indiana Jones and the Temple of Doom* (1984), in which Indiana also saves an entire village (and its children) from the cruel enslavement of a powerful and evil religious cult.

An even stronger evidence of the shift from the claim of authentic national belonging and the search for a national style toward a more flexible Chinese branding is the popular *Pleasant Goat and Big Bad Wolf* series and its two feature-length animated films. The characters and the narrative of *Pleasant Goat and Big Bad Wolf* have become increasingly distant from either socialist or traditional values. Chineseness is no longer a cultural capital recognizable in its essentialized tradition and its variations, but rather a hybrid construct that is subtly embedded in the animation characters' actions and dialogues, no longer requiring a visible protagonist. References to Chinese culture (social behaviors, traditions) are still recognizable but are becoming less specific and, at least potentially, the series could speak to non-Chinese audiences. Paradoxically, it is possibly because of its non-essentialized and non-orientalist Chinese identity that *Pleasant Goat and Big Bad Wolf* has not been seen as a viable export.

In sum, even when animations seem to refer to a quintessentially Chinese identity in their production and marketing strategies, this reference is only on the surface the continuation of the rhetoric on traditional or socialist values that has characterized the official line in the development of animation history for over fifty years (Voci 2010). On closer look, the emphasis on a national style has been replaced by a Chinese-branding that reveals an underlying mixture of hybrid and even clashing perspectives on what being Chinese is supposed to signify. In particular, the Chinese-branding covers up the tension between a globally reaching diffused and adaptable Chineseness and a more inward-looking, self-understood "authentic" Chineseness. The former, similar to the Japaneseness embedded in the global phenomenon of eating sushi (Allen and Sakamoto 2011) is open to transformations and even deformations. The latter opposes and at the same time supports the former by providing the "pure" model against and from which deviations can originate.

It is beyond the scope of this chapter to evaluate the impact that Chinese animation has had in penetrating the world animation market, which is still heavily dominated by Japanese and American production. Yet, we can certainly note that in contrast to the globally oriented Chineseness developed in martial arts film epics, animation is still largely a domestic enterprise and has limited international cultural capital. While one cannot deny the animation industries' declared ambition to conquer the international market and reach non-Chinese audiences, the realities evoked in animated works are much more local than global, often quite inward looking, mostly targeting Chinese audiences in Chinese-speaking localities such as PRC, Taiwan, Singapore, or reaching out to the Chinese diasporas.

Animateur Cinema: Outside the Official Discourse

Despite its rich production and widespread circulation, *animateur* cinema (i.e., independent animation mostly developed after the rise of digital technologies) has received even less academic attention than institutionalized mass-consumed animation. Trying to address this gap and believing that *animateur* cinema deserves serious scrutiny, I have begun to examine gifted (i.e., unmarketed) short animated digital videos that are widely available on small screens, contextualizing them within the scholarship on contemporary visual arts and, more specifically, experimental digital artists such as Bu Hua and Cao Fei (Voci 2010). Following this preliminary investigation, I became convinced that *animateur* cinema is better understood as a cultural practice defined by its production medium and distribution locations rather than its belonging to the "animation" film technique (which misplaces it in the same context as the animation industry). I have proposed that a focus on small screens can help us bring them to visibility and understand their meaningfulness as part of a larger alternative cultural space created by *lightness*. I suggested that *light* cultural practices such as *animateur* cinema expand and challenge the boundaries of "legitimate" cinematic practices (Voci 2010, 12). I use "legitimate" not as a synonym for official, but to describe a type of cinema that, whether conventional or experimental, is more easily regulated, endorsable (and marketable) than the unregulated and often-gifted animated movies I analyze.

Precisely because it is unregulated, unmarketed, unbranded, and not endorsable, *animateur* cinema occupies a cultural space outside, although not fully separated from, the growing animation industry in China. There are, however, some relevant commonalities between the commercial and the amateur animation. The most obvious connection is that many producers who gift their short animations online also are or will become professional animators working in the production of Chinese-branded animation, as briefly outlined in the previous section. The double engagement with dependent (i.e., conforming to the state or to commercial imperatives) and independent (i.e., more experimental or more dissenting) productions is in fact one of the most widespread work patterns for independent Chinese filmmakers. Furthermore, like mass-consumed institutionalized animation, the *animateur* cinema is also deeply contextualized in a Chinese and, even more specifically, PRC context. Even when, as in the case of the escapist *Xiaoxiao* series or the politically dissenting *Grassmud Horse* (*Cao ni ma* 2009), *animateur* movies gain Internet fame and relatively large audiences, they remain local rather than global phenomena.

Besides those commonalities, *animateur* cinema diverges from mass-consumed and institutionalized animation in most other aspects as well. Most importantly, Chineseness is not branded and certainly never marketed. Instead, any specific Chinese belonging is either challenged (even provocatively attacked) or altogether absent. Furthermore, unlike the long narratives (either developed in episodic formats in the TV series or in a feature film) that characterize mass-consumed institutionalized animation, the digital movies on which I focus are short and often fragmented (i.e., a cluster of sketches, rather than a brief linear narrative).

Animateur cinema relies on the aesthetic of playful manipulation to attract and engage, rather than absorb, audiences into an open work (Eco 1962). They are then invited not only to enjoy and interpret, but also to *appropriate*. The notion of appropriation impacts on that of authorship. While in many cases the auteur is declared (although s/he may just reveal a virtual identity and may not necessarily be easily traceable), many other movies may appear to be anonymous creations that are often posted and reposted by viewers rather than their original producer. In either case, these movies are gifts that anyone can claim as theirs; their viewers can easily take, carry, and even modify them. Such appropriation of cinema in one's hands is not unique to these movies. DVDs (whether rightfully purchased or pirated) and illegally or legally recorded or downloaded versions of blockbuster films also take films out of the untouchable space of the movie theaters (or the TV screen) and allow for the same type of ownership of cinema. Yet, even when access to these commercially available films comes at no cost or risk for the viewer, the process of acquisition itself recognizes the original presence of an exclusive authorship and ownership (even if only to cheat it). On the contrary, the digital animations I examine are *true* gifts with no intended or likely market, shared either via public posting or user-to-user sharing.

The very nature of these animations and their screening locations make it almost impossible to identify their viewers; yet it is possible to trace and at least broadly categorize their makers. Three overlapping groups constitute the large majority of *animateurs*: professional flash animators/artists who choose to produce and circulate animation outside the institutional (commercial and/or artistic) channels; animation students, who can also be considered pre-professionals; and nonprofessional moviemakers, who can also be considered occasional *animateurs*. The first important link between *animateurs* and other independent DV makers is therefore their urban identity.[8] Another crucial connection is that, like other DV independent practices, *animateur* cinema also crosses paths with the Chinese "alternative" cultural discourse. Some of the most provocative and experimental animations openly critique mainstream culture and even the CCP government. It is in this "alternative" discourse (traditionally defined by the avant-garde) that nonprofessional and/or amateur practices have begun to play an important role, specific to the Chinese cultural context.

Yet, *animateur* cinema has been absent from the discussion of other digital video developments that have been framed within "alternative" film culture and, more specifically, in the context of independent and/or underground cinema (Pickowicz and Zhang 2006) that circulates in the unofficial (but still recognizable, endorsed by academic and other independent institutions) circuits. While circulating in public domains, *animateur* cinema relies on nonprofessional channels that are even more fluid and unregulated than those generally chosen by independent live-action (fiction and documentary) DV. *Animateur* cinema falls outside the two parallel universes of mainstream/official and independent/unofficial cinema (Zhang, X. 2006) and their established circuits, movie theaters, TV, film festivals, cine clubs, and academic venues, places where films gain most of their exposure, are reviewed, and become endorsed or criticized. Having noted its dislocation from both official and unofficial discourses, it may be in the vicinity of amateur and fan culture that we can uncover some important traits that explain *animateur* cinema's double-folded dislocations and help define its specificity.

Animateur Cinema's Specificity within and beyond the Amateur and Fan Culture

Film scholars have looked at amateur cinema mostly from sociohistorical and anthropological perspectives. Patricia Zimmermann defines amateur films as "records of marginal practices" and "registers of complicated rhizome-like social and historical discourses" (Zimmermann 1996).[9] While she foregrounds amateur cinema's marginality (which she ascribes to its fundamentally private sphere), she also points to its connection with larger social and historical frameworks in order to restore its relevance and establish it as deserving of academic scrutiny. For instance, she examines travel amateur film of the 1930s in close relationship with institutionalized cinema (and Hollywood in particular) and analyzes how amateur films reflected and supported both the nationalist and imperialistic discourses that emerged forcefully in those years. Taking a further step away from the amateur film's private sphere to locate it even more compellingly into the sociopolitical and cultural public space, Stefan Szczelkun proposes that amateur film needs to be examined as an art form in its own right. Through an analysis of home movies produced in the United Kingdom, he offers convincing evidence in support of amateur filmmaking's "aesthetic validation" (Szczelkun 2000, 95). Without oversimplifying the complexity of historical circumstances and personal motivations that have shaped the development of amateur film, it is important to note that this cultural practice has been recognized as both originating in the private sphere (i.e., outside the main institutions of cinema) and participating in the sociopolitical discourses of the public sphere.

In the Chinese context, amateur practices seem to have suddenly emerged in conjunction with the rise of DV culture. Such sudden appearance of the amateur filmmaker is most likely to be at least partly a reappearance, although only historical and archival research—beyond the scope of this study—can show to what extent amateur filmmaking had been present in China before the advent of cheaper means of recording (i.e., VHS and DV cameras). Even lacking such historical evidence, it is still reasonable to assume that at least between the 1950s and the late 1970s, the absence of a sizable middle class, which Zimmermann describes as the essential prerequisite for the existence of amateur film in the USA, may have limited if not altogether prevented the development of amateur film in China. As a result, the 1950–1980 hiatus in home video practices in China (precisely when America and Europe saw home videos booming) makes the explosion of amateur DV practices in the 1990s and, even more noticeably, in the 2000s a radical rupture with the past. In sum, the Chinese amateur has a relatively short life and has strong connection with the DV medium.

Nonprofessional movie-making practices have also been examined as part of fan culture, outside film history and from cultural studies and media anthropology perspectives. Originating in more contemporary contexts than the film studies' examination of amateur film, the emphasis has been on audience ethnography and the subsequent inclusion of fandom and participatory culture in academic discourse.[10] In this area, animation has been specifically examined in the context of Japanese otaku and the subculture developed since the 1990s. In this instance as well, while creativity is acknowledged, it is framed within the fandom discourse, which in turn is closely linked to the idea of a "movement" and a series of institutionalized mass events (Kinsella 1998).[11]

Media anthropology focuses on the conceptualization of the fan (rather than the amateur) as being neither oppositional nor subservient to but rather interrelated with media industries. In *Textual Poachers* (1992), *Convergence Culture* (2006), and *Spreadable Media* (2013), Henry Jenkins has drawn a fluid picture of fans, bloggers, and web users, active both inside and outside "powerful institutions and practices" such as law, religion, education, advertising, and politics (Jenkins 1992, 1–2), creating new content and sharing it freely. According to this participatory model, value and meaning are created and dispersed, in contrast with the old model of "stickiness" on which big companies and corporations have built their marketing strategies (Jenkins et al. 2013). From fanzine practices to blogging, people have created and shared an unsanctioned culture (e.g., creative works, knowledge, and information) that has been ignored, attacked, tolerated, and finally, albeit only partially, absorbed by mainstream media. By theorizing such practices as forms of *participatory culture,* Jenkins has analyzed fans' ability to network, communicate, and relate among themselves, often in transcultural and transnational contexts. Most of the core work on active audiences and fan cultures (including Jenkins' own) therefore has focused on the communal, collective nature of these popular culture practices.[12] The Chinese case is no different. In the China-focused scholarship, the attention given to fan culture has been framed in the larger context of urban culture and celebrity studies (Edwards and Jeffreys 2010) and, in terms of video practices, has mostly focused on *egao* (Barmé 2007; Dang 2009; Gong and Yang 2010; Voci 2010; Yu 2007) and other Chinese variations of *kuso* culture (Li 2010).[13] In most cases, the attention to the parodic, repetitive, communal, collective dimension of *egao* as a clever remake (but not an original creation) has similarly underplayed the more uniquely personal creative, artistic dimension of amateur video-making.

Yet, DV amateur creative practices cannot be simply equated to the collective space of fandom. For instance, the individually defined "auteur" creative impulse shown by the animated movies I examine cannot just be seen as a collective fan response to the popular media. They reclaim a private inventiveness that seeks to be shared publicly but resists inclusion in the main public discourses shaped by mainstream media. At the same time, as noted previously, their small-screen untraceable and not-endorsable location also separates them from avant-garde artists or the unofficial cinema that have found their alternative institutionalized locations in the underground (and slightly above the ground) channels of the various independent festivals, distribution companies (e.g., Fanhall in China and dGenerate in the USA), and at academic events. The specific term *animateur* therefore best embodies the multiple identities of both the makers and viewers of these movies as it points to their creative, original, and even experimental nature as well as their noncommercialized and, above all, noninstitutionalized status.

Chinese Animateur Movies

Now I will zoom into a selection of these movies and, whenever available, provide information about their makers/viewers. The movies I select come from websites that are mostly made for and visited by Chinese-language users and, in some cases, are also included in DVD collections of student works that circulate exclusively in China. It is important to note that, as is the case for all web-circulating movies, not all the digital animation posted online is made in China. However, in my study I searched only Chinese-language websites, and therefore it is reasonable to assume that the viewership is almost exclusively made of Chinese-language speakers who are either located in China or part of the transnational Chinese diasporas, plus the growing but still relatively small number of other (non-Chinese) Chinese-language users, including, for instance, academics.

While my selection is necessarily limited, it is important to emphasize that both the quantity and the quality of the digital animations created and circulated online are relevant to both how and why the movies I discuss were selected. In other words, even when not driven by more traceable consumption desires (as is the case for TV audiences, movie theater goers, or art gallery visitors), viewers (including myself) do not give up agency when they engage with online cinematic practices. Just like the spectators in the movie theaters, once theorized as being passive (or at least passively entrapped into an ideological apparatus where their bodies and minds have been considered as numbed by the mediatic experience), have long been recognized as active, so too web-browsing audiences, though often still assumed to be (if not passive) distracted and almost robotic in their patterns of use, are in fact active audiences.[14] The following are a few examples among the many animated movies that attracted my attention. They inspired my response and my desire to "own," rewatch, and reexperience their creative cleverness, to remake and reinterpret their message. It is indeed in the conceptualizations of repetition (Eco 2005) and remediation (Bolter and Grusin 1999) that we can better understand *animateur* cinema's aesthetics, social and cultural function—in sum, its *experience.*

Ding Meiyin's animation *Holding One's Hand,* aka *Infinity on Your Hand,* aka *Lenient* (*Shouxia liuqing* 2004), is one such animation. As I found out later, this animation is also included in the Beijing Film Academy (BFA) Animation Academy

Award DVD collections. It is a student work (from the 2004 animation class of the Beijing Communication University) that also won the ASIFA (Association Internationale du Film d'Animation) China prize in 2006. I first watched the animation on the popular Chinese-language video hosting service, youku.com.[15] As is often the case with these kinds of smaller-screen videos, I found it accidentally while (purposefully) browsing for animation. *Holding One's Hand* starts with the photo of its author, holding the certificate of her prize, followed by a shot of a whiteboard on which a young woman quickly sketches the title and then, at the pace of an allegro andante classical piece, a series of animated figures (e.g., a rooster, some chickens, a swan, a dove, a deer, a camel, a kangaroo, and a panda) is literally animated from her handprints. In the end, the same young woman, whose hands had initiated the animation, erases the whole fantasy world that had originated from the basic shapes of her palms and fingers. One can easily describe this animation as an exercise of style that entertains and surprises with its simplicity and, at the same time, its sophistication. Yet, in its entertaining inventiveness, the animation conveys a simple but powerful message. At one level, the focus is on the power of imagination and the medium itself; at another level we can even see it as a meta-

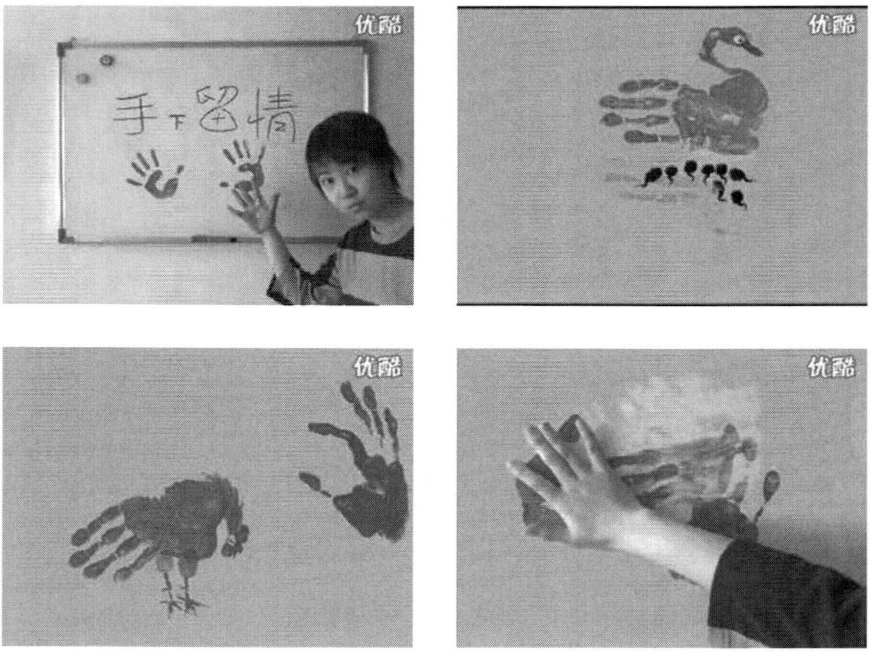

Figure 10.2. Holding One's Hand. Ding Meiyin, 2004.

phor on how the world is in our hands and we can make it or unmake it with our hands. Meaning therefore emerges from what the short movie evokes, rather than what it "says." Reflecting the "animateur" drive of this type of cinema, *Holding One's Hand* invites the viewer to experience the moving image through an intense, momentary, perceptual encounter (rather than a prolonged narrative absorption) in what can be also described as a "brief attachment" (Fowler and Voci 2011).

A bleaker perspective on the possibility for human creativity to imagine or make a new, better world as being ultimately blocked by the impossibility of rising above the constraints of one's urban entrapment is found in *Boundaries, aka Realm* (*Jingjie* 2006) by Yuan Bo. Also a student work, it is posted on youku.com and likewise included in the BFA Animation Award DVD collections. It shows a man climbing a ladder made of clouds and emerging out of the city into the blue nothingness of the sky. At the top of the ladder, a small whiteboard with the characters "境界" is hanging. He grabs it and begins to happily dance with it, jumping from one cloud to the next. A white empty frame interrupts the happy scene. After a few seconds, we see the man, again climbing the ladder made of clouds, but this time the ladder never ends and in fact continues to grow under the frustrated expression and increasingly angry reactions of the man. The man realizes that the ladder is actually curving and bringing him back down. Zooming out, the next frame shows that the man is actually trapped in a bottle and is climbing around the round surface of its walls. Further zooming out, the bottle is shown as rolling back and forth on a street, surrounded by traffic. The final shot looks up from the perspective of the bottle to the blurring bright sky squeezed between the high buildings. The animation credits follow, drawn in pencil and imposed on the bottle. The final dedication appears in typed characters on a black frame: to the people who go around (roll, break) but do not know what they are doing. The short undeveloped narrative aims at capturing a feeling of entrapment rather than telling a story. As was the case with *Holding One's Hand, Boundaries* invites the viewer to connect to the moving image as a carrier of meaning that needs no sustained concentration, but requires him or her to experience a short moment of attraction.

In a similar existentialist tone, I found many other animations in which lonely protagonists are shown on journeys that take them outside urban spaces and toward a nonidentified "other" location. For instance, He Wei's *Hope* (*Xiwang* 2006)—another student work—begins with the image of a flying condor over a deserted land and a backpack on the ground with footprints leading away from it.[16] We then see a young man (likely the one who has lost or abandoned his backpack) walking in a desert and getting nowhere. The final two frames show him looking up and the eagle flying in the blue cloudless sky.

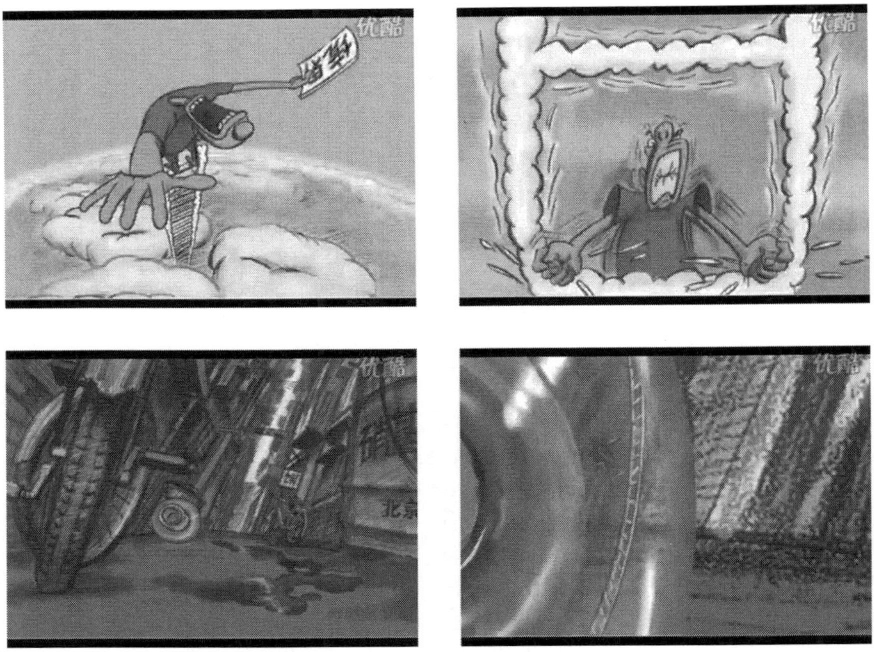

Figure 10.3. Boundaries, aka Realm. Yuan Bo, 2006.

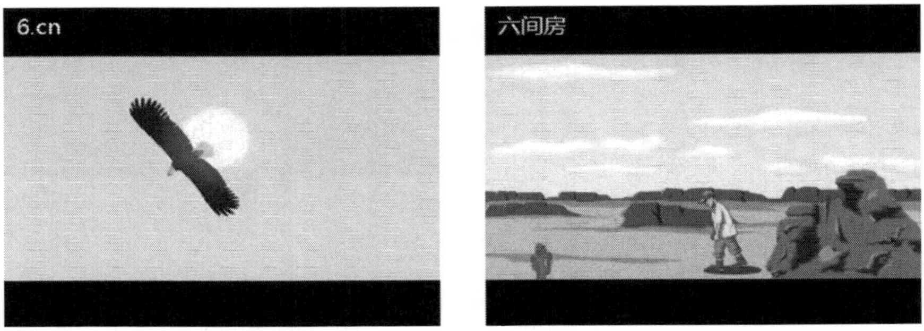

Figure 10.4. Hope. He Wei, 2006.

Much less lyrical and abstract, more satirical and realistic, are the animations dealing with the urban realities in which (most likely) the young animators live.

For example, *University Students' Self-Study Room* (*Daxuesheng zixishi* 2010) produced by Feng Chen and based on the rap by Hao Yu, is an angry satire of the entrapped everyday life of a student moving in and out of his university classroom—or better, "independent study room"—without real hope of getting out anywhere

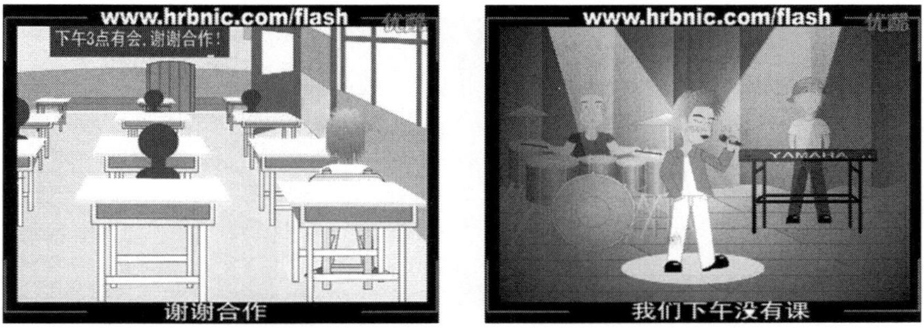

Figure 10.5. University Students' Self-Study Room. Feng Chen, 2010.

that is better than that reality. His life in the classroom is intercut by shots of the same student in a rapper outfit singing about his life. We see the young man finding his assigned seat, surrounded by black figures with whom he does not interact, exploding because of words that he does not understand. A girl he can't get teases him; he tries to read and get ready for an adult life he wants to escape, but can't. He wonders why the other students are there since they show no interest for what the classroom offers them, but ultimately there is nowhere to hide, besides the study room itself.

Also gifted and circulated via the unregulated and noninstitutionalized channels of Internet blogs and video-sharing sites, *Grassmud Horse* and *Little Rabbit Be Good* are much more politically dissenting. These highly controversial videos are most likely made by a combination of professional and nonprofessional animators who, in this case, choose anonymity to avoid prosecution and persecution. *Grassmud Horse* is the protagonist of a series of at least two popular animations and is also featured in live-action videos.[17] The animations (like all the other related visual and verbal creations inspired by the grassmud horse) rely on a series of puns created by homophones in Chinese language in which tone variations allow netizens to use uncensored words to engage in critical debates or simply curse the censors and their ideological oppression. The lexicon, widely used on the Internet, is available with translations and commentaries on the *China Digital Times* website (2014). In particular, the three words for "grassmud horse"—*cao ni ma*—sound very much like "fuck your mother," and the animal is therefore used in endless ways to insult several taboo topics (similarly transformed by puns). In the two animations I have selected (both produced by animators who hide behind safe acronyms), the grassmud horse resembles a llama and lives in a land together with other mythical creatures, among which the most important is its deadly enemy, the river crab (*hexie*—a homophone for the state promoted "harmony"). All sorts of visual variations of the mythical oppositional duo have been circulated on the

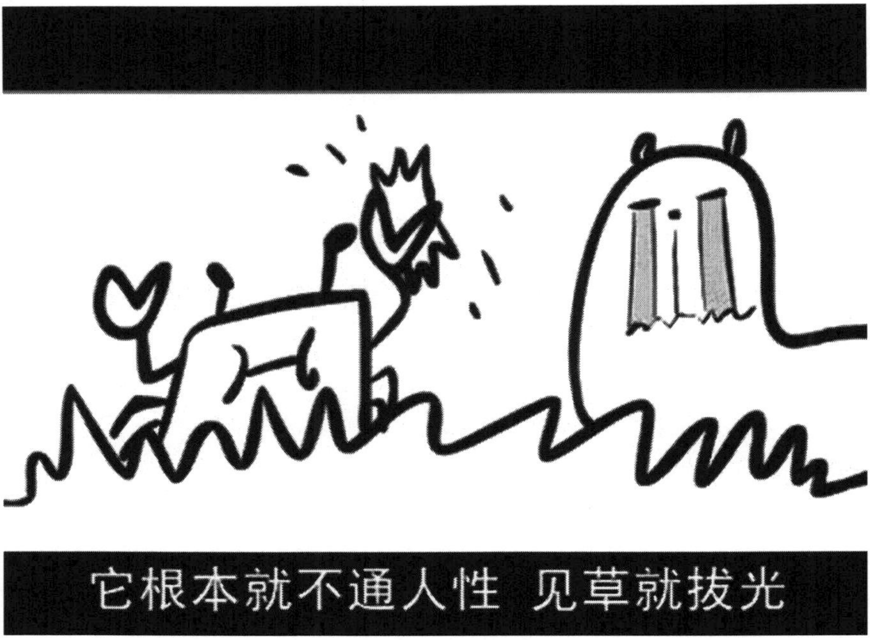

Figure 10.6. Grassmud horse in one of its many variations: The Song of Grassmud Horse (*Caonima zhi ge*), Anonymous.

Internet: the grassmud horse and the river crab have been Photoshopped in many famous images (including a version of the grassmud horse taking the place of the man standing in front of the tanks in Tiananmen Square); they have been reproduced in traditional brush and ink paintings (Brush and Ink Painting of Grass Mud Horses); they have been inserted in music videos and appeared in hundreds of cartoons. Unlike *Holding One's Hand* or *Boundaries,* which reached a limited and also arguably scattered and isolated viewership, *Grassmud Horse* reaches a much larger online community that is characterized by fandom participatory culture strategies and a shared political dissenting stance.

Little Rabbit Be Good (*Xiaotu Kuang Kuang* 2011) by Wang Bo (aka Pi San or Pisan)[18] is an even stronger example of politically dissenting and, in fact, revolutionary *animateur* cinema. An English translation of the video intertitles and song lyrics can be found on the Chinageeks website (Custer 2011). The animation began to circulate as a "year-of-the-rabbit" spring festival video card in January 2011. *Little Rabbit* starts with a disclaimer indicating that the content is not suitable for children and that the video should be circulated only during the spring festival greeting times. Next, we see a child opening a New Year's present; it is a little book titled "Little Rabbit Kuang Kuang," and on the first page we can read, "Far far in the future, there was a beautiful forest. . . ." From the book page, cute little white rabbits become animated. The rabbits are then shown in a series of sketches all referring to widely known Chinese scandals (that have also become big media events) such as the 1994 Karamay fire (Sheridan 2007), the 2008 tragic milk powder deaths (Yardley 2008), and the infamous 2010 car incident involving Li Gang's son (Wines 2010).[19] As was the case for the *Grassmud Horse,* in the *Little Rabbit*'s accompanying song, puns are used to refer to controversial content and comment on the little white rabbits' misfortunes. All these misfortunes are caused by the rabbits' leaders, the tigers, which are not only painted in Communist red, but are also quite obviously shown in a big cave, meeting in a party-congress setting, surrounded by red banners promoting the construction of a "harmonious" forest. After being oppressed by the tigers (and very explicitly killed, poisoned, burnt alive, run over by cars, crushed in illegal demolitions), the little rabbits finally rebel and viciously attack the tigers, biting their necks and making them bleed to death. The

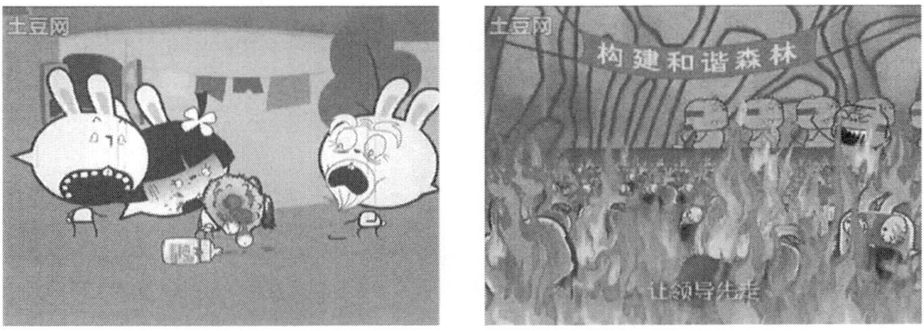

Figure 10.7. Little Rabbit Be Good. The little rabbits, after being oppressed and killed by the tigers, through references to milk powder deaths, the 1994 Karamay fire, and the car accident caused by Li Gang's son, attack the tigers.

animation ends with the little child closing the book, looking visibly upset and scared followed by a final warning: "When they are hard-pressed, even rabbits can bite!"

Despite the wide circulation and the immediate resonance that it had on the various China-bridge blogs, *Little Rabbit Be Good* has arguably had limited visibility because it was almost immediately censored in China.[20] Of course, the Internet savvy in China easily bypasses such censorship, but as a result of this blockage, the animation remains located in a noninstitutional space and outside mass-consumed animation and therefore, not differently from the other *animateur* movies, both practically (de facto) and ontologically (by choice) marginal.

My last example is a short flash animation with no title that seemed very popular on the Chinese Internet. At first I was not able to identify the maker, not because s/he is hiding behind a safe acronym to avoid censorship, but rather because the original producer's name was lost in the various repostings of the animation. In its many postings, the animation is only referred to with phrases such as "birth of a flash animation" or "creation of a flash animation" or simply with a reference to the Chinese website where it was downloaded, for example, "flash animation from Chaoniu website." It took some Internet detective work to find out that its original title was *Animator vs. Animation* (2006), created by Alan Becker, and that the official version was available on the websites Albino Black Sheep and Atom.com.[21] Both the producer and the website are non-Chinese and yet their "foreignness"—or, arguably, their transnational, global cultural location—seems to play no particular role in how and why the animation circulates. I chose this particular animation precisely because of its "absent" maker and the fact that its main belonging, at least in the Chinese Internet, is with the viewers who have chosen it, watched it, and appropriated it. I found that not only was this animation posted on several Chinese video-sharing sites with no reference to its American producer, but it was also included in many personal blogs as a favorite video. The video shows a stick figure literally coming out of its Flash software page and climbing on its command bars and beginning to interact with them, engaging in combat with the Flash drawing board components and destroying several pieces of the board. Finally, several other cloned stick figures appear and take over the frame, winning over the software that was supposed to contain them. The humor of this clever exercise of style is its main attraction. The idea in itself is not new (Bugs Bunny was engaging in fights with its animator's brushes, pencils, and paper in similar ways, long before Flash animation software was developed), but its appeal remains. The Chinese viewers, who chose not only to watch this short, fun and provocative animation, but also to download and/or link it to their blogs and thus share it with many other viewers, are engaging with the cinematic experience

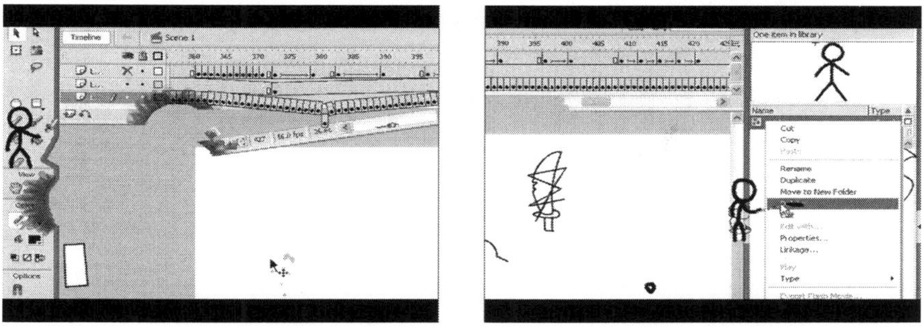

Figure 10.8. Animator *vs.* Animation. Alan Becker, 2006.

in "transnational" ways that are not easy to define but are nonetheless meaningful and certainly increasingly pervasive.

My necessarily limited selection hopefully still shows that *animateur* cinema is a local, Chinese, cultural practice, separate from mainstream animation and contributing to the same "alternative" cultural space of independent DV production. With a few notable exceptions (e.g., *Xiaoxiao, Grassmud Horse,* and *Little Rabbit Be Good*), despite being potentially transnational in distribution because available on the Internet, most *animateur* cinema is not exportable. Such a localized nature originates partly because of language and cultural barriers, but mostly because *animateur* cinema is interested in expressing individual creativity, pushing global identities to the background. Most independent digital animations are closer to *Holding One's Hand* or *Boundaries* than *Grassmud Horse* and *Little Rabbit Be Good.* The latter two works became relatively popular abroad only because their dissenting stance could be framed in the global recognition of the PRC's ongoing violations of human rights and the long-standing international media coverage of the CCP's tyrannical oppression of its people.[22]

Conclusion: Animateur Cinema's "True" Ruptures

In concluding, we should note that the *animateur* cinema's experience goes beyond the specificity of the Chinese context. Whether politically engaged or escapist, *animateur* cinema offers a type of cinematic experience that has also transnational (meaning *beyond* the nation, but not in a globalization sense) relevance. *Animateur* cinema reminds us that, although the cinema experience may have relocated into different media, it continues to be the privileged "eye" of our times (Casetti 2008). Both its forms and locations have taken cinema (back) to a noninstitutionalized space where cinema can still produce new ruptures. *Animateur* cinema is in a transitional space, outside the evolutionary, canonized, and measurable developments of the animation industry. As such, it is closer to the early cinema of attractions with its exhibitionist nature. While the parallel with the earlier cinema of attractions has its obvious limits, I think it is useful to recognize that these movies can all be described as having moved (back?) to animate a reality that is not event-driven and all are—to different degrees—concerned with exhibiting/showing off their own abilities to "do things." The animated movies I have discussed all show a significant departure from both the conventions and the institutions that have defined narrative cinema after its earlier exhibitionist beginnings. In these DV animations, there is indeed a visible degree of experimentation with the medium itself and in some cases even the very self-consciously declared pleasure of surprising—if not shocking—the audiences with what one can do with newly available (and relatively cheap) hardware and software and, most importantly, some creativity.

As Tom Gunning has pointed out, exhibitionism places early cinema at odds with film history (Gunning 1990). Exhibitionism is what makes early cinema profoundly different from "cinema" as it was later understood, and that is why André Gaudreault later would go as far as suggesting the altogether new term "kine-attractography" for it. In the years following the invention of the cinématographe, makers were showing (and viewers were shown) animated photographs or "monstrative attractions" instead of the later established narrative-driven cinema. Unlike a film narrative that creates a self-enclosed text in which the audiences are asked to immerse themselves, the viewer's conscious presence (as witness of the spectacle) was essential, not just complementary, to the making of this attraction. Similarly, digital short animated movies like *Boundaries* or *Holding One's Hand* are "characterized by an implicit acknowledgment of the viewer's presence, a viewer who is directly confronted in an exhibitionist manner" (Gaudreault 2006, 95). *Animateur* cinema's viewers are not asked to immerse themselves into a narrative. Instead, these movies rely on the implicit assumption that the viewers will, first and foremost, enjoy the show and, secondly, position themselves as active (not absorbed) readers/interpreters of a seemingly unconnected series of animated shots. In fact, decoding the subtleties embedded in the entertaining *Grassmud Horse* animation requires a noticeable act of detachment from the movie texts and a very conscious relocation into a much broader sociocultural and political context.

In these DV animated practices, both the maker and the viewer are also very aware of the inevitable and in fact intended manipulations/distortions performed in movies that have almost entirely lost their direct indexicality to the real. The animated movie is recognized from the start as originating from a digital drawing and/or digital programming and encoding. Such awareness of the medium itself often leads to an increased playfulness and to a more exhibitionist dimension of the screening and viewing experience.

André Gaudreault has remarked that "the fundamental point of rupture in film history was not the invention of the moving picture camera in the 1890s (the Kinetograph, the Cinématographe) but rather the constitution of the institution 'cinema' in the 1910s" (Gaudreault 2006, 99). While I agree with Gaudreault about the necessity of separating the moment of technological innovation (in this case the digital technologies that have enabled both the rise of live-action and animated digital videos) from that of the creation of a new cultural, artistic, and media order, I do not think that true ruptures need necessarily to set in motion new orders. They can be just as significant because of their ability to challenge the existing order by focusing on change itself, and possibly because of (rather than in spite of) their disinterest in the making of a new order. While it may not necessarily have led to a "new order," and in fact possibly and precisely because of its resistance to becoming solidified, structured, and institutionalized in a new order, *animateur* cinema has nonetheless brought about true ruptures within Chinese cinema's cultural, artistic, and social space. I have referred to this context as *light* smaller-screen realities (Voci 2010). This *lightness* should not be mistaken with disengagement. Quite the opposite, these *light* practices point to a deeply meaningful need for a noncodified, noninstitutionalized, both entertaining and cognitive act of vision that I believe preexists the acts of video making or viewing. In this sense, digital animation is indeed a crucial technological innovation that has enabled (but not created) such desire to find an outlet previously unavailable.

Animateur cinema's ruptures are deeply linked to its *lightness*. Whether by evoking existential issues (as in the case of *Boundaries*), the possibility of a revolution (as in the case of *Little Rabbit Be Good*), or simply gifting pleasure and spectacle (as *Animator vs. Animation*), *animateur* cinema's cultural critique is consciously reduced to a fragmented, *light*, often humorous display of provocative images rather than constructed in the more ambitious narratives of a philosophical reflection or an oppositional ideology. Both in its escapist or political expressivity, *animateur* cinema remains mostly located in a transitional, temporary, short-lived space of online movie making and viewing practices, in between private and public spheres. In this noninstitutionalized "alternative" space, both individual sensibilities and oppositional stances can still become visible and, most crucially, be shared outside the constraints of profitability, ideology, or intellectualism. Those constraints are not necessarily altogether rejected but rather temporarily suspended so that nonprofitable, nonideological, nonintellectual, non-avant-garde, but still culturally, aesthetically, socially, and politically meaningful realities can become visible.

Notes

1. More specifically, in examining the increasingly large and diversified documentary production, academic attention has focused on how the shift to the digital medium contributes to the creation of a new type of realist aesthetics or *jishizhuyi* (on-the-spot realism) that relied on the contingent effects of presence or *xianchang* (Robinson 2007). Besides supporting and expanding the poetic of *xianchang,* DV was also crucial in closing the gap between professional filmmakers and amateur video makers (Wang 2005; Zhang Zhen 2007).

2. "Animation" and "animating" (literally "putting life into") are conceptually stimulating terms. The term *animateur,* in its French etymology, can refer to both the producer of animation (the animation filmmaker) and the professional or informal animator working in sociocultural (community education and learning) or time-leisure animation activities (from library-based playgroups to commercial holiday villages). Besides its multiple connotations in relation to "animation" as a film technique and a sociocultural activity, I use the term *animateur* because it is a close homophone with two traditionally divergent concepts: the "amateur," another loan word from French, and the "auteur," also a loan word from French, commonly used in English instead of "author" to emphasize the film director's—or, in other instances, the screenwriter's—role as the original creator.

3. *Xiaoxiao*'s author, Zhu Zhiqian, created eight short animations, one video game, and a couple of advertising videos, all based on humorously choreographed and often absurdly violent fights (Xiaoxiao, http://www.flash8.net/user/701.shtml).

4. Some studies have looked at how animation and computer-generated imagery (CGI) have been used in feature films. See, for example, Khoo 2009; Lee 2006.

5. According to Liu Xielin and Stephen White, three main players—primary actors, secondary actors, and institutions—have an important role in the success (or failure) of any innovation in reformed China (Liu and White 2001, 1095). If we were to apply Liu and White's model in the context of animation, the primary actors would include producers, audiences, and animation companies; the secondary actors could be identified in the SARFT as well as other licensing organizations and Ministry of Industry departments. Other larger or peripheral institutions (what Liu and White define as "practices, rules, and disembodied organizations") also exert an important influence on both these primary and secondary actors. For instance, directives coming directly or indirectly from the CCP have the most notable influences. As one begins to look at innovation more closely within the multiple negotiations taking place among these players, issues of authorships and aesthetics are often overpowered and effectively erased by the apparent dominance of the economic and political strategies that seem to be the main concerns of all players.

6. In newspaper articles one often finds reference to the speed of industry growth. "According to the statistics from the Chinese Academy of Social Sciences, China's animation industry is growing at the annual rate of 97 percent." ("Chinese

cartoon industry animated by crisis," *Global Times* 21 [Sept. 28, 2009]: 18). Along the same lines, another report on Chinese animation targeting, more specifically, Canadian investors notes that "[t]he Digital Film and Animation sector in China has been growing rapidly, and it is estimated that there are over 5,470 firms and 100,000 workers in the sector . . . China is in the midst of training over 10,000 animators. There are 447 universities with departments of animation, 1,230 universities with schools related to animation, and an incredible 466,000 students in programs that offer animation as a subject" ("New Media China," http://www.tted.gov.bc.ca/APTI/Documents/China-%20Digital%20Film%20and%20Animation.pdf, an Asian Pacific Market Opportunity Profile issued by the Asian Pacific Trade and Investment division (APTI) of the Ministry of Small Business, Technology, and Economic Development of British Columbia, http://www.tted.gov.bc.ca/apti/Pages/default.aspx).

7. Examples of successful tradition-focused animation are the CCTV animated series *Shaonian Di Renjie* (*Young Detective Renjie*) that takes as its inspiring source Judge Dee as a child, based on the life of Di Renjie, a famous official who served at the end of the Tang dynasty and under Empress Dowager Wu Zetian (Zhou dynasty). The animated film *Butterfly Lovers* (a Mainland/Taiwan coproduction, directed by a Taiwanese filmmaker and produced by the Shanghai Animated Film Studio) similarly takes inspiration from the legendary love story between Liang Shanbo and Zhu Yingtai that dates back to the late Tang dynasty (slightly different versions have continued to be written over the centuries). Among the full-length feature animated films that more directly refer to socialist classics, one finds *Little Soldier Zhang Ga* (*Xiaobing Zhang Ga*) and *Sparkling Red Star* (*Shanshande hongxing haizide tiankong*).

8. Animateur social belongings can also vary quite significantly; however, these groups are all characterized by a strong self-awareness of their belonging to an urban cultural space and urban generation cinema (Zhang Zhen 2007). With possibly only the exception of the *Village Video Project* (sponsored and produced by Wu Wenguang), which literally brought DV cameras to the villages and their dwellers, DV culture has been mostly rooted in the urban context.

9. Zimmermann pioneered this field of research with her book *Reel Families* in 1995, which traces the history of amateur films from its earlier stages to the early 1960s in the American context.

10. Besides the pioneering work on audiences developed by the Birmingham School, other major contributions include the writings of Ien Ang, John Fiske, and James Moran. In the specific "new media" context, studies on the active and interactive audiences have rightly emphasized media convergence and participatory cultures' impact on both creative practices and consumption. (See Jenkins 2006b. For additional examples, see Jancovich, Faire, and Stubbings 2003; Lancaster 2001; Jenkins 1992).

11. The "1992 amateur manga conventions in Tokyo were . . . attended by over a quarter of a million young people" (Kinsella 1998, 289).

12. Maybe the most complex and most extreme development of such a line of analysis is Pierre Levy's utopia of a web-originated collective intelligence. In Levy's theory, new media technology is promoting a "deterritorialization" of knowledge and

will lead to a "cosmopedia" created by self-organized and self-regulated virtual communities that will no longer recognize themselves as part of the still-existing but already porous social groups. Jenkins himself incorporates Levy's theory as a "model for a fan-based politics" in his own reassessment of the impact of digital technology on fan culture (Jenkins 2006b, 134).

13. In Japan, *kuso-ge* originally described a type of video-gaming practice that revolves around flawed, low-quality games. "Since its first appearance in early 2000, both the Chinese and non-Chinese press have reported that the *egao* phenomenon has developed as a variation of Japanese originated *kuso* (literally, "shit") culture" (Voci 2010, 106). For more on the relationship between *kuso* and *egao,* see Voci 2010, 106–108.

14. A discussion on the passive vs. active spectator binary is beyond the scope of this chapter. Different degrees of passivity and agency have been recognized in the interaction with media (and film in particular). They include the effects/hypodermic model developed by the Frankfurt School, the uses and gratification model (Blumler and Katz 1974), screen theory based on the mode of address, and Stuart Hall's encoding/decoding model (and, more broadly, the focus on audience as the decoder of meanings, which was the main focus of the Centre for Contemporary Cultural Studies at Birmingham). Such scholarship on this topic has progressively "emancipated" the spectator (Rancière 2009). Yet even audience studies have not been able to fully address the implications of an individual experience of a medium that falls that outside the "mass audience" framework and includes but also goes beyond a perspective that acknowledges the impact that class, gender, age, and other social and cultural belongings have on the conceptualization of the active spectator.

15. On Youku, as of June 2011, the animation had 3,826 viewers, eleven comments, and seventeen downloads. The animation can also be found in other video-sharing sites under the playlist for the 2006 International University Animation Festival (Aniwow!): for instance, at ku6.com (http://v.ku6.com/playlist/index_1700730.html) or cctv.com (http://space.tv.cctv.com/schedule/SCHE1206426713665378).

16. He Wei graduated from the Guangzhou Fine Arts Institute in 2006. His graduation work *Xiao Pang Jie* can be viewed on the Moho Anime Studio website at http://moho.5d6d.com/thread-548-1-1.html.

17. Its original live-action video appeared in 2009 and new variations (animated and nonanimated) have since continued to be posted.

18. Wang Bo's *Little Rabbit* video card and other subversive digital animations have also been reposted and archived by *China Digital Times,* covered by the *Wall Street Journal* (Chao 2011), as well as profiled in *The World Policy Journal* (Larmer 2012).

19. The Karamay fire (1994) took place in a theater and killed 288 children, while twenty party officials were brought to safety. The fire and its victims are also referred to by quoting the phrase "*rang lingdao xian zou*—leaders first," in reference to the order that was issued once the fire broke out (Sheridan 2007). The 2008 milk scandal, which mostly involved milk and infant formula adulterated with melamine, resulted in an estimated 300,000 victims, six deaths, and hundreds of babies being hospitalized (Yardley 2008). The Tiger Gang car incident (November 2010) is also widely referred to

by quoting the phrase "*Wo baba shi Li Gang*—My father is Li Gang," which was shouted by the intoxicated Li Qiming after he ran over two girls and killed one and sped away in his car, arrogantly claiming that he was untouchable because his father was a powerful deputy police chief. The incident and its legal aftermaths were covered in both domestic and international media (Wines 2010).

20. I use the term "bridge blogs" to refer to large China-focused blogs like *Danwei, EastSouthNorthWest,* or *China Digital Times,* in which social issues, political events, and cultural practices are translated into English, commented on, interpreted, and circulated outside the Chinese-language Internet.

21. Alan Becker also produced two sequels to *Animator vs. Animation,* both available at http://www.atom.com/funny-stuff/animator-vs-animation.

22. An exceptional case of a relatively popular, non-overtly political animateur is Lei Lei (Ray), a twenty-seven-year-old animator who has created (and freely shared) some of the most intriguing and inspiring animations I have personally encountered on small screens. His recently acquired international fame has attracted considerable viewership and media coverage (Sun 2013).

Bibliography

Albino Black Sheep. http://www.albinoblacksheep.com/flash/animator.

Allen, Matthew and Rumi Sakamoto. 2011. "Sushi Reverses Course: Consuming American Sushi in Tokyo." *The Asia-Pacific Journal* 9.5. http://old.japanfocus.org/-Mathew-Allen/3481.

Ang, Ien. 1991. *Desperately Seeking the Audience.* London and New York: Routledge.

Atom.com. http://www.atom.com.

Barmé, Geremie. 2007. "Eating Chinese—a Historical Banquet." Paper presented at *The Future of U.S.-China Relations,* a conference organized by the U.S.-China Relations Institute of the University of Southern California. http://china.usc.edu/App_Images/Barme.pdf.

Blumler, Jay G. and Elihu Katz, eds. 1974. *The Uses of Mass Communications: Current Perspectives on Gratifications Research.* Beverly Hills, California: Sage Publications.

Bolter, Jay David and Richard Grusin. 1999. *Remediation. Understanding New Media.* Cambridge, MA: MIT Press.

Brush and Ink Paintings of Grass Mud Horses. http://chinadigitaltimes.net/2009/08/slideshow-brush-and-ink-paintings-of-grass-mud-horses/.

Casetti, Francesco. 2008. *Eye of the Century: Film, Experience, Modernity.* New York: Columbia University Press.

Chao, Loretta. 2011. "Two New Videos, Two Radically Different Chinas." In China Real Time Report. *Wall Street Journal.* http://blogs.wsj.com/chinarealtime/2011/01/24/two-new-videos-two-radically-different-images-of-china/.

China Digital Times. 2014. "Grass-mud Horse Lexicon." Oct. 15. http://chinadigitaltimes.net/space/Grass-Mud_Horse_Lexicon.

Custer, C. 2011. "'Little Rabbit, Be Good': A Subversive New Years' Video Card." Jan. 24. http://chinageeks.org/2011/01/little-rabbit-be-good-a-subversive-new-years-video-card/.

Dang, Zi 宕子. 2009. "Yinggai qingchude shi 'chengyu egao' beihoude shehui binggen 应该清除的是"成语恶搞"背后的社会病根 (What we need to eliminate is the unsolved social illness behind the 'egao proverbs')." In *Jin chuanmei* 今传媒 (Media Today), July 2009; republished Sept. 15, 2009. http://zhiku.xinwenren.com/2009/0915/3332.html.

Du, Daisy Yan. 2012. "On the Move: The Trans/national Animated Film in 1940s–1970s China." PhD dissertation, University of Wisconsin-Madison.

Eco, Umberto. 1962. *Opera Aperta*. Milano: Bompiani.

———. 2005. "Innovation and Repetition: Between Modern and Postmodern Aesthetics." *Daedalus* 134 (4): 191–207.

Edwards, Louise and Elaine Jeffreys, eds. 2010. *Celebrity in China*. Hong Kong: Hong Kong University Press.

Ehrlich, David and Tianyi Jin. 2001. "Animation in China." In *Animation in Asia and the Pacific*, edited by John A. Lent. Bloomington: Indiana University Press.

Farquhar, Mary Ann. 1993. "Monks and Monkey: A Study of 'National Style' in Chinese Animation." *Animation Journal* 1 (2): 8–15.

Fiske, John. 2011. *Reading the Popular*. 2nd ed. London; New York: Routledge.

Fowler, Catherine and Paola Voci. 2011. "Brief Encounters: Theorizing Screen Attachments outside the Movie Theatre." *Screening the Past* 32. http://www.screeningthepast.com/2011/11/brief-encounters-theorizing-screen-attachments-outside-the-movie-theatre/.

Gaudreault, André. 2006. "From 'Primitive Cinema' to 'Kine-Attractography.'" In *The Cinema of Attraction Reloaded*, edited by Wanda Strauven, 85–104. Amsterdam: Amsterdam University Press.

Gong, Haomin and Xin Yang. 2010. "Digitized Parody: The Politics of *egao* in Contemporary China." *China Information* 24 (1): 3–26.

Gunning, Tom. 1990. "The Cinema of Attractions: Early Film, Its Spectator, and the Avant-Garde." In *Early Cinema: Space, Frame, Narrative*, edited by Thomas Elsaesser. London: BFI.

Hangzhou Hui Huang Animation. 2010. "Company Profile." *HK Film and Television Market*, Mar. 22–24.

Jancovich, Mark, Lucy Faire, and Sarah Stubbings. 2003. *The Place of the Audience: Cultural Geographies of Film Consumption*. London: British Film Institute.

Jenkins, Henry. 1992. *Textual Poachers: Television Fans and Participatory Culture: Studies in Culture and Communication*. New York: Routledge.

———. 2006a. *Convergence Culture: Where Old and New Media Collide*. New York: New York University Press.

———. 2006b. *Fans, Bloggers, and Gamers: Exploring Participatory Culture*. New York: New York University Press.

Jenkins, Henry, Sam Ford, and Joshua Green. 2013. *Spreadable Media: Creating Value and Meaning in a Networked Culture*. New York: New York University Press.

Jing, Xu 许婧 and Yang Wang 汪炀. 2005. *Du donghua: Zhongguo donghua huangjin bashi nian* 读动画：中国动画黄金八十年 (Reading animation: Eighty years of Chinese animation). Beijing: Chaohua chubanshe.

Kang, Helen. 2006. "Shui Mo Donghua: The History and Development of Brush Painting Animation." *Animation Journal* 14: 63–74.

Keane, Michael. 2006. "From Made in China to Created in China." *International Journal of Cultural Studies* 9: 285–296.
Khoo, Olivia. 2009. "Remaking the Past, Interrupting the Present: The Space of Technology and Futurity in Contemporary Chinese Blockbusters." In *Futures of Chinese Cinema: Technologies and Temporalities in Chinese Screen Cultures,* edited by Olivia Khoo and Sean Metzger, 241–262. Bristol: Intellect.
Kinsella, Sharon. 1998. "Japanese Subculture in the 1990s: Otaku and the Amateur Manga Movement." *Journal of Japanese Studies* 24 (2): 289–316.
Lancaster, Kurt. 2001. *Interacting with Babylon 5: Fan Performance in a Media Universe*. 1st ed. Austin: University of Texas Press.
Larmer, Brook. 2012. "Portfolio: Little Rabbit Be Good." *World Policy Journal: Games People Play.* http://wpj.sagepub.com/content/29/2/44.full.pdf+html.
Lee, Vivian. 2006. "Virtual Bodies, Flying Objects: The Digital Imaginary in Contemporary Martial Arts Films." *Journal of Chinese Cinemas* 1 (1): 9–26.
Lent, John and Xu Ying. 2003. "China's Animation Beginnings: The Roles of the Wan Brothers and Others." *Asian Cinema* 14 (1): 56–69.
Li, Fanghe. 2010. "Vidding Kung Fu Panda in China." http://henryjenkins.org/2010/03/vidding_kung_fu_panda_in_china.html.
Liu, Xielin and Steven White. 2001. "Comparing Innovation Systems: A Framework and Application to China's Transition Context." *Research Policy* 30 (7): 1091–1114.
Moran, James M. 2002. *There's No Place Like Home Video, Visible evidence v.12.* Minneapolis: University of Minnesota Press.
Pickowicz, Paul G., and Yingjin Zhang. 2006. *From Underground to Independent: Alternative Film Culture in Contemporary China.* Lanham, MD: Rowman & Littlefield.
Quiquemelle, Marie-Claire. 1985. "Les Frères Wan et 60 ans de dessins animés chinois (The Wan brothers and 60 years of animated film in China)." Centre international du cinéma d'animation. Festival d'Annecy, 1985.
Rancière, Jacques. 2009. *The Emancipated Spectator.* London: Verso.
Robinson, Luke. 2007. "Contingency and event in China's new documentary film movement [online]," University of Nottingham Eprints. http://eprints.nottingham.ac.uk/546/.
Sheridan, Michael. 2007. "China Aghast at 'Sacrifice' of 288 Pupils." *The Sunday Times.* http://www.timesonline.co.uk/tol/news/world/asia/article1752202.ece.
Sun, Yunfan. 2013. "Lei Lei: A Sketch of the Animator as a Young Man." *China File.* https://www.chinafile.com/lei-lei-sketch-animator-young-man.
Szczelkun, Stefan. 2000. "The Value of Home Movies." *Oral History* 28 (2): 94–98.
Voci, Paola. 2010. *China on Video: Smaller-Screen Realities.* New York: Routledge.
Wang, Yiman. 2005. "The Amateur's Lightning Rod: DV Documentary in Postsocialist China." *Film Quarterly* 58 (4): 16–26.
Wines, Michael. 2010. "China's Censors Misfire in Abuse-of-Power Case." *New York Times.* http://www.nytimes.com/2010/11/18/world/asia/18li.html.
Wu Bin 武斌 and Chunyan Han 韩春艳. 2009. *Zhongguo liuxing wenhua sanshi nian: 1978–2008* 中国流行文化三十年： 1978–2008 (Thirty Years of Popular Culture in China). Beijing: Jiuzhou chubanshe.
Wu, Weihua. 2006. "Animation in Postsocialist China: Visual Narrative, Modernity, and Digital Culture." PhD dissertation, City University of Hong Kong.

———. 2010. "In Memory of Meishu Film: Catachresis and Metaphor in Theorizing Chinese Animation." *Animation: An Interdisciplinary Journal* (Apr. 21): 31–54.

Yan, Hui 颜慧 and Yabin Suo 索亚斌. 2005. *Zhongguo donghua dianyingshi* 中国动画电影史 (History of the Development of Chinese Animation). Beijing: Zhongguo dianying chubanshe.

Yardley, Jim. 2008. "Baby Formula Sickened Many More, China Says." *New York Times*. Sept. 17. http://www.nytimes.com/2008/09/17/world/asia/17milk.html.

Yi, Yan 尹岩 . 1988. "Donghua dianying zhong de zhongguo xuepai 动画电影中的中国学派 (The Chinese School of Animation)." *Dangdai dianying* 当代电影 (Contemporary Film) 6: 71–79.

Yu, Guoning 于国宁. 2007. "'Egao' mingzhu dailale shenme? 恶搞"名著带来了什么? (What did *egao* famous works bring about?)" *Jiangsu jiaoyu tongxun* 江苏教育通讯 (Jiangsu Education Journal) 5: 21–23

Zhang, Huilin 张慧临. 2002. *Ershi shiji Zhongguo donghua yishushi* 二十世纪中国动画艺术史 (Art history of Chinese animation in the twentieth century). Xi'an: Shanxi renmin chubanshe.

Zhang, Xianmin 张献民. 2006. "Liangge pinghuang de yuzhou 两个平行的宇宙 (Two Parallel Universes)." In *The Third China Independent Film Festival,* edited by Zou Jing Cao Kai, 38–42. Nanjing: The Museum of Modern Art.

Zhang, Xueying. 2008. "Creating an Animation 'Dream' Factory." *China Today* 57 (6): 12–24.

Zhang, Zhen. 2007. *The Urban Generation: Chinese Cinema and Society at the Turn of the Twenty-first Century.* Durham, NC: Duke University Press.

Zimmermann, Patricia R. 1995. *Reel Families: A Social History of Amateur Film, Arts and Politics of the Everyday.* Bloomington: Indiana University Press.

———. 1996. "Geographies of Desire: Cartographies of Gender, Race, Nation, and Empire in Amateur Film." *Film History* 8 (1): 85–98.

CHAPTER 11

"To Whom Do Our Bodies Belong?"

Being Queer in Chinese DV Documentary

LUKE ROBINSON

Introduction: Documentary, Performance, and Homosexuality in China

Independent Chinese documentary has long been associated with the production of images of the subaltern. While such a focus is identifiable as far back as Duan Jinchuan's first films on Tibet, early DV productions such as Wu Wenguang's *Jianghu: Life on the Road* (*Jianghu* 2000), Yang Lina's *Old Men* (*Lao Tou* 1999), and Wang Jianwei's *Living Elsewhere* (*Shenghuo zai Bie Chu* 1999) expanded the purview of independent documentary to incorporate the socially disenfranchised and the marginal in a multiplicity of different manifestations. Perhaps inevitably, sexual minorities were included. Ying Weiwei's *The Box* (*Hezi* 2001) is usually cited as "the first documentary from the People's Republic that features lesbian subjects" (Chao 2010a, 77). Zhang Yuan's *Miss Jin Xing* (*Jin Xing Xiaojie* 2000)—about the dancer of the same name—featured a gay male protagonist choosing to undergo gender reassignment. Since then, a steady stream of documentaries taking the lives of gay or transgendered Chinese men and women as their critical focus has been produced. Many of these films have been made using digital technology.

What is striking about this early work, however, is its preoccupation with Chinese male homosexuality as performance.[1] This manifests in two clear ways. The first is a focus either on gay male subjects who *are* performers—in particular, although not exclusively, drag queens—or the explicit inclusion in the films of scenes of (predominantly drag) performance, even when the films' protagonists do not make a living this way. Examples here would include *Miss Jin Xing*, Michelle Chen's *The Snake Boy* (*Shanghai Nanhai* 2002), Zhang Hanzi's *Tangtang* (*Tangtang* 2004), Han Tao's *Baobao* (*Baobao* 2004), Gao Tian's *Meimei* (*Meimei* 2005), and Du

Haibin's *Beautiful Men* (*Renmian Taohua* 2005). The second, however, is more indirect and involves the adoption of shooting practices that formally mirror this interest in performance on the part of the films' subjects. These practices include the interpenetration of scripted, reenacted, and unscripted scenes or storylines, with no attempt being made to distinguish between the two; the mixing of actors and "real" people; and the use of camerawork that both pastiches the vérité practices of documentary and reveals each film as a constructed artifact and product of mediation. These techniques, which serve to deliberately blur the line between documentary and fiction, place these documentaries at the intersection of two of Bill Nichols' famous modes: the reflexive and the performative.[2] They are most obviously present in *Tangtang,* Cui Zi'en's *Night Scene* (*Yejing* 2004), and Jiang Zhi's *Xiang Pingli* (*Xiang Pingli* 2005).[3]

This double focus serves to bring Chinese queer male identity and Chinese DV documentary practice into an interesting and mutually imbricated relationship. As Chao Shi-Yan (2010b, 173–174) has suggested in his analysis of *Tangtang,* the presentation of queer men's "real" performance as women serves as a direct challenge to the re-essentialization of gender binaries in post-Mao China, while the reflexive interrogation of documentary style—whether the on-camera interview in *Night Scene* or vérité camerawork in *Tangtang*—similarly serves to "open up" the status of these films as "documents" to broader and more varied interpretations. In this sense, digital video becomes a medium through which Chinese queer identity can be articulated as ambiguous, open-ended, and (in part) self-fashioned. But at the same time, these documentaries make use of the body of the queer performer to interrogate specific understandings of the digital in its Chinese context. Through the practice of *xianchang,* for example, both performance and embodiment have long been understood as central to Chinese documentary, particularly in its more experimental manifestations (Leary 2003; Zhang 2007, 20). The act of shooting live and "on the scene," which came to characterize much alternative cultural production in the 1990s (Dai 1999, 219; Robinson 2010, 180), *xianchang* has been theorized by the artist Qiu Zhijie (2003, 2) as meaning simply "at the time you must be there. Your emotions and your body are all part of *xianchang,* your every action has an influence upon it. You are not outside it, observing, but inside, experiencing it; and you are involved in constituting it." This perception of documentary filmmaking as critically underpinned by physical presence, and produced through the active participation of the filmmaker, was reinforced by the emergence of digital video. Certain practitioners believed that the medium brought one closer both to the body and to the physical world (Zhang 2010, 109): for example, Wu Wenguang (2001, 194–197) detailed his (highly gendered) understanding of the DV camera both as an extension of the body and as an instrument that brings out the unexpected details of the material world in his essay

"Nüxing he DV Shexiangji" ("Woman and the DV Camera"). Zhang Zhen (2010, 101) has also emphasized how Chinese artists and filmmakers have seen the digital as a way of redeeming the physical and the haptic, expressing a "desire to simultaneously document and transfigure the present." It is therefore hard not to see the focus in these films on the body and its transformations—whether onstage or more literally (in the case of *Miss Jin Xing* and *Xiang Pingli*) on the surgeon's table—as a mechanism through which to explore the nature and limits of the "real" in postsocialist China.[4]

The Ambivalence of the "Small Medium"

The performative elements of these documentaries could thus be said to work with, or reinforce, certain specific understandings of the nature of, or possibilities provided by, the digital medium. In other ways, however, these elements could be said to work *against* other presumed qualities of the digital, particularly those associated with its status as a "small medium." A term popularized by Annabelle and Ali Sreberny-Mohammadi (1994), small media are communication technologies that, in contrast to corporate or state-controlled mass media, are comparatively accessible and easy to disseminate. Such technologies are thus often associated with nonprofessional media production and circulation and, in consequence, antihegemonic or unofficial forms and messages (Conway 2008, 62). Video—analog, but particularly digital—is sometimes described as such a technology precisely because of its highly reproducible, distributable format and the portability of the camera.[5] In discussions of Chinese digital video production, these qualities have been subsumed under what Paola Voci (2010) has termed "lightness." This concept signals not simply a playful aesthetic distinct from the solemnity of much mainstream (and indeed independent) media in the PRC, but also a production practice facilitated by the digital camera's size and mobility—the effortlessness with which it can be maneuvered from public to private space and back again, for example, or how quickly the filmed subject can potentially forget about its presence—and the increased facility with which material captured on digital video can circulate publicly through electronic reproduction and dissemination (Voci 2010, 11–17). "Lightness" may be a neologism, but Voci's analysis has a genealogy: the term is consonant with the debates around small media, and from here on, I will thus use it to signify as such.

Chinese independent filmmakers have largely welcomed digital video as a small medium precisely because of its supposedly democratizing impact on media production.[6] From a slightly different perspective, however, some scholars have expressed concern over the potential consequences of "lightness" as a production practice for the documentary subject.[7] I would reiterate such concerns from the perspective of the queer subject of documentary. For such a subject, the outcome of "lightness" in the sense of lower impedance—the increased facility with which the digital video camera can penetrate private space and then make private images public through electronic reproduction and dissemination—should be obvious: greater difficulty in controlling awareness of their sexual identity, and thus the increased possibility of exposure to homophobic violence, whether social or physical. Although performance has often been understood as a way in which the queer Chinese subject can gain access to "public space and public discourse" (C. Berry 2009, 171), in this context it could also be seen as a "survival strategy" (Chao 2010b, 162): a technique that enables the queer subject to fashion a public identity while still retaining a degree of ambiguity about his or her *actual* sexual orientation through the citation of accepted theatrical or operatic codes of cross-dressing. Against the background of this new media ecology, the performative qualities of these documentaries, whether in front of or by the camera, could thus be understood as a defense mechanism against the blurring of the boundary between private and public effected by digital technology. They can be seen as an attempt to preempt the difficulties presented by the medium for the queer subject seeking to control his or her exposure to a less-than-accepting wider world. At stake here is how the queer subject is made visible, to whom, for what purpose, and under what conditions.

Queer identity and Chinese digital video practice are therefore structured in these documentaries in quite particular ways. Both are presented as a performative practice in which the body plays a central role; in turn, this performativity suggests an ambivalence toward the "lightness" also understood as central to the digital as a medium. What is interesting about recent nonfiction productions on queer subject matter, however, is how they have begun to move away from these preoccupations. In contemporary work by Cui Zi'en, Fan Popo, and the collective behind the webcast *Queer Comrades* (*Tongzhi yi Fanren* 2007), the focus has expanded to incorporate a far broader range of issues. Although performance and performers are not excluded, this focus now includes questions of gay history and the emergence of a self-conscious gay community in China; "coming out" (*chu gui*) stories; and the consideration of the everyday quality of gay life in a range of different contexts.[8] Documentary as a genre has been integrated with other, more populist formats: *Queer Comrades*, for example, started by self-consciously adopting the chat show formula, using presenters and a studio format for at least part of every episode. And, finally, the performative and reflexive elements of *xianchang* have been diluted by what appears to be a more traditional broadcasting aesthetic. This is most obvious in the return of the "talking head," a central element in both Fan's *Chinese Closet* (*Guizu* 2009) and Cui's *Queer China, "Comrade" China* (*Zhi*

Tongzhi 2008), and the interview (again a technique critical to the format adopted by *Queer Comrades*)—both practices that were rapidly abandoned by some of the earliest independent documentary filmmakers, in part because they were too strongly redolent of CCTV nonfiction programming.[9] Even a documentary that directly considers issues of performance and performativity, such as Fan and David Cheng's *New Beijing, New Marriage* (*Xin Qianmen dajie* 2009), does so in a far less self-consciously aestheticized manner.

One response to this development might be to argue that it is a form of "mainstreaming." In adopting a more conservative aesthetic, one might reason, the directors of these works aim to reach a wider audience. They therefore abandon any sense of the indeterminacy of gay identity, opting instead for a more "essentialized" vision that may be more in line with broadly held assumptions about gender and sexuality in post-Reform China. One could therefore compare these films to the American documentaries and television programs that, from the 1970s onward, made gay men "visible" by emphasizing their similarity to the mainstream, rather than their problematic difference (Pullen 2007, 5–7). Given the exponential growth and commercialization of queer culture in China in the past decade, this would hardly be surprising.[10] Yet the Chinese media "mainstream" is a more complex creature than its Euro-American counterparts. In China, the term has two meanings: one suggests a product that is commercially driven, while the other indicates material that promotes the CCP political agenda. The question of which genealogy such a "mainstream" aesthetic derives from is therefore an important one to consider. Equally as important, though, is the question of how this aesthetic is being used, and for what purpose. Traditional broadcasting techniques can be appropriated for a variety of different ends, not all of which are either commercially oriented or party political.

I would therefore argue that labeling recent Chinese queer documentary as straightforwardly "mainstream" is too limiting. To do so misrecognizes how many such works modify and adopt elements of both the commercial and political mainstream for quite specific purposes. The directors of these documentaries do not attempt to render queer identity ambiguous; instead, they actively seek out ways to make it both more plural and more publicly visible. They therefore actively embrace the mobility and reproducibility of both digital hardware and software, using these qualities to create new narratives about queer identity in China; establish on- and off-line spaces of queer community; and reflect on how earlier directors have represented homosexuality and the gay male body. These developments can be traced back to their backgrounds as self-identified queer, activist-oriented directors whose entry into nonfiction production has in part been facilitated by the more obviously participatory nature of digital technology. But, given the nature of the Chinese polity, I suggest that these directors do not simply push a rights-based political agenda through films. Instead, I would argue that they use digital's "lightness" to reimagine both how queer Chinese identity might be represented and how it might be effected. The result is the emergence of a queer subject whose sexuality is less performed and documented than incorporated and networked. It is against this backdrop that I would suggest the politics of these works should be judged; and as a point of departure for this analysis, I would like to turn to the documentary *Queer China, "Comrade" China* by Cui Zi'en.

Queer China, "Comrade" China: Voicing Queer History

Queer China, "Comrade" China is a feature-length documentary about the history of the gay community in China. Directed by independent filmmaker and former Beijing Film Academy faculty member Cui Zi'en, the film was distributed with the support of the Li Xianting Film Fund and partly funded through the Ford Foundation. Formally, it is divided into nine sections, each dealing with a discrete element of gay life in China. Composed almost entirely of "talking heads" discussing issues ranging from gay marriage to homosexuality in classical Chinese literature, interspersed with footage of television broadcasts, feature films, documentaries, and amateur or personal video, the documentary avoids the performative mode entirely, making no attempt to mix the fictional and the factual. In comparison with much of Cui's highly experimental oeuvre to date, it is perhaps unsurprising that Bérénice Reynaud (2010) has described *Queer China, "Comrade" China* as adopting "a more traditional form."

However, while some of these techniques may indeed be traditional by association, the use that Cui makes of them in this documentary is often quite distinctive. This is announced at the very beginning of the film. Starting *in media res,* without any contextualization (not even a title), we are thrown into what is clearly the middle of an interview. The screen is filled with the image of a middle-aged man, in three-quarter shot, sitting beside a table, talking. He is discussing homosexuality in China. The man is in mid-sentence when, after a matter of seconds, the image shrinks to a very small window, set against a black screen. As he continues to speak, the screen is suddenly filled with an image of a woman, seated behind a table, also talking. Again, after a couple of seconds, this image shrinks down to a very small window. Now, against a black screen, we suddenly have two small windows, two small talking heads, and two voices: the first man and the woman. This technique is repeated rapidly until the screen is filled with tiny windows of talking heads, each simultaneously discussing homosexuality in China: a mosaic of interviewees. Then, after a couple of seconds, the screen "ripples" from the center outward and this mosaic is replaced by a rainbow flag and the title of the film.

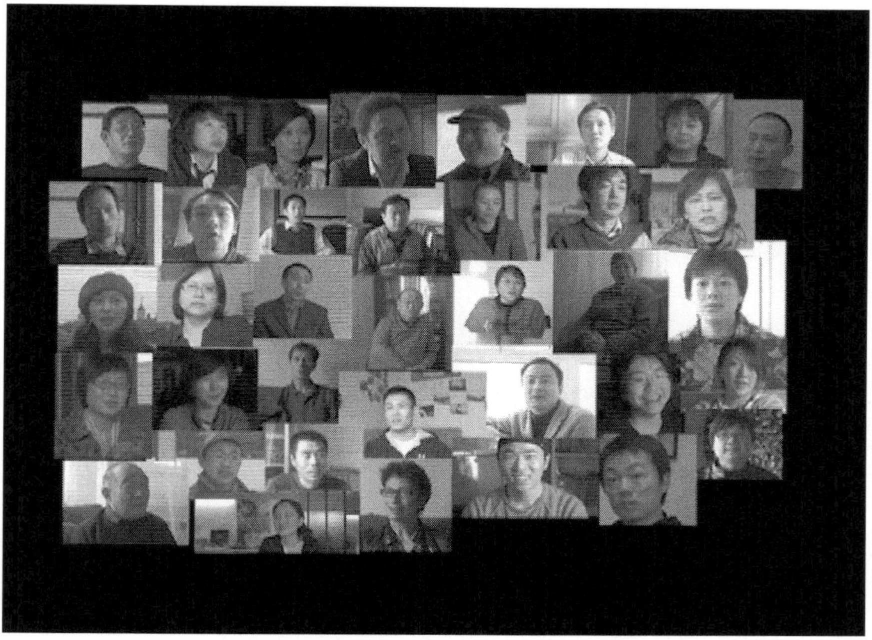

Figure 11.1. Queer China, "Comrade" China. The mosaic of talking heads.

Traditionally, the use of the "talking head" bestows professional authority and gravitas upon a subject. It is often associated with the exercise of institutional power, embodied in the figure of the expert "announcing official policy, imparting official information, or expressing an official attitude" (Halpern Martineau 1984, 256). But in this opening sequence, Cui seems to be deliberately undermining such associations. First, the overall result of this mosaic of tiny windows is not to suggest a single, unified narrative about homosexuality in China; rather, it implies a multiplicity of voices, each adding up to an open-ended narrative in which no single voice is dominant. This is reinforced throughout the film by the director's refusal to paper over the divergent points of view held by certain "talking heads" on particular subjects.[11] Second, no attempt is made in this sequence to identify who these "talking heads" are. In practice, then, no distinction is made between someone who possesses clear "official" standing and someone who does not. Authority in this instance is bestowed not simply through professional recognition, but also through the lived experience of being gay in China. This is why longtime campaigner Zhang Yi, who has no officially endorsed political or social status, is as important to the film as academic Li Yinhe, who does.[12]

The use of "talking heads" in *Queer China, "Comrade" China* thus appears to be less about presenting an official narrative and more about recovering the voice of a particular community. Through this technique the community comes to articulate the narrative of its own past, present, and future. The digital medium, however, plays a crucial role in enabling this narrative to be constructed. In this opening sequence, Cui exploits what Jay David Bolter and Richard Grusin (1999, 44–50) have described as the remediative capacities of the digital: its particular propensity to recycle older media forms. While arguing that remediation is in fact a characteristic of all media, electronic or otherwise, Bolter and Grusin suggest that the relationship of digital to analog media takes a number of specific forms, determined primarily by the degree of competition between "old" media and "new." Thus, in one manifestation an older medium may be represented digitally without any particular emphasis being placed on the "new" medium: for example, when original pictures or paintings are digitized and put online. Here, the digital simply provides access to the older medium. In other manifestations of remediation, however, the digital may attempt to refashion the analog while still retaining some sense of its presence: for example, in the mash-up. This process of decontextualization serves to make one aware both of the older forms of media and their new, perhaps incongruous, context. Finally, new media forms may completely replicate the aesthetic of analog media without acknowledging that this is what they are doing. Bolter and Grusin provide the example of online digital streaming, in which websites replicate the look and function of broadcast television without conceding that this is in fact their goal. This form of remediation, the authors suggest, reflects the particularly intense degree of economic competition between television and the Internet.

In this initial sequence, Cui is clearly "absorbing" an older broadcasting format, but also appropriating it. In making use of the talking head while simultaneously hypermediating it, *Queer China, "Comrade" China* retains a link with a traditional documentary filming practice, but also defamiliarizes it. Cui thus not only reworks the technique for a more radical purpose, but perhaps also encourages the viewer to reflect on the limitations of its original usage in the state television documentary, or *zhuantipian*. Although in the opening section this goal is achieved with original material, the documentary as a whole makes this point even more clearly through its constant sampling of footage from television broadcasts and feature films that touch on issues pertinent to the story of the queer community in China. Sometimes, as with Cui Zi'en and Shi Tou's appearance on the Hunan Satellite TV talk show *Tell It Like It Is* (*You Hua Hao Shuo*), this technique serves to emphasize the social significance of such moments.[13] At other points, it recontextualizes official footage, presenting an alternative position or point of view through the responses of individuals to statements made on television concerning homosexuality.[14] In such instances, the possibilities provided by the digital for the pluralization and democratization of official narratives in China are made very clear indeed.

Queer Comrades: Creating Queer Community

Cui's film thus exploits one element of digital "lightness"—its capacity to reduplicate and reformulate material, both original and sourced—to refashion a distinct history of homosexuality in China. In contrast, the web TV cast *Queer Comrades* embraces the ease with which the digital can blur the boundaries between public and private space to demonstrate how this can be viewed not as a threat to queer identity in China, but as an opportunity. Starting life as *Queer as Folk Beijing* in 2007, *Queer Comrades* specifically addresses aspects of gay life in contemporary China. Formally, it blends elements of the chat show—studio shoots, the use of the host, and informal discussions with guests—with more classic vérité sequences and even elements of the music video. In terms of subject matter, the series is instantly recognizable to the Western viewer, but also wide-ranging in scope: it has addressed everything from gay consumerism to transsexuality, queer artistic production to adoption and parenting. Nor does it restrict its focus exclusively to China, increasingly venturing abroad. Episodes have taken place at the 2010 Gay Games in Cologne, for example, and in Los Angeles, where one of the

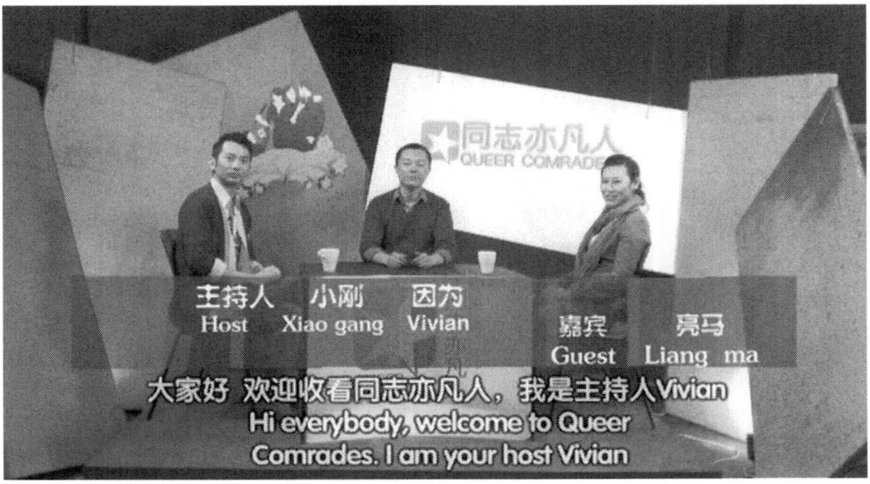

Figure 11.2. Queer Comrades. The chat show format.

presenters was invited to take part in leadership training at the city's Lesbian and Gay Center.

Aesthetically, *Queer Comrades* clearly remediates commercial broadcast television in a much less explicitly critical manner than *Queer China, "Comrade" China*'s appropriation of the *zhuantipian* aesthetic. What is most interesting about the program, however, is how it has exploited the Web not simply as a broadcast medium but as a way of connecting private and public space. Obviously, as a webcast, the program can be watched within the privacy of an individual's home: one can view it without having to publicly demonstrate an interest in queer content. Nevertheless, *Queer Comrades* has explicitly set out to exploit the Web as a community-building mechanism. The website, which has been developed alongside the program, includes a section dedicated to "news," "events," and a blog. While "news" is transnational in scope, covering gay issues at home and abroad, "events" focuses more specifically on social and cultural gatherings, primarily in Beijing. These include gay nights at city bars; club nights; queer film screenings; literary readings of queer fiction; and more obviously political events, such as Shanghai and Beijing Pride. Early episodes of the series sometimes even direct the viewer to the websites of the gay service providers being discussed (commercial or otherwise) by flashing up the web address mid-sequence. *Queer Comrades* is thus embedded in a site that connects the series to multiple actual events in spaces outside the home. In so doing, the producers have exploited the comparative ease with which the digital can move between domestic and public space to generate a virtual sense of the individual viewer's connection to a broader Chinese queer community. That ease also facilitates the actualization of this community through the creation of relationships extending beyond the website into physical social space.

The DV Generation: Advocacy and Queer Documentary in China

What explains this change in direction? One factor might be the pluralization broadly associated with the advent of digital video in the field of Chinese alternative cultural production. Early independent documentary was dominated by professionals from the broadcast media industries, in part because of material barriers to participation. In contrast, the emergence first of Hi8 and then digital video resulted in cameras that were cheap and easy for an individual to operate, and footage which, in the case of DV, could be edited with home computer software (Wang 2010, 75). Zhang Zhen (2010, 104) has thus described video in general, but digital video in particular, as central to the blurring of boundaries between different modes of image-making in China. In the field of independent documentary, this process is usually described as one in which the direct cinema-influenced practices of the earliest directors gradually gave way to more reflexive and performative modes of documentation, as people from backgrounds other than professional broadcasting, including filmmakers and artists, began to experiment with digital documentary filmmaking (Lü 2006, 14). In this particular instance, however, the reverse is true. The directors of the earliest of these documentaries were nearly all filmmakers or artists. Zhang Yuan and Jiang Zhi were both established professionals in their fields when they made *Miss Jin Xing* and *Xiang Pingli;* Zhang Hanzi trained as a sculptor at the Central Academy of Fine Arts in Beijing; Gao Tian graduated from the Directing Department of the Beijing Film Academy; and Han Tao was educated at the Lu Xun Fine Arts Academy in Shenyang (the alma mater of Wang Bing, among others). Only Du Haibin was a professional documentary filmmaker, and even he trained at the Beijing Film Academy. This may in part explain their interest in documentary as the art rather than the act of recording.[15] In contrast, those involved in the more recent work that I have addressed here have more diverse professional backgrounds. Fan Popo, though he studied at the Film Academy, did not pick up a camera until after he had graduated (Collett 2010); Wei Jiangang and Steven Xin Jiang, the first coproducers and cohosts of *Queer Comrades,* trained in acting and broadcasting, respectively; and even Cui Zi'en, whose film practice is the most self-consciously avant-garde of this group, had already diversified into more straightforward nonfiction production prior to releasing *Queer China, "Comrade" China,* as demonstrated by his 2007 documentary *We Are the . . . of Communism* (*Women shi Gongchanzhuyi shengluehao* 2007). The less obviously experimental approach to the genre exhibited by certain of these individuals may thus in part reflect their professional background—or lack thereof.

As important, however, is the fact that these filmmakers all explicitly self-identify as gay. Most are closely involved in Chinese LGBT social activism.[16] Again, this is in distinct contrast to the directors of the earliest documentaries on queer subject matter: a rare example of the social diversification of image production that digital video was supposed to herald. Rather than coming to their subject from the outside, looking in, these filmmakers therefore come to it from the inside, as individuals who identify with their subjects. This relationship perhaps underpins the desire in *Queer China, "Comrade" China* to rearticulate history through the voice of the subaltern, and the manner in which *Queer Comrades* ("Guanyu Women" n.d.) frames itself as presenting stories by and about Chinese queer empowerment. However, it also suggests that the purpose of these films is rather different from their predecessors. Unlike *Tangtang, Meimei, Beautiful Men,* or even Cui Zi'en's earlier films that capture "gay" issues through an experimental lens, these documentaries function in part as a form of community media. As previously suggested, they help to create and support relationships between urban Chinese gay men while simultaneously documenting them. But these films also function as a more self-conscious interface between this scene and society at large, and, as such, they perform a far more explicitly communicative, even pedagogical role, than the earlier documentaries. This in turn is reflected in the way both filmmakers and films position themselves. *Queer Comrades,* for example, lists one of its major goals as raising public awareness of LGBT matters in China ("Guanyu Women" n.d.); *Queer China, "Comrade" China*'s discussion of rights issues and state harassment could be said to function in a similar vein; while Fan (2010) has described *Chinese Closet* as providing a form of "public education" (*gonggong jiaoyu*) for its audiences. All are therefore more concerned with how digital nonfiction can make queer identity publicly visible than they are with exploiting its potential to destabilize that identity. This is mirrored in the efforts made by many of the producers to actively bring these works to a wider audience.[17] The abandonment of the more performative or reflexive elements of the earlier documentaries may therefore reflect a desire to communicate and sustain identity, not simply interrogate it. As Helen Leung (2008, 69) has pointed out, any form of community politics requires the assumption of a recognizable and coherent subject as a point of departure for social action.

In this sense, contemporary queer documentary could be seen as part of the wave of socially engaged media that has swept China in the wake of digital video. At its most radical, this movement also makes use of a "direct to camera" aesthetic, one that has been linked both to the Chinese tradition of "speaking bitterness" and to more global practices of human rights documentation (Jie Li 2010, 39; see also chapter 3 in this volume). It does not follow, however, that the works that I have analyzed here are engaged in the kind of "rightful resistance" (O'Brien and Li 2006, xii) that might be imputed to other forms of activist documentary in China. Historically, LGBT activists in China have been divided about invoking rights-based discourses: while some hope that antidiscrimination legislation will be enacted, others regard it as irrelevant to the more pressing issue of social discrimination (Y. Li 2006, 96–98); still others have viewed rights-based initiatives with deep scepticism, considering them positively detrimental to the relationship of queer Chinese to the state (Ho 2010, 28–29). More practically, the ongoing negotiation of relationships with government has a necessary impact on the discursive boundaries of a regular webcast such as *Queer Comrades,* if less explicitly on documentaries such as *Queer China, "Comrade" China, Chinese Closet,* or *New Beijing, New Marriage.*[18] Instead, I would suggest that this engaged sensibility is manifested in two ways: first, in a self-conscious awareness of how homosexuality is and has been represented on the Chinese screen, and second, through an exploration of how digital filmmaking may itself be used to generate new ways of "being queer" in China. The consequence, however, is the refashioning of the male body from a sign, or a spectacle, into a site through which new forms of queer subjectivity may be produced. This in itself is an act that arguably carries intense political resonance.

Reflecting on Representation: To Whom Do Our Bodies Belong?

The use of the body as a trope through which to explore the nature of reality is not unique to the digital era. Indeed, there is a long Chinese tradition of visualizing the human form as "a site of personal pain, national trauma, and voyeuristic pleasure" (M. Berry 2008, 28) that stretches back to at least the nineteenth century. In this tradition, the body becomes a means to realize the relationship between individual, social, and national identity; it is a sign or symbol through which knowledge about the world may be investigated and organized. The most famous manifestation of this practice is undoubtedly Lu Xun's ([1922] 1994, 2–3) account of his experience as a student in Japan during the Russo-Japanese War, watching a slide show of the beheading of a Chinese spy. In this description, frequently interpreted as the foundational moment of modern Chinese literature, the association of the body, violence, and the gaze has been read in terms of a self-conscious meditation on the nature of representation, action, and witnessing.[19] Critical to such a meditation, however, is the fine line between sign and spectacle: the ease with which such images may encourage an audience not to self-reflection, but to an unreflexive enjoyment of, possibly even a degree of pleasure in, what is being represented. Such affective power becomes particularly problematic when the body visualized is that of the subaltern subject.

The images of surgery captured in *Miss Jin Xing* and *Xiang Pingli* would seem to fit this genealogy most precisely: they both inscribe embodied experience as a form of symbolic knowledge and exert a fascinating yet disturbing power that, for this viewer at any rate, is almost visceral. But other early documentaries also feature scenes in which the body's movement between sign and spectacle is dramatized, particularly during sequences that stage, in different ways, the act of gazing on the body of the cross-dressed performer. Chao Shi-Yan (2010b, 167) has described such a moment toward the end of *Meimei*. In this scene, a friend of the protagonist, called Mr. Lee, has just finished a performance in a beer garden. Backstage, as he undresses, some members of the audience linger, finally catching sight of him partially undressed and out of costume. Chao ascribes this curiosity to a desire to confirm the actual gender of the performer, thus ensuring that "cross-dressing is solely for entertainment purposes and that gender ambiguity is 'properly' limited to the stage" (Chao 2010b, 167). Thus, while performance may indeed endow the queer male subject with a degree of agency in social space, it can also facilitate viewing practices that potentially reduce that subject to the object of audience voyeurism. This process is replicated for the documentary audience by the inscription of such moments on film.

The uneasy power dynamic that such scenes conjure—by whom is this body being displayed, for whom, and to what purpose?—is captured by activist Tong Ge in *Queer China, "Comrade" China*. Discussing the criminalization of homosexual relations in China, he states that "the most important question for me is: to whom do our bodies belong? Do I have the right to use my own body as I wish?" The need, then, for the queer subject to assert control over his body, and through it his subjectivity, is thus articulated as a serious question. It is also one implicitly posed by the film through its constant remediation of Chinese film and television representations of homosexuality—including, among others, the surgery scenes from *Miss Jin Xing*, a sequence from *Xiang Pingli* in which one of the characters is beaten, and scenes of police harassment excerpted from Zhang Yuan's feature *East Palace, West Palace* (*Donggong Xigong* 1996)—and the manner in which these images contrast with those of the documentary's own "talking heads." Poised, clothed, and articulate, in these sequences the documentary's subjects are the very antithesis of spectacular. Nor are their queer bodies distinguished from their straight counterparts: neither dress nor physical comportment necessarily marks these individuals as homosexual. Instead, this is suggested in other ways. In both the interviews with artist Shi Tou and activist Zhang Yi, for example, images of naked men and women—in the former's case, her own paintings—decorate the rooms in which the interviewees sit. These images clearly function to signify desire and the pleasures of the gaze. However, the pleasure here is neither that of the viewer nor of the camera; rather, it is the homoerotic pleasure of the diegetic queer subject. The naked body is therefore not a trope through which the limits of reality can be probed, but rather suggests how *Queer China, "Comrade" China*'s subjects have asserted control both over their own sexual identity and how that identity is signified. This in turn reflects, if indirectly, on one of the documentary's primary concerns.

Queer China, "Comrade" China therefore reappropriates the body as sign, deliberately subverting its spectacular qualities while also suggesting the limitations of such iconography. In Fan Popo and David Cheng's *New Beijing, New Marriage*, however, the significance of the queer body is reworked even more comprehensively. This documentary short chronicles the performance of a gay wedding at Beijing's Qianmen Street on Valentine's Day 2009. Tracking the participants—one female and one male couple, respectively—as they don Western-style wedding clothes and makeup, travel by taxi to the venue, and have wedding photographs taken in full view of members of the general public, the film then turns its gaze outward. The directors and participants question this audience on its views of

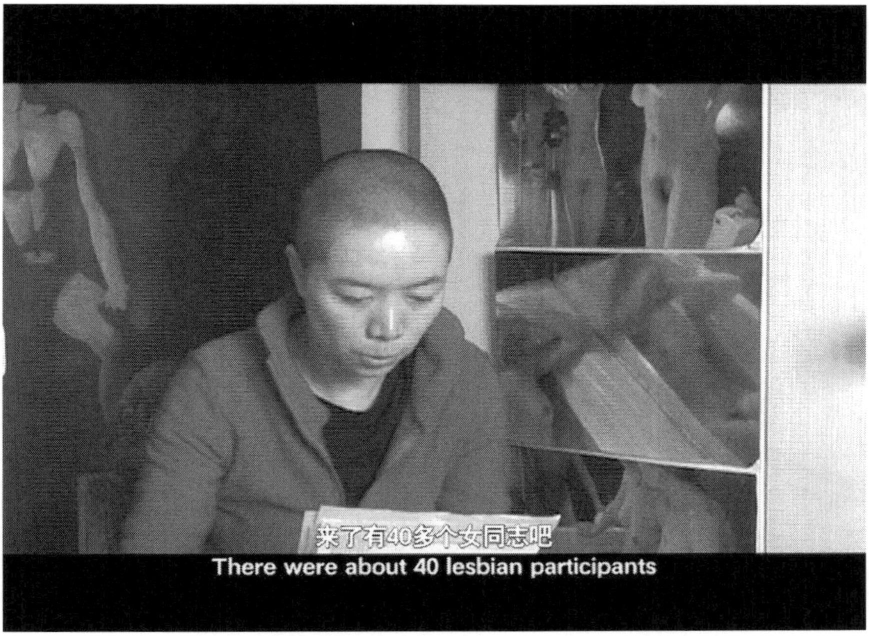

Figure 11.3. Queer China, "Comrade" China. Artist Shi Tou, surrounded by nudes.

homosexuality; ask whether, as individuals, they would accept gay marriage; and finally get people to pose for photographs with the happy couples. The film concludes with a montage of gay wedding stills from around the world and an appeal for the legal recognition of same-sex partnerships in China.

As in *Meimei*, the subjects of *New Beijing, New Marriage* use performance to access public space. The nature of their performance, however, is rather different. The codes borrowed here are not theatrical, but everyday. They do not involve cross-dressing, but rather the appropriation by queer subjects of the gendered identities associated with heterosexual marriage. This facilitates the minimization of voyeuristic bodily display within the documentary diegesis.[20] But, as importantly, it also ensures that any sense of homosexuality as a set of dramatic practices to be adopted or disposed of at will is avoided. Instead, sexuality as a fundamentally incorporated identity, one bound to physical and emotional desire, is emphasized. In the process, not only does the documentary position homosexuality as a constituent part of everyday life, but it also suggests how embodiment is central to the generation of queer selfhood. No longer a sign through which sexual identity—and more—can be read, the body is instead a site through which the day-to-day experience of queer living is enacted.

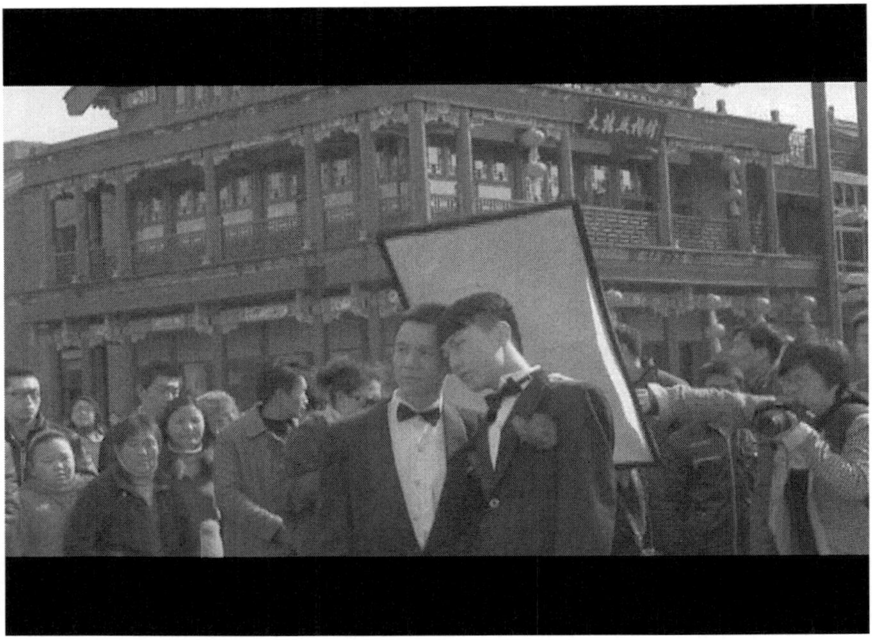

Figure 11.4. *New Beijing, New Marriage.* Homosexuality as quotidian public performance.

If performing the ritual of the modern wedding photograph allows the documentary's subjects not only to appear as identifiably queer in public space, but also to rework the role of the body and performance in the generation of queer identity, so Fan and Cheng use the actual filmmaking process to comparable ends. Presented as a fairly straightforward document of the events recorded, *New Beijing, New Marriage*'s "interactive realism" bears similarities to those American documentaries of the 1970s that captured the first public performances—parades, marches, demonstrations—of gay life in the United States; these were considered interesting enough in and of themselves not to require formal performative supplements (Waugh 1997, 113). As such, the documentary makes no attempt to shroud its subject matter in the veil of aesthetic ambiguity, presenting itself instead as a form of public record. And yet, the filmmakers do not hold back from participating in the event; instead, they use the act of filming as an opportunity to engage with the general public, turning their cameras on the watching crowd, transforming observers into the observed. At the same time they ask questions of these onlookers from behind the camera and off-screen, trying to elicit their opinions on homosexuality and gay marriage. These actions intimate Fan and Cheng's align-

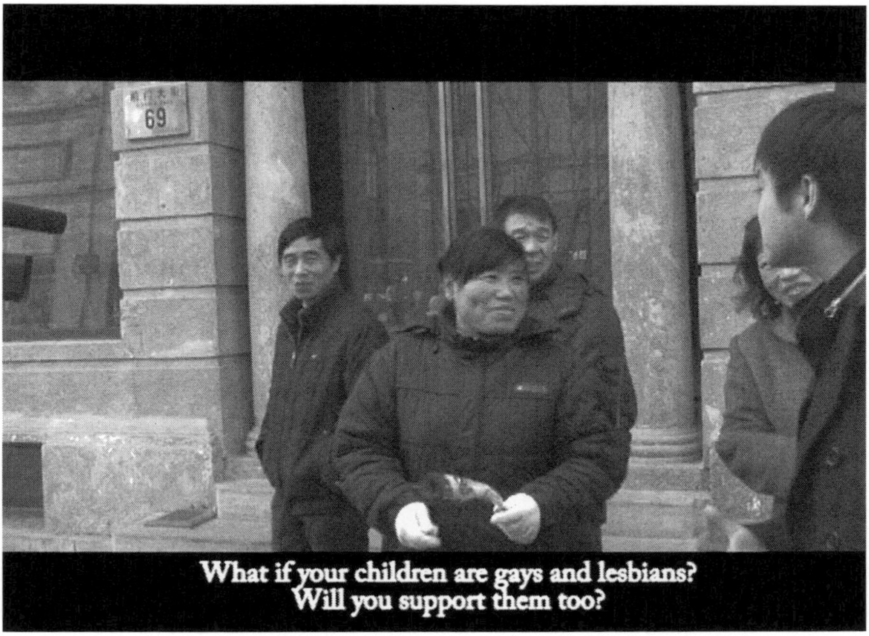

Figure 11.5. New Beijing, New Marriage. Turning the camera on the crowd.

ment with their subjects in a manner that underlines the filmmakers' own politics and sexual orientation. As the couples at the heart of *New Beijing, New Marriage* use performance to enter public space and discourse as queer subjects, so the directors use the act of filming to do the same.

What I am suggesting is that, just as digital video has enabled Fan and Cheng to be incorporated into the field of documentary production, so the directors have in turn used digital filmmaking to incorporate themselves as queer subjects. I use this term here not simply in the sense of a subjectivity rooted in physical and affective experience, but also in that proposed by Paul Connerton (1989, 72), of embodied presence and physical activity as vehicles through which to generate new forms of social knowledge. In *New Beijing, New Marriage,* Fan and Cheng's sexual identity is not so much captured on film as effected through filmmaking: it is this material process that allows the directors to unambiguously constitute themselves as queer individuals in public. The actualization of this identity is dependent on their embodied presence at, and intervention into, the scene of the documentary shoot. However, it also relies on the portability of DV hardware—in particular, the ease of camera movement within and between spaces—that had proved so potentially problematic for the subjects of the earlier documentaries. As with the couples they are filming, Fan and Cheng's own bodies function neither as signs nor as objectified spectacle, but rather as sites through which the queer subject as social agent can be incorporated. Critically, however, it is the "lightness" of the digital that they have exploited to make this possible.

Networking Contemporary Chinese Queer Identity

In the earliest documentaries, then, queer identity is performed, and the queer body appears inscribed as sign or spectacle. In *New Beijing, New Marriage,* the queer body is the site of incorporation: how, then, might one understand the relationship between this body, queer identity and the world, if sign and spectacle no longer suffice? What alternative imaginings, if any, do these works offer? One plausible answer can be found again in the very opening sequence of *Queer China, "Comrade" China.* Aurally, as I discussed previously, this sequence emphasizes a multiplicity of voices and an open-ended debate about the nature of Chinese sexuality. And yet, at the same time, it is also a *visualization* of such discursive diversity and open-endedness. This is achieved through an obviously digital metaphor: that of multiple small screens. As each of these screens shrinks from full-size to bite-size, arranged in intimate proximity to one another, a new vision emerges. It is one of community—a mosaic of individuals, voices, points-of-view and identities, expressed via the layering of tiny windows, one on top of the other. Each of these windows is individually distinct: added together, however, they create much more than the sum of their parts.

As *Queer Comrades* uses the digital to literally "network" the gay community in Beijing, so *Queer China, "Comrade" China* uses a digital metaphor to reimagine queerness *as network.* The identity expressed here is relational as much as performative: a series of affiliations between multiple individuals, constantly shifting and never static, elastic enough to expand or shrink depending on circumstance. Thus, while a stable self appears central to this picture, the individual cannot be understood independently of the community at large.[21] In some ways, such a representation appears particularly Chinese: while certain contemporary scholars note how that notion of "individual" desires is the defining difference between the older and younger generation of Chinese gay men (Kong 2011, 170), most also emphasize how homosexuality in the PRC must be seen as a culturally particular phenomenon rather than as an instantiation of a global sexual culture. In particular, sexual identity is often understood to operate socially, and not "as a separate interior domain that is a constitutive principle of the self" (Rofel 2007, 102). Yet in practice, this networked imagination has interesting consequences. While the early documentaries may reflexively consider gender and sexual identity through the medium of performance, they do not do the same with Chineseness. They may turn their gaze outside the larger cities, but they rarely look beyond the PRC proper. In contrast, these more recent works routinely incorporate non-Chinese into their stories about "Chinese" homosexuality. In *Queer Comrades,* scenes of gay life in urban China often feature foreigners as active participants: as presenters on the program, as subjects to be interviewed, or simply as captured on camera in spaces such as bars and clubs, engaged in everyday socializing. In *Chinese Closet,* one of the subjects is a Taiwanese American with a Caucasian partner, while the film's final scenes, all shot at Hong Kong Pride, are a mélange of ethnicities and nationalities—as are those of *New Beijing, New Marriage.* Finally, in *Queer China, "Comrade" China,* individuals such as Lisa Rofel and Paul Crook feature as talking heads, their commentary, in Chinese, incorporated into the broader history of Chinese homosexuality that is being constructed. Thus, while none of these works explicitly postulate sexual identity as open-ended and socially constructed, they all implicitly normalize its transnational, intercultural dimension. To be queer, they seem to suggest, is to participate in a form of social affiliation that naturally extends beyond national borders.

This perspective may be comparatively new to documentary about Chinese gay men, but it was already nascent in lesbian documentary practice by the mid-2000s. Shi Tou and Ming Ming's *Dyke March* (*Nütongzhi youxing ri* 2004), for example, which records the pride parade in San Francisco from her point of view as a participant, "constructs an identification based on lesbian identity that simultaneously crosses national/cultural boundaries" (Chao 2010a, 89). However, where *Dyke March* tracks the movement of its director out into the (queer) world (or, more specifically, California), more recent documentaries also capture the movement of that world into China. In doing so, they are on one level merely reflecting the fact that foreign nationals have long been involved in gay politics in the PRC, and gay Chinese are constantly involved in a process of negotiation between local conditions and foreign norms in the construction of their sexual identity.[22] But precisely what constitutes these "local conditions" remains opaque. As Petrus Liu (2010, 297–299) has pointed out, while exceptionalism is increasingly taken for granted in scholarly discussion of the history of Chinese sexuality, with Chinese language discourses of homosexuality routinely treated as uniquely culturally untranslatable, "where the borders of [this] exceptionalism . . . begin and end, where these discourses are located, and whose lives they are supposed to describe" (Liu 2010, 298) has yet to be agreed. In harnessing the capabilities of the digital to visualize queer identity as networked, I would argue that these documentaries have precisely begun to formulate the question: what is specifically "Chinese" about Chinese queer identity? In doing so, they articulate a relationship between medium and sexuality that is at least as complex and potentially open-ended as that presented in their performative and reflexive counterparts.

This double move—the visual articulation of a networked yet transnational identity—partly gestures to the ways in which Chinese of all persuasions, but particularly the marginalized, are using digital media to reimagine social solidarity. Ying Qian (2012, 121–122), discussing the work of activist filmmakers Hu Jie and Ai Xiaoming, notes how these directors exploit the participatory possibilities of digital media in their filmmaking. By sharing responsibility for digital film production with their subjects, providing them with cameras and incorporating their work into the final cut, Ai and Hu create, in documentaries such as *The Epic of Central Plains* or *Our Children,* patchwork products that interweave their own live video footage, photographs, and videos taken by their subjects, and even official news clippings. Exploiting the possibilities offered by digital video as a technology and a medium, the filmmakers thus effect a "return to montage" (Qian 2012, 122) that, critically, allows them to connect otherwise isolated events across time and space. In visualizing such relationships on screen *as networked,* these films provide a catalyst for potential social mobilization off it (Qian 2012, 122). While the works discussed in this chapter do not exactly return to montage, the ways they mine the properties of digital media first to visualize, and then to actualize, new kinds of queer sociality suggests clear points of contact with the films of Ai, Hu, and their subjects. This affinity points up how certain social groups in China are using digital media to fashion particular kinds of relational identities, often along activist lines, in distinct yet connected ways.

The particularly cosmopolitan manner in which these films imagine queer identity is, however, unusual. Hu and Ai may use montage to explore the relationships between apparently disparate events, but their focus is primarily translocal or regional. The filmmakers considered here create connections that crisscross China's borders. Such moves are quite deliberate: Cui Zi'en has likened his filmmaking practice to participating in a "Communist International of Queer Film" (Cui 2010), adding, "I rejoice at this kind of globalization" (Cui 2010, 423). And this, perhaps, is the most interesting facet of these works. If the focus of Chinese documentary study has to date been primarily local or national in framing, these films bring a transnational element to the fore. At the same time, this is not the transnationalism of the commercial film industry, governed by market imperatives, nor of the Sinophone, shaped primarily by geo-cultural and linguistic factors. It is instead a distinct form of "minor transnationalism" based on sexual orientation, a "cultural transversalism" (Lionnet and Shih 2005, 6, 8) that connects minority communities across borders without prior mediation through a center, be that national or cultural. Furthermore—and in Cui's case, quite explicitly—it evokes older socialist traditions of social and political solidarity that have now fallen out of fashion. While these contemporary documentaries indisputably demonstrate how queer filmmakers use the digital to generate a new queer filmmaking practice, in doing so they also illuminate digital media's potential to reactivate forms of internationalism, both imaginative and material, that may incorporate or coexist with national and cultural identities, but are never overdetermined by them.

Conclusion

The pluralization of queer documentary practice in China has thus gone hand in hand with an embracing of digital media's small media qualities, or "lightness." Both trends in turn reflect the emergence of a new group of practitioners for whom queer identity is not inherently ambivalent; who are aware of the sometimes problematic history of queer representation in the Chinese media; who see the digital medium as a useful social and political tool; and who are interested in, if not exactly "mainstreaming," then certainly engaging with mainstream society and opinion. The blurring of boundaries inherent to both theatrical performance and formal performativity is not therefore intrinsically helpful for a group of practitioners who appear more concerned with exploring how Chinese queer identity can be articulated and sustained in public spaces, rather than rendered ambiguous. Instead, these directors use the digital to both create and imagine new subjectivities for, and affinities between, queer individuals; these in turn draw upon, and expand the boundaries of, *xianchang*. In the process these filmmakers reconstitute elements of the practice in accordance with their new aims and audiences, drawing on the possibilities of the medium for inspiration. As I hope I have demonstrated, however, the results do not necessarily impose closure on the question of what constitutes queer identity in a Chinese context. Rather, they explicitly complicate other elements of this equation, suggesting not only how these more recent documentaries remain as innovative and sophisticated as their predecessors, but also how digital media more generally has the potential both to catalyze new forms of sociality and to reactivate older forms of solidarity, within and beyond the PRC today.

Notes

1. Interestingly, this is not the case with representations of lesbianism, and as a result this chapter concentrates on gay men. For discussion of lesbian representation in contemporary Chinese documentary, see Chao (2010a).

2. In fact, there is considerable overlap in Nichols's use of these terms, since both modes are ways of complicating our understanding of documentary "knowledge." The crossing of boundaries between the real, the performed, and the imagined is, for example, a critical element of both modes, as is an emphasis on the subjective quality of documentary as a form. See Nichols (2001, 125–138) for more detailed discussion.

3. For close analyses of *Tangtang*, see Chao (2010b, 152–159), and of *Night Scene*, see Voci (2010, 33–35). Cui's film is distinct in not presenting his characters as performers and yet still reflexively considering the way in which they can be said to perform elements of their sexual identity. See also Rofel (2010, 441–453) for discussion of this issue in relation to Cui's *Feeding Boys, Ayaya!* (*Aiyaya, qu buru* 2003).

4. The ways in which this transformation of the real is explored are, however, different. Chao (2010b, 157–159) notes that Zhang Hanzi's use of performance in *Tangtang* destabilizes the assumed correspondence of *xianchang* to reality, thus using the embodied performance of gender to question the very possibility of realist representation. In contrast, other directors use embodied performance as a point of "entry into an understanding of the more general processes at work in a society" (Nichols 2001, 131). Jiang Zhi, for example, has described *Xiang Pingli* as a study of the "third sex"—neither man nor woman, but somewhere in between—but also points out that he feels his protagonists were not engaged in trying to fight gender politics but, as members of the underclass, merely passively trying to survive (Z. Li 2009). In this sense the film uses the transsexual body to explore the boundaries of gender and sexuality, but also to consider how both intersect with personal and class identity under conditions of postsocialist transition.

5. For discussion of analog and digital video as small media, see, for example, various of the essays in Ginsburg et al. (2002), Smith (2010), Chanan (2012), and Battaglia (2014).

6. See, for example, Du (2002) and Jia ([1999] 2009).

7. For discussion of this problem in relation to specific case studies, see Lü (2005, 168) and Zheng (n.d.). Nor is this exclusively the concern of scholars, as the response within Chinese film circles to Xu Tong's documentary *Wheat Harvest* (*Mai Shou* 2008) demonstrates (Nornes 2009, 52).

8. This concentration on the everyday is true of some of the earlier films such as *Meimei* and *Baobao,* both of which consider how gay men negotiate the everyday outside the Chinese metropolis, at the geographical margins. Nevertheless, what is interesting about *Queer Comrades,* for example, is the variety of everyday contexts it chooses to investigate, both geographically and thematically, and the way it radically extends these earlier concerns.

9. For example, Duan Jinchuan, one of the earliest participants in what is sometimes termed China's New Documentary Movement, has specifically connected the use of interviews in independent documentary from the early 1990s with the continued influence of CCTV (Lü 2003, 88).

10. For a brief overview of these developments and their consequences, see Ho (2010, 5–20) and Kong (2011, 143–173). To contextualize them within changes to

mainstream urban Chinese sexual culture since Reform and Opening, see Farrer (2002).

11. A good example occurs in section nine of the documentary, "From Slow Motion to Fast Forwarding." This section focuses on the emergence of what might be described as a contemporary Chinese "Gay Pride" culture and the links forged between rights activists in the PRC and abroad. One segment of this section focuses on the question of gay marriage. Here, a number of different positions are put forward by different individuals, ranging from concern as to whether a heterosexual institution is appropriate for queer individuals, to the belief that, given the overwhelming social prerogative to marry in China, this would only help social integration and acceptance. A whole range of debates about the significance of gay marriage are thus rehearsed, without any single position being validated as the "correct" one.

12. Although individual talking heads are named as the film progresses, their professional status remains unclear: an individual's profession is never labeled in the way that it might be in mainstream television, for example. The refusal to create a hierarchy of voices based on professional standing is thus retained throughout the film.

13. In 2000, both Cui and Shi joined Li Yinhe on the show to discuss homosexuality (Sang 2003, 172). This was the first time a major Chinese TV channel had run a program featuring individuals who self-identified as gay and who were willing to discuss the topic on air. As such, it is considered something of a watershed moment.

14. A good example occurs at the very end of the very first section of the documentary. Here, TV footage of the actor Sun Haiying denouncing homosexuality—itself clearly sourced online and replayed on a computer screen—is remediated on-screen. This is immediately countered, however, with footage of Li Yinhe, academic Cheng Qingsong, and activist Bai Yongbing either decrying Sun's opinions as ill-informed (Li) or describing the actions they took to counter them (Cheng and Bai), which involved blog posts (images of which are presented on-screen) and also consideration of legal action.

15. It may also explain why, of all of these directors, Du Haibin is the most conservative in his approach to his subjects. *Beautiful Men,* while a documentary about performers, is primarily observational rather than performative.

16. Cui Zi'en has of course been a longtime figurehead for the Chinese gay community. However, Fan Popo and Wei Jiangang are also both involved in gay community issues in China and have worked with, or received training from, local and international NGOs operating in this arena.

17. Fan Popo, for example, helped found the China Queer Film Festival Tour in 2008 as a way of bringing films shown at the Beijing Queer Film Festival to an audience outside the capital. The tour has been financially supported by *Queer Comrades,* as well as the Queer Film Festival and the Beijing LBGT Center (Collett 2010). The films are shown in a variety of different venues, from educational institutions to film salons and gay bars, guaranteeing a diverse audience (Fan 2010).

18. Wei Jiangang (pers. comm.) has maintained that one of the reasons for the longevity of *Queer Comrades* is its calculated refusal to directly criticize the government. Nonetheless, the webcast has faced disruption from Internet service providers, who have deleted past episodes from various websites due to concerns about the sensitivity of the subject matter. The strong emphasis the series also places on health and education, which feature prominently in its online rationale ("Guanyu Women" n.d.) also reflects its need to self-present in terms that are acceptable to the government, and also likely to earn it financial support from international NGOs. In contrast, the documentaries by Fan Popo and Cui Zi'en, which are simultaneously too sensitive and insufficiently commercial for domestic cinematic release, have far less to lose by being more explicitly political in tone.

19. Given the multiple audiences built into Lu Xun's description—the Chinese spectators in the photograph, the Japanese students in the theater where the slide show is being screened, Lu Xun himself, both during the screening and years after, describing it in retrospect, and, finally, the reader—Michael Berry (2008, 48) sees this passage as specifically posing the question of *who* is witnessing this scene of primal violence.

20. A good point of comparison here is the opening of the documentary, in which the brides and grooms are made up in preparation for the wedding ceremony. In many ways, this parallels the "backstage" scenes characteristic of films about *fanchuan,* in which the performers prepare to go onstage or unwind off it. However, whereas these scenes often display their subjects in states of semi-undress, *New Beijing, New Marriage* avoids such images. Instead, it focuses on the application of makeup and the careful adjustment of clothing, suggesting how both are central to the identity of "brides" and "grooms," while steering clear of any possible titillation.

21. Indeed, one could argue that a central tension in this image is between the individual and the erasure of individuality that is potentially inherent in any attempt to construct an image of community, crowd, or mass. Ultimately, it is impossible to pick out the words of any single individual from the babble of voices that results from this proliferation of talking heads, although the documentary then proceeds to bring out these individual voices over the course of its narrative. Many thanks to Carlos Rojas for making this point to me.

22. See Rofel (2007, 87–89) for a brief discussion of the emergence of gay identity in China in relation to transnational networks, and the consequences thereof.

Bibliography

Battaglia, Giulia. 2014. "The Video Turn: Documentary Film Practices in 1980s India." *Visual Anthropology* 27: 72–90.

Berry, Chris. 2009. "*East Palace, West Palace:* Staging Gay Life in China." In *Chinese Connections: Critical Perspectives on Film, Identity, and Diaspora,* edited by Tam See-Kam, Peter X. Feng, and Gina Marchetti, 165–176. Philadelphia: Temple University Press.

Berry, Michael. 2008. *A History of Pain: Trauma in Modern Chinese Literature and Film.* New York: Columbia University Press.

Bolter, Jay David and Richard Grusin. 1999. *Remediation: Understanding New Media.* Cambridge, MA: MIT Press.

Chanan, Michael. 2012. "Video, Activism, and the Art of Small Media." *Transnational Cinemas* 2 (2): 217–226.

Chao Shi-Yan. 2010a. "Coming Out of *The Box,* Marching as Dykes." In *The New Chinese Documentary Film Movement: For the Public Record,* edited by Chris Berry, Lü Xinyu, and Lisa Rofel, 77–95. Hong Kong: Hong Kong University Press.

———. 2010b. "Performing Gender, Performing Documentary in Post-socialist China." In *As Normal as Possible: Negotiating Sexuality and Gender in Mainland China and Hong Kong,* edited by Yau Ching, 151–175. Hong Kong: Hong Kong University Press.

Collett, Nigel. 2010. "Getting Behind the Camera: Fan Popo." *Fridae.com.* http://www.fridae.asia/newsfeatures/2010/04/19/9830.getting-behind-the-camera-fan-popo.

Connerton, Paul. 1989. *How Societies Remember.* Cambridge: Cambridge University Press.

Conway, Kyle. 2008. "Small Media, Global Media: Kino and the Microcinema Movement." *Journal of Film and Video* 60 (3–4): 60–71.

Cui Zi'en. 2010. "The Communist International of Queer Film." Translated by Petrus Liu. *positions: east asia cultures critique* 18 (2): 417–423.

Dai, Jinhua 戴锦华. 1999. *Yinxing Shuxie: 90 Niandai Zhongguo wenhua yanjiu* 隐形书写：90 年代中国文化研究 (Invisible Writing: Chinese Cultural Studies in the 1990s). Nanjing: Jiangsu Renmin Chubanshe.

Du, Haibin 杜海滨. 2002. "Ganxie Daoban, Ganxie DV 感谢盗版，感谢 DV" ("Thank You Pirate Copies, Thank You DV"). *Jinri Xianfeng* 今日先锋 (Avant Garde Today) 12: 2–3.

Fan Popo 范坡坡. 2010. "*Guizu:* Fan Popo 柜族：范坡坡" ("*Chinese Closet:* Fan Popo"). Interview conducted at the 7th Chinese Independent Documentary Film Festival. http://v.youku.com/v_show/id_XMTcwOTA5Njgw.html.

Farrer, James. 2002. *Opening Up: Youth Sex Culture and Market Reform in Shanghai.* Chicago: University of Chicago Press.

Ginsburg, Faye, Lila Abu-Lughod, and Brian Larkin, eds. 2002. *Media Worlds: Anthropology on New Terrain.* Berkeley: University of California Press.

"Guanyu Women 关于我们" ("About Us"). n.d. *Queercomrades.com.* http://www.queercomrades.com/about/.

Halpern Martineau, Barbara. 1984. "Talking about Our Lives and Experiences: Some Thoughts about Feminism, Documentary, and 'Talking Heads.'" In *"Show Us Life": Toward a History and Aesthetics of the Committed Documentary,* edited by Tom Waugh, 252–273. Metuchen and London: Scarecrow Press.

Ho, Loretta Wing Wah. 2010. *Gay and Lesbian Subculture in Urban China.* London: Routledge.

Jia, Zhangke 贾樟柯. [1999] 2009. "Yeyu dianying shidai jijiang zai ci daolai 业余电影时代即将再次到来" ("The Age of Amateur Cinema Will Return"). In *Jia Xiang, 1996–2008: Jia Zhangke Dianying Shouji* 贾想 1996–2008: 贾樟柯电影手记 (Jia's Thoughts, 1996–2008: Jia Zhangke's Notes on Film), 32–35. Beijing: Peking University Press.

Kong, Travis S. K. 2011. *Chinese Male Homosexualities: Memba, Tongzhi, and Golden Boy.* London: Routledge.

Leary, Charles. 2003. "Performing the Documentary, or Making It to the Other Bank." *Senses of Cinema* 27 (July). http://www.sensesofcinema.com/2003/feature-articles/performing_documentary/.

Leung, Helen Hok-Sze. 2008. *Undercurrents: Queer Culture and Postcolonial Hong Kong.* Vancouver: University of British Columbia Press.

Li, Jie. 2010. "Filming Power and the Powerless: Zhao Liang's *Crime and Punishment* (2007) and *Petition* (2009)." *China Perspectives* 81: 35–45.

Li, Yinhe. 2006. "Regulating Male Same-Sex Relationships in the People's Republic of China." In *Sex and Sexuality in China,* edited by Elaine Jeffreys, 82–101. Abingdon: Routledge.

Li, Zhenhua 李振华. 2009. "Jiang Zhi Fangtan 蒋志访谈" ("Interview with Jiang Zhi"). *Bjartlab.com.* http://www.bjartlab.com/read.php?139.

Lionnet, Françoise and Shu-mei Shih. 2005. "Introduction: Thinking through the Minor, Transnationally." In *Minor Transnationalism,* edited by Françoise Lionnet and Shu-mei Shih, 1–23. Durham, NC: Duke University Press.

Liu, Petrus. 2010. "Why Does Queer Theory Need China?" *positions: east asia cultures critique* 18 (2): 291–320.

Lü Xinyu 吕新雨. 2003. *Jilu Zhongguo: Dangdai Zhongguo xinjilu yundong* 纪录中国：当代中国新纪录运动 (Documenting China: The New Documentary Movement in Contemporary China). Beijing: Sanlian shudian.

———. 2005. "Houji: Zhongguo jilupian de li yu tong 后记：中国纪录片的力与痛" ("Afterword: The Power and the Pain of Chinese Documentary"). In *Yun zhi nan jilu yingxiang luntan* 云之南纪录影像论坛 (Yunnan Multi Culture Visual Festival Catalogue), edited by Guo Jing, 166–168. Kunming: Yunfest Documentary Archives Series.

———. 2006. "Xin Jilu Yundong de Li yu Tong 新纪录运动的力与痛" ("The Power and the Pain of the New Documentary Movement"). *Dushu* 读书 (Reading) 5: 12–22.

Lu Xun. [1922] 1994. "Preface to the First Collection of Short Stories, *A Call to Arms.*" In *Selected Stories of Lu Hsun,* 1–6. Translated by Yang Hsien-Yi and Gladys Yang. San Francisco: China Books and Periodicals

Nichols, Bill. 2001. *Introduction to Documentary.* Bloomington: Indiana University Press.

Nornes, Abé Mark. 2009. "Bulldozers, Bibles, and Very Sharp Knives: The Chinese Independent Documentary Scene." *Film Quarterly* 63 (1): 50–55.

O'Brien, Kevin and Li Lianjiang. 2006. Preface to *Rightful Resistance in Rural China,* xi-xvii. Cambridge and New York: Cambridge University Press.

Pullen, Christopher. 2007. *Documenting Gay Men: Identity and Performance in Reality Television and Documentary Film.* Jefferson: McFarlane and Company.

Qian, Ying. 2012. "Power in the Frame: China's Independent Documentary Movement." *New Left Review* 74: 105–123.

Qiu Zhijie 邱志杰. 2003. "Xuyan: Zhongyaode shi xianchang 序言：重要的是现场" ("Preface: The Scene Is What's Important") in *Zhongyaode Shi Xianchang* 重要的是现场 (The Scene Is What's Important), 1–2. Beijing: Zhongguo Renmin Daxue Chubanshe.

Reynaud, Bérénice. 2010. "Men Won't Cry—Traces of a Repressive Past: The 28th Vancouver International Film Festival." *Senses of Cinema* 54 (Apr.). http://www.sensesofcinema.com/2010/festival-reports/men-won't-cry—-traces-of-a-repressive-past-the-28th-vancouver-international-film-festival/.

Robinson, Luke. 2010. "From 'Public' to 'Private': Chinese Documentary and the Logic of *Xianchang*." In *The New Chinese Documentary Film Movement: For the Public Record,* edited by Chris Berry, Lü Xinyu, and Lisa Rofel, 177–194. Hong Kong: Hong Kong University Press.

Rofel, Lisa. 2007. *Desiring China: Experiments in Neoliberalism, Sexuality, and Public Culture.* Durham, NC: Duke University Press.

———. 2010. "The Traffic in Money Boys." *positions: east asia cultures critique* 18 (2): 425–458.

Sang, Tze-Lan Deborah. 2003. *The Emerging Lesbian: Female Same-Sex Desire in Modern China.* Chicago: University of Chicago Press.

Smith, Laurel C. 2010. "Locating Post-Colonial Technoscience: Through the Lens of Indigenous Video." *History and Technology* 26 (3): 251–280.

Sreberny-Mohammadi, Annabelle and Ali. 1994. *Small Media, Big Revolution: Communication and the Iranian Revolution.* Minneapolis: University of Minnesota Press.

Voci, Paola. 2010. *China on Video: Smaller-Screen Realities.* Abingdon: Routledge.

Wang, Xiaolu 王小鲁. 2010. "Zhuti jianxian—20nian Zhongguo duli jilupian de guancha 主题渐显—20年中国独立纪录片的观察" ("The Gradual Revelation of Subjectivity—Observations on 20 Years of Chinese Independent Documentary"). *Dianying Yishu* 电影艺术 (Film Art) 6: 72–78.

Waugh, Tom. 1997. "Walking on Tippy Toes: Lesbian and Gay Liberation Documentary of the Post-Stonewall Period 1969–84." In *Between the Sheets, In the Streets: Queer, Lesbian, Gay Documentary,* edited by Chris Holmlund and Cynthia Fuchs, 107–124. Minneapolis: University of Minnesota Press.

Wu Wenguang 吴文光. 2001. "Nüxing he DV Shexiangji 女性和 DV 摄像机" ("Woman and the DV Camera"). In *Jingtou xiang ziji de yanjing yiyang* 镜头像自己的眼睛一样 (The Camera Lens Is Like My Eye), 194–197. Shanghai: Shanghai Wenyi Chubanshe.

Zhang Zhen. 2007. "Introduction: 'Bearing Witness: Chinese Urban Cinema in the Era of 'Transformation'.'" In *The Urban Generation: Chinese Cinema and Society at the Turn of the Twenty-first Century,* edited by Zhang Zhen, 1–45. Durham, NC: Duke University Press.

———. 2010. "Transfiguring the Post-socialist City." In *Cinema at the City's Edge: Film and Urban Networks in East Asia,* edited by Yomi Braester and James Tweedie, 95–118. Hong Kong: Hong Kong University Press.

Zheng, Tiantian 郑田田. n.d. "San Peinü de Bing Shan Yi Jiao: Hu Shu *Wo Bu Yao Ni Guan* Yingxiangji 三陪女的冰山一角：胡庶《我不要你管》影像记" ("The Tip of the Hostess Iceberg: On Hu Shu's *Leave Me Alone*"). *Reelchina.net.* http://www.reelchina.net/chinese.htm.

CHAPTER 12

Toward a Digital Political Mimesis

Aesthetic of Affect and Activist Video

ZHANG ZHEN

Today, everyone can become Ai Weiwei.
I still treat documentary as art, or a kind of art of thought.
—Ai Xiaoming, documentary filmmaker
and feminist scholar

Citizen-generated images are like the ocean, and documentary is a boat. Once such a relation is established, documentary will have boundless vitality and be invincible.
—Hu Jie, documentary filmmaker

Social-politically oriented and activist filmmaking has emerged as an increasingly visible and integral part of the independent documentary in China since the popularization of portable DV cameras, editing software, and Internet-based social media in the first decade of the new century. Yet the thematic and formal attributes of these films as well as manners of their production and dissemination are as varied and complex as the contemporary Chinese social and political life that fuels the filmmakers' sense of urgency, creative passion and action. Many of these films seem to fit well with the tradition of "committed documentary" (Waugh 1984) by virtue of their singular sympathetic preoccupation with subaltern, marginal, and activist subjects and their struggle for survival and recognition within a contradiction-ridden social and political order that rests precariously on an unjust judicial and distributive system. Yet these films are also markedly different in terms of modes of production, distribution, spectatorial address, "authorship," and more. In this chapter, I offer some observations on the variegated activist lens by discussing the works of several prominent independent filmmakers or media activists such as Wang Bing, Du Haibin, Wu Wenguang, Ai Xiaoming, and Ai Weiwei, focusing on their overlap and divergences in the experimentation with DV documentary as a new expressive form and medium for political intervention and social transformation. Ultimately, I am interested in exploring the forms and meanings of a certain *digital political mimesis* as manifested in the fast-evolving independent documentary practice in general and the more radical activist strand in particular in contemporary China.

Anyone who has been following this independent documentary scene since the early 1990s would note the extraordinary variety of subjects and approaches that defy any facile categorization. Based on his festival viewings at the Yunnan Multi Culture Visual Festival (Yunfest) and BIFF in Songzhuang in 2009, Abé Mark Nornes succinctly grouped a wide range of topics into "three inevitabilities: demolition, Christianity, and slaughter of animals great and small" (Nornes 2009). Lü Xinyu, on the other hand, put most if not all films under the rubric of "engagement with the social" while making broad-stroked classifications according to "city and countryside" perspectives and "narratives of the market and the state" (Lü 2010). Yet not all independent documentaries made in the past two decades can be said to have a pronounced "engaged" social and political stance, let alone a radical activist agenda. Stylistically, as Chinese film critic Wang Xiaolu incisively points out, the large bulk of independent documentary from the formative phase in the 1990s to the more recent DV-enabled phase is driven by subjects or topics (*ticai*) that lend themselves well to a direct cinema-style shooting and the long-take aesthetic. A number of filmmakers have ventured into more "subjective" or "constructive" modes of shooting and editing, resulting in more stylistic innovation and variation (X. Wang 2011).

Here I will try to highlight a number of films made in the wake of the DV turn that seem to have gravitated to stances that documentary scholars in the West have alternately termed "committed," "political," "radical," and "activist" vis-à-vis the political and cultural status quo as well as mainstream cinema institutions. They appeared as the so-called New Documentary Movement increasingly disassociated itself from state television institutionally, technologically, and aesthetically and went largely independent in both self-definition and mode of production and dissemination in the second half of the 1990s. After a brief period of the transitional "Hi8 movement" involving a handful of filmmakers including Ji Dan, Hu Jie, Feng Yan, and Zhao Liang (X. Wang 2010),[1] a much larger number of cross-generational independent filmmakers embraced the portable and affordable DV (and nonlinear editing on personal computer) and its social and expressive possibilities. The early Hi8 and DV documentary works by Zhu Chuanming,[2] Du Haibin, and Hu Jie, dubbed the "ninja video warriors" (*yingxiang renzhe*) by film critic Cao Kai (Voci 2010a, 2010b 134), exhibited a politically edgier quality in large part enabled by small cameras that could be more imperceptibly inserted into the social margins and effectively edited with a minimal budget and crew size.

Within a few years in the new century, the contingent of the video-wielding ninjas quickly grew and a series of films with a palpable sense of social urgency and political advocacy appeared one after another, revealing the unjust and oppressed conditions of subaltern or disenfranchised groups (AIDS villages, earthquake victims, the unemployed, migrant workers including sex workers, homeless children) and repressed historical memories, and calling for rectification, redress, and intensified struggle for grassroots democracy. Prominent works include *Along the Railroad* (*Tielu yan xian,* Du Haibin, 2000), *To Live Is Better Than to Die* (*Haosi buru lai huozhe,* Chen Weijun, 2003), *In Search of Lin Zhao's Soul* (*Xunzhao Lin Zhao de linghun,* Hu Jie, 2004), *Taishi Village* (*Taishi cun,* Ai Xiaoming, 2005), *Village Video Project* (*Xiangcun yingxiang jihua,* Wu Wenguang et al., 2006–2007), *Meishi Street* (*Meishi jie,* Ou Ning, 2006), *Fengming: A Chinese Memoir* (Wang Bing, 2007), *The Epic of Central Plains* (*Zhongyuan Jishi,* Ai Xiaoming and Hu Jie, 2006), *We are the . . . of Communism* (*Women shi Gongchanzhuyi de shenglüehao,* Cui Zi'en, 2007), *Though I Am Gone* (*Wo sui si qu,* Hu Jie, 2007), *Bing'Ai* (Feng Yan, 2007), *Who Killed Our Children?* (*Shei sha le women de haizi?* Pan Jianlin and Zhang Lei, 2008), *Prisoners in Freedom City* (*Ziyoucheng de qiutu,* Hu Jia and Zeng Jianyan, 2008), *Buried* (*Yanmai,* Wang Libo, 2009), *Queer China, "Comrade" China* (*Zhi Tongzhi,* Cui Zi'en, 2009), *Disturbing the Peace* (*Lao Ma Ti Hua,* Ai Weiwei, 2009), *Karamay* (*Kelamayi,* Xu Xin, 2010), *To Justify Bu Qinfu* (*Huan Bu Qinfu yi meili,* Wang Yunlong 2011), *Born in Beijing* (*Jingsheng,* Ma Li, 2012), *Juvenile Laborers Confined in Dabao* (*Dabao xiaolaojiao,* Xie Yihui, 2013), and *Detachment of Women* (*Kaifang zhaowo,* Wang Nanfu, 2014). Other films with less artistic and political clout have, to varying degrees, also entered the public arena, particularly online, and pose challenges to the status quo or mainstream media culture as well as academic discourse on independent documentary and media citizenship. The use of the Internet by some filmmakers, notably Ai Xiaoming and Ai Weiwei, who also insert their own bodies and emotions into the documentary *xianchang,* further takes the independent documentary into a broad sphere of civic and media activism.

Poetics of Political Mimesis

In attempting to provide a typology of a nascent independent documentary movement that has achieved certain leverage and a substantial corpus, one is attracted by Michael Renov's seminal study on documentary poetics from the early 1990s. It was a time when documentary (re)merged as a weighty subfield of cinema studies and desperately sought to build a conceptual foundation modeled after classical fashions and contemporary developments in the humanities and social sciences.[3] Renov's well-known scheme, invoking Aristotle's poetics, challenges the old "strictures" of documentary understood as "non-fiction" pure and simple. He presents the "four tendencies" in documentary practices based on "construction, function, and effect": 1) to record, reveal, or preserve; 2) to persuade or promote; 3) to analyze or interrogate; 4) to express (Renov 1993, 21).

At the outset, this scheme seems quite practical for categorizing the Chinese new documentary works made before and after the DV turn around 1999. Many of them are considered "classics" by now; for instance, Jiang Yue's *The Other Bank* (*Bi'an* 1995) and Hu Jie's *Though I Am Gone* (*Wo sui si qu* 2007) are primarily about recording (and thus preserving) an experimental performance by an avant-garde troupe and traumatic historical memory from the Cultural Revolution, respectively. Since the function of propaganda and promotion (with its attendant authoritative voice-over) is explicitly rejected by independent documentary not intended for broadcasting on official TV, very few if any films can be said to squarely fit category 2 (to persuade/promote), though I will raise the case of a unique narrated documentary *Journey of the Tiananmen Mothers* (2009) by the eponymous activist group for its stark critique of an oppressive regime and its rallying cry for swift reversal and change. The large bulk of political and activist works illustrate the impulse to "reveal" (category 1) and to "interrogate" (category 3), such as Zhao Liang, Ai Xiaoming, and Ai Weiwei's investigative or confrontational works. And, obviously, experimental works such as *San Yuanli* (Cao Fei and Ou Ning, 2003) and *Disorder* (*Xianshi shi guoqu de weilai,* Huang Weikai, 2009) (Zhang 2012b), which are more invested in the city symphony form and its rewriting, may sit well with category 4 (to "express"), if one were to employ the typology in a one-dimensional manner for illustrative purposes. While Renov does not mean to separate the four modalities, and indeed stresses their frequent overlap, the implicitly hierarchical scheme clearly proceeds from the (raw) evidential/factual to the analytical and the expressive. The aesthetic, understood mainly as formal effectiveness and lyrical gestures in individual signature works, is placed at a distance from the pulse of the social and political world and suggested to be a mode or stage of refinement. Questions of the body and aesthetic of affect, which I find to be at the center of the independent Chinese social and political documentary, need to be addressed by extending this scheme.

Are existing definitions of "committed" and "radical" documentary in the West applicable in postsocialist China? Often traced to revolutionary Soviet filmmakers Vertov and Eisenstein rather than liberal humanists Grierson and Flaherty, a "committed filmmaker" is "not content only to interpret the world but is also engaged in changing it" (Waugh 1984, xiv). In the wake of the critique of realism (bourgeois or socialist) and the cult of "political modernism" of the 1970s, Thomas

Waugh and other advocates of activist cinema were hardly naive about how one might go about deploying the ideologically charged cinematic medium for "committed" purposes. He stresses that in addition to the "revolutionary principle" and "activist stance," the "subject-centered" orientation or ideal is vital to committed filmmaking. The latter is defined "not by finding and repeating a 'correct' line . . . but rooting them, working *within* actively ongoing political struggles; by making films . . . not only about people engaged in these struggles but also *with* and *by* them as well . . ." (Waugh 1984, xiv, emphasis original). Writing in the Cold War context of the early 1980s, Waugh admits, however, that little has been done in accounting for the "aesthetics of political documentary," the difficulty of which is not unrelated to the fact that "[it] refuses to meet any of the expectations of bourgeois aesthetics, modernist or otherwise."

> Instead of meeting the criteria of durability, abstraction, ambiguity, individualism, uniqueness, formal complexity, deconstructed or redistributed signifiers, novelty and so on, all in a packageable format, political documentaries provide us with disposability, ephemerality, topicality, directness, immediacy, instrumentality, didacticism, collective or anonymous authorship, unconventional formats, nonavailability, and ultimately nonevaluability.
>
> (Waugh 1984, xxii)

These observations are strikingly relevant for describing the politically engaged Chinese documentary, even though world order and global history have changed radically in the last three decades. Waugh and other contributors in the above-cited volume were armed with a passionate leftism of the "First World," and engaged mostly with a "Third World" in Latin America at the time. A post-Mao and China, emerging from the shadow of the Cultural Revolution and poised to embrace a market economy, is conspicuously missing, due in large part to the absence of Chinese film and media studies in Western academia at the time.[4] In terms of documentary production itself, this absence is hardly surprising given that "political documentary" had long been reified into a totalitarian state apparatus for the expressive purposes of propaganda and indoctrination in the form of newsreel, policy, and educational film. An independent documentary movement began to sprout in the crevices of a state television system only when video systematically replaced film stock in production and when the era of reform entered its second decade following the suppression of the Tiananmen democracy movement in 1989. The fervent "Third World" or anticapitalist and anti-imperial rhetoric does not sit well with the historical conditions of a post-Mao China, although the aesthetic strategies that Waugh identifies in "committed documentary" find resonances in socially engaged Chinese documentary works. This seemingly anachronistic reverberation across East and West, the Cold War and post–Cold War divide, could be illuminated by Jane Gaines' observations on the nature and function of radical documentary in response to Jacques Derrida's reflections on the "end of communism" in his *Specters of Marx* (Derrida 1994).

In her article "Documentary Radicality," Gaines takes up Derrida's question on the meaning or continued relevance of "radicaliz[ing]" in an epoch proclaimed as the "end of Marxism," yet one that "still [sees] no end of world suffering." It's an ambitious move to rescue a form of historically embedded radical "realism" from the academic "critique of realism" in vogue since the 1970s (Gaines 2007, 6). Gaines sees Derrida's passionate call "not to neglect" the exponentially multiplied sites of suffering in the contemporary world as a call to reassess the classical Marxist theory of social transformation, or rather the relationship between "the evidence of material conditions and the aspiration to transform the world"(Gaines 2007, 6). Excavating its etymological meaning in radix or "rootedness, as in its botanical or mathematical usage" (Gaines 2007, 6), Gaines develops the concept of "Marxist indexicality" by returning to the early twentieth century and still and motion photography's engagement with capitalist labor relations. She revisits the hand-painted magic lantern slides of the Triangle Shirtwaist Factory fire in New York in 1911 and their effective—and "melodramatic"—use in the radicalization of New York's women's workforce. She writes, "[T]he magic lantern show series elongates the family narrative aftermath of the Triangle Fire, enlarging the impact on the immigrant community." Thus, "[s]ites of suffering rendered as *sights* of suffering are made all the more poignant through a paradoxical supplement to their apparent microscopic factuality" (Gaines 2007, 9). Such an *affective aesthetic* "touched up" by "colorful" fiction and sentiment, in contrast to a "sober" or more "trustworthy" photorealism, illustrates what she calls the documentary "pathos of facts," which Gaines developed after Eisenstein's concept of "political pathos" in an earlier article "Political Mimesis" (Gaines 1999, 92).[5] "The pathos of facts" appeals to and galvanizes the spectators' sensuous perceptions of realities imaged and viewed for *grasping* through photographic indexicality a social "causality" and thereby mobilizes their political consciousness and the desire for change. Gaines elaborates this notion further in "Documentary Radicality":

> Here, we may think of the "pathos of fact" as pedagogical, and it is insofar as radicality is a pedagogy that may be aligned with productive overstatement, that is, with melodrama. The supreme political value of melodramatic hyperbole may be the boost it gives the portrayal of the need for swift change and the possibility of and the hope for awe-inspiring reversal. (Gaines 2007, 18)

So it seems Gaines' object of rescue is not so much realism per se but the melodramatic "roots"—moments of pathos-induced surprise or constructed "verité" (truth) as experienced rather than evidential—operative in documentary realism. This affective dimension associated with a mass culture of sentimentality, she argues, has been too often dismissed by the more sterile "realists" or "moralists" (she names Grierson for one) and later targeted for deconstruction by poststructuralists and feminists invested in modernist reflexive stylistics. Her intervention via the historiography of pre- and early cinema and revisionist melodrama studies boldly revises traditional documentary studies. In particular, Gaines' perspective critically complicates the documentary poetics outlined by Renov. The intertwined roots of radical politics and the mass-mediated aesthetic of affect at the heart of documentary realism reorient the relationships of the four tendencies along a different conceptual axis and *moving*-image tradition. In this sense, Renov's initial understanding of poesis as "active making" remains a useful departure for situating the activist film/video within the documentary field.

My hesitancy in using the term "film/video" points to another tension in grafting Waugh's and Gaines' highly charged rhetoric of Western Marxism or Renov's neo-formalist typology to the postsocialist Chinese context. They base their arguments on documentary's inherent indexicality in the long analog century. What happens to "Marxist indexicality" and "political mimesis" in the digital era? Philip Rosen updates the question in the digital era by developing the pair of terms "digital indexicality" and "digital mimicry," underscoring the hybrid nature of digital temporality and its "radical historicity" (Rosen 2001, 307–309). Bridging the debate on Chinese postsocialism and Rosen's theorization of "digital mimesis," I used Rosen's critique of digital utopia for the sense-making of the "profusion of hybrid images that stockpile the indexical and the digital." These experimental images are heavily "invested in time and body" (Zhang 2010, 100–101), carrying the impulse to change or "transfigure" the present through a range of "expressive" tools and strategies across the analog and digital—still, moving, and composite images. I find it productive to combine Gaines' and Rosen's insights, out of different discursive contexts but related by their shared commitment to "radical historicity" of old and new media, for advancing an experimental conceptual frame, *digital political mimesis,* with regards to the political and activist DV works produced in postsocialist China and circulated locally, transnationally and virtually.

The DV Turn and Activist Tendencies

The DV "turn" in the Chinese independent cinema scene in the late 1990s has been widely commented on by practitioners and critics alike (Zhang 2010, 98). Wu

Wenguang and Jia Zhangke are often credited with earliest, quasi-manifesto-style pronouncements on the democratic promise of DV for amateur cinema and independent documentary. Yet, Wu's account from the time shows a strong reservation about applying the term "movement," which he deems too "grand, spectacular and vigorous" to describing either the earlier analog video-based "new documentary" or the DV phase.[6] He stresses that the " 'new' documentaries did nothing more than return to the basic tenets of documentary filmmaking, focusing on human existence and social issues" (Wu 2002, 133). Yet Wu admits that he did see and sense a significant shift when he encountered Yang Lina's DV footage that was eventually edited into the first DV documentary *Old Men* (*Lao Tou* 1999).

> I was surprised that a young woman should have directed her camera towards the elderly, for it was widely said that busy young people were increasingly neglectful, even the so-called socially-righteous documentary makers. Yang also told me that initially she had hired a cameraman and sound engineer because she had never shot any film before. She fired them a few days later because they kept instructing the old men to sit closer together or altering their positions, making them feel embarrassed. She continued her project using a portable digital video camera.[7]
>
> I did not notice any special relation between the portable video camera and the footage she showed me until after watching for several hours. I discovered that the pictures were unique to a small video camera and an individual point of view. . . . As a veteran, I could not imagine such scenes being seen through the lens of a large intimidating camera. . . . (Wu 2002, 133)

Wu admits that Yang's footage "wrought a change" in him and he "found salvation in DV," resulting in his first DV documentary *Jianghu: Life on the Road* (2000), a semi-ethnographic study of an itinerant peasant entertainment troupe. Wu's account furnishes revelatory clues to the question of how DV facilitated a rupture in the perception and practice of documentary, and the emergence of an aesthetic of digital mimesis geared toward social engagement on a more personal and visceral level.

The proximity between the body of the filmmaker and the filmed subject not only allows the former to get closer to "what lay behind people's public lives," as Wu saw in Yang's footage, but also signaled a shift in the poetics and politics of *xianchang*—as observed by Luke Robinson, from the "public" to the "private," from metaphor or metonymy to contingency and specificity. Robinson rightly observes that the turn to unplanned projects and situations, as in the case of Wang Bing's *West of the Tracks* (2003), leads the "individual" (filmmaker as well as filmed subject) to be "caught up in social and political change, whilst not necessarily symbolic of it" (Robinson 2010, 193).

I would like to suggest further that the nonsymbolic and intersubjective shift in independent documentary also instigated an *activist turn* enabled by DV, more latent at first but quickly embraced by a number of political or cultural activists-turned-filmmakers. Here "activist" does not necessarily equate activism to a preconceived social program and organized action, but rather points to a sympathetic *inter-active relation* and a *pro-active stance* in the production of affective knowledge and the aspiration for social change. DV has not only equipped an increasing number of amateur filmmakers and exponentially widened the documentary field, but also fostered a political mimesis predicated on the active sense-making of social and material conditions, especially those inhabited and energized by disenfranchised and subaltern persons and groups who seek visibility, support, and more importantly, agency in representations and decisions involving their livelihood, rights, and dignity. For Gaines, a large number of documentaries worldwide that in one way or another "melodramatically" expose unjust social and material conditions and agitated political situations would qualify for "documentary radicality." I propose that the new breed of Chinese "personal-political" DV documentary made outside the state and mainstream commercial media systems (the two increasingly overlap) is inclined to generate the dynamism of such radicality precisely through its more direct bodily and affective involvement on the grassroots (*caogen*) scenes of happenings—to echo her emphatic etymological (botanic) use of the term "radicality."

The spectrum of activist tendencies and practices in these videos echo what Ching Kwan Lee and You-tien Hsing describe as a "broad array of modes of activism" and a "*spectrum* of politics" that has emerged since the beginning of economic reforms in the 1980s and intensified after the Chinese government fully adopted an aggressive model of neoliberal market economy in the mid-1990s (Lee and Hsing 2010, 2–3, emphasis original). Faced with the "fragmented, dispersed, and fluid modes of state-society relations that have dominated the reform era," Lee and Hsing outline a typology of activism—politics of redistribution, recognition, and representation, and the attendant forms of actions and discourses, such as "legal mobilization, civic activism, and symbolic forms of subversion"(Lee and Hsing 2010, 2). They name cultural producers including journalists, filmmakers, and artists as "activists" in carrying out the "symbolic contestations." The typology is similar to Renov's scheme in its structural clarity as well as analytical applicability due to its categorical nature and its implicit superstructure-base and form-content binarism. Many of the DV documentaries that I discuss throughout this chapter complicate and enrich this typology not so much by symbolically representing social activism, but by often directly and contingently arising from an affinity with activist experiences. In some instances, the distance between art (of representation) and activism is so radically reduced that the filmmaker becomes the activist or vice versa, as the two bodies overlap in the act of political mimesis. (I'll turn to Hu Jie, Ai Xiaoming, and Ai Weiwei for illustration later in this chapter.)

This particular feature in recent DV documentary helps to differentiate the political and activist videos within a more dynamic structure and spectrum. The tension-ridden kinship between art and activism is very much at the heart of the new documentary since its inception in a chilly or "frozen" (to borrow the title of the Sixth Generation director Wang Xiaoshuai's 1994 film) post-Tiananmen political climate, as evidenced in the early independent films about "artists" on the margins.[8] Elsewhere, I have observed this "built-in" tension in certain institutionalized forms of independent documentary as showcased in Songzhuang, Beijing, where the festival programs and jury selections often strive to balance the political and the aesthetic, the avant-garde and the grassroots.[9] For instance, on the program at the 6th DOC China Festival there in May 2009, while the art-oriented works are hardly nonpolitical (such as Zhang Ming's satiric *Fly* [*Cangying*] set in an artist's studio), the more emotionally stirring films such as Zhao Liang's *Petition* and Pan Jianlin's *Who Killed Our Children?* (about the so-called "57th national minority"[10] and Sichuan earthquake victims, respectively) captivated the audience through the mobilization of a historically and locally grounded "melodramatic imagination" (Brooks 1976). However, these filmmakers, like Wang Bing and Jia Zhangke, are by and large trained professionals in filmmaking, television, and fine art and they carry into their "activist-exposé" lens (Jie Li's term in her chapter on Zhao Liang's work) a received notion of (documentary) film as art (cinema) above all other intentions and purposes. In that regard, their "activist" roles may occupy—more or less—the "politics of representation" end of the typology I've described. However, the heartrending dramatization of the social world of suffering in their works creates a rousing "politics of pathos" that urgently calls for public recognition of the moral dignity, legal, and economic rights of the wronged and victimized.

In my view, a different form of activist and collaborative authorship emerged around 2005, bringing with it attendant new modes of production and dissemination with several parallel developments both above- and underground. China's rapid rise as a global economic power and the spread of digital technology and the Internet were important factors shaping this changed landscape. Wu Wenguang again was a figurehead in this shift by initiating the *Village Video Project* supported by the European Union and China's Ministry of Civic Affairs. Matthew David Johnson perceptively comments that Wu and several other filmmakers' new orientation is inseparable from the "changes in regulation—whether in terms of law, taste, or technology—of the 'cultural marketplace'" (Johnson 2006, 50) under a neoliberal political regime whose cultural policy quickly incorporated the market logic of global capitalism while retaining the postsocialist framework. While the project involves a number of grassroots amateurs from rural China, it is based in the Caochangdi Workstation in Beijing founded by Wu and his partner, choreographer Wen Hui, in 2005.[11] These unusual "students" were trained by Wu and his young urban-educated associates, before they went back to the "field" for filming. The Workstation assisted in the editing of the students' ten-minute short films about self-governance and everyday life in their villages, before sending a few to CCTV or bringing them to campuses and other institutions abroad.[12] Wu serves as the chief curator and producer of the project. The change from the underground director-auteur status to an activist-curator signals Wu's conscious move away from the institution of cinema to a quasi-ethnographic and academic arena, building an expanded platform for documentary practice and its dissemination. His anti-art-cinema stance was already evident in *Fuck Cinema* (2004). At the same time, the dissociation from being a "professional" full-time filmmaker also prepared for Wu's new positioning as a leading member among media activists qua public intellectuals—a trend in contemporary Chinese cultural and

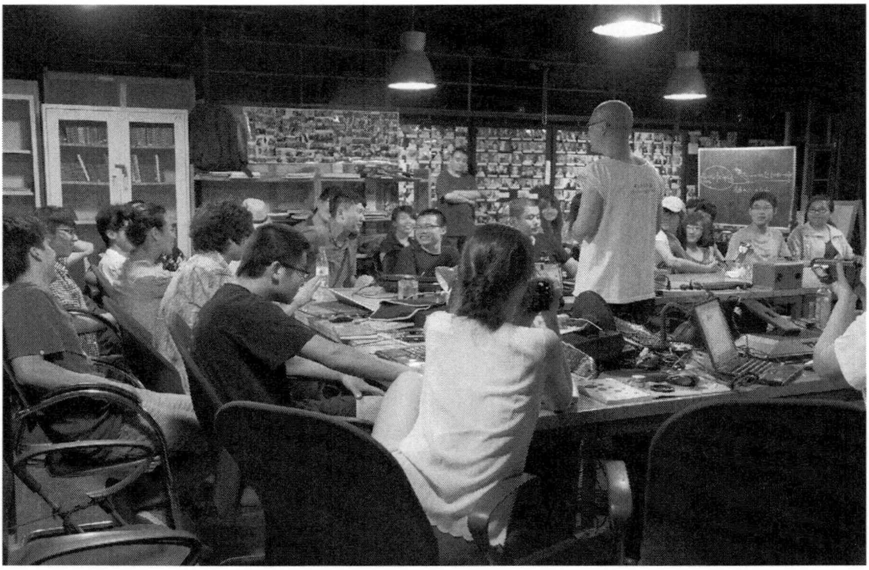

Figure 12.1. Folk Memory Project workshop at Caochangdi Workstation, May 2014. (courtesy of Wu Wenguang)

intellectual politics, in part enabled by the transnational linkages the Internet and social media have made possible. Nowadays Wu devotes most of his time and energy not to filmmaking, but to producing and curating group projects (including the ongoing *Folk Memory Project* synthesizing oral history, documentary, performance, and community activism) and multimedia festivals at the Caochangdi Workstation Art Center/Living Dance Studio (mixing documentary, dance, and performance). The Workstation also has a substantial physical and online archive for Chinese and international documentary performance and other media art works.

Ou Ning is a similar figure in this new expanded documentary domain infused with certain "primitive passions."[13] Whereas Wu moved to the suburbs and envisioned rural China to be the vast location for DV filmmaking, Ou's documentary work was directly concerned with urban forms and themes and took an approach closer to the avant-garde art tradition. His two films, *San Yuanli* (2003) and *Meishi Street* (2006), are in fact collaborative works with members of the U-theque collective, informed by an emerging urban-preservation activism. Similar to the *Village Video Project,* the handing of the camera to ordinary people to film their own lives in *Meishi Street* fosters what Wang Yiman calls an incipient "coauthorship" (Y. Wang, 2010). Yet the intellectual-artist remains in charge of the final product in both form and message,[14] and the agent of its afterlife as the owner of its copyright. *The Dazhalan Project* (which produced the film) as a whole is akin to Wu's project straddling the global, the national and the local, the legitimate culture, and an "alternative archive,"[15] utilizing the new digital media and its democratizing potential. But the ambitious project seems to have been aborted after only one film. Ou Ning has since moved on to other adventures as curator and editor, and more recently joined the new intellectual trend of rescuing culture and memory in rural China.[16]

DV has become an effective means of networking, archiving, and community-building for a burgeoning queer activism as well, which can be traced back to the first China Queer Film Festival in 2001. Cui Zi'en, novelist, film critic, cofounder of the festival, and a professor at Beijing Film Academy ("relieved" of teaching duties until recently), is a pioneer of this subculture and activist movement. While Ying Weiwei's *Box* (2001) is commonly seen as the first video documentary about same-sex relations from a curious yet sympathetic heterosexual point of view, it was not until a few years later that a number of DV films on the subject by queer filmmakers began to appear. Cui's DV works have consistently traversed the fiction and nonfiction border, as exemplified by his first "documentary," *Night Scene.*[17] Lesbian artist Shi Tou also began to make documentaries around 2004. *Dyke March* (2004) is seen as a turning point in the "coming out" of the Chinese lesbian identity via a transnational route, in this case, a gay parade in the United States (Chao

2010). This queer activist-oriented filmmaking trend eventually blossomed fully in the collective project *Queer China, "Comrade" China* (2008), which archives, in a mosaic and testimonial style, a critical and polyphonic history of queer activism (see chapter 11 by Luke Robinson). Cui Zi'en acted as the chief director (*zongdaoyan*) of the project as a group portrait and collective history. More recently, he was an executive producer of *Our Story* (*Women de gushi*, Yang Yang 2013), about the tortuous history of the Beijing Queer Film Festival.

From "Participatory Action" to "Citizen Documentation"

A markedly new activist DV documentary emerged with the work of Ai Xiaoming and Hu Jie in southern China, institutionally and aesthetically quite distant from the avant-garde cultural scene in Beijing. Their collaborative works, including *Taishi Village* (2005) and *The Epic of Central Plains* (2006), shocked the indie film scene with their extremely "sensitive" subject matter and unflinching activist style. When a friend first introduced *Taishi Village* to me, she was apologetic about its lack of formal rigor. My first viewing of the film left me very moved but also somewhat puzzled. Indeed, what kind of aesthetic criteria can we bring to bear on this type of work that seems to recharge the concept and practice of *xianchang* with a raw energy and political commitment? Neither direct cinema or cinema verité that had been borrowed and read into the new documentary would seem adequate enough to describe these films (and many others to come), though the films are definitely *direct* in their manner of inserting the filmmaker into the action being filmed and fearlessly trying to get the truth (*zhenshi*) out loud and clear in most difficult circumstances.

Neither auteur-conscious nor deliberately cultivating an intellectual agenda with a reinvented "going to the people" ethos,[18] Ai Xiaoming and Hu Jie belong to the more militant "ninja video warriors" who espouse a radical dissident politics. They have also made films individually, with Hu Jie's own works more invested in repressed historical memory and an activist-exposé approach in contrast to Ai's direct take on highly controversial contemporary events. However, they share a strong commitment to activist causes using DV and related platforms for rewriting history and intervening in the present. They are also substantially older and intellectually more mature than the new indies or the DV generation, having experienced the Cultural Revolution firsthand and worked inside the "system" (*tizhi*) before embarking on independent filmmaking. They do so not so much for self-expression and realizing the "*cinema paradiso*" dream harbored by younger filmmakers as for urgent social and political intervention. Ai Xiaoming, who is still a card-carrying Communist member and a professor of literature,[19] in particular, openly advocates social and political activism and sees her documentary work as "a form of participatory action" (Ai, 2010a; Zhang 2013). She signed on to Charter 08, initiated by the 2009 Nobel Peace Prize winner Liu Xiaobo (who is still in jail) and other Chinese intellectuals and writers, and was joined by hundreds of ordinary people.[20] Her activism outside the campus has led to police harassments, custodies, and now an indefinite ban on her traveling abroad.

Hu Jie, a veteran member of the New Documentary Movement, has a more "professional" background in art and media work as a painter and a photojournalist for the Xinhua News Agency. While employed, he made several films, including one on Yuanmingyuan artists in Beijing in the 1990s. His career as a documentary filmmaker took a sharp turn when he was forced to resign from his job because of his research on *Looking for Lin Zhao,* about the eponymous young woman who was tortured and died in prison for her audacious criticism of Mao and the Cultural Revolution. It was a subject deemed far more off-limits than the "observational" expositions of contemporary social problems by his peers.[21] Unemployed and based in his hometown Nanjing, he went completely independent and began a series of projects tapping into taboo subjects in Chinese communist historiography.[22] He admits that meeting Ai changed his filmmaking forever: "I used to be

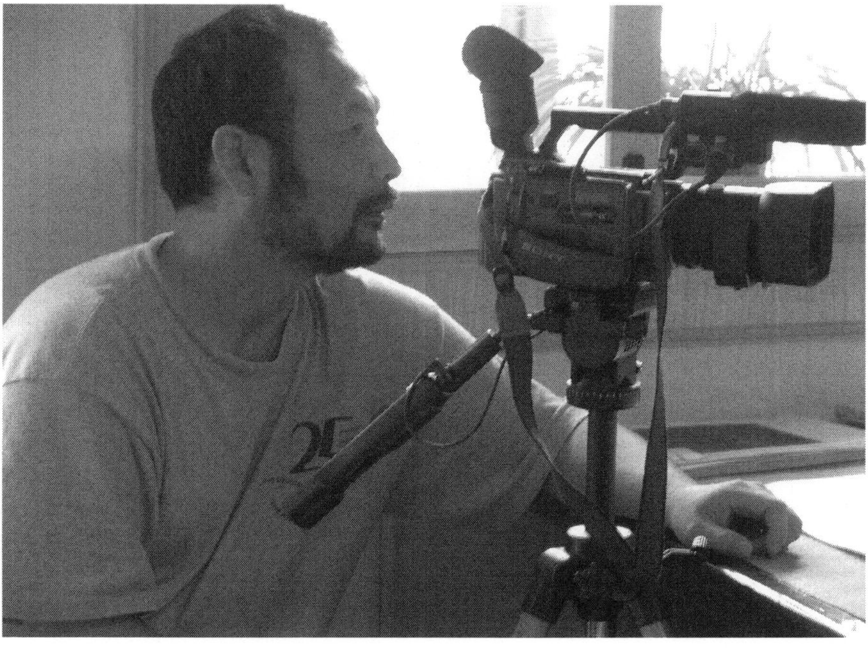

Figure 12.2. "Ninja warrior" Hu Jie. (courtesy of Hu Jie)

like a fly on the wall, making films of the subjects' life in an unperturbed manner. Now I also march toward the front stage while recording, facilitating and intervening in the processes of public events" (Xu 2010).

Their collaboration began in 2004, when Ai invited Hu to show his *Looking for Lin Zhao* at Sun Yat-sen University in Guangzhou where she was a professor of comparative literature. That encounter inspired her to take up DV documentary as an effective form for social and political advocacy as a feminist activist and public intellectual. The result was a cluster of films within two years. Hu Jie assisted her as cameraman and editor on *Paradise Garden* (*Tiantang huayuan* 2005), about an unfair trial surrounding a rape victim and the question of women's rights; *Taishi Village* (2005), about the villagers' heroic battle with corrupt officials and police forces over electoral and land property rights; and *The Epic of Central Plains* (2006), about AIDS victims in the wake of the government-endorsed notorious plasma industry in Henan province. They worked together again on *Citizens' Investigation* (*Gongmin diaocha* 2009), part of Ai's multi-installment project about the victims of the "tofu dregs" school buildings in the Sichuan earthquake of 2008 and the people who try to unearth the truth, especially the compiling of a list of the dead children's names and identities.[23]

To give a full and adequate account of Ai's prolific work—which is ongoing as I write—would be impossible here.[24] Here, for identifying an emerging embodied activist aesthetic derived from direct action and affective affinity in the forging of a political digital mimesis, I will focus on *Taishi Village* and some recurring motifs and strategies in her subsequent works. In hers and other activists' videos, the mobilization of "pathos of facts" (such as showing villagers' wounds inflicted by police and children crying over their arrested parents) is intertwined with an excess of other melodramatic elements such as spectacular action (e.g., protests, physical confrontation) and rhetorical speech (or writing)—both of which include the filmmaker's involvement—concerning rights and justice. More subdued observational and formally conscious documentary rarely deploy such forms of direct action and address, using instead a restrained filming and editing style.

The film documents the villagers' protest to impeach the village chief for illegal land seizure and embezzlement, and the ensuing arrests and harassments by the police sent by the authorities. Ai Xiaoming never hides herself from the subject she films, using voice-over, asking questions, making comments, and increasingly merging herself and her camera into the agitated scenes of conflicts and protests. The manner of such filming in part resembles that of an embedded war journalist,[25] except here Ai takes a stance wielding her camera as both a shield and a spear as a foot soldier among the radicalized citizens fighting with bare fists, slogans, and songs. Yet her films are not just on-scene "reporting," but are innovative constructs that activate and synthesize multiple voices under an unambiguous

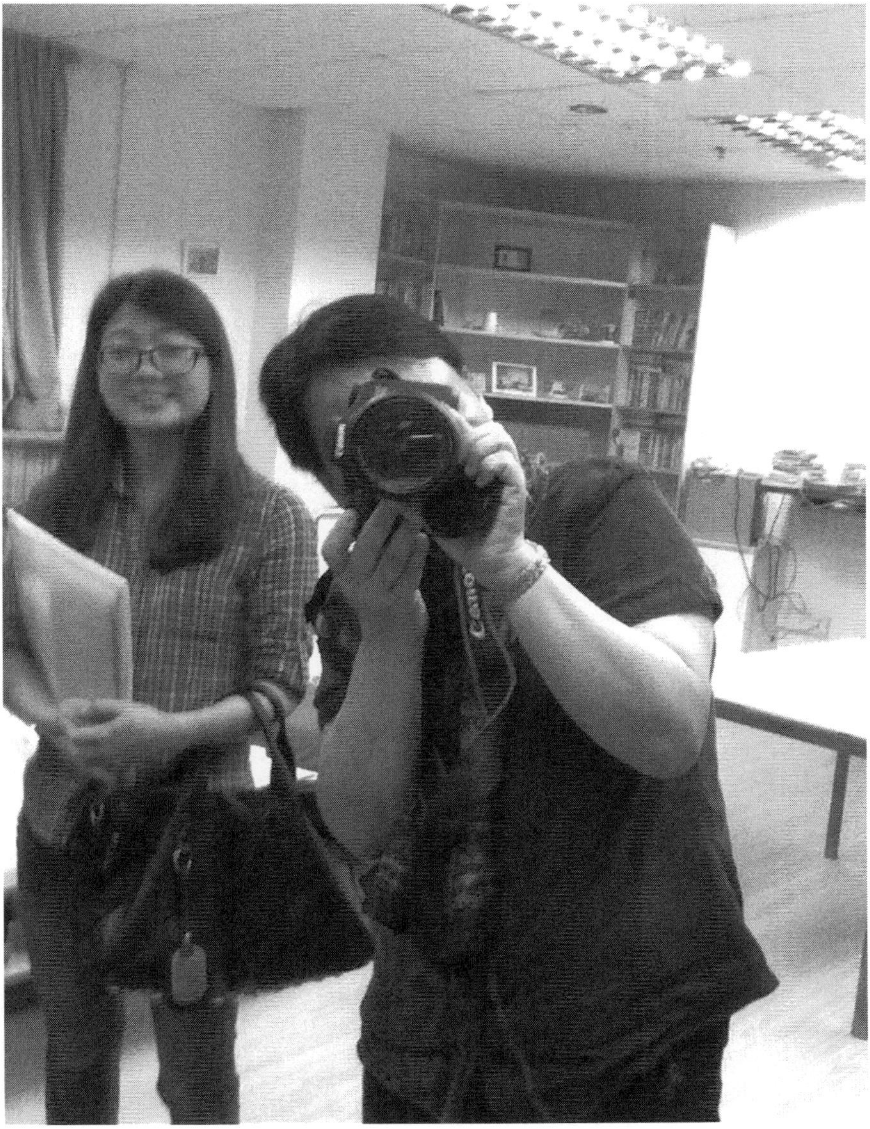

Figure 12.3. Filmmaker Ai Xiaoming, after a graduate seminar conversation with the author at the Center for Gender Studies at Sun Yat-sen University, Apr. 19, 2012. (photo by Zhen Zhang)

activist agenda. Her documentary tale of a dispute over electoral rights in a village escalating into an explosive national event is quite different from the omnibus *Village Video Project* consisting of ten short (ten-minute) episodes "produced and curated" by Wu Wenguang. The latter deals with village election (as mandated by the funding bodies) in a microscopic but inevitably disjointed manner, resulting in an anthology of video diaries on everyday life in postsocialist rural China. While the everyday face of this process as recorded by the villager-turned-ethnographer is unique and heartwarming, *Taishi Village* addresses grassroots democracy with a great sense of urgency and political passion. The protests and violent clashes with the police in Taishi village were sensational news in various Chinese and Western media. The political mimetic power generated by activist documentary, Ai contends, exceeds conventional media—official or otherwise:

> You can gain an understanding of its contributing factors through a great deal of written material and news reportage, but what's important is to *see*—to see the images of the villages, their *emotional state*. Directly facing the range of human emotions, it compels us to try to understand the inner life of the people behind the incident, to understand their *experience and feelings*.
>
> (Ai 2010a, 73, emphasis added)

The "ninja video warrior" and her small "crew" of activist lawyers find themselves literally entering a war-zone of sorts, quickly turning a project of documentation into "participatory action." While acting as her own camerawoman, Ai's presence is never absent from the mimetic space on- and off-screen. Her activist stance and voice are immediately communicated to the villagers and the viewers through her questions and injunctions, as well as the positions and movement of her camera, insistently indicating, "I'm on your side." The film has an agitating pulse as Ai and the legal activists follow and join the villagers' struggles and unexpected twists and turns in the process. Alternating between close shots and overhead long shots, Ai captures the physical intensity, pain, and heroism of the protesting villagers (many are elders and women), as well as the overwhelming high-tech force of state violence. In the midst of a dangerous confrontation, Ai shouts at the police, "No violence! Stop it!" while trying to carry on filming even though all she could capture are wrangled limbs and waving fists and batons. Her own position and body are as vulnerable and defiant as the villagers. The chaotic and shaky framing vividly transmits, via an "awe-inspiring" (Gaines) spectacle pressing for swift change, a radical mimesis shaped by the blurring of the subject-object boundary, and an embodied solidarity. Here the "blurred boundaries" between subject and object, between representation and participation, also illustrate

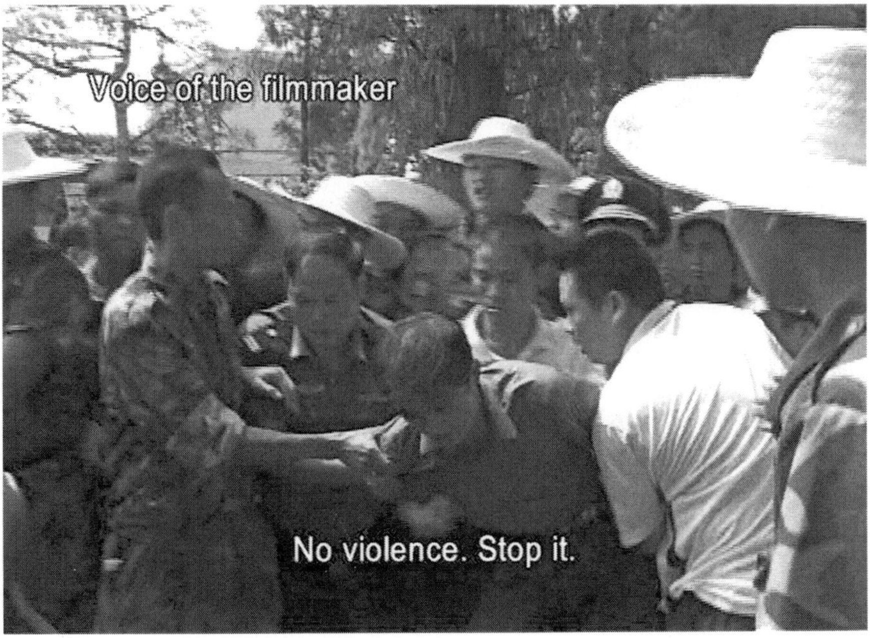

Figure 12.4. Taishi Village. "Voice of the filmmaker."

Stella Bruzzi's negotiation with Bill Nichols' "wariness" of the "performative mode" (for "drawing attention to itself") in documentary (Nichols 1994; Bruzzi 2000, 154).

The "dialect of action and affect" (Williams 1998) ambles compellingly throughout the film. Whenever possible, Ai takes care to yield her camera to the villagers' emotional state behind the front line. She uses ambient music (a feature rarely seen in other independent documentary)—folk melodies from the region—and lyrical imageries of the village's lush natural environment to accentuate the villagers' feelings and contrast them with the harshness and even terror in their everyday reality. Shortly after the confrontation with the police and the massive arrests that followed, Ai and the lawyers return to the village and try to collect further evidence and offer legal aid to the villagers. They encounter two women (Jiao and Xing) resting on the roadside, after just being released from a police detention center, and stop to talk to them. The women first tell them in a matter-of-fact manner where they have just come from and how they were badly treated by police. As the conversation flows and a trusting rapport is established, they get increasingly emotional and tearful, appealing to Ai and her camera to "get more journalists and scholars" to help them. Ai's camera lingers on their faces and the moon cakes on the ground. It's the Chinese mid-autumn moon festival, and the neighbors have offered the cakes to the traumatized, hungry women as both food and sympathy. The juxtaposition of their tearful faces and the moon cakes amplifies the magnitude of their suffering and the dire need for care and redress. For the Chinese, there is nothing sadder than not spending the festival celebrating harvest and earthly happiness with loved ones at home. The roadside "reunion" of the villagers and the activists offers, however, an unusual occasion for affirming their shared belief and destiny.

Jie Li observes that the "activist-exposé mode" in the works of Zhao Liang (*Petition*) and Wang Bing (*West of the Tracks*) gradually gives way to an "empathetic mode"[26] as the filmmakers and their cameras move deeper into their epic scale documentaries about ordinary people's suffering. This is evident in moments like Zhao's role in helping the adopted daughter leaving her crazed mother in *Petition,* or Wang's own heavy breathing and his lens misting up in extreme cold as he shoots in the dying northeastern industrial city. These moments suffused with empathy through intimate contact propel the filmmakers to take part in their subjects' lives and bear not just witness but also certain ethnical and practical responsibilities. Ai's more transparent activist position literally places her and her camera in the same physical danger that has befallen her subjects. Toward the end

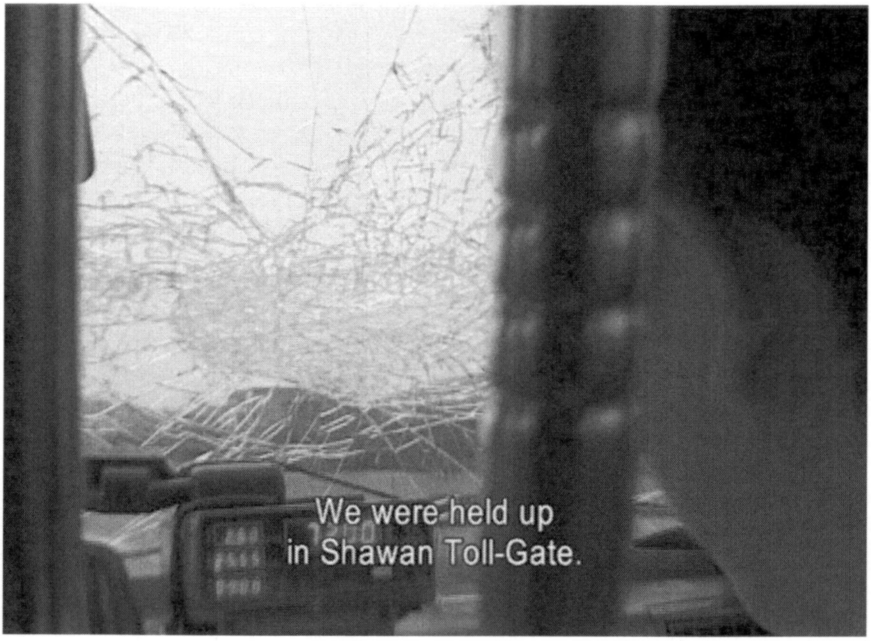

Figure 12.5. Taishi Village. Taxi window, smashed.

of *Taishi Village,* Ai and her activist friends, beaten and terrorized, narrowly escape from the "war-zone." A taxi miraculously comes to their rescue, but as it leaves the village its windows are smashed by a mob of menacing men with unannounced identity. This assault is directed at Ai and her friends' bodies as well as the camera as an activist prosthetic. As the glass fractures and falls off and filming becomes mortally dangerous, the panic-stricken voices of the activists provide the most unusual soundtrack for the blackout screen—like silent film's melodramatic "text of muteness"—with intertitles describing and giving evidence of unlawful state persecution of innocent citizens. In such scenarios where representation is nearly impossible, we witness the overlap and mutual reinforcement of "legal mobilization, civic activism, and symbolic forms of subversion" in activist documentary. In the final title card (or "afterword"), Ai states that after seeing many cameras busy at work in Taishi Village, "I decided that the villagers deserve a camera, too."

Ai's radical practice vividly illustrates "video activism" defined by Thomas Harding: "In the hands of a video activist, a camcorder becomes a powerful political instrument that can deter police violence. An edit suite becomes a means for setting a political agenda. A video projector becomes a mechanism for generating mass awareness" (Harding 1997, 1). Rather than labeling and marketing her filmmaking as "independent cinema" or part of the "New Documentary Movement," Ai Xiaoming has called her documentaries "a part of China's fledgling rights defense movement (*weiquan yundong*)." International festivals and art institutions, which have raised Jia Zhangke, Wang Bing, Du Haibin, and Zhao Dayong to the altar of rarefied art cinema, hardly heed this type of work. Newly emerged small cinephilia or indie-philia distributors in the West show no interest or see no market value in them. Ai's one-woman not-for-profit cottage industry productions rely on her own and volunteers' work and above all her subjects' support and endorsement. She resorts to the Internet (such as YouTube.com and regularly emailing links of her new videos to friends) and other means for free and fast dissemination, a practice increasingly common among media-savvy activists, for which self- and collective piracy serves as a productive means for networking and mobilization. The monetary donations the free videos generate are then channeled to grassroots video-making programs.

Ai's practice and conception of the documentary recently took a new turn in the wake of the death of Wei Wenhua[27] and the great Sichuan earthquake in 2008, joining what she calls the fast-growing phenomenon of "citizen documentation" (*gongmin jilu*). This new orientation pushes political digital mimesis from representing the suffering subaltern to taking part in a broad social movement wherein the disenfranchised populations and their sympathizers strive for political and visual citizenship with a far more visible and consequential degree of media literacy and agency. Coauthorship takes on a more socially salient and multilayered form. In *Our Children* (2009) and *Citizens' Investigation* (2009), Ai worked closely with Tan Zuoren, an environment activist who devoted himself to the investigation of the "tofu dregs" school building and who was arrested in the course of their collaborative project. They use a large number of photographs (especially family albums that survived the ravages) and video footage shot by local people during and after the shoddy school buildings collapsed and killed thousands of children. More than eyewitness evidence,[28] Ai sees the citizens' conscious deployment of media technology in the rights defense process as a "new feature of citizen participation in social movements."[29] The editing of the film has the effect and look of quilting, stitching together material from different sources, media, formats, and sizes, using a host of audiovisual rhetorical devices to generate both argumentation and emotional resonance. If *Our Children,* as the title gives away, still relies heavily on a politics of pathos invested in exposing the magnitude of loss and mourning, *Citizen Investigation,* as the title declares, turns loss into action and mourning into a form of activist labor within a larger context of citizen's rights movement. It clearly articulates its close relation to citizen documentation as a new breed of independent media production outside of the venerated tradition of underground art cinema. As I was writing these lines, Ai's email popped up in the window on my desktop, sharing the news that the film and Ai Weiwei's *Lao Ma Ti Hua* and He Yang's *Days of Hesuoge* (2010) were given the Sunshine Citizenship Award (*Yanghuang gongmin jiang*), an online poll run by Sunshine Satellite TV, based in Hong Kong.[30] The virtual documentary festival without an auditorium and a host of other paraphernalia allowed thousands of viewers to watch hundreds of mostly independent Chinese-language documentaries and compare notes on computers or cell phones.

The new millennium has seen Chinese film and media enter a brave new world with multiple dimensions, especially the fast expansion of independent and amateur practices enabled by new media and related social spaces, physical or virtual. In hindsight, the Sichuan earthquake disaster that ignited the explosion of "citizen journalism" in its aftermath seems to have played a cataclysmic role in consolidating and rapidly expanding an emerging "citizen documentation" movement in the digital era.[31] As new media tools become more affordable and user-friendly, and online forums more accessible and easier to network (despite surveillance and frequent shutdowns), a vast number of Chinese netizens inside and outside of the country have joined this nascent popular movement in various forms and capacities (Yang 2009, 6).

The "Fujian Three Netizens" case in the spring of 2010 pushed the envelope further, as the case itself concerns the rights of netizens using digital tools and platforms to disclose and circulate information suppressed by official channels.

The arrests and trial of the three netizens, who helped to post a video and testimonies surrounding the violent death of a young woman working at a KTV, outraged millions of other netizens. Organized quickly and effectively by activist Wang Lihong,[32] among others, through tweeting, blogging, emailing, and texting, thousands of netizens and activists traveled to Fuzhou to support the defendants and found themselves confronting and recording police harassment. Wang Lihong's courageous filming with a small DV camera recalls Ai Xiaoming's filming in *Taishi Village*. Neither a trained academic/public intellectual nor filmmaker, the retired Beijing businesswoman with severe chronic back injuries and no institutional base seized digital tools as an integral part of her activist cause, using them for evidence-collecting as well as mass mobilization. Ai Xiaoming has since made a series of films about Wang both before and after her arrest, including the series of *Postcards* on the occasion of Wang's birthday, all posted on Ai's blog (which is frequently shut down by censors and thus constantly migrated by Ai) or other sites. Their videos, online for free viewing and downloading, have formed an interlocking chain of documentary as an open and collaborative experience infused with a moving feeling of sisterhood and a shared feminist agenda.

This new phenomenon of citizen documentation has pushed the boundaries of documentary and independent cinema, both institutionally and aesthetically. Indeed, we observe clearly in this new crop of activist DV documentaries the features Waugh attributed to "committed documentary" (in the era of 16mm, super 8, and the beginning of analog video)—"disposability, ephemerality, topicality, directness, immediacy, instrumentality, didacticism, collective or anonymous authorship, unconventional formats, non-availability, and ultimately non-evaluability." Yet the digital turn in activist documentary in a postsocialist China riddled with social and political upheavals has also made many of these features flexible or reversible, such as turning disposability into reproducibility, nonavailability into mass dissemination in cyberspace, and infusing didacticism with affective power and moral persuasion. Activist documentary and citizen documentation are crucial components and extensions of the new "structures of feeling" that have been thoughtfully analyzed by online activism sociologist Yang Guobing (Yang 2009). They are part and parcel of the living experience and everyday struggle now increasingly taking place in cyberspace or mediated by new digital tools, while reconstructing a political mimesis straddling and breaking the boundaries of old and new media, traditional and alternative film practices and institutions. They record, process, and reformulate, in palpable and persuasive audiovisual forms, what Raymond Williams describes as "impulse, restraint, and tone; specifically affective elements of consciousness and relationships: not feeling against thought; but thought as felt and feeling as thought" (Yang 2009, 19).

Beyond Pathos

One of the new additions to the "citizen documentation" movement and challenge to the parameters of the increasingly institutionalized independent documentary (as part of the indie art cinema world) are video works made or facilitated by Ai Weiwei, an "exceptional" citizen by all accounts. He is another iconic citizen-documentarian with whom Ai Xiaoming collaborated both on- and off-screen, starting in the aftermath of the Sichuan earthquake. The "blackout" scene induced by the assault on the filmmaker and other activists in *Taishi Village* received a more aggravated expression in Ai Weiwei's *Disturbing Peace* (*Lao Ma Ti Hua* 2009),[33] which shows Ai's beating by police in his hotel room at night. He and his friends went to Chengdu to support and bear witness to Tan Zuoren's trial but found themselves "house-arrested" at their hotel and then violently attacked. The video quickly went viral online, becoming the most-watched and discussed video online among China's netizens.

Ai is an internationally famous multimedia artist who scandalized the Chinese state by quitting from his advisory role in designing the Bird's Nest stadium for the 2008 Beijing Olympics. Though a latecomer to documentary making, he and his team have made to date over fifteen films.[34] Convinced of the power of the Internet in instigating social change, the films are all posted online (Ai Weiwei 2011, 239–242). While his artistic credentials could have easily set him up for making formally rigorous films ready to be plucked by film festival or art biennial curators, he entered the arena with a direct investment in political advocacy. That his imposing stature in the international art world and his large physical frame would be subject to police's assault and virulent verbal abuse appears to be the central melodramatic spectacle that has galvanized the viewers, who see in his "exceptional" case the permanent state of emergency and the norm of violation of ordinary people's rights and safety. In the face of authoritarian violence, politically interventionist art and artists are rendered as disposable as the needlessly dead children in earthquakes or villagers dying of AIDS. The image of him holding up his cell phone to "shoot" back at the police, and the popular music and song by Zuoxiao Zuzhou, his collaborator, pulsating through the end credits of the film, further amplify the significance of this highly personal political melodrama. Yet in adopting tactics of ironic mimicry and parody in his own performance vis-à-vis the police, and in his other works and acts such as the use of Twitter—a favorite tool of the Chinese activists—and his nude performance art pieces, which are informed by humor and other "popular" elements, critics note a shift in activist representation from "pathos" (*gaobie beiqing*) to "playfulness" (which involves a "cultivated" rough and rogue style resonating with online political jokes and web-spoofs). Ai Xiaoming, who interviewed and filmed Ai Weiwei following the *Laoma Tihua* incident as part of her earthquake series, finds in these tactics a fresh imaginative form that fosters the "quotidianization" of activism and provides daily "gymnastics" for building a democratic society (Ai 2010b). After an initial reticence following his release from a period of detention in 2011, Ai returned to his multimedia creative work infused with even a greater dose of humor, sarcasm, and fun, as evidenced in his gangnam-style dance video (posted on YouTube on October 25, 2012) in which he waved a pair of handcuffs to the dance beat. These and other hybrid articulations or "gymnastics" of political mimesis in the digital era demand new thinking about documentary forms and activist aesthetics. In a post-utopian "post-Reform" China, a new revolution in cinema, art, and society is gathering wind against the heavily polluted air.

Notes

I would like thank (in chronological order) Guo-Juin Hong, Paize, Keulemans, the late Miriam Hansen (my dear adviser), Oksana Bulgakova, Emilie Yeh, Ai Xiaoming, Laikwan Pang, Gina Marchetti, and Dong Bingfeng for providing valuable forums for the development of this chapter, at Duke University, Yale University, University of Chicago, Mainz University (Germany), Hong Kong Baptist University, Sun Yat-sen University in Guangzhou (China), Chinese University of Hong Kong, Hong Kong University, and the Beijing Independent Film Festival, between 2009 and 2013, respectively. An earlier version was also presented at the Visible Evidence 18 Conference at NYU in August 2011 and I am grateful to Jane Gaines' comments there. Above all, my heartfelt thanks go to the many Chinese filmmakers, critics, and curators who have inspired and supported this research in various ways: in particular, Ai Xiaoming, Cui Weiping, Cui Zi'en, Dong Bingfeng, Du Haibin, Hao Jian, Hu Jie, Huang Weikai, Ma Li, Wang Hongwei, Wang Wo, Wang Xiaolu, Wang Yuanlong, Wu Wenguang, Xu Xin, Yang Lina, Ying Liang, Zeng Jianyan, Zhang Xianmin, Zhang Zanbo, Zhao Liang, and Zhu Rikun. This chapter is dedicated to the independent documentary community in China.

1. Wang Xiaolu describes this period as a "neglected movement" that many critics and scholars lumped together with the DV movement. He discusses the markedly different technological and aesthetical differences, arguing that the analog Hi8 is more a part and extension of the early New Documentary Movement while preparing for the coming the DV movement.

2. Because both his critics and his subjects raised ethical issues about *Beijing Cotton Fluffer* (*Mianhua tanjiang* 1999) and *Extras* (*Qunzhong yanyuan* 2001), Zhu allegedly gave up documentary and turned to fiction film.

3. The first Visible Evidence conference took place in 1993; Bill Nichols' *Representing Reality* was published in 1992 (Nichols 1992). Interestingly, the book cover

uses the famous image of the tank-man during the Tiananmen democracy movement, framed in a TV monitor.

4. Other than Jay Leyda's pioneering yet error-ridden *Dianying/Electric Shadows,* Chinese cinema studies outside of China began to emerge in the mid-1980s, in the wake of the Fifth Generation cinema's entrance into international festivals and winning of awards and acclaims (Leyda 1972).

5. In "Political Mimesis," the "pathos of facts" is plainly spelled out: "this happened; people died for this cause; others are suffering; many took to the streets; this innocent victim can be saved if only something is done" (Gaines 1999, 92).

6. Wu's comment was more directed at Lü Xinyu, perhaps the first scholar who systematically used the term to include a range of documentaries made both inside and outside the state television in the 1990s. The title of Lü Xinyu's book, *Documenting China: The Contemporary Chinese New Documentary Movement* (2003), clearly states her view of the "movement" as a pervasive paradigm shift in Chinese documentary history.

7. It was a Panasonic EZ-1. DV was first invented and released to the mass market in Japan in 1997. Incidentally, this was also when several Chinese filmmakers including Wu Wenguang attended the Yamagata International Documentary Festival for the first time. They interacted with, and were impressed by, Japanese filmmaker Shinsuke Ogawa.

8. Films in this "genre" include Zhang Yuan's *Beijing Bastards* (*Beijing zazhong* 1993), Wang Xiaoshuai's *Days* (*Dongchun de rizi* 1993) and *Frozen* (*Jidu hanleng* 1998), Wu Wenguang's *Bumming in Beijing* (*Liulang Beijing* 1990), and Jiang Yue's *The Other Bank* (*Bi'an* 1995).

9. I made these observations in my talk, "Between Art and Activism: The Independent Documentary Scene in China Today," at Workshop on "The Politics of Representation in Documentary," Duke University, Nov. 20, 2009. An expanded version was published in Chinese as "Art, Affect, and Activist Documentary" in *Chinese Independent Cinema* 11 (Zhang 2012a).

10. There are fifty-five officially recognized ethnic minorities such as Tibetans, Mongolians, Yi, and Naxi, while there are many ethnic groups still striving for recognition of cultural autonomy and attendant legal and economic rights.

11. The founding and operation of the Caochangdi Workstation was made possible through the support of Beijing Storm, Kampnagel in Hamburg, Zuercher Theater Spektakel in Zurich, Borneoco in the Netherlands, and Asian Culture Council in the United States, among others. See http://culture360.org/organisation/caochangdi-workstationliving-dance-studio/.

12. For instance, NYU's Center for Religion and Media and Department of Cinema Studies collaborated to invite Wu and his collaborator Jian Yi to show and discuss the first installment of the films abroad in spring 2006. *Village Video Project* was funded by the EU in celebration of the tenth anniversary of village elections in China.

13. I borrow the term "primitive passions" from Rey Chow's well-known formulation in discussing the Fifth Generation's preoccupation with the rural and historical subjects as well as subaltern figures (Chow 1995). While Chow's term is aimed

at the allegorical fictional representation of women, peasants, and children in these films, the "primitive" figures in independent documentary are mostly if not all contemporary and hardly fictional.

14. Chris Berry and Lisa Rofel discuss the ambiguous effect resulting from mixing the filmmakers' observational shooting and the protagonist's often agitated personal shooting. The activist message is not entirely clear as the filmmakers here, as they were in *San Yuanli,* seem "reticent" toward both the protagonist's resistance and the police's aggression (Berry et al. 2010, 145–148).

15. "Alternative Archive," or *bieguan* in Chinese, is also the name of the website for the project as a whole. Berry and Rofel used the term to entitle their article (Berry et al. 2010) and as an inspiration for conceptualizing the new documentary's relationship vis-à-vis the official media or archive.

16. These projects include the literary magazine *Chutzpah!* (*Tiannan*) launched in 2010 and the Bishan Harvestival in Anhui Province.

17. See Paola Voci's reading of Cui's "hybridized docu-drama with the flavor of a film essay" in "Blowup Beijing: The City as Twilight Zone," (Berry et al. 2010, 99–115).

18. "Going to the people" (*dao minjian qu*) refers back to the intellectual and artistic movement in the early twentieth century that tried to reconcile the gap between the high-brow Enlightenment and vernacular movement agenda and the everyday world of popular and oral culture. The impulse resulted in projects to collect folk songs and archive rural vernacular culture, among other things. For its impact on cinema, see my discussion on Tian Han in my *Amorous History of the Silver Screen,* (Zhang 2005, chapter 5).

19. Ai is also known for being the first woman PhD after the Cultural Revolution and a leading feminist scholar. She is professor of literature at Sun Yat-sen University in Guangzhou.

20. The manifesto Charter 08 was published on the sixtieth anniversary of the UN Human Rights Declaration, Dec. 10, 2008, and signed by over 350 Chinese artists and human rights activists and intellectuals. For the full text in English, visit http://www.charter08.eu/2.html (accessed Nov. 21, 2011).

21. My conversation with Hu Jie during Reel China at NYU, Oct. 2008; see also Shen Rui's interview with him in *Senses of Cinema* (Shen 2005).

22. In an STM (short text message) questionnaire on "For Whom Do you Make Documentary?" posted online in 2008, Hu Jie's answer is simply, "For history." More than a few replied, "For myself" or versions of it. http://zgushu.blog.163.com/blog/static/43270469200851515644527/ (accessed July 28, 2011).

23. So far there are five installments: *Our Children* (*Women de wawa* 2009), *Citizens' Investigation* (*Gongmin diaocha* 2009), *Why Are the Flowers So Red?* (*Hua'er wei shen me zhe yang hong* 2010), *River of Forgetting* (*Wang chuan* 2009), and *Enemy of the State* (*Guojia de diren* 2009).

24. At the time of drafting this chapter (November 2010), I received in email her new films about Wang Lihong, the activist who championed a citizen's support movement for the Fujian Sanwan Netizens' case. Wang also took up a camera and recorded

the protests in front of the court in Fuzhou. For updates on her work, especially the making of *Three Days in Wukan* (*Wukan sanri* 2012), see my interview with Ai in 2012 (Zhang 2013).

25. She has been called a "frontline citizen's reporter" (*huoxian gongmin jizhe*) by prominent cultural critics such as Cui Weiping. Ai also says that China needs many frontline reporters, given the country's particular conditions today (Zhang 2013, 155).

26. In chapter 3, Jie Li outlines the evolving cinematic and ethical mode in Zhao Liang's films: from a "voyeuristic mode," to an "activist-exposé mode" (which echoes the "suku" tradition/aesthetic), to the "empathetic" mode.

27. Wei, an innocent civilian (a company manager and party member), was shot to death when he tried to record with his cell phone villagers' protest of illegal dumping of hazardous trash in Hubei.

28. The film was submitted to the court as defense evidence on behalf of Tan Zuoren, "citizen journalist" and activist on behalf of unnecessarily sacrificed and mistreated earthquake victims. Typescript (given to me by Ai Xiaoming), interview with Wu Dongmu of Taiwan public television, Apr. 28, 2010.

29. This collage style derived from weaving archival and found-footage and the collective agency it embodies are also evident in two other ostensibly activist films made under different circumstances in 2009: *Queer China, "Comrade" China* and *The Journey of the Tiananmen Mothers.* In each case, the "directors" or "producers" are leading members of the respective advocacy groups. Huang Weikai's *Disorder,* also from 2009, uses predominantly amateur footage, with some in the vein of "citizen documentation." Collage is thus both the film form and a form of experimental coauthorship, though Huang's imaginative editing assumes and replaces authorship based on directing.

30. But none of the three filmmakers were allowed to go to the award ceremony in Hong Kong. Qi Jianxiang, son of the jailed Wang Lihong, protagonist in Yang's film, went on behalf of He Yang and Ai Xiaoming (correspondence from Ai Xiaoming, Nov. 5, 2011).

31. The "citizen documentation" movement extends and coalesces the video practices of "one-person activism" and "accidental journalism" that Paola Voci describes in *China on Video* (Voci 2010a, see especially chapter 6).

32. For a moving and eloquent introduction to Wang, see Ai's article "Who Is Wang Lihong?" (Ai Xiaoming 2011) at http://www.bullogger.com/blogs/XIAOMINGAI/archives/381136.aspx.

33. The title references the Toufu eatery in Chengdu where Ai and activists gathered for meals and more.

34. These amount to at least sixteen films, including *Fairytale* (*Tonghua* 2007), *Disturbing the Peace* (*Lao Ma Ti Hua* 2009), *Little Girls' Cheeks* (*Hualian ba'er* 2009), *4851* (2009), *Ping'an Yueqing* (2011) which won the Independent Spirit Award at the 10th Beijing Independent Film Festival, *So Sorry* (*Shenbiao yihan* 2011), and *Crab House* (*Hexie fangzi* 2012). For a Western perspective on Ai's artistic and activist engagement, see Alison Klayman's documentary, *Ai Weiwei: Never Sorry* (2012).

Bibliography

Ai Weiwei. 2011. *Ai Weiwei's Blog: Writings, Interviews, and Digital Rants 2006–2009.* Edited and translated by Lee Ambrozy. Boston: MIT Press.

Ai Xioaming. 艾晓明 2010a. Interview. "My Work Constitutes a Form of Participatory Action," *China Perspectives* 1: 71–77.

———. 2010b. "Yingri tihua bieyanghong—Ai Xiaoming da Taiwan gonggong dianshitai Apr. 28, Wu Dongmu xiansheng "映日蹄花别样红"-艾晓明答台湾公共电视制片人吴东牧先生采访 (Ai Xiaoming interviewed by Mr. Wu Dong-mu of Taiwan Public Television). Apr. 28; edited May 4. Typescript.

———. 2011. "Who Is Wang Lihong?" http://www.bullogger.com/blogs/XIAOMINGAI/archives/381136.aspx.

Berry, Chris, Lü Xinyu, and Lisa Rofel, eds. 2010. *For the Public Record: Chinese New Documentary Movement.* Hong Kong: Hong Kong University Press.

Brooks, Peter. 1976. *Balzac, Henry James, Melodrama, and the Mode of Excess.* New Haven, CT: Yale University Press.

Bruzzi, Stella. 2000. *New Documentary: A Critical Introduction.* New York: Routledge.

Chao, Shi-yan. 2010. "Coming Out of the Box, Marching as Dykes." In *The New Chinese Documentary Film Movement: For the Public Record,* edited by Chris Berry, Lü Xinyu, and Lisa Rofel, 77–95. Hong Kong: Hong Kong University Press

Chow, Rey. 1995. *Primitive Passions: Visuality, Sexuality, Ethnography, and Contemporary Chinese Cinema.* New York: Columbia University Press.

Derrida, Jacques. 1994. *Specters of Marx: The State of the Debt, the Work of Mourning and the New International.* New York: Routledge.

Gaines, Jane. 1999. "Political Mimesis." In *Collecting Visible Evidence,* edited by Jane Gaines and Michael Renov, 84–102. Minneapolis: Minnesota University Press.

———. 2007. "Documentary Radicality." *Canadian Journal of Film Studies* 16 (1): 5–24.

Harding, Thomas. 1997. *The Video Activist Handbook.* London: Pluto Press.

Johnson, Matthew David. 2006. "'A Scene beyond Our Line of Sight': Wu Wenguang and New Documentary Cinema's Politics of Independence." In *From Underground to Independent: Alternative Film Culture in Contemporary China,* edited by Paul G. Pickowicz and Yingjin Zhang, 47–76. Lanham, MD: Rowan & Littlefield.

Lee, Ching Kwan and You-tien Hsing. 2010. Introduction, "Social Activism in China: Agency and Possibility." In *Reclaiming Chinese Society: The New Social Activism,* edited by Hsing and Lee, 1–13. London: Routledge.

Leyda, Jay. 1972. *Dianying/Electric Shadows: An Account of the Films and Film Audiences in China.* Cambridge, MA: MIT Press.

Lü, Xinyu. 吕新雨. 2003. *Jilu Zhongguo: Dangdai Zhongguo xinjilu yundong* 纪录中国：当代中国新纪录运动 (Documenting China: The Contemporary Chinese New Documentary Movement). Beijing: Sanlian shudian.

———. 2010. "Rethinking China's New Documentary Movement: Engagement with the Social." In *The New Chinese Documentary Film Movement: For the Public Record* edited by Chris Berry, Lü Xinyu, and Lisa Rofel, 15–48. Hong Kong: Hong Kong University Press.

Nichols, Bill. 1992. *Representing Reality*. Bloomington: Indiana University Press.

———. 1994. *Blurred Boundaries: Questions of Meaning in Contemporary Culture*. Bloomington: Indiana University Press.

Nornes, Abé Mark. 2009. "Bulldozers, Bibles, and Very Sharp Knives: The Chinese Independent Documentary Scene." *Film Quarterly* 63 (1): 50–55.

Renov, Michael, ed. 1993. *Theorizing Documentary*. New York: Routledge.

Robinson, Luke. 2010. "From 'Public' to 'Private': Chinese Documentary and the Logic of *Xianchang*." In *The New Chinese Documentary Film Movement: For the Public Record*, edited by Chris Berry, Lü Xinyu, and Lisa Rofel, 177–194. Hong Kong: Hong Kong University Press.

Rosen, Philip. 2001. *Change Mummified: Cinema, Historiography, Theory*. Minneapolis: Minnesota University Press.

Shen Rui. 2005. "To Remember History: Hu Jie Talks about His Documentaries." *Senses of Cinema* 35 (Apr.). http://sensesofcinema.com/author/shen-rui/.

Voci, Paola. 2010a. *China on Video: Small-Screen Realities*. London: Routledge.

———. 2010b. "Blowup in Beijing: The City as Twilight Zone." In *The New Chinese Documentary Film Movement: For the Public Record*, edited by Chris Berry, Lü Xinyu, and Lisa Rofel, 99–115. Hong Kong: Hong Kong University Press.

Wang, Xiaolu. 王小鲁. 2010. "Zhuti jianxian—20nian Zhongguo duli jilupian de guancha" 主题渐显——20年中国独立电影的观察 (The Gradual Revelation of Subjectivity—Observations on 20 Years of Development in the Independent Documentary) Dianying Yishu 电影艺术 (Film Art) 6: 72–28.

———. 2011. "Zhongguo duli jilupiande qiyue jingshen" 中国独立纪录片的契约精神 (The contractual spirit of Chinese independent documentary). *Dianying Yishu* 电影艺术 (Film Art) 5: 93–98.

Wang, Yiman. 2010. "'I Am One of Them' and 'They Are My Actors': Performing, Witnessing, and DV Image-Making in Plebian China." In *The New Chinese Documentary Film Movement: For the Public Record*, edited by Chris Berry, Lü Xinyu, and Lisa Rofel, 217–236. Hong Kong: Hong Kong University Press.

Waugh, Thomas, ed. 1984. *"Show Us Life": Toward a History and Aesthetics of the Committed Documentary*. Metuchen, NJ: Scarecrow Press.

Williams, Linda. 1998. "Melodrama Revisited." In *Refiguring American Film Genres: History and Theory*, edited by Nick Browne, 42–88. Berkeley: University of California Press.

Wu Wenguang. 2002 "Just on the Road: A Description of the Individual Way of Recording Images in the 1990s." In *The First Guangzhou Triennial: Reinterpretation: A Decade of Experimental Chinese Art (1990–2000)*, edited by Wu Hung et al., 132–138. Guangzhou: Zhuangzhou Museum of Art/Chicago: Art Media Resources.

Xu Xiayin. 2010. "Yuanzi minjiande gongmin yingxiang" 源自民间的公民影像 (Citizen images from the unofficial realm). *Changcheng Yuebao* 长城月报 (Great Wall Monthly). https://cdtnet2.info/chinese/2010/10/源自民间的公民影像/ (accessed in 2011, no longer active).

Yang, Guobing. 2009. *The Power of the Internet in China: Citizen Online Activism*. New York: Columbia University Press.

Zhang Zhen. 2005. *Amorous History of the Silver Screen: Shanghai Cinema, 1896–1937*. Chicago: University of Chicago Press.

———. 2010. "Transfiguring the Post-socialist City: Experimental Image-Making in Contemporary China." In *Cinema at the City's Edge: Film and Urban Networks in East Asia,* edited by Yomi Braester and James Tweedie, 95–118. Hong Kong: Hong Kong University Press.

———. 张真. 2012a. "Yishu, gandongli, he xingdongzhuyi jilupian" 艺术，感动力，和行动主义纪录片 (Art, Affect, and Activist Documentary). *Zhongguo duli yingxiang* 中国独立影像 (Chinese Independent Cinema) 11.

———. 2012b. "Dream-walking in Digital Wasteland: Observations on the Uses of Black and White in Chinese Independent Documentary." *Journal of Chinese Cinemas* 6 (3): 299–319.

———. 2013. "Zhang Zhen duihua Ai Xiaoming: Cong xueyuan dao xianchang—nüxingzhuyi, jilu meixue, shehui yundong" 张真对话艾晓明：从学院到现场—女性主义，纪录美学，社会运动 (Dialogue between Zhang Zhang and Ai Xiaoming: From Academia to Xianchang-Feminism, Documentary Aesthetic, Social Movement). Nü zuozhe zhuanhao 女作者专号 (Special Issue in Women Authors). *Dianying zuozhe* 电影作者 (Filmateur) 4: 156–180.

APPENDIX I

Chinese and Non-Chinese Filmography/Videography

COMPILED BY TING-WU CHO

Chinese Filmography/Videography

Ai Weiwei 艾未未. Fairytale, Tonghua, 童话, DOC, 2007, Color/DV, 152 min.
———. 4851, 4851, DOC, 2009, Color/DV, 87 min. (2012 Taiwan International Documentary Festival)
———. Disturbing the Peace, Lao Ma Ti Hua, 老妈蹄花, DOC, 2009, Color/DV, 78 min. (2009 Hong Kong iSun TV Chinese Documentary Awards iSun TV Citizens Prize)
———. Little Girls' Cheeks, Hualian ba'er, 花脸巴儿, DOC, 2009, Color/DV, 78 min.
———. Ping'an Yueqing, Ping'an Yueqing, 平安乐清, DOC, 2011, Color/DV, 102 min. (2012 Beijing International Film Festival Spirit of Independence)
———. So Sorry, Shenbiao yihan, 深表遗憾, DOC, 2011, Color/DV, 54 min.
———. Crab House, Hexie fangzi, 河蟹房子, DOC, 2012, Color/DV, 12 min.

Ai Weiwei Studio 艾未未工作室. Ai Weiwei Does Gangnam Style, Ai weiwei caonima style, 艾未未草泥马 style, YouTube, 2012, Video, 4 min.

Ai Xiaoming 艾晓明. White Ribbon, Bai sidai, 白丝带, DOC, 2004, Color/DV, 36 min.
———. Taishi Village, Taishi cun, 太石村, DOC, 2005, Color/DV, 114 min.
———. Paradise Garden, Tiantang huayuan, 天堂花园, DOC, 2005, Color/DV, 104 min.
———. Our Children, Women de wawa, 我们的娃娃, DOC, 2009, Color/DV, 73 min.
———. Citizens' Investigation, Gongmin diaocha, 公民调查, DOC, 2009, Color/DV, 64 min. (2009 Hong Kong iSun TV Chinese Documentary Awards iSun TV Citizens Prize)
———. River of Forgetting, Wang chuan, 忘川, DOC, 2009, Color/DV, 86 min.

———. Enemy of the State, Guojia de diren, 国家的敌人, DOC, 2009, Color/DV, 44 min.

———. Why Are the Flowers So Red?, Hua'er wei shen me zhe yang hong, 花儿为什么这样红, DOC, 2010, Color/DV, 76 min.

———. Three Days in Wukan, Wukan sanri, 乌坎三日, DOC, 2012, Color/DV, 100 min.

Ai Xiaoming and Hu Jie 艾晓明 胡杰**.** The Epic of Central Plains, Zhongyuan Jishi, 中原纪事, DOC, 2006, Color/DV, 146 min.

———. The Train to My Hometown, Kai wang jiaxiang de lieche, 开往家乡的列车, DOC, 2008, Color/DV, 59 min.

Cao Fei and Ou Ning 曹斐 欧宁**.** San Yuanli, San yuanli, 三元里, DOC, 2003, B&W/DV, 40 min. (2003 Venice Biennale)

CCTV Animation production 央视动画有限公司, **dir. Kang Baojing** 亢宝晶**.** Young Detective Renjie, Shaonian Di Renjie, 少年狄仁杰, Animation TV Series, 2008, Animation.

Chen, Michelle 陈苗**.** The Snake Boy, Shanghai Nanhai, 上海男孩, DOC, 2002, Color, 90 min.

Chen Weijun 陈为军**.** To Live Is Better Than to Die, Haosi buru lai huozhe, 好死不如赖活着, DOC, 2003, Color/DV, 86 min. (2003 Sundance Film Festival Selection: World Documentary; 2004 Int'l Documentary Film Festival Amsterdam; 2004 British Documentary Award; 2004 George Foster Peabody Awards; 2006 Hong Kong Asian Film Festival 香港亞洲電影節; 2010 Hong Kong Social Movement Film Festival 香港社會運動電影節)

Cong Feng 从峰**.** Dr. Ma's Country Clinic, Ma daifu de zhensuo, 马大夫的诊所, DOC, 2008, 210 min. (2008 China Documentary Film Festival; 2008 Cinema Digital Seoul; 2009 Yunnan Multicultural Visual Festival [Yunfest]; 2009 International Berlin Film Festival Asian Film Awards; 2009 Yamagata International Documentary Film Festival Directors Guild of Japan Award)

Creative Power Entertaining (CPE) production. Pleasant Goat and Big Bad Wolf/Pleasant Goat and Big Big Wolf, aka Happy Sheep and Gray Wolf, Xi yangyang yu huitai lang, 喜羊羊与灰太狼, Animation TV series, 2005.

Cui Zi'en 崔子恩. Feeding Boys, Ayaya!, Aiyaya, qu buru, 哎呀呀，去哺乳, DOC, 2003, Color/DV, 75 min. (2003 Vancouver International Film Festival; 2003 Busan International Film Festival; 2004 Hong Kong International Film Festival; 2004 Q! Film Festival, Indonesia)

———. Night Scene, Yejing, 夜景, DOC, 2004, Color/DV, 80 min. (2005 International Film Festival Rotterdam)

———. We Are the . . . of Communism, Women shi Gongchanzhuyi de shenglüehao, 我们是共产主义的省略号, DOC, 2007, Color/DV, 94 min. (2007 China Documentary Film Festival)

———. Queer China, "Comrade" China, Zhi Tongzhi, 誌同志, DOC, 2008, Color/DV, 60 min. (2009 Shanghai PRIDE opening film)

Ding Meiyin 丁美音. Infinity on Your Hand, aka Lenient, Shouxia liuqing, 手下留情, Animation short, 2004, Animation, 20 min. (2006 Aniwow! Festival; 2006 ASIFA China)

Du Haibin 杜海滨. Along the Railroad, Tielu yan xian, 铁路沿线, DOC, 2000, Color/DV, 100 min. (2001 Yamagata International Documentary Film Festival New Asian Currents, Special Mention; 2003 China Independent Film Festival Best Documentary)

———. Beautiful Men, Renmian Taohua, 人面桃花, DOC, 2005, Color/DV, 98 min.

———. Umbrella, San, 伞, DOC, 2007, Color/DV, 110 min. (2007 Venice International Film Festival Horizons Doc Program Selection; 2007 International Documentary Festival Amsterdam; 2007 Lisbon International Film Festival; 2008 Cinéma du Réel Special Mention; 2008 San Francisco International Film Festival; 2008 Asian Film Festival of Rome; 2008 International Documentary Film Festival of Mexico City Best International Documentary Film)

———. 1428, 1428, DOC, 2009, Color, 117 min. (2009 Dubai International Film Festival Nominated Muhr Asia/Africa Award; 2009 Venice International Film Festival Horizons Documentary Award)

Duan Jinchuan and Zhang Yuan 段锦川 张元. The Square, Guangchang, 广场, DOC, 1993, Color/16mm, 100 min. (1995 Yamagata International Documentary Film Festival Citizen's Prize; 1995 Taipei Golden Horse Film Festival: Films from Mainland China)

Fan Lixin 范立欣. Last Train Home, Guitu Lieche, 归途列车, DOC, 2009, Color/DV, 85 min. (2009 International Documentary Film Festival Amsterdam Best

Feature Documentary; 2009 Montreal International Documentary Festival [RIDM] Best Quebec Film Award)

Fan Popo 范坡坡. Chinese Closet, Guizu, 柜族, DOC, 2009, Color, 88 min. (2011 Hong Kong Lesbian and Gay Film Festival Prism Award)

Fan Popo and Cheng, David 范坡坡 郑凯贵**.** New Beijing, New Marriage, Xin Qianmen dajie, 新前门大街, DOC, 2009, Color, 18 min. (2009 Chinese Queer Film Festival Tour)

Feng Chen 枫晨**.** University Students' Self-Study Room. Daxuesheng zixishi, 大学生自习室, Flash short, 2010, Flash.

Feng Yan 冯艳**.** Bing'Ai, Bing Ai, 秉爱, DOC, 2007, Color/DV, 114 min. (2007 Yamagata International Documentary Film Festival Community Cinema Award; 2007 Yamagata International Documentary Film Festival Ogawa Shinsuke Prize; 2008 Punto de Vista International Documentary Film Festival Punto de Vista First Prize [Spain]; 2008 Nantes Three Continents Festival Silver Balloon Award; 2008 Grand Prix de la Competition International, Filmer A Tour Prix [Belgium]; 2008 Hong Kong International Film Festival Humanitarian Awards for Documentary; 2008 Reel China Film Biennial Grand Award)

Gan Xiao'er 甘小二**.** The Only Sons, Shanqing shuixiu, 山清水秀, FIC, 2002, Color/DV, 100 min. (2003 Vancouver International Film Festival Dragon and Tigers Award Special Mention; 2003 Busan International Film Festival New Currents; 2003 International Film Festival Rotterdam Main Program Features; 2004 Taipei Film Festival New Age of Independence: Global Chinese Films and Video; 2004 Hong Kong Asian Film Festival; 2005 Moving Images of Pearl River Delta)

———. Raised from Dust, Juzi chentu, 举自尘土, FIC, 2007, Color/DigiBeta, 102 min. (2007 Rotterdam; 2007 Hong Kong International Film Festival; 2007 Busan International Film Festival; 2007 China Independent Film Festival Special Award; 2007 Osaka Asian Film Festival; 2008 China New Film Festival)

———. Church Cinema, Jiaotang dianying, 教堂电影院, DOC, 2008, Color/DV, 80 min.

Gao Tian 高天**.** Meimei, Meimei, 美美, DOC, 2005, Color/DV, 82 min. (2006 Berlin International Film Festival; 2006 Guangju International Film Festival; 2006 Madrid International Film Festival; 2006 Reel China Film Biennial;

2006 China Documentary Film Festival; 2006 Pingyao Photography Festival Digital Video Art Exhibition; 2006 International Leipzig Festival for Documentary and Animated Film; 2007 Beijing Independent Film Festival; 2008 Urban Nomad Film Fest; 2009 China Queer Film Festival Tour)

Gu Changwei 顾长卫**.** Love for Life, Zui ai, 最爱, FIC, 2011, Color, 105 min. (2011 Taipei Golden Horse Award Best Film Nominee)

Gu Tao 顾桃. Aoluguya . . . Aoluguya, Aoluguya yanluren, 敖鲁古雅养鹿人, DOC, 2007, Color/DV, 92 min. (2007 Singapore International Film Festival; 2007 China Documentary Film Festival; 2008 Reel China Film Biennial; 2008 China Independent Film Festival Annual Top Ten Film Award; 2010 Shanghai International TV Festival Documentary Magnolia Award)

———. Yuguo and His Mother, Yuguo de jiaqi, 雨果的假期, DOC, 2011, Color/DV, 49 min. (2011 Yamagata International Documentary Film Festival Ogawa Shinsuke Prize)

———. The Last Moose of Aoluguya (Andahan), Zuihou de aoluguya tuolu, 最后的敖鲁古雅驼鹿, DOC, 2013, Color, 100 min. (2013 Yamagata International Documentary Film Festival New Asian Currents Special Invitation Film; 2014 International Film Festival of Rotterdam; 2014 DOXA Documentary Film Festival; 2014 Hong Kong International Film Festival; 2014 Copenhagen International Documentary Film Festival)

Han Jie 韩杰**.** Walking on the Wild Side, Lai xiaozi, 赖小子, FIC, 2006, Color/Digital, 90 min. (2005 International Film Festival Rotterdam Tiger Award; 2006 Hong Kong International Film Festival Silver Digital Award; 2006 Taipei Film Festival; 2006 India New Delhi International Film Festival; 2006 Milano Film Festival; 2006 Osian's Cinefan, Festival of Asian Cinema; 2006 Vancouver International Film Festival; 2006 Tokyo Filmex Festival; 2007 Cinema Digital Seoul)

———. Hello, Mr. Tree, Hello! Shu xiansheng, 树先生, FIC, 2011, Color/35mm, 88 min. (2011 Shanghai International Film Festival Jury Grand Prix and Best Director; 2011 International Film Festival of Asian Pacific Countries in Vladivostok Best Director Award and Best Actor Award; 2011 Vancouver International Film Festival Dragons and Tigers Award; 2011 Hong Kong Asian Film Festival New Talent Award; 2011 Locarno International Film Festival; 2011 BFI London Film Festival)

Han Tao 韩涛**.** Baobao, Baobao, 宝宝, DOC, 2004, Color/DV, 100 min. (2005 Beijing Queer Film Festival; 2006 China Documentary Film Festival; 2006 Xiangshu Independent Film Week, Xi'an)

Hao Jie 郝杰. Single Man, Guanggun'er, 光棍儿, FIC, 2010, Color/DVCAM, 95 min. (2010 Tokyo Filmex Festival Special Jury Prize; 2010 San Sebastian Film Festival; 2010 Vancouver International Film Festival; 2011 Jeonju International Film Festival Easter Jet and NETPAC Award [Asian Feature Films]; 2011 Taipei Film Festival; 2011 Hong Kong International Film Festival; 2012 FIRST International Film Festival Best Director)

———. The Love Songs of Tiedan, Mei jie, 美姐, FIC, 2012, Color/Digital HD, 91 min. (2012 Tokyo Filmex Film Festival; 2012 San Sebastian Film Festival New Directors; 2012 Taipei Golden Horse Film Festival NETPAC Best Asian Film; 2013 FIRST International Film Festival Best Film, Best Director, Best Actor, Best Screenplay, Best Art Design; 2012 Vancouver International film Festival; 2013 International Film Festival Rotterdam)

He Wei 何伟**.** Hope, Xiwang, 希望, DOC, 2006.

He Yang 何杨**.** Days of Hesuoge, Hesuoge de rizi, 赫索格的日子, DOC, 2010, Color/DV, 58 min. (2010 Hong Kong Social Movement Film Festival; 2011 iSun TV Chinese Documentary Awards)

He Yuan 和渊. Apuda, Apuda de shouhou, 阿仆大的守候, DOC, 2011, Color, 145 min. (2011 Yamagata Documentary Film Festival; 2011 Yunnan Multicultural Visual Festival; 2012 Taiwan International Documentary Festival)

Hu Jia and Zeng Jinyan 胡佳 曾金燕**.** Prisoners in Freedom City, Ziyoucheng de qiutu, 自由城的囚徒, DOC, 2008, Color/DV. (2013 Hong Kong Indie Film Festival)

Hu Jie 胡杰**.** In Search of Lin Zhao's Soul, Xunzhao Lin Zhao de linghun, 寻找林昭的灵魂, DOC, 2004, Color, 115 min. (2011 iSun TV Chinese Documentary Awards)

———. Though I Am Gone, Wo sui si qu, 我虽死去, DOC, 2007, Color/B&W, 68 min. (2007 Hong Kong Asian Film Festival; 2007 Vancouver International Film Festival; 2007 Yunnan Multicultural Visual Festival; 2007 Oxdox International Documentary Film Festival; 2008 Reel China Film Biennial; 2008 Chinese Documentary Festival)

Hu Xinyu 胡新宇**.** The Man, Nanren, 男人, DOC, 2003, Color/DV, 113 min. (2004 Singapore International Film Festival; 2004 SHADOW Film Festival in Amsterdam Kodak Award Nominee 2004 Les Ecrans Documentary Festival in Paris)

———. Sister, Jiejie, 姐姐, DOC, 2008, Color/DV, 141 min. (2007 China Documentary Film Festival; 2007 Brooklyn International Film Festival; 2007 Yamagata International Documentary Film Festival; 2007 Jihlava International Documentary Film Festival)

Huang Weikai 黄伟凯. Floating, Piao, 飘, DOC, 2005, Color/DV, 93 min. (2005 Yunnan Multicultural Visual Festival; 2006 Hong Kong International Film Festival; 2006 Reel China Film Biennial)

———. Disorder, Xianshi shi guoqu de weilai, 现实是过去的未来, DOC, 2009, B&W/DV, 58 min. (2008 Busan International Film Festival Asian Network of Documentary [AND] Fund Project; 2009 Yunnan Multicultural Visual Festival; 2009 Cinéma du Réel Special Mention; 2009 Karlovy Vary International Film Festival; 2009 Busan International Short Film Festival Kyobo Prize; 2010 Reel China Film Biennial; 2010 Moving Image Source Top Moving Image Moments; 2010 Hot Docs Toronto selection; 2011 Ann Arbor Film Festival Best Documentary)

Hunan Satellite TV Company production 湖南广播电视台卫星频道(湖南卫视). Tell It Like It Is, You Hua Hao Shuo, 有话好说, TV News Series.

Jia Zhangke 贾樟柯. Xiao Wu (The Pickpocket), 小武, FIC, 1997, Color/16mm, 108 min. (1998 Berlin International Film Festival Wolfgang Staudte Award and NETPAC Award; 1999 Buenos Aires International Festival of Independent Cinema Best Film Nominee; 1998 Nantes Three Continents Festival Golden Montgolfiere; 1998 Busan International Film Festival New Currents Award; 1998 Vancouver International Film Festival Dragon and Tigers Award)

———. In Public, Gonggong changsuo, 公共场所, FIC, 2001, Color/DV, 30 min. (2002 Marseille Festival Documentary Film Grand Prix)

———. Unknown Pleasures, Ren xiaoyao, 任逍遥, FIC, 2002, Color/35mm, 107 min. (2002 Cannes Film Festival Palme d'Or Nominee; 2002 Chicago International Film Festival Gold Hugo Nominee; 2003 Singapore International Film Festival FIPESCI/NETPAC Award, Special Mention)

———. Still Life, Sanxia haoren, 三峡好人, FIC, 2006, Color, 111 min. (2007 Durban International Film Festival Best Director; 2007 Italian National Syndicate of Film Journalists Silver Ribbon Nominee; 2008 Kinema Junpo Awards Best Foreign Film Director; 2007 Venice Film Festival Golden Lion; 2008 Los Angeles Film Critics Association Awards Best Foreign Film)

———. Dong, Dong, 东, DOC, 2006, Color, 70 min. (2006 Venice Film Festival Doc/It Award and Open Prize)

———. 24 City, Ershisi chengji, 二十四城记, FIC, 2008, Color, 112 min. (2008 Cannes Film Festival Palme d'Or Nominee)

Jiang Yue 蒋樾. The Other Bank, Bi'an, 彼岸, DOC, 1995, Beta SP, 140 min. (1995 Hong Kong International Film Festival; 1995 Yamagata International Documentary Film Festival; 1995 Augsberg International Documentary Film Festival; 1995 Cinéma du Réel International Documentary Film Festival)

Jiang Zhi 蒋志. Our Love, Xiang Pingli, 香平丽, FIC, 2005, Color/DV, 78 min. (2008 Beijing Queer Film Festival)

Ju Anqi 雎安奇. There's a Strong Wind in Beijing, Beijing de Feng Hen Da, 北京的风很大, DOC, 2000, Color/16mm, 50 min. (2000 Berlin International Film Festival)

Li Hong 李红. Out of Phoenix Bridge, Huidao fenghuang qiao, 回到凤凰桥, DOC, 1997, Color/ Video, 110 min. (1997 Yamagata International Documentary Film Festival Ogawa Shinsuke Prize; 1998 New York International Documentary Festival; 1998 Festival International de Films de Femmes, Creteil, France; 1998 San Francisco International Asian American Film Festival)

Li Hongqi 李红旗. Winter Vacation, Hanjia, 寒假, FIC, 2010, Color/HD (Sony PMW-EX1), 91 min. (2010 Locarno International Film Festival Golden Leopard Award Golden Leopard Award; 2010 Cinema Digital Seoul Festival Red Chameleon Award; 2010 BFI London Film Festival Nominated for the FIPRESCI Critics Award; 2010 Vancouver International Film Festival; 2010 Melbourne International Film Festival)

Li Ning 李凝. Tape, Jiaodai, 胶带, DOC, 2009, Color/MiniDV, 175 min. (2009 Shanghai Idea Festival; 2010 Reel China Film Biennial)

Li Yang 李杨. Blind Mountain, Mang shan, 盲山, FIC, 2007, Color/35mm, 95 min.

Li Yifan 李一凡. Before the Flood, Yanmo, 淹没, DOC, 2005, Color/DV, 150 min. (2008 International Documentary Festival Amsterdam; 2009 Hong Kong International Film Festival; 2009 Yunnan Multicultural Visual Festival)

Lin Chaoxian 林超贤. Sparkling Red Star, Shanshande hongxing haizide tiankong, 闪闪的红星 孩子的天空, Animation Feature, 2007, Animation, 82 min.

Liu Jiayin 刘伽茵. Oxhide, Niupi, 牛皮, FIC, 2004, Color/DV, 110 min. (2005 Berlin International Film Festival Caligari Film Award and Forum of New

Cinema FIPRESCI Award; 2005 Hong Kong International Film Festival Golden DV Award; 2005 Vancouver International Film Festival Dragons and Tigers Award)

———. Oxhide II, Niupi er, 牛皮二, FIC, 2009, Color/DV, 133 min. (2009 Cannes Film Festival Directors' Fortnight Program)

Lou Ye 娄烨**.** Suzhou River, Suzhou He, 苏州河, FIC, 1999, Color/35mm, 83 min. (2000 International Film Festival Rotterdam Tiger Award; 2000 Paris Film Festival Grand Prize and Best Actress; 2000 Vienna International Film Festival [Viennale] FIRESCI; 2000 Tokyo Filmex Grand Prize; 2001 Belgian Syndicated of Cinema Critics Grand Prix; 2002 Fantasporto Critics Award)

Ma Li 马莉**.** Born in Beijing, Jingsheng, 京生, DOC, 2012, B&W/DV, 240 min. (2014 Reel China Film Biennial; 2012 iSun TV Chinese Documentary Awards)

Ning Ying 宁瀛**.** On the Beat, Minjing gushi, 民警故事, FIC, 1995, 105 min. (1995 Entrevue Film Festival Grand Prix; San Sebastien International Film Festival, Special Mention)

———. Railroad of Hope, Xiwang Zhi Lu, 希望之旅, DOC, 2002, Color/35mm, 56 min. (2002 Toronto International Film Festival; 2002 Cinéma du Réel)

Ou Ning 欧宁**.** Meishi Street, Meishi jie, 煤市街, DOC, 2006, Color/DV, 85 min. (2006 MoMA Documentary Fortnight; 2007 Istanbul Biennial)

Pan Jianlin and Zhang Lei 潘剑林 张磊**.** Who Killed Our Children?, Shei sha le women de haizi, 谁杀了我们的孩子?, DOC, 2008, DigiBeta, 92 min. (2008 Busan International Film Festival; 2009 Vancouver New Asian Film Festival)

Peng Tao 彭韬**.** Little Moth, Xue chan, 血蝉, FIC, 2007, Color/DigiBeta, 99 min. (2007 Locarno International Film Festival; 2007 Asia Pacific Screen Award Achievement in Directing Nominee; 2008 Brisbane International Film Festival Interfaith Award Special Commendation; 2008 Asian Film Award Best Screenplay)

Qi donghua gongzuoshi (Qi Animation Studio) production 柒动画工作室**.** Cute Grassmud Horse Flash Animation, Ke'aide cao ni ma Flash donghua, 可爱的草泥马, Animation, 2009, Flash Animation.

Quan Ling 权聆. Forgetting to Know You, Mosheng, 陌生, FIC, 2013, Color/HD, 90 min. (2013 Hong Kong International Film Festival; 2014 Berlin International Film Festival)

Shi Tou 石头. Women Fifty Minutes, Nuren wushi fenzhong, 女人五十分, DOC, 2006, Color/DV, 52 min. (2007 Chinese Documentary Film Festival)

Shi Tou and Ming Ming 石头 明明. Dyke March, Nütongzhi youxing ri, 女同志游行日, DOC, 2004, Color/DV, 20 min.

Song Fang 宋方. Memories Look at Me, Jiyi want zhe wo, 记忆望着我, FIC, 2012, Color/DigiBeta, 87 min. (2012 Locarno International Film Festival; 2012 Mar del Plata International Film Festival; 2012 Tokyo Filmex Special Jury Prize)

Sun Lijun 孙立军. Little Soldier Zhang Ga, Xiaobing Zhang Ga, 小兵张嘎, Animation Feature, 2005, Animation, 102 min.

Sun Yu 孙瑜. The Big Road, Dalu, 大路, FIC, 1934, B&W/35mm, 109 min.

Tang Danhong 唐丹鸿. Nightingale, Not the Only Voice, Yeying bu shi wei yi de gehou, 夜莺不是唯一的歌喉, DOC, 2000, Beta SP, 180 min.

Tang, Emily 唐晓白. Perfect Life, Wanmei shenghuo, 完美生活, FIC, 2008, Color/DigiBeta, 97 min. (2008 Venice International Film Festival; 2009 Vancouver International Film Festival Dragons and Tigers Award; 2009 Hong Kong International Film Festival Golden Digital Prize)

Tiananmen Mothers Collective 天安门母亲群体. Journey of the Tiananmen Mothers, Tian'anmen muqin, 天安门母亲, FIC, 2009, Color/DV, 95 min.

Wang Baochun 王葆春. Toxicosis, Du zheng, 毒症, DOC, 2010, Color/DV, 88 min. (2010 Tokyo Filmex; 2010 Taiwan International Documentary Festival)

Wang Bing 王兵. West of the Tracks, Tiexi qu, 铁西区, DOC, 2001–2003, Color/DV, 540 min. (2003 Marseille Festival of Documentary Film Grand Prix; 2003 China Documentary Film Festival; 2003 Nantes Three Continents Festival Golden Montgolfiere Jury Documentaire)

———. Fengming: A Chinese Memoir, He Fengming, 和凤鸣, DOC, 2007, Color/DVCAM, 183 min. (2007 Yamagata International Documentary Film Festival Grand Prix)

———. Crude Oil, Yuan you, 原油, DOC, 2008, Color/DV, 840 min. (2008 Hong Kong International Film Festival; 2008 International Film Festival Rotterdam NETPAC Award Special Mention)

———. Coal Money, Meitan, qian, 煤炭，钱, DOC, 2008, Color/DVCAM, 53 min. (2009 Cinéma du Réel, Paris; 2009 Documenta Madrid, Xi Festival Internacional de Documentales de Madrid)

———. The Man with No Name, Wu ming zhe, 无名者, DOC, 2009, Color/DV, 92 min. (2014 AV Film Festival of Art, Music, and Film; 2014 Melbourne Festival)

———. The Ditch, Jiabiangou, 夹边沟, FIC, 2010, Color/DVCAM, 109 min. (2010 Venice International Film Festival)

———. Three Sisters, San Zimei, 三姊妹, DOC, 2012, Color/DV, 153/ 73 min. (2012 Venice International Film Festival; 2013 Fribourg International Film Festival Regard d' Or)

———. Till Madness Do Us Part, Feng ai, 疯爱, DOC, 2013, Color/DV, 220 min. (2013 Venice International Film Festival)

Wang Bo 王波**. Beijing Hu Xiang Animation Ltd production** 北京互象动画有限公司. Little Rabbit Be Good, Xiaotu Kuang Kuang, 小兔哐哐, Flash Animation Short, 2011, Flash, 4 min.

Wang Jianwei 汪建伟**.** Living Elsewhere, Shenghuo zai Bie Chu, 生活在别处, DOC, 1999, Video Art/Documentary, 140 min. (1999 Yamagata International Documentary Film Festival)

Wang Libo 王利波**.** Buried, Yanmai, 掩埋, DOC, 2009, Color/DV, 100 min. (2009 China Documentary Film Festival Outstanding Documentary Award; 2009 China Independent Film Festival; 2009 Hong Kong Asian Independent Film Festival; 2009 South Taiwan Film Festival; 2010 Seoul Independent Documentary Film and Video Festival)

Wang Nanfu 王男栿**.** Detachment of Women, Kaifang zhaowo, 开房找我, DOC, 2014, Color/DVCAM, 60 min. (2014 Reel China Film Biennial)

Wang Xiaoshuai 王小帅**.** Days, Dongchun de rizi, 冬春的日子, FIC, 1993, Color/35mm, 90 min. (1995 International Film Festival Rotterdam; 1995 International Thessaloniki Film Festival Golden Alexander Award; 1995 Taormina Film Festival Best Director)

———. Frozen, Jidu hanleng, 极度寒冷, 1998, Color/35mm, 95 min.

Wang Yunlong 王云龙. To Justify Bu Qinfu, Huan Bu Qinfu yi meili, 还卜琴父以美丽, DOC, 2011, Color/DV, 92 min. (2011 China Independent Film Festival; 2012 Chinese Documentary Festival; 2012 Reel China Film Biennial)

Wei Jiangang production 魏建刚. Queer Comrades (Queer as Folk Beijing), Tongzhi yi Fanren, 同志亦凡人, Webcast, 2007.

Wei Xueqi 卫学奇. Faith, Xinxin, 信心, DOC, 2008, Color/DV, 90 min. (2008 China Documentary Film Festival; 2008 Yunnan Multicultural Visual Festival; 2008 Reel China Film Biennial)

Wen Hui 文慧. Memory, Jiyi, 记忆, DOC, Color/ DV, 2009.

———. Listening to Third Grand-Mother's Stories, Ting sannainai jian congquian de shiqing, 听三奶奶讲从前的事情, DOC, 2011, Color/DV, 75 min. (2011 Vienna International Film Festival; 2012 iSun TV Chinese Documentary Award; 2012 Beijing Independent Film Festival)

Wu Haohao 吴昊昊. Action/Kun 1, Kun1 Xingdong, Kun1/行动, FIC/DOC (Deconstruction film), 2009, Color/DV, 76 min. (2009 Vancouver International Film Festival Dragons and Tigers Award; 2009 Torino International Film Festival; 2010 International Film Festival Rotterdam Session of Bright Future)

Wu Wenguang 吴文光. Bumming in Beijing, Liulang Beijing, 流浪北京, DOC, 1990, Color/Beta SP, 69 min. (1991 Hong Kong International Film Festival; 1991 Vancouver International Film Festival; 1991 Yamagata International Documentary Film Festival)

———. My 1966 (1966: My Time in the Red Guards), 1966: Wo de Hongweibing Shidai, 1966, 我的红卫兵时代, DOC, 1993, Color/DV, 140 min. (1993 Yamagata International Documentary Festival Ogawa Shinsuke Prize)

———. Jianghu (Jianghu: Life on the Road), Jianghu, 江湖, DOC, 2000, Color/DV, 140 min.

———. Dance with the Farm Workers, He Minggong tiaowu, 和民工跳舞, DOC, 2001, Color/DV, 60 min. (2002 Berlin Film Festival International Forum in New Cinema; 2002 Vancouver International Film Festival; 2002 Jeongju International Film Festival; 2002 New Zealand Film Festival; 2002 BFI London Film Festival; 2003 Liverpool International film Festival)

———. Fuck Cinema, cao tamade dianying, 操他妈电影, DOC, 2005, Color/DV, 170 min. (2010 Vision du Réel: Nyon International Film Festival; 2010 Chinese Documentary Film Biennial)

———. Treatment, Zhiliao, 治疗, DOC, 2010, Color/DV, 80 min. (2010 Vision du Réel: Nyon International Film Festival; 2010 China Documentary Film Festival; 2014 Hong Kong Independent Film Festival)

Wu Wenguang et al. 吴文光等人**.** Village Video Project, Xiangcun yingxiang jihua, 乡村影像计划, DOC, 2006–2007, Color/DV.

Xie Yihui 谢贻卉**.** Juvenile Laborers Confined in Dabao, Dabao xiaolaojiao, 大堡小劳教, DOC, 2013, Color/DV, 106 min. (2014 Reel China Film Biennial)

Xu Tong 徐童**.** Wheat Harvest, Mai Shou, 麦收, DOC, 2008, Color/DVCAM, 99 min. (2008 Beijing Independent Film Festival; 2009 Taipei Film Festival; 2009 Cinema Digital Seoul Film Festival Red Chameleon Award; 2009 Hong Kong Chinese Documentary Festival Third Prize; 2009 Yunnan Multicultural Visual Festival Innovation Award and Audience-favorite Award; 2010 Reel China Film Biennial; 2010 Shadows Festival, Paris; 2010 Black Movie Geneva Film Festival; 2010 International Film Festival Rotterdam Bright Future)

Xu Xin 徐辛**.** Fangshan Church, Fangshan jiaotang, 房山教堂, DOC, 2005, Color/DV, 80 min. (2006 Chinese Documentary Film Festival)

———. Karamay, Kelamayi, 克拉玛依, DOC, 2010, Color, B&W/DV, 356 min. (2010 Asia Pacific Screen Award Best Documentary Feature Film Nominee; 2010 Locarno International Film Festival Don Quixote Award, FIPRESCI Prize, Junior Jury Award, and Prize of the Ecumenical Jury, Golden Leopard Nominee; 2010 Hong Kong International Film Festival, Documentary Competition; 2010 Chinese Documentary Film Festival; 2010 Vancouver International Film Festival; 2010 Moscow 2-1 Film Festival; 2011 MoMA Documentary Fortnight; 2011 Cinema du Réel)

Xue Jianqiang 薛鉴羌**.** Martian Syndrome, Huoxing yao zonghezheng, 火星综合症, DOC, 2009, Color/DV, 83 min. (2010 Chinese Documentary Film Festival)

———. When I Was Young I Also Beat a Tiger, Wo Nianqing Shi ye Da Laohu, 我年轻时也打老虎, DOC, 2010, Color/DV, 74 min. (2012 Reel China Film Biennial)

Yang Lina 杨荔钠**.** Old Men, Lao Tou, 老头, DOC, 1999, Color/Video, 94 min. (1999 Yamagata International Documentary Film Festival New Asian Current Award of Excellence; 2000 Cinéma du Réel Jury Prize; 2000 DOK Leipzig Golden Dove Award)

———. Home Video, Jiating luxiang dai, 家庭录像带, DOC, 2001, Color/DV, 65 min. (2002 DOK Keipzig; 2002 China Independent Film Festival)

———. The Love of Mr. An, Lao an, 老安, DOC, 2008, Color/DigiBeta, 84 min. (2008 Amsterdam Documentary Film Festival; 2008 Melbourne International Film Festival; 2008 Vancouver International Film Festival; 2008 San Sebastian International Film Festival; 2008 Hong Kong International Film Festival)

———. My Neighbors and Their Japanese Ghosts, Wo de linju shuo guizi, 我的邻居说鬼子, DOC, 2008, Color/DV, 58 min. (2008 Hong Kong International Film Festival)

———. Wild Grass, Ye cao, 野草, DOC, 2009, Color/DV, 75 min. (2009 in cooperation with Arte Television Vienna Film Festival)

Yang, Ruby. The Blood of Yingzhou, Yingzhou de haizi, 颍州的孩子, DOC, 2006, Color/DV, 39 mins. (2007 Academy Award for Best Documentary Short)

Yang Yang 杨杨**.** Our Story: 10-year "guerrilla warfare" of Beijing Queer Film Festival, Women de gushi—Beijing Ku'er yingzhan shinian youjizhan, 我们的故事 (我们的故事—北京酷儿影展十年游击战), DOC, 2011, Digital, 42 min.

Ying Liang 应亮**.** The Other Half, Ling Yiban, 另一半, FIC, 2006, Color/DV, 111 min. (2006 Tokyo Filmex Special Jury Prize Kodak Vision Award; 2007 Jeonju International Film Festival Special Jury Award; 2007 Singapore International Film Festival Special Jury Award; 2007 San Francisco International Film Festival; 2007 International Film Festival Rotterdam)

———. When Night Falls, Wo hai you hua yao shuo, 我还有话要说, FIC, 2012, Color/HD, 70 min. (2012 Locarno International Film Festival Best Actress and Best Director, Golden Leopard Nominee)

Ying Weiwei 英未未**.** The Box, Hezi, 盒子, DOC, 2001, Color, B&W/DV (DS99), edited with Betacam, 88 min. (2001 First Independent Image Festival; 2002 Reel China Film Biennial)

Yu Guangyi 于广义**.** Timber Gang, Mu bang, 木帮, FIC, 2006, Color/DVCAM, 90 min. (2007 Tokyo Filmex Jury Prize; 2007 Cinema Digital Seoul Film Festival Best Director and Jury Film Prize; 2007 Vienna International Film Festival; 2007 Amsterdam International Film Festival; 2007 Locarno International Film Festival; 2007 Vancouver International Film Festival)

———. Survival Song, Xiao li zi, 小李子, FIC, 2008, Color/DVCAM, 94 min. (2008 Vancouver International; 2008 Vienna International; 2008 Buenos

Aires International Film Festival of Independent Cinema; 2008 Hong Kong International; 2008 Chinese Documentary Film Festival; 2008 Cinema Digital Seoul; 2008 Tokyo Filmex Jury Prize; 2009 International Film Festival Rotterdam Bright Future)

Yuan Bo 袁博**.** Boundaries, aka Realm, Jingjie, 境界, Animation, 2006, Animation Short, 4:52 min. (2006 European Short Film Festival)

Yuan Zhiming 远志明**.** China Soul for Christ Foundation production, 神州传播协会, The Cross: Jesus in China, Shi zi jia—Ye Su zai zhong guo, 十字架——耶稣在中国, Documentary Series, 2003, Color/DV.

Zhang Hanzi 张涵子**.** Tangtang, Tangtang, 唐唐, DOC-FIC, 2004, Color/Betacam SP, 90 min. (2004 Vienna International Film Festival; 2005 Busan International Film Festival; 2007 Chinese Independent Film Festival)

Zhang Ming 章明**.** Fly, Cang ying, 苍蝇, DOC, 2009, Color/DV, 40 min. (2009 Beijing Independent Documentary Film Forum)

Zhang Yimou 张艺谋. The Story of Qiuju, Qiu Ju da guansi, 秋菊打官司, FIC, 1992, Color/Film, 110 mins. (1992 Venice Film Festival, Golden Lion)

———. Not One Less, Yige dou bushao, 一个都不少, FIC, 1999, Color/Film, 106 mins. (1999 Venice Film Festival, Golden Lion)

Zhang Yuan 张元**.** Beijing Bastards, Beijing zazhong, 北京杂种, FIC, 1993, Color/35mm & video 85 min. (1993 Locarno International Film Festival Critics Circle Award; 1993 Singapore Film Festival; 1994 International Film Festival Rotterdam)

———. Sons, Erzi, 児子, FIC-DOC, 1996, Color/35mm, 95 min. (1996 International Film Festival Rotterdam FIPRESCI Prize and Tiger Award)

———. East Palace, West Palace, Donggong Xigong, 东宫西宫, FIC, 1996, Color/35mm, 94 min. (1996 Mar del Plata Film Festival Argentina Best Director, Best Screenplay, and Special Mention for Cinematography; 1997 Cannes International Film Festival Un Certain Regard Competition)

———. Crazy English, Fengkuang Yingyu, 疯狂英语, DOC, 1999, Color/35mm, 95 min. (1999 Locarno International Film Festival; 1999 Filmmakers Film Festival, Milan Best Documentary Award)

———. Miss Jin Xing, Jin Xing Xiaojie, 金星小姐, DOC, 2000, Color/35mm, 31 min.

———. I Love You Boss, Laoban wo ai ni, 老板，我爱你, Mini Movie, 2014, 29 min.

Zhang Zanbo 张赞波. The Interceptor from My Hometown, You yizhoung jingjiao zhuangyan, 有一种静叫庄严, DOC, 2011, Color/DVCAM, 90 min. (2012 Reel China Film Biennial; 2012 International Documentary Film Festival Amsterdam; 2012 Jihlava International Documentary Film Festival; 2012 International Film Festival Rotterdam; 2012 Gothenburg International Film Festival)

Zhao Dayong 赵大勇. Ghost Town, Fei Cheng, 废城, DOC, 2008, Color/DVCAM, 180 min. (2009 New York Film Festival)

Zhao Liang 赵亮. Paper Airplane, Zhi feiji, 纸飞机, DOC, 2001, Color/Beta, 77 min. (2002 Taiwan International Documentary Festival)
———. Crime and Punishment, Zui yu fa, 罪与罚, DOC, 2007, Color/DV, 122 min. (2007 Nantes Three Continents Festival Golden Montgolfiere Award)
———. Petition, Shangfang, 上访, DOC, 2009, Color/DV, 318 min. (2009 Chinese Independent Documentary Film Forum)
———. Together, Zai yi qi, 在一起, DOC, 2010, Color/DV, 84 min. (2011 Berlin International Film Festival)

Zhao Ye 赵晔. Jalainur, Zhalai nuo'er, 扎赉诺尔, FIC, 2008, Color/DV, 92 min. (Busan International Film Festival FIPRESCI Prize; Shanghai International film Festival New Asian Talent Award)

Zheng Dasheng 郑大圣. DV China, DV Zhongguo, DV 中国, 2003, DV Cam, 92 min.

Zhu Chuanming 朱传明. Beijing Cotton Fluffer, Mianhua tanjiang, 棉花弹匠, DOC, 1999, Color/Video, 60 min. (1999 Yamagata International Documentary Film Festival New Asian Currents Award of Excellence)
———. Extras, Qunzhong yanyuan, 群众演员, DOC, 2001, Color/DigiCAM (Sony PD 100), 70 min.

Zhu Wen 朱文. Seafood, Hai xian, 海鲜, FIC, 2001, Color/DV, 76 min. (2001 Venice International Film Festival Grand Jury Prize)

Zhu Xiaofeng 朱晓峰. Hangzhou Jingu Shidai Production Co., Ltd., 杭州今古时代电影制作有限公司, The Legend of a Countryside Hero, Chi Song Weilong, 赤松威龙, Animation Feature, 2008, Animation, 90 min.

Non-Chinese Filmography/Videography

Caouette, Jonathan. Tarnation, DOC, 2003.

Flaherty, Robert J. Nanook of the North, DOC, 1922.

Guzmán, Patricio. The Battle of Chile (La batalla de Chile), Part I: The Insurrection of the Bourgeoisie (La insurreción de la burgesía), 1975. Part II: The Coup d'état (El golpe de estsado), 1976. Part III: Popular Power (El poder popular), 1979, DOC.

Hara Kazuo 原一男. Extreme Private Eros: Love Song 1974 (Kyokushiteki erosu koiuta), DOC, 1974.
———. Emperor's Naked Army Marches On (Yuki yukite shingun), DOC, 1987.

Hitchcock, Alfred. Rope, FIC, 1948.

Klayman, Alison. Ai Weiwei: Never Sorry, Ai Weiwei: Caonima, 艾未未：草泥马, DOC, 2012, Color/DV/HD, 91 min. (2012 Sundance Film Festival Special Jury Prize; 2012 Festival Director's Choice Award Telluride Mountainfilm Festival)

Lanzmann, Claude. Shoah, DOC, 1985.

McElwee, Ross. Sherman's March, DOC, 1986.

Moss, Robb. The Same River Twice, DOC, 2003.

Ogawa Shinsuke 小川绅介. Forest of Oppression (Assatsu no mori), DOC, 1967.

Ophuls, Marcel. The Sorrow and the Pity (Le chagrin et la pitié), DOC, 1969.

O'Rourke, Dennis. The Good Woman of Bangkok, DOC, 1991.

Renoir, Jean. Rules of the Game (La Règle du jeu), FIC, 1939.

Rohmer, Eric. The Aviator's Wife (La Femme de l'aviateur), FIC, 1980.

Wiseman, Frederick. Zoo, DOC, 1993.

APPENDIX II

Tibetan Filmography/ Videography

COMPILED BY ROBERT BARNETT

Part 1: Tibet-related films, dramas, and documentaries by Chinese directors cited in Chapter 5 in this volume

The Dalai Lama (*Dalai lama*). Filmmaker not named. China Intercontinental Communication Center, Beijing. China, 2008. Documentary. Versions in Chinese and English.

The Eight-Petalled Kelsang Flower (*Skal bzang me tog 'dab brgyad ma,* Ch.: *Ba ban gesang hua,* also known in English as Kelsang Metok), dir. Yan Yi and written by Jiang An for CCTV. China, 2001. Television drama series. 6 episodes. In Chinese.

Ganglamedo (*Ganglameiduo*), Dai Wei. China, 2006. China Film Group, Tibet TV and others. Fiction feature. 93 min. Tibetan/Mandarin.

Getag Tulku (or Getag Living Buddha, *Dge rtag sprul sku,* Ch.: *Geda huofu*), dir. Yang Tao for CCTV and United Front. China, 2005. Television drama series. 20 episodes. In Chinese.

Horse Thief (*Daomazei*), Tian Zhuangzhuang. China, 1986. Xi'an Film Studio. Fiction feature. 84 min. In Chinese.

Longing for Lhasa (*Lha sar blo kha phyogs par,* Ch.: *Xiangwang Lasa*), written by Gazang Caidan *(Kalsang Tseten)* and Li Jingzhong, dir. Fan Mingren for Tibet TV and Sichuan TV. China, 1997. Television drama series. 8 episodes. In Chinese.

Love Song of Kangding (*Kangding xinge*), dir. Wang Xiaoli for CCTV. China, 2003. Television drama series. 30 episodes. In Chinese.

Mountain Patrol (*Kekexili*), Lu Chuan. China, 2004. China Film Group, Huayi Brothers, and Taihe Film Investment. Fiction feature. 85, 90, and 98 min. versions. In Chinese with English subtitles.

My Lucky Flower (*Wode gesang meiduo*), Xiong Yu. China, 2002. Emei Shan and CCTV. Fiction feature. 79 min. In Chinese with English subtitles.

No. 16 Barkor South Street (*Ba kuo nan jie shi liu hao*, also marketed as No. 16 Barkhor South Street), Duan Jinchuan. China, 1996. Documentary. Tibet TV. 100 min. In Chinese with English subtitles.

Potala (*Budala*), Chen Zhen. China, 2004. Documentary. CCTV. 94 min. In Chinese with English subtitles.

Prince of the Himalayas (*Hi ma la ya'i rgyal sras*, Ch.: *Ximalaya wangzi*), Sheridan Hu (Hu Xuehua). China, 2006. Shanghai Film Studio and Shanghai Hushi Culture and Media. Fiction feature. 108 min. Versions in Tibetan and in Chinese with English subtitles.

Princess Wencheng (*Rgya bza' kong jo*, Ch.: *Wencheng gong zhu*), dir. Cai Xiaoqing for CCTV. China, 2000. Television drama series. 20 episodes. In Chinese.

Red River Valley (*Honghegu*), Fei Xiaoning. China, 1997. Shanghai Film Studio. Fiction feature. 115 min. In Chinese with English subtitles.

Sacrificed Youth (*Qingchunji*), Zhang Nuanxin. China, 1985. Fiction feature. Beijing Film Academy Youth Studio production. 96 min. Mandarin.

The Secret History of the Potala Palace (*Po ta la'i gsang gtam*, Ch. *Budala gong mishi*), Zhang Yi. Tibet (China), 1989. Emei Films. Fiction feature. 140 min. In Chinese. Not publicly released.

The Serf (*Nongnu*), Li Jun. China, 1963. Fiction feature. 1st August Film Production Studio. 88 min. In Chinese.

Suru Flower (*Suru'i me tog*), dir. Liu Ren for Gansu TV. China, 1984. Television drama series. 3 episodes. In Chinese.

Tales of Lhasa's Past (*Lha sa'i sngon byung gtam rgyud*, Ch.: *Lasa wangshi*), dir. Yang Tao and Cheng Lu for Tibet TV and CCTV. China, 2002. Television drama series. 20 episodes. In Chinese.

Tibet in the Past (*Xizang wangshi*). Audio & Video Publishing house of the Central Newsreel and Documentary Film Studio of China, Beijing. China , c. 2007. Documentary. DVD with versions in Chinese, German, Russian, Spanish, French, and English. (Unacknowledged reissue of Documenting Tibetan Society in the 1950s [*Wushi niandai Xizang shehui jishi*], Fu Hongxing [writer/compiler]. China, 1991. Documentary. 40 min. In Chinese.)

Tibet Wind and Clouds (or The Changing Times of Tibet, *Bod kyi dus 'gyur*, Ch.: *Xizang Fengyun*), dir. Zhai Qunjie for CCTV & TAR Government. China, 1999. Television drama series. 25 episodes (Chinese version); 23 episodes (Tibetan version).

Tibetan Seductions (or Tibetan Temptations, *Xizang de youhuo*), Wang Huaixin. China, 1988. Documentary. 50 min. In Chinese.

The Uprising of *Alag* Tsugu (*A lags rtsib bu'i 'os langs*, Ch.: *Le ba fo chuan qi*, The Saga of Le-ba Buddha), dir. Sun Zhongguang and Liu Ren for Qinghai TV. China, 1989. Television drama series. 6 episodes. In Chinese.

Yeshe Drolma (*Yixi Zhouma,* also called Song of Tibet), Xie Fei. 2000. Shangdong Film, Beijing Film Studio and Beijing Siji Changqing Film and Culture. Fiction feature. 104/108 min. Versions in Chinese and in Tibetan.

Part 2: Additional films, dramas, and documentaries by Tibetans in Tibet—a partial list

The Bet (*Rgyan 'dzugs*), Lobsang (Blo bzang). Tibet (China), c. 2008. Online video. 8 min. In Lhasa Tibetan.

The Biography of the Noble Milarepa (*Rje rtsun Mi la ras pa'i rnam thar*), dir. Choedar Gyatso (Chos dar rgya mtsho). c. 2010. Digital drama series. 18 episodes. Intended for television or for direct sales. In Kham Tibetan.

Blood on the Grassland (*Rtsa thang gi khrag thigs*), Nordreng (Rno sbreng). Tibet (China), 2010. Online fiction feature. In Amdo Tibetan.

The Coral Necklace (*Byu ru'i ske rgyan*), dir. Shide Nyima (Zhi bde nyi ma). Tibet (China), 2006. TV drama series for Qinghai TV. 50 min. In Amdo Tibetan. Reworked as Drolma's Necklace (*Sgrol ma'i ske rgyen,* also described in English as The Dor ma of Coral Necklace), also called *Byu ru'i mgul rgyan*, CCTV early 2011.

Cutting Down Tibet. Filmmaker: anonymous. Tibet Information Network, London. Tibet/UK. Broadcast on BBC-TV, May 13, 1996. Documentary. In Lhasa Tibetan.

Deceive the Text-reciter (*Drongchog pa mgo 'kor*), Rigdan Gyatso (Rig ldan rgya mtsho). Tibet (China), 2008. Short fiction for children. In Amdo Tibetan.

Deji from the Town of Tawa (*THa ba he ba'I bde skyid,* Ch: *Tawa zhen shang de Deji*), Tsewang Norbu (Ch.: Caiwang Naoru). Tibet (China), 2011. Short fiction. 13 min. In Tibetan with English and Chinese subtitles.

The Driver and the Lama (*Kha lo pa dang bla ma,* Ch.: *Siji yu Lama*), Rinchen Drolma (Rin chen sgrol ma, Ch.: Zhuoga). Tibet (China), 2009. Short fiction. 26 min. In Amdo Tibetan.

The Ewe Goes to Central Tibet (*Ma mo'i dbus lam*), Rigdan Gyatso (Rig ldan rgya mtsho). Tibet (China), 2007. Short fiction for children. 43 min. In Amdo Tibetan.

The Fiancé (*Mag pa*), Tenzin (Bstan 'dzin) and Jampa Yonten (Byams pa yon ten), script by Phuntsog Tashi (Phun tshogs Bkra shis). Tibet TV. Tibet (China), 1991. Short television drama/comedy. 16 min. In Lhasa Tibetan.

Fierce Turquoise Mountain (*Gnyen po gyu rtse*), Rigdan Gyatso (Rig ldan rgya mtsho). Tibet (China), 2007. Short fiction. 40 min. In Amdo Tibetan.

A Foolish Brother (*Phun zla glen pa*), Lobsang (Blo bzang). Tibet (China), c. 2008. Online video. 5 min. In Lhasa Tibetan.

Gesar's Horseherders (*Ge sar rta rdzi*), Manla kyab (Sman bla skyabs). Tibet (China), 2004. Comedy sketch, broadcast on Qinghai TV. 18 min. In Amdo Tibetan.

The Girl Lhari (*Bu mo Lha ris*), Rigdan Gyatso (Rig ldan rgya mtsho), written by Mkha' mo rgyal (Khamo Gya). Tibet (China), 2005. Short fiction. 26 min. In Amdo Tibetan.

The Grassland (*Rtswa thang*), Pema Tseden (Padma tshe brtan, Ch.: Wanma Caidan). Tibet (China), 2004. Short fiction. 22/26 min. In Amdo Tibetan with English subtitles.

The Grave-digger (*Shou mu ren*), Drolkar (Sgrol dkar, Ch.: Zhuoga). 1988. Short fiction for Tibet TV. In Chinese.

A Happy Life (*Sprod snang ldan pa'i 'tsho ba*), Writer: Migmar (Mig dmar). Tibet (China), 2008. TV situation comedy series. 5 episodes. In Lhasa Tibetan.

Hope from Disaster (*Nyams nye nang gi re ba*). Filmmaker: anonymous. Tibet (China), 2011. Unauthorized DVD, compilation of speeches and songs. In Amdo Tibetan with some Lhasa Tibetan, with Tibetan subtitles.

Hornig: Beat the Dog, Tsedup Karko. Tibet (China)/UK, 2005. Kula Films production. 47 min. Tibetan.

I Am Tibetan (*Nga ni bod yin*). Filmmaker: anonymous. Tibet (China), 2009. Online video. 5 min. In Amdo Tibetan.

Kokonor Lake (*Mtsho sngon po*), Chenagtshang Dorje Tsering (Lce nag tshang Rdo rje tshe ring, aka Jangbu). Tibet (China)/France, 2008. Documentary. 52 min. In Amdo Tibetan with English subtitles.

Leaving (*Gyes bral*). Nordreng (Rno sbreng) and students of the China Film and Broadcast College. c. 2011. Short fiction. 12 min. In Amdo Tibetan with Chinese and English subtitles.

Leaving Fear Behind (*'Jigs bral*). Dondrub Wangchen, Jigme Gyatso (Don grub dbang chen, 'Jigs med rgya mtsho). Tibet (China)/Switzerland, 2008. Documentary. 25 min. In Amdo Tibetan with English subtitles.

Let's Speak in Pure Tibetan (Nga tsho bod skad cig skyon rogs gnang). Filmmaker: anonymous. Tibet (China), c. 2008. Online poem-video. 5 min. In Lhasa Tibetan.

Lhacham—A Tibetan Nun (*A ne Lha lcam*), Chenagtshang Dorje Tsering (Lce nag tshang Rdo rje tshe ring, aka Jangbu). Tibet (China), 2007. Documentary. 26 min. In Amdo Tibetan with English subtitles.

Life among the People of Choni, Yangdrol Tsongkha (Dbyang sgrol tsong kha). Tibet (China), 2008–2009. Documentary. 110 min. In Amdo Tibetan with English subtitles.

Longing (*'Khreng zhen,* sometimes known as *Nyi ma tshe ring dang Zla ba sgrol ma,* Nyima Tsering and Dawa Drolma), Phagmo Tashi (Phag mo bkra shis). Tibet (China), 1992–1993. Fiction feature for Qinghai TV. 88 min. In Amdo Tibetan.

Love on the Grassland (*Gling dkar stod kyi byams pa*), Padma Tsering (Padma rtshe ring) and Lhamo Tsedan (Lha mo rtse brtan) from Northwest Nationalities University in Lanzhou. Tibet (China), 2011. Short fiction. In Amdo Tibetan.

Milarepa (*Mi la ras pa*), Sonam (Bsod nams). Tibet (China), 2006. Fiction feature. 96 min. In Kham Tibetan with English subtitles.

The Oath, Part 1 (*'Dam bca'*), Lodroe (Blos gro). Tibet (China), c. 2009. Online feature fiction. 46 min. In Amdo Tibetan.

Old Dog (*Khyi rgan,* Ch: *Lao gou*), Pema Tseden (Padma tshe brtan, Ch.: Wanma Caidan). Tibet (China), 2010. Fiction feature. 93 min. In Amdo Tibetan with English subtitles.

The Perfection of Wisdom (*Phar phyin ston mo'i mdzad sgo*), Phagpa Dondrub ('Phags pa don grub, Chinese: Puhua Dunzhu). Tibet (China), 2006. Documentary. 27 min. In Amdo Tibetan with English subtitles.

Red Fragment (or Red Prophecy, *Chag krum dmar po*). Filmmaker: anonymous. Tibet (China), c. 2009. Unauthorized DVD, compilation of songs. In Tibetan.

Return to Lhasa (*Huidao Lasa,* also called Back to Lhasa, originally named Kang Rinpoche), Drolkar (Sgrol dkar, Ch. Zhuoga). Tibet (China), 2008. Fiction feature. Not publicly released.

The Search (*'Tshol,* Ch.: *Xunzhao Zhimei gendeng,* Seeking Drime Kunden, also called Soul Searching), Pema Tseden (Padma tshe brtan, Ch.: Wanma Caidan). Tibet (China), 2009. Fiction feature. 112 min. In Amdo Tibetan with English subtitles.

Shepherd Pig Year (*Lug rzi phag lo*), Wangchog Bhum (Dbang mchog 'bum). Tibet (China), c. 2011. Short fiction. In Amdo Tibetan.

Shepherd Song (*Rdzi glu*), Shide Nyima (Zhi bde nyi ma). Tibet (China), 2008. Short fiction. 4 min. No dialogue.

The Silent Holy Stones (or The Silent Mani Stones, *Lhing 'jags kyi ma Ni rdo 'bum,* Ch.: *Jingjing de mani shi*), Pema Tseden (Padma tshe brtan, Ch.: Wanma Caidan). Tibet (China), 2005. Fiction feature. 95/120 min. In Amdo Tibetan with English subtitles.

The Smile of Xesrob (*Shes rab kyi 'dzum mdangs*) Lhamo Tsedan (Lha mo rtshe brtan), Peltse (Dpal rtsal) and students of Central Nationalities University. Tibet (China), 2011. Short fiction. 13 min. In Amdo Tibetan with English subtitles.

Snow Will Not Forget (*Xueshan buhui wangji*), Drolkar (Sgrol dkar, Ch.: Zhuoga). Tibet (China), 2006. Fiction feature for TV; broadcast on CCTV, 2007. 92 min. In Chinese.

So I Think (*Byas tsang nga,* Ch.: *Suoyi wo*), CYY and Tenchar, for TB films, Lhasa. 2012. Short fiction. 20 min. In Lhasa Tibetan.

Stories of Yesterday (*Kha sang gi gtam rgyud,* Ch.: *Zuotian de gushe*), dir. Dodrak (Rdo grags, Ch.: Duo zhi he), Qinghai TV. Tibet (China), 2009. Television drama series. 8 episodes. In Amdo Tibetan.

Summer Pasture, Nelson Walker, Lynn True, and Tsering Perlo. USA/Tibet (China), 2011. Documentary. 85 min. In Amdo Tibetan with English subtitles.

The Sun-beaten Path (also called The Sun Is Always on the Left, *Dbus lam gi nyi ma,* Ch.: *Taiyang zong zai zuo bian*), Zon mthar rgyal (Sonthar Gyal). Tibet (China), 2010. Fiction feature. 89 min. In Amdo Tibetan with English subtitles.

Sunday (*Gza' nyi ma*), Lhamo Tashi (Lha mo bkra shis) and students of Tibet Nationality Universities. Tibet (China), 2011. Short fiction. 19 min. In Amdo Tibetan.

Taming the Wolf (*Spyang ki drul ba*), Rigdan Gyatso (Rig ldan rgya mtsho). Tibet (China), 2008. Short fiction for children. 40 min. In Amdo Tibetan.

Tantric Yogi (*Sngags pa*), Chenagtshang Dorje Tsering (Lce nag tshang Rdo rje tshe ring, aka Jangbu), Channel 4, UK. Tibet (China)/UK, 2005. Documentary. 50 min. In Amdo Tibetan with English subtitles.

This Is Not a Joking Matter (*'Di btsan bshig slong ba ma red,* popularly known as *Lhag pa ra bzi,* Drunk Lhagpa), written by Phuntsog Tashi (Phun tshogs bkra shis). Tibet (China), c. 1991. Television comedy sketch broadcast on Tibet TV. 23 min. In Lhasa Tibetan.

Tibetan Village Wedding (*Bod kyi gnyen ston mdzad sgo*), Phagpa Dondrub ('Phags pa don grub, Ch.: Puhua Dunzhu). Tibet (China), 2005. Documentary. 35 min. In Amdo Tibetan with English subtitles.

A Tibetan Woman's Life (*Bod kyi bud med kyi 'tsho ba*), Phagpa Dondrub ('Phags pa don grub, Ch.: Puhua Dunzhu). Tibet (China), 2006. Documentary. 52 min. In Amdo Tibetan with English subtitles.

Wailing at Dusk (*Sa srod kyi smre sngags,* Ch.: *Huang hun de mo ai*), Dobha (Rdo bha). Tibet (China), short version 2009; longer version 2010. Online feature fiction. 39 min. In Amdo Tibetan.

The Way Out (*Lam*), Kathub Tashi (Dka' thub bkra shis), Gansu Nationalities Teaching Training College. Tibet (China), 2011. Short fiction. 24 min. In Amdo Tibetan with English and Chinese subtitles.

The Weatherman's Legacy, Pema Tseden (Padma tshe brtan, Ch.: Wanma Caidan). Tibet (China)/Hong Kong, 2005. Discovery Channel Asia. Documentary. In Amdo Tibetan/English.

Yartsa Rinpoche (*Byar rtswa dgun 'bu rin po che*), Chenagtshang Dorje Tsering (Lce nag tshang Rdo rje tshe ring, aka Jangbu). Tibet (China)/France, 2013. Documentary. 100 min. In Amdo Tibetan with English subtitles.

Contributors

ROBERT BARNETT is the Director of the Modern Tibetan Studies Program at Columbia University in New York. His books include *Tibetan Modernities: Notes from the Field* (with Ronald Schwartz, 2008), *Lhasa: Streets with Memories* (2006), and *A Poisoned Arrow: The Secret Petition of the 10th Panchen Lama* (1997). He has published articles on modern Tibetan history, Tibetan films and television dramas, and women and politics in Tibet, as well as on religious policies, political leadership, oral history, and exorcism rituals in contemporary Tibet. From 2000 to 2006 he ran the annual Summer Program for foreign students at Tibet University in Lhasa, as well as training projects in Tibet on ecotourism, teaching, and oral culture. He is a frequent commentator on Tibet-related issues for the BBC, NPR, the *New York Times,* and other media outlets.

TING-WU CHO is a PhD candidate in Cinema Studies at New York University. Her dissertation focuses on trans-Asian exploitation films during the late–Cold War period.

DAN GAO is a PhD candidate at the Department of Cinema Studies, New York University. She has published essays, book reviews, and criticisms on Chinese language cinema, independent film, popular TV drama, and mass culture in both English and Chinese in, among other publications, *Chinese Independent Cinema* (issue 12, 2013), *China's iGeneration* (Bloomsbury Academic, May 2014), and *The Routledge Encyclopedia of Films* (September 2014). As an active translator, she has also been introducing cutting-edge academic works written in English to Chinese readers.

JIE LI is Assistant Professor of East Asian Languages and Civilizations at Harvard. She made the ethnographic film *The Al-Hadji and His Wives* (Documentary Educational Resources, 2006), wrote the book *Shanghai Homes: Palimpsests of Private Life* (Columbia University Press, 2014), and coedited the volume *Red Legacies in China: Cultural Afterlives of the Communist Revolution* (Harvard Asia Center, forthcoming). She has published essays on contemporary Chinese films, Manchurian cinema, and modern Chinese literature in *Public Culture, positions, Journal of Chinese Cinemas*, and various anthologies.

ABÉ MARK NORNES is Professor of Asian Cinema at the University of Michigan. His books include *Japanese Documentary Film, Forest of Pressure: Ogawa Shinsuke and Postwar Japanese Documentary*, and the *Research Guide to Japanese Cinema*. He has worked for the Yamagata International Documentary Film Festival for much of the last two decades.

BÉRÉNICE REYNAUD is the author of *Nouvelles Chines, nouveaux cinémas*, and *Hou Hsiao-hsien's "A City of Sadness."* Her writing has been published in *The New Urban Generation, The New Chinese Documentary Movement, The Routledge Encyclopedia of Contemporary Chinese Culture*, and *Storia del Cinema Mondiale*, as well as in *Sight & Sound, Film Comment, CinemaScope, Senses of Cinema, Cahiers du cinéma, Le Monde diplomatique, Libération, Meteor, Springerin*, and *Nosferatu*. A program consultant for The Viennale and the San Sebastian International Film Festival, she has organized numerous series of Chinese cinema in the United States and Europe. She teaches at the California Institute of the Arts.

LUKE ROBINSON is Lecturer in Film Studies in the Department of Media and Film, University of Sussex, UK. He is the author of *Independent Chinese Documentary: From the Studio to the Street* (Palgrave Macmillan, 2013) and various book chapters and articles on Chinese-language feature film, animation, documentary, and film festivals.

SHUANG SHEN is Associate Professor of Comparative Literature and Asian Studies at Penn State University. She is the author of *Cosmopolitan Publics: Anglophone Print Culture in Semicolonial Shanghai* (Rutgers, 2009) and coeditor of a special issue of *Social Text* on "China and the Human" (2011 and 2012). She has published articles and essays in *MLQ, Modern China, MCLC, PMLA, Xinmin Weekly* (in Chinese), and *Wanxiang* (in Chinese)

J. P. SNIADECKI is a filmmaker, anthropologist, and professor of film and media in the Performing and Media Arts Department at Cornell University. His works are mainly produced in China and the United States and explore the intersection of art, cinema, and ethnography. His filmography includes *The Iron Ministry* (2014), *Yumen* (2013), *People's Park* (2012), *Foreign Parts* (2010), *The Yellow Bank* (2010), *Chaiqian/Demolition* (2008), and *Songhua* (2007).

PAOLA VOCI is Senior Lecturer at the University of Otago, New Zealand. She specializes in Chinese cinema and, in particular, documentary, animation, and other hybrid digital video practices. She is the author of *China on Video* (Routledge 2010, 2012), a book that analyzes and theorizes movies made for and viewed on computer and mobile screens. She has published articles in *Modern Chinese Literature and Culture*, *Screening the Past*, *Senses of Cinema*, and *Bianco e Nero*. Her work also appears in several edited collections of essays, such as *The New Chinese Documentary Movement* and *The Oxford Handbook of Chinese Cinemas*.

QI WANG is Assistant Professor in Film at Georgia Tech. She has written articles on Chinese cinema, documentary, and Japanese anime for *positions: east asia cultures critique*, *Journal of Chinese Cinemas*, *Asian Cinema*, *International Journal of Comic Art*, among other publications. Her book on contemporary Chinese independent cinema and its relationship with (post)socialist historical memory is forthcoming from Edinburg University Press. She cocurated the 2008 Reel China Documentary Biennial.

ANGELA ZITO teaches Anthropology and Religious Studies at New York University, where she codirects the Center for Religion and Media. She has been involved in the Chinese documentary scene for more than a decade as a scholar, filmmaker, and curator, with Zhang Zhen, of Reel China @NYU, a Film Biennial. Her most recent essay on these matters, "*Writing in Water*, or, Evanescence, Enchantment and Ethnography in a Chinese Urban Park," appears in *Visual Anthropology Review*. Find her work at www.angelazito.com.

ZHANG ZHEN is Associate Professor in Cinema Studies and History at New York University. Her publications include *An Amorous History of the Silver Screen: Shanghai Cinema, 1896–1937* and *The Urban Generation: Chinese Cinema and Society at the Turn of the Twenty-first Century* (both translated into Chinese), numerous articles and essays in a number of languages in anthologies, journals, and exhibit catalogs, as well as a book of poems in Chinese. She initiated Reel China Documentary Biennial at NYU in 2001 and is founder and Director of the Asian Film and Media Initiative since 2012.

Index

Page numbers in bold refer to illustrations.